The Italian Renaissance St

This magisterial study proposes a revised and innovative view of the political history of Renaissance Italy. Drawing on comparative examples from across the peninsula and the kingdoms of Sicily, Sardinia and Corsica, an international team of leading scholars highlights the complexity and variety of the Italian world from the fourteenth to the early sixteenth centuries, surveying the mosaic of kingdoms, principalities, *signorie* and republics against a backdrop of wider political themes common to all types of state in the period. The authors address the contentious problem of the apparent weakness of the Italian Renaissance political system. By repositioning the Renaissance as a political, rather than simply an artistic and cultural, phenomenon, they identify the period as a pivotal moment in the history of the state, in which political languages, practices and tools, together with political and governmental institutions, became vital to the evolution of a modern European political identity.

ANDREA GAMBERINI is Professore Aggregato of the Social and Economic History of the Middle Ages at the University of Milan.

ISABELLA LAZZARINI is Professor of Medieval History at the University of Molise.

The Italian Renaissance State

Edited by
Andrea Gamberini and Isabella Lazzarini

CAMBRIDGE
UNIVERSITY PRESS

University Printing House, Cambridge CB2 8BS, United Kingdom

Cambridge University Press is part of the University of Cambridge.

It furthers the University's mission by disseminating knowledge in the pursuit of education, learning and research at the highest international levels of excellence.

www.cambridge.org
Information on this title: www.cambridge.org/9781107460249

© Cambridge University Press 2012

This publication is in copyright. Subject to statutory exception and to the provisions of relevant collective licensing agreements, no reproduction of any part may take place without the written permission of Cambridge University Press.

First published 2012
First paperback edition 2014

A catalogue record for this publication is available from the British Library

Library of Congress Cataloguing in Publication data

The Italian renaissance state / edited by Andrea Gamberini, Isabella Lazzarini.
   p. cm.
   ISBN 978-1-107-01012-3 (Hardback)
1. Italy–Politics and government–1268–1559.   2. State, The–History.
3. City-states–Italy–History.   4. Renaissance–Italy.   I. Gamberini, Andrea.
II. Lazzarini, Isabella.   III. Title.
   JN5231.I73 2012
   320.94509'024–dc23

2011033925

ISBN 978-1-107-01012-3 Hardback
ISBN 978-1-107-46024-9 Paperback

Cambridge University Press has no responsibility for the persistence or accuracy of URLs for external or third-party internet websites referred to in this publication, and does not guarantee that any content on such websites is, or will remain, accurate or appropriate.

Contents

Notes on the contributors	*page* vii
Note on translations and usage	xiii
Italy in 1454	xiv
Introduction ANDREA GAMBERINI AND ISABELLA LAZZARINI	1

Part I   The Italian states — 7

1. The kingdom of Sicily — 9
   FABRIZIO TITONE

2. The kingdom of Naples — 30
   FRANCESCO SENATORE

3. The kingdom of Sardinia and Corsica — 50
   OLIVETTA SCHENA

4. The papal state — 69
   SANDRO CAROCCI

5. Tuscan states: Florence and Siena — 90
   LORENZO TANZINI

6. Ferrara and Mantua — 112
   TREVOR DEAN

7. Venice and the Terraferma — 132
   MICHAEL KNAPTON

8. Lombardy under the Visconti and the Sforza — 156
   FEDERICO DEL TREDICI

9. The feudal principalities: the west (Monferrato, Saluzzo, Savoy and Savoy-Acaia) — 177
   ALESSANDRO BARBERO

10	The feudal principalities: the east (Trent, Bressanone/Brixen, Aquileia, Tyrol and Gorizia) MARCO BELLABARBA	197
11	Genoa CHRISTINE SHAW	220

Part II Themes and perspectives — **237**

12	The collapse of city-states and the role of urban centres in the new political geography of Renaissance Italy FRANCESCO SOMAINI	239
13	The rural communities MASSIMO DELLA MISERICORDIA	261
14	Lordships, fiefs and 'small states' FEDERICA CENGARLE	284
15	Factions and parties: problems and perspectives MARCO GENTILE	304
16	States, orders and social distinction E. IGOR MINEO	323
17	Women and the state SERENA FERENTE	345
18	Offices and officials GUIDO CASTELNUOVO	368
19	Public written records GIAN MARIA VARANINI	385
20	The language of politics and the process of state-building: approaches and interpretations ANDREA GAMBERINI	406
21	Renaissance diplomacy ISABELLA LAZZARINI	425
22	Regional states and economic development FRANCO FRANCESCHI AND LUCA MOLÀ	444
23	The papacy and the Italian states GIORGIO CHITTOLINI	467
24	Justice ANDREA ZORZI	490

Bibliography 515
Index 600

Notes on the contributors

ANDREA GAMBERINI is Professore Aggregato of Medieval History at the University of Milan. He is a member of the editorial board of *Quaderni Storici*. His main publications include monographs: *Oltre la città. Assetti territoriali e culture aristocratiche nella Lombardia del tardo Medioevo* (2009); *Lo stato visconteo. Linguaggi politici e dinamiche costituzionali, Milano* (2005); and *La città assediata. Poteri e identità politiche a Reggio in età viscontea* (2003); as well as edited volumes: (with G. Petralia, eds.) *Linguaggi politici nell'Italia del Rinascimento* (2007); and (with J.-Ph. Genet and A. Zorzi, eds.), *The Languages of the Political Society* (2011).

ISABELLA LAZZARINI is Associate Professor of Medieval History at the University of Molise, Italy, and is currently a Leverhulme Trust Visiting Professor at Durham University. Her research interests focus on the political, social and cultural history of late medieval Italy, with an emphasis on Renaissance diplomacy and the growth of different political languages in documentary sources. Among her main publications are: *Fra un principe e altri stati. Rapporti di potere e relazioni di servizio a Mantova nell'età di Ludovico Gonzaga (1444–1478)* (1996); *L'Italia degli stati territoriali (secoli XIII–XV)* (2003); *Amicizia e potere. Reti politiche e sociali nell'Italia medievale* (2010); (ed.) *Scritture e potere. Pratiche documentarie e forme di governo nell'Italia tardomedievale (secoli XIV–XV)* (2008; www.storia.unifi.it/_RM/rivista/2008–1.htm#Saggi).

ALESSANDRO BARBERO is Professor of Medieval History at the Università del Piemonte Orientale, Vercelli, Italy. Many of his books have been translated: *Carlo Magno. Un padre dell'Europa* (2000; translated in the United States, UK, France, Germany and Spain); *La battaglia. Storia di Waterloo* (2003; translated in the United States, UK, France, Spain, the Netherlands and Romania); *9 agosto 378. Il giorno dei barbari* (2005; translated in the United States, United Kingdom, France, Spain and the Netherlands).

MARCO BELLABARBA is Associate Professor of Early Modern History at the University of Trent, Italy. His main research fields are the political and institutional history of the Alpine area and the history of justice in early modern Italy, and he has written extensively on these topics (*La giustizia ai confini. Il principato vescovile di Trento nella prima età moderna* (1986); (with G. Olmi, eds.) *Storia del Trentino*, III, *L'età moderna* (2003); (with G. Schwerhoff and A. Zorzi, eds.) *Criminalità e giustizia in Germania e in Italia. Pratiche giudiziarie e linguaggi giuridici tra tardo Medioevo ed età moderna* (2001); *Storia della giustizia nell'Italia moderna. XVI–XVIII secolo* (2008)).

SANDRO CAROCCI is Professor of Medieval History in the Department of History, University of Rome Tor Vergata. His main fields of research are the history of the economic and social structure of late medieval Italian cities; the history of rural lordship in Italy and Europe; the history of Italian aristocracies between the twelfth and the fourteenth centuries; the institutional history of the papacy and of the papal state (twelfth to fifteenth centuries). Among his main publications are: *El nepotismo en la Edad Media. Papas, cardenales y familias nobles* (2007); (ed.) *Itineranza pontificia. La mobilità della curia papale nel Lazio (secoli XII–XIII)* (2003); *Baroni di Roma. Dominazioni signorili e lignaggi aristocratici nel Duecento e nel primo Trecento* (1993).

GUIDO CASTELNUOVO, Maître de Conférence HDR at the University of Savoy, Chambéry, France, has worked on the political society of the *principauté* of Savoy in the late Middle Ages (*Ufficiali e gentiluomini. La società politica sabauda nel tardo Medioevo* (1994)) and is now studying the world of the Italian nobilities and their representations from the thirteenth century to early modern times.

FEDERICA CENGARLE is Research Fellow at the University of Milan. She is the author of *Immagine di potere e prassi di governo. La politica feudale di Filippo Maria Visconti* (2006); *Feudi e feudatari del duca Filippo Maria Visconti. Repertorio* (2007); and of several essays on political and institutional history in the fourteenth and fifteenth centuries. She is also the editor of *Poteri signorili e feudali nelle campagne dell'Italia settentrionale fra Tre e Quattrocento* (2005).

GIORGIO CHITTOLINI is Professor of Medieval History at the University of Milan. He has been a co-editor of the series Cambridge Studies in Italian History and Culture for Cambridge University Press. His studies are devoted to the institutional history and the state-building process. He is the author of: *La formazione dello stato regionale e le istituzioni del contado* (1979); and *Città, comunità e feudi negli Stati dell'Italia centro settentrionale* (1993).

TREVOR DEAN is Professor of Medieval History at the University of Roehampton, London. His academic career began with various studies of the Este family and its state in fourteenth- and fifteenth-century Ferrara, (*Land and Power in Late Medieval Ferrara* (Cambridge University Press, 1987) and *Clean Hands and Rough Justice* (1997)), but has focused more recently on the history of crime and criminal justice in Bologna, Italy and Europe (*Crime and Criminal Justice in Late Medieval Italy* (Cambridge University Press, 2007)).

FEDERICO DEL TREDICI is currently Research Fellow at the Università degli Studi di Milano. In 2005 he was Junior Research Fellow at the Istituto Italiano di Studi Storici Benedetto Croce, Naples.

MASSIMO DELLA MISERICORDIA is Lecturer in Medieval History at the University of Milan-Bicocca. He is interested in the history of society, of lay and ecclesiastical institutions, and of political culture in the late Middle Ages, especially in the Lombard area and Alpine valleys. He is the author of: *La disciplina contrattata. Vescovi e vassalli tra Como e le Alpi nel tardo Medioevo* (2000); *Divenire comunità. Comuni rurali, poteri locali, identità sociali e territoriali in Valtellina e nella montagna lombarda nel tardo Medioevo* (2008).

SERENA FERENTE is Lecturer in Medieval European History at King's College London. She has published a book (*La sfortuna di Jacopo Piccinino. Storia dei bracceschi in Italia, 1423–1465* (2005)) and a number of articles on supra-local factional networks and identities in fifteenth-century Italy. She is currently working on two projects: the uses of passion in late medieval political languages and discourses on nature and women's political authority in fourteenth- and early fifteenth-century Italy.

FRANCO FRANCESCHI is Associate Professor of Medieval History at the University of Siena. A specialist in Italian urban history, he has published *Oltre il 'Tumulto'. I lavoratori fiorentini dell'Arte della Lana fra Tre e Quattrocento* (1993) and, together with Ilaria Taddei, *Les villes d'Italie du XIIe siècle au milieu du XIVe siècle* (2004). He is the author of numerous essays on the world of work, the history of guilds, economic policies, the transmission of knowledge, and the *mentalité* of the working classes from the thirteenth to the sixteenth centuries.

MARCO GENTILE is Lecturer in the Department of History, University of Parma. He was Francesco de Dombrowski Fellow in History at

Villa I Tatti, the Harvard University Center for Italian Renaissance Studies (2005/6). He is the author of *Terra e poteri. Parma e il Parmense nel ducato visconteo all'inizio del Quattrocento* (2001), and the editor of *Guelfi e ghibellini nell'Italia del Rinascimento* (2005).

MICHAEL KNAPTON is Associate Professor of Early Modern History in the Languages Faculty of Udine University, Italy. His research centres on the republic of Venice (thirteenth–eighteenth centuries), especially its mainland state. His publications, apart from reviews and encyclopedia and dictionary entries, comprise six books edited singly or jointly, thirty-six essays or parts of books plus others in print, and include lengthy pieces in vol. XII of the *Storia d'Italia* (1986, 1992), the volume devoted to early modern Venice.

E. IGOR MINEO is Associate Professor of Medieval History and History of Medieval and Early Modern Law at the University of Palermo. His principal research interest is the social and institutional history of Italy in the late Middle Ages and, in particular, the problem of aristocracy and the role of the urban elites in the kingdom of Sicily (*Nobiltà di stato. Famiglie e identità aristocratiche nel tardo Medioevo. La Sicilia* (2001)). As well as comparing different forms of social distinction and social display in Italy, he is also interested in the social structure of small cities and communities in some areas of central Italy. Currently he is editing a book on republican experiences in European history.

LUCA MOLÀ is Professor of Early Modern Europe at the European University Institute in Fiesole, Italy. He specialises in the Italian Renaissance, the early modern economy – especially trading communities, artisans and industrial production – and the culture of technological change. His publications include *La comunità dei lucchesi a Venezia. Immigrazione e industria della seta nel tardo Medioevo* (1994), *The Silk Industry of Renaissance Venice* (2000) and the co-edited collections *La seta in Italia dal Medioevo al Seicento* (2000) and *Il Rinascimento italiano e l'Europa*, III, *Produzione e tecniche* (2007). He is currently completing a monograph on the development of the patent system in Italy during the Renaissance, and is the director of the Centre for the History of Innovation and Creativity (CHIC) in Venice.

OLIVETTA SCHENA, having been Temporary Professor of Paleography at the Faculty of Letters and Philosophy, University of Sassari, Italy (1991–2001), is now Associate Professor of Medieval History at the Faculty of Education, University of Cagliari, Italy. She collaborates as research fellow with the Istituto storico dell'Europa mediterranea of the Italian National Research Council. Her research focuses on the political, economic and judicial sources on late medieval Italy preserved in the archives of the crown of Aragon (Barcelona): she has edited volumes III and V of the series *Acta Curiarum Regni Sardiniae*, and is currently editing the royal letters of the kings of the crown of Aragon to the city of Cagliari (fourteenth and fifteenth centuries), forthcoming from the Istituto storico italiano per il Medio Evo (FIS).

FRANCESCO SENATORE is Associate Professor of Medieval History at the Università Federico II di Napoli, and also has teaching and supervising responsibilities in the Doctoral School of History (Dipartimento di Discipline storiche 'E. Lepore'), co-ordinating its section on 'Storia della Società Europea'. Since 2007 he has been co-director of the Rassegna Storica Salernitana. His main research interests focus on Italian diplomacy in the fifteenth century (*Uno mundo de carta. Forme e strutture della diplomazia sforzesca* (1998); *Dispacci sforzeschi da Napoli* (2 vols., 1997, 2004)) and on the Aragonese kingdom of Naples (with F. Storti, *Spazi e tempi della guerra nel Mezzogiorno aragonese. L'itinerario militare di re Ferrante* (2002)) and its urban political society. He is also the author of a synthesis on medieval history (*Medioevo. Istruzioni per l'uso* (2008)).

CHRISTINE SHAW has been Research Officer at the London School of Economics, Senior Research Fellow at the University of Warwick, and Senior Research Associate at the University of Cambridge. She is currently Honorary Research Fellow at Swansea University. Her major publications include *Julius II: The Warrior Pope* (1993), *The Politics of Exile in Renaissance Italy* (2000) and *Popular Government and Oligarchy in Renaissance Italy* (2006). She has published several articles on fifteenth-century Genoa.

FRANCESCO SOMAINI is Associate Professor of Medieval History at the Università del Salento, Lecce. His main research fields are the political and institutional history of the duchy of Milan, the history of the papacy during the late Middle Ages, and the history of the ecclesiastical institutions of the early modern age. He is the author of *Un prelato lombardo del XV secolo. Il card. Giovanni Arcimboldi, vescovo di Novara, arcivescovo di Milano*, 3 vols. (2003).

LORENZO TANZINI is Lecturer in Medieval History at the University of Cagliari, Italy. His works are devoted to the legal and institutional history of Tuscany and political thought in the early Renaissance. He is the author of *Statuti e legislazione a Firenze dal 1355 al 1415* (2004); *Il governo delle leggi* (2007); and *Alle origini della Toscana moderna* (2007).

FABRIZIO TITONE is Ramón y Cajal Researcher at the Universidad del País Vasco, Spain. His research interests centre on urban history in the states of the crown of Aragon. He has published extensively on Sicilian urban history, focusing on different fields such as societies, institutions and economic changes. Among his publications are: *I magistrati cittadini. Gli ufficiali scrutinati in Sicilia da Martino I ad Alfonso V, un'indagine prosopografica* (2008), and *Governments of the Universitates: Urban Communities of Sicily in the Fourteenth and Fifteenth Centuries* (2009).

GIAN MARIA VARANINI is Professor of Medieval History at the University of Verona. His main research fields are the political, economic and institutional history of the Veneto during the thirteenth–fifteenth centuries, but he has also focused on publishing documentary sources (thirteenth–fifteenth centuries).

ANDREA ZORZI is Associate Professor of Medieval History at the University of Florence. His historical interests concern Italian political history during the late Middle Ages, with special attention to Florence and Tuscany. His books include (with W. J. Connell, eds.) *Florentine Tuscany: Structures and Practices of Power* (Cambridge University Press, 2000); (with J. Chiffoleau and C. Gauvard, eds.) *Pratiques sociales et politiques judiciaires dans les villes de l'Occident à la fin du Moyen Âge* (2007); and *La trasformazione di un quadro politico. Ricerche su politica e giustizia a Firenze dal comune allo stato territoriale* (2008).

Note on translations and usage

Elizabeth Alpass (for Durham Translators Limited) translated the chapters written by Fabrizio Titone and Andrea Zorzi; Lucinda Byatt (Edinburgh) translated those by Alessandro Barbero and Marco Bellabarba; Robert Elliott (Ferrara) translated those by Sandro Carocci, Guido Castelnuovo, Francesco Senatore and Gian Maria Varanini; Federico M. Federici (for Durham Translators Limited) that by Francesco Somaini; Theresa Federici (for Durham Translators Limited) translated those by Federica Cengarle, Federico Del Tredici and Massimo Della Misericordia; Amanda George (Florence) translated those by E. Igor Mineo and Olivetta Schena; Susan Scott (Grosseto) translated that by Franco Franceschi and Luca Molà; and Christine Shaw (Swansea) translated those by Andrea Gamberini, Marco Gentile and Giorgio Chittolini.

Other chapters were written in English or translated by the author.

To avoid ambiguity, we adopt the terms '*signoria*' and '*signorile*' to refer to urban proto-princely regimes; the term 'seigneurial', in turn, refers mainly to rural lordships. In line with the most common Italian usage, in this book the term 'modern age' normally refers to the period from the sixteenth to the eighteenth centuries.

ITALY IN 1454

Introduction

Andrea Gamberini and Isabella Lazzarini

Renaissance Italy and its political cultures are a fundamental but controversial topic of Western historiography on the late medieval and early modern state: the political, economic and cultural innovations introduced both by civic humanism and by Renaissance political thought from Marsilio da Padova to Machiavelli, the merchants' and bankers' networks and empirical culture, the rather mythicised artistic, literary and cultural achievements, from Giotto to Michelangelo, from Petrarch to Ariosto, have been considered ever since as some of the most significant steps towards 'modernity'. On the other hand, the concrete political weakness of the Italian peninsula pulled it out of the mainstream leading towards the so-called modern state, leaving to the Italian republics, principalities and political actors only a marginal role in the evolution of the modern European political identity in the crucial period between the sixteenth and the eighteenth centuries. Thus, the Renaissance and Italy, achievements and failures, are deeply linked in a double knot whose components did not precisely overlap and whose combination still provides room for investigation to the community of political, social and cultural historians of Western civilisation.

The Italian Renaissance State: two reasons for a title

Deeply conscious of this apparent paradox, we have devised the present volume to meet two main aims. The first is to provide a synthesis of current Italian research on the political history of Italy, taking into account both a general survey of the transformation and features of Italian kingdoms, principalities, feudal and ecclesiastical *signorie* and republics from the fourteenth to the early sixteenth centuries, and a wide range of key themes that were common to the political experience of all these states.

Secondly, these pages have the ambition to raise once again the theme of the Italian Renaissance with a declared emphasis on politics. Although a great deal of specialised and non-specialised work has been published on these topics, the Italian Renaissance – perhaps better, Renaissance Italy – seems to deserve some sort of reinterpretation *sub specie politicae*, that is, as a founding moment in which political languages, practices and tools – together with political and governmental forms and institutions – grew and proved to be pivotal not just for Italy and its supposed singularity, but rather for the European continent as a whole. Thus, referring to the Renaissance as mainly a political phenomenon shows that the term can define and designate a complex concept of polity and political society. It is no longer limited – or not just limited – to a somewhat technical designation such as 'regional' or 'territorial' state, but is instead a more open-ended concept of structures of authority and power, of frames and patterns of politics.

Historiographical premises

The most recent historical debate in Italy still deals with the elusive puzzle of both the strength and the weakness of the Italian Renaissance political system. In order to put the Italian case study back into the European debate about the origins of the state, Italian scholars have had – and partially still have – to face two different but equally heavily weighted 'grand narratives'. Chronologically, the first of them to appear is what textbooks often refer to as 'the Italy of the cities': being built up during the nineteenth century in order to provide a legitimate historical ideology for the foundation of the newly acquired national identity, its stability is still mostly unchallenged.[1] The second narrative centres on Chabod's model of a 'Renaissance state' made by officials and institutions, which in the 1950s provided the first overall reading of late medieval–early modern Italy in order to draw a possible 'Italian way' to what was then usually defined the 'modern' state.[2]

---

[1] In 2004, John M. Najemy was still assuming that this was the nature of Renaissance Italy, devoting one paragraph of his 'Introduction' to the volume of the short Oxford history of Italy between 1300 and 1550 to 'A world of cities', in J. M. Najemy (ed.), *Italy in the Age of the Renaissance*, 1300–1550 (Oxford University Press, 2004), 3. On this 'grand narrative', see A. Gamberini, 'Principe, comunità e territori nel ducato di Milano. Spunti per una rilettura', *Quaderni Storici* 43 (2008), 243–65, now also in *Oltre le città. Assetti territoriali e culture aristocratiche nella Lombardia del tardo medioevo* (Rome: Viella, 2009), 29–51.

[2] F. Chabod, 'Y a-t-il un État de la Renaissance?' (1956), now in F. Chabod, *Scritti sul Rinascimento* (Turin: Einaudi, 1967), 604–23. To follow the development of this debate, see G. Chittolini, A. Molho and P. Schiera (eds.), *Origini dello stato. Processi di formazione statale in Italia fra Medioevo ed Età Moderna* (Bologna: Il Mulino, 1994; English version, J. Kirshner (ed.), *The Origins of the State in Italy: 1300–1600* (University of Chicago Press, 1996)).

Introduction

In the following decades, two turning points proved to be crucial to start moving forward from those 'grand narratives'. In the 1970s Elena Fasano Guarini and Giorgio Chittolini introduced into the Italian historiographical framework the dualist view of politics they borrowed from German constitutional history (von Gierke, Hintze, Brunner).[3] Both Fasano and Chittolini underlined that the polity developed a more effective regulatory policy not by absorbing or eliminating the scattered and various territorial powers deeply rooted throughout the country, but rather under the aegis of reciprocal pacts and agreements. The prince and the dominant city indeed exercised a discontinuous power over the territories submitted to their formal authority, directly dominating a fraction of them, but mostly ruling the complicated mixture of overlapping institutions that formed their dominions by mediating among different territorial bodies (be they rural communities, lords, subject cities or 'small states').[4]

Moreover, the debate on the origin of the state became lively all over Europe in the 1980s and 1990s, and some challenging research programmes within the frameworks of both the European Science Foundation[5] and the CNRS,[6] as well as a conference held in Chicago in 1993,[7] also provided important landmarks for Italian historiography.

Thus, in 1996, a conference devoted to the Florentine territorial state (in Italian, *Lo stato territoriale fiorentino (secoli XIV–XV). Ricerche, linguaggi, confronti*, translated into English, with a meaningful shift, as

---

[3] The three volumes of E. Rotelli and P. Schiera (eds.), *Lo stato moderno* (Bologna: Il Mulino, 1971–4), represented for Italian scholars a turning point in the crossing of these various historiographical traditions.

[4] G. Chittolini, *La formazione dello stato regionale e le istituzioni del contado* (Turin: Einaudi, 1979) (contributions appeared between 1976 and 1979), and 'Introduzione', in G. Chittolini (ed.), *La crisi degli ordinamenti comunali e le origini dello stato del Rinascimento* (Bologna: Il Mulino, 1979), vii–xl; E. Fasano Guarini, 'Introduzione', in E. Fasano Guarini (ed.), *Potere e società negli stati regionali italiani del '500 e '600* (Bologna: Il Mulino, 1978), 8–47. They resumed their respective theoretical approaches in G. Chittolini, 'Il "privato", il "pubblico", lo stato', in Chittolini, Molho and Schiera (eds.), *Origini*, 553–90, and E. Fasano Guarini, 'Centro e periferia, accentramento e particolarismi. Dicotomia sostanza degli Stati in età moderna?', *ibid.*, 147–76.

[5] See the collection: *The Origins of the Modern State in Europe, 13th to 18th Centuries*, 6 vols. (Oxford: Clarendon, 1994–9).

[6] J.-Ph. Genet and B. Vincent (eds.), *État et église dans la genèse de l'état moderne* (Madrid: Casa de Velasquez, 1986); J.-Ph. Genet (ed.), *Genèse de l'état moderne. Prélèvement et rédistribution* (Paris: CNRS, 1987); N. Coulet and J.-Ph. Genet (eds.), *L'état moderne. Le droit, l'espace et les formes de l'état* (Paris: CNRS, 1990); J.-Ph. Genet (ed.), *L'état modern. Genèse. Bilans et perspectives* (Paris: CNRS, 1990). But see also J.-Ph. Genet (ed.), *Culture et idéologie dans la genèse de l'état moderne* (Rome: École française de Rome, 1985).

[7] Kirshner (ed.), *The Origins*.

Florentine Tuscany: Structures and Practices of Power)[8] offered the opportunity to summarise some lines of research that were already at work here and there, orienting the analysis towards practices of power, factions and client networks, and informal relationships of influence and authority, of grace or service, and focusing the investigation on a whole world of various social bodies and political actors. Thus, the dynamic of state-building and governmental growth in late medieval Italy was more pactist than authoritarian, more reciprocal than vertical. In addition, it involved not only formalised forms of government and institutions, differing merely in scale and purpose, but also actors and practices that did not derive from the public sphere, for example, aristocratic clients or factions. This informal world faced the institutions, forming with them the *unicum* of politics.

Main themes

Firmly rooted in these questions, the following contributions witness a further historiographical evolution, multiplying the perspectives and approaching the more traditional themes in the light of a finer and more comprehensive concept of political power both pluralistic and enclosed by the prevailing institutional, ideological, discursive and communicative frameworks of the time. Freed by the long-lasting idea of the crucial role of cities as the trademark and cornerstone of the political history of Italy, the attention both to a broader range of political players (a real 'geography of power')[9] and to a wider multiplicity of available languages and practices allows the historian to investigate more effectively state-building in Renaissance Italy as a process generated – as summarised by John Watts in a more general framework – by 'pressure from below as well as design from above'.[10]

Given these premises, the volume considers Italy as a whole, aiming to avoid the mostly unconscious assumption that Renaissance Italy comes down to Florence, or Venice, or even Milan. The peninsula provides in fact a wide assortment of political entities that varied greatly in size, form

---

[8] A. Zorzi and W. Connell (eds.), *Lo stato territoriale fiorentino (secoli XIV–XV). Ricerche, linguaggi, confronti* (Pisa: Pacini, 2002; published in English as W. Connell and A. Zorzi (eds.), *Florentine Tuscany: Structures and Practices of Power* (Cambridge University Press, 2000)).

[9] Fasano Guarini, 'Centro e periferia', 156.

[10] J. Watts, *The Making of Polities: Europe, 1300–1500* (Cambridge University Press, 2009), 425. See also W. Blockmans, A. Holenstein and J. Mathieu (eds.), *Empowering Interactions: Political Cultures and the Emergence of the State in Europe 1300–1900* (Aldershot: Ashgate, 2009).

and power. All these territories and powers mutually acted together – not necessarily as perfectly integrated parts of a whole – and shared a huge range of political and ideological tools that they used creatively.

To this mosaic of territories and polities corresponds an even wider array of institutional and constitutional experiments: the political actors were not only 'states' whose authority was legally defined, but also all those that enjoyed even a fraction of political agency and expressed any sort of political culture. The 'state' to which the title refers thus is not reduced solely to duchies, kingdoms, republics, that is, the formal framework of authority and power: the emphasis lies instead on the mutual action of all the different political forces and the complex pattern of their negotiations. Change in political and institutional forms – and the substantial political and governmental growth of this age – may be driven by anybody in political society, and may arise from below or externally as well as from above or internally, according to the assumption that every political actor could elaborate and use creatively his/her own political logic.

This argument also implies that the range of themes and patterns considered in this volume will try to offer an account of the very different fields now investigated by Italian contemporary research on politics: the intersection of cities, rural communities, fiefs, lords and factions; the interweaving of politically and culturally different languages and practices of power; the creation of a shared communication network connecting powers and individuals; the development of a sophisticated system of public records, preserving a written memory in some sort of new political *ordre du discours*; the rise of new social orders based on increasingly rigid distinctions; the gender dimensions of politics and their problematic approaches to late medieval and early modern Italy; and so on. The overall time-scale will vary accordingly.

Dealing with such a definite emphasis on politics, the book will perhaps present the reader with some surprising absences: for instance, no contribution is devoted to humanism or art; but this list could be endless. Again, if some of the contributions do reciprocally relate one to another in harmony, not all of them will present the same – apparently reassuring – uniformity of thinking, and this is perhaps healthy.

Structure of the book

The book is divided into two sections. The first will provide an account of the political and social structure of the various Italian states, presenting an analytic survey of their history and nature in order to emphasise the complexity and variety of the Italian world and to try to provide a meaningful insight into the sometimes frantic and volatile sequence of events and institutional changes.

The second section will focus on structures and patterns, aiming to reveal the consonances and divergences of political languages and ideas, practices of power, territorial and non-territorial networks, governmental strategies and documentary growth. In this section, the aim of the book is to present the most recent and innovative Italian approach to a wide range of relevant topics on state-building, based both on a sophisticated analysis of the sources and on an updated view of traditional and less traditional historiographical fields such as the history of political and institutional frameworks, the history of medieval and early modern political thought, and the history of written communication as a cultural and a social fact. Each part brings together a wide thematic range of concise essays, with minimal footnotes and a carefully selected bibliography, both in English and in Italian, in order to enable English-language readers to follow up the main topics, but also to give them the opportunity for further reading if required.

Acknowledgements

We have benefited from the help of many people in working on this book. First of all, we are most grateful to all the friends and colleagues who improved the hard task of translating by offering – as Anglophones as well as historians – their precious advice: Frances Andrews, Stephen Bowd, Sam Cohn, Bill Connell, Trevor Dean, John Law and Christine Shaw. Moreover, our efforts have been greatly enhanced by Karen Anderson Howes, who copy-edited the volume. Special thanks also go to Edoardo Rossetti for the map. We have also been helped by a number of institutions, without whose support this book would not have been possible: we feel we owe a great debt to Enrico Decleva, Rettore of the University of Milan, and Giovanni Cannata, Rettore of the University of Molise; to Elio Franzini, former Preside of the Facoltà di Lettere, Milan, and Paolo Mauriello, Preside of the Facoltà di Scienze umane, storiche e sociali, Molise; to Grado Giovanni Merlo, Direttore of the Dipartimento di Scienze della storia e della documentazione storica, Milan, and Giorgio Patrizi, Direttore of the Dipartimento di Scienze umane, storiche e sociali, Molise.

Part I

The Italian states

1 The kingdom of Sicily

Fabrizio Titone

Introduction

The success of monarchical power in late medieval Sicily saw several different stages, characterised by different outcomes in the confrontation between king and country. The causes of these transformations in the political geography, as well as the differences and the institutional and economic elements of continuity and rupture, specifically over the fourteenth and fifteenth centuries, will be examined in this chapter.

Following the Aragonese conquest of 1282, a non-vertical relationship between king and country gradually took shape, in which the monarch acted as a co-ordinating force over different political actors endowed with jurisdiction. The establishment of a strong royal role was a gradual, and not always linear, process. It involved significant revisions to the initial ways of co-ordinating the different political forces, as experimented with by the kings. The absorption of Sicily into the crown of Aragon fostered an important circulation of different political cultures, without, however, obstructing the growth and development of distinctive experiences, favoured by the complete autonomy acquired by the region in 1296 and maintained until 1412.

The historiographic debate on late medieval Sicily has long been dominated by an interpretative model that has identified the baronage as uniquely capable of confronting the crown and influencing its actions, and has also judged that the island's economy was largely agricultural and chiefly grain-producing. This depiction of the role of the barons in particular derives from a reconstruction with origins in the studies of Rosario Gregorio (1805),[1] and which has long been upheld in successive studies. Among the more recent findings within this approach, and the most noteworthy, I should mention Henri Bresc's significant research, which has also allowed for a broadening of the analysis in many directions. Indeed, this scholar confirmed the lack of development of the

---

[1] Gregorio, *Considerazioni sopra la storia*.

Sicilian economy, linked to international relations, and the predominant role of the baronage, as well as its strong continuity from the end of the fourteenth century.[2]

Although dominant, this has not been the only interpretative model. A proposal that does not match the analytical paradigms outlined, and one which predates Bresc's, can be seen in the work of Illuminato Peri, with specific reference to the outcomes of the relationships between king and country, economic dynamism in the cities, and demographic calculations. In particular, a primary and important recognition emerges of the existence of different political actors in Sicily.[3] Stephan Epstein's research subsequently defined a new interpretative paradigm for Sicily, particularly highlighting economic characteristics which contradict the argument that the island was underdeveloped with a 'colonial' economy.[4] The image of the kingdom outlined by this and other research reveals a new attention to the urban world and the nature of the economy. Furthermore, it generally highlights an interweaving of common elements and specific characteristics in comparison with contemporary countries, and particularly the dominions of the crown of Aragon.[5]

Aragonese success and the role of the *universitates*

The kingdom of Sicily's position on the European political landscape changed drastically in the second half of the thirteenth century. The investiture of Sicily to Charles of Anjou by pope Urban IV in 1264 and his victory, in 1266, over king Manfred, son of Frederick II of

---

[2] Bresc, *Un monde*, which stands out for, among other things, its extraordinary analysis of notarial documentation. With regard to the nature of the Sicilian economy, Bresc's analysis was partially anticipated by other research, in particular that of Aymard, 'Il commercio dei grani'; and Abulafia, *The Two Italies*. It should be noted that, with regard to the Aragonese era, Abulafia recently emphasised economic, cultural and political contact rather than distinctions between north and south in Italy: Abulafia, 'Signorial power'.

[3] The first of Peri's studies which differentiates itself from the then prevailing paradigms dates back to 1956 ('Rinaldo'); this work was later republished in his book *Villani e cavalieri*. With regard to an initial recognition of more political individuals, see also Moscati, *Per una storia della Sicilia*.

[4] Epstein, *An Island*.

[5] See Mineo, *Nobilità*, with reference to the composition and possible reconfigurations of the political elites; and Titone, *Governments*, with regard to institutions and urban societies. It should be stressed that the recent interest in the urban milieu is characterised by very different research in terms of both findings and methodology; compare Titone, *Governments*, and Pace, *Il governo dei gentiluomini*. With regard to earlier work on the urban milieu, Baviera Albanese's important article, 'Studio introduttivo', should be mentioned. For the royal role, particularly under Martin I, see Corrao, *Governare*.

Hohenstaufen, signalled Sicily's entry into the Guelf league. The heirs of the Swabian aristocracy thus found a natural reference point in the Aragonese court, whose expansionist policies in the Mediterranean created a strong antagonism with the house of Anjou.

The exiles' action suggests that the anti-Angevin revolt known as the Vespers, which broke out in Palermo on 31 March 1282, was preceded by a period of waiting and expectation. Nevertheless, an independent development of the Vespers cannot be ruled out given the immediate establishment, on the day following the revolt, of the *commune civitatis Panormi* and the nomination of certain officials (captains). From the start, the aim was to give momentum to the uprising and its organisation through a confederative plan with Corleone, an inland centre in western Sicily with a strategic role in terms of geographical position and economic production. The plan is of particular interest both for the economic choices made, such as the fiscal exemption for the *cives* in both centres, and for the references to officials and eminent citizens (*probi viri*) who signed it.[6] The organisational structure of the magistracies and the practice of broadening the decision-making base to include individuals outside the ruling class indicate the existence of urban governments capable of both controlling and fanning the flames of the insurrection. In the confederative strategy it is possible to see an attempt to support the economic growth of the Sicilian cities. From the first half of the fourteenth century onwards, this process is more generally confirmed by the gradual control assumed by some large and medium-sized centres over places closest to them and economically most useful (*districtus*).

Like Palermo, other centres also gave themselves leadership through the appointment of captains and other officials. The insurrection was extended from the *commune civitatis Panormi* to the *commune Siciliae*.[7] The dynastic answer from Aragon took shape at the same time, as demonstrated by the rapid involvement of Peter III of Aragon: by 20 August 1282 Peter III was already landing at Trapani. Following a complex diplomatic move and an analysis of the forces in play, and counting on the support of the Sicilian and Iberian nobility, he had decided to intervene. On 4 September, at Palermo, he was elected king by the representatives of the *universitates*, that is, the legally recognised communities.

Peter III responded swiftly to the fall of Angevin dominance: the king established an articulated governmental structure of royal officials, thus

---

[6] Starrabba and Tirrito (eds.), *Assise e consuetudini*.
[7] Bresc, *Un monde*, II, 713–14.

bringing fundamental resources under his control, ratified town elections and appointed royal magistrates to take charge of local government. Managing these officials became the king's principal means of formalising relationships of loyalty and establishing a new network of those loyal to him, consolidating fiscal and legal instruments of control, and searching for balance between the representation of Sicilians and that of non-Sicilians. In this regard, the Aragonese dynasties were characterised by particularly cautious and balanced choices, mindful of developing the forces present on the island without disappointing the expectations of the conquest's Iberian supporters. The structure of offices in certain cases mirrored that of the Angevin and Normano-Swabian periods. The prerogatives of some officials would subsequently be redefined and new positions would be instituted, particularly during the reigns of Frederick III (1296–1337), Martin I (1392–1409), Alfonso V (1416–58) and John II (1458–79).

Among the royal magistrates, justiciars responsible for criminal jurisdiction (*giustizieri*) should at least be mentioned. During the reign of Peter III, jurisdictional districts corresponded in part to the old administrative regions of the Muslim period (val di Mazara, val Demone, val di Noto), and these were partly subdivided.[8] The jurisdictional districts were made gradually smaller over the first half of the fourteenth century until they corresponded with urban centres.

Following the Vespers revolt, local political vitality represented one of the most significant aspects of the transformation: urban centres very frequently appointed their own officials and, in some cases, captains, whose competencies varied and who controlled the city elections from the start. The hopes of the urban milieu found in the king an accessible interlocutor, who was also careful to avoid risking conflict: besides confirming the position of the elected, one of the king's first acts was to control the captains. More generally, one of the most distinctive aspects of the urban milieu, which would strengthen over the following decades, was already emerging during this phase. This is the existence of a significant institutional variety, corresponding to different socio-economic contexts, which can be seen both in the different magistracies in operation and in the variety of criteria for appointment.

Although the dynastic change of 1282 is part of the renewed international polarisation of the Guelf–Ghibelline struggle, the stakes in the conflict between the court of Aragon and that of Anjou were greater control of the Mediterranean area. The protagonists of the Vespers revolt

---

[8] Silvestri (ed.), *De Rebus Regni Siciliae*, provides a rich source of information for these years.

were the *universitates* and those heirs of the Swabian aristocracy still present and in contact with the exiles' front line. Peter III did not disappoint the expectations of the *universitates*, which immediately sought to gain important margins of autonomy, but he did simultaneously restore a structure of royal offices, thus ensuring his control over the territory.

Economic policy and reconstituting the aristocratic framework

In 1285 the key figures in the Mediterranean zone changed simultaneously: the deaths of Peter III, Charles of Anjou and pope Martin IV reopened the conflict. Peter III had established a separation of the two crowns, setting aside the Iberian succession for his son Alfonso and Sicilian rule for his second-born, James, king of Sicily from 1286. In reality the international power balances made control of Sicily difficult for the house of Aragon.

Alfonso III, who died in 1291, had supported the separation, marking out his brothers as his successors, James in Aragon and Frederick in Sicily. In 1291, however, James II took both crowns and returned to Aragon, naming Frederick his lieutenant and viceroy in Sicily. This decision significantly reduced Sicilian expectations. The rupture between the court of Aragon and the Sicilians was sanctioned in 1295: with the ratification of the treaty of Anagni, James II surrendered Sicily to the Angevins. The disparity between the treaty and Sicilian expectations was now too great, and in the parliament of Catania, on 15 January 1296, Frederick was elected Frederick III, king of Sicily. This gave the kingdom of Sicily complete autonomy. Members of the new Catalan and Aragonese political class also took part in the parliament of Catania. Their presence demonstrates that there was scope to maintain a dialogue with the crown of Aragon. This dialogue intensified over the following decades and had important economic and institutional effects, which I will discuss shortly.

The crushing defeats encountered by the Sicilian fleet were probably the cause of a new political strategy whose outcome was the peace treaty of Caltabellotta of 29 August 1302: Sicily was to be reunited with the continent following the death of Frederick, who had taken the title *rex Trinacriae*. In reality, Sicily would not have returned to the Angevins, but the peace treaty of 1302 eased the pressure from the house of Anjou and guaranteed the island, and the new Catalan merchants, better political stability facing Barcelona. Caltabellotta allowed Sicily to interact, in a peaceful context, with the other countries of the crown of Aragon and to benefit from the vast economic circuit promoted by them.

The Aragonese kings intervened significantly in reconstituting the structure of the aristocracy. Indeed, the political transition of 1282 had driven forward a demand to reform the aristocratic framework. On their coronation days, James II and Frederick III installed 400 and 300 knights respectively, and, through the enactment of the laws *Si aliquem* of 1286 and *Volentes* of 1298, they initiated a new feudal constitution and opened up a market in feudal property.[9] In 1286 a dramatic broadening of the capacity to inherit was sanctioned, and in 1298 the principle of alienability was introduced to all types of feudal land-holding, also allowing the possibility of its division. The principal rationale behind this policy was the economic yield guaranteed to the crown through increased mobility of fiefs.[10] At the same time, the royal court appears to have undervalued the significant opportunity gained by the aristocracy to appreciably increase their own dominions as well as their military might. This issue was to emerge dramatically over the following years and profoundly altered the balance of power in the kingdom.

At the same time, the interventions in the structure of the aristocracy triggered a gradual differentiation within the hierarchy: in the wide circle of beneficiaries, those with the title of count were set strongly apart from the rest. With regard to appointments made by Frederick III, the following are of particular note: investiture of the county of Modica to Manfredi Chiaromonte, to whom the king also gave civil and criminal jurisdiction over his dominions; of the county of Adernò to Matteo Sclafani; and of the county of Geraci to Francesco Ventimiglia.[11] The exceptional jurisdictional privilege given to Chiaromonte leads to the identification of a significant difference in the balance of power between king and the high aristocracy compared with the decades that followed. Indeed, large royal concessions such as these to seigneurial dynasties became more frequent from the middle of the fourteenth century, and scope for intervention by the feudal lords became increasingly free of the king's control.

A central piece of political evidence regarding Aragonese domination concerns the fact that the relationship between king and country did not correspond to a vertical policy, instead following a Catalan style of government (*pactismo*) which spread progressively through the lands conquered by the crown. On the one hand, this strategy for government was applied to the different countries, and on the other hand it proved capable of adapting to the different political situations in the various

---

[9] Testa (ed.), *Capitula regni Siciliae*. [10] Mineo, *Nobilità*, 110–11.
[11] For an analysis of the title of count and a detailed list of the counties in Sicily from 1282 to 1392, see Bresc, *Un monde*, II, 808–15.

countries. This style of government would be comprehensively adopted from the end of the fourteenth century, but it already formed an important part of the governmental strategy of the Aragonese kings during the reigns of James II and Frederick III. An analysis of economic policy reveals significant elements: in this phase, the foundations were laid for financial and fiscal policies that were unusual in many ways. In 1286, James II provided for a series of economic guarantees benefiting the *universitates* and the feudal lords, emphasising the way in which these laws were different from the Angevin policies. Also in 1286, he rationalised requests for financial contributions, distinguishing them by purpose.[12] This differentiation would be upheld until the 1460s (the reign of John II).

In general, from the 1320s both indirect and direct taxation increased, due to economic stagnation and declining population levels. Shortly after this, the crown felt obliged to alienate parts of its lands: this action was to be the beginning of a consolidation of important powers, those belonging to the counts, which was to define the balance of the kingdom during the second half of the fourteenth century. From the reign of Frederick III, indirect taxation of the *universitates* increased, with a distinction between central and local government taxes. One of the principal characteristics of the tax system was the possibility of changing the administrator of taxable goods, between the king and the city, a flexibility which would be consolidated over the following decades until it became a central part of the administration of the system of indirect taxes (*gabelle*). Furthermore, from the early fifteenth century, sharing profits of the same imposts became widespread, which made possible rapid and incisive reconfigurations in the possession of revenue according to royal and/or local government need.

In the case of the greatest urban need, sometimes the *gabelle* in force were not sufficient. In these cases, the communities imposed new taxes, including direct taxation, which generally differed according to the people's ability to contribute. The *universitates* could propose direct taxation, but it was the king's responsibility to identify the means of contributions, that is whom and how much to tax. Local governments, then, shared in the decision-making process related to taxation: it was the beginning of a process which would see the cities take on a central role in this sphere.

With reference to urban institutions, Frederick III increased the involvement of the cities in the nomination of local officials and their

---

[12] See, in particular, Testa (ed.), *Capitula*, capitulum XIII, I, 11, and Epstein, *An Island*, 59.

prerogatives. The expansion, in 1309, of the role of the jurats (*giurati*), officials already active in the Swabian period, is the main piece of evidence for this.[13] At the same time he determined that not only officials, but also *caeteri homines* should intervene in local government when the nature of royal mandates required it. At a prescriptive level, the king specified the function of the *homines* deemed worthy of representing the community as a whole, a rule which clearly seems to be a response to growing political confrontation. The governmental body in which these figures operated was soon to be known as the civic council (*consilium civium*). During the reign of Frederick III, the council gradually came to intervene in extraordinary economic policy: a fact that reveals an extension of the 1309 directive. The council began to develop a governing role not only with regard to royal measures, but also in urban politics.[14] More generally, the widespread unrest at local level during these years is demonstrated by the fact that customary documents (private laws) were drawn up by many communities.[15] Nevertheless, the boundaries between local and royal officials remained defined; criminal jurisdiction and financial administration of the crown's wealth remained the latter's prerogative.

From the early fourteenth century, royal policy was characterised by an intense negotiation with the kingdom: the interventions by James II and Frederick III appear to respond to requests from different actors endowed with jurisdiction rather than simply being the result of unilateral decisions. Frederick III, like James II before him, identified a need to pursue the reconstitution of the aristocratic elites, who had been decimated by dynastic change; at the same time Frederick III promoted important normative reforms in response to political unrest in the cities.

Demographic values

According to a strong historiographic tradition, the underdevelopment of southern Italy has its origins in the medieval period. In particular it is claimed that the south's economy was agricultural and predominantly grain-producing from the twelfth century, whereas the economy of the north relied on manufacturing.[16] Trade took place between an 'advanced' area exporting fabrics, the north, and a 'backward' area exporting grain, the south. But this historical reconstruction leaves several problems unresolved.

[13] Testa (ed.), *Capitula*, capitulum CXVI, I, 106–9.
[14] Titone, *Governments*, 17–41.
[15] Peri, *La Sicilia*, 20–1, and Mineo, *Nobilità*, 53–8.
[16] See n. 2.

Studies that support the theory of economic dualism have been useful in alerting us to important series of documents, but in reconstructing the nature of the island's economy they have given greater weight to foreign trade. Grain exports have been considered as the basis of the island's trade policy. On the one hand this scholarship has insufficiently valued the production of grain for the internal market, and on the other it has seen the peaks in exportation as constant, whereas in reality these peaks corresponded to well-contained phases.[17] Indeed, the long-term tendency reveals that foreign trade of grain was not more than 15 per cent of internal production.[18]

By contrast, Epstein has highlighted the central role of manufacturing in the island's economy, the character, advanced in many cases, of the agricultural economy, and the impossibility of considering the south, and specifically Sicily, as an undifferentiated economy. In the middle of the fourteenth century, demographic collapse meant that land unsuited to farming staple crops was converted to a more appropriate and intensive production. This triggered a crucial transformation of the island economy. Moreover, the specialisation of cultivation was aided by the redistribution of revenue, benefiting peasants and wage-labourers. This process contributed to an increase in the demand for consumer goods.[19]

Although the issue is still a controversial one,[20] this analysis clearly presupposes the existence, at the end of the thirteenth century, of significant population levels that would make plausible both the need for the people to turn to more appropriate farming methods and the productive efficiency of the work force involved, even after the losses during the Black Death. It is appropriate, therefore, to look more closely at the reconstructions of demographic data, which have been subject to different analyses.

Epstein's work builds upon Peri's important research on medieval Sicily. Although Epstein's and Peri's calculations differ, they do not contradict each other both because the densities each reconstructs are not irrelevant, and in terms of the demographic fluctuations they identify. For Sicily, there are no data on the relationship between taxation and the number of hearths (family units) taxed, unlike other peninsular parts of the kingdom in the same period. Peri puts forward some figures for the years 1276–7 and 1277–8. Basing these on a rate per hearth

---

[17] Bresc, *Un monde*, I, 523–57, and also Corrao, *Governare*, 84–5.
[18] Epstein, *An Island*, 275.   [19] *Ibid.*, 270–91.
[20] Corrao, 'Uomini d'affari', raises again, albeit in a less decisive way, the dualist theory. This return to the classic dualist paradigm is clearly confirmed by the fact that Corrao does not refer to Epstein's research in his reconstruction of the island's commercial relationships.

recorded for Conversano in the Terra di Bari region of two *tarí* and 15.1/2 *grani* in 1276–7 and of three *tarí* and 5.1/2 *grani* in 1278–9, and attributing to each hearth during those years an average of 3.5–4 people, Peri calculates the Sicilian population for the given years as 567,567–648,648 and 568,675–650,000 individuals respectively.[21] This is the most convincing study of the Sicilian population at the end of the thirteenth century to date.

Moving to later calculations, Bresc puts the population for 1270–80 at around 400,000 units, while Epstein puts this at 850,000 individuals, although both take an average of 4–5 people per family unit. Their opinions clearly differ with regard to the tax per hearth, and their analyses stem from the fiscal declaration of 1277. Bresc considers it more correct to base his calculations on an average rate of six *tarí*, because this, unlike the rate of three, allows for demographic development without excessive margins.[22] His work does not, however, address certain elements, particularly that a high form of taxation appears to contradict Aragon's fiscal policy, which was explicitly more moderate than the Angevins'. Moreover, Bresc estimates losses due to the Great Plague at around 18 per cent, a percentage improbably below the general European average. By contrast, Epstein puts the rate of *tarí* at 3, based on comparisons with the Angevin period and with the reign of Martin (a comparison of very different periods in themselves). Furthermore, he calculates a decrease in population due to the Black Death of 60 per cent.[23] The radical difference in their estimates, including that of losses in the middle of the fourteenth century, results in calculations for this phase that are not dissimilar. Nor do they differ much from Peri's, who calculates 240,000–300,000 people in 1374–6.[24] Bresc and Epstein agree both for the 1430s, when demographic recovery began and population was around 300,000 units, and for the 1460s when it strengthened and grew to 400,000–500,000 units.[25] It is widely held that the greatest concentration of population was consistently found in the demesnial centres.

The sources available, particularly for the end of the thirteenth century, inevitably render demographic calculations uncertain. This

---

[21] Peri, *Uomini*, 244–51, particularly 246–7. Peri puts forward variable estimates for the number of hearths: Peri, *La Sicilia*, 242; Peri, *Restaurazione*, 79.
[22] Bresc, *Un monde*, I, 59–77, particularly 60 on estimates for certain centres before 1277.
[23] Epstein, *An Island*, 33–74. Peri, *La Sicilia*, 246, believes that the losses rose to almost 50 per cent of the population.
[24] Peri, *La Sicilia*, 235–46.
[25] For this phase Peri does not offer detailed calculations, and he places the beginning of recovery from 1434–9: Peri, *Restaurazione*, 66–9.

uncertainty can undoubtedly be reduced by looking at data relating to the phase following the Black Death, which sees greater agreement among scholars. There is no reason to consider that losses were far less in Sicily than those documented in other European states.

The crisis of royal power and the government of the vicars

From the moment Frederick III revealed his unwillingness to surrender the island to the Angevins, the peace of Caltabellotta could not guarantee a solution to the conflict. The nomination of Peter II as co-regent in 1322 (he would reign from 1337 to 1342) indicated the will to ensure dynastic continuity in the kingdom. However, this show of strength against the house of Anjou did not correspond to a royal role that was quite as stable on the island, which would soon be subject to attack by the seigneurial dynasties.

From the 1340s, the balance of the kingdom began to be seriously called into question due to an increasingly weak royal *potestas* and the territorial expansion of the counts' powers. In 1342, Louis succeeded Peter II. However, his young age meant that Peter's brother, duke John, became his regent until 1348. The young age of both Louis and his brother Frederick further damaged the credibility of the royal role. The parliamentary assembly which acclaimed Frederick IV king (1355–77) reflected a divided kingdom: many of the barons and representatives of the demesnial cities were absent. Those years in particular saw a deep economic crisis which continued until the early fifteenth century and was due, as in other European states, to the decline in the seigneurial nobility's revenue which began in the 1330s. This crisis sparked a civil war within the aristocracy which took place between the 1330s and the early 1360s. This resulted in very serious economic damage and caused the collapse of the island's trading system. The most powerful exponents of the aristocracy began to extend their control over the royal demesne, and the region soon fell under their dominion. The great barons managed to control the king with the help of fickle alliances.[26]

In this phase too, control over the king appears to be a fundamental element in the success of those who exercised it: royal *dignitas* legitimised the aristocratic faction protecting the king, showing that royal power had not been completely divested. Frederick's interventions, during the second half of the 1350s, relating to elections in demesnial centres and the exclusion of representatives of the seigneurial nobility, are emblematic

---

[26] D'Alessandro, *Politica*, 92–8.

of this point.[27] Due to poor documentation it is impossible to ascertain the efficacy of these bans, often invalidated by Frederick IV himself with concessions of offices in the cities granted to seigneurial exponents, but it reveals that the king still had some room for intervention at that time. Nevertheless, from the beginning of the 1360s the principal families of counts obtained full control over demesnial revenue, upsetting the pre-existing balance and formalising the island's political and economic rupture.[28] On the death of the king, government of the kingdom was entrusted, at the king's wish, to Artale I Alagona, appointed vicar at the queen's side. It is well known that Alagona preferred to share control with other great barons of equal powers: Manfredi III Chiaromonte, Francesco II Ventimiglia and Guglielmo Peralta.

In general, the government in feudal dominions, even before 1377, was characterised by a reduction in the powers exercised by local officials, due to a greater interventionism on the part of the seigneurial aristocracy, and by the *dominus*'s economic control over revenue. In the feudal dominions, there was no subdivision of the administration of *gabelle*, although this was present in demesnial areas in the first half of the fourteenth century.[29] Based on rare references in documentation for the feudal communities, as well as on indirect comparisons, we know that the *dominus* was considered a tyrant because of his indifference to the common good. Due to the territorial division, on the other hand, the vicars could not guarantee any continuation of trade, causing a slowdown in economic development. Unlike royal policy, vicarial policy was characterised by a significant weakening of the means of subjects' sharing in the government's actions. Gradually, the systems of royal rights and privileges obtained by the communities over the preceding decades were sharply reduced. The vicars were authoritarian in their style of government. They promoted an economic policy geared to hoarding as much as possible and, in the short term, to counterbalancing the crisis of landed revenues, a decision which would soon erode their estates from within.

However, in those years an important change in international balance was recorded: the peace treaty of Naples (1372) resolved the conflict with the Angevins, but vicarial success inevitably reduced the positive effects of this conclusive peace-making treaty.

The vast territorial size of the seigneurs' dominions, associated with their revenue crisis, inevitably caused a polarisation in the clash between crown and magnates. In 1377, a completely distinctive phase in the

---

[27] Cosentino, *Codice*, 165–7, 211–12, 227, 288, 1356.
[28] D'Alessandro, *Politica*, 99, 109–11.   [29] Titone, *Governments*, 41–8.

history of the kingdom of Sicily began: the island was divided into four territories each controlled by a different seigneural 'court', a situation that would soon prove unsustainable.

The restoration of Martin I and the personal union of the crowns

Peter IV of Aragon resolved the interregnum, putting forward the Infante Martin, son of his second-born, the duke of Montblanch, as the ideal husband for Maria, daughter of Frederick IV and heiress to Sicily. Following Peter's death in 1387, Martin of Montblanch became the architect of the reconquest of the island kingdom. This began in 1392 with the coronation of his son as Martin I, king of Sicily.

There is strikingly little documentary evidence available from the years 1377–92. This is probably the result of the bloody clashes between Martin I of Sicily and the coalitions of barons. Among the indirect references, Martin I's statement in 1402 is particularly important as it reports that during the period of the vicars the law nevertheless continued to be regularly applied.[30] The different courts active between 1377 and 1392 in fact kept control of the territories under their jurisdiction. This is a significant statement because it was made by the man who sanctioned the end of the vicarial regime, by the king who reasserted his power but not in a situation of anarchy.

The duke of Montblanch and Martin I predicted that their establishment on the island would not be too difficult thanks to intense diplomatic work carried out previously by the duke. On the arrival of the Catalan army, support for the royal party from the demesnial cities and the homage paid by many of the barons, as well as the rapid elimination of possible supporters of opposition, seemed to show that Montblanch had good reason to be optimistic.[31] Until the close of the century at least, however, the Sicilian aristocracy put up strenuous resistance, the purpose of which was to safeguard their own positions. The unexpected political scene caused a significant change in the royal role: the king ceased attempting to rule Sicily by co-ordinating minor and major lords, and focused instead on choosing some individuals to set above others (following a divide-and-rule policy). This process took place at the same time as an intensification of the dialogue between the king and those parts of the kingdom which were in favour of him.

---

[30] Testa (ed.), *Capitula*, capitulum LVII, I, 177.
[31] Corrao, *Governare*, 74–88, 92–7.

In 1395, Martin of Montblanch came to the Aragonese throne: his coronation signalled a strengthening of the ties between Sicily and Barcelona. This year marked the beginning of a second series of rebellions. The conflict resulted in a complete victory for the king, the breaking up of the landed estates of the counts, and a transferral of aristocratic assets, thus significantly altering the composition of the Sicilian ruling class. The profound change during these years saw Iberian nobles and new Sicilian aristocrats constituting the framework of this renewed Sicilian aristocracy. This new distribution of power would essentially be maintained until the middle of the sixteenth century.[32] At the same time, the king welcomed numerous petitions from the cities, the purpose of which was to restore the balance of power distribution. In this phase, concessions relating to land did not decrease, but the aim was to avoid territorial concentrations. This was in line with the sanctions of the 1398 parliament of Syracuse, which in many ways constituted a rise of the urban milieu in royal politics. In this regard, it should be stressed that during the reign of Martin I the typical parliamentary institution of Catalan origins became established, albeit only after the parliament of 1446 which, as I will show, was evidence of the division of the parliamentary body into branches.

From an economic viewpoint, the political rupture of the vicarial period had caused the crisis in the trade system, which saw a dramatic slowdown in the island's economic growth. From the end of the fourteenth century, however, the situation turned around, and the royal court took full control of the territory and the co-ordination of the different political actors. This process was consolidated in the first half of the fifteenth century. In 1398, Martin I re-established control over the grain trade and eliminated all taxation on exporting grain and other food products by sea from one part of Sicily to another.[33] This decree 'was in fact probably as important as political reunification for establishing a more integrated regional grain market'.[34] At the same time, full stabilisation of relations with Barcelona had revitalised economic relations: this period saw a strong influx of woollen fabrics from Catalonia into Sicily, and an intensification of the different Sicilian exports (grain, cotton, sugar, saltpetre, etc.) to the Catalan principality.

In 1410, Martin I died. In line with his will, the island throne passed to the king of Aragon, according to the principle of personal union. The kings of Aragon always considered their dominions as different entities,

[32] Cancila, *Baroni*, 117–38.
[33] Testa (ed.), *Capitula*, *Capitulum* XIII, I, 145, and *Capitulum* XLI, I, 155, respectively.
[34] Epstein, *An Island*, 141.

in which each country maintained its own legal autonomy. Actual union, created by the fusion of legal autonomies, did not occur: royal policy continued to remain open to differing expectations on the part of the various dominions. With the death of Martin of Aragon, in 1410, the long continuity witnessed by the royal family faded. With the compromise of Caspe in 1412, the dynastic crisis was resolved: the regent of Castile, Ferdinand of Antequera of the house of Trastámara, son of John I of Castile and Eleanor, daughter of Peter III of Aragon, was elected to the throne of Aragon. This election signalled the end of the Catalan influence over the crown of Aragon.[35] Ferdinand confirmed the personal union between the two crowns, and, on his coronation as king of Sicily, the gradual shift towards the governing institute of viceroy on the island began. This was defined by the election of Alfonso V in 1416. Institutional evolution, from kingdom to viceroyalty, did not signal a limitation of the system of island rights and privileges, which, on the contrary, expanded over the following decades through an increase in the confrontation between the royal court and the kingdom.

The rebellion of members of the seigneurial aristocracy had obliged the king to undertake a drastic selection process which appreciably modified the aristocratic framework. The resolution of the conflict in favour of royal authority put in place the necessary conditions for stabilising the structures of the market, guaranteeing a trading network vital for the island's economy and consolidating a policy of negotiation with the kingdom of Aragon. Although the institutional changes following the compromise of Caspe reduced the expectations of autonomy, they found an early and powerful compensation in Ferdinand I's confirmation of the personal union of the crowns.

The outcomes of the confrontation between king and country in the fifteenth century

During Alfonso's long reign and also the reign of John II, processes which had been in play for some time, but had initially been slowed by the royal institutional crisis, were consolidated. The inevitable conflict between the crown and the magnates from the end of the fourteenth century caused a profound weakening of the aristocracy: although in the second half of the fourteenth century the main players in the political balance of power were the magnates, in the fifteenth century this balance was determined by the relationships between the crown and the demesnial communities.

---

[35] Hillgarth, *The Spanish Kingdoms*, 229–38.

Already during the reign of Martin I, but in particular from the reign of Alfonso V, the *universitates* were able to systematically exploit relations with the king, exercising leverage over royal financial and fiscal policies. From Martin I to John II, the royal system of taxation relied only in part on direct taxation: the principal sources of revenue came from indirect taxes and, during Alfonso's reign, from the alienation of demesnial goods.

The increasing fiscal pressure by the king had important institutional and economic effects, which favoured the urban milieu. Economic needs also increased because of the conquest of Naples (1442–3), preparation for which began in 1435. From the earliest years of his reign, and although financial pressure was intensifying, Alfonso V allowed the local governments to decide what forms of taxation to implement and how to collect them. The local system of taxation was largely based on farming of indirect taxes. The centrality of these farms is evidence of the methods of consolidating the local debt, due, in large part, to the advance sale of the right to collect taxes. The sale could be decided not on the basis of the true value of the goods, but on the amount of money the community needed. This process may be seen as anticipating the economic policy of John II. Moreover, this complete autonomy in decisions regarding fiscal revenues saw the growth of proportional and direct taxes.

The fact that the country's political balance depended on the relationship between the king and the *universitates* can be particularly seen in the temporary sale of the latter to feudal lords ordinarily excluded from access to the resources of the demesnial centres. The alienations of the fifteenth century were radically different to those of the fourteenth century: the centres managed to rejoin the royal demesne, obtaining important benefits which had few equals in ordinary political phases. The integration of the market was achieved mainly through exemptions from the *dohana* (duty on trade), obtained, in many cases, by the communities as royal compensation for having consented to the alienation of the *universitates*. With regard to governmental structure of offices, many alienated communities, having rejoined the royal demesne, received the privilege of holding both tribunal courts (*privilegium fori*) and appellate courts for civil and often criminal cases. This process coincided with an unprecedented growth, from the reign of Martin onwards, of graduates in law. This complication of the institutional framework was favoured by social change brought about by the presence of legal experts. The king also very frequently decided to sell the office of captain, the highest royal magistracy in the cities from the middle of the fourteenth century, on whom devolved criminal jurisdiction. Control of this office was sold to representatives of the cities. In general, that Alfonso's policy favoured local autonomy is also evidenced by the concession of the possibility of suspending royal measures, believed to be detrimental to cities' rights, and by the consultation with the king before these were carried out. This step is reminiscent of similar systems in Catalonia, Aragon and Valencia.[36]

As said earlier, significant integration of the regional market was achieved in Sicily through toll franchises during Alfonso's time. It should be added that Alfonso promoted an attempt at interregional integration as well through concessions of toll franchises to some communities on the mainland (Reggio, Scilla, Gaeta and Capua, as well as the Lipari island and Ischia). This policy did not continue after Alfonso's death. The few southern communities that had been granted franchises and the fairly small amount of trade affected do not make it possible to state that a 'common market' had been established among the lands of the crown of Aragon.[37] Nonetheless, the launch of a policy for interregional market integration is evidence of Alfonso's willingness to co-ordinate the territories of the Aragonese crown.

As with other countries of the crown, in Sicily, too, parliamentary activity was particularly important: a *donativum* (donation) was voted in the parliament in return for approval of particular petitions. The functioning of this institution was based on a solid royal *potestas*, capable of co-ordinating the different representatives of the three 'branches' (ecclesiastic, aristocratic and demesnial) and interacting with them. Besides a strengthening of royal authority following the conquest of Naples, the intensification of parliamentary activity from 1446 onwards reveals Sicily's desire to find ways of receiving benefits in exchange for the generous economic contributions it bestowed: the petitions that accompanied the voting of a *donativum* were part of a contractual relationship between king and country, which had been traditional and strongly consolidated.

It is argued that parliament's actions responded to a strategy of local control of the king's activity. However, at the same time, negotiations in the parliament are believed to have been inefficient, given the renewal of requests which, although certainly heard, were not upheld by the king. The contradictory nature of this evidence may be resolved by stating that parliamentary negotiation was a screen for concealing a dramatic change brought about by the birth of a new fiscal system entirely administered at

---

[36] Titone, *Governments*, 123–6.
[37] Del Treppo, *I mercanti catalani*, 600–5, maintains that Alfonso succeeded in establishing a 'common market' among the lands of the crown of Aragon.

the local level.[38] In reality, it must be emphasised that local intervention in the fiscal system dates back to the early years of Alfonso's reign. It was the result of a royal policy crucial to maintaining balance in the country, which thus avoided contrasts in the allocation of requested economic support. The procedure of paying a *donativum* therefore acknowledged a well-consolidated custom. The possible renewal of requests and their lack of application do not point to inefficiency of negotiations, but are a characteristic aspect of the contractual relationship, and in particular of its many applications: renewal of requests constituted significant pressure on royal politics, leading to gradual modifications or, more significantly, to the adoption of new strategies. One of the principal requests put forward in the parliament of 1446 regarded the alienability of demesnial goods considered as a whole (therefore including offices). As the rest of the documentation relative to those years proves, however, the reason for the request was the sale of the *universitates*. This petition was not stringently upheld, although two points should be noted: from 1446 the sale of the communities collapsed,[39] and sales of the royal office of captain increased, due, in the majority of cases, to requests from the cities or their coalitions. Clearly, the petition of 1446 in favour of the inalienability of the royal demesne could do nothing but consider it *in toto*, since the sale of parts of it did not contradict the cities' autonomy. It was, then, a change in the strategy of alienation: the king preferred to increase the sales of the office of captain, thus *de facto* losing control over the principal royal office in the cities. The actions of parliament played an important role in this change.

The role and the structure of parliament's actions provide clear evidence of the existence of standard practices in government similar to those in the different countries of the crown of Aragon: the adoption of a non-vertical strategy of government, however, saw different applications in different contexts. The circulation of different political cultures, which has led historians to affirm the creation of a common identity within the crown of Aragon, did not lose its pronounced pluralistic character.[40] In Sicily, a significant characteristic of the possible

---

[38] See Pasciuta, *Placet regie maiestati*, 208–31, 245–50, particularly 217 on the strategy of control over the king, 245 on the inefficiency of negotiation, 247 on the fiscal system administered at local level.

[39] Bresc, *Un monde*, II, 857, identifies only the sale of Naro in 1453. The 1446 session of parliament is in Testa, *Capitula*, I, 333–58.

[40] Evangelisti, *I Francescani*, asserts the existence of a common identity, with particular reference to economic practices, to which the cohesive attitude of Franciscan representatives in the activities of royal government decisively contributed. This is a wide-ranging interpretative suggestion which needs, however, to be counterbalanced

outcomes of the confrontation between king and demesnial communities concerns the case of the failed application of a royal privilege due to the stabilisation of new local balances, and without royal involvement. More specifically, the regulations of the margins of autonomy of local governments were not always the result of a top-down process; they could be the result of actions from below or, in some cases, actions independent of royal intervention. The institutional differences appeared to strengthen: the local governments altered the magistracies' prerogatives, as well as the nomination criteria, according to their own needs. This continued throughout the reign of John II when, particularly in the small and medium-sized centres, institutional experimentation increased.[41] From Alfonso V's reign, the civic council was strengthened due to considerable involvement of representatives belonging to different taxable socio-professional groups. The civil council decided autonomously which taxes to collect, and, in particular, on cases of indirect taxation when ordinary revenue was not sufficient. The involvement of all of the key players of the urban economy, both small and large, had a further projection in the decision-making process, creating and maintaining open access to the government. In this context, the frequent attempts at closure by some urban coalitions were unsuccessful: the king himself offered his mild support to the majority parties, since he was interested in maintaining a broad agreement with all of the potential contributors.

Even though the second half of the fifteenth century has not been studied in great depth, it is possible to put forward a general hypothesis. Royal openness to political competition did not fade during John II's reign, when the councils' intervention was also maintained. Openness towards feudal communities is also attested, although the *domini* gained control over collective meetings in 1460.[42] The royal concession of 1460 clearly did not signal a new political direction, but it is indicative of a first act of openness to the feudal lords who had seen their scope for intervention reduced. In general, during John II's reign the non-vertical relationship between king and country was maintained, and royal decisions certainly did not conflict with pre-existing equilibria, with the urban communities firmly in a position of power. John II particularly favoured the urban milieu with his concession that cities should be

---

with a concrete analysis of royal economic policies, characterised, in reality, by a profound gap between theoretical intentions and normal practice.

[41] As an initial survey, carried out by the author, on the institutions and urban society in the reign of John II shows.

[42] Testa (ed.), *Capitula, Capitulum* LXIV, I, 464.

exempt from direct taxation. However, due to an increase in revenue from the grain and silk trades, he was able to avoid alienating the property of the crown.

Following the conquest of Naples, Alfonso moved his own residence to the Neapolitan capital, thus emphasising his wish to co-ordinate the southern dominions. Contradicting this policy, however, he resolved that, upon his death, his brother John II would govern the Iberian kingdoms and Sicily, while Naples would be separated from the crown of Aragon and entrusted to Ferdinand, his legitimate son. The balance reached during the reign of Alfonso V was maintained in Sicily through the age of John II, when royal fiscal pressure appeared to generally diminish and the privileges granted during the preceding ages were upheld.

Concluding remarks

A process of ambitious strengthening of monarchical authority in Sicily took shape in the reign of Peter III, only to be thrown into crisis in the 1340s. The island's political geography changed when the opening up of the feudal market favoured the formation of significant seigneurial estates, and the crisis of the nobility's revenue polarised the conflict between magnates and crown. At the same time, the Great Plague and population collapse had significant effects in both demographic and economic terms, diversifying agricultural production and gradually channelling wealth towards the lower and middle classes. Political upheaval and the collapse of the trading system in the second half of the fourteenth century, however, delayed the process of economic specialisation, which recovered only during the reign of Martin I. The reconstitution of monarchical power was characterised at that time by the royal decision to select loyal lineages at the heart of the aristocracy, thus reducing the potential for rebellions. Underlining the defeat of the counts' powers in the late fourteenth century does not diminish the role of the aristocratic dynasties in the late medieval period, but scales down their pre-eminence by drawing attention to the existence of many political actors. In the same way, underlining the circulation, between the countries of the crown of Aragon, of common models of government in no way denies the peculiarities of the relationships between country and king in Sicily.

The political strength of the demesnial communities in the dynamics of the kingdom was thrown into crisis in the second half of the fourteenth century. From the reign of Martin, however, wide opportunities opened up to the urban milieu which, paradoxically, derived its own political fortune initially from the central role exercised by the comital powers, and the subsequent conflict with the crown, and later from strong fiscal pressure during the reign of Alfonso V. Alfonso V allowed local governments the power to establish methods of taxation and considerably increased the cities' autonomy in general. This complex balance did not rupture even when, upon the death of Alfonso V, Charles of Viana, son of John II and Blanche (Martin I's second wife), showed his inclination to be crowned king of Sicily. The island did not lack supporters of autonomy, but Charles of Viana's plan was not met with widespread consensus. The political reality was nothing like that of 1296: Alfonso V had broadened the margins of autonomy as requested by the Sicilians and, upon his death, there was no reason to believe that his successor would take a new direction. Indeed, John II quickly adapted to the pre-existing equilibria.

2 The kingdom of Naples

Francesco Senatore

Introduction

In historical discussion of the kingdom of Naples, for hundreds of years the political framework for the south of Italy, the prevailing judgement is often one of immobility, as if the political and social structures of this part of the peninsula have not changed over the centuries. In order to limit the influence of this view, observations on historiography will be reserved until the end of this chapter. The reader will first be given an outline of the succession of events which will lead to an exploration of: the constants; the points of change; the institutions, remarkably stable, despite serious conflicts; the complex relations between the different territorial and economic powers in the *Regno* – monarchy, feudality, city and foreign merchants.

Anjou and Aragon: the 200-year war

From the end of the thirteenth century to the beginning of the sixteenth, the political history of the kingdom of Naples was marked by a struggle between two dynastic and territorial European powers, the Angevins and the Aragonese, for control of the western Mediterranean. The conflict, ending with the succession to the throne of Ferdinand the Catholic (1503), king of Aragon and consort of Isabella of Castile, continued on into the sixteenth century between the Habsburg empire and France, successors to the Aragonese and Angevins respectively.[1]

In the first period the upper hand was gained by the Angevins, counts of Provence, conquerors of the kingdom of Sicily (1266) led by Charles I, brother of the king of France and allies of the Roman pontiff (the kingdom's feudal lord) who, in the period spanning the end of the thirteenth century to the beginning of the fourteenth, led the

---

[1] Abulafia, *The Western Mediterranean Kingdoms*, 257–8; Galasso, *Il regno di Napoli*, 15–307, 561–729; Vitolo, 'Il regno angioino'.

broad-based Guelf political formation that included southern Italy plus Sicily, the church, the *signorie* and cities of central-northern Italy, the kingdom of Hungary, the dominions in Piedmont, Provence, Anjou and Albania. The bond with Florence was particularly significant for a number of reasons, firstly because the political and financial events of the richest commune in Italy were subject to the influence of the Angevin kings of Naples who, together with the pope, attempted to set up members of their family as *signori* of the city, and secondly because of the extensive financial penetration of Florentine merchant bankers (the Bardi, the Acciaiuoli and the Peruzzi) in the kingdom. These, taking over from the Pisans and Genoese, were the main creditors of the crown, managing its revenue by means of contracts, obtaining licences to export from the kingdom (grain, oil, wine and livestock) and selling the products of the Florentine textile industry.[2] There were numerous Florentines in important public posts, such as the highly powerful grand seneschal Niccolò Acciaiuoli (died 1365).

The power of the Angevins, kings of Naples and counts of Provence – two areas linked by profitable political, economic and cultural contacts – was plunged into crisis first of all by the Vespers revolt (1282), which heralded the beginning of the war against the house of Aragon, the dynasty that was to take over the island of Sicily, and then, in the middle of the fourteenth century, by three concomitant factors: the general demographic and economic crisis, the weakening of the papal see as a result of the Great Schism, and the absence of heirs to queen Joanna I, last descendant of Charles I. In 1377–81, the future succession to Joanna (already the cause of disorder thirty years previously, with the Hungarian invasions of the kingdom and a series of internal conflicts) was claimed by two branches of the family, the house of Anjou-Durazzo and Anjou-Provence. Charles III of Durazzo was supported by the Roman pope (Urban VI) who, despite being Neapolitan, was hostile to the queen, and Louis I of Anjou by the Avignon pope (Clement VII). The war broke out just when plans to reconquer the other kingdom of Sicily (both parts of the original Norman kingdom having kept the same official name) had been finally shelved. The barons and urban aristocracies split into three factions, the Durazzo party, the Anjou party and the Urbanist party, the last being that of Urban VI, who at one point attempted to take over the kingdom, siding against both the other contenders.

In July 1381, thanks to the support of Urban and of Florentine merchants, Charles III took Naples, imprisoning the queen, Joanna I,

---

[2] Yver, *Le commerce et les marchands*, 289–391; Abulafia, 'Southern Italy'. For the Norman period, see Abulafia, *The Two Italies*.

and arranging her death. From then until 1465 the biological and 'political' descendants of the two dynasties met in battle on Neapolitan soil, invaded repeatedly by the Provence branch, often supported by the king of France, Florence and Genoa: Louis I of Anjou fought Charles III of Durazzo (1382–4); Louis II of Anjou fought Margherita and Ladislas of Durazzo (1387–99); Louis III of Anjou fought Alfonso V of Aragon, known as the Magnanimous and adopted by Joanna II of Durazzo (1421–3); René of Anjou fought Alfonso again (1435–42); John of Anjou fought the son of the latter, Ferrante (1459–65). The Angevins of Provence succeeded in governing the city of Naples for brief periods (1387–99, 1435–42), because first the Durazzo and then the Aragonese prevailed. The situation was made unstable, however, by prolonged Angevin occupations of cities and fortresses and recurrent conflicts with barons: the war of Ladislas against the principality of Taranto (1406–7), the rebellion of Antoni Centelles, marquis of Crotone, against the Magnanimous (1444–5) and the conspiracy of the feudatories and court officials against Ferrante (1486–7).[3]

With the conquest of the kingdom by Alfonso the Magnanimous (1442), the crown of Aragon reached its maximum extent in the Mediterranean, ruling over Sicily, Sardinia, part of Corsica and several coastal landing places in Tuscany (a preliminary version of the 'Stato dei Presìdi' of Charles V of Habsburg), together with several significant, even if short-lived, undertakings in North Africa and the eastern Mediterranean. The Aragonese success had important consequences in the economic sphere, firstly because it increased the presence of Catalan merchants (from Barcelona and Valencia), the main financial supporters of the conquest, in the kingdom, thus weakening, although not actually eliminating, the influence of the Florentines. Secondly, it harmed Genoa, which was directly involved in the Angevin-Aragonese conflict, and undermined the hegemony of Venice in the Adriatic and the East.[4] For political reasons, the sovereign had to refrain from expelling the Florentines from his dominions, but, in a proto-mercantilist plan, he encouraged economic integration between the two sides of the western

---

[3] Léonard, *Histoire de Jeanne Iére*; Cutolo, *Margherita d'Enghien*; Cutolo, *Re Ladislao*; Faraglia, *Storia della regina Giovanna*; Faraglia, *Storia della lotta*; Ryder, *Alfonso the Magnanimous*; Nunziante, 'I primi anni'; Senatore and Storti, *Spazi e tempi*. There is an abundant bibliography on the barons' conspiracy – a good starting point now is Scarton, 'La congiura dei baroni'.

[4] Del Treppo, *I mercanti catalani*, 202–61; Del Treppo, 'Il regno aragonese', 89–103. For the Catalans in the administration and their influence on the financial practices of the crown: Del Treppo, 'Il regno aragonese', 107–10, 141–3 and Del Treppo, 'I catalani a Napoli', 86–97.

Mediterranean. Mario Del Treppo insists – though Stephan R. Epstein does not agree – that the Magnanimous deliberately pursued such an economic policy, proven by, among other things, a letter to his wife Maria in which he orders that Iberians should import grain only from Sicily and Naples, and that the supply of cloth to these two kingdoms should be exclusively Aragonese. In shipping, preference was to be given to the ships of the subjects of the crown, which were to be available also when needed for the king's military undertakings.[5]

The end of the Aragonese dynasty of Naples was marked by a dramatic series of events: the abdication of Alfonso II and the conquest of Naples by the French king Charles VIII (both 1495); the premature death of Ferdinand II (1496); the short-lived government of his uncle Frederick, grandson of the Magnanimous, in exile after the kingdom was divided up between Spain and France (1501); and the victory of Ferdinand the Catholic (1503) which brought Naples into the Iberian dominions, dominions that later came into the hands of the emperor Charles V of Habsburg (1516–56).

The monarchy and local powers

This prolonged political instability, common to other European monarchies, had the consequence of strengthening local powers, both feudal and urban, and these powers grew considerably from the end of the fourteenth century and throughout the fifteenth. Many of the monarchy's resources (demesnial land, income from taxes, peripheral offices, etc.) were actually enfeoffed or given to barons and communities, and numerous fixed pecuniary allowances were granted to people (barons, officials, *condottieri*, merchants, etc.), either to reward loyalty and service or as compensation for non-repaid loans, donations or losses suffered in periods of war.

The crown had to take into account the power of some of the major feudal families, most notably the Orsini in Apulia and the Sanseverino in the Principato Citra and in Calabria. There were many other important families (Caetani, Caldora, Camponesco, Caracciolo, Del Balzo,

---

[5] It is 'our wish to [...] reform the trade of our kingdoms and our lands [...] They could practise the reciprocal trade and dealing of products particularly necessary for life [...] the kingdoms here will import from those there, and from no other place, woollen cloth, of which the [western kingdoms] have an abundance; and those there [...] will import from those here, and from no other place, the grain that they require, because these [kingdoms of the East] have an abundance of it, at a very economical price': letter from Naples, 9 December 1451, Del Treppo, *I mercanti catalani*, 603, 534–6; Epstein, 'Storia economica', 105–7.

Marzano, Ruffo, etc.) but, on more than one occasion, the success of either side in the conflict depended on the Orsini and Sanseverino. There was strong solidarity within the two big family clans, sometimes translated into formal bonds (alliances, pacts with claimants or kings, etc.). Often, the Orsini and Sanseverino were engaged in 'private' wars, not to support their party, but rather to procure resources locally along the boundaries of their feudal estates.

In 1443 Alfonso the Magnanimous recognised the full civil and penal judicial authority of all tenants-in-chief in their territories (*merum et mixtum imperium*), thus completing a process begun long ago, albeit by individual concessions. Historiography has asked whether the power of some of the major feudatories can be classed as *de facto* sovereignty, comparable to that of the duke of Burgundy. In actual fact, the principality of Taranto, formerly in the possession of members of the royal family in the fourteenth century, had a considerable degree of autonomy under the Orsini (1399–1463), which manifested itself not only in the judicial, military and taxation spheres (the prince levied direct royal taxation on his own account), but also in the concrete and symbolic way it imitated the monarchy (as seen in, for example, the appeals jurisdiction of the prince's council, the array of officials such as justiciars and *razionali* – accounts clerks – the chancery procedures, etc.).[6] Prince Raimondo Orsini was a determinant factor in the success of the house of Durazzo and his son Giovanni Antonio in the victory of the Magnanimous and the rebellion against Ferrante. It was not by chance that the crown strengthened its alliance with the house of Orsini by marriage (an obvious choice of resource at the time, although the outcome could not always be taken for granted), as in that between Ladislas and Raimondo's widow, the countess of Lecce Maria d'Enghien, and between Ferrante and Isabella di Chiaromonte, niece of Giovanni Antonio.

Like the barons, the cities and towns too, both feudal and public (*demaniali*), benefited from the political upheavals, obtaining many taxation rights (on the transit and sale of goods, exemptions, etc.) and minor jurisdictional bodies, such as the *bagliva* (rural policing and compensation for damages) which, in the Norman period, came under royal jurisdiction. In the event of changes of dynasty and seigneurial pacts, the communities set up their own separate jurisdiction (*ius proprium*), gaining concessions from the sovereign (or feudal lord). The

---

[6] Vallone, *Istituzioni feudali*, 1–31, 129–53 (referring to the debate between G. M. Monti and G. Antonucci); Morelli, 'Tra continuità e trasformazioni'; Somaini and Vetere (eds.), *I domini del principe*.

king's privilege allowed urban and rural governments (*universitates*) to participate actively in law-making, despite not having the *ius statuendi* of a sovereign power. In fact, the text of the privilege included locally drafted rules (marriage and inheritance procedures, election and authority of officials, grain dole of the city, etc.), grouped into items (*capituli*) and approved by the authority with its *placet*. The oldest concessions date back to the time of Ladislas and Joanna II, but most of the *Privilegi, capitoli, lettere e grazie* (this definition indicates that the documents were heterogeneous in form and not collected in homogeneous registers) can be traced back to Alfonso and Ferrante of Aragon. The most important privileges, jealously preserved up to the nineteenth century in university vaults, were reconfirmed by successive rulers and finally included in a 'summary' diploma of Charles V of Habsburg, which some local chancellors simply called *il privilegio*.[7]

The strength of the local powers must not be exaggerated, however. It never matched the substantial independence of much seigneurial or urban domination in other parts of Europe, going from spontaneous, furious development in the twelfth and thirteenth centuries to difficult subjugation by regional or supra-regional powers in the late Middle Ages. In the south, even in the king's weakest periods, the monarchy itself was never called into question. At most, some cities (such as L'Aquila) gave themselves up to the higher feudal authority, the pope, who, in periods of crisis interfered extensively in relations between monarchy, barons and cities.

Recurrent struggles between court factions, barons and communities and continuous shifts in alliances have fuelled a negative judgement of southern Italian people, accused by contemporaries and historians alike of instability and unreliability. Attempting to explain changeability in political allegiances in terms of purely psychological or, indeed, anthropological causes is both banal and an oversimplification. All European states have gone through similar kinds of tension and violence. Which side to choose – either Anjou or Aragon – depended on concrete family and economic interests which, while being well documented in local historiography, tend, for the sake of brevity, to disappear in general treatises written from the point of view of the central power. While barons and urban governments would change sides readily to guarantee control of a wood, water course or pasture or to broaden their sphere of jurisdiction, there were, however, centuries-old political traditions that bound local powers either together or to one or other of the dynasties in a conflict. A rival's

[7] Senatore, 'Le scritture delle *universitates*'. About the *universitas*, see Senatore, 'Gli archivi delle *universitates*', 447–56, disagreed with by Vitolo, 'In palatio communis', 256–75.

choice of sides, on the other hand, would affect one's own: if Onorato Caetani, the count of Fondi, sided with the Aragons, his cousin of the same name would support the Angevins, because of a family quarrel; if Salerno was on one side, Cava de' Tirreni would be on the other.

The sovereign's income was periodically eroded by enfeoffments, exemptions, jurisdictional concessions, earnings from taxation, offices and gratuities, and the actual power of the monarch was much less in areas more distant from the court, either geographically or politically. Theoretically, though, these concessions remained dependent on the good will of the king or queen and could be legally withdrawn at any time, just as allodial property could be confiscated at any time in the event of a rebellion against the sovereign: once the emergency had passed, royal authority could be reimposed and strengthened thanks to the soundly structured administrative machinery, the well-established legal system and regular direct taxation. The effects of important concessions such as *merum et mixtum imperium* or the appeals jurisdiction, granted to a number of feudatories in the Aragonese era, were limited by the always available option of appealing to the royal courts of the third instance or going directly to the royal council. Monarchical power, which had gone through periods of major crisis from the middle of the fourteenth century to the first decades of the fifteenth, advanced steadily in the Aragonese age: Alfonso and Ferrante broke up great feudal estates, undermined the military (we shall see how later) and the economic bases of the local powers by means of public enquiries into the legitimacy of rights and patrimonies (privileges and thoroughfare rights),[8] and enacted institutional reforms, especially in the financial sphere. To be noted here is the setting up of the *percettore generale*'s office to guarantee effective and rational control of all state income and expenditure.[9]

In the event of tactical retreats, if necessary, the king would simply use violence to reassert his authority, characterised by cruel acts of revenge after situations had settled down, such as in the imprisonments, death sentences and murders ordered by Charles III, Ladislas and Ferrante against enemies immediately after reconciliation.[10]

---

[8] Ryder, *The Kingdom of Naples*, 90–124, 136–68; Del Treppo, 'Il regno aragonese', 162–7.
[9] Del Treppo, 'Il regno aragonese', 133–8; Del Treppo, 'Il re e il banchiere', 269–75; Del Treppo, 'Un ritrovato libro', with a reconstruction of relations between *percettoria generale* (supreme body for the control of royal income and expenditure), general treasury and *scrivania di razione* (accounts control office).
[10] Charles III had Joanna I assassinated and her body exhibited in the Neapolitan church of Santa Chiara (1382). Ladislas arrested the Marzano clan at a wedding feast in 1404 and, a year later, slaughtered a number of barons from the Sanseverino family. Ferrante

The state machinery

Neapolitan public institutions were not radically altered by the changes of dynasty and amalgamation into larger bodies, such as the crown of Aragon or the Habsburg empire. There were certainly changes (details of which cannot be given here), but no dramatic breaks in continuity. Those most affected by the wars of conquest were the kingdom's elites, because of the influx of foreign feudatories and officials, changes in political relations and frames of reference, big upheavals in feudal geography and the irreversible downfall of families that found themselves on the wrong side.

The stability of the monarchy dated back to its Norman origins. Unlike other European rulers, the Altavillas (1130–94) and the Hohenstaufens (1194–1266) had stamped a considerable uniformity on the territory, which, on the other hand, had never experienced the breaking down of public power that had occurred in the Carolingian areas. The territory was divided into justiciaries, then provinces, i.e. districts assigned to royally appointed temporary officials (justiciars) with judicial and military authority, chosen preferably from barons outside the province. The justiciars were in charge of a number of local officials (judges, tax collectors and military officials).[11] In Naples, where administrative records have been preserved from the middle of the thirteenth century onwards, the king was backed up by seven grand officials of the kingdom and chancery.[12] All officials, like anyone contracting for a royal appointment, were obliged to keep precise written records of their activities and their accounts were subject to strict auditing. This was done in Naples, by the king's *maestri razionali* (masters of accounts) in the Angevin age and, in the Durazzo and Aragonese periods, by the *regia camera della sommaria*, a sort of audit court with both administrative and judicial authority, also over the fiefs.

The judicial foundations of the kingdom continued to be the constitutions of Melfi (1231), with their clear concept of sovereignty. The proceedings (*ritus*) were those of the central magistracies (*sommaria*, *vicaria* – which is the criminal appeal court), established in the fourteenth and fifteenth centuries, commented on continuously by jurists and printed in the modern period. The 200-year war between the

---

arrested Marino Marzano after the latter swore a feudal oath (1464); he had Giacomo Piccinino killed (1465) and arrested barons and officials during a wedding feast (1487).
[11] Cadier, *Essai sur l'administration*; Morelli, 'I giustizieri nel regno'.
[12] Durrieu, *Les archives angevines*; Kiesewetter; 'La cancelleria angioina'; Delle Donne, 'Le cancellerie'; Palmieri, *La cancelleria*; Vitale, 'Sul segretario regio'.

Angevins and the Aragonese had an effect on administrative organisation. The *maestro razionale*, for example, introduced in Aragon and Valencia in the thirteenth and fourteenth centuries, was an imitation of the Sicilian *maestri razionali* and, in the opposite direction, the Iberian model probably influenced Alfonso the Magnanimous's reorganisation of the *sommaria*[13] after the Aragonese conquest of Naples. A close comparison, carried out over a considerable period of time, of the Spanish Aragonese dominions, the Angevin French ones, the kingdom of Naples and that of Sicily, would reveal quite a few similarities in institutions (chanceries, officials, parliaments, general vicariates, standing army, etc.) and records (diplomas and registers, inquiries, *sindacatus* – i.e. final audits – counting of hearths, income statements, reliefs, etc.).

The power of the monarchy, despite the many compromises it was obliged to make, was a factual reality, as we are reminded not only in the prologues to the diplomas or the limitation clauses of the concessions, but also in diplomatic exchanges and correspondence. Note, for example, the self-satisfied tone of Alfonso the Magnanimous when speaking of his 'absolute power' in the kingdom of Naples, in polemical contrast to the encumbrance of parliamentary consultation in the Iberian dominions (1450), or a letter in which Ferrante asserts his right to revoke any concession whatsoever, no matter how many guarantee clauses it contains, because jurisdictions – he adds, in a comparison based on the *iurisdictio descendens* principle – 'derive from us like streams and water that run swiftly and, nevertheless, always go back to the sea whence they originated' (1492).[14] The expression used by Giovanni Tabacco when he described these two sovereigns as being characterised by a 'cultured and open-minded authoritarianism' is more than apt.[15]

All subjects, both those directly under the king's rule and those ruled by feudatories, with the exception of vassals and clergy, were liable to a direct tax, the *generalis subventio*, introduced by Frederick II of Hohenstaufen and well established by the time of the Angevins, when taxes were also known as *collette*. The levy, repeated several times a year and without prior parliamentary approval (as happened in other monarchies), was reformed by Alfonso the Magnanimous (1443), who fixed both the sum and the frequency (1, then 2 ducats a year per hearth in three four-monthly instalments) and linked it to the enforced distribution of

---

[13] De Montagut i Estrangés, *El mestre racional*; Cruselles, *El mestre racional*; Delle Donne, 'Alle origini'; and Morelli, 'Il controllo delle periferie', 19. Delle Donne, 'Le cancellerie', 375, notes that the text of Aragonese documents for the appointment of pronotaries kept faithfully to their Hohenstaufen equivalents.
[14] Del Treppo, 'Alfonso il Magnanimo', 11; Senatore, 'Parlamento e luogotenenza', 449.
[15] Tabacco, 'Il potere politico', 103.

salt, for which a further payment was required. The taxation was based on a census of the population: royal officials, accompanied by representatives of the *universitates* (the governments of cities, towns and villages), counted the hearths (the units of income production, hence the name *focatico* – hearth-tax) to calculate the amount due for each area. It was then the job of the *universitas* of the area to divide up the sum among the population, and payment was made either by setting indirect taxes or by assessing the income of each individual (by means of the *catasto*, or *apprezzo*, based on income statements). To avoid inequalities, Alfonso ordered the *catasto* to be repeated every three years, but this was not always done.[16]

As well as general taxation, the sovereign had considerable property and fiscal rights, even though these were gradually reduced during the fourteenth and fifteenth centuries. They included woodland areas, hunting reserves, horse breeding and crop farms (*masserie*),[17] customs dues on merchandise in the kingdom's main ports, terrestrial thoroughfares and monopolies on exports. Regarding exports, note that it was the crown that authorised the export of agricultural produce, by means of so-called *tratte* (grants of export). The merchant, baron, urban or rural community that obtained a *tratta* for a certain product in a certain quantity, either on payment or free of charge, had then to pay the dues to the royal officials and the agreed price to the producers or local intermediaries.

In the middle of the fifteenth century, Alfonso the Magnanimous placed regulations on the use of pasture land in Apulia, forbidding enclosures and making the pastures available to flocks of sheep from the Abruzzi in the winter time for the traditional transhumance. The shepherds, subject to special jurisdiction, paid grazing duty to the Apulian *dogana delle pecore*, controlled by the court. With these measures, based on the rational government of a long-standing practice and attuned both to the physical and climatic conformation of the kingdom and to the demographic (a falling population and the abandonment of fields from the middle of the fourteenth century onwards) and economic (the wool trade) conditions, Alfonso obtained a considerable increase in ordinary revenue. The number of sheep passing through the *dogana* rose from 400,000 to 1,000,000 in five years (1445–50).[18]

Like all European sovereigns, the kings of Naples were obliged to alienate their income, pledge it in advance and incur onerous loans in

[16] Morelli, 'Note sulla fiscalità'; Del Treppo, 'Il regno aragonese', 110–16.
[17] Licinio, *Masserie medievali*; Del Treppo, 'Il regno aragonese', 154–8.
[18] Del Treppo, 'Il regno aragonese', 121–2.

order to fund their main item of expenditure: war. In the course of the fourteenth century, mercenary troops were used increasingly to supplement the feudal militias (the vassal military service system was replaced by a money tax, the *adoa*). This improved the efficiency of the army but created a huge hole in public accounts and further complicated political affairs, because of the power of the main *condottieri*, among whom, it should be remembered, were many of the kingdom's barons, attracted by the benefits of military life. To remedy this situation, Alfonso and Ferrante of Aragon created an actual permanent standing army, made up of cavalry (known as *uomini d'arme di casa del re* – the king's men-at-arms – or *genti del demanio*), infantry, crossbowmen, springalders and artillery. Whenever possible, the number of independent *condotte* (mercenary troops led by a *condottiero*) and their combat units were reduced, to prevent any one of the *condottieri* – who were paid per thousand horsemen – from gaining power of veto over the hirer, as had actually happened in the kingdom with Braccio di Montone, Muzio Attendolo and Francesco Sforza, Niccolò and Giacomo Piccinino, and Giacomo and Antonio Caldora.[19] In 1464, Ferrante engaged mercenaries, previously on the payroll of barons, who repledged allegiance to him.[20] It should be noted here that the most powerful baron-*condottieri*, such as the Caldora, never constituted political *signorie* comparable to those of central Italy. What did exist, however (and merit study), were vast clienteles of minor lords (*raccomandati*, *aderenti*) around the more eminent barons.

The political and economic structure of the kingdom

The relationship between central power and local powers, although conflictual, cannot be portrayed as one of opposing forces on the same level, for two reasons: the stability of the public machinery, as emphasised above (the 'composite state' model does not seem applicable to the kingdom, as it was, in overall terms, to the crown of Aragon), and the integration between the royal administrative structure and local ones. Barons were considered public officials with jurisdictional powers. The *universitas*, jointly responsible for taxation, was a terminal of the royal administration system. The royal administration always occupied itself with the solvency of the *universitas* by introducing measures, first individual and then general, that were the forerunners of laws (*prammatiche*) established in the first decades of the sixteenth century

---

[19] Sáiz Serrano, *Caballeros del rey*, 99–138; Storti, *L'esercito napoletano*, 31–49, 134–77.
[20] Storti, *L'esercito napoletano*, 119–34.

The kingdom of Naples 41

(expenditure limits on the executive and fiscal payments taking precedence over all other expenditure).[21]

But above all the kingdom was a unitary political and social space, in which the best way to acquire power and prestige, for the prominent classes, was through contact with the royal court, both when the favour of the monarchy expressed itself in the form of concessions that strengthened the economic bases of the feudal and urban nobility in the provinces, and when it was possible to enter the king's service as officials, *condottieri*, jurists and contractors. Pietro Corrao, in an apt double oxymoron, described this situation as a 'diffused centre' and 'concentrated periphery', referring to the interconnection and superimposition of central power and local powers.[22]

At the middle and lower levels, too, many people achieved social success in public service: captains, castellans, commissaries, tax collectors, tenant farmers, livestock breeders, judges and notaries (*mastrodatti*). The administration of resources, whoever they belonged to, became a perennial market, running from the beginning of the indictional year: every September, in the king's chamber or at the bench of the *sommaria*, at the meetings of the *universitas* executive (the *Eletti*, the *Sei*, etc.) or in the village square, in the baronial castles or in the feudal treasury, offices and *gabelle* were allocated to contractors, both large and small, with notices of sale or summary procedures.

The *pactismo* model, borrowed from Iberian historiography, does not seem pertinent for describing the relationship between centre and periphery. While it is true that the sovereign negotiated both with individuals and urban governments, it should be stressed that his authority over his subjects was never limited by formal constraints like that of the oath before the Iberian *Cortes*. The legitimacy of power, even when based on conquest or the exercise of authority, could be called into question only by the church, which required a feudal oath and the payment of a *census* and gave its permission for the coronation by means of a papal legate. The parliament, in a state of crisis in the Durazzo period and reintroduced by the Magnanimous, did not have the power of other similar European state assemblies and was, according to the Hohenstaufen tradition, more an occasion to demonstrate the legislative will of the sovereign, the guardian of peace and justice, and for approving fiscal measures. Those convoked, first of all just barons and then the mayors of demesnial towns and sometimes clergy, did not decide on the taxes on each occasion, in as much as the

---

[21] Senatore, 'Gli archivi delle *universitates*', 470–1.   [22] Corrao, 'Centri e periferie', 197.

taxa generalis was fixed, but rather approved reforms to the system and presented petitions on behalf of the entire population.[23]

The city of Naples benefited greatly from the proximity of the king: in the Angevin and Aragonese age its growth was unstoppable, although not yet uneven, as it was during the population explosion in the sixteenth century and the beginning of the seventeenth. Being the fixed headquarters of the central magistracies, and thus, to all intents and purposes, the capital from the end of the thirteenth century onwards, it was important not only strategically and economically but also, and above all, from the administrative and political point of view. The urban aristocracy, grouped into territorial associations known as *seggi*, saw entering into the king's service as the road to social and economic promotion, with some families actually gaining important feudal estates. The *Studium*, founded by Frederick II, and the possibility of legal, administrative and military careers had great powers of attraction.[24]

In periods of crisis, Neapolitan nobles formed government commissions, such as the *Otto del Buono Stato* in 1387 and the *Diciotto di Balìa* in 1435, which contested the power of the regency councils. The first occasion of recognition for the sovereign was a cavalcade through the Neapolitan *seggi*. The coronation generally took place in Naples. In the middle of the fifteenth century, the enfeoffment and the appointment of major officials involved a ritual cavalcade through the city.[25]

Periodically, officials and feudatories (or their procurators) would come to Naples, the former to be subject to the final audit (*sindicatus*), the latter to lodge declarations of feudal succession or other procedures (these procedures soon brought homogeneity to administrative records and political language). There were also countless summonses for hearings in the *vicarìa*, *sommaria* and royal council, in so far as some cities, as early as the fifteenth century, had permanent procurators in Naples.

Right from its origins, the monarchy played a major role in the structuring of the kingdom's economic activity. It could be said, using anachronistic language, that it made itself a partisan interpreter of the production potential of the southern Italian regions and interfered constantly in the development and functioning of the market. The monarchy was active in a number of spheres, differing both geographically and temporally. The kings were both entrepreneurs, running agricultural and industrial concerns (cloth manufacturing and alum mining) and

---

[23] Ryder, *The Kingdom of Naples*, 124–35; Scarton, 'Il parlamento'; Senatore, 'Parlamento e luogotenenza', 436–50.
[24] Vitale, *Elite burocratica*; Storti, *L'esercito napoletano*, 83–94.
[25] Vitale, *Ritualità*, 15–78; Senatore, 'Cerimonie civiche', 169.

trading produce on their own behalf, and market regulators, granting fair permits, export permits, passage and boating rights, and tax exemptions and encouraging individuals to set up new industrial enterprises. They were also major clients of merchant bankers, who made their capital and financial infrastructure available to the court (in the Aragonese age, various banks, including the Strozzi of Florence, operated as state bankers).[26] Del Treppo identifies three levels in the economic structure of the kingdom from the thirteenth to the fifteenth centuries: the lowest was that of very short-range production and trade in geographically isolated enclaves, the second was that of intense inter-regional traffic along thoroughfares and in seasonal fairs, and the third was long-distance trade with international credit, dominated by the Florentines, who, together with other foreign merchants, were also active on the second level.

The activities of foreign merchants, often Florentine and Catalan, in the kingdom brought southern Italy into the international economy. The debate on the consequences of this process is still open: traditionally, the monarchy is blamed for encouraging the growth of a dualistic economy, with the exploitation of foreign capital having reduced southern Italy and Sicily to economically underdeveloped colonies. Del Treppo, however, maintains that foreign intervention actually stimulated production and trade, bringing wealth to local traders, lay barons and clergy, and changing their mentality.[27] Epstein has demonstrated that 'late medieval Sicily achieved an unusual degree of market integration and specialisation'.[28]

The territory

The kingdom of Naples covered a third of the Italian peninsula[29] and, evidently, contained a wide variety of natural and human landscapes. The monarchy was aware of this from the outset, adapting its provincial districts to the mountains and communication routes. The main land routes ran along the Apennines or crossed them from east to west.[30] The isolation of some of the regions, such as Calabria, was compensated for by the maritime connections in the form of landing places and the mouths of rivers, very few of which were navigable. These

---

[26] Del Treppo, 'Il re e il banchiere'; Del Treppo, 'Il regno aragonese', 133–40.
[27] Del Treppo, 'Il regno aragonese', 172–83; Del Treppo, 'Prospettive mediterranee'.
[28] Epstein, *An Island*, 402.
[29] This calculation is based on the current surface area of Italy (251,540 km^2), without the islands (49,798 km^2).
[30] Sthamer, 'Die Hauptstraßen'; Figliuolo, 'Profilo di storia'; Dalena, *Ambiti territoriali*.

geographical characteristics must not be forgotten when discussing the institutions and economy of the kingdom.

The economic bases of the monarchy were concentrated in the fertile plains of Campania (the Terra di Lavoro, intersected by the Volturno and the Garigliano, and the Piana del Sele) and Apulia (the so-called Puglia Piana, the present-day province of Foggia). There were many demesnial towns in these areas (Gaeta, Capua, Aversa, Naples, Pozzuoli, Sorrento and Cava; Sansevero, Lucera, Foggia, Barletta and Manfredonia) and the sovereigns had property and important sources of indirect taxation here (maritime customs duties, salt and sheep taxes), together with an abundance of hunting reserves (*difese*). The ancient Appian Way, connecting Apulia and Campania, was thus of enormous strategic importance for the control of the kingdom. Throughout the whole period, there were pitched battles along the Terra di Lavoro-Samnium-Apulia line: Melito (1349), Pietracatella (1383), Troia (1441, 1462), Sarno (1460) and Cerignola (1503), together with the various sieges of Taranto and Naples and the sack of Capua (1501). The successes of the houses of Durazzo and Aragon were made possible partly because of their control of Campania, where the four so-called keys to the kingdom were to be found (Gaeta, Capua, Benevento and Salerno), and partly because of their expeditions into Apulia, where the presence of the king was indispensable for confronting or subduing the local powers.[31] The monarchy tolerated more autonomy in the peripheral regions, such as the Abruzzi, Molise, Calabria and the Terra d'Otranto. The density of royal power depended on this unavoidable geographical and historical conditioning.

Alfonso of Aragon brought a number of innovations to the governance of the provinces, whose different strategic importance he was well aware of. Individual cities or areas containing more than one province were assigned to plenipotentiary officials, already tested out by the Durazzo. Ferrante entrusted the government of these regional areas to his sons, appointing them as lieutenants and giving them territorial councils with judicial and military authority. The first-born, according to Iberian tradition, had the function of vicar-general of the kingdom (in the presence of the sovereign).[32] Duke Alfonso travelled the kingdom not only to suppress rebellions and repel the Turkish invasion of Otranto, but also to make systematic inspections of the fortifications, restructured in the 1480s. The suffocating presence of the monarchy in the daily exercise of jurisdiction, military control and the use of

---

[31] Senatore and Storti, *Spazi e tempi*, 33–57.
[32] Del Treppo, 'Il regno aragonese', 165–7; Senatore, 'Parlamento e luogotenenza', 461–7.

resources lies at the origin of the baronial rebellions of 1459–65 and 1486–7 and perhaps of the final collapse of the dynasty.

As demonstrated by research in recent years, the towns and cities too played an important role in the governance of the territory, although in a way obviously not comparable to the subjection of the *contado* in some Italian communes in the late Middle Ages. The hegemony of a city, be it desmesnial or feudal, manifested itself in many ways: economic centrality (weekly markets, seasonal fairs, city monopolies, etc.), jurisdiction (a judge, with authority in the district in the first and second instance, was based in the city), rituals (processions) and immigration (citizenship applications).[33] Cities, like individuals or monasteries, could exercise seigneurial rights over rural communities (*casali*), sometimes quite big ones, because of property rights or feudal concessions. In these cases the *casali* were defined *non de corpore*, being outside the territory and with inhabitants who did not have the same rights as citizens. These villages had their *universitates*, subordinate to the king for direct taxation, to the city for the appointment of prominent officials and the approval of statutes, and possibly to a feudal lord for minor jurisdiction and various fiscal dues (a cause of continuous dispute).[34] Some cities, such as L'Aquila, Aversa, Capua, Nocera dei Pagani, Cava, Naples, Cosenza and Lecce, governed very large areas. Their territories were almost the size of a present-day province, and there were frequent internal conflicts, related to the hegemony of the city's ruling class and the tendency to heap the main burden of taxes on to the rural communities (known as the *Foria* or the *casali*), which were unrepresented in the central bodies. Apart from L'Aquila, which was punished by having its territory broken up by the Spanish government in the sixteenth century, most of the city 'states' kept their territory until the nineteenth century.

Concluding remarks: the curse of the south

Del Treppo remarked that the history of southern Italy is generally seen as that of a 'missed-out north [*Nord mancato*]'.[35] In other words, it is generally held that in the south (and Sicily), the political-institutional, social and economic phenomena of the north did not manifest themselves (or if they did, it was without positive effects), and that the entire, complex succession of events in the south, from the foundation of the kingdom of Sicily (1130) to the unity of Italy (1861), can be summed up

---

[33] Vitolo (ed.), *Città e contado*; Vitolo, 'In palatio communis', 246–50, 266, 275–8.
[34] Vallone, *Istituzioni feudali*, 179–87.
[35] Del Treppo, 'Mezzogiorno, Nord mancato'.

as a substantial failure, brought about by the institutions and the economy. According to this line of reasoning, the monarchy was too strong for the urban elites and too weak for feudalism, thus preventing the growth of a bourgeois class capable of creating effective economic infrastructures and sustaining the modernisation of institutions and *mentalités* and, paradoxically, in the very European region where it first manifested itself thanks to the mythicised Norman–Hohenstaufen dynasty, the 'modern state' did not form.

This interpretation aims to explain the origins of the economic underdevelopment of the south that manifested itself dramatically after the unification of Italy, when the 'southern question [*questione meridionale*]' was born, and that has apparently remained to the present day. The causes of the 'diversity' of the south have been identified sometimes in geographical and climatic (the poorness of the soil) factors and even racial ones (because of the presumed anthropological defects of southerners); sometimes in historical events such as the non-independence of the cities and the war of the Vespers; and sometimes in structural economic conditions such as the subordination to foreign merchants, encouraged by the monarchy.[36] The search for those to blame for the divide between the 'two Italies' in the contemporary age has gone back as far as Frederick II and the Altavillas,[37] and even the lack of public-spiritedness in southerners has been explained by the fact of missing out on the communal experience.[38]

Many authors have reflected on the aporias of this approach to southern Italian history. For some time now it has become part of the very identity of southern Italians, from intellectuals to the man in the street. What is surprising is that in every piece of research into the kingdom's past, regardless of the subject, the author is tempted to express an overall judgement on the entire history of the south, measured against the yardstick of its current problems. What is even more surprising is that

---

[36] Epstein, *An Island*, 1–14; Del Treppo, *La libertà della memoria*, 111–13. The identification of the Vespers as a breaking point is taken from Croce, *Storia*. For the late nineteenth century on southern Italian anthropology, see Petraccone, *Le 'due Italie'*, 46–87.

[37] Tramontana, *Il Mezzogiorno medievale*. Even though the title brings to mind the debate on southern Italian underdevelopment in the contemporary age, Abulafia, *The Two Italies*, deals only with the twelfth century, concluding cautiously that 'in the very long term the north Italian presence may have had drawbacks for southern Italy [...] Yet in the short term [...] [it] was advantageous if not to the kingdom at least to the king' (284).

[38] Putnam, *Making Democracy Work*: unlike the rest of the volume, which is based on thorough statistics, chapter 5, on medieval origins, is based on a general and inappropriate bibliography.

this judgement is based on unproven postulates: the development of productive urban classes is impossible without political independence; if there had been no kingdom, the communes would have been independent;[39] this is what lies at the root of the cultural and economic underdevelopment over all these centuries; agricultural exporting regions are to be considered as underdeveloped in themselves; landed aristocracies are by definition unproductive and the economic disasters of the middle of the seventeenth century are the inevitable outcome of previous history.[40]

Here are a few examples, in which the reader will recognise the clichés of the southern Italy debate. Emile Léonard (1954) blamed the 'interventionist economy' of Charles I of Anjou, while recognising the efficiency and consistency of his undertakings, and denounced the subjection of the south to foreign merchants; note that this judgement is expressed in a work on political history in which there is no real discussion of the economy, and that the references in the notes are to nineteenth- and twentieth-century volumes on the southern question.[41] Georges Yver, in his book on southern Italian commerce (1903), compares the south of his times (when, in fact, the first books on the so-called southern question began to appear) to that of the Angevin period, arguing that southern Italian history, ever since Greek colonisation, had been characterised by the 'ever precarious and ever dangerous intervention of foreign elements', who, nevertheless, were the only ones capable of guiding the country 'to modern life', given the poorness of the resources and the incapacity of the natives, ever ready to relapse 'into their lethargy' as soon as these good foreign entrepreneurs went away.[42] And, supposedly, from the 'native' point of view, these endless 'foreign dominations' never changed a thing in the social structure of the south, as confirmed in the famous passage from the novel by Tomasi di Lampedusa (*The Leopard*, 1958).

This convergence between historians and novelists comes as no surprise. When talking about southern Italy, thematic overspills between

---

[39] 'I do not want to support any argument that sees southern urban development as "blocked" by the Normans, for such an argument is teleological': Wickam, 'City society', 13.

[40] Based on the argument that the origins of southern Italian and Sicilian underdevelopment date back to the first half of the seventeenth century, related to excessive Spanish fiscal pressure: Epstein, *An Island*, 409–19; Calabria, *The Cost of Empire*.

[41] Léonard, *Les Angevins*, 88–9. As in Putnam, the critical spirit demonstrated in his own field is abandoned when using interpretations taken from other disciplines, whose reliability he is unable to check.

[42] Yver, *Le commerce et les marchands*, 400; Leone, *Ricerche sull'economia*, 23–40.

research, fiction and political propaganda, frequent in other fields too, are the norm. Active in Tomasi di Lampedusa, as in Yver and Léonard, were a number of prejudices, evidently datable to the nineteenth century: anything extraneous (dynasty, merchants, etc.) is in itself a negative factor, in that it prevents the natural historical development of a nation; any state intervention in an economy is to be condemned, as the market must be free.

Now, everything seems to be pointing to the demise of stereotypes such as these, because of the awareness that south and north, or centre-south and centre-north, are abstract entities that conceal a great variety of histories, because of the radical change in cultural and ideological points of reference (medieval vs modern, feudality vs bourgeoisie, centralism vs particularism, and statism vs free market) and because of the renewed historiography of the communes, of that 'north' so envied by southerners. Even so, the 'curse' of the comparison with northern Italy remains, and with it that negative judgement, unwieldy even when – as here – it is an idol to be dismantled.

Even before the southern question was born, historical discourse on the kingdom of Naples was characterised by what could be called serious historical and historiographical traumas, namely, the shattering of Norman–Hohenstaufen unity by the war of the Vespers, and the entry of the kingdom of Naples (and Sicily) into the Spanish empire. When looking at southern Italy's past and present, the dates 1282, 1503 and, lastly, 1861 are as critical as 1990 was for the former East Germany. Just as the annexation of the eastern territories to the Federal German Republic suddenly took the meaning out of an entire state and cultural experience, so that triple break in continuity in the history of southern Italy was an immediate problem for contemporaries, and continues to be so for whoever nowadays reflects on the presumed diversity of the south with respect to the rest of Italy and on its (equally hypothetical) perennial internal homogeneity. Some ideas – on the unreliability of the southern Italian populations, the weakness of the monarchy against feudalism and the unproductiveness of the latifundistas – date back to authors of the modern age, such as Angelo di Costanzo (1507–91) and Pietro Giannone (1676–1748). The conditioning effect of these is evident, for example, in historians of such stature as Giuseppe Galasso.[43]

---

[43] Taken directly from Di Costanzo and quoted abundantly are the 'balance sheet' of the reign of Joanna I and the 'judgement' on Urban VI, and from Di Costanzo and Giannone the 'great balance sheet' of the political and civil government of king Ladislas', etc.: Galasso, *Il regno di Napoli*, 232, 248, 274.

The kingdom of Naples

A second conditioning effect lies in the transmission of the sources. As many of the public written records have been destroyed in the course of time, thanks in particular to an arson incident in 1943, the historian of the south of Italy is forced to work on transmission that is indirect, fragmentary, random and, above all, marked by the personalities of scholars and past historians. Together with the sources, these have also transmitted a sensitivity to certain questions and even a hierarchy of arguments.[44]

Fortunately, the disaster of 1943 greatly boosted the search for new sources, so much so that a peculiar feature of current research into southern Italy seems to be that of complete editions, be they of chancery records recovered from quotations and editions prior to their destruction, Tuscan and Catalan written public accounts records, diplomatic correspondence, notarial protocols or city statutes.[45]

Finally, the stereotypes of the south are ignored by those who, in comparisons with international historiography, introduce new perspectives and methods to the historiography of the kingdom.[46] This, however, is not enough, as it often happens that southern Italian historiography borrows external research models and priorities and superimposes them on its own sources, without sounding them out carefully and respectfully, as Mario Del Treppo would say. I would like to end by quoting this masterful historian, of Istrian origin but who chose Naples as his adopted city. His work and teaching are perhaps one of the major novelties in southern Italian historiography in the second half of the twentieth century.[47] His assessment of 1977, as lucid as it is far-sighted in the research directions proposed, remains to this day an essential requisite for gaining a knowledge of the characters and history of southern Italian historiography.[48]

---

[44] Morelli, 'Il controllo delle periferie', 27–8; Senatore, 'Gli archivi delle *universitates*', 465–77, 496–8; Airò, 'L'inventario dell'archivio', 535–58.
[45] I refer here to the Accademia Pontaniana di Napoli series (*Registri e Fascicoli della cancelleria angioina*; *Fonti aragonesi*), the publications of Jole Mazzoleni, the diplomatic correspondence edited by the Istituto Italiano per gli Studi Filosofici, the Cartulari notarili campani del XV secolo series co-ordinated by A. Leone, and the volumes published by Congedo and Carlone editions.
[46] To be noted here is the work of the Congressi della Corona d'Aragona, two of which were held in Naples (1973, 1997), that of the École française de Rome and that of the Mediterranean History Inter-University Group (GISEM), founded by Gabriella Rossetti and particularly active in the decade 1984–94.
[47] Capitani, 'Medioevo', 291–2; Vitolo, 'Storiografie parallele'.
[48] Del Treppo, *La libertà della memoria*, 109–49.

3 The kingdom of Sardinia and Corsica

Olivetta Schena

Introduction

At the end of the thirteenth century the battle for commercial and political predominance over the western Mediterranean was more alive than ever before. The crown of Aragon had joined the two great rivals Genoa and Pisa in the contention for Sardinia and Corsica. Having gained possession of the Balearic islands and Sicily, it looked on the latter as an indispensible base for maritime expansion.

The battle also involved the papacy, as for centuries it had proclaimed the right of the church of Rome to *dominium eminens* (supreme dominion) over the three large Tyrrhenian islands. And it was indeed from the papacy, when it had seemed that Sicily, Sardinia and Corsica were finally released from its authority, that the initiative came that would place Sardinia, institutionally known as the kingdom of Sardinia and Corsica, inside the state framework of first the crown of Aragon (1324–1516) and then the crown of Spain.

The Trecento: the birth of the kingdom of Sardinia and Corsica

On 4 April 1297 pope Boniface VIII, in order to resolve diplomatically the war of the Vespers[1] – which broke out in 1282 between the Angevin and Aragonese over possession of Sicily – instituted the hypothetical kingdom of Sardinia and Corsica and enfeoffed it to James II, sovereign of the crown of Aragon, in exchange for a feudal fee and pledge of loyalty.[2] The concession of the kingdom was, in reality, a purely nominal act: the islands of Sardinia and Corsica were already politically and institutionally configured and as Casula writes, 'in respect to them the pope gave only a *licentia invadendi* (right of conquest)'.[3] It was necessary

---

[1] Corrao, 'Il nodo mediterraneo'.
[2] Salavert y Roca, *Cerdeña y la expansión mediterránea*, I, 126ff.; II, doc. 21, 22–30.
[3] Casula, *La storia di Sardegna*, 381.

to develop diplomatic and military action to render effective, with or without the consensus of the existing state and judicial bodies, the crown's sovereignty over those territories. In Sardinia these were the overseas possessions of the city of Pisa (represented by the territories of the 'fallen' *giudicali* kingdoms of Càlari and Gallura), the territorial *signorie* of the Doria, Malaspina and Donoratico, and the kingdom or *giudicato* of Arborea; Corsica, contested by Pisa and Genoa, from 1299 until 1769 would belong constantly to the Ligurian republic and the Bank of San Giorgio and would never be conquered by the Catalan-Aragonese.

Possession of Sardinia, perfectly in line with the crown of Aragon's politics of Mediterranean expansion,[4] posed serious diplomatic problems. The strategic position of the island would have facilitated the crown's control of the Tyrrhenian commercial routes. This, in turn, would have disadvantaged the republics of Pisa and Genoa, which had for centuries based their economic fortunes on the use of these routes and had acquired broad political and commercial interests in Sardinia.

Possession of the island undoubtedly offered interesting economic prospects to Aragon:[5] Sardinia was known for its grain production, especially in the *giudicato* of Arborea and in the *curatoria* (district) of Trexenta; for the productive salt fields near Cagliari; rich silver mines in the Sulcis and the Sigerro; precious corals in the seas to the north-west of the island and all the products (leather, cheese, meat, wine, oil, dried fruits) of the farming-pastoral activities of the local populations. But it was the papacy, at least in the beginning, that drew the greatest advantage from the conquest: the feudal annuity from the Aragonese sovereign of 2,000 silver marks (about 500 kg) and the extension to the island of the mechanisms of centralism and fiscalism that had been established by the Aragonese curia. The society and the church of Sardinia were less fortunate as the feudal system imported by the conquerers affected everyone equally and with uniform rigour over the whole island.

The military campaign for the conquest of Sardinia, begun only in 1323, was preceded by a long diplomatic approach, ably conducted by James II to win the greatest possible consensus among the diverse political realities of the island. Alliances and feudal-type relations were established with the *giudici* of Arborea and Donoratico, and with the anti-Pisans Doria and the Malaspina, who offered their various levels of

---

[4] For a good synthesis, see Del Treppo, 'L'espansione'.
[5] On the economic resources of Sardinia, see Manca, *Aspetti dell'espansione economica*; Tangheroni, *Aspetti del commercio dei cereali*; Tangheroni, *La città dell'argento*; Simbula, *Sale e saline*.

support and accepted a situation of feudal dependence that time would reveal to be extremely insidious. In propitiating the Catalan-Aragonese conquest, beyond the favour of almost all the popes – excepting John XXII (1316–34) who did everything to discourage it[6] – an important role was played by a great hostility to the Pisans that was very common in the Sardinian society and church, expressing itself in an almost messianic expectation of the next 'coming' of the king of Aragon.[7] James II's intention was that the military campaign for the conquest of the kingdom would be limited to a battle with Pisa, already diplomatically isolated, for the occupation of its Sardinian territories, the ex-*giudicati* of Càlari and Gallura.

The military operations began in June 1323, with the disembarkation in the gulf of Sulcis of a powerful army commanded by the Infante Alfonso, and ended in 1326: in those three years Pisa lost all of its possessions, including the fortified city of Villa di Chiesa (today's Iglesias) and Castel di Castro (today's Castello, historic quarter of the city of Cagliari). Only the *curatorie* of Gippi and Trexenta remained in Pisan hands, and these also became fiefs of the crown of Aragon until 1365. Even the city of Sassari, a flourishing commune in the north, developed under the aegis of, and governed by pacts stipulated by, the republic of Genoa, was soon turned to the crown's cause. The military campaign was difficult and expensive both economically and in terms of human lives, and allowed James II to occupy three-quarters of the island.[8] These lands composed the first nucleus of the kingdom of Sardinia and Corsica, which was instituted in the Bonaria camp on 19 June 1324 and aggregated in real union to the crown of Aragon.[9]

But discontent and hostility, both on and off the island, were soon apparent. First Genoa, worried about the consequences that might come from a stable Aragonese domination of Sardinia and the surrounding seas, fomented continuous rebellion in Sassari, the 'restless city',[10] and among some Genoese families with deep roots in the island's north, the Sardo-Ligurian Doria and Malaspina. The conflict between Genoa and the crown of Aragon, which exploded openly in 1330, was one of the most important internationally resonant consequences of the Catalan-Aragonese presence in Sardinia.[11] The high state of tension between the

---

[6] Sanna, 'Papa Giovanni XXII'.
[7] Casula, *La Sardegna aragonese*, I, 61–146; Turtas, *Storia della chiesa in Sardegna*, 301–2.
[8] Arribas Palau, *La conquista de Cerdeña*; Casula, *La Sardegna aragonese*, I, 147–211; Cadeddu, 'Giacomo II d'Aragona'.
[9] Casula, *La storiografia sarda*, 9, 15.
[10] Galoppini, *Ricchezza e potere nella Sassari aragonese*, 15–41.
[11] Meloni, *Genova e Aragona*.

two powers contending the Tyrrhenian caused repercussions in the Mediterranean for some centuries, with increasingly continuous activity of hit-and-run attacks, not always distinguishable from acts of piracy, which from the second half of the Trecento and into the Quattrocento occurred often to the detriment of mercantile activity.[12]

The reign of Peter IV of Aragon and the long conflict with the *giudici* of Arborea

During the reign of Peter IV the Ceremonious (1336–87)[13] the war with Genoa reached as far as the seas of Constantinople where the crown, allied with Venice, ruinously defeated its hated enemy in the battle of the Bosporus (1352). The following year this success was renewed in the waters of Porto Conte, off Alghero.

In Sardinia, meanwhile, the delicate political balance that had been put in place just after the conquest had broken down. The centralising politics of the king of Aragon, now also the king of Sardinia and Corsica, had radically modified the political and administrative structure of the island – introducing the feudal system,[14] a method of governing which is well adapted to the maintenance of conquered territories but fatally destined to escape the control of royal power, together with the often uncontrolled activities of those holding offices in the royal administration[15] – creating a strong sense of discomfort in the populace. Ugone II of Arborea in 1325 had already described the situation, writing to Napoleone Orsini that the Sardinians, who believed that they had a new king, found instead that they had as many kings as there were villages in the old *giudicato* of Càlari: 'Sardi qui unum regem se habuisse credebant et modo habent tot reges quot sunt ville in Kallaro.'[16] The poor governance of the royal officials, who at a distance from the centre all became 'little lords', and the absenteeism of the feudal lords from Iberia (above all the Catalans, but also the Valencians, Mallorcans and Aragonese) caused widespread discontent among the Sardinians, and the *giudici* of Arborea expressed it from 1353–4.

Mariano IV of Arborea (1347–75) in particular seems not to have agreed with the politics of the former allies, the sovereigns of the crown

---

[12] Simbula, *Corsari e pirati*.
[13] Schena, 'Pietro IV il Cerimonioso', 457–506, and for the bibliography, 506–12.
[14] Tangheroni, 'Il feudalesimo', 41–6.
[15] Olla Repetto, *Studi sulle istituzioni amministrative e giudiziarie*, 13–70, 121–66.
[16] Arribas Palau, *La conquista de Cerdeña*, doc. 52, p. 430.

of Aragon, and affirmed his political[17] and institutional autonomy with increasing decisiveness, while maintaining his position of personal vassallage to the crown of Aragon (in 1339 young Mariano IV had been named count of Goceano by Peter IV of Aragon). The intolerance of Mariano IV for Peter IV, skilfully stoked by the Genoese, became violently apparent despite repeated attempts by the Catalan admiral Bernardo de Cabrera to intercede after the battle of Porto Conte (1353) and on the eve of the disembarkation of the Catalan fleet, commanded by the king of Aragon himself, at Alghero. The city, founded by the Sardo-Ligurian Doria, had passed to the control of the crown with the conquest of the kingdom and had embraced the Arborense cause, opening its gates to the troops of Mariano IV and Matteo Doria in October 1353. On 22 June 1354 it was attacked by the Catalan-Aragonese and after a lengthy siege the city was reconquered and completely repopulated by Catalans: this solution had been used before at Castel di Castro in 1326 after the Pisans had been driven out.[18] Domination over the two fortified cities and control of their ports would have guaranteed possession of the kingdom of Sardinia to the crown of Aragon, even in the most difficult moments of the war against the *giudici* of Arborea.

Mariano IV's diplomatic ability gave international breathing space to the Arborense 'contestation'. In fact a wise political marriage allowed him to find allies in areas of the Catalan aristocracy that were already in conflict with the monarchy, in French viscounts from Narbonne, in the powerful Roman family De Vico, lords of Viterbo, and on the island itself with the restless Brancaleone Doria.[19] The Arborense *giudice* also succeeded in gaining credit at the pontifical court when it, with Urban V (1362–70), seemed oriented towards retracting the bull with which Boniface VIII had enfeoffed the kingdom of Sardinia and Corsica to the count-king of Barcelona. In 1365 Peter IV, because of the by now decades-old delay in the payment of the fee of 2,000 silver marks, was excommunicated and declared shorn of any right over the kingdom. Around 1370 Mariano IV looked to the pope to obtain, perhaps, a direct

---

[17] Casula, *La Sardegna aragonese*, I, 242–54, underscores the royal status of the Sardinian judges and from this point of view studies the military opposition between the two regnal polities – Arborea and Aragona, placed on an equal judicial plane – that became an encounter between two *nacions*, Sardinia and Spain. For a new reading of the encounter-conflict between Peter IV and Mariano IV, see Gallinari, 'Alcuni "discorsi" politici e istituzionali'.

[18] Conde y Delgado de Molina and Aragó Cabañas, *Castell de Càller*, 9–33; Conde y Delgado de Molina, 'Il ripopolamento catalano di Alghero'.

[19] *Genealogie medioevali di Sardegna*, L. L. Brook and M. M. Costa (eds.), tab. XXXIII, 138–9.

investiture of the whole island or at least of the territories under his control: 'iudex Arboree surgessit summo pontifici et tractavit in curia romana quod dominus rex [Peter IV] privaretur titolo regni Sardinie et quod aplicaretur dicto iudici [the *giudice* of Arborea unsuccessfully appealed to the pope and negotiated with the Roman curia, asking that king Peter IV be deprived of the title of king of Sardinia and that it be conferred upon the *giudice* Mariano IV]'.[20]

The war, begun by Mariano IV in 1349 with the siege of Bosa and after a short armistice sealed by the peace of Alghero (1354) and the more stable peace of Sanluri (1355),[21] continued ruinously until 1364–5 and then with the heirs to the throne of Arborea, the *giudici* Ugone III (1376–83) and Eleonora (1383–1403) – queen regent for her young sons Frederick (died in 1387) and Mariano. Under her regency a new peace was signed in 1388 that altered the balance of the forces in play. It also turned out to be certainly favourable to the Catalan-Aragonese as it restored to them the territories of the Campidano and Gallura which the Arborense had conquered by force of arms with the help of the Sardinians of the kingdom, which by the eve of that ephemeral peace was reduced to the cities of Cagliari and Alghero only.[22] But soon enough the accords were violated and in the summer of 1391 the Arborense Sardinians, led by Brancaleone Doria, husband of Eleonora, and by their son Mariano V, took up arms again, reoccupying in short order the lands lost to the Catalan-Aragonese in 1388. The recurrence of hostilities in Sardinia coincided with the revival of tension between Genoa and the crown of Aragon, following the growing interest on the part of the Iberian monarch in a kingdom of Sicily that was prey to civil war.[23]

With the heirs of Peter IV, John I (1387–96) and Martin I (1396–1410), the projection of the crown of Aragon into the Mediterranean returns to the foreground, and it would result in the definitive acquisition of the kingdom of Sicily, which had already returned to the dynastic orbit of the crown by virtue of the marriage of Constance, Peter IV's first child, to Frederick the Simple, king of Sicily. In 1390 in Barcelona their daughter, Maria – kidnapped in 1382 in the castle of Ursino at Catania and then, after a brief stay at Castel di Cagliari in Sardinia, transported to Catalonia – married Martin the Younger, grandson of Peter IV and son of Martin the Elder. It is significant that, in 1406, in the Catalan

---

[20] Casula, *La Sardegna aragonese*, II, 370–7; Turtas, *Storia della chiesa in Sardegna*, 306–10, in particular 310 nn. 87–8.
[21] Casula, *La Sardegna aragonese*, I, 263–310.   [22] *Ibid.*, II, 384–401, 423–48.
[23] Tramontana, *Il Mezzogiorno medievale*, 115–35.

'courts' reunited at Perpignan, Martin I – in recalling the events that, by means of military campaigns and fortunate marriages, had made the crown of Aragon grand in the Mediterranean – associated the propulsive strength of its Mediterranean expansion to its strong ties with Sicily. That is, Martin believed that controlling Sicily, with its favourable economic and geographical position, granted the Catalan-Aragonese monarchy two benefits: firstly, domestically, the monarchy could ensure the co-operation of the Aragonese aristocracy and the Catalan merchant elites; secondly, the island could play the role of protagonist in encounters with France and with the Italian cities.[24]

During these same years the kingdom of Sardinia seemed instead to elude the control of the crown, and it was precisely in Sardinia that, in 1409, Martin – the young king of Sicily – died. He had answered his father's appeal to help the Catalan military involved in the final phases of the conflict that had opposed the *giudicale* kingdom of Arborea – now governed by the French William III, viscount of Narbonne – to the crown of Aragon. The kingdom of Sicily, which had earlier gone to the aid of Cagliari and Alghero with shipments of grain, financed and supplied the entire expeditionary corps: the ships on which Martin sailed were financed in part by, and wholly constructed in, Sicily. His death marked the end of the glorious dynasty of the count-kings of Barcelona (in 1410 the death of his father Martin I of Aragon and II of Sicily brought about a dynastic crisis which was resolved by the compromise of Caspe in 1412 that assigned the crown of Aragon to Ferdinand I of the Castiglian Trastámara dynasty)[25] and the eve of the "effective" end of the *giudicato* of Arborea: in 1410, during the seige of Oristano, *giudicale* capital, the historic territory of the *giudicato* was transformed into the marquisate of Oristano, the largest fief in the kingdom of Sardinia, and enfeoffed to Leonaro Cubello.[26] The quarrel with William III, last *giudice* of Arborea, was resolved by the crown in 1420 during the reign of Alfonso V (1416–58) by (partial) payment of 150,000 gold Aragonese florins to the viscount and his heir over the course of a decade in exchange for his renunciation of rights to the *giudicale* throne.[27]

The value of a conquest

The enterprise of conquering the kingdom of Sardinia and Corsica, begun in 1323 and ending with the occupation of Sardinia alone in

---

[24] *Ibid.*, 121. [25] Abulafia, *The Western Mediterranean Kingdoms*, 182–9.
[26] Casula, *La Sardegna aragonese*, II, 507–56.
[27] Gallinari, 'Guglielmo III di Narbona'; Gallinari, 'Gli ultimi anni di esistenza'.

1420, 'had become a bottomless pit over time for the human and economic resources of the crown':[28] thus the lapidary and shareable judgement expressed by Tangheroni.

The conflict that bloodied the island for about seventy years had devastating consequences on the economy and, together with the periodic plague epidemics, caused a serious demographic crisis. The historian John Day has calculated that the Black Death alone (1348) would have caused a 43 per cent loss of the rural population,[29] and to this, by the beginning of the Quattrocento, is associated the disappearance of half of the settlements; in Nurra, Gallura, Sarrabus and Sulcis as many as 90 per cent of the settlements were abandoned.[30]

Following the studies of the past twenty years, and especially those of Anatra, Casula, Meloni and Tangheroni, I may in any case affirm that the conquest of Sardinia marks both a high point and a turning point in the expansionist politics of the Catalan-Aragonese monarchy in the western Mediterranean.[31]

It is a high point because it provides the missing link in the 'diagonal of the islands' for the years from 1230 (for the Balearics) and importantly from 1282 in Sicily. This famous imagery, conceptualised by the great Catalan historian Vicens Vives, projected Catalan commerce, especially that of Barcelona, towards the coasts of North Africa and the eastern Mediterranean.[32]

It marks a turning point because the discontinuous war that the monarchy had to wage until 1409 with the *giudici* of Arborea (with its temporary moments of peace in 1355 with Mariano V and in 1388 with Eleonora), with the French viscounts of Narbonne (until the definitive peace in 1420) and above all with Genoa (until the alliance of Andrea Doria with Charles V in 1528) in order to conserve and consolidate the possession of that kingdom was accompanied by a process of institutional reorganisation of all the territories that make up the crown of Aragon.[33]

The Catalan-Aragonese kingdom in Sardinia was reorganised by introducing the administrative model used by the other realms of the

---

[28] Tangheroni, *Aspetti del commercio dei cereali*, 119.
[29] Day, *Uomini*, 63–106, 193–226; on the phenomenon of depopulation, see also Livi, 'La popolazione'.
[30] For the abandoned villages, see *Vita e morte dei villaggi rurali*, especially the contributions by Milanese, Campus, Murgia, Soddu and Serreli, 9–78, 123–60.
[31] Anatra, 'Dall'unificazione aragonese ai Savoia'; Casula, *La Sardegna aragonese*, II; Meloni, *Genova e Aragona*; Tangheroni,'Il *"Regnum Sardiniae et Corsicae"*'.
[32] Vicens Vives, *Manual de historia economica*, 189–90.
[33] For the kingdom of Sardinia, see Lalinde Abadía, *La Corona de Aragón*, 103–97.

crown: control of the countyside by conceding fiefs to those who had aided the conquest of the island; independent administration of the more important economic and strategic urban centres (Cagliari, Iglesias, Sassari, Castelaragonese, Bosa, Alghero and later Oristano), qualified as 'royal cities' and aggregated to the royal domain, integrated by concessions of graces and privileges that for the most part recalled Catalan, and particularly Barcelonese, traditions.[34]

The change in social and administrative organisation with the institution of the kingdom was radical on the institutional, political, social, linguistic and cultural planes. The profound transformation was felt above all in the cities: at Cagliari, and later at Alghero, there was a complete change in the population with the expulsion of the Pisans, Genoese and some Sardinians, and the reassignment of all the buildings to Catalans, Aragonese, Valencians and Mallorcans who at various times had participated in the conquest and whose military contribution had made the kingdom possible.[35] Almost immediately, in 1327, this was extended to the city of Castel di Cagliari, with the privilege called *Coeterum*,[36] the privileged legislation enjoyed by Barcelona: the city was on its way to becoming '*caput totius Sardinie regni* [capital of the kingdom of Sardinia]',[37] described in a Catalan source of the Trecento: 'notoria cosa e certa que.l Castell de Càller sia un dels excellent e nobles castell del món, e sia clau de tota la isla de Sardenya, e sia una de les pus nobles joyes del món [it is known and certain that Castel di Cagliari is one of the most important and noble castles of the world, and is the key to the whole island of Sardinia, but also one of the most precious jewels in the world]'.[38]

Integration of the Sardinian realm into the institutional structure of the crown of Aragon carried another strong point in the introduction of the institute of the Corti: a Catalan type of parliament that was founded on the principle of 'pacting', a contractual concept of relations with the crown that recalled the principle *quid pro quo,* placing in close connection the concession of the gift requested of the sovereign and the approval on his part of the *Capitoli* (petitions) proposed by the *Stamenti* or *Bracci*.[39]

It was for Sardinia a complete novelty that had no relationship to the assemblies of the former states: for Sardinia, and for its specific institutional history prior to the conquest, one must use the term 'imported

---

[34] Casula, *La Sardegna aragonese*, I, 177–99. [35] See n. 18.
[36] Di Tucci, *Il Libro Verde della città di Cagliari*, doc. 41, pp. 145–54.
[37] Urban, *Cagliari aragonese.*
[38] Archivo de la Corona de Aragón de Barcelona, *Cancilleria*, reg. 424, f. 90r.
[39] Marongiu, *I Parlamenti sardi.*

parliament'.[40] The great difference between the Sardinian experience and that of Sicily and Naples lies in the fact that in the latter two the parliaments were local institutions that at least in part represented the community, while in Sardinia the portion of society called to parliament was almost exclusively of Catalan-Aragonese extraction. The parliamentary assembly was, then, at least during the early parliaments, representative of the dominant groups – those which Anatra has aptly termed 'privileged groups'[41] – and the Sardinians could participate only in a very limited way.[42]

The Sardinian parliament, like those introduced by the crown in other Italian domains belonging to the Catalan-Aragonese confederation, was 'stamentale, iuxta lo still y pratica de Cathalunya [according to the style and the procedures of Catalonia]', and formed of three *Stamenti* or branches: the ecclesiastic, which included the bishops, archbishops and abbots of the more important monasteries in the kingdom as well as the representatives of the dioceses' chapters; the military to which were called all the feudatories; and the royal which included the representatives or agents of all the royal cities and the towns which were not enfeoffed. The upper officials of the royal administration also participated in the parliament: the keeper of the royal chancery, the *maestro razionale*, the governors of the *Capi* of Cagliari and Sassari, and the fiscal and patrimonial agents.[43]

The parliament, introduced into the island in the fourteenth century – in 1355 Peter IV called and presided over the first parliament of the kingdom of Sardinia[44] – was perfected in the course of the fifteenth with the assembly of 1421, convoked and presided over by Alfonso V,[45] and that of 1481–5[46] – called by Ferdinand II but presided over by the viceroy Ximén Pérez Escrivá. It reached full judicial and institutional maturity at the end of the last parliament called by the Catholic king – whose labours, preceded by three brief parliamentary meetings (1495, 1497, 1500), began in 1504 and finished only in 1511 after repeated delays and long periods of suspension – a 'miles-long parliament' presided at first by viceroy Giovanni Dusay and then from 1507 by viceroy Ferdinando Girón de Rebolledo.[47] The parliamentary assemblies that in the course of the sixteenth and seventeenth centuries were held every ten years had varying success owing to the political, economic and social

---

[40] Koenigsberger, 'Parlamenti e istituzioni rappresentative', 597 and ff.
[41] Anatra, 'Corona e ceti privilegiati'.
[42] Olla Repetto (ed.), *La Corona d'Aragona. Un patrimonio comune*, 174.
[43] Oliva, 'Il consiglio regio'.   [44] Meloni (ed.), *Il Parlamento di Pietro IV*.
[45] Boscolo (ed.), *I Parlamenti di Alfonso il Magnanimo*, Schena (ed.).
[46] Era, *Il Parlamento sardo*.   [47] Oliva and Schena (eds.), *I Parlamenti dei vicerè*.

events in the kingdom of Sardinia, but in any case they strongly influenced that polity, and became a supporting element in its judicial-institutional history, an identifying mark of the Sardinian people.

The Quattrocento: historical notes

'The history of Sardinian society in the Quattrocento has not yet been written' is the premise for Olla's study in the mid-1980s that offered an absolutely new and extremely interesting picture of Cagliaritan society in the fifteenth century. The author indicated the typology of sources employed and of those available, as well as the tendencies of a certain kind of history of Sardinia as some of the reasons for its unfortunate slowness: a political conception of history that had induced consideration of the Quattrocento as an extension of the preceding century by linking the end of the marquisate of Oristano in 1478 to the end of the *giudicato* of Arborea in 1420.[48] One may perhaps add to these thoughts that, to a certain kind of more recent historiography is due instead a political nationalistic conception of that period that sees it as the last glorious indigenous kingdom, the end of the 'nationalist dream of making Sardinia Sardinian'[49] and the consequent loss of interest in a reality that was becoming 'Catalanised' in the fifteenth century (with the fall in fact (1410) and legally (1420) of the *giudicato* of Arborea).

A different historical view but with identical results can be observed in those who see written in the Quattrocento the final lines of the earlier century and report a progressive marginalisation of the Sardinian ports from the principal maritime and commercial routes, with the consequent provincialisation of the island, aggravated by royal absenteeism, which produced political friction and impatience.[50]

In all of these reconstructions the Quattrocento is seen as a period of hostility and strong ethnic, economic, social and class opposition between the Catalan-Aragonese and the Sardinians, between feudatories and urban classes and between barons and other officials, with a marked accentuation of economic and social decline on the island. According to this historical perspective Sardinia would have been completely removed from the contemporary Mediterranean reality, absolutely extraneous to the political, economic and cultural context that characterised the Italian, and to a somewhat lesser degree the Iberian, Quattrocento.

---

[48] Olla Repetto, 'La società cagliaritana', esp. 19 nn. 1, 6.
[49] Casula, *La Sardegna aragonese*, II; Casula, *La storia di Sardegna*, 372.
[50] Anatra, 'Economia sarda e commercio mediterraneo'.

In this historiographical view there was already counterpoised, as early as the 1970s, a vision of the Mediterranean as an active and lively centre of traffic and commerce, with the Sardinian ports on the principal mercantile routes. The major work of Mario Del Treppo[51] is the basis for this new reading of the history of the Mediterranean Quattrocento, as it restores that maritime activity to Barcelona which had been denied by the backers of the total crisis thesis[52] – whereas the documents show lively activity up until about 1460 – and documents the importance of Cagliari and Alghero as ports of call along the route eastwards.

After commercial relations, scholars have turned their attention to the definition of a Mediterranean cultural area that began to form between 1440 and 1460: the Mediterranean circulation that had its fulcrum at Naples at the time of Alfonso the Magnanimous involved a much larger area including the large islands and, therefore, also Sardinia.[53]

These points, important to more complete understanding and at the same time more open on an international plane, were not immediately accepted by historians of Sardinia. At the beginning of the 1990s, Tangheroni was still in agreement with Olla's analysis when – examining the economic aspects of the role of Sardinia in the Quattrocento – he underscored that 'research in the last thirty years has concentrated much less on this period than on the one preceding',[54] and he recommended a certain caution against negative judgements as well as new investigations.

The proposal of a 'rereading' of the history of the Sardinian Quattrocento and its 'lesser "Renaissance" [...] but extremely important for its history',[55] put forward by Olla and reproposed in an economic key by Tangheroni in the early 1990s, finds confirmation in recent sectorial studies that have undeniably demonstrated that the fifteenth century marked the beginning of an economic, civil and cultural renewal for the island.[56]

Alfonso V and the economic renewal

Between the fourteenth and sixteenth centuries men, experiences and cultures – despite deep institutional, political and social differences – began

---

[51] Del Treppo, *I mercanti catalani*, 159, tab. II, but also 148, tab. I.
[52] Vilar, *La Catalogne dans l'Espagne moderne*; Carrère, *Barcelone 1380–1462*.
[53] Bologna, *Napoli e le rotte mediterranee della pittura*.
[54] Tangheroni, 'Il "*Regnum Sardiniae et Corsicae*"', 72–9.
[55] Olla Repetto, 'La società cagliaritana', 23.
[56] Manconi, 'Catalogna e Sardegna'; Oliva and Schena, 'Il regno di Sardegna', 101–34, and the bibliography, 102 n. 7.

to circulate around the whole of Mediterranean Europe, and this movement became characteristic of the period. Iradiel identified the homogenising elements characterising the western Mediterranean in common global interests and a more cultural than economic aggregation.[57]

The story of the kingdom of Sardinia in the Quattrocento has not been extraneous to and remote from this reality. After the early years of the century and the end of the long war that had opposed the Sardinians of the *giudicato* of Arborea – but also the Sardinians of the kingdom of Sardinia, 'rebellious' subjects of the crown of Aragon – to the Catalan-Aragonese, there began a long period of peace for the island. Interrupted only by the revolt of Leonardo Alagón in 1478, it favoured social and economic renewal. Tangheroni, in considering the role of the kingdom of Sardinia in the new economic picture of the crown in the Mediterranean, recognises the interest of the new dynasty Trastámara for the island, whether in the political action of Ferdinand I (1412–16) or in that of Alfonso V (1416–58) who, after another failed attempt to occupy Corsica,[58] 'initiated his Italian policy by concentrating on Sardinia, and where he moved in 1420 and stayed for a year'. He returned there in 1432, having chosen Cagliari as the departure point for his expedition against the sultan of Tunisia: a natural pretext for beginning the second military campaign in the Mediterranean.[59]

Economic recovery revitalised the exchanges between Sardinian ports and especially between Cagliari and Alghero[60] and other Mediterranean markets; this development would be helped by the Magnanimous's initiatives towards a protectionist, almost autarchic, 'common market' of all the realms of the crown of Aragon, with the aim of a 'reorganisation of trade' so that 'los regnes daça prenguessen de aquelle de allà e no de otra part draps de lana, dels quals habunden [the Mediterranean realms of the crown be supplied only by the continental kingdoms with the bolts of wool that abounded there]', supplying the Iberians from the Italian kingdoms (Naples and Sicily) with those stores that they were now looking for outside the confederation.[61]

Beyond the full and complete inclusion of the Sardinian ports into the commercial traffic in the Mediterranean, particular commercial attention was directed towards the Levant. From the middle of the

---

[57] Iradiel, 'Introduzione'. [58] Meloni, 'Alfonso il Magnanimo e la Corsica'.
[59] Tangheroni, 'Il "*Regnum Sardiniae et Corsicae*"', 74.
[60] Zedda, *Cagliari*; Simbula, 'Il porto di Cagliari'; Mattone, 'I privilegi e le istituzioni municipali di Alghero'.
[61] Del Treppo, 'Il regno aragonese', 97; Tangheroni, 'Trasporti navali', 43.

Quattrocento Cagliari was included in the Atlantic route to Flanders, following a strategy of economic policy set up by Alfonso V: the presence of men from this Atlantic world in Sardinia is witness to these associations.[62]

Cagliari, besides being an obligatory stop on the *ruta de las islas* (island route) since the times of James II the Just,[63] after 1442 became a base for passage, a true 'container' port between Barcelona and the new Neapolitan possessions of the crown of Aragon, the centre of a thick radiating network of both maritime and mainland commercial interests. It was woven by Iberian and Iberian-descent merchants who lived in Castello, but also by the Sicilians and Neapolitans of Stampace and Villanova, who exported grain, cattle, skins, raw wool, cheeses, salt and wood, and imported spices, Flemish and Catalan fabrics, utensils, arms and metals.[64] Apropos of this, Ciro Manca shows us a very interesting image of a Quattrocento Cagliari that he places at the centre of a triangle having Barcelona, Palermo and Naples at its vertices.[65]

The merchant class is certainly emergent in the Sardinian panorama of the Quattrocento. Many members of *companyes* – mercantile societies made up of residents of Catalonia and residents of Sardinia – having accumulated large fortunes, reinvested in the acquisition of lands and feudal titles to protect a part of their earnings. The phenomenon of the 'fief rush' really concerned not only the merchants but also the royal bureaucracy and men in the public view in the patriciate of Cagliari, Sassari and Alghero, who belonged to a closed circle of aristocratic houses and mercantile dynasties.[66] This confirms Del Treppo's theory according to which 'the Catalan merchants constituted a unifying factor in the Mediterranean that was even more powerful than the political factor represented by the crown'.[67]

Tangheroni specifies that economic recovery brought a new, even if limited, migratory movement of merchants of a certain level and specialised artisans from Valencia, Barcelona, Mallorca and Gerona, which was recognised and sometimes aided by the crown.[68] The migratory flow

---

[62] Olla Repetto and Catani, 'Cagliari e il mondo atlantico'; Tasca, 'Portoghesi in Sardegna'.
[63] Meloni, 'Contributo allo studio delle rotte'.
[64] Manconi, 'Catalogna e Sardegna', 43 and ff.; Zedda, *Cagliari*, 24–33, 183–97.
[65] Manca, 'Colonie iberiche in Italia', 5 (preprint). An analogous image comes to us, pictorially, from Bologna, *Napoli e le rotte mediterranee della pittura*, and confirms that the Mediterranean routes were followed not only by merchants but also numerous artists; see also Manconi, 'Catalogna e Sardegna', 50–2, and the bibliography cited in nn. 50–8.
[66] Oliva and Schena, 'Il regno di Sardegna', 126–34.
[67] Del Treppo, 'La "Corona d'Aragona" e il Mediterraneo', 318.
[68] Tangheroni, 'Il "*Regnum Sardiniae et Corsicae*"', 74–5.

may have been quantitatively limited but it was qualitatively varied. We know in fact that, for various reasons, to settle or only stay briefly, exponents of the middle class, professionals and above all members of Catalan-Aragonese society who would take up offices in the royal and municipal administrations came to Sardinia.[69] It is known that, among others, members of the nobility and intellectuals participated in the political action of the crown, especially during the time of Alfonso V the Magnanimous. In the 1420 Sardinian expedition of Alfonso V there was the poet Jordi de Sant Jordi, who became an armed knight in 1420 during his sojourn on the island; Ausias March, a noble of Valencia and author of more than 120 poems, who was in the king's entourage during hunts inland; along with Andreu Febrer and Joan Toralles, who wrote a minor chronicle about Sardinia in the first half of the century.[70]

The royal administration was represented on all levels by Catalan-Aragonese exponents, some of whom belonged to first-rank noble families or the cultured middle class like Ferran Valentí, Mallorcan translator of Cicero's *Paradoxa* and a very able humanist who had studied in Bologna and Florence with Leonardo Bruni, dividing his time between classical studies and the political activity that brought him to serve Alfonso V in Sardinia in 1446.[71]

From the study of the economic and socio-cultural reality of Quattrocento Sardinia, which in recent years was leaning towards prosopographic analysis of the mercantile societies, the middle classes (doctors, notaries, judges, lawyers), the feudal houses and the political-administrative personnel, there emerges a new image of the island whose history is in perfect synchrony with that political, economic and cultural unity desired and attained by Alfonso V in the western Mediterranean.[72]

Ferdinand II and the politics of *redreç* (reform)

The kingdom of Sardinia in the second half of the Quattrocento, with Ferdinand II's rise to the throne, continued to be in the foreground of the crown's strategic plans. From the very beginning the king tried to reconcile traditional Catalan-Aragonese Mediterranean politics with the more peninsular Islamic and North African interests. His political programme envisioned the situation in the Mediterranean in first place: his intentions and political plans envisaged the complete

---

[69] Oliva, 'Il consiglio regio'; Oliva, 'Memorial de totes'.
[70] Carbonell, 'La lingua e la letteratura', 96. [71] Hillgarth, 'Mallorca e Italia'.
[72] Schena, 'Notai iberici a Cagliari nel XV secolo'; Oliva, 'March Jover'.

The kingdom of Sardinia and Corsica 65

enclosure of the Tyrrhenian sea – making it almost a lake – entirely to the advantage of his subjects.

The Ottoman capture of Otranto made the Mediterranean question even more pressing. In the Corti of Toledo in 1480, Ferdinand placed the need to remove the Turks from the Italian coasts above and before Gutierre de Cardenas's proposal to begin the war against Granada. His strategy foresaw the reinforcement of coastal defences and the ports of Sicily and Sardinia, which he asked the viceroys of the two island kingdoms to provide;[73] the consolidation of the Spanish presence at Rhodes, Cyprus, Malta, Gozo, Pantelleria and Djerba which had become hot points; and the training of a fleet to resolve these specific defensive problems under the command of his admiral Bernardo de Vilamarì. Under this strategic plan Rhodes was the defensive forward outpost, the kingdom of Sicily was the true front line and the kingdom of Sardinia the rear guard, but the latter turned out to be incomplete without Corsica, so in 1480 the viceroy of Sardinia Ximén Pérez Escrivá tried, in a failed conspiracy, to occupy Bonifacio. Ferdinand II's attempts to combine the defence of Sardinia and Corsica continued militarily and diplomatically for some years, to no particular effect.[74]

The Catalan-Aragonese society transplanted to the island after the conquest in early Trecento and by now well rooted was well aware as early as 1485 of the strategic role played by the kingdom of Sardinia. In regard to this the comments of Andrea Sunyer – agent of the city of Cagliari in the parliament of 1481–5 – to the sovereign are important: 'los reys predecessors de Vostra Gran Alteza han estimat molt aquell regne de Serdenya, conexent quant comprén, car ab aquell regne poguereu e podeu vós Senyor manassar e maltractar gran part de la Itàlia e de les Barbaries e feu-vos Senyor de aquelles mars [the kings of Aragon, your Highness's predecessors, much appreciated the kingdom of Sardinia – knowing how much it had cost – because from the kingdom they could and you, Sire, can, attack and beat a large part of Italy and the Barbary coast and make yourself lord of those seas]'.[75] Ferdinand II's campaigns in Italy, the conquest of the kingdom of Naples and the later campaigns in North Africa could only accentuate this role.

Even at the time of the Catholic king, Sardinia – in tune with other important points of the crown, Naples and Valencia – continued to attract migrants. The Torella family's experience is emblematic: in the second half of the century their history winds between Valencia,

---

[73] Oliva and Schena (eds.), *I Parlamenti dei vicerè*, 38–52.
[74] De la Torre, *Documentos*, I, docs. 7, 5–8; Suárez Fernández, *Claves históricas*, 195–226.
[75] Era, *Il Parlamento sardo*, 178; Oliva, 'Rahó es que sa Magestat vostra sapia'.

Cagliari, Naples and Rome, a concrete example of that cultural and political aristocracy that contributed to the creation of a unitary society in fifteenth-century Mediterranean Europe.[76]

Ferdinand II's interest in Sardinia is evident also in the setting up of a significant and incisive bureaucratic *redreç* intended first of all to reinforce the weight and authority of the institutions, making their actions effective, but also to reorganise and rationalise some sectors of the administration by eliminating useless offices and introducing new figures. First of all, to resolve the problem of royal absenteeism, he granted the position of *preheminencia real* (delegate of royal power) to the viceroy (1481), increasing his power; he instituted the office of *maestro razionale* (1480) for the kingdom of Sardinia and inserted it legally into the *sacro collegio*[77] (the royal council of the kingdom of Sardinia,[78] which had been created to support the viceroy's governance, a true and proper *alter ego* to the sovereign). In reforming the old royal chancery, he introduced into Sardinia as well the office of the regent of the royal chancery (1487);[79] and lastly, at the same time as the other realms of the crown of Aragon, just after the expulsion of the Jews (1492),[80] he made the tribunal of the Spanish inquisition operable in the island; it was sponsored by the Holy See but controlled by the monarchy.[81]

As Anatra states, 'the *redreç* of the apparatus of state constituted a necessary non-postponable hinge for Ferdinand's entire programme'.[82] Strengthening the apparatus of government allowed the sovereign to have greater control over delegated powers, and especially over those of the cities, so that for their councils and offices during his reign he introduced also in Sardinia the system of election by drawing the so-called *insaculatio* (names were placed into a sack for the drawing) which avoided the 'monopolising' of municipal offices by small power groups. No less important was the attack on feudal jurisdiction, bridled but not reduced, to safeguard the independence of the cities from feudatories and to the advantage of a more attentive royal control. Instead there were the authority and prestige of the corps of nobles, which with Ferdinand obtained the confirmation of the right (already granted by Alfonso V in 1446) of self-convocation – 'per supplicar e reparar greuge, per lo be e

---

[76] Oliva and Schena, 'I Torrella'.   [77] Todde,'Maestro razionale e amministrazione'.
[78] Oliva, 'Il consiglio regio'.
[79] Marongiu, 'Il Reggente la Reale Cancelleria'; Anatra, 'Dall'unificazione aragonese ai Savoia', 419–20.
[80] On the important presence of the Jewish community in Sardinia, see Tasca, *Gli Ebrei in Sardegna*; Tasca, *Ebrei e società in Sardegna*.
[81] Anatra, 'Dall'unificazione aragonese ai Savoia', 420–2.   [82] *Ibid.*, 418.

repos [to forward requests or resolve controversies, for the good and for the peace]' – of the kingdom, with the obligation of communicating to the competent authorities the date of the convocation, but no longer requiring the presence of a royal officer during the assembly.[83]

The policy of *redreç* (reform) had an immediate result and effects that were perhaps more significant for the prestige of the crown in respect to the other more properly Italian kingdoms, Sicily and Naples (dynastically autonomous for the whole second half of the Quattrocento, as the kingdom of Sicily had been in the Trecento), in which the monarchy inevitably battled against a long tradition of independent governing and the strongly independent will of the barons and some urban oligarchies. In Sardinia, instead, the territorial centralisation of government organs had been consolidated at the time of the Catalan conquest and tendencies towards autonomy on the part of the feudatories and the oligarchies were not able to withstand the institutional activism of the Catholic king and thus did not represent a problem for the crown.

Conclusion

From the preceding synthetic account emerges a political, institutional, economic and cultural journey by which the kingdom of Sardinia over the course of two centuries – from its constitution, 19 June 1324, to the death of Ferdinand II the Catholic in 1516 – lives a progessive process of assimilation between the *nació cathalana* (Catalan nation) and the *nació sardesca* (Sardinian nation), which is noticeable mostly in the cities and much less in the farming-herding internal areas, where documentation is particularly scarce or completely absent.

If the Trecento is characterised by a state of conflict, even if discontinuous, between Catalans and Sardinians, and thus the crown of Aragon had to impose itself by force of arms which did not facilitate the integration of the two *nacions*, during the Quattrocento, with the end of conflict and passage from a war economy to one of peace, accompanied by the administrative reform of the kingdom under the Catholic king, one may speak of a process of 'Catalanisation' involving almost the entire island and passing through the integration and pacific cohabitation of the two *nacions*. This process, unstoppable and extremely important for its institutional, economic and cultural effects, may be considered complete only in the full Cinquecento with the rise of Charles of Habsburg to the throne with the consequent extraordinary

---

[83] Oliva and Schena (eds.), *I Parlamenti dei vicerè*, doc. 384, pp. 719–20, 726.

broadening of the political horizons of the crown of Spain. The Catalan-Aragonese subjects felt a need to reassert their historical-political unity in defence of their juridico-institutional independence and, possibly, economic autonomy, and the kingdom of Sardinia is not extraneous to this process that ties it to the fate of eastern Spain. This shows, writes Manconi, 'that the political, economic and also ideological ties to the crown of Aragon [were] by now a reality, and [were] destined to perpetuate themselves even excluding the historical limits established by the kings of Aragon'.[84]

---

[84] Manconi, 'L'identità catalana della Sardegna', 106.

4   The papal state

Sandro Carocci

Introduction

Of all the princes in Europe, the popes alone 'have states, and do not defend them; and have subjects, and do not rule them'. From Machiavelli onwards, the peculiarities and insufficiencies of the papal state have been pointed out countless times. Jacob Burckhardt spoke of 'a thorough anomaly among the powers of Italy', and the most recent research on the Italian Renaissance states as a whole has defined the papal dominions as 'an area of utter peculiarity'.[1] Indeed, anyone who studies the papal state has to reckon with systems of power and institutions which were often unusual and at times totally unique. The very peculiarities of the temporal power of the popes will thus be one of the themes of this chapter. As well as illustrating characteristics and peculiar features, however, I shall also follow a quite different thread, seeking to highlight the many aspects of the papal state which were held in common with other, contemporary states, while at the same time stressing how some important aspects of the Renaissance state were particularly emphasised in that of the papacy.

In order to follow these two major themes, this chapter will be divided into seven parts. Three will sketch an outline of political events, mechanisms of government and territorial assets. The remainder will deal in various contexts with the idiosyncrasy and at the same time the representativity of the papal state. The analysis will focus on concepts of power and of the state: the characteristics of the remarkable double-sided sovereign figure of the pope, reigning at the same time over the universal church and a regional state (a 'double-headed Janus' as this has been termed);[2] the relations between the Holy See and the different subjects of its temporal dominion, in particular the *signori*, the Roman barons and, above all, the communal cities and their ruling elites/groups.

---

[1] Machiavelli, *The Prince*, 40; Burckhardt, *The Civilization*, 81; Lazzarini, *L'Italia*, 105.
[2] Prodi, *Il sovrano pontefice*, 49.

More generally, I will focus in particular on the links between the specific characteristics of papal sovereignty and the composite nature of its territorial dominions.

Fluctuations of power

Not only was the papal state the last territory to join unified Italy in 1870 (this is its first peculiar feature), but it is also, together with Venice, the earliest Italian political entity. The popes took part in the administration and government of the city of Rome and the region of Lazio already from the end of the sixth century. In the centuries to follow, the development of temporal powers proceeded slowly, alternating with periods of stasis. A multi-regional and concrete dominion was not really established until Innocent III, whom many historians define as the 'founder' of the papal state.[3] In the thirteenth century, the reality of temporal power varied greatly, however, according to political and military contingencies, and the papacy attained only a small part of its claims. Yet, despite this, it was able to maintain a stable provincial organisation, permanently exercise some prerogatives (mostly judicial and fiscal) and make important acquisitions, especially in the last three decades of the century.

From the death of Boniface VIII in 1303 to the middle of the fourteenth century, the remoteness of the curia brought with it a serious crisis in temporal authority. The only exceptions were the successes achieved in Bologna and the Romagna by the cardinal legate, Bertrand du Pouget. Sent by pope John XXII to fight the Visconti and Ghibelline forces in 1319, du Pouget obtained the full submission of several cities in Emilia and, above all, in Romagna, thus imposing Guelf–Angevin hegemony on the whole of northern Italy. In February 1327 even the major city of Bologna surrendered unconditionally to the legate. The cardinal intervened in the institutional structures of the subject cities in a fuller and more decisive way than the contemporary *signori*, introducing new concepts of power and new techniques of government, which were later to be adopted by the *signori* themselves. When Taddeo Pepoli became *signore* of Bologna in 1337, for example, he reintroduced the massive use of petitions and pardons, just as they had been used to express and enact autocratic power during the cardinal's regime.[4]

---

[3] The main summaries (which will be referred to for each single event) are: Waley, *The Papal State*; Partner, *The Lands*; Caravale, *Lo stato pontificio*. For all the topics dealt with in this essay, further bibliographical references can be found in Carocci, *Vassalli del papa*.

[4] Vallerani, 'La supplica al signore'; recent research is summarised in Jamme, 'Le Languedoc en Italie'.

A series of defeats, followed by the revolt of Bologna in 1334, put an end to du Pouget's rule and plunged the papal government back into a serious crisis. On various occasions in the past, historians attributed this crisis to a variety of factors, including the corruption of the French administrators sent by the Avignon popes, their lack of familiarity with the Italian situation, the turbulence of the communes and baronial families, or the birth of *signorile* governments. Of all these elements, the main issue was undoubtedly the spread of regimes of a personal and *signorile* character in most of the towns in the state. The numerous vicars and legates appointed to investigate papal administration, pacify temporal dominions and reassert the church's authority produced only modest and transitory results in the first half of the century. Between 1353 and 1367, on the other hand, highly significant developments were introduced by the cardinal legate, Gil de Albornoz. Some *signori* were defeated and deposed, whereas others held on to their dominions by becoming 'apostolic vicars' and thus submitting themselves to a series of undertakings, both political and financial. The papal approach towards the communes also underwent fundamental change, leading to much tighter control than in the past. Anticipating the actions of many fifteenth-century popes, Albornoz now adopted systems of control over urban communities that had been developed by *signori*. Indeed, the legate often himself formally assumed the title of *signore*.

Historiographical judgements on the actions of Albornoz have been subject to periodic revisions. In recent years, evaluations have tended once again to emphasise the strength of his political plan, which, it is argued, was to apply to the papal state governmental schemes developed by the great European monarchies. Indeed, Albornoz has even been identified as the actual founder of the state, and it has been argued that the model of government implemented by popes in the centuries to follow can be traced back to the cardinal.[5] In practice, Albornoz's legateship attests rather to the weakness of a policy which not only left the power of 'tyrants' virtually intact in some areas, but also failed to involve the local elites in the growth of papal territorial authority and taxation. These elements of fragility became evident just a few years after the death of the cardinal, whose work had been forcefully continued by two successors: in 1375–6 several urban revolts undermined papal authority, and then the anarchy and conflicts caused by the schism of 1378 made the situation still worse. In large areas of the state, the popes lost all concrete power.

---

[5] For example, Gardi, 'Gli officiali', 244–6, 254; Jamme, 'De la République', where Albornoz is described as 'le véritable fondateur de l'État' (n. 115); Jamme, 'Forteresses'.

In the last years of the fourteenth century, papal power recovered briefly thanks to Boniface IX and his vast family network.[6] But already in January 1400 a serious crisis was triggered by the expansionism of the Visconti of Milan, the king of Naples and then of various *signori* such as Braccio da Montone, who took possession of a large part of Umbria and neighbouring lands. Of greater impact were the temporal successes achieved by Martin V after Braccio's death in 1424. The end of the schism and, above all, the strength of his kin-group, the Colonna, the most powerful in Rome, played in his favour, guaranteeing the pope greater control over the city and its nobility, the structures of the curia and many areas of the state. The pope conducted an effective temporal policy, motivated by a robust conception of papal prerogatives and, above all, by the need to turn to temporal revenues to compensate for the cuts in spiritual income established at Constance and by the ensuing concordats. The governmental authority and fiscal rights of the Holy See now reached heights never previously achieved.[7]

The death of the pope in 1431 provoked yet another serious crisis, caused by hostilities between the Colonna family and their allies, the invasion of the troops of Filippo Maria Visconti and the establishment of the vast *signoria* of Francesco Sforza in Umbria and the Marche. But once again, papal power soon recovered, and was to continue to increase sharply between 1443 and 1450. In this case, however, there was an important novelty. For the first time in the history of the temporal dominions, arrangements were set in place that were to prove remarkably stable. The *capitula* then stipulated so as to sanction the subjugation of numerous towns often remained in force, with amendments and adaptations, until the beginning of the sixteenth century, and sometimes beyond. Another long-lasting element, with only minor adjustments, was the separation between the lands administered more or less directly by the papal government (*terre immediate subiecte*) and those that continued to be governed by *signori* bound to the papacy by the granting of 'apostolic vicariates', such as the Montefeltro, Malatesta, Manfredi and da Varano (*terre mediate subiecte*). This long-term stability, previously unheard of in the history of the papal state, owed much to the new relations established between Italian states by the treaty of Lodi (1454), which granted a period of peace and the reduction of interference by foreign powers within papal lands. In the first place, though, the stability bears witness to the more solid organisation of the papal government and, above all, its capacity to create bonds with local ruling groups.

---

[6] Esch, *Bonifaz IX*.   [7] Partner, *The Papal State*.

Administrative structures

While the succession of political events over the centuries appears to be a somewhat confused series of fluctuations, the administrative structures of the papal dominions give the opposite impression: one of stability and harmony. Indeed, their basic lines seem to remain almost unchanged from the first half of the thirteenth century to the sixteenth. This impression is partly justified. For the Holy See, continuity and high levels of formalisation in temporal matters, as in many other areas, were part of a deeply rooted culture, a practice of legitimisation and a strategy providing support. Even at times of complete political collapse, the offices of government were always legally occupied. Bureaucratic innovations tended to be concealed by the continuity of names and legal institutions. In practice, though, the actual powers of treasurers, marshals, vicars and other officials underwent profound changes, so that the same office would, from time to time, perform very different functions (a legate, for example, could be a plenipotentiary, a military commander, a political mediator, a governor or an absentee nephew conferred with a lucrative sinecure). Furthermore, new offices were formally established, especially in the fifteenth century.[8]

In the era of Innocent III the temporal dominions were already divided up into four large provinces (the Patrimonio and Campagna-Marittima in Lazio, the duchy of Spoleto in Umbria, and the Marca d'Ancona). In 1278, the acquisition of the Romagna resulted in the establishment of a fifth province. In the fourteenth century, as in the fifteenth, each province had a dual structure, one judicial, the other fiscal. Theoretically, the supreme authority in a province was the rector (called 'governor' in the fifteenth century). As the sovereign's local representative, he was in theory endowed with vast authority and should have been the main point of reference for his subjects. He applied the constitutions and other papal legislation, and issued laws in his own name. Political ideology recognised the full legislative capacity not only of the pope, obviously, but also of the provincial rectors. The most important of the laws made by papal representatives are the *Constitutiones Egidiane*, issued by Albornoz in 1357, incorporating measures from his predecessors. Until the late sixteenth century, these were to remain the principal legal frame of reference in the organisation of the provinces.

---

[8] Gardi, 'Gli officiali', and Partner, *The Pope's Men*, plus the reports from a series of conferences: Monacchia (ed.), *'Ut bene regantur'*; Jamme and Poncet (eds.), *Offices et papauté*; Jamme and Poncet (eds.), *Offices, écrit et papauté*.

The rector was assisted by a small court consisting of judges (usually four, for civil, criminal, appeal and ecclesiastical cases), notaries, servants and small contingents of men-at-arms under the command of a *bargello* or marshal. Financial administration was in the hands of a provincial treasury, this too with its small curia (court), which collected all the revenues due to the papacy and made payments for the provincial administration, submitting the remainder to the apostolic chamber. In each province, the higher nobility, prelates and representatives of the towns were convened in a *parlamentum* (parliament) by the rector. This collegiate body, however, features only rarely, usually deciding on issues contested by subjects and, by the fifteenth century, remained active only in the Marche.

On the periphery, as well as having formal rules and procedures, the administrative structure also appears to have been divided into different departments and constantly developing. By the second half of the fifteenth century, the number of papally appointed officials (excluding the military) in the different regions had reached five hundred.[9] The character of this provincial apparatus was certainly not a given for the papal state: its offices and personnel were entirely separate from the ecclesiastical structures, and had nothing to do with the management of dioceses or local churches. In the Roman curia, on the other hand, all the offices dealt indiscriminately with both temporal and spiritual matters. The scope and complexity of this bureaucratic system, as is well known, were impressive. Originally created to manage and control the ecclesiastical structures of Christianity, from the twelfth century it was also used for the temporal dominions. The most important offices in the temporal administration were the chancery and, first and foremost, the apostolic chamber. Over time, the chamber was divided up into a complex series of offices and colleges. Because of this complexity and because it had to deal simultaneously with very varied matters, the bureaucratic system of the curia was often ill equipped to transmit or carry out the pope's wishes rapidly. For this reason, starting above all from the middle of the fifteenth century, new bodies were set up which were directly subject to the pope and thus suited to promoting his personal power (such as the *Segnatura*, the Datary, the *Rota* and the group of papal secretaries).

Territorial organisation

The areas that made up the temporal dominions had very different histories and characteristics. The differences mainly related to the

---

[9] Gardi, 'Gli officiali', 245.

The papal state

development of towns and the economy, the spread of the seigneurial nobility and the direct presence of the papacy in terms of property and politics. Thus there was extensive urban development in northern Lazio, central and southern Umbria and along the Adriatic coast. After Rome and Bologna, the major population centres, going from west to east, were Corneto, Viterbo, Orvieto, Narni, Todi, Perugia, Spoleto, Assisi, Ancona, Ascoli, Macerata and Fermo, and many smaller towns too were fairly dynamic. Of the cities in the papal state, however, only Perugia and, to a lesser degree, Bologna, had prominent territorial organisational roles, to the extent of being able to structure entire sub-regions. More often, the towns had power over only medium- or small-sized *contadi*. Nor were there clear hierarchies between the numerous towns.[10]

In the interior areas of the Marche, in the Apennines and in central-southern Lazio, on the other hand, territorial organisation was characterised above all by a huge number of rural communities, lively minor centres and lordships belonging to noble families. In all these areas, the deeply rooted seigneurial presence and the development of more or less autonomous local communities were accompanied by the weakness of the towns. Papal demesnes, territorial lordships belonging directly to the pope, were few and far between, apart from in some areas of the Apennines, in southern Lazio and in the Sabina area.

There were many elements of instability in the territorial organisation of this state. The provinces were not based on any effective internal unity and there was little homogeneity in the territories administered by the rectors. It was not by chance that in the fifteenth century, and then even more so in the sixteenth, the number of autonomous administrative districts ('separate governments') multiplied. At the beginning of the seventeenth century in the Marche there were no fewer than thirteen different governors. The large administrative units, although still formally in existence, became ever more difficult to identify. In fact, throughout the modern period, they really were 'unfindable regions'.[11]

In terms of geographical size, of all the Italian states, the papal state was second only to the kingdom of Naples. It covered about 40,000 km^2, was three times as big as the Florentine state and about 10,000 km^2 bigger than the Venetian dominions. Even more than its provinces, however, it too lacked homogeneity and organic integrity. It stretched right across Italy, from the lower Po plain to the river Liri, taking in areas on the Tyrrhenian coast, interior plains, Apennine mountain zones, the Adriatic coast and parts of the Po valley. The lands were diverse and a

---

[10] Chittolini, 'Per una geografia', 15–17.   [11] Volpi, *Le regioni introvabili*.

long way apart, and it was not until the sixteenth century that there was a certain degree of integration. In the late Middle Ages, on the contrary, the economic activities and social and political dynamics of each region were subject to the powerful attraction of the more developed areas outside the papal state. In the Adriatic region, obviously, relations with Venice were predominant, whereas Bologna was gravitating towards Milan and the other big cities of the Po plain, central Umbria towards Florence and Tuscany, and Lazio towards the kingdom of Naples.

Until the establishment of the new balance of power after the wars at the end of the fifteenth and beginning of the sixteenth centuries, the political protectorate of Naples, Milan, Florence and Venice extended over numerous papal territories. Even after the peace of Lodi, these powers did not hesitate to claim the towns and *signori* of the papal state as their 'confederates', 'protégés' and 'supporters', intervening against any papal action thought to be damaging to their own and their protectees' interests.[12]

The idea of power and the state

In the papal state an element common to many other Italian states in the late Middle Ages and Renaissance probably reached its highest level. This was the gulf between political planning, ideologically constructed and expressed in juridical forms, and the effective operativity not just of the many mechanisms of socially pervasive power that characterised political realities, but also of the institutional structures themselves, the languages they expressed, the tools they used and the practices they followed. The main model available to Roman pontiffs for the conceptualisation of sovereignty and temporal administration was influential and ambitious. It consisted of Roman primacy over Christianity, control of ecclesiastical structures, theocratic ideals and theories of *plenitudo potestatis* and papal infallibility. In this model the papacy found not only an immediate ideological framework to which to refer as well as an arsenal of theoretical arguments, but also the availability of practical tools provided by a bureaucratic system without equal in terms of complexity and breadth. The drive to transpose the monarchical and bureaucratic organisation of the church on to a temporal plane was at work behind the scenes throughout the history of papal dominion, starting not just from Albornoz, as is sometimes argued, but from

---

[12] Soranzo, 'Collegati, raccomandati', 28–33, developed in Gardi, *Lo stato in provincia*, 407–8.

at least Innocent III.[13] Periodically it became an explicit, powerful point of reference, which determined temporal policy.

The papacy was affirmed as a monarchy characterised by authority and power at least in the period after the schism. Faced with the threat of conciliarist ideas, stronger European states asserting themselves and the concordats, the reconstruction of the papacy fell into a markedly monarchical mould, both in its ecclesiological models and the organisation of the curia, and in the role of the pontiff within the ecclesiastical structures. In this framework, the monarchical strengthening of papal power over the temporal dominions was portrayed as, and within the space of a few decades actually became, an indispensable source of economic resources and power, and thus the best guarantee of the pope's authority over the universal church and the foundation stone of *libertas Ecclesie*.[14]

Already from the twelfth century, however, there had been a structural divergence between an ideology of the – at times – intransigent assertion of the church's sovereignty and, on the other hand, the opposing tendency of the strongest subjects (communes and major noble families) to consider papal authority as entirely separate and theoretical. Even papal officials and the curia itself were ready to assign an abstract value to many of the sovereign's claims. They saw it as sufficient that papal requests were acknowledged in a merely formal manner, possibly sanctioned with a monetary payment of symbolic or less than symbolic value. The question of the appointment of a city *podestà*, for example, a matter of constant papal claims and continual conflict with the communes was, from the thirteenth century onwards, pragmatically resolved in the bigger towns by delegating the papal right to choose the *podestà* to the commune in exchange for an annual tax.[15]

Other influences, as well as that of the various forms of papal primacy over Christianity, also played a part in the conceptualisation of temporal government. There was the ancient representation of the state as a patrimony and the tendency to portray it, in the language of possession and property, as the *Patrimonium beati Petri* or *apostolicum*.[16] There was also the feudal idea of sovereignty, drawing on the examples of the imperial administration and the Norman monarchy in Sicily. Innocent III, developing tendencies that had existed in the church since the middle of the twelfth century, had advocated a feudal portrayal of papal sovereignty. This view, however, was discarded after a few decades in

---

[13] For a good overview, see Sommerlechner (ed.), *Innocenzo III*.
[14] For an analysis related to the Italian political situation, see Chittolini, 'Papato, corte di Roma'.
[15] Waley, *The Papal State*, 70–3. [16] Carocci, 'Patrimonium'.

favour of territorial and public notions of sovereignty.[17] And it was actually from the kingdom of Sicily that Innocent III took the idea of organising relations with towns. This was not to be in a contractual or diarchic system, where local government was shared between papal representatives and exponents of the local communities. Instead, he ordered that, as in municipal statutes in the kingdom of Sicily, there should be a 'unitary government with a papally appointed magistrate at its head' (whence the previously noted papal insistence on directly appointing the *podestà*).[18] Moving on to the fourteenth century, Castilian ideas of power have been traced in the actions of Albornoz as has the influence of the French monarchic model on the Avignon popes. What can be seen much more directly, however, from the third and fourth decades of the fourteenth century onwards, is the influence of *signorile* regimes, to the point that papal sovereignty was often referred to as a *dominium* or *signoria*.[19] And it is only from Martin V onwards that evidence re-emerges of a notion of papal power which, while never disappearing, from halfway through the previous century had often faded into the background. Rather than portraying himself or, above all, being seen as the *signore* of single towns, the pope was once again conceived above all as holding sovereign power extending over the whole territory. Contractual-style arrangements with towns and other subjects, each having their own sphere of autonomy and privileges, became widespread.

Within the dominions of the Holy See, all these developments assumed a tone that was, for many reasons, unusual. It would, for example, be a mistake to dismiss the emphasis on the particular nature of papal temporal power and the earthly and spiritual well-being that only it could guarantee as mere propaganda, devoid of consequence. From the end of the twelfth century, the political rhetoric of the curia began to associate papal dominion to the 'easy yoke and light burden' of faith in Christ, an emphasis on *libertas*, *pax* and *iustitia* being guaranteed by Roman dominion and theories of the Christian exercise of sovereignty as a mission of God.[20] Halfway through the fifteenth century, preachers in papal lands portrayed the pope as a spiritual monarch and a guarantor of brotherhood and peace.[21] Pius II, when still a cardinal, had exalted

---

[17] Carocci, *Vassalli del papa*, 61–9.
[18] Caravale, *Ordinamenti*, 499; see the detailed analysis by Jamme, 'De la république', which seems, however, to ignore the arguments already clearly expressed by Caravale and other authors.
[19] Carocci, 'Regimi signorili', 245–9.
[20] Maccarrone, *Studi*, 9–22; Petrucci, 'Innocenzo III'; Prodi, *Il sovrano pontefice*, 34–5.
[21] Dessì, 'Predicare e governare'.

not only the superiority of papal sovereignty, which combined priestly wisdom and kingly authority, but also its dissimilarity to other forms of government and especially tyranny.[22] With Paul II, it was this very ideology of the absolute irreconcilability of *tyrannie* and papal dominion that motivated his forceful attack on the privileges of the *Sedici*, the tightly knit oligarchy that controlled Bologna.[23] This is, moreover, one of the cases in which medieval sources are most explicit in attesting to the deep divergence between the royal ideology of a pope who professed 'that he wanted to be totally lord',[24] the political culture of urban autonomy which envisaged relations with the state as merely negotiational and contractual, and the concrete unfolding of relations of authority and government.

In all this, the factor that perhaps more than any other made the papal conceptualisation singular was a tenacious memory, a centuries-old ability to cherish abstract rights and Utopian demands. Many times, the church used the past as a weapon of resistance and a reservoir of new claims more than as a means of legitimation. Guicciardini made a series of caustic remarks on the papal ability to 'resuscitate the already dead reasons of the apostolic see', and on the ability of that immortal institution, the church, to recover in the long term from any political crisis ('though it sometimes seems to stagger, in the end it reaffirms its rights more strongly than ever').[25]

The peculiarities of the sovereign pontiff

The specificities of a sovereign who was also the holder of a highly sacred office conditioned the practice of power in the state. As we have seen, this might be in ways that were, all told, useful to the pope's rule, starting from his position at the apex of political and legal representation and the breadth of the ecclesiastical bureaucratic system. Also undoubtedly positive, at a temporal level, were the ease with which the pope's provincial representatives exercised jurisdictional control over the world of clerics, their capacity to intervene in the provision of ecclesiastical benefices (although this needs to be more fully researched), the content of preaching activity, an undeniable influence of both secular and regular clergy on local institutions, confraternities, *monti di pietà* and so forth. All this meant that the political problems caused in other Italian states by the vast and deep-rooted presence of the church in society were markedly less significant in the papal state.

---

[22] Prodi, *Il sovrano pontefice*, 33–7. [23] Robertson, *Tyranny*.
[24] Carocci, 'Governo papale', 201. [25] Guicciardini, *Maxims*, 49.

But there were also political weaknesses arising from the duality of the pope's figure as a temporal ruler and head of the universal church. The papacy was a sort of monarchy, but elective, collegiate and elderly. The sovereign, usually appointed at an advanced age, remained in office for just a few years, and his geographical and family origins changed each time. The consequences of this were many. In any state, the succession from one sovereign to another raises problems, and poses the question of relations between the entourage of the last prince and that of his successor. But the death of the pope was a much more frequent and profound interruption. 'Battles of memory' commenced between the intellectuals of the curia who, in treatises, pamphlets and poems, sought to cope with the discontinuity on a cultural and symbolic level. A death meant a radical redistribution of power and wealth at the expense of the beneficiaries of the late pope and in favour of the new one. It was often accompanied by changes in political orientation, as much towards Italian and European powers as regarding the internal administration of the state.[26]

Differences in origins, learning and the personal political tendencies of the popes and their closest collaborators all had their effect on this discontinuity. What counted above all, though, were some of the structural aspects of this kind of elective monarchy. There was no lasting bond between the sovereign, his dynasty, a territorially defined power and the local elites. The lands under the direct territorial *signoria* of the sovereign were of modest proportions. Nor was it possible to count on strong kinship networks, marriage alliances or feudal loyalty to the sovereign dynasty to allow the papal power to take root locally.

One of the explanations, and perhaps the most evident, for the massive spread of nepotistic practices that characterised the history of the temporal dominions from Innocent III onwards can be found in these characteristics of the papacy. Nepotism was a complex phenomenon, involving a multiplicity of factors, social behaviours, practices of power and moral values. In nepotism we find love and *pietas* for relatives, the desire to enhance one's own family, the need to keep Rome and the organs of the curia under control, the need for trusted troops and officials and, more generally, an unbridled drive to increase papal power in all ways.[27] Above all, some popes from the great families of the Roman nobility used the power and connections of relatives to control the machinery of the curia and the territory of the state. Of the two recognisable functions of papal nepotism in every era – favouring family

---

[26] De Vincentiis, *Battaglie di memoria*; De Vincentiis, 'Papato, stato'.
[27] Carocci, *Il nepotismo*.

members, but also helping the pope to control the state, the curia and the essential web of formal and informal political relations - the latter, in these cases, developed strongly. The substantial successes in the imposition of temporal power achieved by Martin V depended greatly on the actual military power of the Colonna family, on their being firmly rooted in the curia, on the control over the society and commune of Rome which they had exercised for some time, and on the patronage and factional relations they maintained with many of the state's noble and eminent families. The wars and rebellions that started on the pope's death, however, reveal the impossibility of a system of government in the papal state where consensus and stability were rooted in relations between the prince's family and the dominant families in the territory. In a monarchical or princely regime the sovereign's family was organically linked to the state, whereas in the dominions of the church there was no truly organic link between the pope's relatives and the state, but rather an antagonism that was destined to remain latent during the life of the family's pope, ready to manifest itself soon after his death.

The discontinuous nature of papal power was very evident to contemporaries. Machiavelli worried about its destabilising effect on the Italian political system. But for the pope's interlocutors, both outside and – above all – inside the state, the discontinuity seems to have been seen first and foremost as a resource. On the basis of repeated experience, communes and seigneurial nobility devised recurrent tactics in order to gain from it. Ambassadors sent to newly elected popes, who usually granted an abundance of favours and concessions, would resort to subterfuges such as submitting for confirmation privileges that had actually been contested by the last pope.[28] Even before this, the vacancy presented an opportunity to seize positions of power from which to negotiate advantageous agreements with the new pope. Finally, for nobles under papal attack, the death of a pope not only gave them the chance to reclaim lost dominions even before the end of the conclave but also usually sanctioned the end of hostilities, as newly elected popes only rarely pursued the same policies as their predecessors. And so Roman barons would never fight to the bitter end when defending their territory against attacks by papal troops; it was better to abandon the land before it was ruined, in the certainty of being able to take it back within a short time.[29]

---

[28] Carocci, 'Governo papale', 202–3.
[29] De Vincentiis, 'La sopravvivenza'; Shaw, 'The Roman barons and the security', 320–1; Shaw, 'The Roman barons and the Guelf', 492.

Barons and apostolic vicars

Peculiarities and parallels when compared to other contemporary states can also be seen in relations between sovereign and subjects. Here, too, things need to be greatly simplified. The picture, in fact, seems to be just as complex as the territories, communities, social groups, forms of political aggregation, languages in which they expressed themselves, and ensuing practices and objectives are diversified. Rather than give a comprehensive description, which would necessarily be schematic to the point of parody, I shall limit myself to a few basic outlines, looking first at the great nobles, barons and apostolic vicars, and then at the communes and their ruling groups.

For almost the entire period in question, the Orsini, Colonna and other Roman families enjoyed extremely ample margins of power. From this point of view, parallels in other Italian states are very few, at least in such an accentuated form. None of the other states had such a powerful aristocracy, installed at such a short distance from the capital and capable of keeping the sovereign in a 'state of torment', as Alexander VI put it. In innumerable cases, throughout the entire fourteenth and fifteenth centuries, baronial families incited disorder and even all-out wars which threatened, weakened and sometimes virtually nullified papal authority.

A (partial) limitation to the strength and turbulence of the barons was achieved only in the sixteenth century. In the previous century, starting from Pius II, the attacks made by popes on some of these families produced only short-term results. The Colonna emerged virtually unscathed even from the bitter struggle waged by Sixtus IV, as they regained all their possessions immediately after the death of the pope. As pointed out by Machiavelli and Guicciardini a few years after the death of Alexander VI, the first real containment of the barons took place only under this pope, and especially from 1501 to 1503. With pride, pope Borgia declared that he had 'donated' the defeat of the barons to the church. In truth, after his death, the Orsini, Colonna, Savelli, Caetani and other families repossessed their lands, but the balance of power was, by now, visibly changing.[30]

The barons had numerous factors on their side, giving substance to the threat they posed.[31] They had vast seigneurial dominions and in the fifteenth century they were at the head of the factions in almost all the

---

[30] Shaw, 'The Roman barons and the security', 320; Shaw, 'The Roman barons and the popes'.
[31] There is exemplary analysis of one family in Shaw, *The Political Role*.

towns in Lazio and Umbria. Between them and the pope there were none of the relationships that usually bound a sovereign to the seigneurial nobility. There were no ties of vassallatic subordination to constrain the barons, as their dominions had been allodial properties, not church fiefs, since the thirteenth century. They were given almost no space as advisers to the government or leisure companions in the life of the papal court. And, furthermore, the sequence of popes ruled out any stable kinship bonds between the dynasty of the sovereign and the greater nobles. Related to the instability of these bonds, there was also the lack of any military obligations to the state, a situation in paradoxical contrast to the marked aptitude for war of the barons, who were among the most sought-after *condottieri* of the period.

On the basis of these objective threats and the judgements already formed by contemporaries, historians have often stressed the conflicts between barons and popes. In short, they have identified a structural antagonism between these nobles and papal power: such arguments are undoubtedly justified. What has long been missing, however, is an assessment of how this seigneurial aristocracy also facilitated the assertion and functioning of the papal state. Popes benefited from the network of political relations that allowed the barons to intervene in many sectors: in the machinery of the curia, in the territory of the state, and in relations with other states, both Italian and foreign. In particular, the barons aided the process of political communication between urban societies and the state. They helped their allies in the urban ruling classes find the best intermediaries in the curia and government, while at the same time assisting papal governors and officials in the difficult task of limiting conflicts between the Guelf and Ghibelline factions which, in the papal state too, were a structural feature of the political landscape.[32]

The lack of research is even greater when one turns from the barons to the apostolic vicars and great feudatories of the pope. There has been no systematic work on relations between the church and its vicars, while relations between the state apparatus and the communities, social groups and eminent families living in the dominions of vicars or feudatories have been studied still less. Some developments are, however, clear. The first regards the breadth of the areas involved. From the first half of the fourteenth century, for a long time most of the towns in the papal state, together with many rural territories, were under the rule of *signori* of various types. These *signorie* might embrace entire sub-regions and go on for generations (such as the Montefeltro in the Marche and

---

[32] Shaw, 'The Roman barons and the Guelf'; Shaw, 'The Roman barons and the popes'.

northern Umbria, and the Malatesta in the Romagna), or else be created for shorter periods either by a family (the Prefetti, for example, in the Patrimonio), or even a single individual (the most famous cases being those of *condottieri* such as Braccio da Montone and Francesco Sforza).

Throughout the first half of the fourteenth century, the papacy opposed the development of 'tyrannies'. It attempted to maintain the form of government established in the Duecento, based on central and provincial bureaucratic structures and on the special relationship, albeit often uncertain and conflictual, with the urban communes. An acknowledgement of the change and a radical transformation in political strategy came with the legateship of cardinal Albornoz. On seeing the crisis of the communal regimes, the cardinal and his successors sought to control the development of the *signorie* by the use of apostolic vicariates. In an initial phase, the short duration of the concessions and the heavy obligations imposed on vicars in the military and fiscal fields guaranteed the church's prerogatives and distinguished the vicariate from feudal concessions. From the last twenty years of the fourteenth century, however, the relationship became less binding, resulting in a spread of lifetime vicariates or ones lasting two or more generations, while evasion of the payment of *censi* (duties), the provision of military service and other obligations started to become frequent. In this context, there was also a merging of vicariates and fiefs, with frequent renewals of vicariates as enfeoffments, and vice versa.[33] In much of the state, the main interlocutors of papal government were no longer communal regimes, but dynasties of vicars and feudatories. The favourable conditions of these concessions, however, and, in any event, the difficulties involved in obtaining the respect (theoretically) due, made the pope's capacity to control them very limited.

In this context, it comes as no surprise that some popes pursued a policy of revoking vicariates and opting for the direct government of the towns. In addition to the temporary successes of Boniface IX and Martin V, a massive policy of reconquering territory, regaining vicariates and extending areas *immediate subiectae* to papal power was undertaken by Eugenius IV and Nicholas V in 1443–50. This reorientation did not become exclusive, however, as almost all the popes in the second half of the fifteenth century, while managing to take many towns from vicars and feudatories, immediately regranted them to other *signori*, chosen from relatives or families who were politically closer. It was not until after the death of Alexander VI (and the collapse of the state of Cesare Borgia)

---

[33] Carocci, *Vassalli del papa*, 72–9.

that there was a new wave of even more conspicuous and definitive revocations. Thus, between 1504 and 1510, Julius II obtained the passage to direct papal sovereignty of the whole of the Romagna.

By the middle of the fifteenth century, in the Patrimonio, Umbria and the central-southern Marche, and later on in the Romagna and other areas, with the shrinking of fiefs and vicariates, the towns re-emerged as the main intermediaries of papal power on the periphery.[34] But the picture was totally different to that of the thirteenth century.

Towns and *cives ecclesiastici*

The relations then established between the papal curia and the towns enacted and, at the same time, surpassed a long-standing administrative plan, already existing under Innocent III, which aimed to make the communes almost a peripheral subdivision of the state. The church's claim, advanced since the beginning of the thirteenth century, that the *podestà* and other communal officials be appointed directly by the pope or his representatives, or under their control, had now been accomplished, apart from a few exceptions. But the reality of this accomplishment actually surpassed the long-standing claims: the control over the communes was so intense that it reset the relationship between city and pope on new terms, extraneous to the political culture of the thirteenth century.

Yet again, there is a need to simplify a picture made complex not only by the variety of agreements (*capitula*) sanctioning city obligations and prerogatives, but also by the diverse political tendencies of the different popes.[35] By using a highly schematic approach, however, it is possible to pick out, from among the many variants, two different forms of the church's subjection of the towns. These two different models of state presence in the communes matured gradually from the middle of the fourteenth century onwards, finally becoming evident with the resumption and stabilisation of papal power from halfway through the fifteenth century.

In fifteen or so towns, papal control entailed the dispatch of a governor, the expropriation of the commune's ordinary revenues and, often, the building of a fort.[36] The form of subjection achieved in this way was fairly effective, so much so that the city oligarchies had to seek

---

[34] Zenobi, *Le 'ben regolate città'*.
[35] Carocci, 'Governo papale'. Of the research published subsequently, see especially Mascioli, *Viterbo*.
[36] On the forts, see Nico Ottaviani (ed.), *Rocche e fortificazioni*.

agreements with the Holy See and its officials in order to be able to continue to benefit from the economic resources they had been enjoying for a long time from communal finances. This form of relationship with the sovereign was adopted in almost all the major cities in the Patrimonio and Umbria, and then in a few towns in the Marche and the Romagna. All the other cities of the state, instead, continued to manage their finances independently without resort to resident papal governors; relations with the central power were basically controlled, usually less strictly, by the rector of the province and the officials of his curia.

There were also other control and exaction mechanisms in operation throughout the whole of the state from the middle of the fifteenth century onwards: the annonary system in the Marche and the Patrimonio, and the *Dogana dei Pascoli* in Lazio. These structures, dotted all over the territory, were yet another tool for exerting political pressure on the towns and their elites.[37]

The cases of Ancona and Bologna on the one hand, and Rome on the other, need to be considered separately. The large and relatively wealthy cities of Ancona and Bologna, which were protected, moreover, by their close relations with Venice and Milan, enjoyed substantial autonomy. In exchange for burdensome payments to the apostolic chamber, Ancona avoided all forms of control,[38] and, of all the *capitula* stipulated between papacy and commune, those agreed by Bologna in 1447 were the best for the city, by a long way.[39] Rome, on the other hand, a capital that gained immense privileges from the presence of the curia, was, in return, subject to very strict control of municipal administration and finances.[40]

In this rapid overview, it is also important not to skim over the changes which occurred between the fifteenth century and the sixteenth. Relations between the popes and the towns cannot be interpreted merely as the beginnings of the processes of containment of communal autonomies or the intensification of the presence of the state which were to develop later, in the course of the sixteenth and seventeenth centuries. There was as yet no clear tendency in the Roman curia towards the systematic reduction of particularisms. Above all, the church put itself forward, and was indeed perceived, as a means of co-ordination and pacification between towns, *signori*, factions, foreign powers and other forces active in the lands of the state. The Holy See also appeared as the

---

[37] For the annonary system, see Palermo, *Mercati del grano*; for the *Dogana dei Pascoli*, see Maire Vigueur, *Les pâturages*.
[38] Caravale, 'Lo stato pontificio', 37, 59–60, 64–5, 115, 123.
[39] As well as Robertson, *Tyranny*, see Colliva, 'Bologna', and, for the subsequent period, De Benedictis, *Repubblica per contratto*, and Gardi, *Lo stato in provincia*.
[40] There is an overview of studies in Esch, 'Un bilancio storiografico'.

best defence of traditional freedoms and city privileges. This political order and idea of sovereignty, more even than in other states, attributed great significance to the direct relationship between sovereign and subject towns. Popes and curial offices seem to have entered directly into dialogue with urban communities, which were always afforded the right to refer straight to Rome (either through ambassadors or by starting to appoint their own permanent representatives in the curia).

The continuous ties between the towns and the curia were also, to a significant degree, a consequence of the fragmented structure of power, both in the territory and, especially, at the centre. The choice of a *podestà*, for example, was influenced by complex political and patronage networks. Cardinals, prelates of the curia (and elsewhere), towns of the papal state, both near and far, *signori* and sovereigns of other states all pressed the communes to ask the pope to appoint their clients and protégés. To obtain fiscal alleviation, make special expenditure or for any other need, towns had to increase the numbers of their patrons and supporters to a greater extent than in other states. Also without parallels in other states were the breadth of central organs, the complexity of their bureaucratic culture, the presence within them of interests and forces from different political societies stemming from all over the Italian peninsula and, above all, the number and autonomous power of the men supporting the sovereign at the apex of the entire system, the cardinals. Letters, ambassadors and gifts were sent not only to the pope and *camerlengo*, but also to scores of cardinals, clerics of the *camera*, provincial officials, barons, great nobles and foreign states. A multiplicity of other channels was activated on specific occasions: factional solidarity, baronial networks and the patronage of former governors. Finally, urban solidarity was requested of citizens who were, for whatever reason, active in Rome or the state, such as clerics of the *camera*, apostolic protonotaries, abbreviators, referendaries, prelates, peripheral officials, prestigious doctors and famous jurists.[41]

In this context, the suggestion that there was a 'gradual spreading of papal power at the expense of urban communities which, passively, suffered its effects' should be avoided.[42] On the contrary, one of the more evident characteristics of the new relationships established between the papacy and the towns of the state was the affirmation, in every town, of oligarchical groups which co-operated with the growing presence of state power because the basis of their local prominence, the

---

[41] For a vast range of examples, see Carocci, 'Governo papale', and Mascioli, *Viterbo*.
[42] Mascioli, *Viterbo*, 60 (moreover, misunderstanding the essence of the arguments in Carocci, 'Governo papale').

guarantee of immense revenues and the possibility of careers and social mobility beyond the confines of the town were to be found in the state, within much broader horizons, through either lay officialdom or, much more frequently, an ecclesiastical career. In some towns, this group was defined as that of the *cives ecclesiastici*, an expression which underlined political loyalty to the papacy, but which also made very clear that the origins of the political and social superiority of these urban elites, and the best guarantee of their economic affluence, lay within the power of the church. And thus one of the main weaknesses in the construction of the state undertaken by the popes of the thirteenth and fourteenth centuries – the idea, held by the social groups in power in the towns, that the advantages to be gained from an expansion of state power were far less than the damage that could be caused by the concomitant reduction in the town's autonomy – no longer existed. By now, it was the interest of the communal ruling classes in the efficient functioning of government machinery that provided the best guarantee of the hold on power in the territory. And thus it was that the risk of those general revolts which, in 1375–6, had ended the era of the abrupt assertion of state power inaugurated by cardinal Albornoz became remote.

Conclusion

In concluding, what must be underlined is the composite nature of the political structure created by the church and the breadth of the papal gains. Regarding the first point, it should be remembered that there was a plurality of different territorial protagonists active in the state, and divergent constitutional situations: communal cities and towns both large and small, *signori* of varying origins and importance, seigneurial barons and aristocracies, and rural communities. In the temporal dominions, monarchical, ecclesiastical, princely and aristocratic ideologies of power and political languages coexisted. This variety was greater than in other states of the period. Even more than elsewhere, the greatest driver of the composite character of the state and the spread of non-institutional political logic came from the central organisation itself, from the complexity of a sovereignty such as that of the Roman curia and its – so to speak – collegiate character, shared to a certain extent between pope and cardinals. To act effectively, not only the various state institutions and magistracies, but also the *signori*, patronage networks, clans, factions, urban and rural communities and other actors in the territory, were prompted to develop all kinds of mediation and communication mechanisms, courtly practices, nepotisms, electoral cartels, feuds, corruption, party alliances and municipal solidarity.

The growth of the state broadened the areas and possibilities of intervention for the curia and its organs in the territory; but at the same time it intensified political relations between the different actors and multiplied the different contexts and ways in which they could in turn intervene in the actions of the curia and in the structures of the state. In short, it was the need to shape the expanding institutional presence and its mechanisms which, not in the least paradoxically, stimulated the development of factions, class solidarity, the affirmation of patronage connections, political bodies and more informal groupings. At the same time, it should be stressed that the political structure that had been created so slowly and painstakingly was, in the fifteenth century, able to provide the pope with a temporal principality similar to that of other states. From the middle of the fifteenth century onwards, it was an objective platform of political power and provided major fiscal resources, which were to grow substantially in the following century.[43] It would be difficult to overvalue the role it played in conserving the prestige and independence of the popes in the new political situation, or the contribution that the papal state, developing from the acquisitions of the thirteenth and fourteenth centuries, was to give in the sixteenth century to making Rome the principal court in all Italy.

---

[43] Still of importance is Gardi's summary, 'La fiscalità pontificia'.

5 Tuscan states: Florence and Siena

Lorenzo Tanzini

Introduction

Research into new ways of interpreting late medieval political change has modified the attitude of historians towards Tuscany: traditional topics such as 'Renaissance Florence' have been overtaken by an approach 'beyond Florence', aiming to focus on different models of state-building.[1] This new perspective allows historians to analyse the Florentine model in closer comparison with the experiences of the surrounding city-states, the Tuscan republics of Siena and Lucca.

Following these new approaches, I shall focus on the social and institutional evolution of Florence and Siena at the end of the Middle Ages, comparing them to Lucca in the final part of the chapter: the purpose will be to identify some features of the Tuscan political systems and to underline their contribution to the development of the Italian Renaissance state.

Florence: from *commune* to *respublica*

Robert Davidsohn took his fundamental *Geschichte von Florenz* up to 1328: even if his decision was partially due to the difficulty of extending such comprehensive research to the far too richly documented fourteenth century, Davidsohn's choice provides a useful starting point. The emperor's absence from the Italian political scene and the displacement of the papal court to Avignon in fact gave the most important city-states in central Italy new chances to fulfil their ambitions. The Guelf–Angevin coalition, led by Florence from the 1250s as an alliance against the imperial threat, then lost its primary reason to exist. On the other hand, 1328 was the last year of the formal lordship of Charles of Anjou over the city: after his departure, the Florentine ruling class promoted a reform of the city's major councils that defined the

---

[1] Findlen, Fontaine and Osheim (eds.), *Beyond Florence*.

Florentine institutional system for more than a century. A few years later, Florence succeeded in conquering or peacefully subduing several castles and boroughs towards Pistoia and in the Valdarno previously controlled by Pisa, such as Fucecchio and Pescia.[2]

Following Giovanni Villani's famous praise of Florence in his *Cronica*, Florentine municipal tradition portrays this period as the most prosperous in the city's medieval life. However, prosperity was not the whole story. Even before the bankruptcy of the Acciaiuoli, Peruzzi and Bardi companies shook Florentine finances, the economic crisis of the early 1340s triggered political conflict between the ruling *popolo grasso*, the lower classes and the magnates (excluded from the office of the *Priori* by the *Ordinamenti di Giustizia* in 1293). In 1342, an unorthodox alliance of magnates and lower guilds (*arti minori*) submitted the city to Walter of Brienne, the Angevin duke of Athens. This was the last medieval experience of *signorile* rule over the city: after less than a year, Walter was expelled and the rule of the major guilds (*arti maggiori*) was re-established.

The events of 1343 could be considered the beginning of the Florentine Renaissance period.[3] The territorial growth and the collapse of an entire financial elite in the 1340s gave rise to great social change and shaped a different ruling group composed of newcomers, mostly big merchants and investors. This 'new' ruling class soon split into political factions linked to one or another of the leading families (Ricci, Albizi, Alberti). The main topic of political debate was finance: the new rulers abandoned the *estimo* (the taxation of urban patrimonies abolished in 1315 and reintroduced in 1342) and created the *Monte* (the office in charge of public debt), which became the administrative heart of the city's finances. Very soon, public lending ceased to be normal practice for middle-class citizens, and the ruling elite established its substantial control over the state through a monopoly of shares in the *Monte*.[4]

Internationally, Florence aimed to become the standard-bearer of traditional Tuscan republican values, while most of northern Italy was falling under *signorile* control. Thanks to the efforts of the Parte Guelfa, an oligarchic institution charged with the persecution of public enemies, and increasingly influential in the 1350s, the traditional language of Angevin liberty against Ghibelline tyrants was used to strengthen Florentine hegemony over the whole of Tuscany.[5]

---

[2] For a short survey, see Green, 'Florence and the republican tradition'.
[3] Brucker, *Florentine Politics and Society*. [4] Molho, 'The state and public finance'.
[5] Ferente, 'Guelphs!', 573–83.

In 1353 the Peace of Sarzana defined the political influence of Florence and Milan on both sides of the Apennines. Two years later, Florence bought the imperial vicariate from Charles IV: this title bestowed on its territorial state the legitimation that it had previously lacked.[6] The 1350s represented the most intense years of Florentine territorial expansion. In 1351, Florence bought Prato when Angevin domination over the city ended; in 1348 Colle Val d'Elsa was conquered, followed by San Gimignano in 1353, Volterra in 1361 and San Miniato in 1370, while Pistoia was increasingly subject to Florentine control.[7] Florence was prevented from more extensive conquests to the north by the power of the Visconti; consequently, central Italy became the real target of Florentine imperialism. In this region Florence faced the papal states: the clash between them turned to open war in 1375. The so-called *Guerra degli otto santi*[8] was first and foremost a huge financial effort, because the military campaign caused an extraordinary increase in expenditure, but it soon became an ideological challenge as well. When Gregory XI launched an interdict against Florence, the government confiscated ecclesiastical patrimonies to finance the army. Even if the peace with the pope in 1378 was actually a defeat for Florentine ambitions, the war had substantially strengthened civic ideology within the city; on the other hand, the heavy financial pressures opened up a new phase of internal struggles.

Recent historiography has reinterpreted the events of the famous *Tumulto dei Ciompi* (1378), not only underlining their obvious social relevance, but focusing principally on their political and cultural content and consequences.[9] The Ciompi revolt was in fact the last great struggle for power in the city; after that, a long period of competition between different social factions, institutions and families (the lower classes and the major guilds, the Parte Guelfa and the *signoria*, the Albizi and Ricci), came to an end, and Florence finally found a definite unity. In September 1378, a great Parlamento (the plenary assembly of the citizens) established the *plena potestas populi florentini*: neither internal nor external interventions could limit the power of the *signoria* and the councils in legislation.[10] Moreover, after the experience of the Ciompi, the fear of a social revolt by the lower classes convinced the *reggimento* of the need to elaborate a policy of consent and conciliation under the control of the

---

[6] Fubini, *Politica e pensiero politico*, 17–42.
[7] Connell and Zorzi (eds.), *Florentine Tuscany*; Boutier, Landi and Rouchon (eds.), *Florence et la Toscane*.
[8] Peterson, 'The War of the Eight Saints'.
[9] Lantschner, 'The "Ciompi revolution" constructed'.
[10] Trexler, 'Il parlamento fiorentino del 1378'.

state.[11] Unity and service to the *Patria* were the key-words of this ideology: this period saw the replacement of the ancient title '*commune et populum florentinum*' with the more emphatic '*respublica florentina*' in public records.

Florence: power and government tested

Historians usually refer to the period between 1380 and 1434 in Florence as the age of the Albizi regime, and have mostly focused on the leading figures of Maso degli Albizi and his son Rinaldo. Nevertheless, this period was far more than the age of a family crypto-*signorile* regime. Late Trecento Florence was in fact governed by the *reggimento*: a large group of families whose prosperity was based on commercial activities, banking and great investments in the public debt. Some institutional arenas were crucial for the exercise of power: above all, the *consulte*, informal assemblies to which the *Priori* summoned influential citizens and asked for their advice on public matters. The *reggimento* did not have a defined legal identity, because access to public offices remained widely open in Florence, but at the same time the government of the city was increasingly controlled by an inner circle of leaders of the most important families.[12] These men composed the *consulte*, controlled access to the higher offices, made the urgent decisions in emergency situations; the late Trecento is the age of the great *balìe*, that is the special commissions that were gathered in 1378, 1382, 1387 and 1393 (usually after a Parlamento) to enact extraordinary measures of institutional reform. The *balìe* were also the arbiters of the inclusion of individuals and families in the urban ruling class: the *balìa* of 1434 decreed the exile of Rinaldo degli Albizi and, in doing so, inaugurated the era of the rule of the Medici.

The Albizi period is renowned for a striking display of institutional creativity in reshaping Florence's constitutional framework and innovation in the city's politics. The *Otto di Guardia* were created in 1378 and soon began to submit ordinary justice to political control; in 1384 the *Dieci di Balìa* were given control over military issues; in 1419 the *Cinque conservatori del Contado* were entrusted with administration of Florence's territory; finally, the statutes of the city were rewritten and fundamentally renewed between 1409 and 1415.[13]

The importance and originality of all these elements have been the basis of intense historiographical debate about the nature and character

---

[11] Najemy, *A History of Florence*, 156–87.   [12] Najemy, *Corporatism and Consensus*.
[13] Tanzini, *Statuti e legislazione a Firenze*.

of the late medieval Florentine state: Florence in fact has traditionally represented an ideal model for the so-called *stato del Rinascimento*. Its central role in the Italian political system and its exemplary evolution (not to mention the huge amount of its public and private records) allowed some historians to interpret the late medieval Florentine institutional evolution as a complex but coherent way to a new model of the state. The foundation of a creative legislative power, the growing self-consciousness of the ruling class, the fading of every external influence over political government exercised by the universal powers of the church and the empire from above, and by the lower classes at a local level, have often been seen as evidence of how much the Florentine process of state-building overcame medieval and communal traditions.[14] Other historians stress, on the contrary, the incoherence and partial nature of this supposed process of 'modernisation' of the state.[15] Most Anglo-American scholars emphasise the social basis of oligarchic power: the real fulcrum of Florentine politics was, in this view, the informal links among ruling families, such as the social practices of patronage, and Florentine history is first and foremost the story of the strategies used by an urban patriciate to create and maintain social pre-eminence over the city's political society as a whole.[16]

In spite of these opposing interpretations, nobody could question at least one characteristic of Florentine history in this period, that is, the profound change in its political language. During the war against the papacy, Florence and its famous chancellor Coluccio Salutati tried to weaken the fidelity of the Italian cities to the pope, appealing both to the municipal liberty against tyranny and to Italian pride in the face of French popes and foreign mercenaries.[17] Afterwards, the chancery and the humanist circles of the city created and spread an ideology of republican freedom: its political language was based on classical authors (Sallust, Cicero) but the Latin concepts and words gave voice to the political intentions of the ruling class and strengthened its ambitions. Hans Baron, in his famous book *The Crisis of the Early Italian Renaissance*, has defined this political ideology and its roots: 'civic humanism' grew at the crossroads between a theoretical love for the Latin past and a pragmatic defence of the fatherland. In Baron's view, the long wars against Gian Galeazzo Visconti in 1389–92 and 1399–1402 forced the

---

[14] See the many works of Riccardo Fubini, recently *Politica e pensiero politico*.
[15] Zorzi, 'The "material constitution"'.
[16] For example, Kent and Simons (eds.), *Patronage, Art and Society*, and Peterson (ed.), *Florence and Beyond*.
[17] Witt, *Hercules at the Crossroads*.

humanists to play a public role in defence of the city, reconsidering the ancient values of liberty, the common good, and sacrifice for the fatherland. In spite of the subtlety and the documentary richness of his analysis, Baron overestimated the pressure of the wars against Milan.[18] Of course, in 1401–2 Florence's independence was at stake, but the new political language of freedom, love for the *Patria* and hatred for tyranny employed as an ideological manifesto against the Milanese duke was only the final result of a long tradition that characterised the entire late fourteenth-century era of Florentine imperialism.

The Albizi *reggimento* not only elaborated a particular ideology, but also succeeded in state-building in the Florentine dominion, launching a new phase of territorial expansion. Florence bought Arezzo in 1384, Montepulciano was subdued in 1397 and Pistoia surrendered definitively in 1401, but the biggest achievement was the conquest of Pisa in 1406. Finally, the Florentine economic system acquired the long-desired access to the sea; a few years after the conquest, Florence created the maritime office of the *Consoli del Mare* and its first galley fleet.

It was not just a matter of expansion: in the Albizi age, the regime shaped the institutional framework of the wider Florentine dominion by covering it with a dense network of officials (*vicari* and *podestà*) with jurisdictional powers.[19] The prologue of the city statute of 1415 offers both an idea of this imposing institutional structure, and the impression of coherent and effective control over the whole territory exercised by the dominant city through its laws. In recent years, however, historians have more and more emphasised the weight of the communal and medieval legacy: the Florentine territorial state was a mosaic of hundreds of communities, each of them ruled by local statutes whose relationship with Florentine laws was anything but simple.[20] The network of officials was far from constituting a homogeneous bureaucracy, and the control of such a composite territory was shaped and modelled by the interest of the ruling class in promoting its own power through patronage over subject cities. Even territorial expansion was not always the result of a deliberate project, but rather the reaction to an emergency. This tentative nature of state-building is recognisable even in the most famous achievement of this period, the *Catasto*, a huge description of Florentine households' fiscal incomes composed in 1427 but strongly disputed and then reformed.[21]

---

[18] Fubini, 'Renaissance historian'; Hankins (ed.), *Renaissance Civic Humanism*.
[19] In general, Connell and Zorzi (eds.), *Florentine Tuscany*; see also Chittolini's classic research, 'Ricerche sull'ordinamento territoriale'.
[20] Mannori, *Il sovrano tutore*.
[21] Zorzi, 'The "material constitution"', and Petralia, 'Fiscality, politics and dominion'.

A synthesis of these different features of the Florentine state is difficult; however, at least two main elements can be underlined. Firstly, the Florentine state was the state of Florence, that is the territorial government of a single city and its ruling class. All the officials (*vicari, podestà, capitani*) were deliberately chosen from among Florentine citizens, and communities did not play any relevant political role. Secondly, as a result, the institutional strength and cohesion of the Florentine state were higher than those of any other state of Renaissance Italy. The thousands of minute corrections and cautious approbations granted to local statutes by the central Florentine officers show unquestionably both the variety of the state's facets and the precise control exercised day-to-day by the dominant city.[22]

Predictably, this control was far from being accepted without question and, as a result, the territorial identity of the Florentine state was somewhat controversial. The subject cities were restive under Florentine protection and rule: plots, contacts and secret alliances with external powers as well as open rebellions became real dangers.[23] From a long-term perspective, however, it is difficult to judge whether the heavy hand of the *dominante* over the territory resulted in depressing its prosperity or, on the contrary, whether Florentine control offered new chances to the small Tuscan towns, including them in a wider economic network and granting their elites political stability under the shadow of Florence. The demographic crisis hit the Tuscan towns heavily in the fourteenth century, even before they fell under Florentine rule, but the demographic recovery of the following century was slower in Tuscany than in northern Italy, and Florence often pursued a policy of deliberate humiliation and impoverishment of the cities. In general, Florentine political interests prevailed over a coherent policy of economic integration, and a municipal view was for a long time preferred to a 'regional' attitude.[24]

Florence and the Medici

After the second unsuccessful attempt to conquer Lucca (1426–30), the Albizi regime failed to manage the consequent financial crisis of the republic. As a result, political consensus for the regime declined, and in 1434 a new *balìa* exiled Rinaldo degli Albizi and his supporters, opening the way to Cosimo de' Medici.[25]

---

[22] Tanzini, *Alle origini della Toscana moderna*. [23] Cohn, *Creating the Florentine State*.
[24] Epstein, 'Market structures'. [25] Kent, *The Rise of the Medici*.

Overestimating the changes between the Albizi hegemony and the first period of Cosimo's rule would be a mistake: Rinaldo's overthrow only partially changed the composition of the Florentine ruling class and the structure of the state, and within the *reggimento* Cosimo acted more like a *primus inter pares* than a *signore*.[26] As shown in the classic study by Nicolai Rubinstein, *The Government of Florence Under the Medici*, Cosimo controlled the institutions essentially by influencing access to public offices: a careful choice of the *accoppiatori* (electoral officers), who were in charge of electing loyal men to the *signoria* and other high magistracies, granted him the control of Florence without any open violation of the statutory rules.

On the contrary, Cosimo introduced innovations in traditional Florentine foreign policy in order to provide an external strong support for his internal hegemony, marking a traumatic difference with the past. In his first years of power, Cosimo made the most of his personal friendship with the Venetian pope Eugene IV, offering him Florence as a site for the council which was supposed to unify the Greek and the Latin churches in 1439. The event promptly gave the ruling family a huge advantage in terms of their international image and political prestige. Moreover, in the following decade Cosimo abandoned the pro-Venetian tradition of Florentine foreign politics, in favour of unconditional support of the *condottiere* Francesco Sforza in his claims to the Milanese duchy (which he finally obtained in 1450). Sforza's military strength and political alliance were the strongest support of the Medicean *signoria*: both Piero and Lorenzo de' Medici were forced to make recourse to the Sforza dukes during the crisis that followed the death of Cosimo in 1464, and in the difficult months after the Pazzi conspiracy in 1478. Only after his regime was assured by the Milanese alliance did Cosimo begin to alter the internal institutions of Florence. In 1458 the new *Consiglio dei Cento* was created; its members were all citizens whose names had been drawn for public offices after the 1434 *balìa* – in a word, only loyal supporters of the Medici.[27]

The effectiveness of Cosimo's social influence and political power became clear after his death in 1464: the toughest opposition to the hegemony of his son Piero came in fact not from an unlikely anti-Medicean party, but from some of the most influential and loyal members of the inner Medicean circle. In 1466 Angelo Acciaiuoli, Dietisalvi Neroni, Niccolò Soderini, and the closest confident of

---

[26] On Cosimo's patronage, see Kent, *Cosimo de' Medici*; for the political aspects of his rule, see Fubini, 'Il regime di Cosimo de' Medici'.

[27] Fubini, *Politica e pensiero politico*, 165–85, 227–48.

Cosimo, Luca Pitti, subscribed to a secret (but ultimately unsuccessful) agreement to control the political regime without any dynastic pre-eminence for the Medici family.

The Quattrocento was the great period of the *reggimento*, whose hegemony was also built upon the strategic use of art and culture. The urban *palazzo* replaced the ancient *case-torri* as a material sign of family pre-eminence, and famous architects and artists (such as Leon Battista Alberti, Bernardo Rossellino and Giuliano da Sangallo) were invited to design and build the splendid urban residences of the Florentine patriciate.[28] Humanist culture ceased to be directly linked to public office – as in the time of Coluccio Salutati or Leonardo Bruni – and became a component of the private *paideia* of young patricians.[29] Florence had been a city of big merchants and entrepreneurs; now it was becoming a city of learned statesmen. In this sense, political life became more and more elitist. To obtain a lower public office was still relatively easy for a middle-class family, but only an inner circle of citizens was really able to 'manage the art of ruling the state', according to the city statute of 1415. The various social components of the city were no longer represented in the political arena: statecraft was increasingly an art for carefully selected people.

In Florentine society, however, crossing the social divide that separated the patriciate from the middle class was still possible, and fifteenth-century Florentine history provides several instances of men promoted to the inner *reggimento* from the lower ranks of the world of manufacturing and commerce.[30] The economic prosperity of the city proved an easy way to social mobility: despite the declining fortunes of the wool industry in the fifteenth century, Florentine companies were able to find new economic strategies and different ways to develop flourishing businesses. Far from being limited by guild organisation, the Florentine economy saw a long period of prosperity.[31] Banking was the most famous Florentine enterprise, as the Medici exemplified well; the silk industry became probably the most important manufacture.[32] An effective and powerful merchant court, the *Tribunale della Mercanzia*, offered to this elite of bankers, entrepreneurs and statesmen strong jurisdictional support in defending their interests.[33]

---

[28] Goldthwaite, *The Building of Renaissance Florence*.
[29] Black, *Education and Society*, 462–8.
[30] See the perfect example of the Serristori family: Tognetti, *Da Figline a Firenze*.
[31] Goldthwaite, *The Economy of Renaissance Florence*.
[32] Tognetti, *Un'industria di lusso*. [33] Astorri, 'Note sulla Mercanzia fiorentina'.

The social flexibility of the patriciate does not imply that Florentine society had no means of defining status and disciplining social hierarchies. The fiscal system did not lose its traditional impact as the most effective tool for enlarging or destroying family fortunes.[34] Awareness of the fragility of families and kinships pushed the *reggimento* to elaborate detailed, careful legislation on the family, mostly focused on the transmission of private wealth. As several recent studies clearly suggest, Florentine statutory law was more rigid than in any other Renaissance city in protecting family patrimonies from decay and impoverishment.[35] Women, for example, were completely excluded from the inheritance of their father's goods, with the sole, limited exception of their dowries.[36] The difficulty for young women in finding a good marriage and the high level of dowries (well documented in contemporary private memorandum books and family correspondence) impelled Florence to found the *Monte delle doti* in 1425. The *Monte* was the city's dowry fund: fathers could lend money to the state at a low interest rate, and the amount of money generated by these loans would be available after a few years for their daughters' dowries. Despite a traditional intepretation of Renaissance history as the origin of modern individualism, in Florence as elsewhere family relations and the incorporation of the *amici* in an extension of the kin group were the centre of the social, economic and political life of the patriciate.[37]

The Florentine politics of magnificence

A profound change in the Florentine political structure became evident under the rule of Lorenzo de' Medici, who succeeded his father Piero as the heir to the family fortune in 1469. No historical analysis of the Italian Renaissance could avoid dealing with the great personality of the Magnifico. For that reason, it has been quite difficult to free the Florentine Quattrocento from the enduring myth of Lorenzo as the perfect Renaissance man. In any case, the imposing edition of the entire correspondence of Lorenzo, though unfortunately not yet complete, has provided a huge amount of material and data for a revision of our understanding of the Magnifico and his political experience.[38]

Lorenzo's life marked another, crucial step in the Medici's political trajectory towards a real *signoria* over the city. In order to strengthen his

---

[34] Ciappelli, *Fisco e società a Firenze*.   [35] Kuehn, *Law, Family and Women*.
[36] For an Italian survey, see Kirshner, 'Family and marriage'; for Florence in particular, see Chabot, 'Le gouvernement des pères'.
[37] Connell (ed.), *Society and Individual*, and now Kent, *Friendship, Love and Trust*.
[38] Lorenzo de' Medici, *Lettere*, 12 vols., Florence: Giunti, 1977–2007, until 1488.

personal hegemony, Lorenzo fully exploited the wealth of the family bank and took advantage of the strong alliance with the Sforza, until he exhausted both. He made significant changes to the institutional structure of the state: in 1477 he abolished the *Capitano del popolo*, the official in charge of ordinary justice since the thirteenth century, and strengthened the role of the *Otto di Guardia*;[39] in 1480 he created the *Settanta*, a sort of senate that was given control over appointments to high offices. The Medicean assemblies of the *Settanta* and *Cento* became the new core of the republic, taking powers from the *Priori* and the traditional councils. Lorenzo also devoted great attention to the chancery: integral to its reform in 1483 was the appointment at its highest grade of the humanist Bartolomeo Scala, a loyal Medici client.[40] Even beyond institutional rules, Lorenzo's influential role over Florentine magistracies enabled him to control official appointments and sometimes judiciary matters as well. On top of all these changes, the network of Medici banks provided the Magnifico with a personal diplomacy that was sometimes alternative, sometimes complementary, to the public one. Not surprisingly, the control of diplomatic assignments were at the origin of a crucial conflict between Lorenzo and the Florentine patriciate. As Alamanno Rinuccini's *Dialogus de Libertate* (1479) points out, the old families of the *reggimento* were well disposed towards Medicean rule in so far as it was able to guarantee them their traditional benefits and political privileges (above all a diplomatic career), but they would no longer support it if the regime bypassed them in favour of its clients. Again, the major threat to Lorenzo's rule came from inside: in 1478, the conspiracy that killed Giuliano de' Medici and wounded Lorenzo himself was organised by the Pazzi, a clan of the inner Medicean elite closely tied by blood to Lorenzo, whose electoral and economic ambitions he had frustrated.[41]

The image of the Magnifico as an artist and a poet has for a long time taken precedence over close analysis of his political role. Lorenzo used culture to strengthen his power: he refounded the Pisan university in 1473, and gathered in Florence the best cultural circle of his time, composed of men of the intellectual stature of Cristoforo Landino, Marsilio Ficino, Angelo Poliziano and Giovanni Pico della Mirandola. In pursuing such a cultural policy, however, he was following the tradition of his family and, in any case, in Florence he was acting as just one among many other Florentine artistic patrons.[42]

---

[39] Martines, *Lawyers and Statecraft*; Zorzi, *L'amministrazione della giustizia*.
[40] Brown, *Bartolomeo Scala*.   [41] Martines, *April Blood*.
[42] Kent, *Lorenzo de' Medici and the Art of Magnificence*.

On the contrary, outside the walls of Florence the Magnifico was more ambitious, both in his artistic and his political patronage. He used to spend most of the year in his beautiful country houses, and took a close interest in the building of his princely villa in Poggio a Caiano near Prato. On the other hand, he devoted special attention to the Florentine dominion and subject towns. His official and private correspondence includes a vast number of letters addressed to him from every part of the state: ordinary people asked him directly to cancel a judicial sentence, to arrange a marriage, to lower a tax assessment or appoint an official.[43] In this sense, Lorenzo adopted, albeit informally, a new attitude towards the daily administration of the state; if the city proved to be a difficult arena because of the enduring ambitions of the old patriciate, the territory offered more interesting possibilities and broader spaces.

A similar option influenced his family strategies. Not only did Lorenzo marry in 1469, outside any municipal tradition, Clarice Orsini, a young woman from a powerful feudal family of central Italy, but he also devoted many years of his life to an even more ambitious goal, winning a cardinal's hat for his youngest son Giovanni, in order to acquire the noble status that in a republican context could come only from an ecclesiastical career. Giovanni's promotion in 1489, when he was still a boy, was one of Lorenzo's last, and perhaps most important, successes; he died in 1492.

An uncertain destiny

Lorenzo's death left Florence in a difficult and uncertain situation: the communal tradition was seriously undermined, but a princely regime had not yet been established. The situation could have evolved either way, turning Florence into a principality, or recovering the old republican *reggimento*. The second solution seemed to prevail in the troubled years immediately after 1492. Following Charles VIII of France's descent to Italy in 1494, Lorenzo's young son Piero was forced to leave the city. The restored republic found a new leader in Gerolamo Savonarola, the Dominican friar famous for his violent speeches and his sinister prophecies about the role of king Charles as a tool in the hands of God. Savonarola's political role has often been misjudged: the relation between the religious inspiration of the friar and Florentine political evolution in the 1490s has been widely discussed.[44] Savonarola's

---

[43] Salvadori, *Dominio e patronato*.
[44] Prodi, 'Gli affanni della democrazia', and more recently Fubini, *Politica e pensiero politico*, 249–71.

political project was more complex than the vision of a Christian-inspired republic. The key element of his reform was the creation of the Consiglio Maggiore, a huge council composed of three thousand members; every citizen could be drawn for the council, providing that one of his ancestors had been chosen for a major public office since 1382. Ancient oligarchic factions and the Medicean party were brought together, and popular expectations were satisfied by the extraordinary breadth of the council's composition. The traditional institutional instruments of oligarchic rule were swept away: the *accoppiatori*, investments in the *Monte*, the *parlamenti* and the *balìe* were abolished. However, the political genius of Savonarola could not resolve the deep conflicts between social groups, and the friar himself rapidly became involved in the political struggle. Savonarola was finally brought to his death in 1498 by his Florentine enemies, the '*arrabbiati*', with the support of the pope Alexander VI, who feared the friar's powerful appeal to a council to reform the church.

In the following years Florence seemed unable to find peace. Republican government survived after Savonarola, but in 1502 families of the patriciate (*ottimati*) succeeded in establishing a magistrate at the head of the republic for life, the *Gonfaloniere*, who was supposed to play the same balancing role as the Venetian doge. However, the attempt failed, and in 1512 the Medici re-entered the city. After fifteen years of uncertain rule by various members of the Medici family, the republic was restored once more when another Medici pope (Clement VII) was besieged in Rome by the Spanish army in 1527. The radical popular republic of the late 1520s survived only three years, and finally it was overthrown by the imperial armies, which brought back the Medici in order to include Florence in the new Spanish order in Italy.

Throughout all these political changes, some problems remained unresolved. First was the constitutional form of the state. In the early sixteenth century, an intense debate revolved around the different options: an oligarchic republic (*governo stretto*), a popular regime (*governo largo*) or a mixture of both. Florentine statesmen attentively observed the example of Venice, where a restricted council (Senato) worked together with a larger one (Maggior Consiglio) and a non-hereditary lord (the doge).[45] The great families of the *reggimento* aimed to maintain their hegemony over Florentine society:[46] a strong, definite lordship of the Medici was dangerous, but a popular *governo largo* seemed a much worse solution. Finally, in 1530 most patrician families

---

[45] See the classical study by von Albertini, *Firenze dalla repubblica al principato*.
[46] Najemy, *A History of Florence*, 375–485.

accepted submission to a prince, Alessandro de' Medici. His title was the expression of Florentine contradictions: Alessandro was *dux reipublice Florentine*, duke of the republic of Florence. All these ambiguities finally came to an end in the era of his successor, Cosimo I. Even though he formally became grand duke of Tuscany only in 1569, Cosimo founded an effective monarchy. His strong links with the emperor and the Spanish kings, the creation of a princely court and the building of new ducal institutions provided the city with a solid institutional framework, and granted the patriciate a well-defined political role within an absolutist state.

Another problem was the territorial state. After the passage of Charles VIII in 1494, Pisa rebelled against Florence and remained outside Florentine control until 1509. In the first years of the sixteenth century, Arezzo too freed itself from the *dominante*. The contradictions of municipal rule over a regional state then reached their climax. Only a newly established proper ducal power had the possibility and the strength to start a new era. Cosimo created new territorial offices and inaugurated a policy of favour towards the oligarchies of the subject cities. Local families began, albeit slowly, to find in the wider arena of the regional state room for their ambitions, for so long repressed by Florentine rule: above all, opportunities were found at court and in the ducal chivalric order, the *Cavalieri di Santo Stefano*.[47] Cosimo also created the ducal *bande*, a semi-permanent military force composed of companies of peasants; these bands proved to be a new solution for the old problem of the lack of a permanent army, which the republican tradition (despite Machiavelli's efforts) had not been able to solve.[48]

In spite of the undeniable impact of the reforms of Cosimo's age, historians are nowadays very cautious in interpreting the role of the first grand duke as the true creator of a 'modern state':[49] Tuscany was a composite state, still divided into a wide variety of local communities and settlements governed by thousands of ancient statutes, usages and laws. And outside the borders of the greatest Tuscan state, several independent territories remained: not only the little republic of Lucca with its rural territory, but also the strange enclave of Piombino, controlled by the *signorile* dynasty of the Appiano. The legacy of the medieval past heavily influenced early modern Tuscany.

---

[47] Angiolini, *I cavalieri e il principe*.
[48] On Machiavelli's military project, see Guidi, *Un segretario militante*.
[49] Mannori, 'Effetto domino'; Fasano Guarini, *L'Italia moderna e la Toscana dei principi*.

Siena: a different Renaissance?

Finding the starting date of a history of Renaissance Siena is a difficult task, but 1337 may be seen as the climax of the medieval evolution of the flourishing commune. In that year, Ambrogio Lorenzetti painted the famous frescoes of *Buon governo* in the Sala della Pace of the public palace of Siena. It has proved hard for scholars to determine the philosophical sources of the famous frescoes, but their political message is much clearer. Justice, equal access to the offices of the city, defence from external enemies and the rule of law were the political values of which the frescoes were intended to remind the ruling class gathering daily within the palace. In the very same years, these values were affirmed in the city's statutes.[50]

The frescoes of the *Buon governo* and the statutes of 1337–9 are the best-known symbols of the political regime that had ruled Siena since 1287, the government of the *Nove*.[51] The *Nove* constituted the council that governed the city; turnover of its members was frequent, but it was socially quite homogeneous, being constituted of the *mezzana gente*, that is the large elite of a merchant city. Meanwhile, the Parte Guelfa opted for an alliance with Florence and ensured a long period of external stability. The Mercanzia consolidated the hegemony of trade in the urban economic system. Under the close direction of the *Nove*, the Consiglio Generale continued to ensure wide participation in public discussions, even if the most important functions were frequently assigned to special short-term commissions, the *balìe*.

Despite the proud representation of the *Buon governo*, Siena's political system was in many ways vulnerable. The *Nove* were at the middle of a social chain whose ends were on one side the lower classes, and on the other the ancient nobility of the *Gentiluomini*, the great clans who were excluded from public offices, but who were still powerful thanks to their financial wealth and political networks (the Piccolomini, Salimbeni and Tolomei). Maintaining the internal balance between the different social actors was not an easy task for the *Nove* regime, not least because outside the city walls conflicts over territorial hegemony were worsening in the whole Tuscan region.

The crucial change of Sienese regime took place in 1355, when the arrival of the emperor Charles IV gave to the *Gentiluomini* a chance to reform the state. The *Nove*'s regime was overthrown by a coalition of noble families and guildsmen, whose supremacy found expression in a

---

[50] Ascheri, 'Statuti, legislazione e sovranità'.
[51] Bowsky, *A Medieval Italian Commune*.

new closed council, the *Dodici*. The *Dodici* did not impose a constitutional reform of the city: however, their rule marked the end of a long season of stability and has been usually considered the beginning of Renaissance Siena.[52] The *Dodici* hegemony lasted in fact for only thirteen years, and was followed in 1368 by the regime of the *Riformatori*, a weak coalition soon shaken by a violent rebellion of the urban workers (1371), the *rivolta del Bruco*.[53]

The lower classes were not alone in being concerned about the economic situation of the city. The governments of the *Dodici* and the *Riformatori* were forced to consider attentively the worsening financial situation, because the prosperity of the time of the *Nove* was vanishing. Historians are uncertain about the nature and the reasons for this change: estimates of the Sienese economic system suffer when judgement is biased by the usual comparison with Florence. Apparently, the ruling class soon abandoned trades, manufacturing and banking for a more aristocratic way of life, substantially based on landed property; however, to overestimate this 'conservative' attitude of the Sienese elite in the fourteenth century would be misleading. Even though the economic situation was worsening, the key problem for late Trecento Siena was not the economy, but politics. In the second half of the century the city became increasingly involved in a series of territorial conflicts with its neighbours, first of all Florence and Perugia. Since Siena, like the other Italian cities, was not able to have a permanent army, the commune was forced to pay huge amounts of money every year to mercenary companies, not only for war but also to prevent them from ravaging its territory.[54] The dramatic growth of military expenses threw the city into a deep financial crisis, and the process of decision-making about urgent financial needs was increasingly entrusted to small *balìe*, weakening the authority and the power of the traditional institutions of the city. Consequently, territorial wars forced Siena to exhaust its wealth and erode its constitution.

In 1385, a new regime established another fragile internal coalition, heavily backed by Florence. Siena tried to find an agreement with Florence and Perugia, but its ambitions were frustrated once again in 1397 by the loss of Montepulciano. The revived hostility against Florence and hope of restoring political stability in the city pushed the ruling class to offer the *signoria* of Siena to Gian Galeazzo Visconti. For Renaissance Siena, this was the first experience of an external government, but it would not last very long.

---

[52] Ascheri, *Siena nel Rinascimento*.   [53] Franceschi, 'I "Ciompi"'.
[54] Caferro, *Mercenary Companies*.

In these decades, turning to a *signoria* was not an uncommon solution for a great city to solve a deep crisis of governance. Apart from the case of an external ruler like Gian Galeazzo Visconti, many cities governed by communes, usually under the pressure of financial difficulties, had recourse to a *signorile* solution. Lucca offers a perfect example of this practice: after a long period of instability, in 1400 Paolo Guinigi established his *signoria* over the city, facing Florentine aggression effectively for thirty years.

The Sienese solution was ingeniously different. After the brief experience of Visconti rule, early fifteenth-century Siena showed a remarkable institutional creativity in giving political space to different actors. The ruling class split into different groups, called *Monti*: every *Monte* represented the groups and the families that had previously ruled the city – the *Monte dei Nove, dei Dodici, dei Reformatori*, and finally the *Gentiluomini* and the *Popolo*.[55] Political offices and seats in the city councils were distributed between the different *Monti* according to a well-balanced rotation of appointments.[56] This complicated system allowed the ruling class to keep political struggle under control and to reach and maintain a reasonable concord in the city. At the same time, this agreement, harking back to the fourteenth-century groups, shows how little the Sienese elites proved themselves able to imagine and enact new models of government. This backwards-looking attitude could be considered a general feature of Renaissance Siena: even cultural and artistic achievements were clearly modelled more on the late gothic style of the Trecento than on the classical style so typical of Florentine contemporary art.[57]

Despite these general trends, however, recent studies have strongly rejected contrasting a flourishing 'modern' Florence to a declining 'medieval' Siena. Sienese bankers played a major role in fifteenth-century Italy, mostly at the papal court in Rome, and some of them, like the Spannocchi and the Chigi, built huge fortunes and, learning from their experiences elsewhere in Italy, introduced to Siena examples of Renaissance style, such as the urban *palazzi*.[58] The traditional Sienese concern for the beauty of their city was even more intense during the Quattrocento than in the Trecento, and a Sienese pope, Pius II (1458–64),

---

[55] Ascheri, 'Siena nel primo Quattrocento'.
[56] Although the *Monte dei Dodici* was normally excluded from public charges and the *Gentiluomini* were admitted to some offices only: Shaw, *Popular Government and Oligarchy*, 3–142.
[57] Ascheri, Mazzoni and Nevola (eds.), *L'ultimo secolo della repubblica di Siena. Arti*.
[58] Tognetti, '"Tra compagni palesi e ladri occulti"'.

played a crucial role for both the economic prosperity and the artistic flourishing of his city. In this sense, Siena was definitely not a declining or 'old-fashioned' city.

Nevertheless, 'medieval' pluralism remained a central feature of Sienese politics: many *Monti* shared the decision-making process, and many different semi-independent institutions, such as the Ospedale della Scala, the university or the bishop with his still important feudal territories, participated in day-to-day government. Possibly the coexistence of all these different groups prevented oligarchic or princely projects from being realised, but they also blocked any further evolution of the political structure.

Siena: a simple state

During the late fourteenth and early fifteenth centuries the Sienese ruling class paid increasing attention to the control of the countryside. The *Regolatori* received extensive powers over rural communities including the power to approve their statutes. Sienese territory was growing: even though it cannot be compared with Florentine imperialism, Sienese expansion in southern Tuscany in the early fifteenth century encompassed several small towns and feudal territories.[59] On the other hand, the Sienese *contado*, unlike the major part of the Florentine state, was becoming a land without people. After the catastrophic demographic decline of the 1340s–50s, many communities were unable to recover and return to a significant demographic level; particularly in the south, the rural landscape of Maremma resembled a wilderness of woods and marshes, crowned by a thin web of castles upon the hills.[60] The poverty of rural settlements made the Sienese dominion a 'simple state': without any other episcopal city or important rural community, fifteenth-century Siena had no competitors and controlled every part of its state. Like Florence, Siena established on its territory a network of its own officials, Sienese *vicari* and *podestà*; but because many communities did not develop a basic level of social complexity, usually even local administration was directly exercised by Sienese officials.[61]

The crisis of rural settlements was rather complex. Demographic change in Sienese lands was not only linked to the catastrophe of 1348, but was also the effect of the expansion of citizens' property in the countryside: urban patrimonies undermined the traditional cohesion of rural communities and bound every peasant family to the owner of

[59] Boisseuil, 'La Toscane siennoise'. [60] Ginatempo, *Crisi di un territorio*.
[61] Ginatempo, *Uno 'stato semplice'*.

their fields by the standard Tuscan contract of the *mezzadria* (owner and worker each had half-shares of crops and revenues). The more Sienese-owned property spread in the rural territory, the less the traditional network of local powers and solidarities could survive; in this sense, late medieval change marked the irreversible crisis of a whole social and economic system. At the same time, however, the deserted fields and hills of the Sienese Maremma were converted to highly profitable large-scale sheep-breeding under the control of the powerful *Dogana dei Paschi*, a public guild in charge of the seasonal moving of livestock across the country.

Siena's last century

The system of the *Monti* ruled Siena unchallenged thoughout the fifteenth century.[62] Only in the last decade of the century, in the aftermath of the French descent, did Pandolfo Petrucci, an influential member of the *Monte dei Nove*, succeed in establishing personal rule over the city:[63] during Pandolfo's lifetime, Sienese government avoided factional divisions and survived the Italian Wars, even if Pandolfo's *signoria* was dependent on external support. After his death in 1512, his heirs proved themselves incapable of governing the state, and Siena returned to a republican regime in 1525.

A constant feature of Sienese politics was its never-ending confrontation with Florence. Because of the short distance between the two cities, a military attack against Florence could have found a perfect base in Sienese lands. Alfonso I of Naples followed this strategy in 1447–8, establishing his military camps in the Maremma for several months; thirty years later, during the war after the Pazzi plot, a Neapolitan army moved against Florence from Sienese country.

On the other hand, the survival of the Sienese state depended much more on the external interests of more powerful allies than on its own forces. On more than one occasion, the real protagonists of Sienese politics were the Neapolitan kings, driven by their ambitions against Florence, or the Roman court. A minor change in the political balance of the Italian peninsula could prove disastrous for Siena. In 1555, grand duke Cosimo had the opportunity to take full advantage of such a precarious situation: under the protection of the king of Spain and emperor Charles V, Cosimo was able to move to the conquest of Siena.

---

[62] On fifteenth-century popular or oligarchic regimes, see Shaw, *Popular Government and Oligarchy*.
[63] Recent studies can be found in Ascheri and Nevola (eds.), *L'ultimo secolo della repubblica di Siena. Politica*.

Nevertheless, the fall of the republic was mitigated by the conditions of the annexation, because the Sienese 'new state' was added to the old Florentine territory as a feudal concession to Cosimo, and the city could preserve its integrity. In such a context, some Sienese traditions could survive and even grow. The ancient university of Siena, for example, remained one of the most important cultural centres in modern Tuscany. Even though all political autonomy of the city was revoked, a strong sense of civic identity stubbornly survived: the self-celebration of the urban tradition, and the internal division into *contrade*, each with its own statutes, councils and officers, have been recently re-evaluated as an alternative form of political identity in a great subject city.[64]

Conclusion

After this brief summary of Tuscan history over two centuries, a crucial question should be raised: what had really changed in Tuscan Renaissance city-states? How far had early modern Florence, or Siena, or even Lucca moved away from their communal past? Recent historiography has observed that a sharp opposition between city-states of the communal age and the later 'regional states' is a misleading concept: scholars no longer look for the Renaissance origin of a 'modern state' which has itself proved to be rather problematic. They concentrate instead on more pragmatic themes by investigating the political systems of the Tuscan cities and their evolution, and finally by questioning what the outcome of these changes would be in the long term. We may usefully try to answer these questions by focusing on three main themes highlighted by recent research: territorial rule, internal government and political languages.

Late medieval communal powers were resolute in building and maintaining effective control over their districts and territories long before the most celebrated period of Florentine state-building.[65] The Renaissance had possibly brought to these processes of state-building a higher level of bellicosity due to the collision of different expansionist policies in the same area. In any case, Siena or Lucca ('simple states' from a territorial point of view) did not face any serious opponent in their own territories: their ruling classes were never forced to convert themselves in a more open social group than the original urban patriciate. Florence was a different matter. Even though the Florentine policy of territorial expansion and control was potentially similar, the dimensions and the complexity of the state altered the general picture. The Florentine ruling

[64] Savelli, *Siena*, 59–100. [65] Bratchel, *Medieval Lucca*, 144–69.

class was forced to deal not only with hundreds of rural communities and seigneurial powers, but also with some communal and episcopal cities. The original 'communal' attitude of thirteenth-century Florence had to confront in the following centuries the plurality of the new territorial state and a multiplicity of strong local identities. The strong contrast between an original 'communal' model and an actual composite state – more than the supposed natural effectiveness of the Florentine state-building – pushed Florentine rulers towards the elaboration of new patterns of government and innovative strategies of local control. We should not be surprised by the fact that only the principality, informally under Lorenzo, openly under Cosimo I, overcame this inner contradiction. Lorenzo's policies towards the communities can be interpreted as the beginning of a non-municipal approach to the problem of local control; less than a century later, the ducal state of Cosimo I moved beyond the municipal character of the Florentine dominion.

The turning point of the transformation of the internal constitution of the Tuscan cities is undeniably the second half of the fourteenth century. Under the pressure of prolonged territorial wars and growing military expenses, Tuscan cities experienced, with different results, new forms of concentration of authority and power, such as *balìe*, special councils, executive offices and sometimes *signorile* regimes. In Siena, the exercise of authority and power was restricted to members of one of the *Monti*, whose social composition dated back to the fourteenth century; the *Nove*, *Riformatori* or *Dodici* did not express a particular ideology, but rather represented a collective social identity which stemmed from the municipal tradition of the different Sienese clans or social groups. At the end of Paolo Guinigi's *signoria* in 1430, Lucca restored its communal institutions and reinforced the internal solidity of the aristocratic merchant oligarchy;[66] in the following century a quiet existence under the imperial shadow was the price the city paid for a limited – but solid – freedom.[67] In both cases, the political survival of the city required the enactment of a complex balance between political groups, and strict regulation of participation in governance; this process blocked the evolution of the institutional system and in the end exhausted its vitality. Florentine politics was no less turbulent, nor its final issue less oligarchic. Nevertheless, in Florence the *plena potestas* of the government prevailed over internal divisions or external protection; finally, the erosion of republican liberties generated not political submission but a strong central power.

---

[66] Bratchel, *Lucca 1430–1494*, 290–5.   [67] Berengo, *Nobili e mercanti*.

This feature had an effect on political culture, which was unique to Florence. Not surprisingly, recent studies on the political languages of the Renaissance Tuscan cities have mostly focused on republicanism. Some studies have unmasked the instrumental nature of republicanism: republican values were employed by an elitist ruling class to gain the lower classes' consent by including them in a shared ideology.[68] This sceptical approach has been partially contested, to underline a genuine republican emphasis on collective participation in the *respublica*, and its long-term effects in building a positive institutional culture and civic identity.[69] Nevertheless, republicanism is an ambiguous concept. Participation, the rule of law and good government were (again) medieval legacies, and cities such as Lucca or Siena continued to use this traditional language of freedom and *Buon governo* through the centuries. In Florence something different happened: in spite of any rhetorical (and historiographical) abuse of republicanism, the struggle for power created a background for an innovative debate on the nature of public government. In this sense, Machiavelli and Guicciardini embody in their texts the essential Florentine political experience. The analysis of the relation between their thought and their political background is nowadays one of the most profitable fields of Renaissance historiography.

---

[68] Brown, 'De-masking Renaissance republicanism'.
[69] For example, Ascheri, *Siena nel Rinascimento*.

6 Ferrara and Mantua

Trevor Dean

Introduction: the historiography

Over forty years ago, Philip Jones declared that 'the "Renaissance state" is a fiction to be banished from the books'.[1] He arrived at this provocative conclusion at the end of a review of the policies and achievements of the *signorie* (city-lordships) and principalities of fourteenth- and fifteenth-century Italy, mainly focused on Lombardy under the Visconti, but also referring to the dynasties of the Este in Ferrara, the Gonzaga in Mantua and the Malatesta in the Romagna. The course of his argument was as follows: if the Renaissance state is defined as 'unitary, absolute and secular', there *was* some reality to this description. There was some redistribution of power, as lords determined the activities of civic councils, appointed all important officials and intervened in justice and law. There was also an assertion of princely authority over rural nobles, clans, guilds and clergy, and evidence of movement towards greater equity in justice and taxation 'between different classes and different parts of their dominions'. Nevertheless, such advances were outweighed by two factors, one relating to the power of the lords, the other to the resistance of other centres within their dominions. The *signoria*, Jones argued, was largely conservative, not innovative: it retained inherited forms and institutions of power across the range of its activity (administrative, fiscal, legal, military), and it sought to authorise, not eradicate, privilege. On the other hand lay 'the obstinate survival of diversity and privilege' manifested in strong local sentiment, local statutes and local customs. Between continuity and change, Jones, as in most of his writing, favoured continuity.

Since this first formulation of Jones's argument, it almost goes without saying that the 'Renaissance state' has not been banished. For a long time, a persistent view continued to place the transition from medieval to modern in the Renaissance period and equated modernisation with

---

[1] Jones, 'Communes and despots', 95.

centralisation (concentration of power, limitation of local autonomy, development of capital cities and courts) and with bureaucracy (government by officials with norms, systems and memories). Werner Gundersheimer, who can rightly claim (with Luciano Chiappini) the honour of having pioneered the modern historiography of late medieval Ferrara, retained this model in his influential monograph on that city: in his frequent use of the terms 'absolutism' and 'absolutist style', and his argument that, to control their cities and territories, the Estensi relied on 'a substantial [...] administrative bureaucracy' and 'a highly rationalized, effective and up-to-date administration'.[2] By the late 1980s, however, it was more usual to critique than to celebrate the so-called Renaissance state, but even then James Grubb could propose reusing it and investing it with new meaning, to describe the type of state ('composite, far larger, more sophisticated [...] more lasting') in ways that made it different from both the fourteenth century and the seventeenth–eighteenth, and to describe the behaviour of political actors ('political actors required classical principles for governance').[3] This desire to retain the term 'Renaissance state' is evident in Michael Bratchel's recent book on Lucca: in the title itself and in his discussion of statehood in terms of officials, taxation and centralisation, even if Bratchel is wary of the applicability of the term to Lucca, given that 'there is little agreement over the distinctive characteristics of the so-called Renaissance state'.[4]

Nevertheless, the most important historiographical development in later medieval political history has continued to press Jones's argument that the state in this period was neither absolute nor unitary: Giorgio Chittolini wrote that the first thing we have to do is 'to free ourselves of the image of a state in which the power of the prince radiated, uniform and unchallenged, over all his territories'.[5] And he has elaborated a model for the late medieval Italian state that gives it a particular character, neither medieval-particularist nor modern-centralist, but composite: a state that combined central power with that of semi-independent social bodies and groups. Chittolini began to develop this model through his study of the role of fiefs in the relations between the Visconti dukes and the nobility of their state, and proceeded from there to apply it also to other components of the state, such as officials, small towns and territories separated by the prince from urban control. In this model, central power is based on an accord between the prince and these social

---

[2] Gundersheimer, *Ferrara*, 272–6. [3] Grubb, *Firstborn of Venice*, xv–xvi.
[4] Bratchel, *Medieval Lucca and the Evolution of the Renaissance State*, 146–52 and 203 (for the quotation).
[5] Chittolini, 'Infeudazioni e politica feudale', 37.

groups: they recognised the prince's authority in matters such as war, justice, public order and finance, while retaining legitimate rights of self-government on the basis of agreements (*capitoli*) or feudal investitures.[6] But Chittolini still prefers to retain the term 'Renaissance state', redefining it with new categories, such as the plurality of political classes and centres, the limited capacity of central government, and an institutionalised tendency to recognise areas of immunity and separate organisation.[7]

The dynasties and their territories

The purpose of this chapter is to examine the more recent historiography of the northern Italian principalities, chiefly the Estensi and the Gonzaga, to gauge the balance it suggests between change and continuity in state formation. The first task is to justify the selection of period taken here, namely the last years of the fourteenth century and the whole of the fifteenth. Recent and older histories of the Renaissance in Ferrara and Mantua place the Renaissance and its specific political formations firmly in the fifteenth century.[8] Gian Carlo Malacarne, in his recent series of books on the Gonzaga, includes a chapter 'from the Middle Ages to the Renaissance', which focuses on the second half of the fifteenth century.[9] The early fifteenth century in particular has attracted various historians as a period of significant change in political structures. In an earlier chapter, Malacarne marks the period around 1400 as one of transition in Mantua: 'it was in the years around 1400 that Francesco Gonzaga managed to make an unprecedented transformation, in which consolidation of the borders of his territory was accompanied by intensification of the power of the ruling family'.[10] The same years have been highlighted in Ferrara and the same process perceived. The turn of the fourteenth/fifteenth century, according to Marco Folin, witnessed a change in the relation between the Este family and the citizenry of Ferrara, as made evident in the location, pose and dress of monumental statues of ruling members of the family, and in the absence of meetings of the general council of citizens after 1393.[11] A downplaying of citizen

---

[6] Ibid., *passim*; Chittolini, 'L'onore dell'officiale'; Chittolini, 'Le "terre separate"'.
[7] Chittolini, 'Stati padani, "stato del Rinascimento"', 11, 25.
[8] Salmons (ed.), *The Renaissance in Ferrara*; *Storia di Ferrara*.
[9] Malacarne, *I Gonzaga di Mantova*, II, ch. 3 'I Gonzaga tra Medioevo e Rinascimento', 130–75.
[10] Ibid., I, 315: 'proprio negli anni a cavallo del XIV e XV secolo Francesco riuscì a procedere a una trasformazione senza precedenti, nella quale si verificò il consolidamento dei confini del dominio accompagnato dall'intensificarsi del potere della famiglia dominante'.
[11] Folin, *Rinascimento estense*, 59–60.

participation and an increase in self-projection by the ruling family thus inaugurated a greater political distancing between rulers and ruled. The same idea of intensification also marked Renaissance government in fifteenth-century Ferrara for Gundersheimer: with a focus on the second half of the fifteenth century, he noted 'an ever more highly differentiated and specialized bureaucracy, together with increasingly centralized control'.[12] The 'Renaissance state' for these authors thus means a combination of changes in political relations – borders, bureaucracy, centralisation, visual domination, distancing – that occurred in the fifteenth century, and not before.

This chapter will therefore range across the reign of Niccolò III d'Este (1393–1441) and his three sons, Leonello (1441–50), Borso (1450–71) and Ercole (1471–1505), and that of Francesco Gonzaga (1382–1407), Gian Francesco (1407–44), Lodovico (1444–78) and Federico (1478–84). A second preliminary task is to sketch rapidly the main achievements of each ruler. In Ferrara Niccolò III d'Este's lengthy reign was insecure in its opening years: a military challenge came from a cousin supported by Venice, and he was forced by penury to surrender some territory to Venice in 1395. Perhaps aware consequently of his state's vulnerability, he developed a reputation as a peace-maker among the powers of northern Italy – though this has been linked by one historian to his 'strong and very public religiosity'[13] – and instituted a policy, followed by his sons, of keeping Ferrara out of major warfare in the region. His successor, Leonello, was associated with administrative reform, brought humanistic study to Ferrara and reopened its university (founded in 1391, but in difficulties in the early fifteenth century). His brother, the popular, celibate, display-loving Borso travelled constantly across his territories, especially for the hunt, but also took his duties seriously, revising Ferrarese statute law, reforming his councils and obtaining elevation to the rank of duke. The last of Niccolò III's sons, Ercole, punitively suppressed an attempted *coup d'état* by his nephew (1476), developed the ritual and religious elements of dynastic rule, and, following his preference for alliance with Milan, Florence and Naples, fell into a disastrous war with Venice (1482–4); in subsequent years he promoted a grand urbanistic scheme to fortify, enlarge and embellish the city of Ferrara. The actions of Niccolò III's contemporary in Mantua, Francesco Gonzaga, bear in general terms some similarity to those of his Este neighbours: he acquired new titles and castles, instituted

---

[12] Gundersheimer, 'Toward a reinterpretation of the Renaissance in Ferrara', 276. He does, however, suggest that this 'continued the tendencies begun during the early Trecento'.
[13] Gundersheimer, *Ferrara*, 74.

a practice of serving Milan and Venice alternately as military commander, and focused his building activities on fortifications and the suburban castle of San Giorgio. Territorial gains under Gian Francesco were more numerous, but under the terms of his will they were divided among his four sons (though mostly recovered later), while it was Lodovico, a long-term military commander for the dukes of Milan, who obtained the elevation of a member of the family to the rank of cardinal, and was much more active in promoting public works in Mantua (a new hospital, new churches, a new piazza, a clock tower) and its territory (fortifications, canals, land-reclamation).

In the fifteenth century, the existing city lordships, or *signorie*, of northern Italy evolved into principalities. This was partly a matter of title – the Visconti became dukes of Milan, the Estensi dukes of Ferrara, and the Gonzaga marquises of Mantua – but was mostly a matter of scale and of relations of power, in particular relations with cities. So my broad question is this: what did fifteenth-century principalities do to, or for, cities, and what did cities do to, or for, principalities? Behind this lies the argument of Larry Epstein that, in post-plague Italy, there was urban growth where towns were politically weak and territorial states were strong, and urban decline where towns were strong and central power weak.[14] Cities can obviously be approached from a number of perspectives. They were physical entities, of buildings, streets and squares, public and private spaces, an infrastructure of walls, bridges, fountains, mills and so on. They were aggregates of human population, natives and migrants, property-owners and paupers, producers and rentiers, clergy and laity. They were centres of religious cult, with dedicated personnel, premises, properties and practices. They were centres of power, in its various forms – political, economic, social, judicial – each with its institutions and practices, from the city government and the court, to the marketplace and the banks, the law court and the gallows, the pulpit and the notary's bench. All of these considerations imply, of course, that to speak of 'Ferrara' or 'Mantua' without specification or qualification is inadequate, often reducing the city to its political leadership alone.

Taken as political configurations, the two states in consideration here, Ferrara and Mantua, differed both between themselves and from their larger neighbour, the state of Milan. Mantua was a state with a single city, such that state, city and dynasty fused into one identity. Conversely, the state ruled by the Estensi formed what has been called a 'three-voiced dynamic', comprising the capital in Ferrara, two subject cities,

---

[14] Epstein, *Freedom and Growth*, 95.

Modena and Reggio, and extensive and varied rural territories, encompassing hills and plains, small towns and marshland.[15] They were both different from the state of Milan, which, it has been said, had one capital, but many centres, too strong to be brought into subjection to Milan itself or to the Visconti and Sforza dynasties. The Este and Gonzaga states were, on the one hand, weaker than their powerful neighbours in Milan and Venice, more subject to the flux of political conditions in Italy, more influenced from outside;[16] on the other hand, they achieved what those neighbours did not – stability and longevity of dynasty, large-scale town-planning, or institutional successes such as the creation of a university in the capital.[17]

The two dynasties in power in Ferrara and Mantua shared certain characteristics: feudal origins, longevity, absence of internal rivals, pursuit of titles, professional soldiering.[18] Both families arose from the feudal aristocracy, the Estensi being aristocratic leaders of long lineage in the Veneto, the Gonzaga having more recent and limited origins, but holding the fief and castle of Gonzaga from the late thirteenth century. Both enjoyed long and largely uninterrupted power in their respective cities, from 1240 for the Estensi in Ferrara, from 1328 for the Gonzaga in Mantua, though for the Estensi there were breaks in their rule in Ferrara and Modena in the early fourteenth century, and in Reggio from 1306 until 1409. Plots against these rulers were few, and those there were largely originated within their families; it was difficult now to seize these states 'from the inside'.[19] Both families sought grander titles than those that could be granted by the communes from which they originally derived their authority to rule: Borso d'Este was created duke of Modena and Reggio by emperor Frederick III, and duke of Ferrara by the pope; Francesco Gonzaga obtained the title of count from the pope and that of marquis from the emperor in 1432. Both families also served as military commanders for other states, though the Gonzaga more consistently than the Estensi. The families intermarried: Francesco Gonzaga's mother had been Alda d'Este, Leonello d'Este married Margherita Gonzaga in 1447 and Francesco Gonzaga married Isabella d'Este in 1490. In the second half of the fifteenth century, the Gonzaga were frequent visitors to Ferrara, and official personnel circulated between the two states.[20] There were also contrasting features, however.

---

[15] Lazzarini, 'I domini estensi', 30–1.
[16] Chittolini, 'Stati padani, "stato del Rinascimento"', 10.
[17] Cardini, 'Il libro e il potere'.   [18] Sestan, 'La storia dei Gonzaga nel Rinascimento'.
[19] Mozzarelli, 'Lo stato gonzaghesco', 367.
[20] Chambers and Dean, *Clean Hands and Rough Justice*, 5.

The Estensi were more successful in their territorial ambitions at least in the first half of the fifteenth century: though the Gonzaga retained aspirations to the lordships of Verona and Vicenza, actual additions to their state were on a small scale, whereas the Estensi briefly held the city of Parma (1409–20) and added extensive territory in the Frignano and Garfagnana (1429–30 and 1446–51) and in the Romagna (1437–40 and 1445). The Gonzaga maintained a steady alliance with Venice, the dominant power of north-east Italy, whereas Este relations with that city were often tense and deteriorated into open war between 1482 and 1484.[21]

Contrasts were more evident in the size and complexity of dominion. Gonzaga territory was set in the plain of the Po valley, and mixed agricultural land, woodland and marsh. To Mantua and its *contado* some modest territorial additions were made in the fifteenth century: in the early years of the century, Francesco Gonzaga took the opportunity of the collapse of the Visconti state, following the death of duke Gian Galeazzo, to acquire Ostiglia on the Po, Peschiera on Lake Garda, and other castles towards Verona. Participation in regional warfare brought further acquisitions, some of them temporary, along the borders with Verona, Cremona and Brescia. Meanwhile, surviving rural lordships in Mantuan territory were few, as the Gonzaga acquired Viadana and other castles from the Cavalcabò family in 1420, and Sabbioneta from the da Persico in 1435. They also came to exercise a large degree of control over the important rural monastery of San Benedetto Polirone. Mantuan territory had a simple administrative structure of rural vicariates, though subordinate *podesterie* also existed for newly acquired places such as Viadana and Ostiglia. Indeed the legal act by which the Viadanesi swore loyalty to Gian Francesco Gonzaga contained clauses ensuring that no new taxes would be imposed on them, that they would not be required to perform military service outside their territory and that bandits from Mantua could still take shelter there.[22]

The Este state was more complex, encompassing the pastoral economies of the Apennine hills, rich agricultural plains and coastal communities dependent on fishing, salt-making and river transport. Most of the Ferrarese *contado* formed one jurisdictional unit, as there were no rural lordships. However, at its edges there were settlements with their own statutes: for example, Massafiscaglia, created by the commune of Ferrara in 1219 and endowed with considerable fiscal exemptions; and Pomposa, home to an important Benedictine monastery with a compact

---

[21] Dean, 'Venetian economic hegemony'; Dean, 'After the war of Ferrara'.
[22] Tarducci, 'Gianfrancesco Gonzaga', 49–50.

rural lordship that fell into the administrative hands of the Estensi and their appointees from the early fifteenth century.²³ At Modena and Reggio, the geographical space ruled by civic statutes and jurisdiction was narrower. Their territories contained many places which had their own law-books, their own fully powered judges or their own lords: many castles obeyed local aristocratic families, who appointed their own officials and had their own links, fiscal, feudal and legal, with the Estensi. The lack of civic command over territory is evident in the range of attendance at the feast day celebrations of their patron saints. The Este promoted the St George's day procession at Ferrara, requiring attendance from representatives of communities outside the Ferrarese *contado* (e.g. Comacchio, Bagnacavallo, Lugo), but Niccolò III in 1437 refused to allow Modena to enforce offerings due from its territory to its patron, San Gimignano, while the San Prospero's day procession in Reggio in the later fifteenth century was attended by representatives from only two or three country places.²⁴

Three ways of looking at principalities

The titles of three fairly recent publications may be used as banners under which to marshal some of the evidence and arguments on the relation between princes and cities, starting with the physical, material aspect of the city as a built environment. My three selected titles are these: 'The difficulty of constructing piazzas' (an essay of 1997, by Luciano Patetta about Milan under the Sforza dukes), 'A city in the form of a palace' (a book on Mantua by Marina Romani from 1995), and 'In the shadow of the prince' (an essay of 1997 by Marco Folin about Ferrara).²⁵ These three titles encapsulate three different ways of conceiving of the relation between cities and princes. 'A city in the form of a palace' belongs to an older tradition of scholarship that focused on the prince and on his decision-making power, on his ability to intervene and to shape realities as he desired. 'The difficulty of constructing piazzas' adopts the more sophisticated stance that sees all power as negotiated, all decisions as the outcomes of compromise and all subjects as active participants, whether consenting to, appropriating or resisting the prince's choice. 'In the shadow of the prince' inhabits an area between these two positions, stressing the distance and separation

---

²³ Dean, *Land and Power*, 35–9.
²⁴ Chambers and Dean, *Clean Hands and Rough Justice*, 6–7; Gamberini, 'Una città e la sua coscienza comunitaria', 86.
²⁵ Romani, *Una città in forma di palazzo*; Patetta, 'Milano. XV–XVII secolo'; Folin, 'Ferrara: 1385–1505'.

between princely power and local urban society. Although these three titles relate specifically to three different cities, Milan, Mantua and Ferrara, elements of each approach are present, in varying quotients, in each of the cities.

I start with 'the city in the form of a palace'. What did the author concerned, Marina Romani, mean by this? She readily admits that the words are in fact a misquotation: they come from *The Courtier* by Baldassare Castiglione, and in their original setting refer to the court of Urbino under Federico da Montefeltro.[26] The original meaning was that the court-palace was so well supplied with everything that it *appeared* like a city in the form of a palace. Whereas Castiglione likens the palace to a city, Romani deliberately inverts the phrase to liken the city to a palace. And she applies this idea to the city of Mantua in the fifteenth century, because it captures the significance of a completely new range of urbanistic and monumental interventions by the Gonzaga in the fabric of the city, treating the city as if it were an extension of, or part of, the princely palace. Whereas the Gonzaga in the fourteenth century, and their predecessors as lords, the Bonacolsi, had been content to build up their residences behind high walls in the old part of the city, in the fifteenth they intervened both with specific projects and facilities, and with new routes and alignments. New street-paving facilitated movement around the city, the grant of land by decree to those wishing to build assisted the urbanisation of a barely populated area, a new hospital provided for the relief of the sick, and three new churches demonstrated the prince's concern for religion. Though there might be separate reasons for each of these works – the example of the Sforza inspired the new hospital, the visit of the pope gave urgency to urbanisation of the south-eastern zone of the city – they are connected by Romani to personal events in the lives of the Gonzaga princes: one church was built in fulfilment of a vow by Francesco Gonzaga, another followed a dream experienced by Lodovico. This idea of the city as an extension of the palace has resonance elsewhere: the Sforza spoke about Milan as 'our city', and it has been argued that the notion of the city as ducal property, which emerged under the Visconti dukes, became stronger under their Sforza successors, leading to a very similar range of interventions: street-paving, building licences, church construction and a new hospital. Similarly, the Estensi of fifteenth-century Ferrara followed a step-by-step

---

[26] Baldesar Castiglione, *Il libro del cortigiano*, 82: duke Federico 'edificò un palazzo, secondo la opinione di molti, il più bello che in tutta Italia si ritrovi; e d'ogni oportuna cosa sì ben lo fornì, che non un palazzo, ma una città in forma di palazzo esser pareva'.

appropriation of the 'communal piazza', locating statues of themselves, in increasingly assertive poses, in key positions: Alberto d'Este as a pilgrim on the cathedral facade, Niccolò III (his son) as a mounted commander in the square, and duke Borso as a seated judge in front of the law-court.[27] Ercole d'Este has been presented as an impatient *impresario*, making and imposing his own eclectic choices in architecture and decoration.[28] One can thus see the force of Massimo Miglio's suggestion that urban buildings and spaces became a 'theatre of love and fear' in the fifteenth century, as princes sought to inspire both emotions in their subjects.[29] If the court was the arena for the display of princely power, then princely promotion of schemes such as hospitals, churches and paving projected that display to the whole city.

However, all is not straightforward in love and fear, as 'The difficulty of constructing piazzas' will show us. In his essay of that title, Patetta shows that, although *signorile* Milan had inherited no central piazza from its communal past, both attempts by the Sforza dukes to create piazzas in different parts of the city failed. New constructions – that of the cathedral commenced in 1386, that of the castle in the 1490s – created opportunities for new squares, but although the Sforza granted land for this purpose, and ordered expropriations and demolitions, nothing happened. For Patetta, a combination of existing buildings which could not be demolished, existing interests which could not be displaced or circumvented, and simple non-observance of ducal orders scuppered these plans. Other studies of fifteenth-century Milan have stressed this sort of ducal impotence, revealing the many difficulties and delays that beset all the Sforza building projects. Evelyn Welch's chief argument indeed is that the three major projects in that city – the new cathedral, the new hospital and the rebuilding of the castle – were the site of tensions between duke and urban community.[30] Fifteenth-century Ferrara and Mantua might at first glance show only strong contrast to Milan here: the Gonzaga increasingly intervened in the city, rebuilding churches, realigning streets, incorporating new land; and under Ercole d'Este Ferrara in the 1490s was 'transformed from a little medieval town to a large Renaissance city', by extending the city walls and creating a wide, new urban district, where the duke took deep personal interest in the layout of streets, the creation of a large, monumental piazza and the building of

---

[27] Folin, *Rinascimento estense*, 59–60; Rosenberg, *The Este Monuments*.
[28] Tuohy, *Herculean Ferrara*, 289, 305.
[29] Miglio, 'L'immagine del principe e l'immagine della città', 316.
[30] Welch, *Art and Authority*.

churches and palaces.[31] But even here, this new zone did not follow a rigid blueprint, for the evidence of negotiation with existing landowners and of court influence has been detected in decisions over the location of key elements of the design.[32]

The project also encountered some opposition: chroniclers express incomprehension at Ercole's fervour for architectural projects; existing land-holders resented the way that his plans cut through their properties;[33] the urban patriciate turned their backs on his new residential zone (as did their counterparts to a similar area in Mantua);[34] and an unknown opponent damaged the marble blocks of a planned free-standing column to be topped with a statue of the duke himself.[35] Similarly, an earlier Ferrarese project, to create, endow and construct a new central hospital (the Ospedale di Sant'Anna), promoted by marquis Leonello d'Este in the 1440s, experienced severe difficulties, of maladministration, disappearing resources and slippage of the assistance provided, from the poor and sick to the well-off.[36] Nevertheless, it has been argued that it was the participation of hundreds of workers in the production of cultural artefacts for the court of Ferrara that itself generated a form of consent in Este rule: the court had a massive demand for items of luxury and display, preferred to pursue stable, long-term relations with artists and suppliers, and directly controlled resources and manufacturing.[37]

My third paradigm, 'In the shadow of the prince' contradicts 'the city in the form of a palace' while providing some explanation for 'the difficulty of constructing piazzas'. 'In the shadow of the prince' focuses on the increasing political, social and cultural distance between the prince and the urban populace. In Milan in the first half of the fifteenth century, duke Filippo Maria Visconti abandoned the Visconti palace in the old political heart of the city, and took up residence in a castle at the city's edge: an 'eccentric location', Soldi Rondinini has called it, expressive of a changing concept of princely power.[38] The evolving residential patterns of the Visconti, and then Sforza, dukes of Milan can tell us something of that new concept. Francesco Sforza at first returned to the central Visconti palace, having promised that the castle that he wanted to rebuild would be a fortification, not a residence, i.e. would afford security

---

[31] Gundersheimer, *Ferrara*, 268–9; Rosenberg, *The Este Monuments*, 130–48; Tuohy, *Herculean Ferrara*, 121–41.
[32] Rosenberg, *The Este Monuments*, 137, 141.
[33] Bocchi, 'La "Terranuova" da campagna a città', 177–8.
[34] Lazzarini, *'Sub signo principis'*, 321.   [35] Folin, 'Ferrara: 1385–1505', 375.
[36] Franceschini, 'Il sapore del sale', 93–4, 98–9, 113.
[37] Guerzoni, 'The Italian Renaissance courts' demand for the arts', 66–73.
[38] Soldi Rondinini, 'Le strutture urbanistiche di Milano', 558.

to the city, not protection to the dynasty (thus alluding to the contemporary notion that the edge of the city was a 'tyrannical location' for a castle).[39] His successor, Galeazzo Maria Sforza, tended to avoid Milan, preferring to reside in castles in the territory; and Ludovico Sforza, towards the end of the fifteenth century, based his court at the town of Vigevano, some 30 km to the south-west of Milan.[40] This increasing distance between ruler and city can also be found at Mantua and Ferrara, though in rather different forms. At Mantua, according to one scholar, the division between what he calls 'the city of the prince' (the collection of buildings in the old city near the cathedral) and 'the city of the subjects' deepened under the Gonzaga: following the construction of the castle towards the end of the fourteenth century, much of the old city became the exclusive preserve of the Gonzaga, and the Gonzaga palace was isolated from the rest of the urban fabric, closed and impenetrable.[41] Similar developments are evident in fifteenth-century Ferrara: the Estensi favoured villas, parks and gardens in 'eccentric', edge-of-town locations; their new castle, built in the 1380s, was located at the northern edge of the old town (by which 'the ruling family separated and defended itself from the rest of the city'),[42] and was converted into use as a residence in the 1470s, when Ercole d'Este also carried out various works to separate his palace and the castle from other urban activities, moving a butchery, a market, stables and a bakery, adding gardens and a loggia, to create a dynastic residential island in the heart of the city.[43] However, though Borso d'Este 'travelled extensively' among his country residences, Ercole d'Este gave some of them away, while others were badly damaged in the war against Venice and were not repaired, and for most of his reign Ercole's focus as an architectural and artistic patron was on his city palaces, and only later he did pay more attention to his country seats.[44]

Mid-point summary

From consideration of these three historiographical strands we can abstract three principles of the relation between princes and their capital cities:

(1) incorporation into the court or palace;
(2) opposition of local interests; outcomes as compromises;
(3) domination from the margins.

---

[39] Tuohy, *Herculean Ferrara*, 121.
[40] Lubkin, 'Strutture, funzioni e funzionamento', 77; Welch, *Art and Authority*, 169–77, 192, 203.
[41] Carpeggiani, 'Traccia per una storia di Mantova', 24–6, 32.
[42] Cattini and Romani, 'Le corte parallele', 63.
[43] Folin, 'Ferrara: 1385–1505', 365; Tuohy, *Herculean Ferrara*, 60–120.
[44] Tuohy, *Herculean Ferrara*, 142–8.

The next question is whether these three principles apply to the other areas of city life, in its aspects of human population, religious cult and centre of economic, political and social power. As a starting point it is worth noting the varied response of recent Italian historians to this issue. For Marco Folin, the increasing space opening up between prince and subjects is visible in art, religion, ritual and propaganda, as well as architecture.[45] On the other hand, for Isabella Lazzarini, institutional change was 'more uncertain and nuanced' than princely architectural projects, more marked by compromise and flexibility.[46] So perhaps in these other areas of urban life we should look for different rhythms and emphases among these three elements, rather than any straightforward correspondence between architectural and urbanistic history and institutional, religious and economic history. Leaving aside religious and economic history, I shall devote the rest of this chapter to the institutional development of Mantua and Ferrara in the fifteenth century, focusing on the key element of office-holding, the court and the relations with subject towns.

Offices and officials

Incorporation into court and palace can be seen to have operated at two levels: the merging of roles at court with public offices, and the integration of local elites into a broader class of princely servants. Lazzarini has traced both processes with great precision for Gonzaga Mantua.[47] Around 1400 there were two clearly distinct types of office. The first consisted of public offices inherited from the thirteenth-century commune, their duties defined by statute, their terms of office limited, their holders selected by sortition and appointed formally by letters patent. These were the administrative and judicial officials of city and countryside. The second group consisted of roles in the Gonzaga court and household – servants, courtiers, soldiers – who were recruited and appointed informally, whose roles had no legal definition and who could serve the prince indefinitely. In broad terms, Mantuan families staffed the former, and non-local individuals and families the latter; but there was overlap of native and foreign in financial office and on the lord's council. Mantuan merchant families, for example, were involved with the Gonzaga on many levels: they supplied the court and family, they took financial office, they influenced economic policy. Nevertheless,

---

[45] Folin, *Rinascimento estense*, 165–7.   [46] Lazzarini, '*Sub signo principis*', 321.
[47] Lazzarini, 'Gli officiali del marchesato di Mantova'; Lazzarini, *Fra un principe*; Lazzarini, '*Palatium juris* e *palatium residentie*'.

Lazzarini speaks of 'two levels of involvement of citizens, two senses of belonging, two forms of relation with the holders of power'.[48] During the fifteenth century, the significant evolution in civic offices in city and roles at court was the gradual merging of the two categories, with roles starting to be formally appointed and officials increasingly thinking of themselves as servants of the dynasty, rather than of the urban community. Despite this convergence, Lazzarini insists on the fact that officeholders were far from forming a single, unified body: they continued to differ greatly in geographical origin, social status, property-holding and periods of service.

The importance of these findings for the notion of the 'Renaissance state' needs to be underlined, for officials and officialdom were always essential parts of that construct. Chabod presented officials as expressing a new conception of public life and 'the state of mind of the modern bureaucracy', that is, an impersonal view of office, as something created and defined by law and constitution, in opposition to the nobility's chivalric and personal view of office as a reward from the prince and as a commitment of honour.[49] In place of Chabod's binary opposition, Lazzarini creates a mosaic; in place of his clash of ideologies and the foundation of modern bureaucracy, she sees the gradual victory of personal service to the dynasty.

Similar dismantling of the terms 'office' and 'office-holders' has been performed for Estense Ferrara by Folin, though from a much poorer documentary base (a reminder that principalities, though they might look similar, practised different modes of recording their presence and their activities).[50] He too argues that 'the institutional apparatus, at any one time, seemed composed of discordant strata, each with their own cultural traditions': offices of communal origin, filled by local families, and positions at court, filled at the prince's pleasure.[51] As in Mantua, a range of civic offices was regulated by statute, formally appointed for short terms and paid from civic revenues. The most prominent example is the office of *podestà* or chief judge, held by foreign lawyers. The number of positions in the Este palace administration was much greater: about one hundred and fifty held posts in the finance and estate office, the chancery and the councils. These offices and positions were filled by the same heterogeneous groups: foreigners from outside the Estense state were present as judges, lawyers and courtiers; nobles, merchants and men of more modest backgrounds from the cities of Modena and Reggio held office in or near their cities; but the bulk of offices were held

---

[48] Lazzarini, *Fra un principe*, 154.   [49] Chabod, 'Lo stato di Milano', 169–82.
[50] Lazzarini, 'La nomination des officiers'.   [51] Folin, 'Note sugli officiali', 100–1.

by Ferrarese citizens and noblemen.[52] Few of these office-holders were university-educated: only a quarter of officials were graduates, mainly in law, while most of the nobles and urban patricians were educated in private schools.[53] It follows from the social composition of these groups that 'bureaucracy' is not an applicable term, indeed Folin sees 'corruption', clientage and influence as the main motivations for office-seeking and office-holding. Like Blockmans in his analysis of the Burgundian state,[54] Folin sees the distance that had opened between prince and subjects as creating a need for intermediaries, brokers and favourites, based in the court or the chancery who could link princely power to the wider civic world. Citizens sought office for the income and influence that it brought, and Folin concludes that 'office was a client structure for elites to exchange goods, information and favours'. This is an important, and debateable, conclusion. It expresses an attitude to the state that Chittolini was attempting to counter already in the 1980s: the view that the basic 'institutions' of Renaissance society were not the apparatus of the state, but the informal practices of faction and clientage, kinship and corruption; and that, where they met, it was to the advantage of the latter.[55]

Court and municipality

The model of 'the city in the form of a palace' has also been invoked to denote the changing relation between princely court and municipal government in Ferrara.[56] From the later fourteenth century, it is claimed, the Este lords of Ferrara had adopted a form of government based on close collaboration and connection between, on the one hand, their council and chancery and, on the other, the city government, formed of twelve *Savi* (literally, wisemen) and their president, the *Giudice de' Savi*. Legitimation thus came through urban institutions. A channel of collaboration was the fact that the *Giudice de' Savi* was a member of the lord's council; a symbol of the connection was the fact that rights of appointment at the new Ospedale di Sant'Anna were vested in the city government. However, the trends after mid-century were towards absorption and displacement, not connection and collaboration. The old communal finance office lost its autonomy; the court of the chief judge (the *podestà*, of communal origin) was weakened, as the

---

[52] Folin, *Rinascimento estense*, 190–200.   [53] Folin, 'Studio e politica', 64–84.
[54] Blockmans, 'Patronage, brokerage and corruption', 123–5.
[55] Chittolini, 'Stati padani, "stato del rinascimento"', 21–2.
[56] Turchi, 'Istituzioni cittadine', 150–2, and, for what follows, 132–51.

Giudice was allowed to appoint to some minor judicial posts; though the civic statutes were revised in the later 1450s, procedures for publishing new enactments lost their communal element of public origin. Under duke Ercole (1471–1505), these trends intensified. The ducal administration absorbed the communal finance office. New legal enactments were increasingly made by ducal edict. The work of the *podestà* was now overshadowed by that of a ducal appointment, the captain of justice. A final change, of great symbolic significance, was the transfer of the meeting place of the communal *Savi* from the cloisters of the church of San Romano to the ducal palace itself. By this stage, lordship 'no longer operated in civic form, but the city was identified with the princely court'.

This could not happen at Reggio and Modena, where relations between city councils and the representatives of Este power (the three-man *reggimento* of *podestà*, military captain and fiscal *massaro*) have been described as 'chronically conflictual'.[57] Here the daily conduct of business between ducal and civil authorities kept alive a 'plurality of political mechanisms'. Indeed, the image has been created of lord and cities speaking different political languages, the one informed by courtly chronicles, manuals for Christian princes (*specula principum*) and allegorical tapestries, the other by statutes, negotiated agreements and *capitoli*.[58] The status of the lord's decisions related to the city, the methods of appointing the city council (the *Anziani*) and its officials, judicial relations with rural peasantry through the operation of the court for criminal damage, the activity of the *reggimento* as judges-delegate: all acted as points of tension at various times in the middle of the fifteenth century. Though Niccolò III had assured the city government that his orders from Ferrara would be registered in the communal chancery, the *reggimento* created its own chancery for this purpose, creating a rival or parallel method of ratification. Though Niccolò III took control of the appointment of the city council of *Anziani* in 1435, because of unspecified 'rumours and suspicions', he restored the traditional method, by sortition, in 1439; but he moved the procedure from the hall of the communal palace to the chancery of the *reggimento*, and imposed an oath of secrecy on incoming *Anziani*. When the same Niccolò took up complaints from the Reggian countryside and ordered changes to the procedures for hearing and punishing accusations of criminal damage, the *Anziani* modified his proposal to the city's advantage. Under Borso, who was created duke of Reggio and Modena by the emperor in 1452,

---

[57] Turchi, 'Riflessioni su statuti e politica', 371, and generally for what follows.
[58] Turchi, 'Una piccola modifica', 351.

the balance shifted; not only were the city's requests for reintegration of its *contado* brushed aside, as before, but Borso also began to enfeoff castles there to his courtiers, and sent a commissioner to the city who transferred some judicial and fiscal functions from the municipality to the ducal governors.[59]

At both Ferrara and Mantua, such displacements were accompanied by expansion of the size and functions of the princely court. In a suggestive comparative study, Cattini and Romani sketched three phases in the evolution of princely courts in the Po valley.[60] The first phase was the domestic or family court of the thirteenth and early fourteenth centuries, in which the dominant presence was that of the lord's extended family and the economic basis was that of dynastic resources in lands, properties, financial investments and military contracts. This phase was succeeded in the late fourteenth century by the lordly court, marked by a growing distance between lord and subjects, as lords acquired new titles, built urban castles and expanded the territories under their control. At the same time, the court became a public space, a site of social mobility and a place for the literary and artistic representation of the lord. Finally, from the later fifteenth century, the court became a space of bureaucracy and ritual, as the administration was professionalised and the ritual representation of power increased. Although the lines between these phases are not as firm as the authors would like to suggest, this sketch does represent a plausible evolution from private household, sustained by private resources, to public court, maintained with public resources.

However, local interests expressed opposition to the authority of duke and court. A focus on opposition and compromise has formed an essential part of the revision in the later twentieth century of the Chabodian definition of the 'Renaissance state'.[61] An extraordinary exercise in opinion-seeking in Mantua in 1430 uncovered popular unease at the perceived decay and weakness of the city in its physical, economic and institutional aspects. Asked to suggest policies that would be profitable to the Gonzaga and useful to the common good, a variety of merchants, lawyers and officials responded by arguing for changes to fiscal, commercial and official policies. To stimulate trade and attract foreign merchants, they suggested improvements to the commercial infrastructure and measures to increase the quantity and affordability of foodstuffs on the city's markets. To increase the population, one advised instituting a fund from general taxation to subsidise immigration: 'because of its

---

[59] *Ibid.*, 353–4, 364–5, 371.   [60] Cattini and Romani, 'Le corti parallele', 48–51.
[61] Mozzarelli, 'Corte e amministrazione', 248–9.

little traffic, the city is large but has no rich citizens, as other cities have'.[62] To facilitate the repair and building of houses, several participants recommended reducing the tax on building materials. To remove the discontent of native Mantuans at the numbers of foreigners holding office, terms of office should be limited, circulation enforced and restrictions imposed on foreigners. To improve the administration of justice, the office of *podestà* (currently replaced by a cheaper substitute) should be restored and the judicial activity of sundry lesser officials curbed. These opinions give the impression of a city lacking in population, in a wealthy elite and in well-stocked markets, with a horde of resented foreigners taking all the best offices. In addition to the content of the suggested measures, the mode of argument of the participants is also revealing: a number make unfavourable comparisons between Mantua and other neighbouring cities; and others express a strong desire for the return to a previous state of affairs, when Mantuan cloth had a good reputation, when the laws disciplining trade and manufactures were observed, when offices were distributed to citizens. As Mozzarelli put it, they evince 'nostalgia for a disintegrating old order'.[63]

The rapid enrichment of individuals by princely favour drew even more resentment, as seen by the comments of chroniclers in both Mantua and Ferrara.[64] Moreover, Ferrarese chroniclers showed a clear lack of interest in the territorial state, mentioning Modena or Reggio only in connection with dynastic events, expressing resistance to princely and courtly innovations including the sale of office, new ceremonies, prestige projects, favourites.[65] And this resistance can be taken as expressive of the political system as a whole, which, for Folin, was 'enduringly urban, oriented to maintaining the privileges of civic authorities'.[66] Paradoxically, the Este lordship seems to have had the effect of promoting such civic privilege in its subject cities. At Reggio, a clear division separates that city under Este rule from its history in the fourteenth century, when it was dominated by rural noble families and their factions, which stifled civic identity, as expressed for example in the festival of the patron saint, San Prospero.[67] With the decisive action of Niccolò III d'Este against some of the rural nobles, the urban elite was strengthened and greater civic consciousness emerged, such that the city could mount stouter defence of its statute laws and of appointments to its offices and councils.[68]

---

[62] *Mantova 1430*, 97.   [63] Mozzarelli, 'Lo stato gonzaghesco', 375.
[64] Folin, *Rinascimento estense*, 13.   [65] Ibid., 9–30; Dean, 'Ferrarese chroniclers', 182.
[66] Folin, *Rinascimento estense*, xxi–xxii.   [67] Gamberini, *Oltre le città*, 95–6.
[68] Ibid., 97–101.

The contractual state

The contractual nature of the state is made evident in the number and range of *capitula* and *conventiones* submitted by, negotiated with and registered for noble families, villages and small towns. With noblemen in the Modenese and Reggian territories, Niccolò III d'Este made accords in which they promised obedience and access to their military resources, while he promised exemptions, protections and pensions. The context varied according to the bargaining position of individuals and families – to nobles who 'returned to obedience', the marquis granted favours; with nobles who retained some independence of property and position, the marquis negotiated bilateral contracts. Both types of arrangement – of 'obedience' or 'adherence' – were couched in terms of the marquis's 'friends and enemies' and his 'honour and state', and rarely mentioned the cities.[69] To small towns and villages that had newly submitted to Este rule, Niccolò III routinely offered tax exemptions and reliefs, along with a range of other emancipations (from vassalage to local lords, from the bishop's rent-collectors) and made assurances that they would not be returned to *signorile* possession.[70] When the town of Rubiera was acquired in 1423, the marquis approved its petitions 'not to be constrained to give obedience to any other city', to have only citizens of Ferrara as its appointed officials, and to have assurances regarding local mills, markets and waterways.[71] Such contracts with noblemen and villages damaged the interests of cities: it was their tax revenues, the jurisdiction of their courts, the power of their markets, and the monopoly of their notaries to authenticate legal transactions that were undermined. No wonder that the city of Modena repeatedly petitioned the marquis for the reintegration into its domain of territories that he had acquired. Amid a set of sixteen *capitula* which Modena submitted to the marquis in 1425 were three requesting that castles acquired by Niccolò III in Modenese territory be returned to its control: 'because it is unsightly and damaging to the city to keep its *contado* separated from it, which has happened to this miserable city, because no castle in the world obeys it, by which it is desolate and grows weak, not being able to support itself. And because in the case of well-governed cities, as are Bologna and Ferrara, the whole *contado* obeys them.'[72] Niccolò III consistently refused, advancing his opinion that now was not the time

---

[69] Archivio di Stato, Modena, Archivio Segreto Estense, Cancelleria, Leggi e Decreti, B III, cc. 227, 232–3, 264–5, 282–3; Dean, *Land and Power*, 166–78.
[70] Leggi e Decreti, B II, cc. 144–6, 328, 332–7; B III, cc. 217–19, 230, 321–5.
[71] Ibid., B IV, cc. 87v–88.   [72] Ibid., B IV, c. 129v.

Ferrara and Mantua

for change, or that the places concerned were 'ready to perform his commands'. The lord's attitude to such petitions is summed up in his response to the request that the citizens of Modena should not be dragged to Ferrara by litigants, but that their cases should be heard in Modena: 'the lord replies that it does not seem to him that this should be granted as he does not intend to deprive himself of his *arbitrium*'.[73]

Conclusion

The language of such responses – couched in terms of *dominium*, command and princely preferences – takes us straight back to a model of the state that privileged the prince's decision-making power. That, however, should not be the final note, because, as this chapter has attempted to show, elements of formal state power were mixed with negotiation and compromise, with informal powers and practices. Whether that mix had anything particular or distinctive about it, deserving a label of its own, must remain open to challenge.

---

[73] *Ibid.*, B IV, c. 130v.

7 Venice and the Terraferma

Michael Knapton

Introduction: from 1300 to 1530

In 1300 Venice was one of the largest cities in Europe, its population about 120,000 – or 160,000 if we include the lagoon settlements of the *dogado*, the only Italian territory it then controlled. In 1530 population figures were similar, after recovery from plague mortality.[1] In both 1300 and 1530 Venice possessed vast wealth connected mostly with trade: its port and shipping, its merchants and market were key intermediaries especially in long-distance dealings linking Europe to the Mediterranean, the centre of world commerce in the late Middle Ages. In political terms, however, much altered over those 230 years. Venice had developed communal government from about the middle of the twelfth century, curtailing the doge's authority, superseding his curia with more numerous conciliar bodies and collegiate magistracies. From 1300 to 1530 its regime remained republican, but there were major changes relating to the broader context (Italian, Mediterranean and European), to the territory it controlled and to important features of the state, government and politics.

In the fourteenth century, rivalry with Genoa in Levantine maritime trade caused alternate tension and open warfare, and so too the development of state-owned and -organised galley convoys as part of tighter regulation and security in sea trade beyond the Adriatic. Foreign policy also sought to consolidate or recover control over northern Adriatic coastal territory via relations with local communities and with hinterland princes. Possessing ports there supported Venice's hegemony in Adriatic trade and the logistics of all its merchant shipping, and the same strategy, mingling commercial and military features, was also served by more distant coastal and island colonies in this fragmented overseas dominion (*stato da mar*), especially Crete and other, lesser Aegean holdings, taken

---

[1] For this section, see *Storia di Venezia*, III–V; Cozzi, Knapton and Scarabello, *La Repubblica*, I; Lane, *Venice*; Finlay, *Venice Besieged*.

in the early thirteenth century from the Byzantine empire. Then in the 1380s–90s fears due to Ottoman Turkish advance helped Venice occupy other Greek and Albanian territory, especially Corfù, and assert full control over Negroponte.

During the fourteenth century, lordly regimes replaced communal governments in north-east Italy, and the city-states were gradually absorbed into larger, albeit unstable political units amidst territorial rivalry especially between Verona's Scala lords, Padua's Carraresi, Milan's Visconti, the Habsburgs and the kings of Hungary. Venice's policy there was mostly limited to vigilance and diplomacy, although it fought an unsuccessful war (1308–13) to occupy Ferrara, situated on the Po and a potential rival for trade links between the Adriatic and inland areas, and in 1338 it annexed Treviso, strategically sited for mainland communications, though losing it briefly (1381–8).

In previous centuries Venice's relations with a multiplicity of governments had promoted trade flows and routes linking the city to both the hinterland and inland destinations further afield. But the post-1300 trend towards fewer, larger territorial blocks enabled lordly rulers to divert or damage trade, and even threaten Venice's very survival. This risk was dramatically apparent in the 1378–81 war of Chioggia when Venice nearly succumbed to an alliance between land-based enemies, mainly the Carraresi and the king of Hungary, and Genoa (this was the last major conflict with Genoa, whose priority trading interests then shifted to the western Mediterranean).

In the political melée after the death of Gian Galeazzo Visconti (1402), Venice broadened the buffer area under its control and thwarted potential aggressors, occupying Padua, Vicenza and Verona (1404–6). By 1420 it had extended this Terraferma dominion northwards and eastwards – to Rovereto, in the southern Trentino; to Belluno and Feltre; to almost all Friuli – and also occupied most of the Dalmatian coast, where it had lost long-standing holdings to the king of Hungary in 1358. Turkish pressure in the south-east Balkans facilitated scattered territorial gains east of Dalmatia, some ephemeral, but from the 1420s Venice was primarily committed to expanding its Italian dominion, especially by annexing territory previously subject to the Visconti – Brescia and Bergamo (1426–28), Crema (1449) – and Ravenna (1441), strategic gateway to the Romagna region.

Though extensive and rapid, mainland expansion was no abandonment of Venice's maritime, Mediterranean interests, and evolved as an empirical process of progressive involvement, not from a pre-ordained plan. However, as shown by the sharply diverging views in the early 1420s of doge Tommaso Mocenigo (1414–23) and his successor

Francesco Foscari (1423–57), it did develop governmental awareness of the rationale and potentiality of territorial acquisition in Italy in this final phase of regional state formation. Creation of the Terraferma dominion also settled the political geography of most of north-east Italy, severely limiting both the influence earlier exercised by transalpine dynasties (Austria and Hungary) and Milan's eastwards ambitions.

Shock at Turkish conquest of Constantinople (1453) inspired calls to crusade, but European rulers' indifference matched the ambiguity of the *Realpolitik* for which Venice was often criticised, in reconciling defence of Christendom against the infidel with Levant trade with Muslim states. The same shock combined with military stalemate between the Italian powers to usher in the uneasy peace of Lodi and the Lega Italica (1454–5), with Venice now the strongest among them, and consequently feared – a reputation it then justified by partial success in the War of Ferrara (1482–4), when it annexed Rovigo.

The sea empire's vulnerability to land attack grew with Ottoman advance from mid-century in the Balkan hinterland, resulting in losses of coastal territory during the two Turkish wars of 1463–79 (especially Negroponte, and Scutari in Albania), and 1498–1503 (Modon, Coron, Lepanto in Greece). There was, however, consolidation of island holdings: annexation of Zante (1482) and Cephalonia (1500) in the Ionian, and first control (1473), then formal annexation (1489), of Cyprus. Heavily dependent on its navy for defending maritime colonies, and inclined to see the Turkish naval threat more in terms of piracy, Venice learned from failures to halt Ottoman fleets, in losing Negroponte (1470) and especially at the drawn battle of Zonchio (1499), that it could no longer count on naval superiority – despite major expansion of the Arsenal from 1473, and the ability to mobilise huge forces (sixty-five galleys and about sixty other vessels at Zonchio, with 20,000–25,000 men). The balance of sea power swung further against Venice after the Turks' absorption of the Mameluke sultanate of Egypt (1517), which gave them continuous control over the Mediterranean coastline from Albania round to north-west Africa.

During the Turkish war of 1498–1503 Venice was greatly stretched by simultaneous military commitment in Italy, one of the many rounds of the Italian Wars (1494–1530). It initially gained territory in this contest for predominance in the peninsula, with its frequently changing alliances, but was then defeated at Agnadello (May 1509) by the League of Cambrai, a coalition including all the main European states and its Italian rivals, so losing almost all the Terraferma to French and imperial forces. Only in 1516 did it recover full control over the mainland, though suffering marginal permanent losses, especially the Trentino and

Romagna holdings. After the concluding peace of Bologna (1529–30) Venice was the only major Italian state to escape direct control by or strong dependence on the Habsburg victors, but lost much European and Mediterranean political standing, especially in relation to the Habsburg and Ottoman superpowers. In the early sixteenth century, moreover, its economic future was dramatically threatened by Portuguese development of the sea route to Asia and direct shipping of the spices whose transit via the Mediterranean had made Venice's commercial fortune – though later events showed that in the sixteenth century the Atlantic seaboard paralleled rather than displaced the Mediterranean in patterns of world trade.

Taken together, defeat in war and difficulty in recovering from it, the fragility of control over the dominions (quite unexpected in the Terraferma), the prospect of major economic downgrading, and shortcomings in governmental capacity especially to handle diplomacy and war all contributed to a deep sense of general crisis affecting the Venetian state in the early sixteenth century, which triggered important changes in the working of the state and politics.

The city-state: myth and reality

What historians call the 'myth of Venice' is a long-running tradition of praise of the city, mingling Venetians' own civic pride and foreigners' admiration; it developed further in the decades before and especially after 1509, when it was part of reactions to crisis.[2] Describing Venice in 1493, the patrician Marin Sanudo emphasised political and social features of an idealised polity: welcoming and harmonious, proudly independent since birth, well governed; superior to pagan, classical Rome (a comparison suggested by humanist culture) owing to its founders' greater dignity and Christian faith, to divine favour associated especially with its patron, the evangelist St Mark, and to its centuries-long duration.

In Renaissance Venice such messages were assiduously communicated in words – from preambles of laws to speeches in the councils; from chronicles to treatises, to visitors' guides – but also and especially in non-verbal form. This meant recurrent public ritual mixing civil and religious elements, rich in symbolism and material splendour – thus the yearly renewal of the city's 'marriage of the sea' on Ascension day, as well as occasional rites, e.g. for the enthroning and funerals of doges and, by the fifteenth century, for the *dogaressa*'s entry to the ducal palace. The myth

---

[2] For this section, see Raines, *L'invention du mythe*; Casini, *I gesti del principe*.

involved many of the performing and visual arts, themselves often part of ritual: music, theatre, painting, sculpture, architecture and the overall aspect of the city. Much of this focused on the St Mark's area, Venice's civic and religious heart, whose government buildings and ducal chapel were perennially embellished (and where the *renovatio urbis* fostered by doge Andrea Gritti in the 1520s–30s as part of the reaction to Agnadello introduced new classical architecture and ideological messages). Similar beliefs also emanated from individual patrician families especially via their palaces, libraries and funerary monuments.

The myth is a cultural phenomenon which can distort or sublimate features of Venetian public life that were really more banal or less flattering, and blur change over time into timeless immobility. The dialectic myth–reality is a component of Venetian government and politics, and it is sterile merely to contrast the two, while the myth's claims about Venice's singularity have often hindered adequate comparison linking its experience to a broader Italian and European context.

The city-state: institutions and patrician politics

In late thirteenth-century Venice there was considerable diversity among the governing aristocracy (here generally described as patriciate), but significantly less than in many Italian city-states, where mercantile wealth mixed with land-based patrimonies and urban political culture with conceptions and practices of power linked to the surrounding *contado* and lordly authority exercised there. If Venice remained republican after 1300, this was essentially to do with how the relationship between aristocracy and government evolved, promoting the right to participate in public life to primacy among the criteria of aristocratic status and identity.[3]

Reforms of the Maggior Consiglio – begun in 1297, largely in place by 1323 and misleadingly later called the *serrata* (closure) – transformed it into an assembly to which all adult male members of the aristocracy had right of access for life, with the prerogative to elect and be elected to magistracies and other councils of state, and also with hereditary transmission of that status to their legitimate male heirs. This was the formal confirmation of a *de facto* definition of the ruling group already largely evident in office-holding and council membership over the previous half-century, and indeed tended partly to broaden it. It reassured the families involved of their role in public life, as did – for most bodies other than

---

[3] For this section, see *Storia di Venezia*, III–IV; Chojnacki, *Women and Men*; Romano, *The Likeness of Venice*.

the Maggior Consiglio – practices favourable to power-sharing and access to office, such as the collegiate responsibility of a plurality of office-holders, short tenure and restrictions on individuals' immediate re-election to any given body or on the excessive concentration in it of single families' members. If the *serrata* had any intent to exclude, this concerned foreigners, whose previous access to fully fledged Venetians' rights caused diffidence at a time of international trading difficulties. But it cannot be considered a manoeuvre serving the sort of faction rivalry, linkable to Guelf and Ghibelline labels, which so undermined communal institutions elsewhere. In the decades before and after 1297 rivalry at least partly resembling this did appear in Venice and was repressed, and the *serrata* may best be seen as a radical ploy to pre-empt it.

Definition of the patriciate was further reinforced by laws of the early fifteenth century, modifying and tightening access procedures to the Maggior Consiglio, and of the late fifteenth and early sixteenth centuries, especially to enforce the registration of patricians' births and marriages. These latter norms both reasserted the patriciate's traditional values and emphasised governmental concern with key aspects of its private life (the laws of a century earlier had already addressed marriage), further strengthening endogamy as well as the patriciate's established patrilinear orientation. Apart from the co-optation of thirty new families to reward patriotism after the 1378–81 war, and very occasional conferment of honorary patrician status, the patriciate remained closed until 1646.

The decades immediately after 1297 were also essential for the evolution of the main institutions of government and their respective functions. From partially discontinuous membership of about 400 per year and a major role in law-making, the Maggior Consiglio became the plenary assembly of the patriciate (about 1,100 members in around 1320), its members perennially and primarily engaged in voting and standing for election to other councils and offices; it retained little other ordinary government activity, though remaining the ultimate seat of sovereignty, debate and justice. In the course of a few decades, following on from earlier practice by the Maggior Consiglio in empowering it to debate and shape policy, the Senate was upgraded to the main legislative body, and its numbers rose progressively from the initial 60 to around 300 in the later fifteenth century. The Forty (*Quarantia*), which before the *serrata* had paralleled the Senate in receiving delegated powers albeit over different issues, quickly lost most such activity to the Senate, of which its members also became a component. Temporary councils were occasionally created for exceptional needs like the conduct of the 1378–81 war, but this practice died out in the following decades, confirming the Senate's central role in policy-making. A new, fundamental, permanent addition to state institutions was the Council of Ten: created in 1310 after a conspiracy and rapidly made permanent, it wielded very extensive power – legislative, judicial, policing – over all matters concerning the security of the state.

After the *serrata*, the main co-ordinating executive body initially remained the *signoria*, comprising the doge, six ducal councillors and three Heads of the Forty. The Senate's emergence as main policy-making body was accompanied by its designation of panels of *Savi* with steering and executive functions. By the early fifteenth century three such panels had become permanent: six authoritative *Savi Grandi*, five *Savi ai Ordini* and five *Savi di Terraferma*, responsible respectively for government in general, matters maritime, and the mainland. Meeting together, as became frequent practice, the Signoria and these *Savi* formed the Collegio, which became the main executive body.

After 1297 additions continued to the already numerous magistracies handling more specific matters; much growth in Senate numbers was due to *ex officio* membership given to holders of the more important posts, and there was a roughly 50 per cent overall increase in patrician offices in Venice itself from about 1400 to 1493. More numerous magistracies partly reflected – certainly from the late fourteenth century – patrician expectations of reward for serving the state (significant pay characterised these offices much more than prestigious posts such as ducal councillor), but increasing government activity did also reflect ongoing assertion of public interest, sometimes independently of significant new institutions. An example of this is policy concerning the lagoon, urban development and the general relationship between human settlement and the environment in and around Venice. Once out of post-Black Death stagnation of urban development, and before more systematic sixteenth-century policy choices and new, permanent magistracies (starting with the *Savi alle acque* in 1501), government authority in often temporary form spasmodically but progressively increased the quality and quantity of attention to urban form and structures and lagoon management, asserting stronger control over private initiative.

Some stimulus to evolving government activity also came from its extension to new territory and subjects in the regional state. Though involvement by institutions in the capital in mainland government developed more intensely after 1530, an overall increase in such activity was evident earlier for larger bodies: in 1440 the registration of ordinary Senate deliberations separated into series eloquently entitled *Terra* and *Mar*, and there was gradual, empirical accumulation of Terraferma competence by the Council of Ten, while judicial appeals from the dominions influenced the cloning of the Forty into two and then three courts (1441, 1493). Some magistracies already competent for Venice also developed significant mainland business, especially the state attorneys (*avogadori di comun*), guarantors of respect for legality in public life, and there were rare new bodies with solely mainland duties like the *Provveditori sopra le camere di terraferma*, set over provincial exchequers in 1449.

Much actual working of government depended on long-term, non-patrician officials, subordinate to patrician office-holders but essential for their continuity of service and often expertise, particularly in the ducal chancery. An increasing proportion of such posts went to Venetian *cittadini*, a small elite subordinate to the patriciate defined by birth, residence and tax-paying, and similar to the patriciate in developing cohesion – albeit less strongly – through a mix of formal rules and informal group identity. Prominent in these rules was the nexus with government service, with the ducal chancery (1478) and then other important posts (1517) reserved to the sub-category of native Venetian citizens, their status subjected to formal checking (1487).

The whole apparatus of government was very complex – more admired than understood by outside observers – and not necessarily efficient, since more numerous magistracies more often meant duplication or overlap in single sectors than clear assignment of competence favouring specialisation and hierarchy of functions. If present, rationality was mostly empirical – e.g. the Forty, originally a policy-shaping legislative body, became the highest ordinary law-court and lost most of their extra-judicial mandate. Many offices mingled sectorial executive or administrative competence with some judicial power in enforcing their authority, as well as autonomous money-handling. However, the system succeeded reasonably in marrying the principles and practices of a republican system, in terms of power-sharing and turnover in office, with continuity, stability and firm government. As well as in effective vigilance by the Ten, these traits emerge in features such as Senate members' re-eligibility for continuous terms, the *de facto* concentration of key posts such as ducal councillor in the hands of a minority, and also the permanence provided by the doge. His authority was everywhere beset by limitations, but his term of office was quite exceptionally for life rather than for a few months, and his very election required broad consensus around a seasoned politician.

Despite the richness of Marin Sanudo's diaries,[4] Venice's historiography suffers from a deficit of information with which to flesh out terse

---

[4] Excerpts in English in Labalme, Sanguineti and Carroll, *Città excelentissima*.

government records, and analyse many issues underlying the functioning and malfunctioning of the state. Not surprisingly, much historical attention has focused on a few major phases of difficulty, either crisis periods of warfare with tension fuelled by military near-failure and concomitant heavy tax demands – thus the 1378–81 war, and the aftermath of defeat in 1509 – or traumatic moments especially concerning doges: a failed plot against doge Pietro Gradenigo (1310); an abortive conspiracy involving doge Marino Falier, resulting in his trial and execution (1355); the deposition of doge Francesco Foscari (1457). But such episodes pose broader questions: the implications of rivalry between leading families (Gradenigo and Dandolo vs Tiepolo in 1310, and Foscari vs Loredan in the fifteenth century), and the role played by the Ten – created after 1310, decisive in 1355 and 1457 – in relation to general issues of power-sharing within government and the patriciate.

Further key issues concern differences among the patriciate, especially between but also partly within the extended family groups bearing the same surname, often described by historians as clans: differences of antiquity and prestige, of amount and type of wealth, of interest and involvement in public life, of numbers (obviously important in voting). The political implications of such differences could extend from one family or clan to another via alliances generated or cemented especially by marriage, but also through patron–client relations. Diversity along these lines was present before the *serrata*, and while a single clan's destiny could alter over time, there was a gradual increase in its overall incidence. Patricians further from real power could show resentment openly: thus, especially at the end of our period, poorer patricians but also younger men impatient with gerontocratically gradual access to high office, at a time of greater competition for elections and more blatant breaking of the moralistic rules against electioneering. But already in the fourteenth century patterns of participation in public life and access to office show concentric circles in the patriciate, with about a quarter of all clans dominating elections to key posts. Nonetheless, despite the stratification of access to power, with major offices monopolised by patricians described at the end of our period as the *primi* (first), the top layer was far from compact, and its individual components competed hard for electoral support.

Moreover, while political rivalry – between individuals, clans, broader groups – could marry clashing ambitions with differing opinions on single policy issues, there was nothing resembling more permanently structured and broadly based factions or proto-parties. Shifting majorities on key policy choices might represent a gradual groundswell of changing views, as over the extension of Terraferma conquests west of

Verona in the 1420s, or rapidly altered perception of contingent circumstances, as in abandoning initial caution to take Papal Romagna lands on the collapse of the Borgia papacy in 1503. Even in the Ten's decision to depose doge Foscari, pragmatic evaluation of his failing ability to do his job perhaps weighed more than Loredan vindictiveness.

The 1509 crisis altered power-sharing significantly. In many post-Agnadello elections candidates were encouraged to pledge money to government as proof of patriotism (an emergency revenue measure), and application of this practice to a Senate facing vital foreign policy issues strengthened many senior patricians' diffidence towards a body which could seem overpopulous and short on wisdom and secrecy. The Ten had already extended their competence in piecemeal fashion, especially from the middle of the fifteenth century (e.g. taking over monetary policy from 1472), and from 1509 a smallish elite was able to circulate continuously at the heart of power between the Collegio, the Ten and its Zonta. It transformed the Zonta, exempt from restrictions on eligibility, from one or more small, temporary co-opted panels created for specific issues, towards permanence and general competence, and short-circuited the Senate on a growing range of sensitive matters. The Senate–Ten dialectic, representing the tension between opposing political priorities of broader-based decision-making and authoritative government, remained a key issue after 1530.

As far as 1300–1530 is concerned, though, there were important, interlinking factors of cohesion in the patriciate, which tied with an overall robust commitment to the working of the state: a fairly strong sense of group identity, reinforced in the post-*serrata* period; widespread interest in public life, albeit significantly threaded with material motivation, and thus endemic risks of corruption in seeking and holding office; substantial acceptance of what became increasingly differentiated career paths, in terms of prestige and income; consequent conformity with the self-effacing political behaviour required for electoral consensus (what the myth presented as patriotic altruism and modesty); common experience of political apprenticeship through office-holding which did foster expertise and sense of the state – even though crises such as Agnadello proved Venetian politicians to be as fallible as any others, and showed up weaknesses in policy-making specific to a republican rather than a princely regime.

The regional state: similarities and differences

Within the *dogado*, Venice – the islands round Rialto – had become the main settlement during the ninth century but, although the *dogado* retained important traits of common identity with Venice, the subordination and separateness of the other localities such as Murano and Chioggia gradually emerged, especially during the post-*serrata* period.[5] These communities were under the jurisdiction of Venetian patrician governors, but much local government depended on their own councils and norms. A similar mix of subjection and autonomy characterised Venice's relations with its coastal and island colonies in Istria and Dalmatia; treaties asserting its higher authority over them dated from the tenth century, though Venetian dominion long remained partly precarious.[6]

Beyond the Adriatic, colonies of Venetians lived under other rulers, often with considerable autonomy and headed by a patrician official (thus especially the Venetians of Constantinople with their *bailo*, under Byzantine and then Ottoman rule), and there were small Greek territories held by patrician feudatories in their own right, over which Venice exercised a sort of protectorate. In the Greek territories it controlled directly, Venice's authority related to societies, institutions and norms generally mingling Frankish crusader and Byzantine elements; power was shared between Venetian patrician governors and combinations of urban institutions and feudatories, with ample recourse to local law. Peculiar to Crete was the further, capillary presence of a feudal aristocracy of Venetians, settled there since the thirteenth century and partly Hellenised but preserving rights of access to the Maggior Consiglio in Venice itself.

The timing of Venice's acquisition of maritime and mainland territories overlapped, and there are other analogies between the two dominions: economic motivations for annexation, to guarantee security and support to trade flows serving Venice; the empirical approach to acquiring much territory, assessing and exploiting opportunities as they occurred; the often major element of voluntary subjection, rather than mere imposition of annexation; procedures solemnising their passage under Venice. Particularly important were the flexibility of power-sharing between Venice and its subjects and the major degree of delegation to the latter, but also the clear separation between their respective spheres of influence, rigid in almost totally excluding provincial political elites from mainline government activity in the state as a whole – a fundamental, lasting characteristic of its experience of dominion. This choice expressed the patriciate's conviction that its corporate identity and monopoly of mainstream power preserved the nature of the state

---

[5] Orlando, *Altre Venezie*.
[6] On the sea empire, see Ivetic, *L'Istria Moderna*, and Arbel's chapter in *Storia di Venezia*, V.

and quality of government, rationalising its application of a city-state mentality to the regional state.

Despite such similarities between the Terraferma and *mar* dominions, and others concerning more specific aspects of government, there were major differences.[7] The sea empire was scattered, often weeks of travel time from the capital and at recurrent risk of Turkish attack, so requiring perennial priority attention to its defence, and there might also be major cultural and linguistic distances involved: e.g. many subjects' Greek Orthodox religion complicated their relations with Venetian authority. In its permanent shape the mainland state was a fairly compact area of over 30,000 km^2, mostly densely populated (the first aggregate datum available gives 1,417,000 inhabitants in 1548). Despite more rural and/ or feudal fringe areas – especially Friuli, the south Trentino, later the Polesine – it had largely experienced the economic, social, political and cultural development of the later medieval Italian city communes, as was evident from cities large or very large by European standards: in around 1500 Verona had about 40,000 inhabitants, and Brescia nearer 50,000. This experience left a lasting imprint on such sectors of government activity as law-making, control over territory, organisation of defence, public finance and justice and, although fourteenth-century lordly rulers marginalised civic councils, they built on many communal policy aims. They tightened jurisdictional control over the *contado* and preserved many posts and procedures generated by communal government. Their choices of political supporters and officials favoured significant turnover among the families of the elite, but the result was mostly to strengthen its cohesion and its identification with the city and with residence there, even if *contado* land was usually its main basis of its wealth.

However, despite some fourteenth-century amalgamation into larger units – thus e.g. Visconti rule over Brescia, Bergamo and (briefly but significantly) Verona – each territory came under Venetian control with specific connotations it largely preserved. As well as overall socio-economic characteristics – Verona, vastly populous and rich, was a crossroads between major north–south and east–west trade routes, and Feltre a quiet hill town the tenth of its size – this specificity concerned basic features of public life such as statutes (the primary source of law), councils, magistracies, law-courts, procedures and instruments of

---

[7] For this section, see Castagnetti and Varanini, *Il Veneto*; Collodo, *Società e istituzioni*; Grubb, *Firstborn of Venice*; Law, *Venice and the Veneto*; Ortalli and Knapton, *Istituzioni, società e potere*; Varanini, *Comuni cittadini*; Viggiano, *Governanti e governati*; Zamperetti, *I piccoli principi*; and essays by Mallett and Viggiano in *Storia di Venezia*, IV. See, too, surveys of mainland historiography in Grubb, 'When myths lose power'; Knapton, '"Nobiltà e popolo"'; *Intorno allo stato degli studi*; Varanini, 'La Terraferma veneta'.

government. In a broader sense it covered aspects of the organisation and sharing of power such as the overall degree of cohesion of local elites and the extent of their identification with cities and city-based authority, and the balance between urban institutions and other jurisdictions in control of the *contado*.

The provinces' relationship with Venice in the new mainland state introduced other variables into this political geography, starting from the circumstances of their annexation, which affected the extent of concessions favourable to local prerogatives. Treviso, conquered early (1338), and Padua, taken after a bitter war to defeat its lordly rulers, got a weak start: Treviso's city council was shadowy, and named no vicars or *podestà* to minor *contado* jurisdictions, while its Paduan counterpart shared them half and half with Venetian patricians. Both then experienced relatively earlier and stronger government action from the capital, favoured by proximity, which also subjected these areas – unlike those further afield, until the sixteenth century – to the pull of the Venetian market in basic foodstuffs. Akin to this was the greater presence there of individual Venetians' private interests, especially in the form of land-holding and church benefices.

Definitions of dominion

The 'myth of Venice' extended to its dominions too.[8] While the patriciate's collective memory, e.g. chronicles compiled during the fifteenth century, began to incorporate pride in possession of the mainland and military events relating to its acquisition or defence, stereotype images of wise, beneficial Venetian government permeated the political language used by both Venetian and Terraferma institutions. They were also projected via material symbols such as the winged lion of St Mark, a regular presence in mainland cities' public buildings and squares.[9] The patrician Marin Sanudo, already mentioned, wrote an enthusiastic description of the mainland and Istria when he toured them in 1483 with a cousin, one of three *Sindici Inquisitori* sent from the capital on a periodic inspection. His pride in Venetian government and general superiority included comparisons with the provinces' misfortunes under previous, lordly regimes, and attention to his own family's role, especially his paternal uncle Francesco (recently deceased while in charge of troops attacking Ferrara, and remembered for his governorship of Verona and other cities by inscriptions and a portrait).

[8] For this section, see works indicated in n. 7, especially those by Grubb and Law.
[9] Humfrey, *Venice and the Veneto*.

By Sanudo's time the mainland dominion was well established, but neither Venetians nor subjects had produced much explicit analysis of its standing within the state, although its traumatic temporary loss after Agnadello did stimulate reflection. Its status is discussed in a few treatises and in legal *questiones, consilia,* etc. formulated by jurists; albeit unsystematically, it figures in diaries, chronicles, historical writings and a few letter collections of the time, and in a variety of public documents. Significant among the latter is the preface written by Silvestro Lando, Verona's humanist chancellor, for the 1450 revised edition of his city's statutes, marrying celebration of its past with praise for current Venetian government, including respect for local autonomy. Overall reticence by Venetian patricians was consistent with their buttoned-up approach to public life, but also convenient in tacitly allowing differing notions about the Terraferma state to coexist, together with diversity of language describing political relationships. Behind this ambiguity were major differences between Venetian and mainland elites in both general political culture and attitudes to the heritage of ancient Rome, with whose empire Venetians might favourably compare their own dominions,[10] while its legal tradition could support their subjects' defence of local prerogatives.

Much attention to the nature of the mainland state by both contemporaries and later historians deals with an important but limited question – the legitimacy of the republic's annexations and subsequent exercise of government. Shaded with ambiguity, the issue gained importance with the development of propaganda hostile to Venetian 'imperialism' by other Italian rulers from around the middle of the fifteenth century, drawing answers e.g. in the humanist Bernardo Giustinian's funeral oration for doge Francesco Foscari. There was indeed a humanist cultural matrix to much justification of Venice's mainland dominion and of its overall policy towards the Italian peninsula in the fifteenth and early sixteenth centuries, just as humanist historical writing became a more general political tool: Marcantonio Sabellico's *Rerum venetarum ab urbe condita* ... (1487), inaugurated a long series of Venetian 'public historiography', although much of its ideological ancestry lay in medieval chroniclers including the authoritative doge Andrea Dandolo (d. 1354).

In justifying Venetian possession of mainland provinces, mere right of conquest was often near the truth, but tact towards subjects curbed reference to it. Jurists' opinions divided over the need to recognise the

---

[10] Fortini Brown, *Venice and Antiquity.*

German emperors' rights over territory belonging to the *Regnum Italicum*; in 1437 Venice obtained partial, belated imperial investiture with the Terraferma lands (excluding ex-Scala Verona and Vicenza), but later drew no attention to this, though tolerating subjects' display of affection for the emperors' prestige. Claims for the legitimacy of annexations and dominion were often generically framed: God's favour towards the republic, its right to self-defence, its commitment to freedom and peace, its altruism towards Terraferma communities earlier crushed by tyranny. And the most significant specific source of *de iure* sovereignty lay in subjects' spontaneous acceptance of Venetian rule, formulated in language which came to prefer the binding term *deditio*. Such acceptance was usually part of a broader initial exchange of requests by new subjects and concessions by Venice, whose tone was largely that of a pact or contract, although negotiated between parties of *de facto* disparate status. Such agreements could coexist politically with higher recognition of Venetian authority, like the 1437 imperial investiture or a 1445 pact by which the patriarch of Aquileia ceded temporal jurisdiction over Friuli. Though many single issues named in them were superseded, they maintained lasting political value, on an increasingly symbolic plane, as confirmed by periodic Venetian pronouncements, careful to prevent their overgeneral application and to distinguish them from rights of other sorts.

As to the terminology used to describe the mainland state, new, extensive territorial power was one of the factors behind the transition from 1423 on in Venetian official language, from reference to the state as a whole as '*comune*', towards '*dominium*', or '*signoria*' in Italian – words expressing a principle of authority, the political body exercising it, and also the territory concerned. Later in the century similar meanings were conveyed by the vernacular '*imperio*' and Latin '*imperium*', though implying no recognition of German imperial rights over the mainland. None of these terms, nor the polyvalent '*status*', in any way assimilated Terraferma subjects as participants in the Venetian political order or the authority with which it was invested, and they made no request for representation in mainline Venetian government. Both they and Venetians might use the same political metaphors (parents/children, patrons/clients, head/members of the same body), but a mainland city would call itself *civitas*, meaning a political body with its own laws, authority and jurisdiction over a '*districtus*', while Venice did not necessarily consider '*civitas*' as implying such rights, and in referring to a subject city might use more modest, generic terms such as '*communitas*', or the non-committal multiple '*terrae et loci*'.

Finally, neither this terminology nor *de facto* political practice signified any meaningful perception of the mainland provinces as a common entity by virtue of subjection to the republic. Subordination to higher authority, which did little to assimilate them into its conception of the state, delegating much local administration, married with a carry-through from each territory's specific experience of government and politics into a series of overwhelmingly one-to-one relationships between Venice and individual subject communities. Despite a slow accumulation of Venetian laws and policy directives concerning the whole Terraferma, this meant – even much later than 1530 – no prospect for it of anything like a single law code, a uniform tax system or even common rules for citizenship rights.

Venetian policy and authority in the Terraferma

Among the sectors of government activity drawing most attention and direct involvement by Venetian authority, an unsurprising priority is defence organisation.[11] The republic already had a long tradition of arming both warfleets and regular peacetime naval patrols, with only occasional use of citizen militia and hired professionals when land war required forces larger than peacetime garrisons. With conquest and lasting occupation of extensive territory it developed a standing army which by the middle of the fifteenth century had become arguably the strongest in Italy. Whereas galley and fleet commanders were Venetian patricians, and crew members ordinary Venetians and *mar* subjects, command and service in this land army were the preserve of non-Venetian professionals, including an increasing proportion of Terraferma subjects, occasionally supported by militia raised in the provinces. But all major policy decisions and appointments and general supervision of the army were reserved to Venetian authority and Venetian-named personnel.

With defence and public debt generated by their swallowing the majority of public income, equally unsurprising was the Venetian takeover of the receipt and disbursement of most mainland revenue, especially from indirect taxation, the source of the great majority of income, but also from direct tax, which became regular in the mainland during the first half of the fifteenth century (*dadia delle lanze* or *colta ducale*).[12] This preceded its introduction in ordinary form in Venice itself in 1463 (*decime* and *tanse*): cycles of war spending and forced loans, in use there

---

[11] Mallett and Hale, *The Military Organization*.   [12] Pezzolo, 'Stato, guerra e finanza'.

since the thirteenth century to fund extraordinary expenditure, had so inflated the republic's consolidated debt as to destroy confidence and impose a pause in forced loans. In peacetime in the later fifteenth century, the mainland's incomes more than covered the ordinary costs of its government and defence, contributing about 420,000 ducats to the republic's total revenue of about 1,150,000 ducats (two to three times the other leading Italian states' income). Strong mainland defence therefore reflected not only the wealth of the dominion, but also Venetian adroitness in gauging how much and how to tax. Politically delicate matters such as the sharing and collection of mainland direct tax were left to local bodies, which also handled much public spending and taxraising extraneous to state finance proper. Connected with public finance, but important for the economy in general and also the symbolism of dominion, was monetary policy, over which Venice established full control, though making concessions to local identity e.g. in minting coins for Verona with the image of its patron saint, Zeno.

In dispensing justice and in the laws it was based on, Venetian policy was complicated by markedly diverse legal cultures.[13] On the one hand, the Roman law-based tradition of Terraferma statutes (their validity everywhere confirmed by promises made to new subjects), sources of law in general, and judicial practice – a tradition much dependent on the legal expertise of jurists organic to local elites. On the other, Venice's own, separate legal and judicial tradition, among whose key features were the space for empirical, informal, 'political' criteria of equity in judging, and the assignment of judicial posts to patricians with no requirement of legal training. Although much mainland judging remained the business of local courts with local judges, the uneasy reconciliation of these two cultures was evident in the dual options of mainland governors (very few of whom had studied law at university, like the patriciate in general): they used an entourage of legal professionals, judging by local law, but were also empowered by their commissions to override the usual priority in sources of law. A similar contrast and compromise affected subjects' appeals to courts in the capital like the Forty: though desirable in underlining Venice's reputation for good justice, as too for single litigants and for patricians holding judicial posts happy to increase their business, appeals were often incompatible with defence of Terraferma courts' prerogatives and local elites' contentment – issues Venetian authority was also sensitive to. As to the relationship between local and Venetian law, single statutory traditions continued

---

[13] Viggiano, *Governanti e governati*; Povolo, 'Un sistema giuridico'.

essentially intact, with periodic renewal of statutes subject to Venetian approval, which entailed no drastic interference. Such codes were generally not significantly updated by new laws formulated by mainland legislators once under Venetian dominion, nor did they include as statutory norms the heterogeneous accumulation of Venetian laws and rulings, referring to single territories or (more rarely) to the whole mainland. Both these facts pointed towards the eventual partial superseding of statute law, though this long-term trend extended well beyond 1530.

In economic policy, Venetian authority imposed no drastic changes, and left much regulation of production and commerce to local bodies, partly owing to the strong imprint already given by treaties with the area's previous rulers.[14] Directives thus formulated already favoured the flow of goods to and from Venice (e.g. wool imports for mainland cloth production and exports of the quality textiles resulting), placed Venetian-supplied salt in mainland monopolies with major gains for both merchants and government, and eased Venetian access to inland supplies of timber and other raw materials for ship-building. In other ways economic policy remained *laissez-faire*. Distances, logistics and political muscle did not allow Venice to exercise serious constraint on the central and western mainland cities' long-distance trade flows and business links, so that no integrated economic region emerged, no 'common market', no specialisation of roles, no hierarchical dependence on Venice. Each city jurisdiction basically maintained rules and tax tariffs protecting its local trading circuits and manufacturing (and guaranteeing the local Venetian exchequer's revenue). Such protection included control over the movement of locally produced foodstuffs, though with exceptions for the areas near Venice, anticipated by earlier treaties' provision for Venetian land-owners' freedom to export crops.

Ecclesiastical policy extended to the mainland the identification of the republic's destiny and authority with divine favour and approval, represented especially via St Mark, and its attention to the church's well-being and efficacy.[15] Policy could include support for projects of a primarily spiritual character, as given to the Paduan monastery of S. Giustina whose gradual regeneration from the 1420s nurtured widespread Benedictine reform. But, as under previous lordly rulers, much policy concerning churchmen, their benefices and property had immediate and strong political and/or material implications, and extended to the Terraferma contentious issues already open between Venice and the Roman curia. This meant limiting church courts' competence and protecting

---

[14] Lanaro, *At the Centre*.   [15] Del Torre, *Patrizi e cardinali*.

but also taxing church property, and seeking to influence the assignment of benefices (whose revenues statewide were reckoned to total about 240,000 ducats per year in the middle of the fifteenth century), especially via regular Senate designations for dominion bishoprics. These latter were considered to need safe nominees – where possible Venetian patricians – to guarantee good use of their spiritual authority as a sort of back-up to secular patrician governors.

There has been debate over how much, if at all, the fifteenth-century Terraferma experienced expansion, planned or haphazard, of government activity by Venetian authority, especially from the capital. Indications of some sort of growth have been given above, but for much of the period up to 1530 it is also clear that Venetian authority was often feeling its way, and not always familiar with issues it had to face (Marin Sanudo wrote his 1483 description of the Terraferma aware that many other patricians knew little about it). Any expansion of more direct government was much more casual than planned and primarily concerned the provinces nearer Venice. Equally evident, though, and often successful especially for the more distant provinces, was local institutions' defence of their prerogatives against interference by Venetian authority. These contrasting trends were manifest in the matter of appeal justice mentioned above, in the often contradictory action of magistracies and courts in Venice, in uncertainty and overlaps of competence, in clashes between different organs of government and policy priorities. Another sign of the rather confused situation was the periodic despatch to Venice of mainland representatives, especially by city councils seeking to defend prerogatives; although central government sought to limit it, it became enough of a habit and necessity to require stays extending over days or weeks, and the use of regular quarters in the capital by single cities' delegations. Linked to this was subjects' development of patronage networks for lobbying in Venice, often involving patricians who served in dominion posts, and Marin Sanudo (treasurer in the Verona exchequer in 1501–2) also performed this function.

The Italian Wars gradually reoriented this balance, leading mid-term to greater attention to mainland government by Venetian authority. The preservation in Venice of written reports by returning dominion governors, ordered and begun in 1524, anticipates later trends towards the creation of new central magistracies with specific competence for Terraferma matters (fiefs, common property, etc.), especially from the middle of the sixteenth century.

Direct Venetian government of the mainland was chiefly the responsibility of patrician officials, sent to eleven main urban governorships and a number of smallish but often strategically important towns, some largely separate from dependence on bigger cities' jurisdiction over *contadi* (e.g. Bassano and Rovereto).[16] These officials consisted of one or two governors with broad responsibility, from civil to military, from judicial to executive and administrative; one or two treasurers in charge of the Venetian exchequer (*camera fiscale*); and a few castellans, their posts completely bereft of jurisdictional powers, essentially sinecures for patricians with modest ambitions and income. They were assisted by a not very numerous mix of mainland subjects and non-patrician Venetians serving as governors' judges, chancellors and police, exchequer staff, minor castellans and garrison troops. In the more prestigious governorships (Padua, Vicenza, Verona, Brescia and Bergamo), responsibility was shared between a *podestà* and a captain, the first with primarily civil authority and the second mainly concerned with the exchequer, defence and the *contado*. Patrician officials' terms in office were usually brief, settling at sixteen months, and many had neither specific aptitude nor career specialisation in Terraferma posts. A partial exception to this were a small but quite influential minority of mainly humanist patricians, who also served as Venetian ambassadors and army commissioners, e.g. Francesco Barbaro and Ludovico Foscarini, respectively seven and ten times mainland governors.

In 1493 the patricians serving in Venice itself and the sea empire totalled respectively 514 and 138; mainland posts then totalled 112, 30 of them in the Padovano and Trevigiano, while 39 of the 112 were mere *castellanie*.[17] This very scant presence of ordinary patrician functionaries in the mainland was sporadically and temporarily increased by extraordinary officials, generally patricians, sent from Venice with a variety of mandates – among them the *Sindici Inquisitori* like those with whom Sanudo toured in 1483, empowered to investigate, judge and report on matters concerning justice and good government. As further examples of more occasional posts, if the army was mobilised, it was mostly managed by various grades of patrician commissioner (*provveditore*), while particular financial stringency stimulated the despatch of officials to inspect and galvanise the exchequers.

Patrician governors of the main Terraferma cities were important political figures, such posts a significant stage in their *cursus honorum*. They answered for the dominion's external security and inner harmony, and collected and spent much revenue; they represented Venetian sovereignty; they were guided by a commission from the doge, and by directives and norms from Venice in general – responsibilities not unlike

---

[16] On smaller towns, see Bellavitis, 'Quasi-città'.
[17] Varanini, *Gli ufficiali*; Zannini's essay in *Storia di Venezia*, IV.

those earlier discharged by lordly officials in relating to surviving communal bodies. But just as lordly regimes had left much power to such bodies, in the Venetian mainland state both central authority in Venice and patrician governors in the dominion had no alternative to collaboration with local elites and institutions. The delegation to them of vast responsibility for government, visible in the numerical imbalance on the ground between Venetian and local officials, deeply influenced patrician governors' actions, making them perforce a point of intersection and mediation, an institutional element of flexibility. They had to respect local statutes and privileges, to understand and handle tensions in provincial society, to communicate its moods and needs to Venice, to pass on information and evaluations to higher authority – if possible while enhancing their authority locally, and without siding with any single interest. The ritual associated especially with their entrance and departure from office – speeches, parades, commemorative inscriptions, etc. – was a thermometer of their skill in relating to local society, and repeated Venetian laws attempting to restrain this ritual testify to its lasting importance.

Local decision-making and power-holders in the Terraferma

The previous section's analysis of Venetian policy choices and government activity by Venetian authority also suggests how much they did not deal with, or did not deal with exclusively, as compared with matters delegated wholly or partially to local decision and local power-holders.[18] These latter may be summarily indicated in partly overlapping categories: civic councils, their status generally revamped by the republic after decline under lordly rulers; the many executive, judicial and administrative bodies and officials depending on them or linked to them; legal professionals, especially judges and notaries; a plethora of civic bodies concerned with what we would call social issues, such as hospitals (the big, rich Battuti hospital was especially important in Treviso, where early Venetian annexation had confirmed the already weak profile of communal institutions);[19] holders of rural jurisdictions – lords and feudatories, valley or mountain communities (e.g. the valleys north of Bergamo, or the *Sette Comuni* in the northern Vicentino) – more or less independent of and/or antagonistic to urban authority, more thickly present in Friuli and mountain areas in general; and rural communities, the basic unit of all government activity.

---

[18] For this section in general, see works indicated in n. 7.
[19] D'Andrea, *Civic Christianity*.

Between them, all these local power-holders coped with the great majority of government, producing norms, dispensing justice, handling taxation and public finance and myriad other administrative tasks. The existence of Venetian higher authority to invoke was a perennial stimulus for them to seek to alter balances of power between them, especially the extent of cities' control over their *contadi*, but Venetian fifteenth-century decisions mostly confirmed pre-existing urban jurisdiction. Particularly strong in the Padovano, Vicentino, Veronese and Bresciano, this was functional everywhere to city interests and citizens' privileged status. Nonetheless, after timid fifteenth-century beginnings in the Padovano, Veronese and Bresciano, during the sixteenth century higher-level *contado* representative institutions (*corpi territoriali*) would partly alter this balance between *contadi* and cities, especially in matters fiscal; their emergence both favoured and benefited from the rise of *contado* political elites, based primarily in small towns.

While the Venetian patriciate was tightly defined by the fifteenth century, Terraferma urban political elites – as well as varying from place to place – had a looser, more composite collective identity: prevalently aristocratic, but including newer families whose rise to eminence dated from the fourteenth or sometimes the fifteenth century; mainly city-dwelling, primarily land-owning, active in honoured military and civil professions (especially those connected with the law), but with no preclusion yet of wealth acquired through mercantile or manufacturing activity; strongly linked to power-holding via civic institutions, which indeed they dominated and with whose dignity they identified – as symbolised materially by new civic buildings such as the council chamber started in late fifteenth-century Padua.[20] Historians no longer credit Ventura's hypothesis that Venetian authority pressed for 'aristocratic closure' of these elites via similar mechanisms to those defining the capital's patriciate, making councils smaller and more tightly regulated, their membership determined by co-optation or inheritance and denied to the low-born.[21] Change in these terms did develop, but gradually and spontaneously, with the general slowing of social turnover – though such turnover did not cease. Among the major cities only Bergamo was characterised, like largely rural Friuli, by deep divisions within the local elite according to factional loyalties, the continuation of earlier splits; this generated political instability and security risks, since faction conflict also meant antagonism over loyalty to Venice and favour received from it.[22]

---

[20] Varanini, 'Nelle città'.   [21] Ventura, *Nobiltà e popolo*.
[22] Cavalieri, *'Qui sunt guelfi'*; Muir, *Mad Blood Stirring*.

The elites included families important enough to count beyond their local context, and particularly prone to embellish that context with such status symbols as urban palaces, funerary monuments and – much more in the sixteenth than in the fifteenth century – villas: thus e.g. the Veronese Bevilacqua and Maffei, the Vicentine Thiene, all families which had come to eminence in the fourteenth century. Such leading families, their previous generations important in lordly courts and councils, were most affected by the change of political horizons with passage under Venice. Exclusion from the Venetian patriciate – with very few exceptions like the Savorgnan, Friulan feudatories made patricians in 1385 as a diplomatic gambit before Venetian conquest of Friuli – downgraded mainland elites to a basically 'municipal' sphere of power-holding, with few, limited opportunities to serve the republic in a broader dimension. These opportunities were offered very rarely in diplomacy, more often as judges in the retinue of patrician Terraferma governors (who, however, did not prefer members of leading families), and in the army as cavalry captains – thus e.g. the Brescian Martinengo – or administrators. Very few mainland aristocrats, though, developed careers serving other rulers.

Disappointment over the lack of opportunities for service and prestige which a princely ruler would have given did not generate seething resentment in mainland urban elites, and the overall tone of their relations with Venice was fairly harmonious, with a strong element of mutual *laissez-faire*, especially after initial uncertainty over the Venetian regime's solidity (a phase of wars and scattered plots which continued for the western provinces until the 1440s). Here too proximity to Venice made a difference. The Paduan aristocracy was periodically irritated by the tax status of Venetians' property, law-courts in the capital damaging local prerogatives, reduced access to posts in Padua university, and individual Venetians' massive occupation of middle- to low-rank church benefices – a problem mixing material interests with sensitivity about local identity as expressed through civic religion, also felt in Treviso.

This irritation lay behind Paduan noble acrimony in the 1509 crisis of Venetian control over the mainland, but chafing at Venetian authority was then evident in other civic elites too. Hopes of greater local autonomy and of gratification in serving other rulers married with the need to reconcile advancing armed enemies and to maintain local pre-eminence, orienting many mainland aristocrats towards interest in a change of regime – though the new rulers generally sharply disappointed them. The Agnadello crisis also revealed raw tension in Terraferma society in general, especially in the loyalty to Venice shown by significant parts of the urban *popolo* and of the rural population, resentful of the aristocracy's pre-eminence. Though Venice took advantage of such support in the short term, after the emergency its political choice could only be to resume its priority relationship in government with the civic aristocracy.[23]

Conclusion

In editing essays reviewing Venetian historiography since about 1973, John Martin and Dennis Romano noted in 2000 that despite the undermining of a 'unilinear reading of Venice's past', 'American scholars, with very few exceptions, have been concerned, at least until recently, with the capital city only' (something true of all English-speaking historians), and that, 'alongside the rather triumphalist history of the Venetian republic celebrated primarily by American scholars, Italian scholars in the postwar period have looked harder at the realities of Venice as a regional state'. But their volume included only one piece addressing the regional state, and overall leant more towards another aspect they identified as new in Venetian historiography – 'the intrinsic role of art, music and literature in fashioning the way Venetians understood and viewed themselves' (still centred on an essentially urban, inward-looking vision of Venice).[24]

This chapter has aimed to redress the balance, giving Venice itself proportionately less attention and presenting to non-Italian readers the results of scholarship concerned especially with the Terraferma. Need for concision and this whole volume's focus on Italian history have elbowed out the sea empire – though no discussion of the republic of Venice should ignore it. As outlined above, the evolution of Venetian state structures between 1300 and 1530 was constituted by a mixture of factors, partly a confirmation of the city-state matrix of those structures but also, to a significant extent, new elements deriving from the acquisition of a territorial state, much more juxtaposed than assimilated, but no less important in its overall implications, and destined to last well beyond the period considered here.

---

[23] Del Torre, *Venezia e la Terraferma*.
[24] Martin and Romano, *Venice Reconsidered*, xi, 6, 7, 27.

8 Lombardy under the Visconti and the Sforza

Federico Del Tredici

Introduction

Cautious victor, gentle orchestrator of peace. The archbishop Ottone Visconti appears thus in the Angera cycle of frescoes celebrating his victory, and that of the Milanese nobles, over the Della Torre and the Milanese *pars populi*, the harbinger of Ottone himself being proclaimed lord of Milan by the general council (22 January 1277). Unarmed, Ottone saves the lives of his enemies starting with his arch-rival Napo Della Torre, calms the situation and distances himself from the factious conflict to which his ascendancy was linked.

The *pax* of the Visconti covered Milan and its surrounding area. The events depicted in the Angera frescoes narrate an exclusively Milanese story centred around concluding and overcoming the conflict between the nobles and the *populares* of Milan. Some elements, however, refer to larger areas. The defeated Della Torre are taken to a prison near Como, and it is the hand of a nobleman from Pavia, ready to kill Napo Della Torre, that is stopped by Ottone. These details serve as a reminder that for a long time events in Milan had an effect on a wider scale, beyond that of the city itself. Examples can be seen in the central role of the Milanese commune in the alliances opposed to the undertakings of the emperor; in the extensive travel of the Milanese to be *podestà* in nearby towns; and the nature of the influence of the Della Torre, which already extended beyond the city of Milan.

'The alternate dominance of the Visconti and the Della Torre', Francesco Cognasso wrote, is 'a totally accidental phenomenon, within Lombardy, with the hegemony of Milan being the only defining feature'.[1] This is an affirmation that nowadays cannot be fully adhered to given, for example, the recent prominence placed on the different styles of government of the two dynasties. This affirmation, however,

---

[1] Cognasso, 'Note e documenti', 28.

invites scholars to consider the fortunes of the Visconti *signoria*, within the evolving context of political areas establishing themselves on a regional scale, in which many Lombard cities and territories had, for a long time, gravitated towards the Milanese metropolis. Within this context, it is important to bear in mind that the continuing gravitation of cities and territories towards the Visconti was rather difficult and by no means automatic.

The fifty years following Ottone's victory were dedicated to problems other than those of overwhelming expansion. Far from faithfully following the serene image proposed by the Angera frescoes, the Milanese reality forced Ottone (d. 1295) and his successor Matteo to confront returns of the Della Torre, rebellions of the nobles, internal rivalry within the Visconti family, and uncertain relations with popular organisations. Further problems accumulated in the times of Galeazzo, the son of Matteo: the difficult conflict with pope John XXII, with accusations of heresy and the proclamation of anti-Visconti crusades, and the ever-changing relationship with the newly crowned emperor Louis IV, on whose order Galeazzo was incarcerated shortly before his death (1328).

In this troubled context, other hegemonic dynasties, such as the Angevins to the west and the Della Scala, lords of Verona, to the east, seemed to be endowed with more vitality. Lombardy was not entirely composed around the Visconti's rule: towards the end of the 1320s even substantial sections of the Milan *contado* slipped from their control. Once a firmer relationship with the emperor had been established, the Visconti were able to restrain the ambitions of the Della Scala, while, following the death of Robert of Anjou (1343), new opportunities presented themselves in the direction of Piedmont. It was, therefore, with Azzone (1329–39) and his heirs Luchino and Giovanni (1339–54) that the Visconti *signoria* could really assume a supra-local dimension. This was achieved by the acquisition of Novara, Vercelli, Bergamo Cremona, Como, Lodi, Piacenza and Brescia; then – with Luchino and Giovanni – of Asti, Alessandria, Tortona, Alba, Cuneo, Parma, Genoa and Bologna. Clearly, these were not long-term gains in all cases. Following the death of Giovanni (1354), Genoa, many Piedmontese territories and, in light of renewed hostilities with the pope, Bologna were lost. However, under the brothers Bernabò and Galeazzo II, Giovanni's successors, a dominion of a regional scale remained, to which they also added Pavia (1359) and Reggio (1371). The brothers governed the dominion by dividing it clearly: Galeazzo II had the western part of the state and Bernabò the eastern part. It was Bernabò, nevertheless, who was the true leader, and this was more true when Galeazzo (died 1378) was succeeded by his son Gian Galeazzo 'believed by all to be a shy youth'.[2]

The results of this situation are well known: treacherously capturing and poisoning his uncle (1385), the 'shy youth' assumed control of the entire state, negating any rights of Bernabò's heirs. This was the beginning of a final phase of great territorial expansion. Verona, Vicenza, Padova, Feltre and Belluno fell within the space of a few years. In addition Pisa, Siena, Perugia and other Tuscan cities also fell to Gian Galeazzo, to the point that, on his death in 1402, even Florence seemed close to surrendering to the armies of the Visconti. To his sons, Giovanni Maria and Filippo Maria, Gian Galeazzo left not only a state of never-before reached dimensions, but also a legitimate title, something that none of his predecessors had been able to achieve. The title was that of duke, obtained by the payment of a significant sum to the emperor Wenceslaus in 1395. This marked an important turning point. Not only was it useful to consolidate Gian Galeazzo's power base, but it also, with some uncertainty, sanctioned the union of the territories within dominion in new terms. The dominion was no longer an accumulation of single bodies united in their dependence on a lord, but a 'duchy', an autonomous, institutional entity and, as such, theoretically indivisible.

The events following the death of the first duke conspired to show the extent to which this indivisibility was, in reality, only theoretical. The state fractured after 1402, prey to factional in-fighting in the centre, separatist forces in the periphery, renewed activity by old aristocratic houses, initiatives by powerful military men. On the assassination of duke Giovanni in 1412, the task of recapturing part of the lost territory fell to his brother Filippo Maria, who became the protagonist of a patient work of recomposition that was crowned with success. The territories in Tuscany, in the Veneto and in Brescia and Bergamo, were lost to Florence or the republic of Venice (the latter had by that time become a fully fledged land power on the banks of the river Adda not 30 km from Milan). The power of the Visconti, however, was reaffirmed in the heart of the previous dominion of Gian Galeazzo, establishing borders that were barely altered until the end of the fifteenth century.

Following the death of Filippo Maria (1447) the major change was, clearly, that of the ruling dynasty. The main line of the Visconti dynasty had no male heirs, and from the competition for the succession the victor who emerged was the *condottiero* Francesco Sforza, husband of the only descendant of the late duke, Bianca Maria. With difficulty,

---

[2] According to Bernardino Corio, who lived around a century after those events: Corio, *Storia di Milano*, 879.

Francesco established his control over a state that was once more fragmenting, and on 26 February 1450 he entered the capital: a Milan that, following the death of Filippo Maria, had experienced a republican government. However, Francesco Sforza could not obtain acknowledgement by the emperor. As the investiture of 1395 excluded the possibility of succession through the female line, Frederick III claimed the duchy to be devolved to the empire. By appealing to the right of Milan to choose its own rulers, the new prince was content with legitimation 'from below'. He obtained the title of duke by a general assembly of the people and received the symbols of the office during a public ceremony in the presence of the highest ranks of Milanese aristocracy.

This solution provided a legal cover under which to govern the city of Milan and its territory, but it could not guarantee to Francesco the same legitimation outside the capital. As Jane Black noted, the rest of the dominion 'consisted of multiple separate communities so that there was no one body that could be assembled for the purpose of electing a new duke'.[3] The lack of imperial acknowledgement, thus, remained a serious problem for Francesco and his heirs until the investiture obtained by Francesco's son, Ludovico, in 1494. Together with hostilities from the Milanese political elites and a constant shortage of resources, this defect contributed significantly to keeping the new princes in an uncertain condition.

However, skilful in securing his own position by using politics based on mutual guarantee between the states of the peninsula, which had resulted from the Lega Italica (1455), combined with a prudent link to France, Francesco eventually died of natural causes in his own bed in 1466. The same cannot be said about his son and successor Galeazzo Maria. He attempted a more authoritarian affirmation of his power and, having exhausted all the possibilities of reciprocal support from within the Italian states, orchestrated a much more decisive and dangerous alliance with France. Killed by Milanese noblemen in 1476 as a result of an accumulation of internal and external tensions, Galeazzo Maria left a legitimate heir, though still a child, Gian Galeazzo Maria, and a wife, Bona of Savoy, who would have taken on the regency of the state albeit under the strict control of the powerful secretary Cicco Simonetta. At this point, the figure of the late duke's brother emerged. Ludovico, who from 1480 was able to assume responsibility for the government in his role as lieutenant, obtained the title of duke legally only in 1494. From the 1480s, however, Ludovico accentuated the more authoritarian and despotic characteristics of his government, increasingly relying on

---

[3] Black, 'Double duchy', 18.

homines novi who owed everything to him and taking every decision on himself. This can be considered a progressive 'deformation of the state system'.[4] Rather than a sign of strength, however, this is a sign of a profound weakness derived from the illegitimate nature of Ludovico's role and from the fact that survival was becoming difficult for the rich, but small state of Milan, in a context in which the large European powers' interest in Italy was becoming ever stronger. This weakness was destined to be dramatically exposed in the final years of the century, firstly on the descent into Italy of Charles VIII, when Novara surrendered to Louis of Orléans; and again in 1499 when the same Louis who had then become Louis XII, descended to Milan with his army to lay claim to the duchy. Easily caused to flee in the summer of 1499, and conclusively defeated in the April of the following year, Ludovico thus lost the duchy and the duchy lost its autonomy. Two other members of the Sforza family, Ludovico's sons, in the turbulent decades that followed managed in some way to salvage the dominion. Massimiliano (1512–15), however, regained the dominion in the capacity of *duchetto* (little duke: his ironic nickname of the times) and was controlled by the Swiss. The other son, Francesco II (1521–35), did so only as a ward of Charles V, into whose hands, on the death of Francesco, the state definitively passed.

The apparatus of government and the role of the cities

Some of the princely interventions that accompanied the conquests of the Visconti included: the construction of fortresses and military citadels; the dispatching of armed garrisons; and the reform of the statutes of newly acquired cities. These interventions can be noted from the very first conquests, from the 1330s onwards. Alongside them, slowly but surely, came the definition of an extensive administrative and bureaucratic system both in the centre and in the furthest-reaching periphery.

An immediate consequence of conquering cities was that the *podestà*, who were the highest judicial magistrates in the urban areas of the dominion, were integrated into the ranks of princely officialdom. From the 1350s, however, new officials began to arrive in the various cities, sent by the Visconti in order to strengthen their hold on the extremities of the state. Initially, these officials held the roles of *referendari* or treasurers, that is, magistrates charged with keeping a town's income and expenditure under increasingly stringent surveillance so as to keep the town under the full control of the Visconti. Later, officials charged with

---

[4] Covini, *'La balanza drita'*, 293.

combating contraband or with monitoring the movements of men and livestock (*capitani del divieto* and *ufficiali delle bollette*) were sent, along with fortress and garrison leaders. From the rule of Filippo Maria onwards, these figures were also flanked by *commissari* to whom the task of supervising the more typically political aspects of local affairs was assigned in areas where the Visconti's control proved to be important or difficult.

In the meantime, the central judicial systems strengthened and became more precise. During Gian Galeazzo's rule in particular, a new office of *magistratura delle entrate* (revenue office) began to be defined which was destined to control state finances. From 1389 this office was split into two branches: one dedicated to general revenue, *entrate ordinarie*, and one to extraordinary revenue, *entrate straordinarie*. At the same time the two major advisory and executive bodies were created: the *consiglio di giustizia*, justice council, and the *consiglio segreto*, secret council. The jurisdiction of these bodies comprised the main judicial functions and mediation on behalf of the duke in the management and debate of the most important questions of state, including public order, legislation, foreign policy and fiscal policy.

Once in power, Francesco Sforza had to deal with a 'dense and coherent' administrative network,[5] which would not experience structural change for a long time. Any of these offices could, of course, be given new mandates, or see their importance diminished. An example of this can be seen in the rule of Galeazzo Maria, who preferred to consult groups of selected advisers who were close to him rather than the secret or justice councils. What is more, when called upon by financial necessity, he could attribute supplementary judicial competences to the office of extraordinary revenue. From the time of Francesco onwards, the consistency and importance of the chanceries linked to the various offices grew and became more central to public administration. This is particularly true for the *cancelleria segreta*, secret chancery, which handled the most important affairs of state. New offices were also born, the most notable being the office of auditor, whose role it was to deal with the numerous pleas that came from individuals and communities within the dominion. It is, however, only with the rise to power of Ludovico, and particularly from the late 1480s, that the original Visconti administrative structure met with radical changes: the authoritarian and personalised 'subversion' noted above. Long-standing sectors of the administration such as the *magistratura delle entrate* made room for new organisations that were wholly dependent on the will of the duke, such as

---

[5] Leverotti, 'Gli officiali'.

the *deputati al denaro*, in charge of the income and expenditure of the state. The activities of the councils became totally devalued, while Ludovico and his trusted advisers handled all affairs of state. Even the *cancelleria segreta* diminished in importance in favour of the personal chancery of the Sforza.

It is clear that, despite the autocratic intentions of Ludovico, there is also no comparison in terms of size and complexity between the bureaucratic and administrative apparatus of the late fifteenth century and that of the first conquests of the Visconti in the middle of the fourteenth century. The importance of the diplomatic machine had also grown exponentially and, from the middle of the fifteenth century, comprised permanent ambassadors in the main courts of the peninsula and also the court of France. It is impossible to compare the sheer size and luxury of a court like that of Galeazzo Maria, hundreds of people strong, with the courts of the Visconti, respectable as they were. Such complexity clearly came at a cost, and was offset by the continuous and at times anxious search for money by means of new taxes, confiscations or alienations. The growth in government structures also gives a point of comparison. The disparity between the revenue of Luchino Visconti and that of Gian Galeazzo barely thirty years later is already great: Luchino did not reach even a twelfth of the revenue of Gian Galeazzo. These figures are incomparable to the state revenue of Francesco Sforza, according to a famous balance sheet of the Sforza's dating from 1463.

Despite the clear growth in the power of state apparatus, the Visconti–Sforza state, as with any political state in Renaissance Italy, inevitably remained a 'light-touch approach government'. This approach lay in the necessary engagement in constant dialogue with outlying territories. Thus, it lay in the recognition and legitimation of the role of local bodies, which a long tradition of historiography identifies primarily with the urban communes that, in the twelfth and thirteenth centuries, were able to dominate using the strength of their political and territorial setting, eliminating or subjugating other centres of power such as rural lordships or smaller communities. Giovanni Tabacco, emphasising the enduring vigour maintained by local forces in the Visconti dominion, intended to underline this mainly urban particularism, thus portraying a state perceived as 'a *grouping of cities* under the same lord'.[6] Tabacco, however, also drew attention to research current at the time suggesting at least a partial reconsideration of this urban-centric perspective, by highlighting the high number of exceptions to this supposed urban control of

---

[6] Tabacco, *Egemonie sociali*, 385.

territories, and also the 'doctrinaire' rather than the actual nature of the predominance of cities.

The new historiographic research to which Tabacco referred was primarily the studies that Giorgio Chittolini had brought together in the volume *La formazione dello stato regionale e le istituzioni del contado* (1979). In Chittolini's view, areas such as that between the Apennines and the river Po at the close of the age of the communes appeared to be significantly different from the traditional view: they were less marked by the hegemony of the city and instead pervaded by 'forces of the particularism of the rural lords [that] seem to be organised in a solid and robust fashion'.[7] When larger political systems of regional scale appeared, new forms of particularism came into play alongside the urban system; in particular, for the Lombard region these local forces were the rural *domini* which were impenetrable to the pretension of urban superiority, were rather active politically and militarily, and were charged with effective control over villages and territories. The ducal government tended to liaise with them using a flexible approach, not necessarily through mediation by the city, but rather through the exploitation of other instruments of control and discipline, such as the fief.

Despite having multiplied the number of actors on the scene, Chittolini himself in his introduction to the volume nonetheless depicted an overall order in which cities remained the protagonist. The legacy of the communes could indeed be considered in terms of a lesser centrality of the city-state; particularly in the Visconti–Sforza duchy, there were clear signs of an initial openness on the part of the centre to acknowledge as its interlocutors clusters of power outside the city context. In the long term, however, the cities continued to come out as the winners, protected as they were by the prince exercising his superior power while largely preserving the cities' privileges and prerogatives, albeit in a subordinate position. The mechanisms of fiscal charging favouring the *cives* and penalising the rural communities were also preserved, as were a series of benefits and competences in terms of property, grain supplies and road maintenance. The city retained high jurisdiction over the *contado*, together with the maintenance of the city statutes, in which the decrees of the prince must be recorded in order to be enforced. Within the state of Milan, the potentially anti-city nature of the dukes' feudal politics is considerably limited from the 1441 decree *del maggior magistrato*, of the highest judicial court, which recognised a degree of superiority of the city courts over the feudal courts: no real signs of a weakening of the cities. Furthermore, Chittolini could conclude by

---

[7] Chittolini, *La formazione*, x–xi.

saying that overall the aspirations of cities, which had not been able to impose themselves over their *contado* in the age of communes, seemed to be fulfilled precisely within the context of the new regional states. In Lombardy, relinquishing freedom and independence appears to have been a reasonable price for the urban communities to pay in exchange for the guarantee of opportunities to fight off 'those elements of concern and instability consisting of rural seigneurs and all those clusters of autonomous political and military action that had made dominance over the countryside very precarious in the Middle Ages'.[8]

The line of interpretation defined in the aforementioned introduction was destined for great success over the following years, so much as to be reinstated by Chittolini on the publication of a second collection of essays entitled *Città, comunità e feudi negli stati dell'Italia centro-settentrionale* (1996). In comparison to his previous research, the spectrum of local powers investigated had expanded; together with cities and fiefs, with varying degrees of success and in different ways, large non-urban communities of the plains or of the mountains came to the foreground demanding to escape – *separarsi* (to part) – from city control; sometimes they succeeded in becoming direct intermediaries of the prince. However, the background picture was not different from the one outlined in 1979. Significant as they may have been, the fractures introduced into city control over the territory from the 'parting' of the fiefs or some rural communities, the diarchy prince–city continued to characterise the state of Milan. The 'primitive order centred around the city' did not appear to be subverted, nor the city's influence annulled or drastically weakened. In particular, over the fifteenth century the city commune fully restored its prominence, its ability to act as privileged intermediary of the dukes and its fundamental role within the political system.

Francesco Somaini's essay followed a few years later along the same lines.[9] In his contribution, the special consideration in which the role of the city was held allowed the author to suggest a clear periodisation of the institutional organisation of the state of Milan over three phases. The first phase, at the beginning of the fourteenth century, was characterised by the overall centrality of the city. The second phase, in the late fourteenth century, is marked by a conscious intention of the *signoria* to favour – with the concession of fiscal exemptions and jurisdictional privileges to the rural seigneurs, non-urbanised communities and entire Alpine valleys – the definition of a less city-centred and more multifaceted state. The third phase saw this configuration disappear from the

---

[8] *Ibid.*, xxxii.   [9] Somaini, 'Processi costitutivi'.

end of the fourteenth century and especially under Filippo Maria (1412–47), when it was replaced by the duke's preference for towns. The fifteenth century witnessed a 'new alliance with the cities',[10] mainly motivated by the increased financial needs of the dukes, as a fiscal model based upon the role of urban organisations responded to the augmented needs of the princes better than a scheme in which it was always necessary to negotiate with hundreds of subjects.

A debated diarchy

Massimo Della Misericordia observes that the prince's planning needs and rational calculations were the protagonists in Somaini's reading of the history of the Visconti–Sforza state. The initial predominance of the cities, the subsequent emergence of a multiplicity of other protagonists, and the final confirmation of the centrality of cities thus became first of all the result of centralised politics, of conscious choices made by one or other of the Visconti *signori*. It is on this point that he seems to disagree, by emphasising, beyond the prince's calculations, the 'strength with which, independently or even notwithstanding the plans of the *signori*, these protagonists managed to impose themselves'.[11]

At a time in which the polemical debate against the 'grand narratives' was gaining force, the background to these observations within Italian historiography was the consistent assertion of readings that were careful to avoid state-centric teleologisms and tended to stress the crucial position of peripheral actors rather than the presumed linear processes of centralisation driven from above. Therefore, for Della Misericordia it becomes important to pinpoint deep discontinuities in the political and institutional parabola of the Visconti–Sforza state and to illustrate that this journey had been 'eventful' and 'interrupted' by emphasising the way in which such important discontinuities were due not only to changes of mind of the centre, but also to the force and energy of peripheral clusters of powers, not just those of cities: rural seigneurs and feudatories, kinships, factions and rural communities. As a matter of fact, when Della Misericordia's essay was published, research was trying to abandon the temptation of 'explaining' all of fourteenth- and fifteenth-century history of the state of Milan in terms of the long relationship between the prince and the city, in favour of piecing together a picture of the socio-political context that was characterised throughout the fifteenth century by less distinct equilibria, the 'highly complex and articulated' features of which had to be captured in full.[12]

[10] *Ibid.*, 755. [11] Della Misericordia, 'La Lombardia composita', 634.
[12] *Ibid.*, 615.

Around the same time, a contribution by Marco Gentile underlined that the renunciation of a 'hierarchy of relevance', acknowledging the factors that were more meaningful than others in certain times and places, was not the issue in point.[13] The issue lay in the need effectively to assess these hierarchies by avoiding the attribution of evaluations based on hindsight, for instance, assessing whether, at the time of the reconstruction under Filippo Maria, the relationship between the prince and urban communes was the only relevant factor or whether the relationships with aristocrats and factions were also important. Even though the aristocracy and factions were later considered irrelevant in Milan, in 1420 they still had a place.

At the end of the 1990s, the interpretative paradigm of the diarchy prince–city opened to another debate, destined to remain the underlying context for many later studies focused on the various protagonists of the political scene in the state of Milan in the fourteenth and fifteenth centuries. A brief overview of these studies is warranted at this point, beginning with the urban environment.

Far from disappearing from current historiography, several cities of the Milanese territories have been investigated in recent years although, with studies now careful to assess with more caution the actual substance of civic identity, and the possibility of identifying the political body of the city as a real and functioning entity. A multilayered scenario has emerged whereby the communal identity often appears as a fragile container under the surface of which more substantial clusters of power and identity acted. Pavia was different, as shown by recent studies; well into the fifteenth century, the city is indeed characterised by the existence of substantial divisions within the civic organism, of factions that impose 'precise rules in the division of positions and offices'.[14] However, Pavia remained something far more complex than and different from the mere sum of its parts. The sharing of communal offices among factions is frequently disregarded and the preservation of some fiscal privileges, the support of the prerogatives of the city court, and the attempt to make the university part of the commune become the subject of compact and often successful civic fights.

Also with regard to Tortona it is possible to speak of the 'prevalence of council-public' aspects and of a greater importance given to the city identity than to identification with a faction,[15] but the case of other cities in the dominion was different. In Reggio Emilia, a Visconti city between 1371 and 1409, there was not a strong sense of civic identity. Local

---

[13] Gentile, 'Leviatano regionale'. [14] Covini, 'La balanza drita', 232.
[15] Arcangeli, Gentiluomini di Lombardia, 365–419, 385.

society was organised around powerful aristocratic families, rich in land and jurisdictional power. At the same time, the common sense of belonging to the *civilitas* did not become the prevailing identity over the faction identity; 'the faction system determined the political field of action of individuals and oriented their choices'.[16] As a consequence, there are no signs here of a 'civic religion', whereby a strong city identity was reflected in the religious sphere; equally scarce were instances of polemical opposition to the rural lords with the intention of regaining the city's jurisdiction over the *contado*. Similarly, from the end of the fourteenth century in the nearby city of Parma, the political scenario of the city seems to be formally dominated by four local factions (*squadre*), here too controlled by members of aristocratic families who were powerful in the countryside that generally managed to avoid being controlled by the city. Positions, offices and posts within the council – reduced to a *parlamento delle squadre* – were divided among factions. Throughout the fifteenth century the figure of a chancellor of the commune was missing, replaced by four chancellors, one for each faction. It is, therefore, very difficult to perceive the community as anything more than a simple sum of its parts in this case: Parma was the *place* in which clusters of local powers met, but as a civic community, it was characterised by a peculiar 'political tenuousness'.[17] The voice of the community can sometimes be heard; for example, when Parma returned within the territories of the Visconti (1420), the council presented a substantial petition against the rural seigneurs. However, this struggle was aimed only against those lords who were not included among the aristocrats who dominated the communal institutions through the factions; thus their requests of a seemingly communal nature held the vested interests of the factions. With regard to the capital, Milan, its factions, in contrast to those of the other cities in the territories, have appeared 'amorphous', 'untraceable' and 'elusive'.[18] Rather than bodies whose constant presence could be recognised in the rather weak municipal institutions, they were 'court parties' and as such they can be distinguished by their more fluid and unstable nature, together with their strong relationships with people who came from outside Milanese society. However, the weakness of the factions does not correspond to the force and cohesion of a compact urban oligarchy. Several studies by Letizia Arcangeli, starting from her pioneering research on Gian Giacomo Trivulzio,[19] show that even within Milanese political society aristocratic figures emerged who could

---

[16] Gamberini, *Oltre le città*, 83–107, 93.   [17] Gentile, *Terra e poteri*, 187.
[18] Somaini, 'Il binomio imperfetto', 142.
[19] Arcangeli, *Gentiluomini di Lombardia*, 3–70.

be entirely comparable to the principal lords and feudatories of the state, who could not be reduced to the dimension of urban patricians. From these figures, networks of alliances able to cut 'vertically' through the civic organism began, yet not in the stable forms of institutional factions, but in terms that did not allow a patrician system to emerge throughout the fifteenth century.

Indeed, the vertical divisions of urban society into factions were not the only divisions in the cities of the duchy, nor were they the only focus of recent attention. Party divisions were sometimes intertwined with or replaced by horizontal levels related to social class or profession. Divisions of a territorial nature, by quarter or other division within settlements, could also assume great importance. Far from drying up at the arrival of the Visconti *signoria*, the initiatives of lower 'popular' classes of Milanese society – which in actual fact were important in the first phases of the *signoria* – continued to be expressed long into the future, at the time of the Ambrosian republic as well as at the fall of Ludovico Sforza when a *università popolare* devised its own *capitoli* (agreements) and emerged on to the political scene by virtue of its rioting. Also, in places where the relevance and importance of factions in the organisation of the local political life were fully acknowledged and calmly accepted, the weight of social and economic divisions could lead the dukes to support an equal representation within the faction. For example, Gian Galeazzo did this in Parma in 1388, by imposing a larger portion of *artifices* in an administration whose composition was already defined in terms of factions. Galeazzo Maria Sforza behaved in a similar fashion a century later with Cremona, when he supported a principle of equal social representation within each faction. Nonetheless, it is undeniable that the significance of city factions may explain the way in which civic identity could fade away in the Visconti–Sforza state. This is clearly a point of crucial importance in the context of the renewed discussion on the role of the city in the regional state, thus explaining the interest driven by the theme of the factions in recent research. It must be said that this interest has also allowed scholars to study the 'normal' and not necessarily episodic, violent or seditious existence of parties and factions even in contexts in which the sense of belonging to a faction did not end up obscuring the identity of the city.

Therefore, if currently few doubts remain regarding the 'public' relevance and the institutionalised character of factions in the state of Milan and their inclusion among the active actors, recent studies more cautiously assess the real existence and relevance of the Guelf and Ghibelline factions at a higher level than that of the city. Several scholars indicate that, although this level of 'partisanship' or 'meta-factiousness', as it has been described, remained more elusive, it consisted in a 'reality that would excite people even if only evoked, activate networks of contacts, put in contact distant areas, make available an enormous legacy of immaterial resources that materially translate into political action'.[20] In Lombardy, too, it can be affirmed that at the beginning of the fourteenth century the game played between 'meta-factions' (as a system of connections not based on territorial proximity) and the territorial state to guarantee political integration on a regional scale was won by the latter. However, within the framework of the state the Guelf and Ghibelline channels continued to present themselves as crucial instruments of connection, able as they always were to 'guarantee and smooth political and social exchanges'.[21] Therefore, for instance, belonging to one faction or the other could be important in the selection of an officer; the dukes considered the political leanings of candidates, as did their subjects. The neighbours (*vicini*) of Bellinzona demanded from Francesco Sforza in 1450 that in their area only men of 'Ghibelline and not of Guelf hue' ought to become *castellani* and constables. Needless to say, the 'interstatal' value of faction identity was always susceptible to reignition, ready to re-establish its importance in favouring changes and mutations within the established state and territorial system despite no longer being able to break up the system. They could encourage such changes by promoting the passage of one city or a territory under a different domination or by favouring the accession of Francesco Sforza over his challenger Giacomo Piccinino.

Bearing in mind the specific circumstances of each case, an 'inextricable nexus' has been established between parts, factions and great aristocratic and feudal families.[22] In recent years, much attention has been dedicated to the weight of rural seigneurs and feudatories, allowing, in turn, the phenomenon to be 'quantified' in a new light confirming that it was not limited to the peripheral and marginal corners of the dominions, but was widespread in 'unexpected' areas. With regard to the *contado* of Milan itself, for instance, the surprisingly large presence of castles in the fourteenth century has been observed; furthermore, over the fifteenth century, large portions of Milanese territory were characterised by the presence of lords who were mainly connected with lateral branches of the Visconti family.

Needless to say, extreme differences underlie the expression 'clusters of seigneurial-feudal power': the geographical sizes of the individual lordships, with all the correlated issues in terms of administrative

---

[20] Gentile, '"Postquam malignitates temporum"', 257.
[21] Della Misericordia, 'La "coda"', 371.   [22] Gentile, 'Aristocrazia signorile', 153.

management, could be very different, as could the origins and antiquity of those powers and their ability to protect jurisdictional and fiscal privileges maintained by the various *domini*. 'Small states' of lords, of traceable origins and endowed with an independent title of legitimacy, as well as complex bureaucratic-administrative structures, were completely different from newly formed dominions whose existence was justified merely by a feudal investiture and possibly whose feudatory mainly considered them to be sources of income. Important differences have also been identified between situations in which the *dominus/homines* relationship appeared to be qualified on purely territorial terms – at times mediated by solid structures of the community – and cases in which the lordship took the form of a relationship between the lord and his individual protégés without a precisely defined territorial dimension. Referring to the precise issue of assured protection, the need to carefully verify the long-term solidity of the relationship between the lords and their subjects has led to an acute observation of the times of crisis for this relationship: situations in which either through incompetence or disinterest the lord's authority displayed an attitude that did not correspond to expectations, even ending up by being openly contested. Nevertheless, studies have more frequently underlined the effective military, fiscal and jurisdictional tutelage that they guaranteed to the *homines* and the lasting interest that the latter demonstrated in supporting their lords and recognising in them the privileged channel enabling a relationship with the broader political picture. Such recognition and support – if necessary even military – represented the 'treasure' of the great aristocratic families, being the primary resource to maintain their role and have their role acknowledged in the state and by the prince. Marco Gentile has recently reasserted that this role was not marginal, but that on the contrary it was a 'deep structure' in the Milanese state of the fourteenth and fifteenth centuries. Gamberini has emphasised that, both in the Visconti and in the Sforza eras, the power of the aristocratic families was essential in determining the impossibility of interpreting the dominion as a privileged relationship between the princes and the cities.[23] The great aristocratic lineages were able to stand out as instrumental in integrating the political places of the state of Milan; they were not 'flaws' in an otherwise established structure.

Studies in the first decade of the twenty-first century, mainly those of Massimo Della Misericordia, have added an important piece to this complex puzzle by emphasising the role of protagonists in political mediation that rural communities in significant areas of the state had

---

[23] *Ibid.*, 155; Gamberini, 'Ottre la città', 47–8.

gained by the end of the fifteenth century. For instance, at the beginning of the fifteenth century in Valtellina, rural lords and faction leaders played a central role as intermediaries between the city and local society. At the end of the century, though, they 'had to give precedence to a generation of new mediators, including influential people of lower social standing (notaries, pettifoggers, small merchants, money-lenders and so on)', 'common' men whose political course developed within the councils of individual communities and in the federation that brought together all the communes of the valley and who interpreted their role of political mediators not as 'built on independent, personal power, but as taking up functions upon formal delegation from the community'.[24] Elsewhere, events took a different course and communities struggled to have their voice heard or to have recourse to civic or noble mediators to be heard. In the Milanese *contado*, for example, the existence of stable federative organisations for the communities, equipped with representatives still active at the end of the fifteenth century, did not coincide with the emergence of a new social class of intermediaries born in the communities: this role was for people from outside the communes, city-dwellers or rural nobles. However, that some communities undoubtedly assumed an active role in supra-local mediation is no longer a marginal fact destined for a footnote to robust paradigms centred around the city, but represents a significant stimulus to debate those paradigms.

The centre

One of the most relevant aspects of recent research dedicated to the various actors within the political scene of the dominion is, without a doubt, the attention given to the idealistic perspectives in which they operated. Through an investigation of a full range of documentary and non-documentary sources, the various political languages to which subjects referred, as a framework of reference for the appropriateness of their practices, have emerged. Such a level of ideas was not an empty theoretical postulation, but possessed a performative nature: in other words, it could construct and transform reality; it could strongly condition action. This position within historiography leads indeed to restored significance at the level of 'discourse' but, within the field of Visconti–Sforza historiography, it remains a long way from constituting an escape into the 'world of ideas'. Those who have focused on this type of analysis are careful not to offer a reading in which the important place of the performative nature of languages is transformed and the relationships

[24] Della Misericordia, 'La "coda"', 374–5.

between these languages and the practical actions proceed univocally from the former into the latter. As a consequence, reference to a dialectical relationship between the level of representation and the level of practice, between the politics of actions and political actions, remains stable.

From this theoretical framework of reference, it has been possible to unearth, for instance, the terms of pacts, and of contracts, according to which communities or great aristocrats perceived their relationship with the prince; also 'more or less coherent fragments of a republican language'[25] have emerged from the petitions of the rural communes, often noting the duke's opposition or proposal of alternative discourses instead of sharing these ideals. Yet, recently, the attempt to restore vibrancy to the portrayal of state organisation has often focused on the 'pictures of power' put forward from the centre. There is no lack of new studies on 'events' of government focusing on the evolution of central and peripheral magistrates' courts, legislation, financial and fiscal policies, the army, diplomacy, control over ecclesiastical institutions and so on. It is nevertheless true that such studies gradually overlapped with a growing attention to the princes' 'discourses' so as to suggest a stronger reading of the role of the *signori* and the dukes, of their ability to have an impact on political and institutional equilibria. As an illustration of this, Nadia Covini highlighted the way in which the appropriate attention to the 'weak effects' sometimes obtained by the legal decisions of the dukes should not overshadow the fact that those degrees 'expressed high ideological and political values and represented crucial moments in the construction of the relationship between rulers and their subjects',[26] thus deserving of study also from this perspective. 'With the aim of understanding how [...] the Visconti and the Sforza themselves interpreted their authority and status', Jane Black, however, focused on the references that, from the time of Azzone onwards, the rulers made to their 'plenitude of power', as well as the contemporary debate on this very issue spreading among jurists.[27] Federica Cengarle has devoted in-depth study to those principles upon which the role of the *signore* was legitimised over time, again emphasising the way in which the 'rhetorical construction' of power was not extraneous to its 'real exercise' but was one of its fundamental components.[28]

The determination not to make the study of government and administration into 'a sum of acts and deeds'[29] has long characterised the

---

[25] Della Misericordia, 'Decidere e agire', 377.   [26] Covini, '*La balanza drita*', 121.
[27] Black, *Absolutism*, 2.   [28] Cengarle, 'Le arenghe', 57.
[29] As is well known, this expression was coined by Angela De Benedictis: *Repubblica per contratto*, 399.

historiography on the Visconti and the Sforza. The great attention dedicated to the theme of legitimisation of power of the *signori* by studying the titles, imperial vicar and duke, which the Visconti and the Sforza held, suffices as an example. These titles were not considered as frills of an otherwise established authority but as essential moments attesting to the 'separation' of the central power from the conditioning of the subordinate society. However, as already mentioned, the increased interest in the changeable theoretical scenarios in which the Visconti and the Sforza affirmed their role and actions in the course of the fourteenth and fifteenth centuries must be noted. The significance of these approaches is noteworthy because the state was no longer interpreted as a 'neutral field' in which the demands of several actors were ranged against each other, but instead was seen as a fully fledged protagonist in its own right. Together with studies more directly linked to government practices, the many interests in the 'centre' indeed contributed to stress the multitude of orientations and political approaches that characterised the *signori* and dukes of Milan. The difference in style of government of the two brothers Bernabò and Galeazzo II Visconti in the second part of the fourteenth century, for example, has been recently highlighted. The former, inspired by an authoritarian concept of the dominion, was prone to intervene energetically regarding its structure by reasserting his will over everything. Galeazzo II and after him his son Gian Galeazzo showed themselves to be careful in maintaining the established equilibria and by respecting pacts and customs.

New aspects and more nuanced observations now emerge regarding individual princes. For example, Filippo Maria was traditionally regarded, at least during his last years in power, as a restorer of city privileges and an enemy of noble and seigneurial powers. An opposing reading gives us the image of a duke indeed committed to fighting the ancient aristocratic families, but not attentive to the restoration of a political and territorial structure centred around the role of the city. On the contrary, it seems that in the 1430s Filippo was busy 'correcting it by partially eroding more or less substantially the old *contadi* of the cities',[30] by granting to a large number of feudatories land that was then 'separated' from the urban district, which no longer benefited from it financially or politically. The jurists close to the prince willingly recognised that these fiefs held the rank of 'province', previously reserved for city districts; this demonstrates that a more pluralist polity developed not just because of a change in practice or because of a change in theory, but from both types of change simultaneously.

[30] Cengarle, *Immagine di potere*, 96.

Conclusion

From several perspectives, the necessity, expressed a decade ago, of investigating the 'highly complex and articulated features' of the Lombard political picture of the fourteenth and fifteenth centuries – both its centre and its periphery – appears to have been considerably fulfilled and, even more importantly, attained with results that suggest different overall pictures in comparison to the paradigm of a definitively victorious alliance between princes and cities. This is not to say that by looking 'beyond the cities', to recall the title of a recent study by Andrea Gamberini, these disappear from the stage. However, it seems to be increasingly difficult to recognise, in the agreement between the dukes and urban bodies, the largely prevalent, if not unique, lever of integration within the regional political space. Throughout the fifteenth century, together with the *cives*, members of the feudal aristocracy could still retain a role of mediation, possibly as chief of a faction or as representatives of rural communities. Ultimately, in this longevity of the polyphonic dialogue, in the irreducible plurality of the networks of relations, the specificity of the Lombard political structure both in the Visconti and in the Sforza age seems to be identified.

In the presence of this multilayered landscape, there is indeed a feeling not only of having gained but also of having lost something. In particular, lost is the possibility of identifying in a clear way the different 'phases' of evolution of the political scene, which the assumption of the relationship prince/city as the main interpretative line allowed. In a scenario in which the pluralist rather than urban-centric system of the dominion is no longer restricted to the fourteenth century but becomes a 'persistent tradition'[31] still alive at the end of the fifteenth century, it is difficult to identify points of discontinuity and to propose linear timescales. It is as though the tradition of a pluralistic state has no starting or ending point, and therefore has no 'history' at all. As soon as it is acknowledged that the role of the feudal and aristocratic component in the material constitution of the state is still decisive, it becomes difficult to identify in the promulgation of the decree *del maggior magistrato*, or, in more general terms, in the rule of Filippo Maria traditionally seen as a watershed in periodisations, the signs of a turning point. Chittolini's recent observations come back to mind, the points he made regarding the possible risks that are connected with research focused on 'horizontally widening the plurality and multiplicity of the objects of study, of the active actors, of the identities and of the practices put in place'.

---

[31] Della Misericordia, 'La "coda"', 379.

Such risks included the loss of the 'temporal dimension, in the sense of the long term within which subdivisions and lines of evolution can be stressed' and the transformation of the past into some kind of 'immobile repertoire of various and different cases, a sum of unconnected and unrelated moments'.[32]

Leaving aside an initial disorientation, the widening of analyses at a 'horizontal level' of the Visconti–Sforza historiography of the last decade did not coincide with the exclusion of the 'time factor' from the research area. 'Discontinuity' of dynamic evolution is indeed a term that is increasingly linked with the institutional 'plurality' of the dominions. However, this approach does not translate into the assumption of a 'composite Lombardy', which is immutably equal to itself, a quiet sea in which both all and nothing happens: Chittolini's 'immobile repertoire of various cases'. The discussion of the multiple political actors who are always active on the stage has continued to be accompanied by a feeling of the progressive growth of their interrelations. The Visconti–Sforza state, beyond the mutable equilibria of its clusters of power found within, continues to appear as a key moment in the slow but decisive expansion of the political spaces which characterised the late Middle Ages. The Milanese formation crumbles in 1402 and 1447, no longer, however, at the death of Francesco Sforza or at the murder of Galeazzo Maria. With the beginning of the Italian Wars, its 'constituent elements' – cities, communities, factions, aristocratic families – found 'new spaces in which to act and negotiate'; they display a new vitality. Nonetheless, the same aspirations of independence of the beginning of the century do not emerge in 1499. Pavia offered to Louis XII some chapters in which it seems intent in deleting 'the very memory of extra-city relationship and of the existence of a regional state'. However, Pavia is the exception, in a context in which 'autonomy or even independence from the capital'[33] no longer seemed to be questioned.

With regard to the longevity of the constituent elements, it is clearly noticeable that the new emphasis laid on this vitality has not led to it being postulated as immutable between the fourteenth and fifteenth centuries. Identifying the influence of the territorial aristocracy as one of the 'deep structures' of the state – which continues to operate under the waves of dynastic changes – continued to make the introduction of chronological turning points necessary, assessing the moments and places in which this power increased or decreased. Attributing importance to the role of the rural communities in the architecture of the state does not imply the renunciation of a careful reconstruction of the period in which their political initiative could show. Yet, it is important to

---

[32] Chittolini, 'Un paese lontano'.   [33] Arcangeli, *Aggregazioni*, 396.

highlight the actual depth of the 'temporal dimension' in current scrutiny into the multiplicity of actors in the political arena, that is, when the focus is on the identity of these actors. Extending these investigations to suggestions coming from lines of historiography particularly concerned with the theme of praxis has undoubtedly brought more careful considerations on the evolving and dynamic nature of the social and political identities to the fore. The various bodies of Lombard society of the fourteenth and fifteenth centuries are currently considered in a less static perspective; care is taken not to consider them as points of departure, as if the groups' borders and their respective sense of belonging have been established once and for all. The emphasis moves towards identifying the *process of becoming* of the collective political actors – cities, communities, factions and so on – and the changes in relation to the concrete actions of the individuals that belonged to them, while at the same time considering reciprocal interactions thus truly and ultimately assessing the 'vertical', temporal value of these actors.

Nevertheless, the increased attention to the evolving nature of the forms of social life seems to be far from reaching reductionist results. Perhaps this is the last common and firmly rooted trait of the recent historiography on the Visconti–Sforza state on which to expand. Not reifying institutions and social bodies does not imply the negation of their autonomous importance. Small seigneurial states, cities, rural communities, the very frame of the state are considered as products of acts and deeds, but also as something different and larger than their sum; they are considered, in other words, as structures that are capable of direct choices and individual behaviour. I believe this theoretical option is rather widespread, which understandably explains why recent historiography is interested in political languages, in 'discourses'. Needless to say, this option does not coincide with the necessity of recognising certain identities – those of citizens, faction members, community members – as important even when they were not. From a theoretical perspective, it is significant that, in the study of both the centre and the peripheral areas, the attitude is to include among the subjects of the investigations the 'weight' of the institutions, and the willingness to focus, once the real display of power has been brought to light, on 'the "unique form" in which that system organising power is shaped'.[34] Having lost some of its ancient 'communal chromosomes', to use this famous expression of Gian Maria Varanini's, even in its most recent readings, the history of the Visconti–Sforza state continues to present robust 'institutional chromosomes'.

---

[34] Chittolini, 'Considerazioni conclusive', 598.

9 The feudal principalities: the west (Monferrato, Saluzzo, Savoy and Savoy-Acaia)

Alessandro Barbero

Introduction: the importance of a definition

In the late Middle Ages most of the territory making up modern Piedmont was controlled by three princely dynasties: the counts of Savoy (dukes from 1416), the marquises of Monferrato and the marquises of Saluzzo.[1] The Savoy dynasty, which also ruled over vast possessions on the other side of the Alps, was undoubtedly the strongest: between the thirteenth and fifteenth centuries, its domains underwent a period of steady expansion, while, in contrast, the marquisate of Saluzzo shrank considerably and that of Monferrato struggled to defend its possessions. However, the Savoy state was itself squeezed between two far more powerful rivals: the kingdom of France and the Visconti–Sforza state. These curbed its expansion and created the political circumstances in which both marquisates were able to survive.

There is a technical justification for defining these states as feudal principalities. Count Umberto, the founder of the house of Savoy, and marquis Aleramo, the antecedent of both the Monferrato and Saluzzo lineages, were public officials working in the kingdom of Burgundy and the Italic kingdom, respectively, during the tenth and eleventh centuries. Their successors continued to recognise feudal loyalty to the emperor: this was still true in 1530, when the duke of Savoy, Carlo II, took precedence as the most senior imperial prince at Charles V's coronation in Bologna. All three dynasties came from what were essentially rural roots; as counts and marquises, they were accustomed to governing the territory through feudal investitures to families of vassals. They used

---

[1] A fourth dynasty, the princes of Acaia, was founded in the late thirteenth century through an agreement between count Amedeo V of Savoy and his cousin, Filippo, in which the latter was granted a prerogative over most of the territories ruled by the Savoy in Piedmont. However, the Acaia remained a cadet branch, subordinate to the main dynasty, which severely punished its occasional attempts to implement an independent political line and, when the last prince of Acaia died in 1418, duke Amedeo VIII reabsorbed the principality into the Savoy state.

feudal investiture with greater juridical awareness, were stricter in controlling its forms, and showed less of a tendency to experiment than other Italian potentates.[2]

These circumstances justify the use of the category of feudal principalities, provided that it is clear that it is not exhaustive. The relationship between the prince and the territory he controlled was far from being exclusively feudal: equally importantly, a number of towns and villages swore loyalty to the prince and acknowledged him as their *dominus* without feudal intermediaries. Therefore, this definition does not imply any absolute distinction between these principalities and their neighbouring Italian states. Indeed, over time, the long struggle between the Savoy state and the Visconti emphasised their similarities: the Visconti dynasty learned to make more widespread and confident use of feudal practices and relied less on urban *contadi* as the organisational backbone of its territory;[3] in turn, the dukes of Savoy learned to wage war using professional Italian *condottieri*, rather than relying on recruiting men-at-arms through vassals and community levies, as they had done before.[4]

Lastly, in terms of typology, the uniqueness of the Savoy state lay in its bipartite nature, part French and part Italian; while the marquisates of Monferrato and, above all, Saluzzo can be classified as 'small states' whose princes survived in the fifteenth century by offering their services as *condottieri* to their more powerful neighbours. However, apart from these differences, all three come under the general heading of princely state, or *état princier*.[5]

The structure of the territory

A distinguishing factor of the territories governed by the Piedmontese principalities was the presence of numerous small towns, mostly without a *contado*, and a dense network of rural communities. The pattern of

---

[2] Castelnuovo, 'Omaggio, feudo e signoria'; Del Bo, *Uomini e strutture*, 37–45.
[3] Cengarle, *Immagine di potere*. For the distinction between principalities 'with a feudal base' and those 'with an urban base', see Chittolini, 'I principati italiani', and Varanini, 'Governi principeschi e modello cittadino'.
[4] Barbero, 'L'organizzazione militare'. On the organisation of war, in general, which will not be discussed further in this chapter, see, for Savoy, Castelnuovo, 'Les maréchaux en Savoie'; Barbero, 'I soldati del principe'; Biolzi, *Avec le fer et la flamme*. For Monferrato, see Settia, '"Sont inobediens et refusent servir"'.
[5] Savy, 'Gli stati italiani del XV secolo'; Gentile and Savy (eds.), Noblesse et *états princiers*. The marquisate of Saluzzo in the Quattrocento included about seventy communities, some held in fief by around twenty vassals (Barbero, 'Appannaggi, infeudazioni, riacquisti'); the marquisate of Monferrato had 110 vassals with 170 enfeoffed communities, many fewer under direct lordship (Del Bo, *Uomini e strutture*, 42, 45).

rural settlement took the form of villages, grouped around a parish church and dominated by the seigneurial castle. The spread of the *appoderamento*, essentially a fifteenth- and sixteenth-century phenomenon, did not undermine this network of village communities, all of which were robustly organised and capable of obtaining franchises or statutes through continuous political dialogue with the lords. Contrary to the situation in the rest of northern and central Italy, few of these farming communities depended on a city. By far the greater proportion were controlled by noble families, whether rural magnates or even urban nobility, and much more rarely by a bishop or monastery; others depended directly on the prince and were governed by an official representative.

The aggregate number of communities making up a state was not fixed: it was enough for a noble family or a community to decide to change loyalty, for whatever reason, and the boundaries would change. This resulted in a certain degree of territorial discontinuity because the outcome of negotiations, and the pressures exerted on various individual subjects, could lead to different results. Communities and lords who recognised the sovereignty of one or other prince would frequently alternate, above all along the borders or in areas of friction between one state and another. In the Canavese, where for years the loyalty of the local nobility was disputed between Monferrato and the Savoy, the matter was finally resolved in 1389 through the arbitration of Gian Galeazzo Visconti when he assigned the homage of some nobles to the marquises. However, the solution did not always respect geographical constraints, with the result that some villages, albeit completely surrounded by Savoy possessions, became part of the marquisate and remained so until 1630. Instead, in the Biellese and Vercellese, areas that were contested by the Savoy and Visconti for over half a century, there were even *villae mixtae*, in which some inhabitants were under the jurisdiction of the Savoy, and others under the Visconti.

This did not mean, of course, that the frontiers were not well defined. The inhabitants of any given area would have known precisely what jurisdiction they came under. But there were no linear frontiers, based on geographical features and easily shown on a map. Perhaps the first example of the need for rationalisation, where acquired rights were sacrificed in order to obtain a more clearly defined linear frontier, was the case of Vercelli: in an agreement of 1427 duke Amedeo VIII of Savoy ceded to Filippo Maria Visconti a number of localities on the east bank of the Sesia which Vercelli had always claimed as part of its own district. In this way, the river became the frontier between the two states. But any cartographical representation of a principality in this period should, in general, portray a hotchpotch of communal territories rather than a single homogeneous territory.

The nature of relations between each community and the prince constitutes one of the key matrices for the organisation of the state. Administrative documents distinguish between *comunitates domini*, whether domain or direct lordships, and *terre nobilium*, feudal or mediated. The latter belonged to the state as a result of the homage paid to the prince by the local lord, while the former depended on the prince because of bilateral agreements that were technically not feudal at all and, in most cases, had been negotiated more or less freely. Of all three principalities, Monferrato could certainly claim a higher proportion of vassallatic relationships, with more than 110 families of vassals by the late fifteenth century, while it had fewer domain lands;[6] in the Savoy territories, on the other hand, the influence of the powerful feudal aristocracy was offset by the importance of the communities under the prince's direct lordship.

There was no fixed separation between mediated and unmediated localities, because a prince could decide to alienate crown lands to create new fiefs. This policy was systematically implemented by the marquises of Saluzzo, who formed feudal appanages for various cadet branches of the dynasty in the fourteenth and fifteenth centuries and alienated an Alpine valley on each occasion.[7] However, generally speaking, investitures of domain lands were a limited phenomenon: many communities that depended directly on the prince held privileges that guaranteeed their non-alienability, and a large proportion of land remained under direct control. Contrary to the situation in southern Italy, towns had never been assigned in fief to vassals. Although unwritten, this rule was so widely applied that it leaves no doubt as to the strong leverage applied by towns when negotiating submission to the prince.

Taking precisely this aspect as a starting point – the contractual capacity of local communities in their relations with central power – we can analyse the bipartite nature between domain communities and enfeoffed communities still further. Among the former we find communities that had depended on the prince from time immemorial, or had become subordinate without negotiating preferential conditions, granting him full overlordship and undertaking to pay tributes solely in exchange for protection; and stronger communities, both urban and rural, which had obtained franchises at the time of submission and

---

[6] Del Bo, *Uomini e strutture*, 38, 42, 45.
[7] Barbero, 'Appannaggi, infeudazioni, riacquisti'. The custom was rarer in Savoy and Monferrato: Del Bo, *Uomini e strutture*, 196.

therefore enjoyed a degree of power-sharing, retaining a quota of the fines and even controlling the fortifications. Among the *terre nobilium*, on the other hand, were places whose lord was a vassal to the count, and who therefore had received the investiture and held the entire jurisdiction in fief, and others, albeit much rarer, where investiture only granted the local lord rents, honours and seigneurial rights, while the prince reserved all or part of the jurisdiction.

Then there were localities whose jurisdiction lay in the hands of bishops or monasteries, which technically, at the start of our period, cannot be regarded as part of the state, but which became so, *de facto*, to the extent that the prince could hand out benefices and intervene to curb the jurisdictional monopolies held by the ecclesiastical authority. Lastly, there were rural localities that depended on an urban centre that, in turn, was subject to the prince; this was a category whose limited diffusion highlighted a marked difference between these feudal principalities and their more powerful neighbour, the Visconti–Sforza state. It was often the case that a number of immediately adjacent villages were regarded as being dependent on a town, and indeed there were also castles in the countryside that controlled several villages. But it was quite rare for the submission of a small urban community to bring an entire, ready-structured *contado* in miniature under the prince's dominion, this *contado* constituting in itself one of the elements of the state. Such cases appeared to be decidedly secondary in the structure of the feudal principalities: while *terre separate* (separate lands) appeared to be an administrative exception elsewhere, here they were the rule. In conclusion, at least six different forms of dependence can be identified binding a locality to the ruling house with the result that its territory was deemed part of the state.

Alongside these juridical distinctions, the administrative structure of the princely states was influenced by both geographical and historical factors. Built up through the gradual expansion that brought increasingly vast territories under its control, at different stages and using varying juridical forms, the Savoy state, or rather the half that lay *citra montes* (on this side of the mountains), was seen by its administrators as comprising various heterogeneous sectors. The accounts detailing subsidies granted in the fifteenth century by the *patria Pedemoncium* follow a repetitive format: first of all, there was the *terra vetus*, the lower Susa valley and the Lanzo valleys, home to the first territories of the Italic kingdom that the Savoy's forebears had inherited by the late eleventh century (this was the only area to form a *balivato*, following the usual pattern in the dynasty's transalpine domains). Then came the *terra principatus*, or the lands that formed the appanage granted to the

Acaia princes until 1418. Then there were the *lancee spezate Pedemontis*, namely those towns, Cuneo, Chieri and Mondovì, subjugated only during the fourteenth century: since they contributed a reasonably sized *contado* and enjoyed extensive tax exemptions, they were therefore calculated separately. The possessions of the Canavese nobility, who were obliged, not without difficulty, to pay homage to the Savoy during the fourteenth century, were also regarded as a separate entity. Lastly, there were the *terre ultra Duriam*, also known as the *terre Lombardie patrie ducalis*, the result of a recent push towards the Sesia river, which at times were administered by a captain-general appointed specifically for this area, and which in particular included the *capitanato* of Santhià, the *podesteria* of Biella and what remained of the vast urban district of Vercelli.[8]

The internal structure of the marquisate of Monferrato appears to have been dictated instead more by geography than historical events. When the parliament of vassals and communities met in 1305 to decide who would inherit the legacy of marquis Giovanni I, who had died with no male heir, it listed, with no particular qualification, the representatives of the localities that made up Monferrato, and still do so today. The list then went on to include the representatives of the lands *de ultra Burmidam*, beyond the Bormida; *de ultra Tanagrum*, beyond the Tanaro; and finally, for the lands *a Pado citra et de Canapicio et Val de Matis*, which included the communities on the far side of the Po that had been taken from the Vercellese and the nobles of the Canavese and the lower Lanzo valley, where the marquis had to compete for homage against the count of Savoy. A charter from emperor Sigismund dated 1414 refers to an older territorial division, one that had not existed for centuries, which identifies the marquisate with the two counties of Acquesana – based on the episcopal city of Acqui – and the Canavese; the former included all the localities, jurisdictions and homages held by the marquis *in toto territorio citra Tanagrum deversus ripariam maris*, and *ultra Tanagrum deversus Pedemontem et Astam*, and therefore using the Tanaro river as the main reference point for an internal division of the area, to which the localities *in Canapitio et toto territorio ultra Padum*[9] were added later.

The local offices

Each community, whether urban or rural, was governed by a local executive authority based in the castle, which maintained public order,

---

[8] Barbero, 'La struttura amministrativa', 10–12.
[9] Bozzola, *Parlamento del Monferrato*, 3–5; Moriondo, *Monumenta Aquensia*, 83–7.

collected fines and tributes, and approved the drafting of statutes, save in cases where it shared part of these responsibilities and profits with the communal bodies. In the *terre nobilium*, the lord himself, or a *podestà* or castellan appointed by him, held these powers, above all in those all too frequent situations where the lordship was not vested in a single individual but in a consortile. In domain communities these same functions were delegated to an official appointed by the prince, who was almost always called a castellan in rural situations, while in towns he was known by a variety of names: *vicario*, *podestà* or *capitano*. Depending on the situation, and above all in the more complex urban situations, he was flanked by receivers, tax collectors or *clavari*, who were responsibile for managing the finances and accounts, and by judges of the first instance. Directly above these local officials were the prince and his council; in the Savoy state, however, given that the ruler was more often than not on the far side of the Alps, his role was filled by a *capitaneus Pedemoncium*, or later by a lieutenant-general, an office of considerable political stature whose functions ceased as soon as the prince crossed back over the mountains.

The local functionaries were appointed using letters patent, remained in office at the prince's pleasure, and were paid a stipend. They had to provide detailed accounts for all revenues and expenditure; in the case of the Savoy, their accounts were always audited, albeit sometimes many years later, by the Audit Chamber (Camera dei Conti) based in the castle of Chambéry. However, the appointment of a castellan was a very different matter in political terms from the appointment of a public civil servant in a modern state. It was always the outcome of personal relations between the prince and a man who had many different ways of obtaining the post. When the official was the prince's vassal, as was often the case, it is reasonable to assume that trust played an important role in the choice; but it is also true that every official had to pay an advance when he took possession of the post and it was therefore difficult to remove him without settling this debt. In some instances, offices were awarded directly as security for a large sum lent to financiers who were not even native to the country.[10]

In other cases, which became increasingly frequent over time, offices were obtained through cash advances and political recommendations from men with shared local interests, who owned or were seeking to create a seigneurial domain, if it was in a rural setting, or a hegemonic position among the urban notables. Public office became a stepping

---

[10] On this and what follows, see Barbero, 'La struttura amministrativa', 26–30, and Barbero, 'La venalità degli uffici'.

stone to achieve this purpose: Ribaldino Beccuti, a doctor in law, Turin's richest citizen and head of the city's most aristocratic family, held the post of judge of Turin without a break from 1499 to 1533. Over time it also became increasingly common to find that a community obtained the right to present a list of candidates from which the prince would then choose the official. In these cases, the official would then act as a broker between local interests and central government requirements, rather than the latter's representative. The network of offices spread across the territory should therefore not be thought of as a passive instrument at the prince's disposal, but rather as an area of constant negotiation between the prince and the elites, in which each party had something to gain.

The mechanism of loans backed by offices did not yet count as full-blown venality, at least for the highest offices with real political influence; the swarming ranks of minor offices (tax collectors, toll collectors, secretaries in the local courts) were instead regularly farmed out to speculators, much like a *gabella* would be farmed out. Officials managed the appointment of their own deputies in the same way; the tendency for the most influential figures at court to accumulate offices resulted in an increasingly widespread presence of these 'farmers' (*appaltatori*), who exercised the office in practice and pocketed the revenues after having paid an agreed portion to the office-holder. To start with, however, these were purely private agreements but, by the middle of the fifteenth century, they had become so widespread that the prince had to intervene. An attempt was made to regulate the practice in the duchy of Savoy by responding to the generalised complaints from the lowest tiers about the absenteeism of officials and the robbery of their substitutes. Then, in response to a specific request made in 1478 by the Three Estates, it was decided that the prince would appoint the deputies himself. This resulted in a real duplication of territorial offices whereby in practice an office-holder enjoyed only the title and a pension, while his deputy negotiated the terms of appointment directly with the duke.

The widespread presence of these deputies turned the mechanism of office-backed loans into an explicit and organised venal system that anticipated that of the *ancien régime*: candidates were no longer asked for a *prestanza* (loan), but rather a *censo* (bond), which for the most important offices could amount to thousands of *fiorini*; in exchange the holder would retain not only the agreed remuneration, but also all the other revenues generated by the office. Territorial offices, which from the outset were relied on by the great aristocratic families as a means of confirming their own local political influence, offered an attractive route that enabled men capable of managing money to rise through the social ranks. While on paper the network of offices continued to be the main channel through which the duke or marquis imposed their authority locally, in practice the early decades of the sixteenth century led to a sort of 'capitalisation' of offices which were managed indefinitely by real committees of local notables.

The institutions of central government

The main decision-making and judicial body of each state was the prince's council, an extension of the ancient vassallatic court.[11] This body varied in composition since the prince could convene whomever he wanted; the rank of *consiliarius domini* was granted widely, reducing the office largely to an honorary title, while in practice meetings were regularly attended by a select group of leading figures: a few powerful vassals, a bishop or abbot, the financial office-holders and the highest-ranking courtiers. Jurists became an increasingly stable addition to the council, and they were responsible for preparing the cases brought before the council in its capacity as the supreme tribunal. Although tied to the person of the prince, the council could also be convened and take decisions in his absence, give orders in his name and operate to all purposes as a government. In this case it was chaired by the chancellor, the keeper of the seals, a post that was becoming increasingly less technical and more political, given the growing size of the duchy of Savoy and the frequent absences of the prince. Whether held by a great baron, an ecclesiastical figure or a jurist, the post of chancellor of Savoy in the fifteenth century can be regarded as the foremost state office. Appointments were carefully scrutinised; candidates were a focus for lobbying by neighbouring powers, as well as attracting fierce competition between rival factions: in 1462 chancellor Giacomo di Valperga was sentenced to death in a mock trial and drowned in Lake Geneva on charges of attempting to bring the duchy under French rule.

The dual functions of the council, governing the state and acting as an appeal court, became more distinct over time as the judicial procedure became increasingly complex and codified. Those council members who were graduates met to discuss legal affairs separately from the politicians, so occasionally two separate council meetings are recorded on the same day, but in different venues and with different participants. Towards the end of our period the judicial section started to need a permanent seat where its documents could be housed. The jurists in the

---

[11] For a summary, see Barbero, 'La struttura amministrativa'; Castelnuovo, 'Quels offices'; Del Bo, *Uomini e strutture*; Grillo, 'I gentiluomini'.

council became increasingly established in Turin, which was also home to the Studio, the university from which most had graduated; at this point, even if the council remained formally united, contemporary records habitually draw the distinction between the Secret or State Council, and the Council of Justice, with its own president. In Monferrato the council separated into two parts at the end of the fifteenth century, following the constitution of the Senate of Casale based in the small city that acted as the state capital; the minute marquisate of Saluzzo had a single council right to the end.

The greater complexity of the Savoy state led to a further division of the council, this time on a territorial basis. A second council had already been formed in the fourteenth century to supervise legal affairs beyond the Alps: this was comprised solely of jurists and was known as the Council of Chambéry. In turn, the captains and later lieutenant-generals, who had operated in Piedmont since the late fourteenth century, set up their own council, which became a permanent body based in Turin during the fifteenth century, known as the Cismontane Council. Unlike the Council of Chambéry, the Cismontane Council was, to all effects, a replica of the supreme ducal council and was vested with political as well as judicial prerogatives. Moreover, during the frequent emergencies of the late fifteenth century, it acted as a real governing body. By the early sixteenth century the duke of Savoy's council had therefore been divided into four distinct branches; the small nucleus of politicians who assisted the prince in the decision-making process were flanked by a preponderant number of jurists, most of whom resided permanently in Turin, the *de facto* state capital.[12]

Therefore, from the late fifteenth century on, the multiplication of councils and their graduate members marked the emergence of a new power base. The offices of *collaterale*, procurator fiscal and, above all, president of one of these councils were among the most prestigious in the state. Although they were often held by members of the leading aristocratic families, the fact that they were open only to graduates made them an important channel of upward social mobility. The arrival of new men who held major state offices as a result of their own legal qualifications was also a feature of the marquisates of Monferrato and Saluzzo, but on a more limited scale given that there the councils had not multiplied: one or more vicars-general flanked by two or three doctors, holding posts of *collaterale* or simply councillors, sum up the juridical

---

[12] Barbero, 'Un governo per il Piemonte'. On the role of capital played by Turin, see Barbero, 'Il mutamento dei rapporti'.

and political responsibilities granted in the duchy of Savoy to a multiplicity of councils and their presidents.[13]

Another office which became gradually more complex and formalised grew up over time around those responsible for producing documentation. From the fourteenth century onwards all the princes used a body of notaries who went by the title of *secretarius domini*, or also chancellor (*cancelliere*) in Monferrato, following Italian custom. These notaries were also allowed to provide services to private clients, and therefore they were not exclusively public officials. However, they kept special registers for government documents, and these began to form an embryonic archive. During the fifteenth century there was a clear trend for princes to retain secretaries for their sole use; the number of these posts was fixed by special ordinances from time to time and rose steadily. This resulted in the creation of a real governing body, known as the secretariat in the duchy of Savoy, or more usually the chancery in the marquisates. Both had their own rooms in the prince's residence and their own internal hierarchy.

A first secretary appeared sometime in the fifteenth or sixteenth century, a direct forerunner of the secretaries of state under the *ancien régime*. This was not only an executive figure, but also an influential minister through whose hands passed much of the business of government, while, below the secretaries, who were now the holders of enormously prestigious offices involved in political decisions and diplomatic negotiations, were a growing number of scriveners and assistants. Like the council, the secretariat became an important rung on the ladder of power and upward social mobility, and its composition was a sensitive political matter and the subject of public debate. Attempts at reform were frequent in the duchy of Savoy, as were conflicts between the duke and the Piedmontese parliament: the estates pressed for an increased number of secretaries, as well as the separation between those following the duke and those based with the local councils, while, in contrast, the ruler attempted to reduce their number and keep them concentrated in a single body.[14]

The development of financial offices was much more chaotic. In general, all officials and all government bodies were authorised to collect and spend on the prince's behalf, and they therefore kept their own accounts, albeit minimised to a list of revenue and expenditure, with

---

[13] Del Bo, *Uomini e strutture*, 150–6; Gentile, 'Le carriere di Galeazzo e Francesco Cavassa'.
[14] Barbero, 'La struttura amministrativa', 38–41; Castelnuovo, 'Cancellieri e segretari'; Castelnuovo, *Ufficiali e gentiluomini*, 109–13; Del Bo, *Uomini e strutture*, 97–122.

their respective descriptions. From the late thirteenth century the prince was flanked by receivers, whose task was simply to collect the balances paid by the various officials and to keep cash on hand. Towards the middle of the fourteenth century, as revenues – including extraordinary revenues – expanded, treasurers appeared in both Savoy and Monferrato who managed significantly larger cash flows, yet they continued to be based on the same principle as all the other officials: they received income of all kinds and spent monies for various purposes, in accordance with instructions received from the prince.

There was more than one treasurer, and the fact that in the duchy one of them held the post of treasurer-general of Savoy should not lead us to overestimate the rationalisation of the system. The fact that both extraordinary expenditure, in the event of war, and extraordinary revenues, linked to the granting of subsidies by the Three Estates, played an important role in the balance sheets of the time encouraged the creation of *ad hoc* receivers and treasurers: for example, each military campaign of any importance was managed, in financial terms, by a war treasurer; each subsidy was collected by a receiver appointed for the purpose, and all of these officials recorded revenues and outlays in their books that never reached the accounts of the treasurer-general. In short, the situation that Beatrice Del Bo rightly defined as the 'promiscuity of responsibilities'[15] held by financial officials was never resolved and consequently, among other results, it was impossible to forecast budgets, or even to obtain a clear idea of revenue and expenditure.

Inevitably, this led to the burgeoning use of credit, a race in which the treasurers themselves were among the front runners. As far as the prince was concerned, the treasurer was still obliged to keep the necessary cash on hand whatever the circumstances, which meant that if the coffers were empty he had to advance his own. Therefore, treasury offices were always held by financiers with solid cash positions, in a spiralling overlap between public and private interests that guaranteed huge profits to the office-holders, but at the price of enormous personal risk. It was no surprise, therefore, that during the middle years of the fifteenth century, when the duchy of Savoy was embroiled in a disastrous war against Milan and it suddenly realised how dramatically short of cash it was, various reform projects were put forward by these financiers highlighting the deficiencies of the system. It was suggested that the treasurer-general should remain in office for at least six years, in order to provide the necessary continuity; that only he could collect subsidies and donations;

---

[15] Del Bo, *Uomini e strutture*, 180–1, 195.

that all other financial officials should be appointed by him and report to him; that the duke should not collect any direct revenues; and furthermore that the duke could not oblige the treasurer to honour his instructions for payment unless there was sufficient liquidity. These proposals were widely discussed at court but, for the most part, were never implemented. Instead the government created a new office, a general of finances, whose remit was to think up new ways of making money.[16]

The finance officials were also responsible for auditing the accounts submitted at more or less regular intervals by the various governmental bodies and by local officials. In the marquisate of Monferrato, the audit seems to have been carried out sometimes by the treasurers, at other times by the secretaries or the masters of revenues, a generic figure with broadly similar responsibilities. It was some time before a *cancelleria delle entrate* (chancery of revenues) was set up. In the Savoy state, on the other hand, from the late thirteenth century the Camera dei Conti was one of the most important administrative bodies and guaranteed the complete centralisation of the audit process. Accounts were often submitted late and audits could drag on for years; disputes were not easily resolved and there were cases where the heirs of officials finally received payment of outstanding sums decades after they had been due. However, the activity of the chamber, with its staff of auditors managed by a president, a structure clearly distinct from the treasury, was undoubtedly one of the key strengths of the Savoy state. It did not augur well that the expansion of directly farmed offices in the late fifteenth century translated into a drastic reorganisation of the auditing process, given that the *appaltatori* now managed their own revenues and expenditure and were responsible for paying the duke only the agreed *censo*.[17]

The production and preservation of government records by all the offices described above are particularly well illustrated in the case of the Savoy state, the largest of all three and the only one to survive until the unification of Italy. Indeed, its archival collections continued, without a break, to form part of the archives for the court and the chamber throughout the *ancien régime*. Today, the largest *fondi* in the State Archive of Turin are those that were produced by the secretariats, known as *protocolli dei notai ducali e camerali* (registers of the notaries to the duke and chamber, 468 volumes, fourteenth–early sixteenth centuries) and the *conti dei ricevitori e tesorieri generali di Savoia* (accounts compiled

---

[16] Barbero, 'Progetti di riforma'; Barbero, 'L'organizzazione militare', 88–92; Castelnuovo, 'Quels offices'; Del Bo, *Uomini e strutture*, 177–98.
[17] Barbero, 'La struttura amministrativa', 41–5; Demotz, 'Une clé de la réussite'; Del Bo, *Uomini e strutture*, 5–26, 64, 108.

by the auditors and treasurer-generals of Savoy, 152 volumes covering the period 1297–1500). However, the most unusual source, in view of its direct links to the territory, is unquestionably the castellans' accounts, namely the hundreds of parchment rolls from the *castellanie* that were audited and then archived by the Camera dei Conti. While sources for administrative and accounting history abound, very few offer a more narrative slant, such as diplomatic correspondence and letters of remission.[18]

Documentation for the marquisates of Saluzzo and Monferrato has survived in rather more patchy form, primarily because both territories ceased to exist as independent states in the sixteenth century. The former was absorbed into the Savoy duchy after a short-lived personal union with France; the latter was annexed to the duchy of Mantua under Gonzaga rule, before also joining the Savoy state in 1708. In both instances, the documentation finally converged in the State Archive of Turin, but not before it had been moved, selected and reordered, thereby destroying the original organisation. In any event, the analysis of the surviving documentation shows that the output was smaller and less rigidly structured than the records of the Savoy administration.[19]

Courtiers and officials

A common constraint in all historical work on late medieval states is the difficulty of distinguishing between the court in the specific sense of the term, namely the personnel assigned to the domestic service of the prince and his family, and the court understood, more generally, as a bureaucratic organisation made up of the officials employed by the prince who constitute the central state government. The custom of using this wider definition of the court, rather than confining it to merely describing the hierarchy of household officials and servants, runs the risk of underestimating the importance and specificity of the latter, which became increasingly complex and acquired even more pronounced political significance during the late Middle Ages. This confusion can be justified only by the fact that many noblemen simultaneously held posts both in the court hierarchy and in the government; therefore, the distinction becomes secondary in the case of sociological research and prosopographical studies of political groups.[20]

---

[18] Castelnuovo and Andenmatten, 'Produzione documentaria e conservazione archivistica'.
[19] Del Bo, *Uomini e strutture*, 17–31; Grillo, 'Comunità e signori', 223.
[20] I will not discuss the historiography of the court on this occasion; readers should refer to Barbero, 'Corti e storiografia'; Barbero, 'La storia ufficiale'; Castelnuovo, 'Nobles des champs ou nobles de cour?'; or, for questions of ritual and heraldry, to Gentile, *Riti ed emblemi*.

The Savoy court was the largest of the three and was divided into a number of separate 'services' or units.[21] The first, and most important, was the ducal household, which was also known as the *hôtel*; run by the masters of the household (*maggiordomi*), it included gentlemen who served the prince in the official capacity of ducal equerries (*scudieri*), as well as subordinate kitchen and dining-hall staff. The second unit was the chamber which was run by the chamberlains and included, among other offices, those responsible for the duke's body, such as doctors and barbers. The third unit was the stable which was run by the stable equerries who managed the grooms (*palafrenieri*), the stableboys (*stallieri*) and the whole hunting retinue. The ducal chapel and the company of archers were separate units. Moreover, this structure was not fixed and the balance between the various units altered at different times. For example, in the early sixteenth century there was clearly a trend to bring the officials of the chamber under the control of the master of the household, and therefore to see the chamber as part of the *hôtel*. Another relatively important variable was the size of the court assigned to the duchess, a question that also depended on political factors. For example, the household assigned to Beatrice of Portugal, who married Carlo II in 1521, reflected her own status as a king's daughter: her court cost as much as her husband's. It is revealing in this sense that the numerous Portuguese courtiers in her retinue received higher salaries than the locals, and that the women were paid more than the men.[22]

During the period in question it is evident that the numbers of court officials, and their relative stipends, tended to rise: this meant that the court assumed an increasingly important role in the process of binding the nobility to the prince, to use Elias's concept – or, as it is more usually put today, it became a place for negotiation and exchange between the prince and the elites. Some offices acquired purely honorary status, such as the chamberlain who was comparable to the post of ducal councillor; others, like the key post of master of the household (*maggiordomo*), who could sign payment instructions for the largest of all the units within the court, multiplied in number, to the extent that it was necessary to appoint a *grand maître d'hôtel* to whom all the others reported. This inflation of court officials also meant that, by the early sixteenth century, 'shifts' were introduced whereby officials were required to serve three months a year (*quartieri*). This became typical of all

---

[21] Bianchi and Gentile (eds.), *L'affermarsi della corte sabauda*; Barbero, 'La corte ducale sotto Carlo II'.
[22] Barbero and Brero, 'Genre et nationalité'.

ancien régime courts: for example, of the sixty equerries who held office under duke Carlo II, only fifteen served during a given quarter.

The courts of the marquisates of Monferrato and Saluzzo were structured along the same lines, but with less ambitious propagandistic aims and a more modest structure: there were never more than eleven equerries in Monferrato, while, before its expansion in the late fifteenth century, the tiny court at Saluzzo was reduced to a single *maggiordomo* and five *scudieri*, at most. The marquisate courts also lacked any division into separate units, which tended to be replaced by a single hierarchical organisation. In Monferrato, the *scudieri* were at the bottom, then the *camerieri* or chamber courtiers, and the *maggiordomo* at the top. In the late fifteenth century there was a change in terminology, mirroring that found at the Sforza court, whereby the *scudieri* became known as *aulici*, and the *maggiordomo* was called the *siniscalco*; moreover, the appearance of a *primo siniscalco* and a *primo cameriere* was a sign of further hierarchisation. However, all were gentlemen, even if at the court of the Saluzzo the *scudieri* were often foreign aristocrats because there were so few local nobility. This would have been inconceivable at the Savoy court where, if anything, the main issue was to maintain a balance between the traditionally more numerous Savoyard nobility and the Piedmontese.[23]

For these reasons the court was not only a place of negotiation and confrontation between the prince and the nobles, but also of competition and at times even conflict between the factions.[24] In this regard, an analysis of the court, in the narrower sense of the term, can be expanded to include the governing elite, namely those men who had no compunction in combining the posts of ducal chamberlain or *maggiordomo* with territorial offices or those in central government. The research done by Guido Castelnuovo has illustrated the dynamics of this relatively stable, but not sclerotic political society in which there was competition, but not antagonism, between the feudal elite, on the one hand, and the urban and professional elite on the other. The judicial offices were often held by the graduate members of leading noble families, while the holders of the top financial offices passed in a single generation from moneychangers in the *bottega di cambio*, to the feudal nobility. The pathways of social mobility passed through the sale of deputyships and offices, but they regularly culminated with the acquisition of lordships; the number of posts that could guarantee power and wealth, while at the same time requiring more technical financial, and, above all, notarial and juridical

---

[23] Grillo, 'I gentiluomini'; Gentile, 'Il cerimoniale'; Del Bo, *Uomini e strutture*, 76–88, 212–13.
[24] Barbero, 'Le fazioni nobiliari'. On the clash between the Piedmontese and Savoyard factions, see Marini, *Savoiardi e Piemontesi*; Barbero, 'Savoiardi e Piemontesi'.

qualifications, grew over time, yet the political society remained one. In the same way that there was no opposition between centre and periphery, the same people held both local and central offices. If anything, purely local interests coalesced around the deputyships, and the latter's growing importance after the middle of the fifteenth century also pointed to a dislocation between the central institutions, in which by now offices resembled court appointments, and the local institutions over which central control had become increasingly slack.[25]

Relations with the country: statutes and assemblies of the Three Estates

The importance of the communities in the Piedmontese principalities can also be gauged from the wealth of local statutory legislation. As the product of bargaining between the community and the local lord, or directly between the community and the prince in those instances of direct lordship, statutes could not be amended unilaterally. Therefore, for centuries they regulated the framework of everyday life. A particular community could pass from being enfeoffed to being a domain territory, or even pass from one ruler to another, without any change whatsoever to its statutes, unless the community itself wished to make alterations in order to obtain more favourable conditions. Not all communities possessed statutes; many rural localities only achieved them over the years, while others had to make do with more limited immunities and privileges, and many never obtained them, remaining in complete subjection to the lord's power. However, where such statutes existed, they could not be infringed.[26]

The obligation to respect local statutes represents the principal limit to legislative activity undertaken by princes from the late fourteenth century and, above all, during the fifteenth century. The most notable result of these efforts were the *Decreta Sabaudie Ducalia* issued by Amedeo VIII of Savoy in 1430 and those passed a century later by duke Carlo II, although their application remained limited due to the French invasion of 1536. On the contrary, the marquises of Monferrato approved collections of decrees that were less unified and ambitious, while the marquises of Saluzzo issued only isolated edicts. The area of

---

[25] Castelnuovo, 'Quels offices'; Castelnuovo, *Ufficiali e gentiluomini*; for Monferrato, see Del Bo, *Uomini e strutture*; for Saluzzo, see Grillo, 'I gentiluomini'.

[26] These rural statutes and autonomous communal rights have been recently analysed, above all for the marquisate of Saluzzo: Grillo, 'Comunità e signori', 212–22, and Mongiano, '"Predecessorum suorum"'.

greatest innovation was in justice, detailing the procedures used by the appeal courts and extending their responsibilities. These courts represented the main lever available to governments in order to expand their own area of intervention and undermine local autonomy, whether seigneurial or communal. But the Savoy *Decreta* went beyond these procedural aspects. The dukes tried to outline an organised vision of state administration in which they laid out the responsibilities and personnel required in all the component offices; moreover, they devised methods of regulating society, aimed at promoting moral conduct and consolidating social hierarchies, in line with the general trends of society between the late Middle Ages and the early modern period.[27]

Another arena of dialogue between the prince and the country was at the assembly of the estates. As mentioned earlier, the first occasion when the vassals and communities of an entire principality met to deliberate was at the parliament of Monferrato in 1305, which was convened after marquis Giovanni I had died without heirs. On that occasion the marquisate was offered to his nephew, the Greek prince Theodorus Palaeologus. After that, assemblies of the estates met frequently in the marquisate, in the principality of Acaia and in the Savoy state where separate meetings were held for the Savoy *patria* and the *patria Pedemoncium*. Joint meetings involving the whole duchy were more rare. The main role of these assemblies was to authorise the extraordinary contributions demanded by the prince on a variety of occasions; this meant that the government had to explain its intentions to the country and also justify the size of the sums requested. The large number of communities, not only urban, which depended directly on the prince meant that leading members of the peasant farming communities also attended the assemblies, giving them a particularly broad nature.

At times of emergency, like those experienced by the duchy of Savoy on various occasions in the latter half of the fifteenth century, the assembly took on proper governmental functions: it intervened in the struggles between ruling princes, and guided ducal foreign policy. A respected councillor and ducal captain, Luigi Tagliandi, commented to the Sforza ambassador, Gioan Bianco, in 1476: 'although they [the Piedmontese] have a prince, nevertheless, in every important case, it is the Three Estates which deliberate, make decisions and govern this country'. These meetings were therefore important opportunities for open public political debate, a testbed for the prince's leadership and

---

[27] Comba, 'Il progetto di una società'; Patriarca, *La riforma legislativa*; Del Bo, *Uomini e strutture*, 143–9; Grillo, 'Comunità e signori', 224 and note; Mongiano, '"*Predecessorum suorum*"', 101–4.

his government, as well as a considerable curb on their freedom of action. For example, the assembly's reluctance to authorise payments to maintain permanent military forces was undoubtedly damaging to the credibility of duke Carlo II in the dramatic events of the Italian Wars.[28] It is no surprise that the refusal to continue to summon the parliament and to impose new taxes without asking for the country's approval were among the most significant measures – together with traumatic shows of strength, like the unilateral decision taken by the duke of Mantua not to recognise the privileges of the commune of Casale and to abolish its communal council[29] – that allowed the princes of the middle and late sixteenth century to move towards absolute rule by radically altering the power structure on which the political life of these feudal principalities had previously been based.

Conclusion

Anyone who studies the evolution of public administration cannot fail to note the artificiality of the traditional periodisation which imposes a clean break at the end of the fifteenth or start of the sixteenth century. In practice, instead, it is clear that, in this regard, the four centuries from the Trecento to Seicento form a relatively compact period during which the organigram of state institutions, the organisation of taxation and warfare, the internal dynamics of the office-holding class, the princely ideology and the theatre of court all undergo a remarkable evolution, while remaining within a system of shared reference points. It is no coincidence that the traditional view, which sees the Savoy state being completely rebuilt on new foundations laid during the reign of Emanuele Filiberto (1559–80) has been largely corrected by recent research: many of the structural innovations attributed to this duke – ranging from the choice of Turin as his capital to the introduction of *servizio a quartieri*, or quarterly shifts for courtiers, and the creation of a rural militia – had already been established by his predecessors, or at least were based on political and cultural conditions that had emerged in earlier decades.

At the same time, an analysis of the Piedmontese principalities highlights the concentration of particularly significant changes between the second half of the fifteenth century and the middle of the sixteenth. In the case of the Savoy state, the most studied of all three and the only one

---

[28] On the activities of these assemblies, see Koenigsberger, 'The Parliament of Piedmont'; but, above all, the vast collection of documents assembled by Tallone, *Parlamento sabaudo* (cited here, vol. V, 180) and Bozzola, *Parlamento del Monferrato*.

[29] Raviola, *Il Monferrato gonzaghesco*.

to survive as an independent state after the Italian Wars, the principal changes can undoubtedly be identified as the expansion of the farming out of public offices and their patrimonialisation, the abolition of the assemblies of the Three Estates immediately after Emanuele Filiberto's return, and a far-reaching reorganisation of the production of records. Indeed, during the course of the sixteenth century, the latter resulted in the abolition of the main series of documents produced by the public administration during the previous two centuries, and their replacement with new forms characterised, among other aspects, by the use of the vernacular instead of Latin. Therefore, while there is no justification, when using a more extended periodisation, for continuing to contrast the 'late medieval' state with the 'early modern' state – as if the Quattrocento princes, court, officials and offices had more in common, paradoxically, with Charlemagne than with the *Roi Soleil* – a closer analysis of the period from the fourteenth to the early sixteenth centuries does reveal sufficiently uniform traits to justify the notion of a 'Renaissance state' put forward by this volume.

10 The feudal principalities: the east (Trent, Bressanone/Brixen, Aquileia, Tyrol and Gorizia)

Marco Bellabarba

Introduction: the medieval background

During the early Middle Ages the eastern Alps comprised large swathes of territory assigned to ecclesiastical rulers who also enjoyed temporal sovereignty. The repeated involvement of the Holy Roman emperors in Italian politics, and therefore the need to defend communication routes between Germany and the peninsula, had led to the creation of the ecclesiastical principalities of Trent, Bressanone/Brixen and Aquileia, whose original function can be traced back to controlling stretches of the roads through the southern Alps.

Having been granted sovereign rights over the counties of Trent, Bolzano/Bozen, Venosta/Vinschgau and parts of the Val Pusteria/Pustertal between 1027 and 1034, the bishops of Trent and Bressanone/Brixen effectively controlled the roads that led south from the Resia and Brenner passes, or crossed the Val Pusteria/Pustertal to follow the line of the Roman road, the Claudia Augusta, on to the plains of the Veneto. Likewise, when the patriarch of Aquileia was granted the counties of Friuli, Istria and Carniola by the emperor in 1077 (albeit not permanently), a vast ecclesiastical dominion was formed to protect the roads over Monte Croce, in the Carnic Alps, and the Iron Road (the *via vel strata Hungariorum*), the best routes at the time for travellers heading for the Adriatic ports or for eastern Europe.

In all three cases, notwithstanding the bishops' close links with imperial policy, the institutional development of these principalities was influenced by their relations with the powerful secular lords invested with the title of *advocati*. In keeping with Carolingian customs, the *advocati* were obliged to protect the ecclesiastical lords – who were denied the right to declare war or vendetta (*Fehde*) – and to defend them in law against any damage to their property. In practice, in all three centres – Trent, Bressanone/Brixen and Aquileia – it was not long before the office was appropriated by leading local vassals who completely reversed the original function of the *advocatia*.[1]

---

[1] Riedmann, 'Vescovi e avvocati'.

From the early decades of the twelfth century onwards, the counts of Tyrol and Gorizia unscrupulously used their role as hereditary *advocati* of the churches of Trent, Bressanone/Brixen and Aquileia to augment their own possessions (fiefs, rights of transit, levies on agricultural revenues and so forth) to the detriment of the ecclesiastical princes through a skilful combination of military raids and alliances with other aristocratic families.

However, the counties of Tyrol and Gorizia had other aspects in common: the two comital lineages descended from the numerous noble families who had originally moved from the ancient duchy of Bavaria in the high Middle Ages to settle south of the Alps. These settlements had spread haphazardly, dotted here and there between the upper Adige river and the Isonzo valley. The counts of Tyrol held rights and jurisdictions in patriarchal Friuli, while the counts of Gorizia expanded their feudal possessions as far as the duchies of Carinthia and an extensive area of land in eastern Tyrol. The ramification of these feudal powers had also encouraged repeated marriage alliances between the two families, culminating in 1253 when Meinhard III, count of Gorizia, inherited all the lands belonging to the counts of Tyrol.[2]

In 1271 the possessions of the two lineages were again divided, but this did not mark the end of their common policy. For many years Meinhard, *comes Tirolis et Goricie*, and his brother Alberto, *comes Goricie et Tirolis*, continued to share military defence, the minting of their currency and the levy of tolls on produce crossing their borders. By the middle of the thirteenth century the *comites Goricie et Tirolis* ruled over a string of territories stretching along the ridge of the Alps from Swiss Engadine to the Karst plateau and Istria. It was a vast dynastic domain, although none of the individual possessions were contiguous. On the one hand, the *dominium* or *terra Tirolis*, further to the west, stretched over both sides of the Alps, thereby imposing greater jurisdictional uniformity; on the other hand, the Gorizian territories were more fragmented because, in addition to the Tyrolean lordship of Lienz, in the eastern Tyrol, there were also lands around the county of Gorizia and jurisdictional enclaves of varying sizes scattered in Friuli, Carniola and Istria.[3]

'Pass-states' or 'frontier states'?

The territories ruled by the two counties therefore grew at the expense of the ecclesiastical principalities, but the aggressive strategies of the counts

---

[2] Wiesflecker, 'Die politische Entwicklung'.
[3] For a detailed description of Gorizian possessions and their subdivision, see Niederstätter, *Die Herrschaft Österreich*, 247.

of Tyrol and Gorizia were not the only threat to the powers of the prince-bishops. The tendency to disperse and fragment their power through feudal instruments generated a second, even more insidious, form of weakness. A myriad of medium- and low-level aristocratic nuclei, which had emerged as castellan lordships in the episcopal territories during the twelfth and thirteenth centuries,[4] later successfully exploited the conflict between bishops and *advocati* to become firmly established. When the bishops assigned – or were obliged to assign – rights and land to the most powerful noble families, the dispersion of ecclesiastical powers among the ranks of the *nobiles terrae* became unstoppable. In practice, as had happened in the case of the advocatial investitures, the granting of fiefs ended up by sanctioning the princes' renunciation of the ownership of castles, land or monasteries that were instead permanently assigned to noble houses.

Therefore the precocity and solidity of these bishoprics had turned into a condition of weakness already by the early decades of the thirteenth century. The 'actual possession of lands and peasant families, castles and parishes, patrimonial and tax revenues was in the hands of a plurality of ecclesiastical institutions and lay elites'[5] throughout the area, while the power of co-ordination exercised by the prince-bishops was little more than a formality. Moreover, their rivals' dominions were no more homogeneous, indeed quite the opposite. Both Tyrol and Gorizia were newly formed territories that had expanded by piecing together, bit by bit, rights, fiefs and allodial property in a mosaic that still lacked any overall cohesion. While relatively uniform at first sight, Tyrol was still known in the fifteenth century as the county of Tyrol and other lordships (*Grafschaft Tirol und die übrigen Herrschaften*), a definition that was used in documentary sources to highlight its special structure compared to the older and more compact Austrian *Länder*. Moreover, the county had to deal with the existence of a large number of castle lordships within its territory, as well as the continuing mediation of episcopal officials. Similar conditions could also be found in the *dominium Goritiae* which, in practice, was little more than an aggregation of distant fiefs over which the patriarch and his noble allies could still claim rights of sovereignty.

Both the principalities and the counties were therefore characterised by scant territorial uniformity and a series of intersecting areas under different dominion. There was not even a proper political border to provide a clear-cut separation: 'not only were there no physical borders between territories, there were also no monetary or customs barriers, no

---

[4] Cammarosano, 'L'alto medioevo', 75–7. [5] *Ibid.*, 116.

restrictions on owning property in areas belonging to different lords or obstacles to the movement of people and assets'.[6] The fact that the Trentino-Tyrolean area formed part of the ancient *Regnum Teutonicum*, while the *Patria* of Friuli belonged to the *Regnum Italicum* had done nothing to curb the gradual process of osmosis between these territories and their inhabitants. Similarly, the formation of an ethnically 'mixed' group of officials and dignitaries serving the episcopal courts had been encouraged by the transnational composition of the dioceses of Trent, Bressanone/Brixen and Aquileia (the latter, in particular, occupied the whole of Friuli and parts of Carinthia, upper Styria and Slovenia). But the tendency to mix different national origins was even more visible among the ranks of the aristocracy. On the one hand, the expansive policies of Tyrol and Gorizia had fostered the settlement of loyal transalpine families with the result that the bishoprics were dotted with small feudal nuclei of officials or men-at-arms of German origin; on the other hand, over time these families had established ties of loyalty with the episcopal courts, for reasons of either political prestige or personal gain, thereby making the ethnic divisions among the nobility even more blurred and interconnected.

Understanding this broad, but at the same time indefinite 'frontier of inclusion'[7] along the eastern Alpine arc has always given rise to disputed historical interpretations. In a climate of growing national tension in the late nineteenth and early twentieth centuries, German historians coined the term 'pass-states' (*Paßstaaten*) to describe these territories as a succession of antique districts established to protect the border between the *Regnum Italicum* and the *Regnum Germanicum*. Writing after the defeat of the First World War, Albrecht Haushofer saw the counties of Tyrol and Gorizia merely as the remnants of territories that had once belonged to the Germanic area but extended either side of the Alps as ideal 'frontier bodies' (*Grenzkörper*) dating from the first medieval empire.[8] Italian historians usually countered the geopolitical theories of the *Paßstaaten* with the theory of 'natural boundaries', seeing the Alps as a geographical, cultural and political frontier. The ecclesiastical principalities were perceived as territories that had originally stretched as far as the foothills, but that then shrank as a result of continuing Germanic military aggression: the principle of the Alpine watershed as Italy's natural frontier became a classic example of one of the many 'frontiers of exclusion' that fascinated European historians in the early twentieth century.

---

[6] Degrassi, 'Frontiere, confini e interazioni', 216–17.
[7] Lattimore, *Studies in Frontier History*.   [8] Haushofer, *Pass-Staaten in den Alpen*.

Delayed feudalisation

Theories regarding *Paßstaaten* and 'natural borders' evoke a methodological nationalism now luckily forgotten; however, the difficulties of tracing the rapid changes in rule that characterised this area in the late Middle Ages and the tendency of these alternations to ignore modern national boundaries are still very real.

For the ecclesiastical principalities, for example, the absence of any form of dynastic succession was an objective weakness. Every time a bishop died, disputes regarding succession led to fierce struggles in which the various political players (the cathedral chapters, the feudatories and the *advocati*) immediately took sides, and this then spread to their political contacts outside the principalities: the papacy and the empire. Aquileia, Trent and Bressanone/Brixen were therefore exposed to the clash between the Roman curia and the German rulers, two hostile universal powers that nonetheless found themselves at the centre of relatively similar 'translocal multipolar organizations'[9] based on extremely volatile networks of personal and military alliances.

The co-ordinating function originally played by the ecclesiastical figures and their links with either the papacy or the empire set the regional situation within a political horizon that in the end inevitably influenced its stability. Moreover, some characteristics of the internal structure of power – common to both the ecclesiastical principalities and the counties – could be traced back to medieval origins. Perhaps the most striking outcome of the control exercised by the Germanic emperors over the ecclesiastical territories was the weakness of the towns. Given that public sovereignty had been delegated to the bishops since the earliest investitures of the eleventh century, a very close symbiosis had been formed, and indeed strengthened over the centuries, between the German emperors and *Germania sacra*. Under the aegis of the empire, the prince-bishops had succeeded in curbing any tendency towards political emancipation along the lines of the Italian communes.

An evolution of this kind had never taken place in any of the episcopal sees: instead, the three cities resembled the typical Germanic *Residenzstädte*, important administrative and economic hubs but populated by *cives* who were firmly bound to the bishop's court and incapable of escaping his control. Even the absence of any external projection of the land owned by citizens, which never stretched further than a few miles beyond the city walls, reflected the persistent bond of subjection to the

---

[9] Sassen, *Territory, Authority, Rights*, 39.

bishop. In Trentino and Friuli, the only towns were politically weak ones where a strong influence continued to be exerted by the bishop or by a powerful aristocratic family which had moved into the city, as in Udine or other walled *borghi* in Friuli (Cividale, Sacile, Gemona).

In practice, the weak or late urban development of these areas was reflected by the existence of a vast, and much more solid, network of feudal lordships. One effect of the absence of towns capable of following the experience of the communes was that the whole area of Friuli, Trentino and Tyrol was covered by a series of castles and fiefs that gave these territories a typically seigneurial appearance. It was not until relatively late, during the course of the thirteenth century, that the aristocracy who resided in these castles affirmed their status after the bishoprics and patriarchate had had to concede ever wider margins of public authority to their vassals. In the case of the principalities of Trent and Bressanone/Brixen, the rise of a new class of rural lords depended on the investiture of fiefs (including the custody of castles, jurisdictional rights and the collection of tithes) granted by the episcopal chancery, irrespective of the fact that the nobility did not own large tracts of land.[10] The systematic spread of fiefs as an organisational model had been the only weapon that the bishops of Trent could use to limit the power of the rural nobility within a more tightly ordered framework. The development of the aristocracy under the patriarchate was completely different: here its power rested on a vast network of landed estates rather than on jurisdictional practices. Friuli was covered by large noble possessions, for which villages and *mansi* served as the basic production units, and the proliferation of castles built by the local nobility during the thirteenth and fourteenth centuries was based on this widespread ramification of landed estates. The acquisition of judicial prerogatives and a public role therefore followed a different route compared to the Trentino and Tyrol: in Friuli it happened as a result of noble families being included within the structure of patriarchal official posts and also due to the dual (urban and rural) 'roots' enjoyed by some of these families; however, it was an equally effective way of occupying a number of Aquileia's public offices.[11]

Although the link between 'land and power' had different origins, an unbroken network of fiefs became established along the entire eastern Alpine fringe and, having initially been a means of co-ordination between the sparse seigneurial nuclei, it came to symbolise a political

---

[10] Varanini, 'Il principato vescovile nel Trecento,' 478.
[11] Zacchigna, 'L'inclinazione signorile', 194, and Zacchigna, 'Il patriarcato di Aquileia', 93.

sovereignty fragmented between too many players. Constrained by an inability to use military force – which had been appropriated by the *advocati* – on the one hand, and compelled to tolerate the rebelliousness of the nobility and their armed supporters, on the other, the ecclesiastical rulers could repress the most manifest abuses, cases of felony or violent attacks on their persons but were not in a position to completely alter what had become the consolidated balance of power.

The feudal contract, an 'instrument that, on the one hand, conceded or legitimised local powers, and on the other subordinated them to and disciplined them through the superiority of the *suzerain*', proved a very effective means of defining relations between the old and new centres of seigneurial particularism.[12] Its rapid spread throughout the eastern Alpine regions was entirely due to efforts made to regulate a distribution of powers that was still fluid and disorderly compared to the situation that had evolved in city-states. By delegating the public powers enshrined in the imperial diplomas, the prince-bishops derived authority from their position as overlords to their vassals. However, the image of a well-organised chain of power, as conveyed by the registers of the episcopal chanceries, was, for the most part, true only in theory.

The transcription of the investitures said little or nothing about the actual capacity of the bishops to control and rule their feudatories; for example, some who were granted seigneurial rights over towns and offices then exploited them to enhance their family prestige virtually unconstrained by subordination to the bishop. Forms of personal obligation or economic ties imposed by the castellans on the rural inhabitants of their fiefs further reinforced these processes of seigneurial independence. But above all, the feudal documents concealed the ease with which ties of loyalty tended to grow slack so that other bonds could be formed with some nearby *dominus*, or increased so that they existed in parallel. The web of feudal oaths was unevenly shaped and could be traced back to more than one source. The original starting point was the episcopal curia where the oldest investitures were kept; these had then given rise to the concessions made by the *advocati* who could independently create a second layer of feudal clientage thanks to the margins won through their territorial pre-eminence; lastly, a third network of ties had been forged with neighbouring powers – Italian lordships, Austrian duchies, the Germanic empire, the kingdom of Hungary – who had managed to superimpose concessions of lands or nobility on those already made by the local *domini*.

---

[12] Chittolini, *Signorie rurali e feudi*, 644.

Having developed with such inherent juridical contradictions, the stratification of feudal bonds made this area a tangle of 'geographical space' and 'membership spaces',[13] where the latter tended to be more resistant and to count for more than geographical proximity. The frequent conflicts over land ownership, the 'land-war offences',[14] which regularly broke out between castellan lineages, were a consequence of this unravelled feudal network. For example, the proverbial unreliability and turbulence of Friuli's ruling families were well known to fourteenth-century Italian chanceries: *'pessime observant conventionem et foedera colligationis'*[15] affirmed a letter from the Veronese Antonio della Scala to the Venetian Senate, alluding to the ease with which Friulan nobles, lacking a point of reference at Aquileia and often in economic difficulty, were attracted by nearby principalities (whether German or Italian). The Trentino aristocracy were no different, and the ongoing *'partes, discordiae, malitiae'*[16] constantly prompted its members to look for support from the Tyrolean court or, in the opposite direction, from the da Carrara and della Scala *signorie*.

The fourteenth century: between the German empire and the Italian states

It was above all this weak feudal framework that compelled Trent and Aquileia to mould their 'geographical space' in keeping with the rapid transformations of the Italian political contexts in the early fourteenth century. The creation of new territorial structures, 'either as more cohesive republics or as lordships that were legitimately and formally recognised by titles derived from the emperor',[17] exposed the two ecclesiastical principalities to a series of wars that far exceeded their capabilities. While Trent managed to establish a form of acceptable coexistence with the Tyrol in the early decades of the century, by contrast Aquileia found itself on the point of ceding its sovereignty to the Gorizian *advocati*.

After the death of pope Boniface VIII, who had included the patriarchate within the Guelf and papal camp, the Aquileian *advocato* Henry II of Gorizia forcibly renewed his political claims, especially after his marriage in 1297 to Beatrice of Camino made him heir to the

---

[13] Very pertinent also, in this case, are the comments made by Rokkan, in his collection of essays, *State Formation, Nation-Building*, 104.
[14] Bellamy, *Bastard Feudalism and the Law*, 10–56.
[15] Varanini, 'Venezia e l'entroterra', 195.
[16] Varanini, 'Il principato vescovile di Trento', 360.
[17] Lazzarini, *L'Italia degli stati territoriali*, 64.

signori of Treviso. His aspirations to build a territorial *signoria* with regional influence prompted Henry to enter Italian politics: in 1305 he symbolically moved his residence from Gorizia to Cividale and then to Treviso, where the king of the Romans, Frederick the Handsome of Habsburg, invested him with the vicariate; the following months saw him conquer Monfalcone and add the title of *podestà* of Trieste, which guaranteed a major outlet to the Adriatic and access to the Gorizian possessions in Istria. Having disposed of his Caminese ally, he forced the patriarch Ottobono de' Robari to sign an agreement on 25 November 1313 guaranteeing his position as captain-general of Friuli for five years and granting him full administration of patriarchal jurisdiction together with considerable revenues from a number of cities.

Within the space of a few years, Henry II's conquests had made him one of the most powerful lords in eastern Italy. However, Gorizia's newly won territories were lost equally suddenly. The appointment by pope John XXII of two Guelf patriarchs, Gastone Della Torre (1316) and Pagano Della Torre (1319), forced Henry II to side with the papacy against the imperial vicar Cangrande della Scala, as well as committing himself to an anti-Ghibelline military campaign in Padua and Treviso. Separated from the heart of his possessions, the count of Gorizia was unable to counter the rebellions of much of the Friulan nobility with any real efficacy. Even the support of the elector-princes who had backed the imperial election of Frederick the Handsome (1314) proved unsuccessful; first of all the stiff opposition to the Habsburg candidate by Louis of Wittelsbach, who disputed his election, and then Frederick's military defeat (at Mühldorf in 1322) undermined any protection that might have been offered to the Gorizian territories.[18]

Henry's sudden death in 1323 threw the count's family into severe difficulties: his second wife, Beatrice of Wittelsbach, and his underage son, John-Henry, were placed under the guardianship of his uncle Henry, count of Tyrol and duke of Carinthia. The financial troubles caused by the wars against Venice meant that Henry of Carinthia and Tyrol was unable to enforce his claim to the possessions around Treviso and Padua, which shortly afterwards passed to the Della Scala family). Free from the tutelage of the *advocati*, the patriarchate then focused its energies on combating seigneurial particularism. This renewed strength of the patriarchate, especially during the fifteen-year rule of Bertrand de Saint-Geniès (1334–50), was partly the result of the diplomatic tensions agitating central-eastern Europe. The conflicts were aligned principally

---

[18] For a careful political and diplomatic reconstruction of these events, see Brunettin, 'Una fedeltà insidiosa'.

along two fronts: first, the war between emperor Louis the Bavarian and the king of Bohemia, John of Luxemburg, who after conquering Silesia between 1327 and 1329 had tried to expand his territorial possessions to include the Austrian duchies and the Italian regions.

By setting his sights on the Austrian lands king John opened a second battlefront against the Habsburgs, who were intent on defending the Austrian duchies, although uncertain whether to side with the Luxemburgs or the Wittelsbachs. The dispute between Wittelsbach, Luxemburg and Habsburg, a dynastic dispute that would influence the political situation throughout Europe for more than thirty years, involved the Friulan patriarchate and the bishoprics of Trent and Bressanone/Brixen. In some ways it was an indirect involvement, the result of the constraints of *advocatia* and the geographical proximity of the Habsburg provinces. This was true in the case of Trent and Bressanone/Brixen, both of which were forcibly included in a game of marriage ties devised by the Prague court to absorb Carinthia and Tyrol.

In 1330 Henry of Tyrol and Carinthia's only female heir, Margarete, married John-Henry of Luxemburg, king John's second son. Without being nominally imperial vicar, the king of Bohemia used the Tyrol as a base to consolidate his power over the northern Italian cities, and in 1333 he launched the first military expedition against them. In spite of a number of defeats in Italy, John of Luxemburg's strategy proved successful in April 1335, following the death of duke Henry, when he inherited the duchy of Carinthia and the county of Tyrol. Although Margarete had already started to rule as *Landesfürstin* and her father's legitimate successor in Tyrol and Carinthia, in May, in Linz emperor Louis invested the Habsburgs with the duchy of Carinthia and those areas of the county of Tyrol south of the frontier gatehouse known as the Chiusa di Rio Pusteria.

Having never recognised Margarete and John-Henry's marriage as legitimate, Louis of Wittelsbach's reaction was the result of a secret agreement with the dukes of Austria, Albert II and Otto of Habsburg, both of whom had taken the emperor's side on this occasion. Within a few months Carinthia (together with the Slovenian lands of Carniola) passed to the Habsburgs, but not the Tyrol where John-Henry and Margarete's resistance, strengthened by the arrival of margrave Charles of Moravia – the future emperor Charles IV – further complicated the political and military situation. Initially both the Habsburgs and the emperor recognised Luxemburg rule over the Tyrol, and also over the possessions won in the Veneto in 1337 (Agordo, Cadore, Feltre, Belluno). The election of Matthäus Kunzmann, John-Henry's chaplain, as bishop of Bressanone (1336) and of Nikolaus von Brünn, chancellor to margrave Charles, as bishop of Trent (1338) and '*capitaneus in comitatu Tyrolis*' helped to strengthen their hold on the county.

But the growing opposition of the Tyrolean nobility and the emperor's political manoeuvring – he successfully arranged a second marriage between Margarete and his son, margrave Louis of Brandenburg – led to a direct military confrontation in Tyrol in 1347. In spite of being helped by the Visconti and da Carrara rulers, Charles of Luxemburg, who was elected emperor in 1346, was forced to yield to Louis's army which was supported by the leading Tyrolean feudatories. At this point, the imperial defeat and the defence of Charles IV's hold over the cities in the Veneto drew the Tyrol and ecclesiastical principalities of Trent and Bressanone within the radius of Bavarian influence. However, the new political structure sanctioned by Margarete's marriage to the margrave Louis was as brief as the previous one had been. The desire to claim the county as part of the kingdom of Bavaria, thereby creating a southern appendix with access to Italy, did not outlive Meinhard III's sudden death in January 1362, aged barely 23. The hereditary rights of succession claimed by the Habsburgs (Meinhard III had married Margarete of Austria, duke Rudolf IV's sister, in 1358) were decisive and in January 1363 the nobles of the county ratified the transfer of the Tyrol ('*die Land und Gegende an der Etsch und daz Intal mit der Burge ze Tyrol*'), together with the Bavarian jurisdictions of Rattenberg, Kufstein and Kitzbühel, to Rudolf IV. A year later emperor Charles IV invested the Habsburgs with fiefs that had belonged to Meinhard III, thus effectively extinguishing the Tyrol lineage.

A similar sequence of diplomatic agreements, military conflicts and dynastic alliances was also played out during this period in the Friulan territories. The political players were the same: Wittelsbach, Habsburg, Luxemburg, with the addition of Venice and the Italian *signorie*. When Carinthia and Carniola were reabsorbed into the Habsburg lands after the death of duke Henry in 1335, the patriarchate and the county were caught up in the conflict. It was the Gorizian *advocati* who paid the highest price for this military competition and, having been weakened by the division of family properties between the three branches (1342), they slowly faded from the scene. Charles IV's plans to turn the patriarchate into a sort of link between the Danubian countries and Italy[19] initially gave the Aquileian lords new scope for manoeuvre: Bertrand de Saint-Geniès and his immediate successor, the patriarch Niccolò of Luxemburg, Charles IV's half-brother, played their cards skilfully under

---

[19] Cusin, *Il confine orientale d'Italia*, 46.

the protection of the Luxemburg rulers to reinforce patriarchal authority. The emperors' interest in protecting the integrity of the patriarchate, 'not merely in order to underline the empire's ancient presence in the *Regnum Italicum* and, above all, its control of the Alpine passes, but also to call upon the patriarchate to fulfil its role as an imperial pawn both in the increasingly lively affairs of the upper Adriatic – a conflict centred on predominance in Dalmatia and Zara – and in the tricky Italian situation',[20] guaranteed a political standing for the Aquileian church that the dioceses of Trent and Bressanone/Brixen had already lost years earlier.

However, in practice, even imperial protection could not prevent the intervention of the most aggressive and closest territorial powers. As had already happened in the Tyrol, marriage agreements between the Gorizian *advocati* and the dukes of Austria (who were also lords of Feltre and Belluno during this period) gave the Habsburgs an opportunity to become more closely involved in Aquileian affairs. At times of uncertainty for the patriarchate, for example after the violent death of Bertrand of Saint-Geniès, the Habsburgs managed to obtain the capitancy-general of the *Patria* during the *sede vacante*, an office normally reserved for the *advocati*, as well as control of the main patriarchal fortresses. On that same occasion, according to the description given by the *Chronicon Spilibergense*, Albert, duke of Styria and Carinthia, travelled to Friuli in person to order 'the nobility of Friuli to make truces among themselves' and to ensure that they swore to keep them.[21]

These closer ties with the imperial camp gained only a momentary respite against the Habsburg threat;[22] the fact that Charles IV raised the counts of Gorizia to the rank of imperial princes did not stop the gradual dismemberment of their inheritance in favour of the Austrian dukes.[23] Nor did it prevent the ongoing transformation of local power structures that was taking place in Friuli. The 'princely' aspirations of Saint-Geniès and Niccolò of Luxemburg, combined with the increased Habsburg pressure, completely altered relations between the Aquileian government and the nobility. The collage of already fragile ties collapsed when the patriarchs called on the aristocratic groups centred on Udine, the

---

[20] Brunettin, 'Una fedeltà insidiosa', 328.   [21] Paschini, *Storia del Friuli*, 117.
[22] After the patriarchal office had passed to Ludovico Della Torre following Niccolò's death (1358), duke Rudolf IV, Albert's eldest son, declared war on Aquileia. The conflict ended with a series of agreements that were very damaging to patriarchal authority, and Ludovico soon declared that they had been extorted by Rudolf '*dolo et fraude*'; for extensive documentation on these clashes between the patriarchate and the Habsburgs, see *Austro-Friulana*.
[23] For example, in 1374 the dukes of Austria acquired possession of the fiefs on the Karst, the counties of Pisino, Möttling and other Istrian territories from the counts of Gorizia.

largest urban nucleus in eastern Friuli and for some years the patriarch's real residence, to bolster their own political ends. Of all these groupings, the Savorgnan, who owned a large number of castles and had maintained a presence in Udine for many generations,[24] took the greatest advantage of patriarchal support to extend their influence even further.

The patriarchs showed their support for the Savorgnan on numerous occasions. The family frequently backed the patriarchs' financial requests and helped them in conflicts against other Friulan *potentes*. For their part, the patriarchs recognised that Udine and the Savorgnan formed 'a nucleus of extraordinarily influential power that would help to centralise the co-ordination of local powers'.[25] It represented an abrupt simplification of the political picture that upset and rearranged the seigneurial geography of Friuli on new terms. As a Friulan chronicler noted, in 1349 the count of Gorizia was obliged to return to the *Patria* as *advocatus*, accompanied by a 'large company of people – the nobles of Castel Porpeto, Della Torre, de Portis, Spilimbergo and representatives of the municipality of Pordenone di Cividale – because patriarch Bertrand, backed by the Savorgnan and the city of Udine, was dealing with matters concerning the Friulan nobility'.[26] The rise of the Savorgnan and the move towards centralised princely rule led to an explosion of hostility among other castellans in the *Patria* whose sympathies lay with the empire, opposing any centralisation of patriarchal power.

At an ideological level these families, who were mainly concentrated in western Friuli, 'saw themselves as protecting the most authentic traditions of the *Patria*; by emphasising the value of a form of state modelled on the centrality of the feudal castellans and the importance of ancient lineages of *milites*, there was an implicit rejection of the political experience that had grown up around the nucleus of Udine'.[27] At a political level, precisely this resistance to the alliance between the patriarchs and the Savorgnan encouraged the castellan faction, led by the Della Torre family, to approach the Gorizian *advocati* and later, when the power of the latter started to wane, to turn to the newly emerging Habsburgs. Two large groupings slowly took shape during the second half of the fourteenth century: on the one hand, the Della Torre family and its supporters (the so-called *comites* of *citra Tulmentum*), and on the other, the patriarch and the Savorgnan faction. A relatively vast and fragmented array of jurisdictions, representing families from both chivalric and

---

[24] On all aspects of the evolution of the Savorgnan's possessions, see Casella, *I Savorgnan*, 25–67.
[25] Zacchigna, 'Il patriarcato di Aquileia', 99.   [26] Paschini, *Storia del Friuli*, 104–5.
[27] Zacchigna, 'Il patriarcato di Aquileia', 103.

military traditions, opposed the more dynamic mix of urban and seigneurial traditions formed by the nobility centred on the city of Udine.

This split into two factions affected both the networks of political allegiance and the marriage market. 'The Della Torre confined their choices to a very restricted marriage market. In contrast, the Savorgnan progressively expanded their alliances to families in the dominant city of Venice and other towns in the Venetian Terraferma while they still retained a strong commitment to other castellans within Friuli. The Della Torre acted defensively, the Savorgnan expansively and opportunistically.' Moreover, the Della Torre *consorteria* 'largely consisted of an association of aristocrats who were at least formal equals', while that of its rivals 'followed a vertically arranged clientage system with the Savorgnan indisputably at the head'.[28] The struggles that shook the patriarchal structure during the second half of the century, seen by nineteenth- and twentieth-century historians as the decidedly negative result of an 'extremely agitated political life',[29] developed against the background of an increasingly precarious balance between the factions.

A careful reading of the documents describing the situation of the *Patria* in the late fourteenth century clearly shows how the factions managed to mould the institutions to suit their particular aims.[30] At this stage, it may be useful to compare the breakdown of relations between the two Friulan parties with the political conditions in Trent and Bressanone during the same period. A number of similarities emerge at the outset: a weakened ecclesiastical authority, a robust network of fiefs and a geographical location that attracted both German and Italian rulers. The significance and sequence of some events were almost identical: in 1363, after acquiring the Tyrol, duke Rudolf IV's attempt to extend his range of action towards Italy involved the bishopric of Trent. In this instance, the outcome was not territorial possession, but the drawing up of special legal agreements (the *compattate* or *Verschreibungen*) that subordinated the prince-bishop's military responsibilities – to recruit soldiers and, if necessary, to declare war – to Tyrolean control.

By signing these agreements, the principality was forced to accept restrictive limits on its foreign and military policy, and this was immediately reflected in the social composition of the aristocracy. By forcing the castellans to repudiate any bishop who had not sworn allegiance to the convention and to obey, *sede vacante*, the count of Tyrol's orders, the text of the *compattate* 'institutionalised the many ties that had bound the

---

[28] Muir, *Mad Blood Stirring*, 86–7.   [29] Leicht, *Il parlamento*, lx.
[30] Or, to put it differently, how 'the exercise of authority was inseparably connected to its social substratum': Holenstein, 'Introduction: empowering interactions', 5.

Trentine nobility to the county since the thirteenth century: in other words, it strengthened the patrimonial, feudal and matrimonial relations between the Trentine and Tyrolean nobilities, making them a group whose interests frequently coincided'.[31]

Fresh evidence appeared in the clashes between the prince-bishop, the feudatories and the urban patriciate on the cusp of the fourteenth and fifteenth centuries. The duke of Austria and count of Tyrol, Frederick IV of Habsburg, had good reason to support the claims for independence advanced by the capital city of the bishopric, and by exploiting his position as *advocatus* of the *ecclesia Tridentina*, he had occupied Trent when it rebelled against the prince-bishop George of Liechtenstein. This marked the start of a confused period of military campaigns, attacks and small urban and rural uprisings during which the battle for the city's sovereignty, waged between the bishops and the Tyrolean overlords, gradually involved all the feudatories in the principality and the county.

A few months before the Trentine revolt exploded in 1407, twenty or so of the leading Tyrolean aristocrats signed a defensive league (*Bund*) to protect themselves in the event that Frederick IV ignored the ancient privileges of the county. Another assembly of nobles also gathered early the following year, in Bolzano on 28 March 1407, under the name Bund an der Etsch (the Adige League, later also known as the Falkenbund or League of the Falcon). Headed by the county's most distinguished noble, Heinrich von Rottenburg,[32] the league united most of the feudatories in the Austrian Tyrol and the ecclesiastical principality who had sworn to stand together for ten years to guard their territorial right (*Landrecht*).

Similar associative phenomena were recorded throughout this decade in many other southern areas of the empire: the noble leagues (*Einungen*) or companies of nobles (*Adelsgesellschaften*) founded in Franconia and Swabia shared a common trait of providing mutual defence against external threats from the free cities or their own princes.[33] The agreements underwritten by the *societates* of the Elephant and the Falcon also contained very similar defensive provisions. However, the charters of these early fifteenth-century Tyrolean aristocratic leagues all emphasised one particular point: namely, infringement of their territorial right (*ius terrae*, or *Landrecht*) was cited as grounds for resistance to the prince. In practice, this *Landrecht* consisted primarily of the privileges the

---

[31] Bettotti, 'L'aristocrazia nel tardo medioevo', 427.
[32] Bellabarba, 'Statuti, "Landrecht", leghe aristocratiche', 241–51.
[33] On the aristocratic leagues in imperial provinces during the early fifteenth century, see Zmora, *State and Nobility*; Zmora, 'Feuds for and Against Princes'; Algazi, *Herrengewalt und Gewalt der Herren*.

Tyrolean nobles had received from their territorial rulers during the Middle Ages, such as guarantees regarding investiture, tenure of hereditary ownership of fiefs, and assurances regarding the personal character of noble rights. This territorial right therefore comprised, above all, aristocratic liberties and privileges, but this did not prevent the aristocratic leagues from presenting it in public as a *Landrecht* that had always been respectfully observed by all the county's inhabitants.

The dispute between duke Frederick IV and the king of the Romans, Sigismund of Luxemburg, kept these aristocratic feuds alive for years. Under the leadership of Ulrich and Wilhelm von Starkenberg, two brothers who became the most powerful feudatories in the Tyrol after Rottenburg's death, the leagues of Trentine and Tyrolean feudatories began to imagine a new territory without a prince. In a surprise move, on 6 May 1416 the assembly of estates gathered at Bressanone, under the guidance of the Trentine nobleman Peter von Spaur, proposed plans to unite county and principality in a single regional territory stretching either side of the Alps and divided into five districts, each headed by a noble *capitano* and elected councillors.

However, it did not take long for the dream of a *Land* governed by the nobility alone to evaporate. Their appeal to the rural communities and to the Tyrolean towns and bishoprics – who preferred ducal protection to that of the aristocratic leagues – fell on deaf ears. Although king Sigismund tried to rally the aristocratic opposition, within the space of a few years the rebellion was quashed. Frederick IV's military successes were helped significantly by the urban patriciate and the rural jurisdictions, and in return their representatives were admitted to the county's parliament (*Landtag*), an institution that by the early fifteenth century had started to meet at regular intervals. But their appearance at the diet did not undermine the overall importance of the castellan feudatories who continued to be the prince's preferred interlocutors. With occasional exceptions, such as the ban placed on the Starkenberg brothers, none of those who had taken part in the earlier feuds paid the price for rebelling against Frederick by forfeiting their fiefs. A group of Trentine noblemen – Vinciguerra Arco, Paride Lodron, John and George von Spaur – who had formed a new '*liga facta contra dominum nostrum ducem Fedricum*' in 1423 became the last to lay down their arms and were allowed back into the duke's graces immediately after being defeated by the Habsburg army,[34] and subsequently admitted to the noble *Stand* of the county.

---

[34] Bettotti, 'L'aristocrazia nel tardo medioevo', 431.

Conclusion: moving towards a new genealogy of power in the fifteenth century

The formalised creation of an order of Trentine–Tyrolean nobles registered in the county's rolls was the most lasting legacy of the fifteenth-century feuds. In some ways the end of the aristocratic revolts corresponded to the 'socio-genesis'[35] of a different kind of nobility, one that now had more uniform boundaries, ignored linguistic or geographical differences and enjoyed a stable legal status, anchored to the possibility of sitting on the aristocratic benches in the diet. Those nobles residing in the original fiefs of the county quite readily acknowledged the court of Innsbruck and the *Landtag* as the arenas where they could exercise their social pre-eminence. On the other hand, there was greater resistance in the episcopal territories where the early fifteenth-century changes had marked a more profound caesura with the previous regime. This undoubtedly marked the start of a completely new period for the episcopal aristocracy: the noble order that 'became established during the second quarter of the thirteenth century following the integration of the various juridical positions of the Trentine aristocracy as part of the general vassalage relationship to the prince-bishop'[36] had had its day. Feudal links to the bishop were dissolved, the urban patriciate sought greater margins of freedom through the diets of Tyrol, and the feudatories began to see themselves in a network of political, matrimonial and economic relations that no longer revolved purely around the bishopric.

Some episcopal families whose lands lay close to the Italian boundaries refused to become part of this new horizon of political loyalty. The lords of Castelbarco, whose fiefs had occupied the lower part of the Vallagarina for nearly a century, remained aloof from the early fifteenth-century feuds and preferred to seek alliances with or military backing from the Della Scala in Verona or the da Carrara in Padua. When the hold of the da Carrara *signoria* over Verona collapsed in 1405 as a result of Venetian aggression, the Castelbarco barons replicated this relationship with the *Serenissima*. It was these friendly relations that allowed Venice to gain its first foothold in the Trentine region. Taking advantage of the testamentary wishes of one of the Castelbarco lords, in 1411 Venice occupied the feudal possessions of Avio, Ala and Brentonico lying immediately beyond the frontier at Verona. The

---

[35] Morsel, 'Die Erfindung des Adels', 322–7, contains very cogent arguments for understanding the processes of material and 'discursive' formation of the imperial nobility in the fifteenth century.

[36] Bettotti, 'L'aristocrazia nel tardo medioevo', 433.

decision to garrison these castles and despatch small armed contingents to other fortresses held by the Castelbarco aimed, at least initially, to achieve a temporary goal. Above all, the republic was concerned that 'communications between the lagoon and the major northern markets should remain open and secure, and therefore, having added Verona to its dominions in 1405, Venice inherited and became an interested custodian of those territories for which the route up the Adige valley was of primary strategic importance'.[37] But in 1416 a rising led by Aldrighetto Castelbarco, lord of Rovereto, forced the republic to alter its strategy. Having besieged and then destroyed Aldrighetto's own base, the Venetians embarked on further territorial acquisitions: in 1426 they conquered the Ledro valley and Tignale, bordering with Brescia, and then in 1439 the lakeside village of Riva del Garda, a key addition that consolidated communications with its new possessions in the Terraferma (Brescia and Bergamo, both captured from the duke of Milan).

As soon as they had secured a foothold in southern Trent, the Venetians immediately dismantled the seigneurial structure left by the Castelbarco. The decision to transform these fiefs *ex novo* into possessions dependent on the two *podesterie* of Rovereto and Riva confirmed the Venetians' propensity to use city-centred models of government wherever possible. The situation of the *Patria* during the same period was much more worrying since it continued to be rife with civil unrest and disturbed by threats of an imminent war with the new king of Hungary, Sigismund of Luxemburg. It seems likely that the speed with which Venice stabilised its possessions in Trent can be explained by the urgent need to concentrate all its efforts on the eastern frontier. 'The threat posed by the Hungarians and the influence acquired by the rulers of da Carrara, the Visconti and even the Florentines in Friuli during the closing years of the fourteenth century were among the chief reasons for the republic's fear of being surrounded. Moreover, Friuli was a valuable source of food and timber.'[38] Following lengthy preparations, the war against Sigismund broke out in 1411 following a sudden attack by the Hungarians. After nearly ten years of war, the armies of the *Serenissima* were eventually able to control the whole of the *Patria* by the summer of 1420.

---

[37] Ortalli, 'Federico IV Tascavuota', 153.

[38] Mallet, 'La conquista della Terraferma', 189. Moreover, the patriarch of Aquileia agreed to recognise Venetian rule officially only in 1445 in return for an annual payment of 5,000 ducats and continued sovereignty over Aquileia, San Vito and San Daniele. As for the counts of Gorizia, they received confirmation of their fiefs from doge Francesco Foscari in 1424, who declared them to be of patriarchal origin, thereby implicitly making the counts vassals of the republic.

A significant part was played in the Venetian victory by Friuli's internal divisions, as well as by Sigismund's other military commitments in eastern Europe. The closing decades of the fourteenth century had already witnessed closer links with the Savorgnan counts who controlled many of the castles and fiefs lying along the road arteries leading to the German territories, and in 1385 they were granted the status of Venetian patricians. 'These objectives led to the creation of an explicit Venetian "protectorate" that, from 1404 onwards, financed the strengthening of the Savorgnan family's operations and position in military terms.'[39] Moreover, in 1407 the patriarch appointed Tristano Savorgnan to the captaincy of Cadore, another key territory positioned between Friulan, Venetian and Germanic lands. Venice did not object to the counts and city of Udine establishing a temporary alliance with the dukes of Austria since, if anything, it would add to friction between the Luxemburgs and Habsburgs. Indeed, after Udine was occupied by the Hungarians and a ban was imposed on Tristano Savorgnan, relations and financial support were stepped up and it was precisely the resistance of the Savorgnan castles that eventually compelled Sigismund to sign a truce with Venice from 1413 to 1418.

Venice used greater caution in its dealings with nobles who owned lands to the west of the Tagliamento river, namely the rivals of the Savorgnan. Even before the end of the conflicts, the Senate signed a series of *recomandatio et adherentia* pacts with the '*nobiles de citra Tulmentum et alii in Patria Foroiulii*' (the Prata, Porcia, Spilimbergo, Polcenigo, Ragogna-Torre and Valvasone nobles) who undertook to act as '*boni amici, adherentes, colligati et recomendati*' of the republic, and, clearly, enemies of its adversaries. Venice was at liberty to fortify river crossings wherever it saw fit, even if located within their fiefs, and in turn the *recomandati* nobles would provide Venetian men-at-arms with everything they required.[40]

The republic had signed the same sort of diplomatic agreements in another tricky frontier zone: southern Trent. But contrary to what happened in the former bishopric's lands, signing these Friulan agreements did not lead to any territorial reorganisation. Indeed, the last revisions of the *recomandatio* agreements, drawn up after 1420, did nothing to change the jurisdictional boundaries and kept the same fragmented situation of feudal, civic and communal districts that had characterised the patriarchate before its disappearance. As soon as they swore loyalty to Venice, all the *domini locorum* obtained confirmation of

---

[39] Casella, *I Savorgnan*, 41.   [40] Ortalli, 'Le modalità di un passaggio', 17.

their ancient prerogatives, except for the counts of Prata who paid for having switched sides to the Hungarians with the confiscation of their possessions and exile.

Retaining control over the *Patria* depended almost exclusively on collaborating with the local forces who, after decades of civil crisis, had joined the new state between 1418 and 1420. That 'the need for continued support and points of reference in Friuli rested above all on agreements and treaties with individual feudatories had been fully accepted in Venice for some time, and the Marcian government had always respected this requisite in the past'.[41] This explains why the republic granted much more to Friuli than it had conceded to any other province within the dominion: the inviolability of feudal borders, guarantees of land ownership, and the validity of inheritance customs. The numerous concessions of 'rights and freedom' granted when they swore devotion authorised the castellan nobles to give a wide-ranging and arbitrary interpretation to their own titles, claiming jurisdictional faculties, the right to levy rental revenues or rural *corvées* that very often were not legitimised by genuine investiture charters.

But claims to possess a seigneurial tradition of ancient standing, as asserted by the Friulan feudatories, had little or no foundation. Most of the lay and ecclesiastical seigneurial districts in the area were of recent origin; or at least the connection between their landed base and the jurisdictional rights claimed by the aristocrats, above all the exercise of *merum et mixtum imperium*, was recent. Once the frenetic phase of the war against Sigismund was over and after the dedication of 1420, Venice relied on the mediation of local elites, perhaps also to make up for its precarious legal claims to conquest. Together these conditions triggered a decisive change in Friulan aristocratic society, almost a process of 'socio-genesis' similar to that undergone by the Trentine–Tyrolean feudatories. On the one hand, the form of territorial powers did not change in either area; the feudal system survived and if anything, in the case of Friuli, it became even more pervasive. On the other, however, the end of ecclesiastical rule inevitably changed the methods of dialogue used by local nobility with the new princes and, consequently, the forms of 'political coalitions'[42] within them.

As has been seen, for episcopal and Tyrolean castellans the end of the fifteenth-century cycle of feuds led to a clearer delimitation of their powers; in a juridical and material sense, the nobility created an exclusive identity, protected by requisites that were now defined by their

---

[41] Zamperetti, *I piccoli principi*, 193.   [42] Spruyt, *The Sovereign State*, 25.

membership of the *Landtag*. In the absence of an urban counterweight, feudal codes also became a criterion of social distinction and a means of communication between the prince, his court and the assembly of estates. Moreover, the degree of uniformity achieved by the Trentine–Tyrolean aristocracy also explains the absence of factional groups or divisions between aristocratic families during the course of the fifteenth century. The re-emergence of violence that occasionally ignited the Trentine–Tyrolean landscape, following the rules of vendetta, were residual episodes that were relatively quickly quenched. Towards the end of the fifteenth century even the ethnic differences between the episcopal aristocratic kinships (mostly Italian) and their German-speaking Tyrolean neighbours faded away: a newly composed list of feudal families admitted to the Tyrolean diet allowed the Trentine ecclesiastical principality's greatest lords to enter a common *Adelstand*, thus obliterating the ethnic origins of the noble *nationes*. The feudal vocabulary proved capable of spreading a single political culture and guaranteeing orderly mechanisms for the social reproduction of the aristocratic class, even if the territorial geography remained unchanged, subdivided into parcels of seigneurial jurisdiction of varying size that made up a 'particular type of assemblage of territory, authority, and rights'[43] characterised by its weak centralisation.

Territorial and seigneurial particularism merged into something completely different in the *Patria*. At the time of the Venetian conquest, as Edward Muir writes, the unity of the patriarchal lands became 'a legal fiction, and government at all levels failed to function effectively as subjects and officials alike wandered through a labyrinth of discordant institutions and procedures'.[44] Local chronicles record disputes between the aristocratic families and the outbreak of openly anti-magnate peasant protests that spread like wildfire through the countryside. For their part, the dispatches of the Venetian rectors hark on about the difficulty of governing a province fragmented into dozens of different jurisdictions: implacable bad blood and 'mortal enmities' between noble lineages helped to give the *Patria* a 'grim and violent reputation and its physical setting, these provincial territories with their harsh, wild and mysterious landscapes, made it even gloomier'.[45]

That the lands were divided between dozens of feudatories was just one factor in the Friulan crisis, and perhaps not even the most influential. Rather, in spite of Venice's obstinate denial, it was the start of

---

[43] I have borrowed this expression from Sassen, *Territory, Authority, Rights*, 73.
[44] Muir, *Mad Blood Stirring*, 32–3.
[45] For a detailed picture, see Bianco, *La 'crudel zobia grassa'*, 22.

Venetian control that had broken the pattern of its fourteenth-century institutional structure. First, it coincided with the decline of the parliament as a representative assembly for the Friulan nobility. Even in the middle of the sixteenth century, the nobleman Girolamo Porcia would remember when parliament had been a sovereign body under the patriarch, one that made the *Patria* resemble more 'a form of republic than a principality'[46] (something very akin to the federation of noble cells dreamt up by the Trentine–Tyrolean leagues of the early fifteenth century). But the republic had refused to allow the assembly to take part in institutional dialogue or to act as judicial 'peace-maker' between the estates. Stripped of its legislative responsibilities, the parliament had degenerated into an arena for clashes between the noble factions of the *Patria*. Face-offs between the two consorteries were a regular occurrence: the first led by the Della Torre, also known as the *strumieri* and Ghibellines (like the fifteenth-century label), was a federation of feudal and land-owning families with pro-Habsburg political loyalties that managed to dominate the assembly purely by outnumbering its rivals; its opponents were the so-called *zamberlani* (or Guelf) party, led by the Savorgnan, who fuelled their 'princely ambitions'[47] with wealth derived from countless fiefs, trade, public contracts and, above all, the political support of Venice.

The Savorgnan, who posed as the guardians of Udine and of the interests of the peasant classes, were used by the republic as 'leverage in order to pressurise and intimidate the feudatories',[48] and in doing so it sought to recalibrate the powers of the parliament. The Venetian decision to support the *zamberlani* was a calculated move prompted by the need to establish a preferential dialogue with the noble party who gave proof of having solid urban roots. It was no coincidence that the imbalance between the wealth of the Udinesi and that of other Friulan territories became increasingly marked[49] and that, especially in the second half of the century, the city could claim, for itself and its nobles, 'an authority and superiority that seemed fitting' after the arrival of Venice.[50]

Over the years the friendships and protection given to the Savorgnan consorterie aggravated the extent of this conflict, which took the form of 'a long series of dualities':[51] in addition to the traditional rivalry between

---

[46] Porcia, *Descrizione della Patria*, 19.   [47] Muir, *Mad Blood Stirring*, p. 39.
[48] Bianco, *La 'crudel zobia grassa'*, 22
[49] Zacchigna, 'Il patriarcato di Aquileia', 109–10.
[50] Corbellini, 'Udine capitale della Patria del Friuli', 243.
[51] As Viggiano clearly states in 'Politica e giustizia', 428.

the pro-imperial and pro-Venetian factions, there was now also attrition between a system of urban values, on the one hand, and, on the other, the culture of the castellan nobility who were still ideologically tied to the link between land ownership and power. The widening gap between the two parties contributed to an unsettled and restless situation in Friuli. The division certainly predates 1420, but it was exacerbated by the Venetian conquest. After all, even the division of the *Patria* into the various factions owed its continuity to the need to unite against an external force; but this upheaval of the internal balances within the aristocracy was now the outcome of a genealogy of powers imposed by Venice. The comparison with republican political culture and with a dominant city, which, it should be added, had no court or parliament where the subordinate aristocracy (like the Tyrolean nobility) could be represented, served to crystallise the factional divisions within the *Patria*. It was this crescendo of accusations and tensions that laid the foundations in Friuli for Renaissance Italy's largest popular uprising in 1511.

11 Genoa

Christine Shaw

Introduction

The republic of Genoa was renowned for its political instability, and its reputation was justified. Between 1300 and 1528, when the constitution was radically reformed under the aegis of the great Genoese naval commander, Andrea Doria, it has been calculated, there were seventy-two rebellions and changes of regime.[1] Several of those regime changes were the submission of the republic to an external lord, generally either the king of France or the duke of Milan, or rebellions in which the Genoese shook off their subordination and recovered their independence. The city of Genoa did not have an extensive territory in mainland Italy, and its government had considerable difficulty in asserting control over what there was. But for all its political turmoil and its weakness as a territorial power within the Italian state system, Genoa was a major commercial power in the Mediterranean and beyond, and had colonies in the eastern Mediterranean and on the Black Sea coast until the advance of the Ottoman Turks in the middle of the fifteenth century. In the Casa (or Banco) di San Giorgio, the city had one of the most stable and trusted public financial institutions in Renaissance Italy.

'The absence of the state'

It has been Genoese commerce, the activities of Genoese mariners and merchants, rather than the Genoese state, that has been the favoured subject of historians of Genoa. The state has been dismissed as weak and chaotic, barely worthy of the name. 'The absence of the state' is 'the primary characteristic of Genoese history' according to a standard modern account of the history of Genoa in the Middle Ages.[2] The most authoritative historian of the Genoese colonies, Roberto Lopez, described the medieval Genoese republic 'as never quite emerging from

---

[1] Epstein, *Genoa and the Genoese*, 325–7.   [2] Airaldi, *Genova e la Liguria*, 109.

the cocoon' to develop the form of 'a permanent state, transcending individuals'.[3] In his monumental study of the economic and social history of Genoa in the fifteenth century, Jacques Heers attributed the chronic instability of Genoese political life to 'a striking divorce between an archaic constitution and a different social reality'; he blamed it on the power of the landed nobles, responsible for 'this republic of businessmen', being nothing more than 'a city-state, and a weakened state'.[4]

Another leading modern historian of Genoa, Geo Pistarino, summarised the negative commonplaces and the criticisms that have been levelled at the medieval republic in a long-standing historiographical tradition. One theme has been that a state 'organised as a free commune' should have been ready to ally with 'feudal forces' (landed nobles, the emperor of Byzantium) against townsmen; and to accept the lordship of the king of France or duke of Milan. Then there was 'the incomplete formation of the regional state' that Genoa might have been expected to develop in Liguria, as though, Pistarino commented, distracted by colonial expansion, 'the republic had not fulfilled its precise and principal historical duty'. It has been judged surprising that a maritime power should not have formed its own fleet, but relied on individuals, often acting on their own account, to wage its naval wars, and how often in relations with other powers, including the Ottomans and the Byzantine empire, the commune left so much to the initiative of citizens acting in their own interests. And there has been much emphasis on 'the scarce sense of the state' that characterised the citizens of Genoa, the direction of government by whichever of the rival families was dominant at the time, the mingling of private business with public interests in financial matters 'as though this was the norm, not the exception'.[5]

This image of a culpably weak government and state has not been derived from detailed analysis of how it actually functioned; indeed, it may well have deterred historians from devoting much attention to the workings of such an inadequate polity. The dearth of studies meant there was little Steven A. Epstein could draw on for the political sections of his survey of Genoa and the Genoese in the Middle Ages, for those periods when there are no surviving chronicles. A lack of contemporary chronicles is one reason, he believes, for the particular neglect of the fourteenth century, although Giovanna Petti Balbi's work on the government of Simone Boccanegra, the first doge of Genoa (1339–44, 1356–63), has made an important contribution to filling that gap.[6] For the fifteenth

---

[3] Lopez, 'Venise et Gênes', 40.   [4] Heers, *Gênes au XVe siècle*, 611.
[5] Pistarino, 'Genova medievale', 73–4.
[6] Epstein, *Genoa and the Genoese*, 188–9; Petti Balbi, *Simon Boccanegra*.

century, Riccardo Musso has made valuable contributions, particularly in his analyses of the government of Genoa under Milanese rule in the middle of the fifteenth century, and I have written on various aspects of Genoese political life, including the working of the government councils, Genoese political language, and attitudes to political liberty and independence.[7] Our knowledge of the significant events and reforms of the early sixteenth century has been immeasurably increased by the work of Arturo Pacini.[8]

In the light of this recent work by these and other historians, it is now possible to look at the Genoese state in the later Middle Ages from a different perspective – to attempt to understand what it was, and how it functioned, rather than decry it for what it was not, and did not do.

Political instability and commercial power

Genoa in the fourteenth century was a major Mediterranean power. In the eastern Mediterranean, although not quite such a force as they had been in the later thirteenth century, the Genoese held their own. They continued to dominate maritime trade in the Black Sea, and had several trading colonies on its shores, the principal one being the city of Caffa. At the entrance to the sea was Genoa's flagship colony, the thriving trading settlement of Pera, near Constantinople. New colonies were still being acquired, notably the island of Chios in the Aegean, taken definitively in 1346, and the city of Famagusta in Cyprus, ceded by the king of Cyprus in 1373.[9]

Their gains did not please the Venetians, and there was a series of wars between Genoa and Venice.[10] The most notable episode of all of these wars was an ambitious assault by the Genoese on the Venetian lagoon itself when, in collaboration with Francesco da Carrara of Padua, they took the city of Chioggia and held it for nearly a year before surrendering to a Venetian siege in June 1380. While the Venetians managed to hold on to most of their colonies after the conquest of the Byzantine empire by the Turks in the fifteenth century, the Genoese lost nearly all of theirs.

---

[7] Musso, 'Le istituzioni ducali'; Musso, 'Il dominio sforzesco'; Musso, 'Lo "stato capellazzo"'; Musso, '"El stato nostro de Zenoa"'; Shaw, 'Counsel and consent'; Shaw, 'Principles and practice'; Shaw, 'The language of Genoese political pragmatism'; Shaw, 'Bartolomea Campofregoso'; Shaw, 'The French signoria over Genoa'; Shaw, 'Concepts of *libertà*'.
[8] Pacini, 'La tirannia delle fazioni'; Pacini, *I presupposti politici*; Pacini, *La Genova di Andrea Doria*.
[9] Lopez, *Storia delle colonie genovesi*; for Chios, see Argenti, *Occupation of Chios*.
[10] Ortalli and Puncuh, *Genova, Venezia, il Levante*; Surdich, *Genova e Venezia*.

Pera had no option but to submit after the Turks took Constantinople in 1453; the Black Sea colonies were taken by the Turks in 1475. Phocaea on the mainland of Asia Minor and the island of Lesbos were lost; only Chios remained in Genoese hands, but had to pay tribute to the Ottomans. Famagusta was taken back by the Cypriots in 1464.[11]

These losses were naturally a blow to Genoese commerce, but the economy was not crippled by them. Compensation could be found by increasing their already susbstantial trade in the western Mediterranean and on the Atlantic coast routes up to England and Flanders. In the Tyrrhenian sea the Genoese had gained the upper hand over their longstanding rivals there, the Pisans, in the late thirteenth century; the destruction of much of the Pisan fleet at the battle of Meloria off Porto Pisano by a Genoese fleet in 1284 had been a decisive victory. More threatening to Genoese interests in these waters in the fourteenth and fifteenth centuries were the subjects of the crown of Aragon, particularly the Catalans, and the expansionist policies of Aragonese kings. Alfonso IV of Aragon invaded Sardinia in the 1320s, driving out the Pisans who claimed dominion over the island. The Genoese had a strong presence in northern Sardinia, and members of the Doria family, who held substantial estates there, resisted Aragonese rule on the island for a century and more.[12] If resistance to the Aragonese in Sardinia was generally left to private initiative, defence of the island of Corsica against the Aragonese was considered a public interest. Keeping some semblance of control over Corsica even when it was not under attack was no easy task:[13] the Genoese persevered, because they could not afford to let the island, situated at the mouth of the Ligurian sea, fall into enemy hands and be used as a base from which Genoese shipping could be harassed in its home waters.

Genoese territory on the mainland of Italy was restricted to Liguria. Much of it was mountainous; the city of Genoa itself was hemmed in by mountains, hence the tall buildings and narrow streets that still characterise the medieval centre of Genoa. Most of their subject towns there – Savona was the only one that could really be considered a city – were on the coast, and access to them was easier by sea; some could scarcely be reached at all by land routes. The commune's control over large parts of this territory was tenuous at best. Power there was in the hands of noble families – the Grimaldi, Doria, Spinola, del Carreto, Fieschi and

---

[11] Lopez, *Storia delle colonie genovesi*, 317–18, 327, 338–9; Pistarino, 'La caduta di Costantinopoli'.
[12] Pistarino, 'Genova e la Sardegna'.   [13] Franzini, *La Corse du XVe siècle*.

others – and the factions that divided every coastal town, every valley and mountain community.

Four of these noble clans, the Doria, Spinola, Grimaldi and Fieschi, known as the *gentes*, had dominated the political life of the republic for much of the thirteenth century. From the 1260s to the 1330s, the Spinola and Doria had supplied the heads of government, usually with two captains, a Spinola and a Doria, holding office in tandem. After the institution of the office of doge in 1339, members of the *gentes* could no longer be at the head of the government, but the Doria and Spinola played a crucial role in the choice, maintenance and change of regimes. Usually, they were on opposing sides: if the Doria were backing a regime, many of the Spinola tended to leave the city, and vice versa.

The Fieschi were just as influential, but in a somewhat different way. While some members of the clan lived in the city and sat on the committees and councils of civic government, as members of the Spinola, Doria and Grimaldi also did, often the heads of the Fieschi family preferred to live on their estates, yet claiming the right to a share in the government, sometimes to a share in appointment to offices, especially those in the eastern Riviera where their lands were. The Grimaldi clan became less prominent in the political life of the city. Although individual members could be figures of great authority in civic affairs, the major focus of their political interests came to be their estates on the western Riviera, particularly Monaco, which they ruled as an independent lordship.

The Spinola and Doria were Ghibellines, the Grimaldi and Fieschi, Guelfs. In the network of Guelf and Ghibelline alliances that linked the states and communities and major families of Italy, Genoa was generally considered Ghibelline in the fourteenth century. But the Genoese Guelfs retained control over much of the territory of Genoa, and were not driven out of the city. In the fifteenth century, offices would be divided equally between Blacks (Guelfs) and Whites (Ghibellines). Every Genoese citizen who held political office did so as a Black or a White. It was possible for individuals or families to change their designated colour without controversy. There was no fighting between Guelf and Ghibelline factions in the city in the fifteenth century; in some parts of Liguria it was a different matter.

Divisions between Guelfs and Ghibellines gave place as the main fault line in the political life of the city in the middle of the fourteenth century to that between nobles and *popolari*. The turning point was 1339, the year of the election by popular acclamation of the first of the 'perpetual' doges, the doges for life, Simone Boccanegra. Until then, Genoa had been governed largely by a group of families associated with the foundation and development of the commune, who came to be known as nobles. Breaking into this circle for those born outside it could be difficult, even for rich merchants, although not impossible.

One way to be assimilated was to to be accepted into one of the noble *alberghi*.[14] These were groups of families, often near neighbours, who adopted a common surname, had property in common (often including a defensive tower and a loggia where members could meet), and had recognised leaders who could speak and act on their behalf (the only '*popolare*' *albergo*, the Giustiniani, was formed by business partners who held the island of Chios). Social and economic distinctions between the *alberghi* and the rest of Genoese society should not be exaggerated. Membership could be accorded as a favour to clients and neighbours, who were not necessarily rich; and not all members of the original families prospered; there could be a wide range of levels of wealth and social prominence among the members. The *popolo* was not wholly excluded from government before 1339. 'Captain of the people' was the title of the noble who headed it; and the *popolo* had an association with a council and an elected 'abbot', who had a subordinate role in the government.[15] Yet they lacked the institutions and the degree of organisation that made the *popolo* in other Italian cities the dominant political force.

Simone Boccanegra's election as doge in 1339 came about when the crowd assembled outside the government palace where the election of the abbot was taking place acclaimed a suggestion shouted by one of them that Boccanegra should be abbot. Hesitating to accept designation as abbot, Boccanegra agreed to be 'doge', a title hitherto not used in Genoa for the head of the government. Another, larger assembly held at the cathedral a day or two later confirmed his nomination as doge for life. Behind this ostensibly spontaneous election can be discerned a group of *popolare* families, including wealthy merchants who wanted a share of power, if only to bring an end to the wars between the noble factions which had been troubling the city for decades.[16]

The new office of doge took root, becoming a permanent part of the Genoese constitution. Theoretically, doges were elected for life, but in practice only a handful lasted more than a few years before they resigned or, more often, were driven out by rivals. Doges had to be *popolari*; no more Genoese nobles headed the government of their city until the

---

[14] Hughes, 'Kinsmen and neighbors'; Grendi, 'Profilo storico'; Grendi, 'Problemi di storia'; Heers, *Gênes au XVe siècle*, 564–76; Heers, *Le clan familial;* Heers, 'Consorterie et alberghi', 55–7.
[15] Epstein, *Genoa and the Genoese*, 157.
[16] *Ibid.*, 203–5; Petti Balbi, *Simon Boccanegra*, 24–33.

reform of the constitution in 1528. In the fifteenth century two families, the Campofregoso and the Adorno, came to monopolise the dogeship. Their rivalry provided yet another and increasingly significant strand in the complex pattern of factions in Genoa.

Part of the doge's title was 'defender of the people'. At times, doges could assume the role of champions of the *popolo* against the nobility as Pietro Campofregoso (1450–8) did in 1454.[17] At times, in the fourteenth century, nobles were excluded from other political offices, including the main executive committee, which governed with the doge, the *Anziani*. Socially, economically and – through their factions, clients and *alberghi* – politically, nobles were much too powerful to be excluded permanently. Should the doge of the day find it politically expedient, these exclusions might be waived, as Antoniotto Adorno did in 1394, during what was his fourth term of office since 1384.[18] From 1413, their right to a half-share in all political offices, committees and councils was enshrined in the *Regulae*, the reformed constitution promulgated under doge Giorgio Adorno (doge 1413–15).

Throughout the fourteenth and fifteenth and into the sixteenth centuries, periods when first captains of the people and then doges were at the head of the government alternated with periods when the republic was subject to a lord from outside Genoa: to the emperor Henry VII, from 1311 to 1313; Robert, the Angevin king of Naples, 1318–35; archbishop Giovanni Visconti, lord of Milan and then his nephews and heirs, 1353–6; Charles VI, king of France, 1396–1409; Theodorus Palaeologus, marquis of Monferrato, 1409–13; duke Filippo Maria Visconti, 1421–35; king Charles VII of France, 1458–61; the Sforza dukes of Milan, 1464–77 and 1487–99; and then the French kings Louis XII, 1499–1512, and Francis I, 1515–22 and 1527–8; in the interval between these last two periods of French dominion, Genoa under doge Antoniotto Adorno had been dependent on, though not formally subject to, the emperor Charles V.

Sometimes, the Genoese had little choice but to submit, as in 1499, when Louis XII regarded Genoa not only as belonging to the French crown by right, because of the submissions to Charles VI and Charles VII, but also as an adjunct of the duchy of Milan which he had just conquered from Ludovico Sforza, and the Genoese were in no position to argue with the victorious king. More often, the Genoese did have a choice, and they chose to accept the sovereignty of a prince. They might do this because they hoped for protection against their enemies, as when

---

[17] Borlandi, 'Ragione politica'; Shaw, *Popular Government*, 156–7.
[18] Epstein, *Genoa and the Genoese*, 245.

they submitted to archbishop Giovanni Visconti, when a war in which they were engaged against the Venetians and the Catalans was going badly for them. Usually, the citizens were acquiescing in a decision taken by a doge for his own personal reasons to give the city over to a foreign prince, as Pietro Campofregoso did in 1458, and Paolo Campofregoso in 1464 and again in 1487. While it was not uncommon in fourteenth-century Italy for cities to submit to lordships, only to recover their independence after some years, Genoa was unusual in continuing to do so in the fifteenth century. By the end of the century, with both the dukes of Milan and the kings of France considering that they had a hereditary right to rule Genoa, the Genoese were in real danger of losing the independence of their republic for good.[19]

Genoese, of all social groups, who had been hoping for respite from the disruption and fighting that arose out of competition for the doge-ship under the rule of a prince, could find themselves faced with demands for men, ships, and money to fight in the wars of their lord. Sooner or later, they would grow weary of the lords and their officials, who found the Genoese a difficult people to govern if they did not agree with the policies and the aims of their rulers. The attraction of holding the lordship of Genoa was the prospect of access to Genoese wealth and shipping. Genoese galleys and ships did not belong to the commune, however, but were in private ownership, and if they were to be used to wage war, their owners expected them to be hired, not requisitioned.[20] And if Genoa was a wealthy city, little of its riches came into the coffers of the commune.

A peculiar form of organisation of the public finances had developed in Genoa, which resulted in the majority of tax revenues not going to the commune, but to share-holders in the *compere*. These began as associations of state creditors who had provided funds (willingly or not) when large sums were needed for extraordinary expenditure, generally to pay for war. Revenue from taxation, often customs dues or taxes on sales of various commodities, were assigned to pay interest on debts that there was little prospect of the commune ever being able to redeem. Shares in the *compere* could be bought and sold in the open market, as a relatively safe form of investment. In 1407 – during a period of French government, but on the initiative of the adminstrators of the *compere*, not at the suggestion of the French – all the *compere* were brought together into the Casa di San Giorgio. Governed by a committee of eight Protectors and a council, all of whom had to be share-holders, the Casa di San Giorgio

---

[19] Shaw, 'Concepts of *libertà*'.
[20] See Heers, *Gênes au XVe siècle*, 267–320, for a detailed discussion of Genoese shipping.

(which until 1444 also operated as a bank) became one of the most respected financial institutions in Italy, and a pillar of the Genoese state.[21]

When colonies or other territories were threatened, and the commune was unable to defend them or hold on to them, they could be entrusted to San Giorgio, as Famagusta was in 1447, the Black Sea colonies and Corsica in 1453, the stronghold of Pietrasanta in the Lunigiana in 1446 and Sarzana in 1484, the Ligurian port of Lerici in 1479, Ventimiglia in 1514 and Levanto in 1515. On occasion, as during the dogeship of Pietro Campofregoso in the 1450s, there were even suggestions that the government of the whole republic of Genoa should be given over to the Casa di San Giorgio, in the hope of providing more stability at the head of the government.[22]

By the late fifteenth century, many Genoese longed to find a permanent solution to their chronic political difficulties, especially to find a way of making their state less vulnerable to disruption by factions. Various schemes and projects to bring 'union' to Genoa finally bore fruit in reforms promulgated in 1528, after the French had been driven out. All those considered eligible to take part in government were brought into twenty-eight reorganised *alberghi*, and the structure of councils and committees was radically changed. Doges were to hold office for two years only. No account was to be taken of Blacks or Whites, of Campofregoso or Adorno, nobles or *popolari*. All members of the new *alberghi* were to be considered noble.[23] If the measures proved successful in eliminating the Campofregoso and Adorno factions and, largely, the distinction between Blacks and Whites from Genoese politics, the division between 'old' nobles and the 'new' nobles (the former *popolari*) would persist, and the reorganisation of the *alberghi* brought these divisions into them. But on the whole the constitution of the 'new republic' – for this was how it was seen – was a success; and under it the Genoese republic, 'La Superba' (the Proud), lasted for three more centuries.

Public and private spheres

The complexity of Genoese political life and the peculiar nature of the Genoese state may be easier to comprehend if analysis is based on the

---

[21] Sieveking, *Studio nelle finanze genovesi*; Marengo, Manfroni and Pessagno, *Il Banco di San Giorgio*; Felloni (ed.), *La Casa di San Giorgio*.
[22] Marengo, Manfroni and Pessagno, *Il Banco di San Giorgio*, 475–517; Shaw, 'Principles and practice', 60–3.
[23] Pacini, *I presupposti politici*, 324–46.

premise that the Genoese had a distinctive perception of the relation between the public and the private spheres.

Like many medieval Italian city governments, the republic of Genoa began as an association of individuals coming together to protect their personal interests and their common interests. To a much greater degree than other civic governments, it kept that character. Their primary interests were commercial and Genoese power came from trade, from the capital resources of its citizens, not from territorial power or the deployment of armies by the state. To protect their commercial interests, the Genoese commune could organise powerful fleets by mustering vessels owned by its citizens; but if they were not at war, they were reluctant to pay for, at most, more than a galley or two to patrol their home waters.

The Genoese saw no need even to try to keep control over their colonies, as the Venetians did. Historians have come to describe the Genoese colonies as a 'commonwealth', rather than an empire. Pera, Caffa and the other Black Sea colonies were largely left to govern themselves (although some appointments to major offices were made in Genoa) and to make their own arrangements as to how they would coexist with their neighbours and trading partners. In general, the administration of Genoese colonies was left to those who had founded them or settled there or invested in them. Chios was held by the shareholders in a fleet raised at government behest but sponsored by private individuals and syndicates in 1346, and sent to protect Genoese interests in the eastern Mediterranean. On their own initiative, they took the island and neighbouring Phocaea, and the ship-owners, organised as the '*Maona*' of Chios, were granted the rights by the Genoese government to administer their conquest and exploit its resources.[24] The fleet that forced the cession of Famagusta from the king of Cyprus was a joint venture between the doge and commune and private share-holders, and the commune figures as just a share-holder in the *Maona* of Cyprus that was instituted in 1374 to exercise jurisdiction over Famagusta.[25] Entrusting threatened colonies to the Casa di San Giorgio was consistent with this approach to colonial administration and government.

In Liguria, geographical constraints militated against the establishment of a unified, centralised administration of Genoese subject territories. All the Genoese could realistically aspire to was to keep key routes through the mountains and key harbours along the coast out of the hands of those who would impose tolls on trade goods, and even that

---

[24] Argenti, *Occupation of Chios*, 86–146.   [25] Petti Balbi, 'L'opzione su Cipro'.

was not easy to achieve. In the case of Savona, the Genoese were wary of the potential of the port to attract merchants away from Genoa. Savona's potential was evident to the lords and their officials who governed Genoa, and tended to view it as an opportunity, much to the consternation of the Genoese, who tended to see it as a threat. Eventually they resolved the problem in the winter of 1525–6 by ruining Savona's harbour, throwing the stones from the demolished wharves into the sea to prevent large ships docking there.[26] Strong objections by the Genoese to the grant by their Milanese or French princes of places in Genoese territory, either to outsiders or to Genoese, were maintained in large part because the lands that were granted tended to be sought after for their situation on trade routes.

Local wars fought to protect their commercial dominance in Liguria or naval wars against their commercial rivals, such as the Venetians or the Catalans, were the only wars the Genoese entered into with any enthusiasm. They took little part in conflicts between other Italian states. Any doge or lord who wanted to involve them in conflicts or alliances with Italian states, unless Genoese interests were directly concerned, found it very difficult to raise money in Genoa to pay for them.

Perhaps because protection of Genoese commercial interests could be seen as the primary function of the Genoese state, wealthy Genoese were not obliged to seek political office in order to protect their own interests. It was not illegitimate in Genoa for citizens who believed their private concerns would be harmed by a proposal or a decision that had already been taken by the government to go openly to the palace to put their case. It was not felt necessary to protect the *Anziani* from such lobbying by keeping them sequestered during their term of office. The *Anziani* in the fourteenth century were obliged to reside in the palace during their four-month terms of office, but there were provisions for a few to be absent for short periods, and in the fifteenth century they did not have to be resident at all. Frequently, the government actively canvassed public opinion; commissions might be sent to sound out opinions on the problems of the day in the squares and in the banking quarter; or anyone who wanted to give their views might be invited to come to the palace to speak privately if they wished. Sometimes, councils would decree that the policy to be adopted on a certain issue was to be determined by what emerged from such canvassing as the favoured option.[27]

Whatever factions were striving for power, Genoese citizens did not have to choose sides. Indeed, there was clearly a role, an important role,

---

[26] Scovazzi and Noberasco, *Storia di Savona*, III, 89–91.
[27] Shaw, 'Counsel and consent'.

in Genoese public life for individuals not strongly identified with any faction, whose social station, judgement and powers of argument earned them the respect of their fellow citizens. Such men could sway the decision of a council, against the wishes of a doge or a prince's governor.

Those who chose to stay out of politics were not in danger, as they could be in other states such as Florence, of suffering discrimination in taxation. Forced loans were used to help pay for wars in the fourteenth century, but they were compensated by shares in the *compere*, which came to be seen as sound investments. Theoretically share-holders would be paid interest until the debts were redeemed, but the government was rarely in a position to make substantial repayments and the *compere* continued in existence, decade after decade. As most of the indirect taxes levied were assigned to paying this interest – and many of them had been devised specifically for that purpose – this was a source of discontent to those who had to pay taxes on necessities, but did not have cash to spare to buy shares in the *compere*.

With the foundation of the Casa di San Giorgio, this sense of grievance seems to have diminished; San Giorgio became the investment of choice for widows and orphans, and for religious institutions: a safe place for smaller savings. Richer investors still held shares in it, although there were probably better returns to be earned elsewhere. Forced loans became no longer acceptable as a means of raising extraordinary revenue in the fifteenth century. If desperate, doges might resort to detaining wealthy men, presumably targeting known opponents of their regime, to force them to lend, but this proceeding aroused more ill-feeling than any yield was probably worth. For the commune to borrow money from the citizens came to be considered wasteful, because any loans made were expected to be short-term and at commercial rates of interest. The Genoese expected their government to be run on quite a small budget, and an efficient committee kept a close eye on ordinary expenditure. Agreement by the councils to extra levies of the main direct tax, the *avaria*, from which many, including the poor, were exempt, was given only reluctantly. Expenditure of any extraordinary revenue that was voted was scrutinised closely, to check that the monies were spent only for the purposes for which they had been raised. Lords and their officials had to face the same problem as the doge. Nor was an easy option to be found in drawing on the funds of San Giorgio, at least after it ceased to act as a bank (the problems caused by lending money to the commune were the major reason for the Casa di San Giorgio ceasing to be a bank).[28] The

---

[28] Epstein, *Genoa and the Genoese*, 261.

government could not borrow from the Casa at will; the consent of the administrators was needed and that was by no means automatically given. (The nature of the relations between the Casa di San Giorgio and the commune have yet to be properly studied and understood.)

Holding political office was not seen as being crucial to the social prestige of an individual or a family. Election to serve on the *Anziani* or on a *balìa* or other extraordinary commission, or representing the republic as an ambassador brought no special status, and there is no evidence of competition for such posts. Doubtless some citizens enjoyed the opportunity to take part in public affairs, to feel they were at the heart of government. To others, serving a term as *Anziano* or on an executive commission with responsibility for administering a war, or finding a way to raise money, was undertaken as a duty, something of a chore rather than an honour. After an arduous term in office, the members of special commissions could ask, as a reward for their labours, not for another appointment but for a period of exemption from being called upon to serve again. Once both nobles and *popolari* were given equal shares in power, access to political office does not seem to have been controversial. There was no social group that felt entitled to play a part in government that was excluded. Nor were there any barriers to men from the subject towns who settled in Genoa holding executive offices or being summoned to councils. Fourteenth-century councils have not yet been studied in detail, but in the fifteenth century there was no fixed membership, and the numbers summoned might vary from a few dozen to several hundred. All councils, like government committees, had to be constituted with set proportions of half Blacks, half Whites, half nobles and half *popolari*, and among the *popolari*, half merchants and half *artefici* (tradesmen or members of professions such as notaries and physicians).[29]

The only exception to the lack of competition for office was the dogeship. Elaborate regulations about how the doge should be elected by a procedure involving several stages and electoral commissions were generally ignored. Aspirants fought or intrigued their way into power, with legitimation coming from a council summoned after the victor had emerged. On one occasion, in 1393, two contenders, Antonio Guarco and Pietro Campofregoso, were said to have settled which of them should be doge by playing dice; the winner, Guarco, had his 'election' ratified by a council of sixty citizens the next day.[30] He did not last long. Few doges did hold office for long, for all that it was supposed to be held

---

[29] Shaw, 'Counsel and consent'.   [30] Basso, 'Antoniotto Adorno', 294.

for life. The family whose members held it more frequently than any other was the Campofregoso. By the early fifteenth century, this family came to believe they had a quasi-hereditary right to the dogeship, and some – notably Tommaso Campofregoso (doge 1415–21, 1437–42) and Pietro Campofregoso (doge 1450–8) – saw their position as approaching that of a prince.[31]

But the powers of the doge fell far short of those of a lord. They had a very limited budget, and that would not pay for many troops: one reason doges found it so difficult to entrench themselves in power. They had to act with the *Anziani*; in fact, there was not much that the doge could do without them or another executive commission. All major decisions – such as making peace or war, or raising taxes – had to be approved by a council. The electoral procedures for the *Anziani* were such that it would have been very difficult for the doge to pack the committee with his supporters. He might have a freer hand in choosing who would be summoned to a council meeting, but still had to observe the proportions of Blacks, Whites, nobles, merchants and *artefici*. Councils were conducted in an unusual way; they were summoned to discuss problems and to make proposals for dealing with them, not merely to approve proposals put to them by the executive; there was no guarantee they would do as the doge wanted. When Genoa was subject to a lord, his officials would be expected to abide by the same constraints. Attempts to evade them, to manipulate the councils or to bypass them, would cause resentment and arouse resistance. Ready to acquiesce in whatever doge the factions might present to them, or to surrender the independence of their republic to an external lord as the Genoese might appear to be, they were not prepared passively to leave the direction of public affairs to them. At least by the fifteenth century, a broad spectrum of Genoese citizens, from nobles and merchants to *artefici*, had a sense of the government as something in which they shared, for which they had a common responsibility, and which should be conducted according to certain principles.

How can this perception be reconciled with the prevalence and power of political factions in the Genoese state? Contemporaries from outside Genoa might struggle as much as historians have done to make sense of the interplay of factions and their function in Genoese political life. Given the current state of knowledge of the factions, especially for the fourteenth century, any generalisation can only be tentative. It does seem as though the power of factions in the city of Genoa changed and

---

[31] Basso, 'Tommaso Campofregoso', 326; Borlandi, 'Ragione politica'; Shaw, *Popular Government*, 207–8.

lessened from the fourteenth to the fifteenth centuries, even if it is not possible as yet to say precisely when, how or why this happened. Political life in Genoa in the middle of the fourteenth century, with hostility between Guelfs and Ghibellines, antagonism between nobles and *popolari*, and co-operation between the Doria and the Spinola, was very different from political life in fifteenth-century Genoa, where the most significant division was between the Campofregoso faction, backed by the Doria, and the Adorno faction, backed by the Spinola. The Campofregoso, originally Ghibellines, vied for leadership of the Guelfs in Liguria with the Fieschi, but this did not mean they could claim to lead or represent the Blacks in Genoa, any more than the Adorno could claim to represent or lead the Whites.

Antagonism between nobles and *popolari* was still evident at times, as in debates over whether they should continue to be assessed separately for the *avaria*, and how the burden should be divided between them. There was a perception that the nobles were readier to welcome and support the duke of Milan or the king of France as lord of Genoa, a perception heightened when nobles appeared to be favoured under these regimes, being allowed to extend their lands and power in Genoese territory in Liguria.[32]

The best-known instance of hostility between nobles and *popolari* was the uprising by the *popolari* in 1506–7, directed against the nobles who were accused of behaving arrogantly. The long-standing equal division of offices was altered to two-thirds for *popolari*, one-third for nobles, but most nobles refused to take up offices under this arrangement, and many left Genoa. This took place while Genoa was subject to Louis XII: the *popolari* insisted their quarrel was with the nobles, not the French, and initially had the support of the lieutenant governor, but the nobles had the support of the king, and a military expedition led by Louis himself brought the uprising to an end.[33] Should this episode be seen as a fundamental conflict, usually suppressed, emerging into the open, or as an exceptional episode in a generally uncontentious relationship? The fact that this was the only occasion in which the equal shares of nobles and *popolari* in government offices established by the *Regulae* of 1413 was challenged points to this episode being an exception.

When the reforms of 1528 incorporated *popolari* into the reorganised *alberghi*, the desire was to create a new, homogeneous political society; it did not succeed in this, but, had there been visceral enmity between nobles and *popolari*, it is inconceivable that the new *alberghi* could have

---

[32] Shaw, *Popular Government*, 155–9.
[33] Pandiani, *Un anno di storia genovese*; Taviani, *Superba discordia*.

seemed a feasible remedy for it, or that they should have survived for fifty years. This reform was long seen as a classic example of the formation of a closed oligarchy, but it has been convincingly shown that its purpose was to bring union among the Genoese, not to exclude many *popolari* from government.[34] It was intended to eliminate factions from Genoese political life, above all the Campofregoso and Adorno factions. Contenders for the dogeship had always been willing to look for the support of other powers, either to win the office or to maintain themselves in it. In the circumstances of the Italian Wars, the stakes in this game became higher, and added to the risk the Genoese were running of the permanent loss of their independence, if they allowed it to continue.

The success of the reforms in purging the Campofregoso and Adorno factions and the instability they caused from the political life of the city was complete. The new constitution soon became regarded as the bulwark of the republic and its independence. Arguments about whether it required some modification or adjustments did not detract from the loyalty it generated among the Genoese. The constitution and its success were the fruit of the commitment to their republic, which had been burgeoning during the period when the primary loyalty of many Genoese seemed to be to a faction, rather than the state.

Conclusion

If the Genoese state was weaker, the institutions of government less sophisticated than those of some other Italian states, it cannot be put down to some congential incapacity of the Genoese to come up with anything better. The basic institutions of civic government, the executive committees and commissions and the councils, were very stable, and carried on with their work whatever the regime. It was at the very head of the government that change came so frequently. On the whole, the Genoese seem to have been content with how their institutions worked, and felt no need to change them, except for the head. A few experiments were made, in between the doges and the external lords, with collective leadership, such as the eight Captains of the *Libertà* of Genoa, elected in December 1442 or the four *artefici* elected Captains of the People in May 1462; none of these lasted for very long.[35] But, by the early sixteenth century, dissatisfaction with a system of government that could not prevent the wearisome succession of regimes had grown to the point where proposals for radical reform could attract general support.

---

[34] Pacini, *I presupposti politici*, 347–413.   [35] Shaw, 'Principles and practice', 66.

The Genoese have been criticised by historians for their deficient sense of the state, for their failure to develop – or even to seem to want – political power to match their commercial power, for being overmaterialistic, too concerned with their own business affairs, for their lack of an elevated concept of the virtue of political participation. Nor can the Genoese or their state be fitted easily into the matrices that have been imposed on the history of the political society and the institutions of government of cities in the 'Centro-Nord', northern and central Italy. There is much still to be discovered about the Genoese state, but this intriguing political society and the state it expressed can be better understood if they are accepted as being not ineffective or underdeveloped, but simply *sui generis*.

Part II

Themes and perspectives

12 The collapse of city-states and the role of urban centres in the new political geography of Renaissance Italy

Francesco Somaini

Introduction

Innumerable aspects of fourteenth- and fifteenth-century Italian cities and city-states have been studied recently. Research has focused on political and institutional contexts, fiscal systems and normative structures, but also on political discourses (both those of the cities as collective actors and those of their internal components), the forms of production of documentary evidence, factions and their presence or absence in different urban contexts and so on. Justice, both its forms and procedures and the effects of these on social and political dynamics, has been investigated too, as have practices and forms of relationship between social and political actors in the cities (and between urban and countryside actors); and individual social groups – the elites, the poor, Jewish communities, clergymen, monks. Research into urban identities, their construction and representation, has been carried out, by investigating, for example, ideologies and mindsets. Studies have focused on the forms of religious life, especially with investigations of the 'civic religion' and on the relationships with both secular and regular local ecclesiastical institutions: on hospitals, for instance, focusing on their distribution in the fourteenth century; on sacred places; on brotherhoods; and on devotional activities and activities of care. Moreover, anti-clericalism and the emergence of both popular and elitist forms of lay sensibility and culture have been investigated. Urban spaces have been studied, both those utilised by the various economic, political and social actors and those imagined and modelled by urban politics; these were considered in the light of their functional values, as well as their underlying ideological values of propaganda, power or struggle for power. The analysis of artistic and literary patronage has gone together with research on moments of collective sociability such as both lay and religious celebrations, festivals and rituals. Finally, more 'traditional' themes have been investigated: demographic trends, economic and productive life, the role of corporations and merchants, capital, investments, gains, types of production, consumption and prices. The relationships between social dynamics and political equilibria, or between cities and countryside, have not been overlooked either – thus including issues relating to the management of the territories, to the processes of *comitatinanza* and their efficacy, or to control over forces outside the cities.

Overall, the number of studies is truly significant and they are often of high quality. Investigations have frequently opened new problematic research avenues that suggested readings of great interpretative flair or new ways of dealing with the primary sources. Substantial efforts of comparative or synoptic nature also abound – not only on various Italian cities, but also comparing the Italian situation with other European regions.[1]

Nevertheless, the historiography on cities was not exempt from the underlying limitation of most contemporary historiography, which is the tendency to adopt descriptive rather than explicative approaches. In other words, even in studies on the cities it is possible to notice a penchant for analyses that privilege the description of past phenomena over their explanation.

These 'idiographic' tendencies may have emerged from the necessity of moving away from pre-constituted models of interpretation, or from universal readings of history – possibly affected by teleologism, that is, the notion that history must forcibly tend towards certain endings. At the level of understanding, nonetheless, this renunciation of explicative historiography has had consequences that cannot be underestimated. Mainly, it is possible to perceive some reluctance in establishing explicit nexus of causality. The very notion of causality seems to have disappeared from many current studies, thus making unclear the motives behind the historical facts and the phenomena that are being described. The perception of change has sometimes been blurred, by overlooking the causes or frequently emphasising the 'how' over the 'why'. Perhaps under the influence of social sciences and anthropology, scholars have lost sight of the historical dimension of time passing. As a result, studies have not only erased the surface changes and the much abused *histoire événementielle* (which is at times still bound by old ostracisms), but also the deepest dimension of history that Lucien Febvre once called the *changements de climat*.

Obviously, it would be unwise to generalise; there are in fact many important exceptions, but the underlying feeling of descriptivism remains.

---

[1] Berengo, *L'Europa delle città* and *Città italiana e città europea*. See also Jones, *The Italian City-State*.

In any case, it is impossible here to offer a critical literature review of the most significant studies dedicated to the topic of city-states in the last decades.[2] Thus, in order to adopt an explicative approach, the focus will be on four fundamental themes: the crucial issue of the ending of the city-states of northern and central Italy and its possible causes; the changes to the territorial expansion of the cities and their relationship with the countryside; the political and social governance of different cities and the oligarchical closures; the political and social dynamism of southern and Sicilian cities in the fourteenth and fifteenth centuries and its implications, which constitutes one of the most innovative themes of current historiography.

The collapse of the city-states

Undoubtedly, the end of city-states in central and northern Italy is an essential point of departure to grasp the significance of the transformation of the status of cities in the Renaissance.

Formally part of the *Regnum Italicum* and of the papal territories, over the central centuries of the Middle Ages, the northern part of the Italian peninsula saw the unique phenomenon of cities that flourished not only because they had gained political independence (appointing specific forms for self-governance) but also because they had conquered large parts of the surrounding territories, thus creating territorial states based upon the city. They were small, yet not minute, sovereign states that, apart from a formal dependence on the emperor or the pope, did not recognise any superior authority. Around 1350, when several of these communes had already surrendered or were close to doing so, the famous jurist Bartolo da Sassoferrato coined the formula of *civitas sibi princeps*, so as to indicate the *de facto* sovereignty of the city-states. Yet, between the fourteenth and the fifteenth centuries, the majority of these city-states disappeared.

Evidence speaks for itself. At the beginning of the fourteenth century, the Italian city-states numbered more than eighty. One century later when the political landscape of the peninsula reached a partial stabilisation after the peace of Lodi of 1454, there were fewer than fifteen city-states remaining. After the peace of Cateau-Cambrésis in 1559, sanctioning Spanish dominion in Italy, their number had shrunk again. Only one remained of the old city-states of communal origins that

---

[2] It is impossible to indicate an essential bibliography; for essential references, see Ginatempo, 'Le città italiane'; Franceschi and Taddei, *Les villes d'Italie*; Ascheri, *Le città stato*; and Gamberini, *Oltre le città*.

comprised a single city, the republic of Lucca, maybe a maximum of two if the marquisate of Mantua, which had joined dynastically with the Montferrato in 1530, is included. Through several events, other institutions emerged replacing the city-states: principalities of feudal origins (as the Savoy dominions); ecclesiastical principalities (such as the papacy); and mainly new configurations emerging from the city-states transformed in larger territorial formations that held together many of the existing communal entities and various other territories. The mosaic of independent city-states was replaced by new geopolitical configurations. For the smaller states, two, three or four subordinate cities converged into a new aggregation as was the case for the territories controlled by the Este, the republic of Siena, the states of the Malatesta or those of the Montefeltro. For larger, regional or supra-regional states, even more cities were driven into the new configurations. The Visconti, for instance, at the peak of their expansion at the end of the fourteenth century, ruled over thirty ancient communes.

Over the course of the fierce struggle to survive that changed the traditional geography of the city-states between the beginning of the fourteenth and the first half of the fifteenth century, the small states were not always absorbed by the larger and growing potentates. For instance, Ferrara managed to fight off Venice in 1308–9; Mantua resisted several attacks from the Visconti and the Della Scala over the fourteenth century; Lucca frustrated the attempts of Florence to annex its territories between 1429 and 1431. Furthermore, some city-states that lost their independence sometimes managed to regain it. There were even times when city-states made a comeback, thus challenging the hegemony of larger and stronger powers. For example, following the death of Gian Galeazzo Visconti in 1402, the state of the Visconti, which seemed to have affirmed its control over the central and northern regions of Italy, collapsed. Centralised leadership seemed to slip away and soon almost all the cities of the dominion regained their *de facto* autonomy. Similar phenomena, though on a much smaller scale, happened again in Lombardy after the death of the duke Filippo Maria Visconti in 1447, when the Milanese state, which this duke had managed to restore between the 1410s and the 1420s, was left without a rightful heir and at the mercy of many pretenders. After its defeat by the League of Cambrai in 1509, Venice's inland dominions (conquered over the fifteenth century) fell apart too; the cities of eastern Lombardy, Brescia, Bergamo, Crema and Cremona, gravitated towards the French (who had owned the Milanese area since 1499), whereas the cities of the Marca Trevigiana (especially, Verona, Vicenza and Padua) gravitated towards the Holy Roman emperor, Maximilian of Habsburg, in the hope of regaining their lost sovereignty under the aegis of imperial authority. Similar hopes were also held by the citizens of Pisa when in 1494 they rebelled against Florence, which had ruled over them since 1406. In other words, even at the beginning of the sixteenth century, not only could the notion of a possible return to a political order different from the regional states arouse enthusiasm and passion but it also seemed to be a feasible option.

However, all these events were short-lived. The Milanese state, dismembered at the death of Gian Galeazzo, was restored, as mentioned above, by Filippo Maria; and again years later by Francesco Sforza who entered Milan victorious in February 1450. The regained independence of the 'second republic of Pisa' lasted only fifteen years, until 1509 when the Florentines once again took control over the city. By 1517, eight years after the defeat of Agnadello, Venice regained control over a large part of its *Stato di Terra*, including most of the cities it had lost. These events confirm that the crisis of city-states was not easily reversible.[3]

The demographic shock of the first half of the fourteenth century seems to be the primary identifiable cause of the end of the city-states. The Black Death of 1348 brought many Italian cities to such a breaking point that it impeded their survival as independent entities. Between the 1350s and the 1360s, for instance, several communes in Umbria and the Marche ended up submitting to the papal legate Gil Albornoz because, devastated by the Black Death, they realised that they could no longer retain their autonomy. A similar fate was reserved to such communes of Tuscany as San Gimignano, Colle Val d'Elsa, Prato and Volterra, which Florence absorbed into its dominions between 1349 and 1361 (further extending to Arezzo in 1384).[4]

All the same, in several other cities, in the Veneto region, in Lombardy, in Emilia and even in Tuscany, the end of the independence of many cities in actual terms pre-dated (even by several decades) the pandemic of 1348. Clearly, other factors beyond the demographic decline were at play.

The crisis of city-states began at the end of the thirteenth century; one of its causes lay in the difficulties of the communes in the late thirteenth century to resolve their internal tensions of a political and social nature.

---

[3] Of fundamental importance when discussing these events, see Valeri, *L'Italia nell'età dei principati*, and Simeoni, *Le signorie*. In English, see also Larner, *Italy in the Age of Dante*; Hay and Law, *Italy in the Age of Renaissance*; Mallett, 'The Northern Italian States'; Law, Green and Abulafia, 'Italy in the age of Dante and Petrarch'; Najemy, *Italy in the Age of Renaissance*. On the Italian Wars, see Pellegrini, *Le guerre d'Italia*.

[4] For studies of demography, see Ginatempo and Sandri, *L'Italia delle città*.

Indeed, in comparison to the bloody civil struggles of the thirteenth century, several communes had managed to reach more balanced situations before the beginning of the fourteenth century. In areas in which, for instance, a single *dominus* or a family established a personal government, the arrival of *signorie* overall produced pacifying results, diminishing private violence and clamping down on the struggles of factions. At least, regarding public order, the development of *signorie* had a moderating effect, as did the creation of new structures and apparatus of government leading to political control. The experiences of 'extended government' were equally effective (though obtained with different solutions). These also had stabilising effects, for instance by devising peace-making ideologies, tied to values of civic harmony and of good government, or even by stimulating institutions and judicial practices based on the notion of *bonum commune*, which were thought of as instruments leading to more impersonal forms of government. It is no accident that this tendency was termed the affirmation of a 'culture of the institutions' of the regimes of the *popolo*. The same happened to some extent with the first *serrate* (closures) of the oligarchies (for example in Venice).[5]

The political structures which appeared around the late thirteenth century seemed to succeed in limiting internal conflicts. However, social stability was not usually achieved by overcoming or settling social and political tensions but foremost by ostracising opponents. Whether it concerned members of families and lineages hostile to the power of a *signore* or of his dynasty, or magnates exiled from the cities or excluded from political office by the proscriptive policies of the regimes of the *popolo*, or even the supporters of a party of a faction opposed to the prevailing oligarchy, the common result was to assist the flight of the dissidents from the cities. But this approach did not resolve the issue of internal stability, because these political exiles regularly tried to return to their homeland so as to eject those who had exiled them. Moreover, the fragmentation of the overall political frame allowed them to find refuge, allies and support abroad. The phenomenon of extromission undermined the preservation of the city-states at its very base; this issue did not have solutions, unless a remedy to the overall geopolitical fragmentation was to be found.[6]

Many communes, unable to sustain this situation, ended up submitting to the political tutelage of stronger potentates. By the second half of the thirteenth century, for instance, several cities of the *Regnum Italicum*

---

[5] Crouzet-Pavan, *Enfer et paradis*; Hyde, *Society and Politics*.
[6] Heers and Bec, *Exile et civilisation*; Milani, *I comuni italiani* (with an updated bibliography).

submitted themselves to the Angevin kings of Naples, conferring on them extraordinary powers; a solution taken once again in the first half of the fourteenth century. In Lombardy, too, over the second part of the thirteenth century, the Della Torre family, *signori* of Milan, devised a similar system with the main difference being that they did not establish a more or less temporary *signoria* over far-away cities, but over closer ones. After them, the Visconti, especially Matteo (between 1295–1302 and 1311–22), did the same.

In general, the cities did not see submission to a lord as a danger to their republican status. Urban communes were mostly interested in regaining and maintaining their internal stability; moreover, the *signori* were not necessarily supposed to monopolise power and authority for a long time. Nevertheless, the final outcome of a change of regime to the advantage of a larger potentate was often a substantial loss of political independence by the city-states.

Another answer to the instability was to bring to life forms of political co-ordination at a higher level. Referring to the Guelf and Ghibelline ideologies allowed the various actors to join together in political groupings of wider scale. Thus, the tendency towards alliances, leagues or other supra-local forms of agreement extended not only to towns but also to territorial lords, consortia and even the *extrinseci*, the exiled political figures of one faction or the other. These alliances were indeed strong factors of political polarisation and created contrapositions between blocks – that is, Guelfs against Ghibellines – which often exacerbated local conflicts by interconnecting them in a simplified way. As a result, the tensions were not resolved but amplified; at the same time, new networks of solidarity and protection, which introduced some ordering principles into the general anarchy of the system, came into existence. In a chain reaction, new motivations of a hierarchical nature emerged: weaker actors had to submit to the will of stronger ones.

However, crucially, the efficacy of these leagues as co-ordinating factors remained rather limited. In 1310, for instance, the league of Guelf *signori* of Lombardy could not join forces to oppose Henry VII; neither did the *tallia Tuscie*, the league of Guelf Tuscan communes, prove to be more effective when, a few years later, it showed its military weakness in the battles in Montecatini (1315) and Altopascio (1325).

In the context of Italy, pervaded by a powerful political individualism, the supra-local alliances or even forms of submission to a larger potentate that were to a greater or lesser extent temporary did not manage to guarantee a durable stability. Around the 1320s a drive towards the construction of power systems that would fully supersede the city-states began to emerge. The papal legates Bernard Gui and Bertrand de la Tour sent a famous report to John XXII in Avignon in which they insisted that the cities of Lombardy were ready to give themselves into the hands of 'any king' who would put an end to the disorder in these territories. Between 1330 and 1331 many communes and *signorie*, converging into a large multi-city aggregation, in a surprisingly swift decision submitted to the king of Bohemia, John of Luxembourg.

Although this phenomenon remained ephemeral, it revealed the need for higher-level political and territorial co-ordination. Soon afterwards, with this experience fading away, the same drive was taken up by others, such as the Della Scala family, who between the 1320s and the 1330s joined together the vast majority of the Marca Trevigiana (even with some attempts to expand into Lombardy, Emilia and Tuscany); or the Visconti family that, with Azzone (1329–39), ensured their *de facto* control over Lombardy.

In short, within few decades, many city-states disappeared, to be replaced by wider, bigger and more powerful states that could better face the issue of general stability. Soon enough the new potentates who chose this path entered into battles against each other. The 'war of Lucca' (1336–9), which also downsized the Della Scala's aspirations, established a significant precedent that was followed by the conflict between Milan and Florence (1351–3); the long wars of the 1350s, 1360s and 1370s between the papacy and the Visconti – which expanded the theatre of war in a series of secondary areas; the War of the Eight Saints between Florence and the papacy (1375–8); and so on. As these conflicts spread, becoming ever more extensive and consuming, many city-states (as well as several minor *signorie*) ended up submitting to the sphere of influence of the major potentates, through the pacts of *accomandigia* and of *aderenza*, which began to spread around the second half of the fourteenth century.[7]

Furthermore, the growing scale of conflict created in turn an additional factor of crisis for the city-state system: the 'military crisis' of the commune. In few decades, the traditional communal militias based upon citizens' mobilisation became entirely inappropriate. The new conflicts demanded specialised armies of considerable size and able to remain in arms for long periods and operate over long distances. Yet the traditional communal armies were not capable of performing these functions (in addition, the city governments tended

---

[7] Tabacco, *Egemonie sociali*; Lazzarini, *L'Italia degli stati territoriali*; Fubini, '"Potenze grosse"'; Somaini, 'The political geography'.

to disarm their inhabitants rather than keep them in arms). Therefore, making recourse to mercenary troops had already become more frequent at the end of the thirteenth century and the beginning of the fourteenth, at the time of the Guelf and Ghibelline coalitions and city leagues. However, maintaining armies of mercenaries had huge costs. In commenting on many fourteenth-century communes' devotion to the Angevin *signoria*, Pietro Azario of Novara, chronicler and witness of the Lombard events between the second half of the thirteenth and the first half of the fourteenth century, observed that 'cives non patiebantur expensas guerrarum supportare [the citizens did not tolerate the fact that they had to sustain war expenses]'. Over the fourteenth century, when large mercenary armies appeared, attracted to Italy by this escalating situation of conflict in the peninsula, the cities had to come to terms with a financially unsustainable situation. Enrolling and maintaining military companies was unthinkable for those who did not have vast economic resources, but resisting an enemy attack from this type of army was almost impossible. In 1377, for instance, during the War of the Eight Saints, the city of Cesena, allied to Florence against the papacy, had to face the Breton mercenaries commanded by the English captain John Hawkwood and the cardinal Robert de Genève – later to become the pope of the Avignonese obedience after the schism of 1378. The citizens of Cesena refused to accept the mercenaries' demands, which was an ill-advised decision. The city was taken by storm and the retaliation against its population of 6,500 led to carnage in which thousands of people were massacred.

Individual city-states did not have the means of sustaining the boom of military expenses, nor could they resist the up-and-coming powers and their (often uncontrollable) armies of this new kind that had been attracted to Italy. City-states often had to accept the changed situation and let the new regional states absorb them into the new structures that were forming around actors who were more entrepreneurial and possessed more resources. Their independence was thus definitely lost. As mentioned above, there were nonetheless some attempts at returning to the model of the city-state in the fifteenth as well as in the sixteenth centuries. However, this model was no longer feasible at a military level. For instance, episodes such as the sack of Piacenza perpetrated by the Sforza troops in 1447, or the sack of Volterra of 1472 by Federico of Montefeltro's soldiers (paid by Florence), or the infamous sack of Brescia of 1512, by French troops, did not reach the brutality of the carnage in Cesena of 1377, but they demonstrated that in the age of large regional potentates, of professional armies, of conflicts between great powers, the time of armed citizens and independent cities was gone forever.[8]

The separation of the *contadi*

The end of the city-states of the central and northern regions did not imply the end of the centrality of the urban role. With the exception of some mountainous areas in the Alps and in the Apennines, and of some geopolitical areas of feudal and seigneurial majority (such as Friuli and, partially, Piedmont), northern Italy remained, together with the Low Countries, the European region with the highest concentration of cities and with the highest rates of urbanisation. The Italian cities were numerous, important and crowded. With their level of manufacturing production, their substantial trading and financial activities, and their consumption, they continued to be the economic driving forces, as well as the main centres in which wealth accumulated and circulated in vast quantities. As a result, they were also places of high sociability and significant clusters of cultural, artistic and religious life.[9]

Losing their political independence did not alter this embedded feature. The cities maintained their role, not least because the new territorial states – with specific exceptions, such as the position of Florence with regard to Pisa – did not adopt punitive policies against the subjected cities. The status of citizen, albeit of a subjected city, continued to imply substantial advantages as it had done in the past. There were fiscal privileges – citizens benefited from fewer costs than others, the cities maintained some power in the subdivision of fiscal burdens both internally and externally in managing the dependent rural communities. There were jurisdictional privileges tied to the citizens' right to be judged by city courts – normally closer to their interests. There were also privileges regarding food supply – the cities had rights over farming surpluses in the countryside – or of many other kinds such as the freedom to purchase houses and properties in the city, to join a corporation and so on.

Nevertheless, the transition from a city *sibi princeps* to a subjected city was not painless. The possibility for subjected cities of maintaining real financial autonomy was reduced, and the loss of independence corresponded to a drawback in terms of city planning, as the

---

[8] Mallett, *Mercenaries and Their Masters*; Grillo, *Cavalieri e popolo in armi* (with an updated bibliography).
[9] Crouzet-Pavan and Lecuppre-Desjardin (eds.), *Villes de Flandre et d'Italie*.

construction of forts, castles and fortified *cittadelle* passed to the new higher powers. Even more evident were the effects in relation to control over the dominion.

The end of the city-state often translated into a change in the conditions of the rural areas, that is, the territories that the city-states had previously considered as directly relevant to them and that they had submitted to their own rule (or attempted to submit). City–*contado* relationships changed: the territory was no longer entirely submitted to the city, and more actors negotiated with a superior authority (the prince or the dominant city) in order to obtain concessions and specific privileges.

The so-called process of *comitatinanza*, that is, the submission of the *contadi* to the city-states of the twelfth and thirteenth centuries, had not been entirely effective everywhere. In several instances, this process had succeeded only modestly, partially or even disappointingly. The *contadi* of the cities in the Marca d'Ancona, for example, were of small if not minute sizes; whereas the Lombard and chiefly the Emilian cities had not managed to impose their authority at all in large areas; here the autonomous rural lordships survived, often favouring the creation of fighting factions in the cities, whose vitality was explicitly based upon the relationship with these fierce rural seigneurs.

When larger states replaced the city-states, the new governments had to face the problem of having to deal not only with the cities but also with those political-territorial components that had managed to avoid being subject to urban communes. Moreover, they had also to enter into dialogue with all those forces that, precisely because they were under the cities' tutelage, intended to have the primacy of the cities reconsidered and to be liberated from any submission to them. Boroughs aspiring to more or less marked forms of autonomy – the so-called quasi-cities, the rural or mountain communities of very diverse identity and size, the *domini* of small or medium-sized rural lordships (lay or ecclesiastical) were all interested in maintaing dialogues with the new central powers in order to have recognised, confirmed or conceded *ex novo* rights and privileges that would ratify their 'apartness' (*separazione*) from the old city districts. Having lost their independence, several cities thus found themselves forced to operate in political contexts in which the new authorities, even if they were not necessarily hostile to them, had to negotiate with several actors with different interests and demands.

The newly formed states at times had to re-establish the internal borders of their territories, thus upsetting geographies constructed earlier by the cities. Florence, for instance, had accompanied its expansion over the fourteenth and fifteenth centuries with solid reorganisations of the *contadi* of the subjected cities, thus expanding its own *contado* (at least over a certain period). After the Visconti obtained the ducal title in 1395, the Milanese state witnessed the substantial creation of fiefs – assigned to courtesans and *condottieri*, as well as to established *domini* rooted in the territory – thus arguing against the previous districts of the cities. The same happened, at least partially, to the territories that submitted to Venetian control. Not only did Venice often recognise the rights and jurisdictions of the various *domini locorum*, who were in place at the time of the conquest, but it also favoured the creation of separate areas to be assigned, for instance, to those captains whose loyalty needed to be consolidated.

In reality, no regional state, not even Florence, would have ever assumed positions similar to those of Henry VII of Luxembourg (1308–13) in relation to their subjected cities. He reached the point of postulating the illegality of the institution of the urban *contadi*. From his perspective, which was one of reconstructing the *Regnum Italicum*, all subjects had to be equally submitted to the royal authority; therefore, the *contadi* had to become part of the crown's estate.[10] In stark contrast to such a view, the new Italian states held a moderate line. Venice, for example, attempted to assume the role of arbiter among its subjected cities and territories, whereas it is possible to see, with regard to the state of Milan, a timeline in the dynamics of the relationships between the Visconti (and, later, the Sforza) and the cities of its dominion. Periods characterised by the intention to disaggregate the cities' *contadi*, so as to weaken the commune (and also, in part, the *contado* of Milan itself), were followed by times in which the dukes looked after (in actuality, for fiscal motives) the interests of these cities and of their ruling classes. Thus, where on the one hand, starting at the end of the thirteenth century, they had recourse to the fief, on the other hand, over the following century, there were interventions of a corrective nature intended to limit, for instance, the autonomy of the feudal courts in comparison to those of the cities. However, the cities unavoidably experienced a certain loss of control over the *contadi*, even though this phenomenon did not stop the economic expansion of the citizens, who consolidated their presence in the country especially by purchasing land mainly to the detriment of small peasant holdings.

The emergence of the oligarchies

Among the factors contributing to the loss of independence of many communes or, at the opposite end, to the transformation of a few urban

---

[10] Somaini, 'Henri VII et le cadre italien'.

settlements into capitals of new multi-city states, the internal institutional events within the various cities did not seem to have a particular impact.

It is impossible to establish exact links between the crisis of republican order and the survival of cities as politically independent actors. The birth of the urban *signorie*, that is, of new political structures grounded in the concentration of power in the hands of only one person or one family, did not seem to have much impact either on the probabilities of survival of city-states or on the differing propensity of a city to commit to expansionistic politics. In fact, in several cases, the transition from republic to *signoria* was anything but irreversible. Lucca, for example, between 1314 and 1341, saw a succession of various *signori* from Uguccione della Faggiola to Castruccio Castracani – and even external *signorie* such as those of John of Bohemia, of Marsilio Rossi, and of Mastino Della Scala – until the republican state was reinstated. The city then went through a new phase as a *signoria* during the regime of Paolo Guinigi (1400–30), followed by a second and durable return to the republic. Florence, until 1532, kept the republican institutions, at least formally, but over the fourteenth century, it had, in reality, known several 'experiments' in terms of *signorie* (such as the well-known case of the duke of Athens, Walter VI of Brienne, in 1342–3). Additionally, in the fifteenth century, Florence was characterised for a long time by the crypto-*signorile* hegemony of the Medici (dominating the political scene from 1434 to 1494, then from 1512 to 1527, and definitely from 1530).

Even those cities that had seen a more decisive or earlier development into a *signoria* or a principality (when feudal titles were given to the *signori* either by the emperor or the pope) might experience restoration of a republican form of government. The city of Milan experienced this between 1327 and 1329 – that is, between the deposition of Galeazzo Visconti and the arrival of his son Azzone – and especially between 1447 and 1450 – with the extinction of the Visconti family line and the arrival of the Sforza. In this second interval, which corresponded to a temporary disaggregation of the regional state of Milan and to a momentary return to independence of some cities, a republican form of government was restored. Similar restorations of an ephemeral nature also happened in Parma and Tortona. Camerino, long-time capital of a city-state that had maintained independence for a long while (until 1540 with a few short interruptions at the beginning of the sixteenth century), experienced the restoration of a republican form of government in the first half of the sixteenth century. A temporary crisis of the Varano (*signori* of the city from 1266) led the city government to return to the communal institutions for a decade (1434–44).

At times, moreover, more ambiguous solutions appeared in which the institutions of a republican government survived only formally. As mentioned above, the Medici's dominance in Florence is considered as a crypto-*signoria*, with the precise intention of emphasising that the Medicean authority was *de facto* a type of *signoria* that manipulated the republican constitution while remaining formally faithful to it. In other instances, the term ought to be 'para-*signorie*', that is, regimes that allowed a partial formalisation of the prominence of a semi-*signore*. The Bentivoglio's power in Bologna, for instance, falls into this category – especially after Giovanni Bentivoglio was granted a perpetual gonfaloniership in 1463. The same applies to the Baglioni in Perugia in the fifteenth and sixteenth centuries, to the Petrucci in Siena at the beginning of the sixteenth century, and to other families in several cities of the papal state between the fourteenth and the fifteenth century, such as the Gatti in Viterbo, the Vitelli in Città di Castello, the Monaldeschi in Orvieto, the Mulucci in Macerata and so on.

The crisis of communal institutions produced different outcomes at institutional level. However, it is impossible to identify one outcome that more than others would guarantee the survival of a city as an autonomous political actor.[11]

The closure of the participative bases of the political life of the cities is significant, even though it is not appropriate to establish rigorous comparisons between events that were extremely different from each other, such as for instance the establishment of the Venetian patriciate after the famous *serrata* of the Maggior Consiglio of 1297 (or the 'second *serrata*' of 1323), or the events that led to the constitution of a type of agro-mercantile block in Milan under the protection of the Visconti. In Venice a stable and unchallenged social hierarchy, led by a circle of nobles which was almost a type of 'collective prince', emerged whose primacy was never seriously contended. In Milan, in contrast, where there was only one prince, a court 'nobility' emerged, which was more open and composite but, at the same time, was not internally compact nor surrounded by a clear social consensus. Additionally, whereas the Venetian nobles had a strong 'sense of the state' and a deep devotion to their own institutions, the Milanese ruling classes did not entertain good relationships with the power of the *signorile* or later ducal court, which they served (and benefited from) but with which they did not identify. It was no accident that in the fifteenth century two dukes of Milan out of seven were murdered (Giovanni Maria Visconti in 1412 and Galeazzo Maria

---

[11] Chittolini, *La crisi degli ordinamenti*; Capitani, *et al.*, *Comuni e signorie*; Dean, 'The rise of *signori*'.

Sforza in 1476) as a result of conspiracies of the Milanese nobles; a third, Ludovico il Moro, ended up being overthrown in 1499 by Louis XII, king of France, who arrived in Milan with an army led by the Milanese nobleman Giacomo Trivulzio. The Genoese and Florentine situations were different again. In Florence the city oligarchy was strongly involved in public life, just as in Venice, but it was less compact and joined. Internal conflicts were frequent and visible, even if there were some periods of (relative) political stability, such as the time of the Medicean dominance. Genoa, however, was characterised by the total inability of its own ruling class, consisting of people from both noble and popular origins, to find a peaceful coexistence. For its continuous internal tensions, Genoa had long periods of foreign rule in the fourteenth and fifteenth centuries (continuing until 1528): the city ended up under a Milanese government, under Angevin (then French) tutelage, and also, for a short while, under the marquis of Montferrato.

There is no scope here to scrutinise these different situations in detail; the contributions in the first part of the volume deal with them in depth. Nevertheless, it is possible to notice a common denominator in these events, the overall shrinking of participation. The political society of the different Italian cities began to shrink considerably, a countertendency to the previous experiences of wide-participation government. These experiences of the governments of the *popolo*, between the second half of the thirteenth and the beginning of the fourteenth century, were characterised by the involvement of various groups of citizens in the government of common goods and by attempts to overthrow many forms of privilege (whether political, economic, social or fiscal) of the traditional ruling elites of the first period of the age of the communes. Albeit in different ways and times, the inverse trends appeared in the fourteenth century and were to be consolidated over the following century.

In the cities of Veneto, of Lombardy and of Emilia, these inverse tendencies emerged early with the birth of the *signorie* (even when the founding families were of popular origin, such as the Della Scala in Verona). In Tuscany, the timing was different. The first phase saw the rise of what could be termed as popular oligarchies, or 'nobility of the people' (such as the *Nove* in Siena). In the second half of the fourteenth century, the reaction became more apparent, especially after the explosion of proletarian rebellions – such as the Compagnia del Bruco rebellion in Siena (1371), or the Ciompi rebellion in Florence (1378) – which seemed to threaten the entire social apparatus and the very position of those *populares* who had become rich. At this time, the end of forms of wide-participation government followed swiftly: its demise was obvious in the Florentine reforms that in 1382–7 rejected the old artisan structures, based upon the role of the *Arti*.

The extromission of the *populares* from the decision-making process, though with different timings and in different ways, was indeed a tendency common to many cities (regardless of the forms of constitution of the different governments). In the fifteenth century, the phenomenon had already spread to all the Italian cities; the government of state had become an affair for the few. There were some exceptions: even Florence, for example, after the expulsion of the Medici in 1494 experienced a restoration of forms of wide-participation government (especially at the time of Girolamo Savonarola in 1494–5), whereas Milan, during the Ambrosian republic (1447–50), witnessed the *populares* taking control of the city. The Florentine experience was extremely short-lived (virtually ending with the burning of Savonarola at the stake). The rise of the *populares* at the helm of the Milanese republic even provoked a shift to an anti-republican position of those ruling groups of the city that two years earlier had given birth to the republic. The Milanese elites surrendered to Francesco Sforza – the *condottiero* who had been trying to overthrow the republic and restore the principality with himself as prince – rather than be ruled by artisans or other components of the lower-middle classes of the city. This episode may be taken as a paradigm.

Moreover, the tendency to shrink the composition of the ruling classes was clearly evident not only in the cities that remained independent but also in those that slid into the condition of subjected cities. This tendency was visible in the Lombardy of the Visconti in the fourteenth and the fifteenth centuries, but also in the Marca Trevigiana, as well as in the Este's dominions (Modena and Reggio Emilia) and partially in Tuscany. Effectively, in the subjugated cities the dominance of the local oligarchies became gradually apparent; they were legitimised in their hegemony precisely because they had managed to impose themselves as the main interlocutors with the central power. The various governments of the states born over the ruins of the city-states endorsed the local supremacy of such elites in exchange for their submission. Shrinking the potential pool from which the city councils took their members (a phenomenon that became more widespread during the fourteenth century) proved to be the evidence of this process. In this perspective, the elites of the cities were rewarded for renouncing their independence.

Not all urban elites, however, gracefully accepted this compromise. In Pisa, for instance, the Florentine occupation of 1406 resulted in the migration of the most eminent local families. On the other hand, even elsewhere, though in a much more contained fashion, the phenomenon of *fuoriuscitismo* continued well into the sixteenth century and beyond.

In other circumstances, there were forms of internal dissidence that at times, in moments of crisis, could be heard once more (as in Novara in 1495, when the city rebelled against the Sforza and gave itself to the duke of Orléans). It could even happen that the local ruling groups were still internally organised into the old factions. Normally, the central government tried to pacify or eliminate the factions by attempting to join them together. This endeavour did not always succeed, especially if there were autonomous seigneurs outside the cities, who to some extent fuelled conflicts in the cities (a typical, but not unique, example was that of Parma). On the other hand, the survival of factions does not necessarily imply strong conflict; often they found ways of resolving their struggles with the division as well as the subdivision in equal parts of the city offices (such as the redistribution in equal measure of the city offices that occurred in some Lombard and Emilian cities, or in Belluno).

The fact remains that, whatever the internal structure, these restricted groups of *cives* accumulated in their own hands the levers of power at local level. They dominated the city council (which had been remodelled following the government's top-down changes); they managed what was left of the communal fiscal system; they had control over the local ecclesiastical institutions (clearly not of the bishopric but certainly over the cathedral chapter, the convents of nuns, and many ancient *pievi* in the territory); they ruled hospitals, sacred places, and charitable and devotional institutions; they controlled the main rituals, such as festivals and processions, that marked the calendar of the city life.

In other words, not only the social, political and economic direction of their community appertained to the *cives*, but also its ideological direction. In terms of mindset, ambitions and social attitudes, this role made the *cives* closer to aristocracies of the capitals, thus transforming them into the natural contacts for the central governments. By now, the attitude within the new states was one of dialogue between higher powers and subjugated cities; the local oligarchies were at ease in this context because of their ability to deal and network informally (in terms of clientage and patronage) with the courts of the princes, with groups, with parties and with influential people of the dominant cities.[12]

---

[12] Bertelli, *Il potere oligarchico*; Varanini, 'Aristocrazie e poteri' (with a large bibliography); Chittolini and Johanek (eds.), *Aspetti e componenti dell'identità urbana*; Chittolini, '"Crisi" and "lunga durata"'; Gentile (ed.), *Guelfi e ghibellini*; and Zorzi and Connell (eds.), *Lo stato territoriale fiorentino*.

The vitality of southern and Sicilian cities

Southern Italy and Sicily had not witnessed the rise of the city-states. The cities had been organised, from the twelfth century, within the frame of the *Regnum Siciliae*. Royal power, especially in the Swabian period (1194–1266), had clamped down on any aspiration of independence. The hypothesis of city-states, in this part of Italy, was no longer debated. Not even the creation of two different kingdoms of Sicily – 'on this side' and 'on that side' of the Faro (the lighthouse of Messina), according to the denomination that emerged at the time of Alfonso of Aragon (1416–58) – modified this situation, since the revolt of the Vespers in 1282 ratified the separation of Sicily from the southern regions of the Italian peninsula, but did not alter the condition of the cities. It is true that during the first phase of that rebellion the Sicilian cities asked the pope to acknowledge them as independent communities subjugated only to the church, yet this proposal was not accepted and was never taken up again, either in Sicily or in the *Mezzogiorno* (the southern part of the peninsula). Only L'Aquila among the cities of the continental kingdom, the so-called kingdom of Naples, had at some point plans for emancipation. In 1485, for example, the citizens of L'Aquila rebelled against the crown and with an *atto di dedizione*, a sworn oath of submission, to the papacy they separated from the institutional body of the kingdom. It was, however, an exceptional case.

During the fourteenth and fifteenth centuries, in the cities of the two kingdoms, there were nonetheless some substantial phenomena of energetic political and social activity. The southern and Sicilian *universitates* managed to enter into a dialogue with their respective crowns, also showing an ability to develop real processes of construction of an identity as civic communities. There was, in other words, a real phenomenon of urban awakening. The political role grew in parallel with an economic and demographic recovery, which was partially produced spontaneously as an outcome of the increased dynamism of the cities. This phenomenon was, however, also induced, that is, the process was endorsed and encouraged by royal power, which realised that the cities were fiscal resources to strengthen, and at the same time saw in the cities a political counterbalance to, the feudal elite (often unmanageable and keen to rebel).

In the kingdom of Naples, the tendency towards establishing new relationships between the crown and the *universitates* emerged at the beginning of the Angevin era (from the last decades of the thirteenth century). Together with a marked policy of feudalisation (which brought the enfeoffment of several cities), for those cities that had remained demesnial there was a substantial increase in functions and powers delegated to the city's own administrative offices. The phenomenon became explicitly marked during the Aragonese age, after the conquest of the kingdom by Alfonso the Magnanimous in 1442 and even more during the kingdom of his son, Ferrante (1458–94). The crown's tendency to support the cities became more explicit while the two large rebellions of the barons in 1458–62 and 1485–6 demonstrated that relations with the feudal elites were becoming more difficult and more conflictual.

For example, after the 1463 dissolution of the large feudal aggregation of the Orsini Del Balzo (princes of Taranto, counts of Lecce, dukes of Bari, counts of Matera, *signori* of Brindisi and so on), several Apulian cities entered into a new relationship with the crown, by agreeing solutions that allowed the city to exercise substantial forms of control over the surrounding areas and remarkable financial autonomy. This included the direct management of the income from the *bagliva* (the jurisdiction of first-degree civil law) and those of the *capitania* (the jurisdiction of criminal law). Similar developments also occurred in other regions of the continental kingdom; for example, Campobasso in Molise became demesnial again in 1464. The renewed collaboration with the Aragonese monarchy encouraged many cities to provide personnel for the bureaucracy and the apparatus of government of the kingdom, possibly in the understanding that increased autonomy at local level did not contrast with the area of intervention of the central state or with its institutional reinforcement.

In Sicily, the turning point in the relationship between the crown and the cities occured between 1392 and 1410, in the age of the two Martins (Martin the Elder and Martin the Younger). Previously in Sicily the penetration of barons in the life of cities had been acknowledged. The feudal system had often taken control over fortresses and demesnial castles, thus affirming some form of monopoly of the political, legal and administrative life of the cities and also, therefore, claiming a monopoly over their social and economic context, and even urban planning (see, for example, the dominance of the Palizza in Messina, of the Alagona in Catania, of the Chiaromonte in Palermo and so on). The two Martins quickly changed things. Upon the arrival on the island of Martin the Younger, many Sicilian cities presented the king with some *capitoli* (petitions), to which he gave his *placet*. In many cases, for example Messina, these were relevant concessions. The cities entered into a dialogue with the crown, thus becoming political actors (this was also registered in some Sardinian cities, such as Sassari, Cagliari, Alghero, Bosa and Iglesias, which were embedded in the kingdom of

Sardinia which over the fourteenth century had been in turn aggregated to the dominions of the Aragonese crown). Overall, this new activism of the cities increased the level of involvement of urban groups in public governance.

In some cases, this involvement translated into an increase in internal conflicts between different groups and components of urban society. In the cities of the kingdom of Naples, the crux of the matter usually lay in the assessment of the *apprezzo* (the evaluation of wealth from real estate for the purpose of taxation) or in the competition over the elective offices (*apprezzatori*, evaluators, mayors, judges, *maestri giurati* and the like). Opposite sides often converged into the *nobiles* and *populares* parties. The solution of taking decisions away from the general councils of the citizens, that is, the parliaments of the cities, in order to assign them to more compact bodies avoided harsher conflicts. Various cities of the kingdom witnessed the creation of bodies such as the council of Six in Naples, the council of Four in Trani, the council of Twelve in Salerno and so on. This approach favoured the rise of an urban patriciate. In Naples, the council of Six (or the court of San Lorenzo) was dominated by the urban aristocracy connected with the six seats of the city (*Sedili*), that is, the six lodges or squares (Nido, Porta Capuana, Porta Nuova, Forcella, Porto and Montagna) in which the noble families of the city districts gave their verdicts. Each seat had its own administrative competences over the relevant district or gate (and to an extent over the territories outside the city) and was in turn managed by a closed council consisting of five or six knights. In 1420, Giovanna II established the seat of the People, consisting entirely of representatives of the *populares*; however, Alfonso of Aragon suppressed it in 1442. In L'Aquila, the artisan corporations of the city still dominated the council of Five in the fourteenth century. By the end of the century, an aristocratic hegemony emerged with the rise of two rival families: the Camponeschi – champions of the popular interests – and the Pretatti, followed by the Gaglioffi. In the fifteenth century, the Camponeschi prevailed, to the point of having a para-*signoria* with Pietro, known as Lalle I, and Pietro Ludovico, known as Lalle II. The arrest of Lalle II ordered by king Ferrante was in fact one of the factors contributing to the 1485 secession mentioned above.

In the Sicilian kingdom, however, there was the issue of weakening the barons' influences in the cities. To this purpose, over the fifteenth century, the crown encouraged urban forces outside the feudal potentates, or even animated by anti-baronial sentiment. In many cities of Sicily, these processes were favoured by gradual rise of the *giuranzie* and of their elective system. Between the age of the two Martins and that of Alfonso the Magnanimous (from 1394 to 1458), then, a recognisable social structure came into existence subdividing society into *nobiles* or *gentilomini*, *borgesi*, *magistri* and *populares*. The prevailing tendency was a convergence towards a single ruling class, some sort of patriciate, an expression of the aristocrats, the merchants and of the *togati* – magistrates, lawyers and so on – thus excluding the popular components.

Overall, the Sicilian cities also managed to restore, through their relationship with the crown, significant leeway in terms of action. In comparison to the kingdom of Naples, they did not have the opportunity of expanding their control over surrounding territories and also had many fewer opportunities to operate in terms of internal regulations. Nonetheless, they had the chance to make themselves heard in the parliament, which was of central importance on the island. Usually, they did not work as a united body or as a collective and joint actor; on the contrary, they competed against each other and were animated by reciprocal jealousy and mistrust (in particular between Palermo, Messina and Catania). In the inland kingdom, the role of the cities within the parliament was significantly more marginal. They remained characterised by their focus on their particular and individual interests; and their relationship with the crown was mainly regulated via bilateral agreements with royal power. This feature, which was also visible in the central and northern states of Italy (in which the parliamentary institutions did not exist, with the exception of the Savoy dominions and in Friuli, that is, areas with fewer cities), did not impede the development of a political conscience and, to some extent, of real civic ideologies in some southern and Sicilian cities.

Analysis of the political language adopted by the very cities, of the way in which they defined themselves in absolute terms and in relation to other actors, such as the crown and its officers, or the barons, or other cities and communities, confirms this process. In other words, whereas oligarchic restrictions and forms of patricians' closures seemed to prevail in those areas of Italy that had seen a predominance of city-states, the vitality of the city-states in southern Italy, at times, appeared to be able to revive civic ideals and values of engagement in city politics.[13]

---

[13] For further studies on the southern cities, see Cirillo, 'Città e contado nel Mezzogiorno', and Vitolo (ed.), *Città e contado nel Mezzogiorno* (both with comprehensive and updated bibliographies). For the Sicilian cities, see Epstein, *An Island*; Bresc, *Un monde méditérranéen*; Corrao, *Governare un regno*; Titone, *Governments*.

Concluding remarks

To conclude, the picture of the Italian cities at the time of transition between the Middle Ages and the Renaissance appears very multi-faceted; some general points can nevertheless be made.

The *époque* of the city-states of the *Regnum Italicum* and of the pontifical dominions came to an end. New realities of a regional nature, with fewer capital cities and numerous subject cities, replaced the city-states. Three factors caused the loss of sovereignty: the overall lack of stability of the geopolitical system of the central and northern regions (aggrieved by the *extrinseci* and not contained by the Guelf and Ghibelline co-ordination); the demographic collapse of the middle of the fourteenth century; and the military crisis of the city-states. Separately, or in relation to each other, these elements contributed to the weakening of many cities, leading them to fall. At the same time, they allowed other – larger, wealthier, stronger – cities to emerge as new forces exploiting the weaknesses of others. Significant consequences ensued in some instances: the cities' pretext to exercise absolute powers over their *contadi* was challenged, whereas at the same time oligarchies imposed themselves on the local scene (a development also appearing among the cities that had maintained their independence).

Similar tendencies towards the formation of local oligarchies also occurred in the south and in Sicily, where the cities, because of their ability to create a more serious relationship with royal authority, experienced an era of remarkable dynamism. In this view, possibly the most significant element of this age was that the older gap in conditions between the southern cities and those of the centre and northern Italy diminished. With respect to cities, too, the Renaissance was the age in which the peninsula witnessed the growth of an Italian and mainly homogeneous space. This space was soon to face the arrival of European powers to fight for hegemony over Italy, which clearly had further impact on life in the cities.

13 The rural communities

Massimo Della Misericordia

Historiographical considerations

Renewed interest

The interest shown by Italian historiography in the subject of rural communities has varied greatly over the past century. At the beginning of the twentieth century, rural communities became a favoured topic of research which absorbed some of the greatest historians of the time, from Gaetano Salvemini to Romolo Caggese, from Gioacchino Volpe to Gian Piero Bognetti, and became the source of animated debate between Italian and transalpine, particularly German, historiography. This debate developed into a sounding board for significant interpretations and methodological approaches. The origins of the rural communes became the prism through which historians confronted the crucial issues concerning the history of Italy, such as class conflict, relations between cities and their countryside, the combination of Roman, or pre-Roman, heritage with Germanic contributions in forming a specific national culture, and the strength with which ecclesiastical structures at a local level united groups of people settled within their territory. In the same context they also debated the relationship between sociological theory and history, between generalisations and erudite foundations of research.

In the second half of the twentieth century, interest in this topic notably diminished. Only a small number of medievalists were undertaking research into communities and their sporadic contributions were rarely central to the historiographical debate. Research into Italian rural areas privileged dynamics of possession and transformations of the countryside and settlements, leaving politico-institutional organisation in the shade.

The climate altered again towards the end of the last century, due to the convergence of several lines of research. Since the 1980s, historians of the modern age have dedicated special attention to communities. The first wide-scale research project took place in the Veneto. This was followed by a co-ordinated project that led to a series of monographs on local identities in Tuscany. Aside from these important case studies, microhistory, especially the work of Edoardo Grendi and Angelo Torre, formulated epistemological reflections that provoked wide debate and proved to be stimulating for researchers working on earlier ages. The debate concerning the origin of rural communes came to the fore once more in 1995, thanks to Chris Wickham's monograph dedicated to the social and institutional processes in the area around Lucca in the eleventh and twelfth centuries. The much-discussed pan-European summary by Peter Blickle in 2000, accompanied by a series of detailed studies, proposed the model of 'communalisation' to scholars of late medieval Italian society that is again drawn upon in this chapter. Contributions multiplied in the following years to the extent that this line of research can now be described as one of the most dynamic areas in national historiography (see the bibliography).

Such reinvigorated concern, however, is connected to a cultural context wider than the spectrum of specialised studies. This interest is connected firstly in terms of some general reflections that, despite not always being made explicit among historians, are ever present in their research, particularly reflections on the crisis concerning the paradigms of modernisation in the West. Current doubts about representative democracy and impersonal market economies, as well as the individualistic premises on which they are based, and the recognition of the untarnished vitality of local micro-identities in a globalised world have served to fuel scepticism towards the overarching narratives of the modern age that centred on the origins of the state, the broadening of the market and the growth of the individual on the ashes of the previous kaleidoscopic world of intermediary bodies, community affiliations and seigneurial enclaves. Conversely, these reflections have stimulated an interest in the forms of political participation at a local level and in collective action, in reciprocal exchanges between small groups of people, in the assumption of responsibility and social conditioning to which an individual's search for success and profit are subjugated. The past offers up a vast and rich array of similar situations which it is ever more urgent to explore.

Secondly, the promotion of research into communities is one of the tangible signs of the strength of identity and of local institutions in contemporary Italy. Many organisations, such as local, provincial or regional administrations as well as banking institutions, are investing significant resources in the support of research carried out on the areas that they govern or in which they operate, and in the publication of this research. Such funding enabled the publication of important monographs and the activity of research teams, assembled into collective works or brought together for stimulating and serious debates such as the conference dedicated to *Lo spazio politico locale* held in 2004. In an era of low turnover of research-active academics and insufficient public funding for universities, compounded by the difficulties faced by universities in Italy in creating a dialogue with society and politics, such commissions have led scholars to apply their specialised expertise to the study of local history by becoming involved in research projects in provincial archives or into specific issues of historical events in territories.

Institutions

The research questions posed in the 1980s were far removed from those faced by historians at the beginning of the century. For this reason, recent publications rarely proceed from the questions that were dear to the tradition of the studies from the last century, referring rather to methods from new European social history and to themes of social sciences, particularly anthropology.

To the contemporary historian, the rural commune in the most-dated studies appears to be too cohesive a unit, defined firstly as an institutional entity engaged in confrontation with external political competitors (from cities to local seigneurs), but little studied in terms of its internal tensions; entangled, furthermore, in the age-old continuity of identity, boundaries and customs in the utilisation of collective goods, too unreactive to change in historical situations. Individual people, conversely, were almost lost in those pages, swallowed up by territories and their political structures. As a consequence, research in the last thirty years has changed the focus from the commune to the community, from the institution to its social components. The preferred subjects have become the elites who were able to bend to their own thirst for power the workings of the normatively governed bodies, groups (families, kin or residential units) and individuals able to interlace strategies of personal affirmation both within and outside official political places. Informal relations and the fleeting powers *de facto* executed were seen as more interesting than the description of human coexistence as envisaged by laws. Rather than the statically determined territories and administrative districts or the statutory norms, then, attention has moved to the factions, the clientelage or the networks of friendships, to people able to cross boundaries due to their physical mobility or the wide range of their economic and political drive. Conflict and precariousness have become the characteristic features of the historical reconstruction of relationships between individuals, groups and local institutions; sociological or historiographical frameworks that rendered an image of stable and harmonious cohabitation among members of medieval communities have been charged with naivety.

The interpretation that emphasised the elusive political and social fluidity to the point of dissolving into it the unifying elements of institutions and of class stratification has only very recently shown signs of weakness. Today, scholars are re-evaluating the relevance of institutional structures in permitting or proscribing access to resources, in granting recognition of status, in offering the opportunity of public affirmation, in creating the conditions for mobility, in influencing the range of amicable links and the economic bonds in relation to the borders that these drew on the territory.

In the fourteenth and fifteenth centuries, in particular, it is of benefit to distinguish at least three levels of organisation of communities. The subject that is normally the most visible in primary sources, the oldest form and the most deeply rooted was the 'commune' (in central and northern Italy) or the *'universitas'* (in central and southern Italy). Generally established in the eleventh and twelfth centuries, they were led by a single official or a small committee, flanked by one or more councils, the largest of which overlapped with the assembly of the heads of the families. In the late Middle Ages the personnel expanded, especially in the larger centres. There was a dramatic increase in the number of representatives of the community before the state authorities, of people responsible for the administration of money, of collective goods or of churches, or for taking emergency resolutions in times of war or plague, and so on. Joining these were others with technical or executive functions such as rural guards and those in charge of the duties of the police force broadly speaking, evaluators and chancellors.

When a commune was not made up of a single village, but of a larger, more populated centre (*borgo*), or of more than one settlement, other collective figures operated at a sub-communal district quarter or *contrada* level. These configurations saw themselves as a part of the superior unity of the commune, but at the end of the Middle Ages they developed their own organisation (leading a life centred around assemblies, controlling certain resources, electing officials) and held more solid aspirations of autonomy. Next to these formed neighbourhoods of co-terminal properties that bordered on to the same wood, or of beneficiaries of the same summer mountain pasture. Again, co-residency, be it only seasonal, or adjoining properties united, on a minute scale, temporary communities, which, however, followed written rules and shared responsibilities such as policing the countryside and negotiating with institutions one level up from themselves.

Lastly, there were communities made up of many communes, federations of varying size (a *pieve*, a single jurisdictional district, a valley or a lakeside area, an entire satellite *contado* to a city) that normally operated as representatives before the state authorities. Equipped with statutes, and with councils on which sat delegates from the individual elements that constituted the federation (communes or, in more extensive organisations, lesser federations), and sometimes a guiding leader, they assumed the duty of representing territories, particularly in the regional dominions of Milan, Venice and Florence, in which parliamentary bodies were not formed.

Members of these communities with full rights were defined with appropriate, if rather varied, terms: *uomini* (men: from time to time of a small *contrada*, a commune, or of a federation), *vicini* (for inhabitants of *contrade* and communes that were not of noble extraction), *terrigeni*, *citatini* and so on.

Clearly the experiences brought together here would have differed greatly. The communes themselves did not conform to a homogeneous reality. The habitats of Italy varied significantly: there were isolated houses and farms in the countryside; small villages with a few families; *borghi* with populations in the thousands, which, in terms of wealth, had a variety of trades and services available to residents and lacked nothing compared to many urban centres in Italy and in Europe, except the formal title of *civitas*, which most of them sought to attain. When referring to the latter, the adjective 'rural' is used in an imprecise way. Rural is used simply to mean 'not truly urban' as they did not have that rank officially (nor did they have a bishopric whose presence sanctioned this rank). Also, towards the end of the Middle Ages there were centres that boasted centuries-old continued settlement, whereas others were founded *ex novo* through urban, seigneurial or princely initiatives. Appropriate nomenclature (*comune di villa*, *borgo* or *castello*, *università di terra* or *di casale*) attempted to hierarchically order this multitude of settlements, making distinctions according to the varying institutional levels. At the same time, the flexibility of terminology in documents is significant: a *universitas*, for example, was a district, a territorial body comprising more than one commune, but also in other cases a single commune, either a village or a *borgo* (mainly but not exclusively in central and southern Italy). The vocabulary of the primary sources clearly recognised the unitary paradigm of all these institutional structures: a community organisation, founded, in all cases, on the co-operation of inhabitants with full rights, by direct participation or participation mediated by select bodies, in every responsibility pertaining to the institution.

The highly formalised nature of these functions has already been alluded to. All the subjects identified – even a village made up of a small number of houses, over and above the informal networks of friends, neighbourhoods and consanguinity that could be integrated within them – were formed legally. Not just the communes or the federations, but even the *contrada* could produce a statute. Where there was no chancery to register and preserve the acts undertaken in the name of the community, notaries were brought in; they ratified the legality of the work of the assembly and of administrative decisions with formulae suggested from law and from custom.

Recent historiography has, therefore, underlined the way in which local politics, both within and external to these procedures, was the monopoly of a small number of men, whose strength came not only from the role bestowed upon them in the assemblies, but also because of their own personal authority, their followers and the links they maintained with one another. In reality, regardless of the undoubted social polarisation that occurred towards the end of the Middle Ages, which will be discussed later in the chapter, the emptying of local institutions by oligarchic groups and the freeze on circulation of political personnel, which were presumed in the past, did not occur. Not only notaries and lawyers, merchants and land-owners, but also more modest craftsmen and peasants who, presumably, could afford to divert some of their time and energy away from providing for their family, continued at the helm of communities. The decisions that leaders made in vital areas (the destination of undivided property, the acceptance of new members) often needed to be sanctioned by assemblies. Finally, due to customary procedures, the thirst for power of the worthies was held at bay. If they betrayed the mandates received, they had their role as political mediator withdrawn.

Research has also emphasised the conflictual nature of relations within communes, between kin-groups and *contrade*, and concerning boundaries and politics, between communes within a federation. In contrast to the conciliatory models that perpetuated the idealised image that communities offered of themselves, it has come to light that communities were permeated by harsh competition pursued with the goal of guaranteeing themselves the wealth of the territory and public offices. On the other hand, it is true that the flexibility of these organisations was able to absorb rivalries. Thanks to the divisions of offices and resources between the various institutional members, often determined by the statutes themselves, the portions of local society based both on social class and on geography could find a balance to enable cohabitation. The logic behind the division of offices in some valley communities in the fifteenth century remained unchanged throughout the centuries of the *ancien régime*. In many regions of Italy the inter-commune boundaries have remained, in substance, from the Middle Ages to today. For these reasons, the longevity of relations as defined in normative texts or in compromises between communes, kin or *vicini*, therefore, is worthy of consideration equal to that paid to the rapid reconfiguration of relationships of solidarity and conflict within these communities at a specific moment in history.

Lastly, it is important not to forget the persuasive efficacy that corporative models held in the culture of the time. They were useful not to contrast pluralism with unity, but to harmonise the differentiation of social roles, or the fragmentation of settlements within a united organism. These models circulated in academic reflections that elaborated them conceptually, in the true social and political pedagogy that friars carried out in their homilies to the large audiences, and in the linguistic forms and graphic layout of the pragmatic documents written by notaries. These views idealised the federations as co-ordinating bodies over the communes, the communes as a mosaic of social classes, families and *contrade*, a synthesis of different parts each imbued with its own recognisable and distinct features but at the same time potentially willing to co-operate.

Identity

The subjects concerning rural communities that have been examined so far in this chapter from a social and institutional perspective have been recently reconsidered in the light of a new category, that of 'identity'. This word is new to historiography on the subject and has been used to bring the cultural dimension of the community to the fore (that is, the community as a place for belonging) and the symbolic vocabulary (words, religious and civic ceremonies) used to show it.

From this viewpoint, the tendency to accentuate the problematic and frayed nature of communities, rather than the cohesion and solidarity of community members, is expressed by an insistence on plurality, contingency and conflicts of identities. Even adopting this viewpoint, however, the deconstructionist reading seems to be showing its weaknesses. An individual living in the late medieval countryside would certainly feel himself not only to be a member of his own commune, but also, looking only at loyalties of immediate social and political impact, to be a noble or a *vicino*, a member of a kinship group, the friend of a powerful lord.

Nevertheless, the view is being put forward that the sense of belonging to a community was often a decisive factor in the driving forces motivating individual actors on the public scene of Italian *borghi* and villages, able to impose, in conflict or in the daily search for personal affirmation and networks of contacts, demanding choices that were not easily revocable.

This pluralism of identity leads once more to the exploration of the pragmatic potential of the previously mentioned organicistic models, capable, thanks to the order observed in processions or in the lists of the heads of families contained in the documents of notaries and chancellors, of creating harmony and hierarchy among the various sentiments of affiliation alongside, or often within, the sense of belonging to a community.

An interpretive hypothesis: the processes of communalisation in late medieval rural Italy

Chronologies

Using the approaches adopted in this chapter, it is possible to see a capillary process of communalisation from the late Middle Ages that will become the unifying theme adopted in this section. The process will be approached from two perspectives: the investigation of the conditions of access to a wide range of resources and essential services, and the analysis of the identity of the individual. From both perspectives, this age, in contrast to the preceding and following periods, is characterised by the role assumed by the community as a crucial form of organisation in rural Italian society.

Clearly it is beyond the scope of this chapter to reconstruct even a summary of the rural environment's various walks of life and their relative changes in more than one thousand years of history. This chapter will instead focus on the economic, social, religious and political functions that were concentrated into community organisms in the late Middle Ages. Going further back in history, these same environments are occupied by entirely different actors: the holders of public power, extensive property and seigneurial prerogatives. Prior to the eleventh century, for example, free land-owners in rural areas had the right to uncultivated lands as fiscal assets; they had to maintain public roads and bridges and to obtain justice ensured by functionaries of the king. With the later discontinuity in the organisation of the state, the formation of the *signorie di banno* (the territorial lordships) forced the *homines* to use, and in onerous conditions, mills and other infrastructure organised by the *dominus* of the castle, and to negotiate with the lord in order to gain access to woods and pasture. The lordship also imposed restrictions on the mobility of their subjects, their choice of spouse, and the buying and selling of land for those under the same curia, thus contributing to the limitation of their horizons. Rural inhabitants, furthermore, attended churches that were directly under episcopal or monastic authority, or founded by aristocrats. In cases of extreme poverty, peasants would have resorted to begging at a monastery or a bishopric.

In the modern age, conversely, the incisiveness of the powers held by the church and the state grew. They were able to remove from local communities some of the fundamental competences that the latter had appropriated. The curing of ills and the salvation of the spirit, schooling, environmental protection and the maintenance of various infrastructures are emblematic here. Through such activities, the state and the church's powers channelled the sense of belonging that linked a person to local affiliations towards new, wider religious and national identities. In our times, notions that affirm the universality of human rights – from instruction to health – are currently gaining in importance, although they are much debated. In contrast, in the late Middle Ages, they were often determined in a particularistic way, for example when the school in the commune was open only to the children of residents or the right to beg was reserved to the needy of that particular place. At the same time, the opportunities for the affirmation of individuals gradually grew in the fields of politics and economy, which were heavily controlled by collective initiatives.

Over the long course of European history, the late Middle Ages, as a whole, is seen as the period in which lasting community-based institutions were being devised, able to execute a far-reaching range of competences that, in other periods, had fallen to the state, the church, local lords or individuals. This was a period, therefore, of strong interdependence between inhabitant and community, and of the related identification of the former in the latter.

Within this timeframe, the twelfth and thirteenth centuries have always received more attention, and perhaps continue to do so. Italian historiography has long considered the origins of rural communes and the struggle against the nobility as the most compelling moments of a period that, in substance, ended with the regulation of the countryside by the urban regime well into the thirteenth century. According to this historiographical tradition, thus, urban governments of the time intended to transform the rural communes into mere instruments suitable only for the division of the fiscal load and other exacting burdens imposed from above, such as the maintenance of river banks, bridges and roads, and of obedience and public peace. In the meantime, economic penetration by the urban capital and peasant indebtedness drastically impoverished the countryside. The brief phase of rural freedoms then ended; the emergence of the regional states seemed to exacerbate the economic and cultural subalternity of rural areas to the cities, and the impoverishment and political debasement of communities.

Some undeniable transformations, which occurred in the rural world in the later Middle Ages, have been interpreted as critical moments for the experience that communities had already gained in the previous era. Social and economic processes of clear differentiation can be seen: in the largest communities, wealth tended to concentrate in the hands of just a few individuals; political leadership was taken on, but not necessarily monopolised, by the elite of rentiers, merchants, money-lenders and notaries. At a territorial level, analogous processes of polarisation can be seen: an increase in the distance between market towns and *borghi* living on manufacturing activities, which were attractive due to the many opportunities for economic growth and political career offered to individuals, and the farming villages. The richest, most cultured or most entrepreneurial people in the smaller centres transferred to the major communities or to cities, leaving behind them rural entities that were impoverished both materially and in terms of services provided. Such processes certainly supplied communities, in particular the richest and most populous, with new ruling groups with enough strength in knowledge and in personal prestige to carry out the activities of mediation with the state and to challenge the local lords. At the same time the traditions of participation and wide-scale redistribution of collective resources that had defined community life were put to the test. Often in order to cope with fiscal pressure and debt, parts of the collective patrimony were sold to members of these elites; the assemblies of the heads of families had to concede important decision-making faculties to restricted councils, manned by the same influential people. Princes and republican oligarchies supported these closures. The aristocratic culture that prevailed as public language largely shared with the Renaissance significantly added to the diffidence felt towards the tumultuous public lives of groups of peasants who, in a rut of traditions of a republican hue, laid claim to room for autonomous decisions. This diffidence persuaded the central authorities and their local agents to prefer instead as their interlocutors those notables who were gaining strength locally.

Despite these issues, it cannot be said that the fourteenth and fifteenth centuries represented a hiatus in the process of communalisation, which made progress in important areas. The rural population, almost in its entirety, reached the legal status of liberty. Community institutions elaborated the most stable and defined functions. The liquidation of communal patrimony that historiography had once supposed is not to be found; indeed common goods continued to exist and occasionally expanded, thanks to new investments in woods, pastures, tithes from churches, or the surrender of seigneural prerogatives. If the administration did change, it was when, for example, the direct tenure of a wood or a mountain pasture by *vicini* was replaced by a more remunerative rent from investors and shepherds from other parts.

The territorial states accepted the rural communities as interlocutors. In the Italian parliaments there were mayors from non-urban communities, as long as they were part of the *demanio* (that is, were not subjects of a feudatory). In Friuli, where there was no rural representative in parliament, in the years 1518–19, and after a bloody revolt, a regional representation of rural dwellers was recognised and known as *Contadinanza*. Similar ranked assemblies did not develop in the dominions of Milan, Venice and Florence. There, an analogous function was assumed by the federations of communes, who took on fiscal commitments, which were shared among members, housing provision, and the provision of supplies for armed forces or the recruitment of infantrymen. In all the states of late medieval Italy, then, a daily interaction between those governing and those governed took place through other channels: the stipulation of *capitoli* (agreements) that defined the privileges of local institutions and legitimised their position within the corporate order of the state; the writing of letters and pleas; the issue of ambassadors of the people to the central authorities. The princes and ruling cities, furthermore, deployed a network of officials throughout the territory, with responsibility for local government and the administration of justice. These representatives of the state also became valuable mediators between the centre and the periphery, as they allied with the *homines* and were sensitive, formally or *de facto* whether they desired to be or not, towards the needs of the local councils. The dense web of peripheral magistrates, the generalised concession of immunity, and the attention paid by ruling cities and monarchs to the petitions of their subjects – that is, to the written records that explained the requests, and to the mayors who presented them – allowed local communities regular access to communication with the central power.

At times, furthermore, the Renaissance states favoured the communities over their long-standing competitors, and in some way this served to balance relations. They mediated legal cases with local lords, if they did not arbitrate them in favour of the *homines*, adjudicating to the latter control of communal lands, tolls and other rights. In central and northern Italy, characterised by a deep-rooted urban tradition, the new rulers conceded economic privileges that city powers had always denied, consenting to, for example, the multiplication of fairs and markets. Thanks to the widespread presence of local officials, they relieved some of the rural inhabitants of the need to refer to urban courts of law. They especially promoted the federal co-ordination of rural communes, which the urban regime had discouraged or prevented. Desired by rulers in order to increase subjects' responsibilities with regard to taxes, the military and the legal system, from another point of view they became the place in which subjects could discuss these issues and plan the battle against urban privileges. They also assumed prerogatives that city-states had executed in the age of their hegemony over the *contado*, such as regulation of the notary's office, or supervision of the weights and measures used in commerce.

The communities worked with determination, well beyond the support of the state and its courts of law, resorting to violence or to transactions with their adversaries, and trying to gain the favour of other authorities further afield, such as ecclesiastic authorities. Thus, in the fourteenth and fifteenth centuries, they obtained tithe rights, rights of patronage for local churches, and ownership of land previously held by local seigneurs.

Resources

Communes and sometimes *contrade* controlled a noteworthy variety of economic resources that were essential to the various ecological contexts. They held not only possession of pasture and woodland, which in historiography feature as collective goods *par excellence*, but also of coastal forests, marshlands, cultivated land, wells, fountains and equipment such as mills, sawmills, olive presses, furnaces and forges for ironwork, and kilns for bricks and for lime, as well as hostelries, hotels, thermal baths, butchers' shops and pharmacies. They held rights over river ports and water rights (which varied from fishing to using water for agricultural purposes); they collected tolls and duty on the sales of foodstuffs, taxes on fairs and markets. Along some Alpine routes, the communities whose territory wound across the roads monopolised the ability to carry out the profession of transporters, reserving it for their own members. The list could go on, and the list of administrative procedures would be just as long: emphyteusis for parcelled-out funds, direct access to woodland and pasture for *vicini*, but also the temporary concession of rights to fell wood and to have access to summer pasture in exchange for a *fictum*, the rent of mills and other facilities, the contracting out of tolls, and buildings for the reception of wayfarers.

Services

With secure incomes, communes could cover at least a part of the fiscal burden imposed by the state, and they were ready to take on a wide range of services. They supported people who were experiencing serious difficulties such as orphans, widows, the ill poor. To this end they dispensed private pious bequeathals, with occasional alms-giving, or used donations from public funds for the foundation and running of hospitals. They offered seed to peasants at advantageous prices; in times of famine they bought enough grain to sustain families. They could keep a bull for the use of local livestock farmers. They employed schoolteachers, doctors, barbers and prostitutes, who were paid at least a partial salary, while another part was often paid by the clients.

Communes and *contrade* had a role in the spiritual health of their inhabitants: they founded, embellished and maintained local churches; provided the living allowance for a curate; and established the conditions of his ministry, subsidising individual ceremonies, votive masses and processions. The investment of small centres in places of worship that were self-sufficient in the provision of sacraments contributed decisively to the creation of a capillary network of parishes, long before the ecclesiastical hierarchy concerned itself with normalising and rationalising it. The larger communities also supported the settlement of mendicant friaries and the building of impressive shrines. In addition, the brotherhoods, when they were not directly managed by the communes, received financial support from them.

The federations of communes often did not have the same resources. As intermediary bodies between the state and local society, they managed to temper military and fiscal requests from the rulers, to negotiate with magistrates sent from the centre, to defend land privileges and to submit to the rulers the requirements that were locally most crucial.

Many tasks were divided between the federations and the rural communes, either because they fell ambiguously into either or both camps or because the federations worked with state authorities in order to carry out tasks that then had to be divided among the constituent institutions. Such tasks included the maintenance of bridges and roads, defence of the territory, and the locating of a work force and the materials needed in the construction of forts. The administration of justice was traditionally a prerogative of public power, which the Italian states of the late Middle Ages executed by means of peripheral magistrates nominated from above, as previously discussed. Communities did not limit themselves to carrying out support functions, such as informing judges about crimes committed in their territories or contributing to policing operations (for example, the capture and custody of criminals and the handover or at least the expulsion of bandits). Minor cases and damage to crops were normally within the competences of officials elected by the *homines*; local officials promoted reconciliation, punished or moderated the judgements, and occasionally flanked the state judges in the verdict of sentences.

The attributes identified here should not be taken as elements of an entity that was defined *a priori* and in an unquestionable way, but as areas of participation in a collective body that, thanks to actions achieved and prerogatives claimed, defined its own features. It was not always a pre-existing community, for example, that founded and funded a church: on occasion a group of residents achieved their own institutionalisation through building initiatives and the formation of the benefice. In order to construct a place of worship, *vicini* had to gather publicly, in the presence of a notary who had the responsibility of articulating the majority or unanimous decision made by the assembly, of conferring an explicit mandate on the most highly regarded of them, acting in the name of the whole *contrada*, to follow the fortunes of the building and to negotiate with ecclesiastical authorities and the priest. The donations that communities managed on behalf of private benefactors were a formidable instrument in promoting local identity, when the men and women who bequeathed the distribution of wine, bread, foodstuffs, clothes and so on to the poor stipulated that the fruits of their generosity could be reaped only by the needy of the commune or of the *contrade*. It was not by chance, then, that separatist tensions existed between *contrade* and the communes to which they belonged. These tensions often surfaced firstly as a drive towards a separate organisation of charity and towards parochial emancipation. This is true, however, on a general level for all the functions carried out by the community, which determined the nature it assumed and its membership regulations, which consolidated the customs of the assemblies and which defined the elites able to take on leading roles.

Even the city communes and the territorial states sought to forge unity, assigning exacting duties to communes and federations and appointing the residents as jointly responsible for the breaches. In order to ensure upkeep of bridges and roads, for example, local officials had to summon all able-bodied men from the village to form a collective work force. If a crime was committed in the territory of a commune and not reported, or if the party guilty of a robbery could not be found, the entire *homines* had to answer for it. If a commune did not contribute to a work of fortification or any other financial burden imposed on the federations, other organisations were forced

The rural communities 275

to pay that commune's share. In this way, even the most exacting duties had the result of forcing inhabitants towards solidarity.

Individual and collective identities

From the perspective of a single individual, communities guaranteed resources and essential services. They offered peasants the opportunity to cut wood, an indispensable fuel and construction material, and to allow livestock (whose produce was a vital supplement to income from leased or owned lands) to graze in shared pastures. They permitted and sometimes obliged *vicini* to use their mill, they set up hospitality services and facilities for land and river transport for travellers and merchants, and they looked after markets and fairs. They helped the poor and procured food supplies in times of famine. They protected individuals from the invasive presence of the state in fiscal, military and legal matters.

They often represented the interests of individuals (*particolari*) – the unsatisfied creditor, the merchant who had been robbed but not compensated – who needed to be defended outside their area of jurisdiction.

Due to the extension of their powers, communities were able to intervene in many aspects of daily life in a prescriptive way. Statutes imposed urban regulations and the proper disposal of waste; they established the observation of liturgical feast days and the rules that were to be observed for funerals; they imposed a detailed agrarian calendar, forbidding, for example, hay-making, grape-harvesting or transfer of livestock from mountain pastures before a certain date, forcing land-owners to open their lands for shared pasture for some months of the year. Local councils prohibited certain uses of woodlands or waters; they established the prices for the retail of wine, bread and meat; they supervised the weights and measures used in the exchange of goods; they established educational programmes; in times of epidemic they banned travel and isolated those infected.

Clearly there were some privileged individuals, literally *uomini fuori dal comune* (men out of the community):[1] citizens who, thanks to their status and despite living in the *contado*, benefited from certain fiscal and jurisdictional advantages. The most powerful nobles, who did not need the protection of local institutions, did not participate in the assemblies of the heads of the families, and did not share the tax burdens to which the heads of the families were subjected, also fell into this category. The majority of the inhabitants of villages and *borghi*, in contrast, were

---

[1] Politi, 'Rivolte contadine', 166.

subject to duties and benefited from rights granted to the *uomini del comune* (men of the commune). The *poveri del comune* (poor of the commune) and the *figlie del comune* (daughters of the commune, girl orphans who were provided with food) were given relief in their poverty. The *prete del comune* (priest of the commune) was charged with the salvation of the *anime del comune* (souls of the commune), while the physician was committed to the health of the *corpi degli uomini del comune* (bodies of the men of the commune).

Other identities, constructed on foundations different from territorial belonging, such as consanguinity, faction loyalty, personal ties and class equality, coexisted and conflicted with that of *vicino*. The man of the commune was also, and at times especially, a member of a kinship group, or of a social class, dependent on a lord, Guelf or Ghibelline. In certain entities, or in certain situations, these other identities could even prevail. In the long term, however, the control of local resources and the legitimation selectively offered by the state in the late Middle Ages, in general, privileged community organisation.

Political actions such as party struggle and affiliation, which in the fifteenth century were assailed by a generalised campaign to discredit them, were reduced. Over the centuries, the dualism or pluralism of the social orders of many castles and population centres was overtaken: the nobles or knights, and *vicini* or *homines*, who in the past had not readily integrated, tended to become mixed within a single entity, although they were still separate parties; and even the privileged nobles of long lineage became incorporated into a class of *nobili del comune* (nobles of the commune). Other social configurations, such as corporations, did not flourish in the rural environment as they did in cities; where they did form, however, they enriched the political dialectic of the *borghi* without necessarily damaging cohesion. Even aggregations formed on bases that were initially different adapted to the successful model: when the established kinship group of an area within a commune strove to become an autonomous commune, or when a group of peasants dependent on an important ecclesiastic or lay land-owner separated from the *vicini*, setting up a commune of farmers of that particular church or that particular aristocrat.

A systematic investment of a symbolic nature strengthened the processes of social integration. *Case del comune* (houses of the commune) were constructed, which made the abstract entity of the commune more concrete by assigning it a place of residence, as well as, where the ambitions of jurisdictional autonomy were strongest, *palazzi* (palaces), traditionally known as the seat of public power. Coats of arms were painted on the walls of these buildings and could also be found on the seals of documents, affirming the identity of the community. These were the buildings in which the heads of the families met, the elective magistrates operated, contracts and compromises between people in litigation were entered into.

Chiese del comune (churches of the commune) were built which, thanks to their imposing architecture and the beauty of the works of art held inside, represented the unity of the people who came together there for religious ceremonies, but also for civic meetings, and displayed their prosperity compared to the accomplishments of neighbouring communes.

On the occasion of patronal festivals, and religious ceremonies in general, or on the day commemorating the founder, either at the founder's house or at the doors of the church, the giving of alms was a festival of the redistribution of wine and food. When donations arrived from the officers of the commune destined for the poor of the commune or *contrada*, or if they were available to all residents, this created a group unity in which benefactors and beneficiaries could feel a part.

The documents compiled by chancellors or notaries had more than a pragmatic function. Norms of cohabitation or the tax declarations of residents could be collected in beautifully compiled codices, showing the prestige of the institution to which they belonged. The formulae of the minutes of assembly meetings and the lists of councillors and heads of the families who participated, ranked by individual standing, by *contrada* of residence, by kin or more rarely by gender or by age, or, indeed, unranked constituted essential occasions in the search for and the local debate on the shape to give to each experience of communal life. The focus was at times on the unitary and impersonal nature of the community, at others on its aggregate character occasionally made up of individuals, social classes, kinship or lesser territorial unities. Even the most humble fiscal or proprietary entries preserved by notaries or in the communal archives that were stratified towards the end of the Middle Ages served to remind families of their local origins and their continued belonging, over generations, to the *universitas*.

In some areas, among the names that could be given to a child was the name of the commune in which he or she was born. Thus personal identity and the deep-rooted sense of belonging to a community would be united from birth.

Essere di – to belong to – a commune, a *contrada*, or a federal community became a fundamental characteristic in individuals, and was specified as such in written documents and in the conversations among people meeting who presented themselves or spoke about their acquaintances. If, therefore, and on good grounds, one of the roots of modern individualism can be found in Renaissance Italy, it must be taken into account that at the same time other anthropologies existed, expressed in documentary sources or in certain festivals, assembly discussions or conflicts (such as revolts or boundary disputes). When all the members of a community took up arms against the usurpers of a pasture, or when they shared out food on the patronal feast day, in plenary assemblies in which the voice and the gestures of an individual became confused with those of the people around them, the reciprocal relationship between the individuals and the community to which they belonged strengthened, to the point of converging into a collective of the same *being* of individuals, as the highly significant formulae described above and located in sources from the time attest.

Territories

The territory in turn was moulded by the communities within it. All their attributes, in reality, were localising: the responsibility of the police which the central authorities assigned to the communes and the federations; the areas of quarantine set up during epidemics; the investitures of tithes, or the dominion extending over pasture and woodland that the *homines* had taken from the local lords; the spiritual care (*cura d'anime*) of the parish all created rights and duties that extended towards delineated horizons. At the cost of interminable litigation and agonising compromises, boundaries were marked, recorded and made sacred with periodically renewed religious references, which attempted to attribute, in the least controversial way possible, areas of responsibility or use of the people belonging to the one side or the other (even if these were not exclusive). Within these areas the communes were furrowed with densely woven boundary lines, carved out by the statutes or council orders that regulated an ideal countryside by dividing it into areas reserved for different kinds of cultivation, for pasture in certain seasons, for the use of local or external livestock farmers. So deep, then, was the imprint of these institutions, that the written records of certain cultural areas resulted in a significant degree of assimilation: the 'territory of the commune of ...' became then, concisely, the 'commune of ...', that sanctioned the sense that the territory belonged to a legally defined group of people that dwelled therein.

Outsiders

A confirmation of the growth of the economic, social, political and cultural importance of the community can be found in the evolution of the condition of those that did not belong to it. A wide range of figures fall into this category that had one thing in common: *not being* from the commune, *contrada* or jurisdiction in which they lived. In the late Middle Ages these *extranee persone* (people from outside) experienced a serious deterioration in their position.

The *forensis* was a person who did not live in the territory of the commune but who could work in it. The *habitator* was a person who had recently moved to the commune and had not acquired the full rights of their neighbours. The statutes did not cease to introduce new injunctions against the *forenses*: banning them from using collective pastures, removing wood and acquiring property or livestock. For some infractions, he would have paid a fine that was double that charged to residents. Attitudes towards the *habitator* also changed. If the first rural communes had seemed rather open institutional entities, ready to integrate new arrivals and grant them the right to major responsibilities and a share of the local resources, communes of the fifteenth century and later rarely rapidly welcomed those who moved to them. Two separate groups existed in many entities: the original or long-standing *vicini* who benefited from the income of the commune and who held public responsibilities; and the so-called *non vicini* or even the *forenses*, who, even after generations of residency, were excluded from full participation in its economic and political life.

An even further level of extraneity was reached by another group: the gypsies. They could not belong to this network of local communities, as they were even more *forenses* than those coming from a different territorial community. Arriving in Italy in the first half of the fifteenth century, they became the target of a specific politics of expulsion to the extent that communities hurried to accompany them to the boundaries of their territory, perhaps, if necessary, encouraging them with alms.

Jewish people, on the other hand, were accepted with specific agreements as they practised medicine or were money-lenders or craftsmen. These pacts could not avoid resistance, but recognised Jewish people as a component of the population, in some entities given their own *universitas*. In the second half of the fifteenth century, however, the relations between this religious minority and the Christian majority began to rupture, fuelled by the anti-Semitic preaching of the observant friars, often accepted by local authorities, who adopted harsher sanctions of marginalisation within the community or of expulsion.

There were disadvantaged members even within the community, although their situation was not directly comparable to that of these excluded figures. The poor were normally excluded *de facto* from public life; women and young people were excluded in terms of their legal status. The *vicina*, in particular, is a more elusive figure than the *vicino*: she had fiscal responsibilities only if she was single or a widow, a giver of and, in times of necessity, a receiver of alms. Only in certain entities and in certain circumstances was she invited to the council meetings of the *vicinanza* and it can be said that she was not called to undertake tasks of administration or representation. In the fourteenth and fifteenth centuries her economic and proprietary role was further weakened: she was excluded from the use of collective resources; the statutes forbade her to marry outsiders on pain of losing all or part of her inheritance. These measures led to new circuits of matrimonial alliances being formed, driving her to seek a spouse from within the local community and therefore further strengthening relational and patrimonial value, and increasing the closed exclusivity of the local commune.

The Italy of rural communities

Of course, in the late Middle Ages not all rural Italian communities executed all the functions detailed here. The aim here is to present an initial inventory of the material and symbolic resources that there may have been and that, in some areas more than others – especially in the most prosperous places – were effectively communalised. The overview here provided does not rest on an equal body of research, as not all the Italian rural communities have been studied in equal depth. In recent years, detailed research into rural communities has taken place in Tuscany, in the Po valley and especially in Lombardy; less research into rural communities in other regions has taken place. The new focus on the *universitas* that enlivens studies on Sicily and the south of the peninsula, for example, concentrates mostly on urban environments. The current issue is to define fields of possibility and to discuss a research hypothesis, which awaits the findings and more precise evidence that may come from further investigations in different regions.

The interpretations that contrasted northern and central Italy, the Italy of local communities, and the Italy of the south and the islands – which were characterised by different historical protagonists (monarchies or barons) as having two opposing civic traditions – however, are no longer acceptable. Neither is it necessary to continue with the current tendency of reducing the area of greatest strength of rural communities to the Alpine or Apennine valleys or to other marginal areas in the Italy of the cities, gentlemen and princes.

It is of fundamental importance to bear in mind the various Italian political and social configurations. The layout of settlements is not homogeneous, and it is impossible to suppose that there would be identical institutional developments in those parts of the Po valley that were dotted with a myriad of small villages, in those areas of central Italy where peasants lived in isolated farms, or in settlements around a castle, or in those southern regions where in the late Middle Ages dramatic environmental selection reduced the number of settlements and concentrated inhabitants in a small number of centres, often called cities even when they were predominantly farming areas. The final centuries of the Middle Ages were not favourable to medium-sized rural entities everywhere in Italy: in Tuscany they went through a critical phase, whereas in Lombardy they developed. The resources controlled by the communities were also more or less wide-ranging. The quality of the groups of ruling elites also differed: not everywhere was an aristocracy of knights and jurists assimilated who then assumed leadership and strengthened the initiative, as happened in the central Alpine valleys. Lastly, analogous phenomena – from the emancipation from servile duties to the complete institutionalisation of public life – did not happen synchronously.

Nevertheless, these nuances need to be introduced into a unitary framework, which, next to other actors, recognises the fundamental role that the communities of villages or *borghi* played in Renaissance Italy, regulating the economy, supplying vital services, representing the population politically, confirming the personal identity of men and women. On the one hand, the new approaches that analyse the social construction of local identities and of political institutions have been tested only in a small number of regional entities, as mentioned earlier. The reconstruction of the spectrum of more general attributes of the community, on the other hand, can indeed benefit from a large number of recent and more dated studies, and from any number of editions of primary sources. It emerges that the institutional organisation of the inhabitants aimed at least at preventing the profligate use of natural resources, maintaining the upkeep of churches, and resolving disputes among *vicini*, and dialogue with the state was generalised. Some areas were clearly more subjected to urban and seigneural power than others, but the intermediary through which the *homines* negotiated with stronger political powers and attempted to resist overly heavy burdens was always the community. Where autonomy could not be gained, communities sought to mitigate subjection. Even in medieval Sardinia, for all that it has been recently reasserted that 'it never experienced rural communes',[2] the collective organisation of village representatives and the use of undivided land were not ignored. One of the proofs of increased political strength of

---

[2] Ferrante and Mattone, 'Le comunità rurali', 149.

communities, the ability to create stable supra-local committees, almost exclusively studied with reference to the north of Italy, has its counterparts elsewhere, such as the federations of the villages (*casali*) of Cosenza or the castles in the *contado* of L'Aquila, which were able to act co-operatively with, but at times also against, the city.

Conclusion

The discussion so far leads us, in closing, to seek an answer to a question that continues to be raised in research into late medieval Italy: why was there no peasants' revolt in Italy akin to those in other European countries at the same time? In recent years, many episodes of rebellion have, in fact, been researched further; in many cases, communities stood up to local lords and, by means of open violence, the threat of resistance or recourse to trial, frequently achieved their aims. It is true that these rebellions cannot be compared in scale to those in France, England and Germany. The frequency or infrequency with which these rebellions occurred, the range and the co-ordination of this extreme form of political demonstration by peasants constitute a relevant indicator of political development in the rural environment. This gap in Italian history has been explained by reference to the weakness of local communities. It is said that the penetration of the urban capital into the countryside destroyed the solidarity in villages that could have supported mass movements of protest. This is a persuasive hypothesis particularly for the areas of Tuscany that were reorganised into *poderi* (farms); these were mostly self-sufficient in terms of produce and entrusted to one family for cultivation, and were linked more to their land-owner, to whom the family had to give half the produce, than to other peasant families. Furthermore, it is held that the persistent force of the urban political control over the *contado* quashed even their will to rebel. None of these phenomena, however, would have been able to induce a generalised disintegration of the vicinal bonds on a national scale. The most plausible explanation, therefore, must be the opposing one. The Italian rural communities, in their political and economic strength, in the rights that they exercised over churches, in the tithes they collected and so on, enjoyed a role that is not inferior to but, in fact, is often superior to those from continental Europe. In order to create a comparison, the requests formulated in the Twelve Articles by German peasants in 1525, the most famous document produced over the course of a wave of revolts that was even felt on the Italian side of the Alps, can be examined. In the German countryside, they demanded, among other things, the possibility of electing a curate or a pastor and of administering the tithe; freedom from servitude; the cession of hunting rights, water rights and woodland retained by lords; and an end to judicial abuses by lords. Among the aspirations of this rebellion, furthermore, was to create a recognised corporate group and therefore have a voice within the state. It has now been shown that, in many regions of Italy, rural communities in the late Middle Ages had, in substance, empirically fulfilled the political programme of 1525, extending the prerogatives exercised and defined in an ever clearer way the group who were to share it. These communities would also have had a privileged status; like the cities, noble families and clerics, they formed representative bodies and occupied a recognised place within the constitution of the territorial state. At least the luckiest among them did not have any reason to aspire to a radical transformation of social and political order, and they acted periodically in order to consolidate their own rights over a wood, to restore commons usurped by a baron or to remove a priest nominated by a bishop but undesirable to the parishioners.

14 Lordships, fiefs and 'small states'

Federica Cengarle

Introduction

In the fourteenth century the Italian peninsula was fragmented into medium-sized, small and very small political entities.

Within this panorama kingdoms and principalities could be found (both lay and ecclesiastical) that historiography generally labels as 'feudal', that is to say, as elsewhere in Europe, in which the political role of cities was weak and relations between lords and vassals and the rural nobility represented the principal forms of aggregation within a dominion. Within Italy, many examples of this typology existed: the Angevin kingdom, following the death of king Robert, was devastated by battles for succession that, for over a century, provided ample room for the ambitions of the barons and that led to a continuous redefining of the balance of local politics; Aragonese Sicily was also a stage for continuous conflict; the princely bishopric of Trent was progressively worn away by the ambitions of the Habsburgs, the *advocati* of the Tridentine church; the patriarchate of Aquileia had a parliament, mainly composed of lords and feudatories, with wide-ranging decision-making powers; the county of Savoy was a hereditary dominion that the counts, due also to dynastic continuity, began to organise into more centralised forms, heavily involving the rural aristocracies.

Long-established historiographical interpretations hold that a marked decline in seigneurial relations and of the feudal institutions influenced, on the contrary, central and northern Italy. In western Piedmont, Lombardy, the Veneto (with the exception of the Trevigiano), Tuscany and Emilia-Romagna cities had for a long time attempted to present themselves as the organising element of the surrounding territory. The same is true, but to a lesser extent, in Umbria, the Marche and Lazio.

In the late 1970s, however, Philip Jones was already proposing a rereading of the political culture of medieval Italian communes. He underlined the conspicuous influence of rural aristocracy on city-states that was and remained linked to forms of political organisation from the rural nobility.[1]

Partially entering into dialogue with Jones's suggestions, Giorgio Chittolini's studies have shown that, in the fourteenth and fifteenth centuries, the reality of strong seigneurial and feudal relations was difficult to disregard even in a highly urbanised context such as that of Lombardy.[2] This interpretation fully engaged with a new reading of the emerging regional states and stressed the 'prudence and adaptability' with which the new orders imposed themselves over local political figures, accepting and recognising their existence but, at the same time, attempting to discipline them or, at least, putting themselves forward to arbitrate their differences.[3] Other studies followed that analysed the economic and social implications, in addition to the political and institutional implications, of the transition of seigneurial and feudal relations within the new regional political systems.[4]

But it is only in recent years that 'the significance of the phenomenon of rural lordship in the fourteenth and fifteenth centuries'[5] has once more become the source of more comprehensive considerations, extended to a geographical area that is not limited to the central area of the Po valley. In the light of the survival of the seigneurs, as confirmed by documents, a rereading has begun of the coherent and well-structured organisation of districts in which the city-states had extended their hegemonic ambitions on to the surrounding territory. What becomes clear is that in reality, alongside and frequently in opposition to the cities, there coexisted 'at length forms and organisations of power that did not originate from the city-states and the existence of which has been previously undervalued first and foremost due to a lack of research in the area'.[6]

When faced with a more or less widespread presence of rural lords, this has been a very profitable approach in reconsidering the actual political and territorial composition not only of some *contadi* that came under the dominion of Venice (Verona, Bergamo, Brescia), but also of those *contadi* governed first by the Visconti and then by the Sforza (Vercelli, Novara, Pavia, Piacenza, Parma, Reggio, Cremona, Como,

---

[1] Jones, *Economia e società*.
[2] Chittolini, *La formazione dello stato regionale*. For a contemporary historiographic overview on the subject, see Chittolini, *Signorie rurali e feudi*.
[3] Chittolini, 'Introduzione', in Chittolini (ed.), *La crisi degli ordinamenti*, 35ff.
[4] Dean, *Land and Power in Late Medieval Ferrara*; Visceglia, *Territorio, feudo e potere locale*; Vallone, *Feudi e città*.
[5] Varanini, 'Qualche riflessione conclusiva', 250.
[6] Zamperetti, *I piccoli principi*, 42.

286   Federica Cengarle

Milan) and even of the Florentine territory.⁷ The aim of this line of research was certainly not that of negating the peculiar and lasting role of the cities of central and northern Italy as strong elements in the organisation of territory. Indeed, the aim was more that of attenuating an overly urban-centric reading that, grounded in studies of medieval communes, it remains difficult to move away from.⁸

During the fourteenth and fifteenth centuries, the lordship did indeed constitute a common and widespread element that, sporadically arising in scholarly debate, unites the Italy of the city-states with the Italy of the feudal principalities, even within the specifics of individual contexts. Still within a political and institutional context that, in Italy as in Europe, was showing a tendency to be organised in a vertical way, developing a more mature state system, the bond of mutual reciprocity that linked the seigneurs of the castle to their *homines* continued to constitute a factor that united society in various rural areas. This link was horizontal, not vertical, and it was not formalised. Within it the dominion was born out of consensus, and the fealty of the *homines* was, and remained, rigidly counterbalanced by the effective protection of the *dominus*. Thus, as political and economic horizons gradually widened, the actual power and autonomy of the lord were tightly bound to his ability to mediate the interests of his people in the presence of old and new actors on the wider political stage who, with increasing frequency, peered in on individual rural situations.

'Lordship' (*signoria*) and 'fief' are two terms that have been employed indifferently by historiography since the 1960s, and still today they are often used indistinctly. It is not, however, merely a question of selecting one word or the other. It is, indeed, a question of attempting to identify and distinguish the powers exercised informally by the seigneur by virtue of the reciprocal and personal relationship that bound him to his territory (lordship), from the functions officially delegated by a prince or a ruling city, for example, to that very same lord (fief).

From at least the twelfth century the fief was a relationship of a mutually obligatory, contractual nature which established the delegation of the possession of goods or the exercising of a right on the part of a

---

⁷ For the Veneto, see Zamperetti, *I piccoli principi*; for the Lombardy of the Visconti and the Sforza, a selection of monographic works and reference texts includes: Greci, *Parma medievale*, in particular 1–42; Della Misericordia, *La disciplina contrattata*; Gentile, *Terra e poteri*; Gamberini, *La città assediata*; Cengarle, Chittolini and Varanini (eds.), *Poteri signorili e feudali*; Gamberini, *Lo stato visconteo*, in particular 153–99; Cengarle, *Immagine di potere*; Della Misericordia, *Divenire comunità*; Gamberini, *Oltre le città*. For the Florentine area, refer to the works of Paolo Pirillo.
⁸ On the opportunity to reconsider this urban-centric paradigm, see Gamberini, *Oltre le città*, 34–7.

concessor in exchange for fealty and service. From the second half of the fourteenth century, in the emerging regional states, the fief was used, not exclusively but with ever increasing frequency, to delegate the exercising of public functions in exchange for an oath of fealty by the vassal to the *senior*, whether a prince or a dominant city. In many cases the fief was a formal expedient used to legitimise and, at the same time, discipline the effective administration of a power that, at a local level, continued still to construct and maintain itself through a purely seigneurial logic. The *homines*, it seems, were not always prepared to accept the authority granted by a prince to a feudatory, if this particular feudatory was not able to interpret and mediate its own interests.

In order to define some of the largest rural lordships, at times recourse was made to a category borrowed from modern-age historiography: the 'small state'. This term has been used to define the attempt, made by some seigneurs, to survive on the margins of the new regional configurations and to maintain their own autonomous role, allowing them to enter into dialogue with the *potenze grosse* (large powers) at equal level. Both 'small' and 'large' are adjectives used to measure and quantify the concrete extension of a territory, but also describe the level of visibility and autonomy of the political entity that they are describing.[9]

At this juncture, it is opportune to highlight that, in the thirteenth and fourteenth centuries, in the lordship, the fief and the 'small state', there seems still to have been a common and essential foundation that enabled the effective execution of power: the contractual nature of the relationship between lords or feudatories and their *homines*. This line of research has received differing levels of scholarly attention; however, it is frequently sacrificed in order to attempt to assess the political weight of individual seigneurs or feudatories within the emerging regional configurations.

Yet the *homines* themselves are often active interlocutors, both with the lords and feudatories, and with the princes and dominant cities. On the one hand, the agreement that allows lords and feudatories to *congregare homines* is one of the instruments used by the lords to assert their own political role within regional states, or even in the fragmented political landscape of the whole peninsula. On the other hand, however, the dissatisfaction of the people with their lord is one of the factors used as a lever by princes and ruling cities in order to contain and discipline seigneurial powers, exercising not only *de jure* but also *de facto*

---

[9] On the multifaceted meanings of 'small' and 'large' with reference to the state, see Raviola, *L'Europa dei piccoli stati*, 11.

control over the nobles, who were by their very nature forces pulling away from the new regional states.

In this summary, the role carved out by the *homines*, therefore, can be considered as the common denominator that links together very diverse political entities (lordships, fiefs and 'small states'), constantly changing over time and in dimension.

Lordships

Throughout the fourteenth century, Italy was witness to continuous conflict: internal struggles within cities; the exile from towns of the ringleaders of one faction, then of another; the connection of these local conflicts to the opposing allegiances to the pope in Avignon or to the emperor; the growing ambitions of the Angevins and of some city-*signori*, for example the Scaligeri and later the Visconti, to extend their power and influence; the distance from the papal see; and, later, the battles for succession to the throne of Naples generated a permanent state of war throughout the peninsula (without even mentioning the incessant internal conflict that characterised Aragonese Sicily).

In many regions the degree of political and military instability during those years led to a widespread need for protection on the part of those living in the countryside. This need for protection was readily satisfied by seigneurs of long lineage and new seigneurs alike, who ably exploited these favourable circumstances to further their own ambitions of dominance. They restored old castles and had new ones built, with the effect of altering the political balance in rural regions.

Over and above any title flaunted to other political actors (titles based on customary law and immemorial possession or later titles that had been bought), the power of the seigneur of a castle first of all had to be legitimised by the *homines*, who were constantly negotiating their fealty and service commensurate to the level of effective military, economic and fiscal protection guaranteed by the *domini*. In this way seigneurs gathered a conspicuous number of *fideles* around their castle. An important resource of the *dominus castri*, the *fideles* were engaged at one moment to affirm and extend the lord's power throughout the local area and the next to play a role further afield within the political patchwork of a region, linked with other lords or even with cities or princes.

But who are these 'small lords'? How does their role change in the fragmented political landscape of the peninsula? To what extent does their relationship with their *homines* favour or condition their autonomy? There is no single answer as the small *signorie*, which in late medieval Italy bought or retained a political role of note, were many and of various origins. The seigneurs were first of all from rural families of long lineage and who, for centuries, had passed down *pro indiviso* various rights and prerogatives over the local population (varying levels of jurisdiction, taxation, control of collective goods, ecclesiastical patronage). These families became established particularly in the areas of the Apennines (the Del Carretto, the Busca, the Ponzone in the Langhe; the Fieschi, the Malaspina from Lunigiana and those from the Oltrepò; the Roberti, the Da Dallo, the Fogliani, the Boiardi, the Ubaldini, the Ubertini and the Guidi; the Aldobrandeschi and the Visconti from Campiglia nel Senese; etc.), but not exclusively (the Visconti in the Seprio; the Collalto and the Camposampiero in the Trevigiano; etc.).

There were also noble families whose power originated in castles within the *contado* but who moved to urban areas, weaving themselves into the social fabric of the city and personally intervening in the political organisms of one city or more, in order to defend or strengthen the interests of their own title, family or faction. Families who followed this path include the Avogadro in Vercelli, the Landi, the Scotti, the Da Correggio, the Pallavicini and the Rossi in Piacenza, Parma, and Cremona; the Rusca in Como; the Da Dallo and the Fogliani in Reggio; the da Camino and the Tempesta in the Trevigiano; the da Stenico, the Roccabruna and the Madruzzo in Trent. The list could also extend to the Savorgnan in Udine and the de Portis in Cividale or, in the context of the significant weakness of the papal monarchy, the Orsini and the Colonna in Rome.[10] It was because they could count on their possession of men and castles in the countryside that, in the second half of the fourteenth century and the beginning of the fifteenth, many small seigneurs in Umbria – such as the Baglioni in Perugia, the Trinci in Foligno, the Monaldeschi in Orvieto, the Gabrielli in Gubbio, the Vitelli in Città di Castello – even managed to temporarily gain lordship of their city, obtaining apostolic vicariates confirming these 'short-lived' urban and semi-urban *signorie*.[11]

Alongside these families with deeply rooted history in their area, another type of family can be added who occasionally managed to

---

[10] On the Avogadro, see Barbero, 'Da signoria rurale a feudo'; on the Pallavicini, see Arcangeli, 'I Pallavicini'; on the Rossi, see Gentile, 'Giustizia, protezione, amicizia'; Arcangeli and Gentile (eds.), *Le signorie dei Rossi*; on the Fogliani, see Gamberini, *La città assediata*; on the Trevigiano, see Canzian, 'Signorie rurali nel territorio trevigiano'; for Trentino, see Bettotti, *La nobiltà trentina*; on the Roman barons, see Carocci, *Baroni di Roma*; Allegrezza, *Organizzazione del potere*; on the Savorgnano and the de Portis, for a recent and effective rereading on the Friulan situation, see Zacchigna, 'L'inclinazione signorile'.

[11] For central Italy, see Maire Vigueur, *Comuni e signorie in Umbria, Marche e Lazio*; Nico Ottaviani, '*Statuta sive leges municipales*'; Regni, 'I Gabrielli di Gubbio'.

supplant older families at a local level. These families had not had titles for countless generations but often, after having built up riches in cities through commercial and financial activities, bought land in the countryside and gained the voluntary obedience of the *homines*. This is true, for example, of the Scarampi and the Guttuari in Asti, the Falletti in Alba, the Anguissola in Piacenza, the Salimbeni in Siena, etc.[12]

Ecclesiastical lords were, on the other hand, in steady decline over the fourteenth and fifteenth centuries, if the lords, be they bishops, abbots or members of chapter, were not energetic people, able to refer to a wider network of relatives and those from the same faction in order to defend their independent political role. For similar reasons the rare lordships held by soldiers of fortune and *condottieri* were short-lived as they were reliant only on their own leadership and did not have an original nucleus of noble power (as, in contrast had, for example, the Alviano in Umbria, the Orsini in Pitigliano and the counts of Santafiora in the Siena region).[13]

How did their role change in the fragmented political landscape of the peninsula?

It has been shown that, over the first few decades of the fourteenth century, these lords played an important role in the confused and divided political landscape of the peninsula, carving out autonomous areas for themselves particularly in the centre and the north. Able to recruit soldiers, they offered their lands as a gateway for external political forces that wanted to pass through to gain a presence or strengthen one in hostile territories. The Falletti in La Morra, *foederati* of Robert I of Anjou in Piedmont, for example, took this course of action.[14]

But around the middle of the fourteenth century the political structure of the peninsula began to have a hierarchy. *Signorie* and cities able to accumulate greater numbers of men and lands emerged, a prelude to the new political configurations of a regional nature. In central and northern Italy the expansionist politics of the Visconti progressively included the inland Veneto, the territory of the papal state and even Tuscany, provoking reactions from the pope, Florence, and the Carraresi, Scaligeri and Este dynasties. Particularly in border areas, small seigneurs continued to oscillate between the large powers, from time to time negotiating offers of men, weapons and personal or family networks in exchange for immunity, exemptions and recognition of their autonomy.

---

[12] On the nature of this obedience, see Chittolini, *La formazione dello stato regionale*, 36–100; for the Astigiani, see Sisto, *Banchieri-feudatari*.
[13] Chittolini, *Signorie rurali e feudi*, 627–31; Covini, *L'esercito del duca*.
[14] Del Bo, 'Un itinerario signorile'.

Some lords obtained formal recognition of independence, appearing in peace treaties as *foederati, adherenti, collegati, complices* and *raccomandati*. Common in the fourteenth century, these contracts that regulated relations between greater powers and minor powers (*aderenza, accomandigia, foederatio, colleganza*, etc.) have recently begun to catch the attention of scholars once more.[15] These agreements were of a rather flexible nature; they ratified promises and established reciprocal advantages of all natures for both parties. The lesser power could, for example, obtain recognition of a series of ill-defined rights and privileges that it exercised *de facto* rather than *de jure* by offering allegiance in exchange for a formal legitimation (for example, the seemingly highly sought-after *merum et mixtum imperium*) and another set of commitments and promises. At the same time the greater power, thanks to this legitimising action, could, in turn, expand both land and ambitions into areas that did not fall under its jurisdiction. These agreements offered the lesser power an ambiguous position somewhere between allegiance and subjection. Many seigneurs had recourse to these agreements, even well into the fifteenth century, in an attempt to affirm or reaffirm their independence in times of temporary uncertainty concerning the power of princes or ruling cities.

In order to safeguard their autonomy, the smallest powers did not look exclusively to this form of 'international' recognition. Other lords strenuously defended their free rule over their dominion, for a number of years, by appealing to the same source of legitimation to which princes and ruling cities had recourse in order to continue to communicate with them on an equal footing, at least formally: the emperor. The Collalto in the Trevigiano used this approach: they were imperial feudatories and *adherenti* to Venice until 1481, when Venice forced them to accept the status of vassals to the *Serenissima*.[16]

From the final decades of the fourteenth century, the contractual power of these seigneurs was severely undermined by a number of factors. The continued easing of conflicts, peace agreements being signed between the major powers, and the peninsula-wide reorganisation process of land and political power all had an impact.

Some seigneurs then renounced their independence and accepted feudal investiture or inclusion in the apparatus of government as a necessary counterpart to maintaining *de facto* autonomy at a local level.

---

[15] Gamberini, *La città assediata*, 128–31; Fubini, '"Potenze grosse"'; Somaini, 'Le *declarationes colligatorum*'; Arcangeli, 'Piccoli signori lombardi'; Chittolini, 'Ascesa e declino'.
[16] Zamperetti, *I piccoli principi*, 57–8.

As feudatories or officials of the princes and ruling cities, the rural seigneurs were formally legitimised by a higher authority to exercise various public rights. These rights, of low, medium or even high jurisdiction, were generally the same as those that their *homines* had previously spontaneously recognised as a counterpart to military or fiscal protection from external political actors. The exercising of these rights now had to be granted to the lords in exchange for subordination, at least at a formal level, to the new regional states.

Furthermore, others divided their own personal conditions in relation to the various locations of their territories. In the 1420s, for example, Uguccione Contrari, tutor and adviser to Niccolò III d'Este, at the same time as recognising himself as a loyal subject of Niccolò III for some of his properties, declared himself to be the free land-owner of other territories situated in the area of Parma and, as such, attempted to lead autonomous negotiations with the duke of Milan, who had just become ruler of Parma.[17] In 1468, Manfredo da Correggio was at the same time feudatory to the duke of Milan, autonomous lord of Correggio, and loyal to the duke of Modena.[18] These complicated, tangled webs of privilege and subordination were far from uncommon. Their existence is attested in court records and seigneurial cartularies that, with ever increasing frequency from the beginning of the fifteenth century, show a growing necessity to define, guarantee and protect the prerogatives and the immunities of lineage.

Neither was it an infrequent occurrence for lords temporarily dispossessed of their territories to return as rightful lord, following a change in political circumstances, and to repossess their dominion, their only strength being the support of the *homines* who still recognised them as their *dominus*. This was frequently the case for the Orsini and the Colonna who, taking advantage of frequent papal successions and subsequent changes in retinue from one pope to the next, could constantly reassert possession of their properties which had temporarily been bestowed on papal favourites.[19]

Both the changing of the geopolitical structure within the peninsula and the effective maintenance of the relationship between a lord and his *homines* contributed to the loss of, or indeed the preservation of, autonomy. Recent research in historiography has greatly focused on this informal basis for exercising power.

---

[17] Cengarle, 'Gerarchie e sfere d'influenza'.
[18] Arcangeli, 'Piccoli signori lombardi', 411.
[19] Shaw, 'The Roman barons', 105; on the temporary resurgence of the ambitions of the Lomellini lords in the delicate years of transition between Visconti and Sforza rule, see Covini, 'In Lomellina nel Quattrocento'.

Studies such as that of Paolo Pirillo into the Ubaldini and Guidi dynasties show that it was indeed the solidarity of the *fideles* towards their *domini* that delayed for some time the departure of the *domini* from the Italian political stage. Despite having taken control of some of the land belonging to the Ubaldini and taking over the jurisdiction, the commune of Florence was not able immediately to break down the network of actual and personal duties that linked the *homines* to their *domini*. In the middle of the fourteenth century, following a number of attempts at victory by force, Florence, under threat from troops of the Visconti, finally recognised a *districtus Ubaldinorum*, promising, however, lighter taxes and political immunity to those who abandoned the territory of the Ubaldini to enter Florentine territory.[20]

Following a general appeasement of conflict and reorganisation of territory, the rural families of long lineage without an adequate network of relations outside the local area seemed destined to pass into extinction. The possession of lands, frequently dispersed, was no longer sufficient to guarantee a lord control over his *homines* who were, at that point, emancipated from their servile status. Weakened and divided by internal power conflicts, over time the families increasingly struggled to fulfil the requests of their *homines* or the promises used to entice them away from other political actors in their lands (princes, cities, seigneurs or larger communities).

These moments of crisis for seigneurial power demonstrate that the exchange of protection and obedience could be based on a political culture that was not common to both *homines* and *domini*. In some areas, such as the erstwhile dominions of Matilda of Canossa, lords attempted to slow down defections by asserting jurisdictional functions and competences over a defined territory and, therefore, those living in it. The *homines* countered this principle of 'territoriality' with a different political culture, in which obedience was established as an individual and voluntary act and was, therefore, rescindable at any time: the *confugere ad castrum* (taking refuge in the castle). This culture generated the political fragmentation of some villages in which, in times of war, those loyal to the lord could take refuge in his castle whereas others found refuge in different forts (and were loyal to the owner of that fort).[21]

Defection from land and from obedience to a lord was only one of the possible outcomes of the conflict between the *homines* and their *domini*. Faced with an economic offensive from external competitors, which

---

[20] Pirillo, 'Signorie dell'Appennino'. A temporary resurrection seems to have been felt by the Visconti di Campiglia in the Siena area: Dean, 'The dukes of Ferrara', 366.
[21] Gamberini, *Lo stato visconteo*, 203–30.

included the steady stifling of the seigneurial markets, the most entrepreneurial social and economic elements (merchants, craftsmen, the men of the *masnada*) led ever harsher litigations between the communities they represented and the seigneurs, no longer able to fulfil the necessities of their economic and social growth. In different ways and at different times a pulling together of community solidarity can be noted: people began to see themselves not just as individuals exclusively linked to the *dominus*, but also as a collective of people who lived in the same territory, defended common interests and took common political action.[22] From the many instances that could illustrate this point, the example of some communities in the Reggio area is emblematic: in the 1420s they autonomously decided to remove their allegiance from the *domini loci*, the Da Dallo and the Fogliani, and give it to the Este marquis in exchange for privileges and tax exemptions.

Despite growing pressure from both external factors (competition from princes, cities, seigneurs and larger communities) and internal factors (hereditary fragmentation of the land and the weakening relationship with the *fideles*), the lords managed to maintain an important role if they were able to make themselves representative of the community on a wider political, social and economic horizon. Again, this is a long and inconsistent process in which changing circumstances played a crucial role. However, whether a lord wanted to retain his independence or whether he decided to become part of the emerging regional states, and not necessarily with an act of feudal subordination, he had to move away from a local perspective and extend his network of connections in order to perform the economic, fiscal, and later political necessities of his *homines*. He had to transform himself from a patron into a mediator, exercising functions of protection, of representation and of guarantee towards his men in the face of possible external competitors and before the prince and his public office.[23] The link between the failure of this role and the disappearance of the lordship of the Ubaldini from the Italian political stage has already been mentioned. Ably playing on their privileged and ambiguous position within the duchy of Milan, some branches of the Visconti del Seprio, however, continued to consolidate their lordships, procuring exemptions and fiscal advantages for their *fedeli* throughout the fifteenth century.

---

[22] For the Alpine area, see Della Misericordia, *Divenire comunità*; for the Apennines and the plains, in addition to the work of Pirillo, see Cengarle, Chittolini and Varanini (eds.), *Poteri signorili e feudali*; for the southern *universitates* of *cives*, and also of *habitatores*, see Galasso, *Il regno di Napoli*, 394; Massaro, *Potere politico*. On the continued friction between lords and rural communities in Trentino, see Bettotti, *La nobiltà trentina*.

[23] Della Misericordia, 'Dal patronato alla mediazione politica', 208.

Fiefs

During the gradual process of reorganisation of territory in fourteenth- and fifteenth-century Italy, the emerging regional configurations increasingly had recourse to the fief as a means of political and territorial co-ordination. The fief allowed princes and ruling cities not only to increase their clientelage through the concession of goods and rights, but also to obtain at least formal recognition of their superiority over local lords who had renounced their independence.

In a seemingly ordered vertical hierarchy of power, through a fief the prince could grant to a feudatory property, goods, offices and various rights (of passage, concerning water, fiscal, etc.) and, increasingly, delegate full jurisdiction over a territory and its inhabitants. It has already been noted that, by means of feudal homage, many rural lords recognised the authority of princes or of ruling cities in exchange for confirmation of their status. The extent to which these enfeoffments were able to corrode the concrete bases and prerogatives of noble power seems to have varied in different states and over time.

These formal subordinations did indeed relatively undermine the prerogatives and the *de facto* power exercised by the *domini* if the following criteria were to be found: areas in which the presence of the city was weak, if not entirely absent; areas in which landed property was and remained a source of power and control over the *homines*; and areas in which the institution of vassalage itself had been used for a long time by sovereigns and princes (lay and ecclesiastic).[24]

The *suzerain* did not always have sufficient strength and/or will to control and discipline all his feudatories. In this sense, but for different reasons, a substantial weakness characterised both the princely bishopric of Trent and the patriarchate of Aquileia, where 'Forms of personal obligation or economic ties imposed by the castellans on the rural inhabitants of their fiefs further reinforced these processes of seigneurial independence.'[25] For much of the fifteenth century, the marquises of Saluzzo had only minimal recourse to the fief, fearful that a coalition between the populace and the feudatories would oust them from control of the territory.[26] Elsewhere,

---

[24] On the strengthening of the noble character of the Neapolitan barons in the Angevin–Aragonese era, see Galasso, *Il regno di Napoli*, 369. On the continuing attachment, at least in Val d'Aosta, of the aristocracy to local privileges and peripheral autonomy when faced with the feudalisation of the Savoy dynasty, see Barbero, 'Principe e nobiltà negli stati sabaudi'.

[25] Bellabarba, 'The feudal principalities: the east', 203, in this volume.

[26] Cengarle, 'La riduzione dei diritti feudali'; Barbero, 'Appannaggi, infeudazioni, riacquisti'.

even in the papal dominion, after the schism, the clauses that guaranteed the sovereign control over his feudatories, introduced in the times of Albornoz, began to disappear. Straddling the fourteenth and fifteenth centuries, the papal fief only sporadically performed functions of public co-ordination, demonstrating rather 'the weakening of papal power compared to the various forces present in such vast territories which were difficult to control directly'.[27]

Elsewhere, however, Italian princes adopted practices that allowed them to marginalise their vassals' political autonomy, subordinating it not only to their formal authority but also to their increasing *de facto* power.

Firstly the princes forced the vassals' fealty by multiplying their personal obligations to the princes and their obligations towards the territory. To the bond of vassalage, perhaps due to its contractual nature perceived as too precarious an instrument of coercion, they added and merged the concepts of personal service to the prince and innate obedience based on belonging to a territory and a jurisdiction. Thus, in the fourteenth and fifteenth centuries, in the county of Savoy, local lords were called upon with increasing frequency to cover the administrative functions of the Savoy principality, receiving duties (castles, etc.) even with feudal titles. In the middle of the fifteenth century in the Lombardy of the Visconti, and possibly also in the kingdom of Naples, feudatories were at the same time, in a complex and far from continuous or linear process, subject to an affirmation of affiliation to the territory as the authoritative grounds of the new regional state.[28]

In this respect the heavily researched Lombard situation is particularly significant. At the end of the fourteenth century, after the imperial investiture had conferred on the new duke, Gian Galeazzo Visconti, a legitimate title that allowed him to set out jurisdiction, he and his successors began to use the fief as an indirect instrument of government over the territory. Using feudal concessions, the prince delegated the execution of jurisdictional and fiscal functions to the local lords of long lineage and newly enfeoffed lords alike, obtaining their subordination and thus linking their individual fate to his. In the first half of the fifteenth century, various legislative measures issued from the Visconti: the inclusion of particular clauses in the contract of investiture and the transformations made to the form of the contract itself show that the duke was trying to assert increased control over the actions of the feudatories. It is the form of the contract in particular that suggests that

[27] Carocci, 'Vassalli del papa', 79.
[28] Cengarle, 'Vassalli et subditi'; Vitolo, 'Linguaggi e forme', 57.

the prince intended to remove from feudal relations those last remnants of political autonomy that derived from its contractual nature. Vassals, then, pledged fealty to the duke not only in his capacity as ruler, but also as subjects and inhabitants of the territory; this type of obedience, as the *Libri feudorum* show, proved to be much more coercive than vassal fealty.[29]

The situation was much more complicated in the southern kingdom. Studies on noble and feudal institutions, numerous for the Normano-Swabian era, became much less abundant for the Angevin-Aragonese period. A rapid, initial reading of the feudal texts produced by Martino Caramanico and by Andrea d'Isernia appears to reveal a new and emphatic interest, already visible in the jurists of the first Angevin era, for a form of coercion different from vassal fealty and subjection. There is no evidence in documents produced by the Angevin chancery, however, confirming that these are anything but theoretical reflections, probably born out of political exigencies from the new French sovereigns. In this perspective, a recently proposed study on the possible equal status of vassals in the middle of the fifteenth century compared to other subjects bound to the sovereign is considerably more attractive and full of possibilities.[30] Such parity may be deeply rooted in an earlier and autonomous tradition compared to the previously mentioned Lombard situation.

In general terms it is perhaps not too risky a hypothesis to suggest that the princes of the peninsula attempted progressively to weaken the political role of the feudatories, by trying to make frequent changes of feudatory into an incentive and preventing feudatories from embedding themselves within a territory. This hypothesis does not exclude the possibility that, rather than a conscious authoritarian project, this mobility is due to growing financial necessities: the fiscal burdens that weighed down the transition of feudal possession constituted an important source of income for tax revenue.

Certainly, the frequent turnover in the fief of noblemen from outside the local area did limit the capacity of feudatories to put down roots, as they were not able to establish enduring relations with their subjects. Furthermore, a reading of relations between seigneurs and vassals that overly focuses on the continuous nature of this relationship has been brought into question recently even in Sicily where the fief is a deeply rooted institution. The fief does indeed have deep roots in Sicily; however, the lineages that circulated among portions of territory taken from the dominion of the sovereign and traditionally enfeoffed did not.

[29] Chittolini, *La formazione dello stato regionale*; Cengarle, *Immagine di potere*.
[30] Vitolo, 'Linguaggi e forme', 57.

Often these feudatories had no links whatsoever with the local environment. After the Sicilian Vespers, the high rates of circulation both in the higher and the lower military aristocracy and among the lesser urban feudatories could be explained, in the view of Igor Mineo, only through 'a tendency towards low levels of dynastic organisation and of seigneurial settlement'. With a small number of noteworthy exceptions (the Ventimiglia and the Chiaromonte), this fragility in the structure of the seigneurial nobility did not seem to fade throughout the fourteenth century. This confirms the occurrence of circulation linked to the endemic conflict that characterised the Sicilian political stage and forced the aristocracy to create alternative strategies to balance out the precariousness of territorial rooting.[31]

Moreover, in the Savoy area, in the fourteenth and fifteenth centuries, the great mobility of the feudal market in terms of fiefs, land and offices leads to considerations of the difficulties the new feudatories faced in establishing themselves. These new feudatories did not come from the rural aristocracy but were officials, money-lenders and merchants.[32] Using the jurisdictional fief as a means of temporarily rewarding or compensating military leaders, money-lenders or loyalty was a frequent practice too in newly formed principalities such as the duchies of the Visconti, Sforza and Este.

The feudatories' precarious situation, both in Sicily and in Lombardy, was desired and encouraged using legislative measures and legal clauses. However, although vassals were not able to integrate into local communities for more than two, or at the most three generations, the prince was and remained a constant figure of reference for enfeoffed communities within the fiefs. Those princes who, more than others, consistently and deliberately strove towards subjugating territory for themselves, though not necessarily to govern themselves, explicitly confirm that the fealty shown by the *homines* to their vassals was conditioned by the fealty that the same *homines* showed towards the prince himself. Over and above being subjects of the feudatory, therefore, the people remained subjects of the prince.[33]

For all that this discourse resembles law, it had prominent practical implications: subjects could refer directly to the central government in

---

[31] Mineo, *Nobiltà di stato*, 101–2, 168ff.
[32] Castelnuovo, 'Omaggio, feudo e signoria'. The effective duration of the political claim of many families of officials in the Angevin kingdom is still to be ascertained. These families were able to take root in local areas, especially in the Durazzo era, having obtained feudal concessions of land and castles confiscated by Ladislao: see Vitale, *Élite burocratica e famiglia*.
[33] Cengarle, 'La riduzione dei diritti feudali'.

the case of malpractice and acts of misrule by feudatories, on occasions even obtaining the removal of the feudatory. In the second half of the fifteenth century, during the tumultuous events that pitted the barons against Ferrante in the kingdom of Naples, enfeoffed cities and communities increasingly referred to the sovereign, either asking to be annexed to the kingdom's domain, or asking for increased guarantees from the feudatory, occasionally using their fealty as a negotiating tool if it suited their cause.

The behaviour of the new feudatories towards their enfeoffed communities and their ability to meet the needs of local society became determining factors less for the survival of the fief (which could subsequently be sub-enfeoffed) and more for the survival of the feudatory. Feudal concession was only a formal delegation of authority and did not necessarily correspond to the direct execution of power. In order to retain a fief, the feudatory had to abandon all language of authority with his subjects, relying instead on the customary role of seigneur, as a provider of protection and defence, a role his subjects still understood and accepted.[34] In real terms, his power was directly proportional to the consensus he was able to gain among his *homines* in his role as mediator for their interests with the central government. His role was to obtain exemptions and fiscal privileges for the community and to defend it in controversies with cities, communities or bordering territories under the jurisdiction of other seigneurs.

Not all feudatories, however, managed with equal levels of success to balance the needs of the prince with those of the community. The prince expected feudatories to use their local influence to maintain fealty, to resolve internal disputes and to collect taxes. It was on this final point that the feudatory met the most opposition from communities.

From the Alps to Sicily, influence at court became a fundamental factor for both seigneurs of long lineage and recently enfeoffed seigneurs alike. Their task of mediation was made considerably more difficult if, isolating themselves in their distant territories, they did not encourage the prince's favour towards their subjects. There were a good number of cases of sons or descendants of *condottieri* who, having given up arms, took up residence in their remote dominions and, after a while, lost influence over their subjects (Dal Verme, Sanseverino). Furthermore, in the court, where few were interested in upholding the defence of these marginalised lords, grievances and complaints arrived from the community, lamenting the poor government of the feudatory. These complaints, at times, led to the temporary

---

[34] Cengarle, Chittolini and Varanini (eds.), *Poteri signorili e feudali*.

or permanent revocation of the fief due to the opposition of all, or a part of, its subjects (Mandelli, Balbiani in Valchiavenna).

The case was different for those feudatories who did not make their relations with their *homines* their only link to power. Such feudatories did not isolate themselves in their dominions but entered into the wider political dynamics, interacting with the court and with other political actors both internal and external to the regional state. Dynasties such as the Borromeo in Lombardy, the Orsini Del Balzo in Puglia and the Chiaromonte and Ventimiglia in Sicily used these techniques to create large uninterrupted seigneurial and feudal dominions.

It can be concluded that the delegation of government established in the feudal contract in no way dried up the relationship of protection and defence that, from the perspective of the community, exclusively justified and legitimised the feudatories' execution of power. In order to defend their own interests, the community, *mediate subiecte*, discovered means of direct communication with other political and economic actors, and with the central government itself. Feudatories, whether old aristocracy or *homines novi*, needed to intercept these communications and champion the communities' interests themselves; if not, they risked the loss of the fief or, in extreme cases, its depopulation.[35]

'Small states'

During the 1970s, a period in which historiography recognised only cities as having a leading role in the constitutional dynamics that created the history of Italy, Giorgio Chittolini applied the term 'small state' to a number of seigneurial configurations in the countryside of Emilia which, in the fourteenth and fifteenth centuries, established themselves as autonomous states. These states had well-structured internal administration and formal external recognition from larger powers and, furthermore, were strengthened by a strong sense of *publicum*.[36]

A recent and ongoing debate aims to establish the political entities in the fourteenth and fifteenth centuries to which the label 'small state' can be applied. In a recent volume, in particular, the contrasting views are clearly stated. One side argues the politological view: this perspective favours a broad notion of the term that, irrespective of formal contracts, focuses on the concrete execution of autonomous and structured

---

[35] On the progressive waning of influence of rural aristocracy in Lomellina in the fifteenth century, see Covini, 'In Lomellina nel Quattrocento'. On the true extent of depopulation in the old *signorie* in the Este duchy, see Folin, 'Feudatari, cittadini, gentiluomini'; on the Terra d'Otranto, see Visceglia, *Territorio, feudo e potere locale*.
[36] Chittolini, *La formazione dello stato regionale*, 254–91.

seigneurial power in a local base (through a network of castles and officials, and the administration of justice). The contrasting argument sustains a narrower view of this autonomy, seeing it in terms of formal jurisdictional and institutional powers (both *de facto* and *de jure* recognition from within the 'system' of Italian states).[37]

What are the characteristic elements of the 'small state'?

Giorgio Chittolini himself has recently highlighted the 'uncertain and elusive' appearance of these 'small states', given that 'their characteristics not only differ from state to state, but altered according to changes in political and institutional circumstances, that is, the circumstances in which they received recognition of their condition'. It was the relationship between a *dominus* and his *fideles* that was at the heart of these clusters of power. When a lord decided to plan and organise his territories in a uniform way by constructing a bureaucratic system for the administration of justice and the collection of taxes, however, this relationship took on a territorial dimension, not just a personal one. Other elements that characterised the 'small state' can be found in the lord's ability to create and maintain complex networks of relationships with other political actors at a local and wider level, by taking part in the military and diplomatic campaigns of the peninsula, and by receiving '*de facto* and also *de jure*' recognition as a part of that 'system' of states that was emerging within the Italian peninsula between the fourteenth and fifteenth centuries.[38]

Frequently discussing elements of '*de facto* and *de jure*' to filter and distinguish between lordships and 'small states', Chittolini has thus circumscribed areas to which the category may be applied. He has individuated the presence of 'small states' over the course of the fourteenth century in the Apennines of Liguria and Tuscany, in the Marca Trevigiana and especially in western Emilia.

In the border area of western Emilia, political entities such as the Rossi, Fieschi and Pallavicini dynasties were able further to maintain an international presence even in the fifteenth century because of the endemic political instability that characterised the area. They were also able to organise themselves into configurations that were more definitely territorial and 'state-based', thus enabling them strenuously to defend their autonomy from external interference.

---

[37] Arcangeli and Gentile (eds.), *Le signorie dei Rossi*, in particular Arcangeli and Gentile, 'Introduzione'; and Somaini, 'Una storia spezzata'. For a wide interpretation of 'small state', see also Varanini, 'Aristocrazie e poteri', 182–5.

[38] Chittolini, 'Ascesa e declino', 476.

Towards the middle of the fifteenth century, however, the emergence of more stable territorial and political structures signalled the decline of much of the contractual power of these lords and their eventual absorption into the *potenze grosse*. From that time, they no longer appear in peace treaties or in alliances as *aderenti* or *raccomandati* of the larger powers, that is, in a subordinate but formally autonomous position.[39] They were also subject to a substantial reshaping of their political and military role. When the Rossi family, from 1482 to 1483, demonstrated their ability to mobilise their *homines*, engaging at length the forces of the dukes of Milan before being defeated, they were considered rebel feudatories and not autonomous seigneurs.[40]

The 'small states' that managed to survive until the peace of Lodi and the Lega Italica were rather few in number and included the Pio, Pico and da Correggio in Emilia and the Appiani in Tuscany. The survival of these small states was sometimes short-lived: the Pio di Carpi, for example, witnessed the definitive end of their autonomy during the Italian Wars at the very moment in which other small lords were able to profit from the new state of uncertainty and attempt to raise their heads once more, seeking an autonomous political claim within the divisions of the peninsula.[41]

The definition of 'small state', therefore, appears to comprise not only the execution of *de facto* power but also a formal legitimation of that power, that is, strictly in terms of public governance of the territory. This definition, too dogmatic from a politological point of view, seems to exclude from the category of 'small state' the previously mentioned configurations that were at the same time both seigneurial and feudal; despite being large and territorially homogeneous, they were *mediate subiecte*. Such configurations included those that *condottieri* (the Dal Verme, the Sanseverino, the Colleoni, the Orsini Del Balzo, etc.), and bankers or money-lenders (the Borromeo, etc.) constructed or that old aristocracy maintained (the Rossi in the second half of the fifteenth century) *within* the regional states. The structured internal organisation of their lands, the complex networks of personal, family and faction loyalty, and the ability to *congregare homines* did not cancel out the fact that these lords had given their own *sudditanza* towards the sovereign, princes or ruling cities. They were important political actors and often problematic for the duke of Milan (Dal Verme, Sanseverino, Borromeo, Rossi), the republic of Venice (Colleoni) and the king of Naples

---

[39] Important considerations of the condition of adherents in Lombardy in the second half of the fifteenth century are found in Arcangeli, 'Piccoli signori lombardi'.
[40] Arcangeli, 'Principi, *homines* e "partesani"'.   [41] Varanini, 'I Pio di Carpi'.

(Orsini Del Balzo, the princes of Taranto);[42] however, they did not succeed, if indeed they tried, in obtaining '*de facto* and *de jure* recognition' within the 'system' of Italian states.

Conclusion

During the fourteenth and fifteenth centuries the widening of political and economic horizons also drew in the rural areas, bringing about profound changes to rural lordships. The relationship of protection and defence that a seigneur had towards his *homines* continued to develop alongside the economic, social and political ambitions of the community. In order to maintain his ascendancy over his *homines*, a lord had to intercept their communications with an increasing number of economic and political actors (lords, communities, cities, princes) and widen his own networks of relationships so that he could be an effective mediator for their interests. This could happen if seigneurs were able to maintain their own autonomy, formally recognised by the other political actors of the peninsula (as a 'small state') or if they were able to obtain a delegation of authority from one of the emerging regional configurations (as a fief).

The persistence of this contractual logic which permeates the political mentality of the *homines* appears to constitute an almost anthropological connecting tissue that is subject to individual historical events and that outlives them. Certainly, profound differences are determined by the various geographical, politico-institutional and socio-economic circumstances within or surrounding a particular lordship or fief. A number of scholars prudently stand guard against the dangerous 'isomorphisms' that strongly point out the differences between the Italy of the north and the Italy of the south, the Italy of the feudal principalities and the Italy of the cities. Others, however, though not insensitive to individual peculiarities, value the application of new interpretative categories that allow the inception of a comparison between entities that are certainly different, but not, however, too distant.

Yet for the moment this comparison appears rather difficult to implement, given the clear lack of homogeneity among studies with regard to the various geographical areas and the insuppressible variety of questions and interpretations with which historians have approached, approach, or may well return to approach the lordship, the fief and the 'small state' in the late medieval era.

---

[42] Morelli, 'Tra continuità e trasformazioni'; Abulafia, 'Signorial power'.

15 Factions and parties: problems and perspectives

Marco Gentile

Introduction

During the past two decades, the forms of political organisation that generally come within the definition of 'faction' or 'party' have without doubt acquired new importance in Italian historiography. While this theme, previously visited mostly by historians of the era of the communes, has come on to the agenda of early modern historians, and largely from there has been transmitted to the historiography on the late Middle Ages, the approach to factions as a subject for study has also undergone some significant changes, from the point of view of both methodology and conceptual and interpretative categories. The wealth of studies resulting from this new attention to the theme is in reality still very unevenly distributed: the bibliography is rich in contributions on northern Italy between the fourteenth and sixteenth centuries, while historians of southern Italy in the same period have only recently shown signs of interest in it. Partly for this reason, a detailed reconstruction of the geography of factions in late medieval Italy is not an objective of this brief synthesis, which aims instead to emphasise some significant core themes.

Beyond evil and disorder

Tackling late medieval factions as a specific subject of enquiry often implies coming to terms with poor sources, rarely explicit about their nature. About thirty years ago Jacques Heers, still the author of the only attempt at a comprehensive treatment of 'parties' in medieval western Europe, noted that factions escape the usual procedures of historical enquiry: they were spontaneous formations, held together by tacit or at least informal bonds, the moment of their birth is generally unknown, and there are no pacts, written contracts or statutes that furnish information about their aims and social composition.[1] In part, the difficulties

---
[1] Heers, *Parties*, 13, 89–92.

arise from the fact that the types of documents traditionally most used to gather information on factions can produce severe distortions of perspective. This consideration applies above all to narrative sources, because chronicles speak of factions almost exclusively in relation to the most violent moments of political confrontation, and at the same time take for granted how they functioned and their very existence. Public documents, including those produced by central governments, are often reticent about organised political groups, which they tend to mention on the occasion of repressive interventions. From these factors derives the singular opacity in the documents of the features of faction as a form of political aggregation, despite its effective importance; and the situation worsens when the object of interest is the Guelfs and Ghibellines, although this pairing is an essential element for the comprehension of the Italian political system, at least until the 1530s.

As if all this is not enough, there are strong prejudices against factions in the wider sense: commonly, the term 'faction' evokes a picture of disorder, of anarchy and of irrationality, and designates groups who, in the shadows, plot subversive projects against the common good, emerging into the open only to unleash senseless violence. These prejudices are connected to the refusal to recognise the rationale of forms of political and social organisation that lost out to the 'territorial state'[2] which, between the end of the Middle Ages and the beginning of the modern era, asserted a monopoly on the output of legitimating political discourses and produced categories that continue to shape our 'pre-comprehension of the political'.[3] The criminalisation of association in factions or parties, which underwent a decisive acceleration during the Cinquecento in state legislation, in juridical treatises and in the practices of social discipline by states with the backing of churches of all confessions, can be traced back to at least three principal causes: the vertical social composition of late medieval factions and parties that cut across barriers of social rank that were tending to become more rigid in the Europe of the *ancien régime*; their inability to be contained within the principle of territoriality that was becoming the constitutive element of forms of government and sovereignty; and the self-evident fact that the presence of parties implied a division of the political body, incompatible with dawning monarchical absolutism in particular. It was not by chance that in western Europe the party re-emerged as an authorised or at least tolerated form of political association only in England under the constitutional monarchy, although Whigs and Tories were considered an aberration long after they had appeared; and then with the clubs of

---

[2] Spruyt, *The Sovereign State*.   [3] Hespanha, *Introduzione*.

revolutionary France, ancestors of our contemporary political parties, which were born at a moment of a complete break with the preceding political and institutional framework.

In the last two decades of the twentieth century, the historiography on the origins of the modern state in Italy has demonstrated a marked capacity for assimilation. If on one side historians have developed a new attention to the pluralism of institutions, judicial systems and political subjects in late medieval Italian society,[4] on the other they have partly distorted the sense of that pluralism, presenting it as a functional element in the processes of state formation.[5] The evolution of the perspectives of research on factions provides a typical example of this attitude. The liberation of factions from the sphere of disorder, in effect, is the fruit of a long and contradictory process that still cannot be said to have been concluded:[6] in the historiography on politics and institutions, in fact, the adoption of a 'top-down' perspective has often conveyed that very political discourse which should have been the object of enquiry, and which considers the pluralism of bodies and their capacity to act as political subjects as residues, rearguard actions or pathological phenomena – with the result that these subjects are denied, even implicitly, that same sense of purpose that tends to be conceded to the state on the basis of its own self-legitimating discourses.[7] The persistence of a real 'ethical prejudice' and the difficulty historians have had in recognising the ordinary, physiological, not just pathological, traits of conflict have thus affected various studies on cities and territories in which the particular intensity of factional dynamics and the pervasive influence of the parties on social relations, sometimes for long periods, has aroused in some respects pioneering attention to the theme: on the papal Romagna, above all (where there was still talk of Guelfs and Ghibellines at the end of the Cinquecento), but also on Pistoia and Genoa.[8] In other cases, factions have been promoted as a compliant instrument of government in the hands of the prince or the dominant city,[9] and considered as a phenomenon not opposed to, but functional in, the affirmation of the state. In a monograph innovative in many respects, Daniele Andreozzi has argued that the 'birth of factions' in the Val Nure in the early

---

[4] For example, Connell and Zorzi (eds.), *Florentine Tuscany*.
[5] See in general Chittolini, Molho and Schiera (eds.), *Origini dello stato*.
[6] For example, as in the value-laden and moralistic approach of Bruni, *La città divisa*.
[7] Benigno, '*Reductio ad unum*', and Zorzi, 'I conflitti nell'Italia comunale'.
[8] On the Romagna, see Casanova, *Comunità e governo*; Casanova, 'Da "parziale" a "buono ecclesiastico"'; Casanova, 'Potere delle grandi famiglie'; Gardi, *Lo stato in provincia*. On Pistoia, see Connell, *La città dei crucci*; on Genoa, see Pacini, 'La tirannia delle fazioni'.
[9] Dedola, '"Tener Pistoia con le parti"'; but compare Milner, 'Rubrics and requests'.

sixteenth century created an instrument useful to the papal government for political control of the zone and to local elites for social control of the peasants.[10] Another strategy of assimilation advanced in the historiography is that which recognises in the factions an autonomous capacity for social organisation at moments of marked acceleration of political dynamics, such as those produced by a dynastic crisis or a war. In essence, such an approach tends to emphasise the relation between factions and conflict, in close connection with the system of vendetta and the feud,[11] or even to conceive of it by definition as the typical form of aristocratic conflict.[12]

The 'informal' paradigm: agency and the individual

What should be understood by 'faction' remains in many ways an open question. Up to about fifteen years ago, the historiography on factions in the late Middle Ages and early modern period tended, by and large, to refer to two principal theoretical paradigms – models in some degree convergent, despite one being considerably older than the other, and despite their having their origins in very different disciplines. I am referring first of all to the outcomes of the so-called polemic between Nicola Ottokar and Gaetano Salvemini on the conflicting social and political groups in late thirteenth-century Florence, where (to simplify) Salvemini's interpretation in terms of class struggle (1899) was set against that of Ottokar, of a competition for power between oligarchies that were part of the same elite.[13] John Najemy has recently underlined the effects of Ottokar's legacy on the historiography of succeeding decades, in particular on US scholarship on Florence. This was essentially an expansion of the concepts of 'political' and of 'political history' in the direction of informal ties, of clienteles, of ritual, and a consequent attention to groups, parties and factions, which has appreciably widened the horizons of research on political and institutional themes. The side effect of this expansion, however, has been the restriction of the social area that has been the object of analysis almost exclusively to the ruling classes, in part because of the greater availability of information on elites compared to the lower classes. According to Najemy, the idea that the political can

---

[10] Andreozzi, *Nascita di un disordine*, in a theoretical frame of reference that refers to Blok, *The Mafia of a Sicilian Village*; in general, for example, see Schmidt, Landé and Guasti (eds.), *Friends, Followers and Factions*; Briquet, *Clientelismo*.
[11] Bianco, *La 'crudel zobia grassa'*; Baja Guarienti, 'Le "guerre civili" di Reggio'.
[12] For example, Berengo, *L'Europa delle città*, 322–3, 329–32.
[13] Salvemini, *Magnati e popolani*; Ottokar, *Il comune di Firenze*; see the introductions of Ernesto Sestan to the two volumes and, in addition, Artifoni, *Salvemini*.

in the ultimate analysis be reduced to family relations, the nexus between patrons and clients, ties of dependence that only elites had the resources to establish in the framework of a consciously pursued strategy, has led to the removal of class conflict from the horizons of research: the effect is particularly evident in US historiography on the Italian Renaissance, which in this way has found an alternative to Marxist models that were clearly not acceptable in the United States.[14] The success of the Ottokarian paradigm, in itself, implied a marked tilt towards informality as the common denominator of socially isomorphic political groups that confronted one another in the urban arena in the communal and *signorile* eras.

To this approach should be added the influence exercised by British social anthropology in the 1960s and 1970s: in the context of a more general reaction to structural-functionalism, the new emphasis on process in the study of politics resulted in a marked attention to individuals and their capacity to manipulate norms, links and memberships, and in a tendency to analyse groups from the perspective of individual strategies. The *Theory of Action* opened up new and broad spaces to the study of factions, seen not so much as a destabilising element of the political system, but as a form of aggregation that is characterised – in contrast to groups such as political parties or lineages, characterised by fixed structural elements – by informal ties and acute sensitivity to political contingency, and by the absence of an ideological centre, which hinders the heads of factions from exploiting completely the available resources. The partly generational nature of this strand of research – which saw, among other things, the birth of the notion of factionalism, originally understood as defining groups or contexts in which factions constituted the dominant mode of political organisation – can be observed through a simple quantitative check: a search of the Anthropological Index Online, which indexes all periodicals held in the library of the Centre for Anthropology at the British Museum, reveals how a marked increase in studies dedicated to factions in the 1950s and 1960s was followed by a rapid falling-off of attention in the 1980s, with a weak recovery beginning in the 1990s.[15] In any case, the idea of faction that results from these theoretical premises envisages a fluid grouping, which adapts to changing circumstances and whose main purpose is the organisation of conflict during periods of rapid social change, which is formed in opposition to other similar groups and which dissolves when the immediate objective is achieved or its leadership fails.[16]

---

[14] Najemy, 'Politics, class and patronage'.
[15] See http://aio.anthropology.org.uk/aio/ (link active in May 2010).
[16] In general, see Lewellen, *Antropologia politica*, 147–9.

This definition of factions as aggregates of cliques, of action-sets and of ego-centred networks has been taken up by sectors of historiography more eager for dialogue with the social sciences, and in Italy by the 'micro history' of the 1980s and 1990s, in particular.[17] According to Angelo Torre, in the imperial fiefs of the Langhe in the early modern era, conflict was manifest in a multiplicity of episodes: 'the protagonists are groups of close relatives – fathers, sons and sons-in-law – in a play of constantly changing alliances that continually refashioned the framework'. The factions, which appealed to supra-local political points of reference, were only 'labels of convenience, used when they might be of service'.[18] In Val Fontanabuona, studied by Osvaldo Raggio, there were present 'factional formations [. . .] not drawn together by circumstances alone'; but the local groups that in moments of general political crisis tended to rally around traditional symbols and names (Adorni and Fregosi, Verdi and Turchini), once quiet had returned to the wider political theatre assumed their own 'natural' features once more, resting on lineages and feud. The local political dialectic was thus fragmented into many micro-conflicts, which only occasionally borrowed the languages of high politics, manipulating them to legitimate their own activities. The factions, therefore, had little sense in themselves: they were a form of political communication between the state and local society, and floated suspended at an intermediate level between the only two planes – the lineage and the Genoese government – in which sense of purpose and self-awareness were evident.[19]

This quickly sketched anthropological paradigm is also the theoretical frame of reference for Edward Muir in relation to the Friulan factions of the *zamberlani* and *strumieri*, protagonists of a bloody conflict that exploded during the War of the League of Cambrai. Muir describes configurations characterised by a very high degree of fluidity, to the point that 'membership in the factions was so transitory that their composition can usually be discerned only at the moment of confrontation when participants revealed allegiances by attacking members of the other side. One knows the factions by discovering who killed whom.'[20] Another example coloured by the historiographical approach prevalent in the late 1980s and early 1990s, although less explicit at a theoretical level, is a study of Cesena at the time of Cesare Borgia, where, in the words of Ann Katherine Isaacs, 'in the kaleidoscopic changes in the orientation of the civic factions [. . .] individual alliances

---

[17] Palumbo, 'Scuola, scala, appartenenza'.
[18] Torre, 'Faide, fazioni e partiti' (quotation at 794).
[19] Raggio, *Faide e parentele*, 159–93.   [20] Muir, *Mad Blood Stirring* (quotation at xxv).

remained fluid, and were decided moment by moment according to anticipations of personal advantages that varied with the evolving situation'.[21]

Rediscovering institutions: factions and government

The influence exercised by some of the research mentioned above on the studies from the second half of the 1990s onwards dedicated to the material constitution of the Lombard regional state is undeniable, in particular as far as the theme of the relations between centre and periphery is concerned. In these studies, however, the need to resolve some problems of interpretation linked to the role of parties and factions in the *Verfassung* of the duchy of Milan under the Visconti and Sforza has led to a rethinking of the assumption of the informal and contingent nature of factions, which proved unable to grasp the peculiarities of these political aggregations. From the analysis of some Lombard instances in the fourteenth and fifteenth centuries have come clear indications pointing beyond the 'informal paradigm'. In the Valtellina under the Visconti factions were not the prevalent form in which local conflicts were expressed, partly because belonging to the Guelf or Ghibelline party coincided with belonging to a place: a community was either Guelf or Ghibelline. The factions of the Valtellina had a well-defined public profile even in times of peace, because they organised relations with the central power, and guaranteed equilibrium in elections to local magistracies and in the division of tax burdens. They were, in effect, guarantors of the normal course of political life, without being reduced to a docile instrument of government in the hands of the dukes of Milan. Starting from the example of the Valtellina, Massimo Della Misericordia has brought into question a 'weak' use of the term 'faction', insofar as it is used to define 'every form of segmentation of society'.[22] A situation in some ways similar to this has been shown in fifteenth-century Parma: the four civic factions, called *squadre* as in other cities in the Po valley, defined themselves as *universitates* and for long periods exercised an institutional role recognised by the ducal government.[23]

In effect, one of the principal results of recent research on Renaissance Lombardy consists in the recognition and evaluation of the not exclusively conflictual function of local factions. The factions did not appear only to perpetrate more or less ritualised massacres (which indeed were rather rare) or street-fighting: they were also a widespread way of

---

[21] Isaacs, 'Cesena agli inizi del Cinquecento' (quotation at 24).
[22] Della Misericordia, 'Dividersi per governarsi', 757. [23] Gentile, *Terra e poteri*.

organising political representation, in forms often explicitly recognised by the prince. This verdict can be extended to vast areas of northern Italy between the second half of the Trecento and the beginning of the Cinquecento, where the factions were able to exercise a regulatory function in political life, determining the distribution of public offices and, in some cases, presiding over the allotment of the burden of extraordinary taxation.[24]

Another very important element is the problem of the distinction between the planes on which the factions operated. Normally, there was a local level in a single city or territory where the factions often appeared as vertical groupings that encompassed diverse social strata and that were guided by the major families of the landed nobility. In the cities political competition among these groups was not necessarily polarised around two formations, and even when there was a dyadic opposition, recourse to the labels of Guelfs and Ghibellines was not automatic. The landscape of Lombard faction in the Visconti and the Sforza eras, for example, is very varied and instructive from this point of view.[25] If the old names of Guelfs and Ghibellines were used to define the politicised groups of Lodi, Brescia, Bergamo, the Valtellina and the Lago Maggiore, at Como and on the Lago di Como people spoke of the Rusconi and Vitani, while at Pavia they referred to colours, 'Whites' and 'Blacks'. At Alessandria, to the split between Guelfs and Ghibellines was added the division between *popolari* and nobles, which saw the latter excluded from the executive committees of the commune, while at Cremona from the early fourteenth to the early sixteenth centuries there were three factions, Ghibellines, Guelfs and Maltraversi. In the cities of western Emilia, the *squadre* (the 'squads', a term that evokes the notion of an armed following) took the names of the major families of the landed aristocracy, who held powers of jurisdiction and fortresses in the territory. At Piacenza there were five and then four squads, but only the partisans of the Landi and Anguissola families defined themselves as Ghibellines, while the Scotti, Fontana and Fulgosi were Guelfs. At Reggio, too, at the end of the Trecento there were five squads, four of them Guelfs (Manfredi, Canossa, Fogliani and Roberti) and one Ghibelline (da Sesso). At Parma only the Pallavicini squad was

---

[24] Apart from the studies cited above, see, for example, Arcangeli, *Gentiluomini di Lombardia*, 303–420; Arcangeli, 'Tra Milano e Roma'; Bellosta, 'Le "squadre" in consiglio'; Gamberini, *La città assediata*; Gamberini, *Lo stato visconteo*; Gentile, 'Casato e fazione'; Gentile, 'From commune to regional state'.
[25] In general, see Gentile, '"Postquam malignitates"'; Gentile, 'Discorsi sulle fazioni'; Arcangeli, *Gentiluomini di Lombardia*.

Ghibelline, while the partisans of the Rossi, the Sanvitale and the Correggio supported families that were traditionally Guelf.

The case study of Parma, in particular, has shown the pressing need for a rethinking of categories. In fact the squads – which defined themselves as *collegia* and *universitates*, which fulfilled an institutional function recognised by the ducal government and which, from the late fourteenth to the early sixteenth centuries, constantly called upon the leadership of the same families of lords – do not fit the definition of faction as the fluid grouping shaped by circumstances described by the social sciences. They were, rather, proper corporate groups, for which anthropologists and sociologists consider the notion of a 'party' more pertinent, even in the absence of an ideology and a defined political programme.[26] In general, an individual's political membership had structural bonds: normally, one was born into this or that faction, and factional identity tended to become more binding the higher up the social scale one stood. In fifteenth-century Parma it was very rare for members of the most important and influential urban families, or even of families that had a tradition of membership of civic councils, to change squads; and it was even rarer to see a family change faction to suit the material and individual interests of a single member. Circumstantial factors tended to be overridden by a structural given: membership of the faction was a integral part of the identity of the family. At the end of the fifteenth century these traditions, with a century and a half behind them, still created an envelope constricting the initiative of the individual. This is true also for a relation between cause and effect that has often been taken for granted, that is, that a feud between two families 'generated' the factions. In reality, it was difficult for a blood vendetta, in an urban context, to succeed in structuring around itself new political configurations. The path led from faction to feud, not in the other direction. Only at the lowest social levels did the cohesion of a squad tend to break down into individual and voluntary membership. At Parma, in effect, there existed 'proper' factions as well, that is, volatile aggregations, oriented from time to time to the pursuit of practical political objectives: but these were structured in groupings that cut across the squads, in the second half of the Quattrocento could be defined as pro- and anti-Sforza, and did not coincide with Guelf or Ghibelline political traditions and identities. These last, for their part, persisted and fulfilled their own function at still another level, but one that was always eminently supra-local.[27]

---

[26] Boissevain, 'Factions, parties and politics'; Nicholas, 'Factions'; Bosco, 'Faction versus ideology'.

[27] Gentile, *Fazioni al governo*.

Guelfs and Ghibellines: a resilient code for long-distance communication

Up until the late Cinquecento, the old pairing 'Guelfs and Ghibellines' continued to be used in practice in many areas of the Italian peninsula: in particular in the Visconti and Sforza duchy, in the Romagna and in vast areas of the papal states, in the Lombard cities subject to Venice (Brescia and Bergamo), in Genoa and Liguria. It is possible to understand Guelfs and Ghibellines as two 'meta-factions' or, from the perspective of political languages, as key terms of a widely diffused idiom, one spoken throughout the later Middle Ages and the beginning of the early modern era. To comprehend the reasons for the longevity of the two names (which became established in the political vocabulary of Tuscany in the second half of the thirteenth century but were diffused through northern Italy only during the reign of the emperor Henry VII), it is of little use to insist on their meagre 'ideological' content and on the fact that already by the middle of the fourteenth century Guelfs and Ghibellines no longer signified the partisans of church and empire. From the start, the 'Guelf party' designated a much wider grouping than the *pars Ecclesie*, comprising the papacy, the Angevins and that part of the Florentine ruling class linked to them politically and financially. It should also be borne in mind that the partisans of the empire (and Henry VII himself) for a long time refused the label of Ghibellines, which was originally adopted by the Guelfs as a defamatory epithet to undermine the legitimacy of their adversaries.[28] Only recently has the long prevalent idea of an obligatory correspondence between supporters of the church and Guelfs, and supporters of the empire and Ghibellines, been brought into question. To imagine a pure 'Guelfism' and 'Ghibellinism', from the innate 'ideological' presuppositions of the two parties, leads to the paradox, difficult to explain, of their 'survival' from the middle of the fourteenth to the middle of the sixteenth century as meaningless labels.[29] This paradox, I believe, has two principal causes: the well-known tendency unwarrantably to apply Tuscan and Florentine models to other Italian realities (above all for the period defined largely as 'Renaissance') – hence the irrelevance of Guelfs and Ghibellines after the age of Dante; and the common notion of Guelfs and Ghibellines derived from nineteenth-century schematisation, like the equivalence so readily taken up by Italian political commentators today, between Guelfs and clericals and Ghibellines and secularists.

[28] Dessì, 'I nomi dei guelfi e ghibellini'; Varanini, 'Nelle città della Marca'; Gentile, 'From commune to regional state'; Ferente, 'Guelphs!'
[29] In general, see Gentile (ed.), *Guelfi e ghibellini*.

The problem of the ideological coherence of late medieval or Renaissance Guelfs and Ghibellines is, in reality, badly put. We should rather ask ourselves how and why contemporaries continued to refer to the old pairing to denominate politicised groups. For the whole of the Quattrocento and throughout the Italian Wars, Guelfs and Ghibellines remained effective in establishing political co-ordination at supra-local and interstate levels, and even in international relations. The heavy symbolic weight of the two names could be exploited by those major seigneurial families sufficiently powerful to be able to utilise this kind of intangible resource to construct and legitimate their dominant position in a city or a territory. Normally, the great families of the landed nobility tended to 'invest' in tradition and in the political identity of the family more than minor families did. To emphasise their own role at the head of the local Ghibelline or Guelf party could serve to establish preferential relations with the central government, or relations with external regional powers interested in destabilising or annexing a city or a territory.[30] But the language of Guelf and Ghibelline was a means of communication used in international relations as well. A few examples will suffice: the duke of Milan considering it appropriate to turn to the emperor to ask for help against Florence and Venice in 1430 in the name of Ghibelline solidarity;[31] the renewed Ghibelline enthusiasm that pervaded Siena during Sigismund of Luxemburg's stay there in 1432–3;[32] the fact that, according to Philippe de Commynes, in 1494 the Orsini and the Colonna took sides for or against the king of France in accordance with their respectively Guelf and Ghibelline traditions.[33]

In Lombardy, the political traditions of the great families took shape during the fourteenth century; a fundamental stage of this process was probably the canonical proceedings for heresy directed against the Visconti and their supporters by pope John XXII. City by city, the names of the families involved sketch a geography of Lombard Ghibellinism still valid on the whole in the fifteenth century: the Lanzavecchia and Inviziati at Alessandria, Opizzoni and Guidoboni at Tortona, Beccaria at Pavia, Tornielli and Caccia at Novara, Tizzoni at Vercelli, Rusconi at Como, Suardi at Bergamo, Vistarini at Lodi, Benzoni at Crema and so on. The formation of the regional state implied, in cities and territories subject to the Visconti, the abandonment of the model based on the

---

[30] Arcangeli, 'Appunti su Guelfi e Ghibellini'; Gentile, *Terra e poteri*; Shaw, *The Political Role*.
[31] Gentile, '"Postquam malignitates"'.   [32] Pertici, 'Uno sguardo in avanti'.
[33] Commynes, *Mémoires*, 533.

exclusion and expulsion of the losing party in favour of an inclusive model, which provided for factions living together under the prince.[34]

In the Milanese state, the success of the terms 'Guelf' and 'Ghibelline' as a supra-local political language suggests the transition to a regional dimension, where Guelfs and Ghibellines were functional in the construction of a 'space of membership';[35] this very success, however, implies greater difficulty in the process of territorialisation and the greater importance of personal and 'vertical' links. Certainly, episodes of exclusion and of expulsion for political motives continued to occur in the Visconti dominions, in particular during the convulsive period following the death of Gian Galeazzo in 1402, but in general these were residual and therefore circumscribed phenomena. A greater degree of informality of the parties was characteristic of the capital as compared to the cities and territories of the dominion, either because of the presence of the ducal court with its changeable lobbies, or because a substantial majority of the great Milanese families were traditionally Ghibellines, quite apart from the vast and many-branched Visconti lineage, which remained very powerful in the city and the countryside even after the extinction of the principal branch in 1447.[36] But in general in fifteenth-century Lombardy the Guelf–Ghibelline idiom continued to be used in communication between centre and periphery, and the factions as a form of social and political organisation and as an element of connection between city and territory continued to prosper up to the devolution to the empire (1535) and the insertion of the duchy of Milan in the Spanish imperial system.[37]

Longevity of factions in general and of Guelfs and Ghibellines in particular was also characteristic of the papal states, an ecclesiastical principality of a peculiar nature both in the extent of its dominions and in the elasticity of the territorial control exercised from the centre. Running throughout the composite aggregation of cities and territories that made up the papal states was a dense supra-local network of party solidarities. The Romagna, where the political framework was especially fragmented and unstable and where the names of Guelfs and Ghibellines survived in the political lexicon longer than in the rest of the Italian peninsula, constituted a case apart.[38] More integrated was the factional

---

[34] Gentile, 'From commune to regional state'.   [35] Rokkan, *State Formation*, 104.
[36] Somaini, 'Il binomio imperfetto'.
[37] Arcangeli, *Gentiluomini di Lombardia*; Arcangeli, 'Appunti su Guelfi e ghibellini'; Arcangeli, 'Les Ytaulx qui désirent franchise'.
[38] On the Romagna, besides the bibliography cited above in n. 8, see for example Bombardini, *Il diavolo nel tamburo*; Isaacs, 'Cesena agli inizi del Cinquecento'; Casanova, 'Ai vertici della società'.

configuration of the central block of provinces subject to papal dominion: in particular, in Campagna and Marittima, in Sabina, in the Patrimony of Saint Peter and in Umbria the local factions looked to the powerful Roman baronial families of Orsini and Colonna, the undisputed leaders of the Guelf and Ghibelline parties, lords of fortresses and fortified villages and holders of very extensive landed estates and jurisdictions.[39] In the towns of Umbria and Lazio the factions often kept their local names (Gatti and Maganzeschi at Viterbo, Chiaravallesi and Catalaneschi at Todi), to which were added the names of Guelfs and Ghibellines, which were also known as Orsini and Colonna respectively. In these provinces, the Guelfs were by no means considered natural supporters of the pope, nor the Ghibellines automatically his adversaries. The papal government could when necessary utilise the barons as intermediaries with the local factions, and the links between the Orsini, the Colonna and their partisans could be seen as a way to organise conflict but also as a way to keep the peace and guarantee political equilibria in many cities and provinces. Up to the end of the pontificate of Clement VII at least, the factions constituted 'one of the most enduring political structures of the Renaissance Papal States'.[40]

In their extreme diversity, the Visconti and Sforza duchy and the papal states had two elements in common: they were both principalities, in which the prince normally acted *super partes*, implying that Guelfs and Ghibellines should live together; and in Lombardy as in Lazio the rural lordship, at the end of the Quattrocento but also in the Cinquecento, was still a widely diffused form of social organisation, on which basis the great aristocratic families continued to be able to dispose of robust and numerous armed clienteles that nourished the factions. The situation was very different in Florentine Tuscany and in the republic of Venice. It is not my intention to propose a schematic opposition between principalities and republics: the cases of Genoa and Siena, both characterised by political systems with highly complex configurations of party and faction (which I shall not discuss for lack of space),[41] suffice to show it

---

[39] In general, see Shaw, *The Political Role*; Shaw, 'The Roman barons and the security'; Shaw, 'The Roman barons and the Guelf and Ghibelline'. On the Colonna, see Serio, *Una gloriosa sconfitta*; on the Viterban factions, see Mascioli, *Viterbo*. On the factions in Rome in the fourteenth century, see Rehberg, *Clientele e fazioni*; for the sixteenth century, see Visceglia, 'Farsi imperiale'.

[40] Shaw, 'The Roman barons and the Guelf and Ghibelline' (quotation at 493).

[41] On Genoa and the Genoese state, besides the bibliography already cited, see Musso, 'I "colori" delle Riviere'; Shaw, 'Counsel and consent'; Shaw, 'Principles and practice'; Ferente, 'Gli ultimi guelfi', 153–216; Taviani, *Superba discordia*. On Siena, see Ascheri, 'Siena nel Quattrocento'; Ascheri and Pertici, 'La situazione politica'; Isaacs, 'Cardinali e "Spalagrembi"'; Pertici, 'Uno sguardo in avanti'; Shaw, *Popular Government*.

is pointless to search for a form of faction typical of republican states, any more than for a republican form of state.

At Venice the formalisation of an oligarchy or patriciate – that is, the typical alternative to government by vertical groups based on factions – happened very early on, in 1297, with the *serrata* of the Maggior Consiglio which circumscribed participation in the organs of government to a closed group of families: the political life of the *Serenissima* was thus characterised by the substantial absence of formal factions. Even in the cities of the Venetian Terraferma, in the early decades of the Trecento, structured parties, visible and disposed to open contests for power, were no longer to be found. Groups of this type were found only in the cities and provinces that were strictly outside the Veneto, at Brescia and Bergamo in the west and in Friuli to the east, with the exception of minor and peripheral centres such as Feltre and Belluno. In the Veneto, the 'death of the factions' in the fourteenth century had two principal causes: the establishment of robust *signorile* regimes at Verona, to which Vicenza was long subject, at Padua and at Treviso (the same could be said for Mantua and Ferrara, but not for the western provinces ruled by the d'Este); and the affirmation of strong control by the cities over their respective territories, with the weakening of rural lordships and the consequent 'unravelling of the social relations of personal dependence' that constituted the basis of the factions. In the Veneto, Guelf and Ghibelline would never have great success as party names, except for a brief period during the first half of the Trecento. It is significant that the pairing appeared at Belluno, where it had not been used before, just at the turn of the century, during the years of Visconti domination. The advent of Venetian domination, at the beginning of the Quattrocento, encouraged the process of oligarchic closure and the formation of patriciates in the cities of the Terraferma. In the cities of the Veneto, mirroring Venice, could be found politicised groups acting mainly at an informal level, as lobbies and electoral cartels, while Guelfs and Ghibellines or factions structured around aristocratic clienteles were present and still active in the first decades of the Cinquecento in Brescia, Bergamo and Friuli.[42]

Structured factions similar to those in Lombardy, the Romagna or Umbria were not particularly evident in fifteenth-century Florentine

---

[42] In general, see Varanini, 'Nelle città della Marca' (quotation at 583); on Belluno, see Law, 'Guelfs and Ghibellines'. On Bergamo, see Mainoni, *Le radici della discordia*; Cavalieri, *'Qui sunt guelfi et partiales nostri'*; on Brescia, see Pagnoni, '"Il trattato che fessemo"'; Merici, 'Luigi Avogadro'. On Friuli, see Muir, *Mad Blood Stirring*; Bianco, *La 'crudel zobia grassa'*.

Tuscany, either, for reasons only partially the same as in the Veneto.[43] In Tuscany, the nuclei of seigneurial power had almost all been broken up, and the cities, even before they became subject to Florentine dominion, had established firm control over their respective territories.[44] The well-known exception is Pistoia, where the division in the city and its territory between the Cancellieri and Panciatichi, which often became open conflict, represented a 'model of enduring opposition', only definitively suppressed by Cosimo I de' Medici.[45] In contrast to Venice, however, at Florence Guelfism (and consequently Ghibellinism) still counted for much. The Florentine ruling class had chosen to identify with the tradition of the Guelf commune, imposing a single-party model and continuing to make use of procedures to exclude the losing political party that were typical of popular communal regimes; the Parte Guelfa survived as an institution with its own officials, having important ceremonial functions and endowed with noteworthy financial resources.[46] At Florence, in effect, one had perforce to be Guelf: only below this level, which represented the essential condition for the exercise of political rights, did the Florentine elite split into informal lobbies, dubbed Albizi, pro- and anti-Medici, and so on.[47]

Between the end of the Trecento and the early decades of the Quattrocento, Florentine Guelfism not only continued to provide material for the ruling class's discourse of self-representation, but also constituted a powerful force of attraction in the construction of political links on a vast scale: this is shown by the capacity to affect and (through significant financial incentives, among other methods) to give direction to the political actions of numerous aristocratic houses in northern Italy after the death of Gian Galeazzo Visconti.[48] It is commonly accepted that 'the War of the Eight Saints between Gregory XI and the Florentines in 1376 marks the end of the traditional Guelf political theory in Florence'.[49] This, however, does not mean that a Guelfism different from that based on the Florentine-Angevin-papal axis was not practicable: above all because – it should be emphasised again – to identify the opposition between Guelfs and Ghibellines with the conflict between the papacy and the empire means giving too simple a solution to a complex

---

[43] Various case studies can be found in Connell and Zorzi (eds.), *Florentine Tuscany*, 207–332; see also Mazzoni, 'Dalla lotta di parte'.
[44] Zorzi, 'The "material constitution"'.   [45] Connell, *La città dei crucci* (quotation at 54).
[46] Brown, *The Medici in Florence*, 103–50.
[47] On Florentine political networks between the fourteenth and sixteenth centuries, see, for example, Brucker, *The Civic World*; Kent, *The Rise of the Medici*; Ansell and Padget, 'Robust action'; Ferente, 'Gli ultimi guelfi', 96–151.
[48] Gentile, *Terra e poteri*; Gentile, '"Postquam malignitates"'.
[49] Partner, 'Florence and the papacy', 381.

problem, or imagining a Platonic idea of 'the' Guelf and 'the' Ghibelline identity. The fact is that things changed. By 1942 Nino Valeri had recognised that 'the word remained the same, but the content was radically changed, to the point where it became the sign of an ideology promoted and spread no longer by the papacy, but by the Florentine republic': in effect, a Guelfism that, becoming detached from its original meaning, came to symbolise *libertà*.[50] To speak of Guelfism and Ghibellinism, instead of Guelfs and Ghibellines, obviously shifts the discourse from the ground of practice to that, much more slippery, of political ideas: but in any case, the evolution in Florence between the Trecento and the Quattrocento from a pro-church Guelfism to a markedly pro-French Guelfism cannot be considered a mere rhetorical device.[51]

That the Italian Guelfs of the fifteenth and early sixteenth centuries completely identified with an ideology of *libertas* is difficult to demonstrate, just as the equivalence between membership of the Guelf party and connection to the vast network centred on the Bracceschi and the *condottiero* Jacopo Piccinino is based, all things considered, on circumstantial evidence. Indeed, to consider as 'Guelf' any nucleus of political power that was opposed to the stabilisation of the political framework imposed on Italy by the Lega Italica[52] would lead to the classification as Ghibelline of various aristocratic lineages of Lombardy and the Po valley (and the factions that depended on them) whose Guelf identity is beyond doubt.[53] Moreover, in this context, the 'liberties' of the landed nobility as a relevant declension of the concept of Liberty must be taken into due account: '*Moi, je suis guelfe et féodal*', the duke d'Auge proclaimed, around the time of the Council of Basle, in Raymond Queneau's *Fleurs bleues*. What can be said is that the first half of the Quattrocento was a period in which the Guelf and Ghibelline parties were much in evidence, helped by a constantly shifting political framework, a period during which the nuclei of local power could exploit the opportunities granted by a highly unstable situation.

These spaces were closed by the formation of the Lega Italica in 1455: the league was in effect an agreement between mutually supporting regimes, whose spine was the axis between Florence and Milan (or rather, between the Medici and the Sforza).[54] The convergence of interests between the two traditional political points of reference brought

---

[50] Valeri, *La libertà e la pace*, 43–4. The theme was developed by Baron, *The Crisis*. See also Ferente, 'Guelphs!'
[51] Fubini, *L'umanesimo italiano*, 334 and note; compare Gilli, 'Guelfisme et mémoire'.
[52] Ferente, *La sfortuna*; Ferente, 'Gli ultimi guelfi'.
[53] As, for example, in the case of the Rossi of Parma: see Gentile, *Fazioni al governo*.
[54] Fubini, *Italia quattrocentesca*.

an eclipse of Guelfs and Ghibellines at the level of interstate relations, both because the strange alliance between the old rivals changed what could be defined, in the weakest sense of the term, the 'ideological' framework, and because the states adhering to the league acquired greater capacity to control and exert pressure on the nuclei of local power within their borders.

A third phase, during which the Guelf and Ghibelline parties came into the limelight for the last time, opened with the Italian Wars, from Louis XII's expedition in 1499. The exemplary research of Letizia Arcangeli on the structures and political dynamics of Lombardy in these turbulent times, characterised by a permanent state of war and continual changes of regime at the centre and the periphery, has brought to light the density of the political ties of the great aristocratic families, principal depositaries of Guelf and Ghibelline traditions in the long term, and clarified the rationale of the superficially eccentric behaviour of some lineages, such as the Ghibelline Pallavicini siding with the French. Such episodes do not demonstrate that the two names were (or had become) mere labels to be exploited at will: indeed, 'presenting themselves to the French as effective heads of a coalition of forces ranged with them was a way for the Pallavicini to secure for the Ghibelline faction under the dominion of Francis I the favour and legitimacy they had already enjoyed in the time of Louis XII'.[55] This, at bottom, is the clue to the unstable equilibrium reached by the Guelfs and Ghibellines in their cohabitation in the regional state.

Concluding remarks: developments

In his renowned *Tractatus de guelphis et gebellinis*, written in the first half of the Trecento, Bartolo da Sassoferrato granted the legitimacy of the parties, provided that their aim was to foster the public good, including resistance to a tyrannical regime.[56] The legitimacy of the parties was, however, systematically denied by later doctrine, with rare exceptions. In the Cinquecento, the evolution of legal and political doctrine on factions led to the equation of *crimen laesae maiestatis* with mortal sin: to be a member of a party meant to be damned.[57] It is no coincidence that, besides the theories of jurists, the most intransigent opposition to the presence of political groups organised in factions came from religious

---

[55] Arcangeli, 'Appunti su guelfi e ghibellini' (quotation at 443).
[56] Quaglioni, *Politica e diritto*.
[57] Abbondanza, 'Franco Gaeta'; Gentile, 'Guelfi, ghibellini, Rinascimento'; Gentile, 'Bartolo in pratica'.

preaching, in particular that of observant Franciscans, foremost among them Bernardino da Siena in the first half of the Quattrocento and Bernardino da Feltre in the second. The consonance of legal and political theory and religious preaching with the processes of state formation in progress is an accepted fact and, moreover, it is well known that in the modern era absolutism was theorised before it was realised (if it ever was realised): Jean Bodin came before Louis XIV. It should be borne in mind that criminalising factions through an emphasis on the violence that accompanied competition for political power was functional in the acquisition of that monopoly on legitimate public violence to which the state was inclined. It should also be borne in mind that the efflorescence in the scholarly literature on factions of pathological, value-laden metaphors – such as plague, infection, cancer, wasting away – derives from contamination of the language of politics resulting from the demonisation by the state of alternative (which does not mean 'better') forms of political organisation.

On the political and social plane, the decline of civic governments structured around power-sharing by parties who got along together with more or less tension between them generally led on to a greater rigidity in the composition of the ruling groups, or rather the patriciates: this argument is valid (to take up a classic theme of Italian medieval historians in the second half of the twentieth century) for republican states and for princely states alike, at different times and in different ways.[58] In the early fifteenth century Bernardino da Siena, looking about for a solution to the plague of the cursed factions, would have liked all Italian cities to be like Venice.[59] Bernardino saw far ahead: a century and a half later, the desire for oligarchic closure had spread to all Italian elites, decisively displacing the political discourse founded on respect for *equalitas* and the custom underlying the practice of division of offices among the factions, or on the 'constitutional factionalism' of the city.[60] The oscillation between systems of political representation that were 'vertical' (personal, factional, of clientship) and 'horizontal' (in the sense of belonging to a social rank, but also to a territory, from a parish to a community to a state)[61] is not the only suggestive perspective that recent work connected in various ways to the theme of factions has revealed. I shall mention some themes briefly, and not systematically. First of all, the history of emotions seems to be a promising perspective, given that factions, which

---

[58] Tabacco, *Egemonie sociali*.   [59] Gentile, 'Discorsi sulle fazioni', 408.
[60] Schiera, 'Il *Buongoverno* melancolico'; Zorzi, '*Fracta est civitas*'.
[61] Della Misericordia, 'La "coda"'; Della Misericordia, *Divenire comunità*; Gentile, 'Fazioni al governo'; Arcangeli, 'Tra Milano e Roma'.

were for Bartolo *affectiones* adhered to through nature and will, became for political science in the modern era passions to be repressed; and also, because it is high time to move a step further a scientific paradigm that is basically a variant on the theory of rational choice, and that has much overvalued 'strategies' and the calculation of costs and benefits as compared to the affective components that melded to form group identities.[62] Secondly, we have the active role (not only as an object of exchange on the marriage market) of women in the factions, which has already yielded extremely interesting results for Renaissance Italy, at least concerning the attitude to party leadership by some women.[63] Last but not least, there is the south of Italy, because both the kingdom of Naples and Sicily, although very different worlds from one another in the organisation of social groups, offer a luxuriant but barely known panorama of factions.[64] As for the supra-local level, in the kingdom of Naples 'the Guelf and Ghibelline names were not in use'.[65] Nonetheless, the relationship between the two names and the Angevin and Aragonese parties in the fifteenth century (obliquely referred to by a sharp observer such as Philippe de Commynes),[66] as well as interesting factional environments, such as L'Aquila,[67] has yet to be thoroughly investigated. If until some time ago the concern not to perpetuate stereotypes and mythologies about the contrast between barons (and factions) on one side and the state on the other directed attention mainly to the disciplinary function of monarchy, there is no reason now not to explore such vast and promising territories: and there are some encouraging signs.[68]

One thing in particular seems to me to be the most important: either in order or disorder, to try to distinguish forms.

---

[62] Muir, *Mad Blood Stirring*; Ferente, 'Gli ultimi guelfi'. There are interesting politological points in Green, Palmquist and Schickler, *Partisan Hearts and Minds*.
[63] Arcangeli, 'Un'aristocrazia territoriale'; Shaw, 'Bartolomea Campofregoso'; Casanova, 'Mogli e vedove'.
[64] See, for example, Corrao, *Governare un regno*; Mineo, *Nobiltà di stato*; Delille, 'Marriage, faction and conflict'; Titone, *Governments*.
[65] Ferente, 'Guelphs!', 581.
[66] Commynes, *Mémoires*, 533.
[67] Elements in Ferente, 'Gli ultimi guelfi', 218–79.
[68] Vitolo, 'Linguaggi e forme'; Vitolo, '*In palatio communis*'.

16 States, orders and social distinction

E. Igor Mineo

Introduction

Early in the sixteenth century Niccolò Machiavelli, in a famous chapter (I, 55) of the *Discorsi sopra la prima deca di Tito Livio*, set out one of the fundamental criteria marking the difference between republics and kingdoms. He thereby created a long-lived image of the diverse Italies as unitary and coherent. According to this criterion, monarchies are such because they need the presence of nobility, while on the contrary republics exist on the principle of the 'equality' of the citizenry. Where there is a republic there must be no gentlemen, and wherever there is a king there must be lords. The geometrical simplicity of this scheme appears in a different light if compared with at least two other passages from the *Discorsi*: one (I, 6) notes that in Venice – by then considered the perfect model of a republic – not all of the citizens participated in governing the city and that the gentlemen were exactly those who were 'allowed to take part in administration'; the second (I, 16) states that in every type of republic it was a small minority that in reality governed and that for the majority it was 'enough to live safely'. Seen this way, the dichotomy kingdom–republic is heuristic and normative rather than descriptive of the complicated mosaic in the peninsula. It corresponds to a substantial symmetry: maintaining the 'orders' would require the social configuration to be congruent with the type of constitution; but the 'equality' of the republic is not and cannot mean equality inside the community, just as the presence of nobility may not be considered a prerogative of kingdoms.

Machiavelli opens a valuable perspective on how mature the processes of constructing social hierarchies were in the Italian states at the end of the Middle Ages: while offering the basis of an image for the political geography of an earlier Italy which had become part of the common perception – the three-part image of republics, principalities and kingdoms – he suggests a way of questioning it. Indeed, recent historiography seems to follow this path, suggesting a minimal criterion of orientation: the most classical pictures of political geography do not precisely correspond to real societal forms. In order to find our way through this labyrinth we must break down the bi- or tripartite political spaces and adopt a different perspective to seek out the resulting social spaces.

City, state and the logic of distinction

Machiavelli worked at the time of a chronological divide, and so will we: that is, the era of the wars that traversed Italy in the early sixteenth century and radically changed the internal equlibrium of the peninsula. The other chronological limit is the middle of the thirteenth century, and is marked by two major changes: on the one hand the failure of the imperial and Swabian project, and on the other the solidification of 'popular' regimes in the communal towns. All the other factors that determine the specificity of the era that was beginning – from the construction of Guelf hegemony and the Angevin presence to the formation of two separate monarchies in the south – may be related to these two great political upheavals.

It is not difficult to justify the reasons for this chronology and particularly its *terminus a quo*. In the first half of the thirteenth century in communal cities the *popolo*, that is, the 'middle' ranks of urban societies or the non-noble citizens, by means of specific associative and corporative processes, established itself as an autonomous political and institutional subject: a phenomenon that accelerated a reformulation of what social pre-eminence meant. In the earlier consular and *podestarile* times governing groups had a relatively clear identity generally defined by carrying out the duties of governing or the militia and sometimes by exhibiting lordship or vassalage. But from the middle of the century these signs of identification rapidly became more complicated and caused a crisis in the schemes commonly in use in urban/communal contexts: society appears increasingly less able to fit into the traditional, pigeonholed dichotomies *milites/pedites*, *maiores/minores*,[1] and the spectrum of differences becomes enriched by many nuances both within and outside the aristocracy.

Outside the cities, the end of the Swabian project certainly did not stop the ongoing decline of the feudal aristocracy, which was not entirely Ghibelline. Tuscany shows the clearest examples of this experience: on the one hand there is, in Pisa, the role conservation of the great noble families which derived from their ability to integrate into the commune;

---

[1] Cammarosano, 'Élites sociales'; Maire Vigueur, *Cavaliers et citoyens*.

on the other, the paradigmatic decline in the first half of the thirteenth century of a great comital lineage, the Aldobrandeschi, in the face of the growth in Siena's power.[2] Elsewhere – in the Romagna, Emilia, the Veneto, Piedmont – the parabola of the 'feudal' *consorterie* was different and often characterised by greater continuity; nevertheless, even there the social laboratory that the city was becoming worked a change not so much in the relations of power as in the very nature of the actors. The 'feudal' or military nobility that preserved its identity, as in the case of the Paduan dynasties described by Giovanni da Nono in the early fourteenth century, was assimilated into the citizenry and was conditioned by its institutional codes, beginning with fiscal responsibility and the need to renounce former privileges and immunities.[3]

It is thus misleading to assume the presence of nuclei of the older aristocracy as a phenomenon of resistance to changes. An overview reveals not only the political centrality of the cities, but also their nature as the places in which the basic meanings of social distinctions are set: even the meanings that evidently emerged before the development of communes, such as those relative to the feudal values and lordly superiority, or those of a religious-theological type that were often framed within the organic and functional representations of society, were filtered by the institutional and economic fabric of the urban world. Urban centrality is furthermore a key to connecting (not for separating) north and south. The cities were well-developed realities within the Norman-Swabian kingdom, at least in some regions (Sicily and Campania especially), but in the second half of the thirteenth century their function appears clearer. Thus, in the south too the major phenomena of distinction and classification of social elements seem in the fourteenth and fifteenth centuries to be produced in urban space.

That said, the reinforcement of the cities as places central to politics should be placed within the much more articulated context of the political systems and government that was taking shape during this same period. These systems are generally characterised by the affirmation of public authorities of a territorial kind that tended to be more extensive and complex. The ruling classes and their political arenas, and more generally all the social roles, came to be defined within these spaces (which I shall simply call 'states'). This territorial framework is not a uniform characteristic of political structures in the late Middle Ages, because it presupposes the pluralism of the many autonomies present in the space that is developing: not only large and small cities, but also rural

---

[2] Bordone, 'L'aristocrazia territoriale', 31–3; Collavini, *'Honorabilis domus'*.
[3] Jones, *The Italian City-State*, 421; Maire Vigueur, *Cavaliers et citoyens*, ch. 5.

dominions, communities and villages and so forth; not to mention the non-territorial forms of political organisation such as personal service, patron–client relationships or networks of solidarity, family and faction. In sum, the processes of distinction and classification develop in this phase on different scales, and definitions of hierarchy and status are very uncertain and discontinuous: from the local scale of the small community or the landlord–peasant relationship, to the complex system of a state of medium or large dimensions, which may or may not have a princely court, a feudal nobility, a senate, a bureaucracy, a parliament and a *popolo*.

Supra-local government and the exercise of sovereignty within a determined area, for all their many configurations, offer possible criteria to help us to get our bearings in this apparently chaotic universe made up of different forms of society and practices of classification. It is not only the ruling classes – their composition, borders and legitimacy – that are touched by the formation of territorial states. The game of social classification enters into a community and segments it, just as it signals the differences between communities. It is not enough, in other words, to analyse the upper social segment, even if our sources push us in this direction and for the most part describe the differences in relation to the degree of political capacity. The distribution among individuals and groups of this resource – political capacity – establishes relationships and consequently mechanisms of competition and imitation.

Making the development of territorial states, and the complications of institutional scale, into our chief analytical concern inevitably involves taking other forms of demographic and economic expansion into consideration. The new lexicons of legitimacy developed in a setting that was not exclusively political; indeed these lexicons may be read as the political translation of much more complicated dynamics of differentiation and social segmentation brought by economic growth and changes in institutional scale. It is easy, for example, to include in this framework well-documented phenomena of specialisation and division of labour, and also the increase in the technical complexity of administrative and governing activities. It will be useful to start from these phenomena in trying to understand the concrete consequences of the rise of the *popolo*. The *popolo*'s rise sets off a process of stratification that can then be tied in with the more classical problem of aristocracy and the nature of privilege.

The division of labour and corporations

The division of labour is in turn intimately connected to the development of the guilds, one of the most important social and economic phenomena of all late medieval and modern Europe. From a political point of view their birth, or more often their transformation into something greater than a society for mutual aid or devotional practices, coincides in most European cities with a broadening of participation in local government. The political emergence of the guilds constitutes one of the decisive elements in the making of community's autonomy. Particularly in the Italy of the *comune*, this very process is often tied to the formation of the *popolo* – understood as the entirety of the components of the city's society that did not dominate the city during the first phase of communal self-government. But the *popolo* does not include the whole of the urban population which was excluded from the government of the consular commune: its formation and solidification during the thirteenth century produced new distinctions both inside the city and between town and countryside, transforming the entire range of social roles.

If we read the statutes of two important 'popular' communes – Padua in the 1270s and Bologna in 1250–80 – we can see how participation in governmental space was formalised. These normative exercises, brought about by the need to define political power, in fact contain a summarily descriptive scheme of the complex range of lay society.

In 1274 the basic rules of elections to councils and offices were established by the Paduan commune: legal age, a certain continuity in residence in the city, enrolment in the fiscal lists (perhaps the most important factor: a wealth assessment of 100 *lire* was required for the right to vote, of 200 *lire* for a candidature, and moreover landed property estimated at 500 *lire*). Shortly after, in 1277, the norms dealing with the election of the *Anziani* showed a more accurate system: in fact they included a list of the subjects that could not enter the office: 'mariners, gardeners, agricultural labourers, cowherds, workers and employers in mechanical arts, servants, fishermen, jesters, those who do not reside autonomously, those who have not any income or who get clothes, old or new, from someone else'.[4] In 1251 the statutes of Bologna limited the range of people eligible to sit on the councils of the *popolo*: bakers, porters, workers in transport services and servants could not participate in elections.[5] Because of the need to fix the composition of the Council of the Two Thousand, in 1289 this list took on, in a new statute, a more definite content. The lower status of trades connected with bread and flour was confirmed, as was that of transport trades and small retailers; but now a similar disadvantaged condition was explicitly applied to individuals stigmatised by a (too) poor urban identity: the people residing more often in country than in town, or coming from rural

---

[4] *Statuti del comune di Padova* 132 sg. (I, rubr. XXXII).   [5] Gaudenzi (ed.), *Statuti*, 531.

households, as well as farmers. Finally, the same active discrimination was imposed on strangers, that is, new inhabitants who had not resided continuously in Bologna for almost twenty years, and those not enrolled in the *estimo*, or who were obliged to pay tax outside the town.[6]

On the basis of these two cases we may assert that certain, rather precise social categories (farmers, recent immigrants, some types of labourers or artisans, the poor) were excluded from the *popolo* and above all from its ruling ranks. Moreover, another necessarily marginalised social pole, reveled by the statutes of Bologna, was made up of those whose reputation was damaged: pimps, assassins or 'whoever is publicly reputed to be assassin or pimp, or anyone with a bad reputation'.[7]

Thus when we attempt to answer the question 'who is the *popolo*?' in Italian cities in the thirteenth and fourteenth centuries we must focus on the formation of a double barrier. There was certainly a line dividing the new institutional entity (and its composite social base) from the often highly militarised elite who had dominated and governed the commune in its early stages and who were often the object of specific discriminatory measures because of their pre-eminence.[8] This was a distinction entirely internal to the city even though the magnates may have had earlier power bases or lordships in the countryside. This distinction elaborated the common perception of nobility as knightly dignity or lordly authority and endowed it with a new institutional value. In some important cities an act of classification determined the condition of the magnates, a listing of the families considered to be – because they were too powerful and independent – outside the *popolo*, if not indeed its enemy.[9] The space thus created could not easily be homogeneous; some statutes, like those in Pistoia, drew up lists that did not include the less dangerous 'nobles'; or sometimes the excessively 'strong and outrageous *popolari*' could be – as Giovanni Villani writes about Florence – 'worthy of inclusion with the *grandi* for the good of the *popolo*'.[10]

It is, however, also necessary to find the other border that separated the *popolo* not only from the nobles and magnates but also from those who moved in the broad space made up of the true outsiders (foreigners and strangers/visitors) and those who came to make up a different, internal outsidership. In the dynamics of mobility that in this phase disturb the relations between a city and its satellite communities, these figures remain halfway between urban and rural – especially the more

---

[6] Fasoli and Sella (ed.), *Statuti*, II, 1, p. 41; II, 3–4, p. 52.
[7] Gaudenzi (ed.), *Statuti*, 535.
[8] Maire Vigueur, *Cavaliers et citoyens*; *Magnati e popolani*.
[9] Milani, *L'esclusione dal comune*; Castelnuovo, 'L'identità politica', 211–14.
[10] Giovanni Villani, *Nuova Cronica*, X, 287.

manual labourers who are not shielded from poverty and contact with the danger zone of disreputable activities and identities.[11]

We then see another border forming inside the city that separates the subjects of thirteenth-century political conflict (*popolo* and magnates) from the great mass excluded from the *popolo* itself and from any sort of participation. Naturally it is especially the identity of the *popolo* which is directly affected by the definition of this border and by the delimitation of the mass of the incapable (or less capable), who are variously described as *plebe, popolo minuto, minores*, etc.

Association in guilds established itself as a decisive instrument of stratification; when it became one of the privileged channels of access to government, one of the more important prizes of the political game came to reside in the power to create new guilds and install a principle of equal dignity among those already existing. This is clearly shown by the history of Florence between 1293 (the year of the *Ordinamenti di giustizia*) and 1378 (the year of the Ciompi revolt): in this period Florentine history was riven by a tension between the enlargement of the political space of the twenty-one corporations, and the imposition within that space of a precise hierarchy at the top of which those who represented the elite of the great merchant-businessmen excelled.[12]

Hierarchical discipline as a shared principle and the lack of any notion of equality between the corporations emerge clearly from a famous passage in which Giovanni Villani, virtually the official chronicler of the Florentine *popolo*, shows his scorn for the minor guilds that are inept at managing the common weal and for the other categories of inferior subjects (strangers, rustics, low-ranking labourers): 'let's consider the government of the towns, when the rulers are artisans and manual workers and idiots: most of twenty-one chiefs of the Arts that now govern the *Comune* were small artisans from the countryside and foreigners who had little idea of the state and even less of leading it'.[13]

The distinction between honourable crafts and socially ambiguous activities produced, then, a series of demarcations by which the part of society fully able to govern the *res publica* was defined, together with the social actors who had this ability to a lesser degree or not at all. The economic cleavages presupposed the existence of a system of nearly universal rules (active even when not formalised): citizenship and political participation were tied to contribution to the collection of taxes, an ability based on the absence of poverty. And in this context poverty was understood 'as lack [...] as privation not only of wealth [...]

---

[11] Todeschini, *Visibilmente*, 137–47, ch.7.   [12] Najemy, 'The dialogue of power'.
[13] Giovanni Villani, *Nuova Cronica*, XIII, 43.

but also of physical, mental or social abilities, or as an absence of recognisability', as 'a suspect condition' that impeded full autonomy and participation in the public sphere.[14] This social weakness was produced, in general, by the humbler trades, confused with those having a partial or suspect condition of dependency or servitude (in the Bolognese *statuto* ex-servants were excluded from the electorate); it limited, for example, the full credibility of these subjects as witnesses in proceedings. The rule, already present in Roman law,[15] that excluded not only women and minors but also the poor from testifying in court alludes in fact to a universal limit to speech that the political systems of the *comune* of the *popolo* in northern Italy did not violate. The poor man, who – says Thomas Aquinas – is among those '*quibus imperari potest*',[16] is not free, or is so only in name; therefore he is vulnerable to blackmail and does not have the right to make formal accusations. From this standpoint there was no difference between the urban communal world and the 'feudal' world that emerges from the norms of Frederick II's *Liber Augustalis* wherein it is expressly forbidden to the *rustici* or the *villici* and generally to anyone of *umilis conditionis* to testify against counts and barons or simple *milites*. By contrast, the *burgenses bonae et honestae opinionis*[17] did have the power to testify.

Thus the institutionalisation of the arts represents a decisive factor not only in the broadening of political participation but also in new forms of hierarchisation and exclusion. In fact in the places where corporative dynamics were weaker, that is, where the public importance of trade and professional solidarity were less evident or completely absent, the mechanisms of selection were different and usually less marked.

The example of a large non-communal city such as Palermo offers more insights. In an article of its *consuetudines*,[18] it is stated that the 'artificers of all mechanical arts', whether *cives* or *exteri*, may freely exercise their trade, and the following trades are mentioned: barbers, bankers, *venditores rerum*, blacksmiths and farriers. But the list also includes the *pauperes mulieres* permitted to bake bread, the prostitutes, tavern-keepers, butchers and Jews, all free to exercise their activities free of tax 'even though they conduct a dirty and sordid existence'. Business thus seems free, there is no formalised corporate organisation, and the distinction between honourable and dishonourable trades has no political effect. This does not mean that there were no trade associations, but

---

[14] Todeschini, *Visibilmente*, 211.
[15] Dig. 48.2 and Nov. XC, 1; Todeschini, *Visibilmente*, 205ff. and 230.
[16] *Summa Theologiae* II–III, q. 70 a. 3 co.   [17] *Liber Augustalis*, II, 32.
[18] La Mantia, *Antiche consuetudini*, 214ff.

we have few sources and they only let us state that their public role, if there was one, was restricted to the ritual and devotional area: when artisanal or professional activities needed regulation, it was handled by local officials.

This is by and large how things stood in the second half of the fourteenth century. Later, between the end of the fourteenth century and the century following, the city's autonomy increased gradually: the political class consequently tended to broaden and to divide into distinct groups: their internal borders, when a more accurate distinction was needed, were often borrowed from the composite and still fluid world of the corporations. In Palermo and other Sicilian cities the sources from not earlier than the first decades of the fifteenth century reveal a scheme of distinction based on criteria that are not all decipherable. Around 1450 the citizens' council in Palermo appears to have been composed of groups that were able to contribute fiscally: that is, (1) the *gentilhuomini*, or the upper segment of the social scale: land-owners and businessmen, those who acceded most often to town offices; (2) the *mercanti*, meaning 'great merchants', men involved in regional or international trade; (3) the *borgesi* or small and medium-sized land-owners; (4) the *magistri* (in other places called *artisti* or *ministrali*), or the artisans and professionals who were members of the guilds.[19]

Work was thus very important in these summary distinctions of the parts of the population that could participate in a city's institutions. But the *popolo* was not included in these groups even though it is mentioned frequently in the sources, and this complicates the issue of its definition. Nevertheless, framing the *popolo* is necessary in order to understand the configuration of the social hierarchy. If we consider other Sicilian cities, we might imagine that the *popolo* corresponded to a less defined social space that included salaried workers and artisans, but this would show its physiognomy only in the negative, i.e. as those workers who cannot be numbered among the *magistri*.[20]

The year 1450 was an unusual one for Palermo. The revolt that broke out stimulated an increase in the precision of the social map as a result of the dialogue between city and crown (and by means of a series of statutes emanating between 1448 and 1472).[21] The rules for conferring local offices became more selective, starting with a new and more restrictive definition of the term 'citizenship'. In particular the measures relative to the *maestri di piazza* – one of the principal offices – ordered that these be 'important citizens, serious and of great authority and wealth' and not

---

[19] Epstein, *An Island*, 358–65; Titone, *Governments*, 175–81.   [20] Titone, 'Il tumulto'.
[21] De Vio, *Felicis et fidelissimae*, 306–13, 313–24, 382–91.

'common men, and ignorant of town customs': thus the competition for the offices had intensified and could concern also segments of the lower and *less* defined society between *magistri* and *popolo*. The idea that universal representation should be entrusted to the 'principal men', meaning only officials, gentlemen and *borgesi*, emerged in 1451. Not only were the artisans not included, but immediately after the revolt they suffered a partially successful attempt to exclude them from office.

Later on, in 1472, these processes, as well as the logic of local politics, apparently stabilised. Access to offices was now regulated in a much more defined way. In particular, the public role of the guilds was finally recognised. At the same time the honoured and 'low' trades were polarised, and so the old article 77 of the *consuetudini* was definitively superseded. Indeed, people such as pimps, tavern-keepers, butchers 'and other low and dirty persons' who plied a dishonest trade could no longer run for the office of *maestro di sciurta*. But it was also the case, more importantly, that when it came to establishing the rules for the offices of *giudice idiota* and *maestro di piazza*, for which 'neither mechanics nor artisans may run' and which were explicitly reserved for gentlemen, lawyers and 'honoured citizens', the field of pre-eminence, and its borders, was defined, and the corporations were removed from the upper ranks of politics and the more important offices. One of the faces of the aristocratic dimension then did not coincide with the administration of the city as such but with its upper segment.

This long example shows how the construction of the *popolo* and trade corporations produced mechanisms of social distinction within a heterogeneous urban reality, and even in different times. In particular, while these mechanisms were not directly determined by the public affirmation of the guilds (as we have seen, this was not so in Sicily), the integration of the guilds themselves into the political space was often a symptom, in late medieval society, of the phenomenon in question: it revealed the existence of dynamics of distinction between groups that were until then not so clearly separated. It is not community or corporate autonomy that engendered phenomena of exclusion but rather the possibility of shaping this autonomy, that is, of stipulating who may or may not be *universitas*.

To return to the communal area, we are struck by the fact that it is precisely in the contexts in which the ideological investment of the *popolo* is more pronounced that the distinctions not only do not diminish but instead are no less exact than those in the places in which an urban *signoria* has matured. Of course it is easy to think of the case of Florence and the republican ideology that began to form in the early fifteenth century. This ideology rested, among other things, on the increasingly precise separation of political elite from common citizen;[22] those described by Matteo Palmieri in mid-Quattrocento, who in theory (like the shoe-makers) had the right to participate in the making of the 'civil law' but in reality had to leave these offices, for the good of the community, to the more qualified.[23] And even in those places, such as Bologna in 1376, where there was an attempt to re-establish a 'popular' government, society seemed to be neatly split into hierarchically ranked groups: in fact a man called Tommaso di Pietro '*Galixi*' in a speech to the council asserts the existence of four '*partes seu genera hominum*', all nominally involved in the governing of the city: '*magnates*', '*homines divites populares et doctores*', '*homines medie conditionis*' and '*homines de parva conditione*'.[24] As in other cities the oligarchic process was already underway. The magnates, a far from neutral term in the communal social lexicon, were reintegrated into the government: prosopographic analyses, like those on the Florentine magnates, show us how much the composition of this group changed over the course of a century and a half.[25] This helps to throw more light on the sense of consolidating an order founded on the progressive separation of the governing groups from the rest of the *cives*, and on the intensification of the significance of the opposition between 'nobles' and 'people' in the political systems in which the tradition of the popular party had been important. This opposition became more and more frequently assumed to be a condition of nature between the thirteenth and fourteenth centuries in Florence as well as Bologna, Siena and of course Venice.[26]

Nobilities among the local ruling groups

The distinctions that stratified the upper levels of society should be placed in an appropriate context: often this is the new practice of classification created by institutional transformation. The operations of formalisation and identification were very different, but had a common content: how to construct and define the rights of individuals who took on public roles, from the elementary ability to speak in assembly or in court, to the assumption of government offices and representation of the community. Even the nobility, its definition, the ideological and juridical elaboration of its statute, are part of the same dynamics of construction of a legitimate order inside the new territorial states, whether monarchic

---

[22] Najemy, 'Civic humanism'.   [23] Palmieri, *Vita civile*, 68.
[24] Castelnuovo, 'Vivre dans l'ambiguïté', 96–102.   [25] Klapisch-Zuber, *Retour à la cité*.
[26] For Bologna, see Castelnuovo, 'Vivre dans l'ambiguïté'; for Siena, see Shaw, *Popular Government*, 44–5.

or republican. When we speak of aristocratisation, of the mechanisms of formal separation of a nucleus of families above the rest of the community, the reference is to phenomena that are principally institutional: procedures of the criteria of access to the decisional sphere, rather than actions finalised in the *recognition* of pre-existing identities, or the legalisation of predefined conditions of social leadership.

This explains why the processes of aristocratic selection in this phase are not movements of unification and why 'noble status' remains vague and hard to grasp despite the tendency towards objectivisation and naturalisation: thus as corporate geography tends towards complication, we do not see the confluence of the aristocracies into a single institutional edifice. 'Nobility' was an abstract ideal or a theoretical canon, never an institutional subject (and, of course, never a coherent social dimension).

It is difficult then to reduce local distinguishing factors to a few general lines; one may attempt to single out those that appear more frequently and move towards formalisation, and sometimes towards legalisation of social superiority. In particular we may refer to two modes of recognition of the superiority that we encounter in all the political realities of the peninsula: one represented by the civic councils and their 'closure'[27] and the other by the multiple forms of service given to the territorial governments and especially by of the ennoblement function of relationships with a prince (or the ruler of a republic). The tendency to close the councils, even to listing those families who had the right to belong, manifested itself fairly early on, for example in the Veneto. The case of Venice is emblematic. But it is exactly Venice that shows us how the tendency to oligarchic closure does not immediately bring a homogeneous leadership class. Viewed from the lagoon, where the process began explicitly in 1297 with the so-called *serrata* of the Maggior Consiglio and continued for at least a century and a half, the aristocratisation of the *consiglio* determined differing levels of pre-eminence: Venetian nobility as a compact collective actor is a modern myth whose roots in the late medieval time are quite ambiguous.[28] This despite the fact that, in the fifteenth century, when the process was completed, it was precisely the Venetian grand council, 'closed' and strictly controlled by a certain number of families, that for its contemporaries constituted a model of 'popular' or 'mixed' but certainly not noble[29] government: the model, within the world of communal tradition, of a political class emancipated from the control of the common *cives* but on the basis of

---

[27] Varanini, 'Aristocrazie e poteri', 164–8. [28] Chojnacki, 'La formazione'.
[29] Shaw, *Popular Government*, 174–5.

recognition of the 'sovereignty' of the organic body of these same citizens. In this way, the governing oligarchy took over the function of fully representing the *popolo*, that is, the unmediated role of who *is* the sovereign community. A new aristocratic identity arose from this new constitutional order.

The Venetian case must be compared carefully, in the same period, to the multiplicity of similar situations in very many cities. Yet, it is clear that it loses a (not decisive) part of its meaning. Indeed the quality of these transformations varies with the scale of the community: even the smallest or most peripheral of them experienced similar dynamics, but the exclusion of the governed (or not-nobles) was, in the cases we know, much more tempered and the emergence of more formalised aristocracies did not necessarily imply that participation was weaker.[30] When the scale and complexity increase, up to the upper level of the medium-sized territorial state (such as Venice), we can observe the inverse tendency to close channels of participation, to interpret pre-eminence as a right to govern the communal institutions (with the councils as central places), and to be part of bureaucratic and military apparatus in the princely states. In the rapport between various institutional and community levels the phenomena of osmosis and imitation were strong forces, but scale and levels of social complexity were equally so.

The dimension I speak of intersects with another which was determined by the relationships between public power and a number of subjects and actors: relations that could assume the form of service in offices or courts or that of the noble or feudal function disciplined by the political relation with the ruler. Often this relation was reinvented or renegotiated in order to strengthen both the faithfulness of the vassal and his aristocratic legitimacy: it is a fact that 'feudalism' as a method of control and local government in this period grew in concomitance with the reinforcement of the states and their capacity to co-ordinate the territories, both in the north and in the south of the peninsula. Savoy at the end of the Middle Ages, for example, shows clearly the increasing presence of 'an elite [...] characterised by seigneurial control of the territory, by individuals faithful to the prince and by participation in an administration perceived as an organ of political co-ordination':[31] an elite in which administrative activity had become an essential instrument of promotion and ennoblement.

These intersecting processes produced social stratifications and maps, and new representations: for example, the stability of the Venetian

---

[30] See, for the Lombard mountains, Della Misericordia, *Divenire comunità*.
[31] Castelnuovo, *Ufficiali e gentiluomini*, 365.

republic and its leadership; or Sforza Lombardy as a land of lords more than of cities[32] (an image on which Machiavelli would impress his mark). These processes could give rise to the reinvention of a *popolo* with a theoretical first place in the chain of legitimacy, as well as to the construction of a 'nobility'. In fact, as we shall see, even 'nobility', perceived either as a more or less traditional code (feudal or noble) of social distinction or as a space of concrete political capacity, could be framed in the light of these institutional phenomena.

Thus, local aristocratic universes show their specific complexities as much as their common matrices. Let us consider some examples that indicate more clearly the composite character of the aristocracies and their dependence on the processes of state construction.

In Milan and its territory many spaces of variously privileged distinction took shape in the second half of the fourteenth century. There were the residual communal institutions and their councils, by now in fact controlled by the lord (and later the duke). There was the world of the offices and of the court, and here the ducal councils took on an increasingly crucial function in the selection of the upper tiers of Lombard society. There was also, still in the capital, another more exclusive area made up of a well-defined ecclesiastical community (the chapter of the cathedral) which claimed the prerogative of calling together the *capitanei* and the *valvassori*: those who were reputed to be descendants of the vassals of the archbishop of the first communal period. The book (*matricola*) of the families that were allowed to participate in the chapter was written not later than 1377. However, there was not only Milan. Outside the walls of the capital, and even as the *signoria* was consolidating, the power of territorial lords seemed to increase in the fifteenth century: often they were interested in having a continuous presence in the city, but almost always their strategies were influenced by the dialogue with the prince, fed by loyalty or antagonism, according to political contingency.

Inside another large popular commune like Siena which, unlike Milan, had not undergone a precocious transition to the *signoria*, the fundamental distinction between magnates and *popolo* is clearly evident. Nevertheless, we have already seen that the two groups were not at all homogeneous. Indeed, records of the popular government, throwing light on the whole space of social pre-eminence, can reveal the fractures in the magnates' camp and how deep they were. In 1341, for example, when the council approved a petition addressed to the government of the Nine not only is the conflict between *popolo* and magnates mentioned, but also that between greater and lesser magnates, and a request is made

---

[32] Arcangeli, *Gentiluomini di Lombardia*; Gentile, 'Aristocrazia signorile'.

to protect the latter from the violence of the former.[33] A case of this kind lets us understand the concrete, if not immediate, effects of anti-magnate politics. It certainly limited and excluded the aristocrats, but often ended by favouring the formation of a collective subject destined to be reintegrated into the governing space.

A complicated but rather transparent process transformed the diverse regimes governing Siena from the second half of the thirteenth century: the members of the ruling elite, their descendants and families became part of five distinctly leadership bodies, called the *Monti*, who were destined gradually to monopolise the public offices. The phenomenon manifests itself at the end of the fourteenth century and shows how social and institutional memory was stratified: the regimes of the late thirteenth and of most of the fourteenth centuries, all of them expressions of the *popolo*, were the bases of the *Monti* of the *Nove* and of the *Riformatori*. But a *Monte del Popolo* made up of the more recent members of the council formed separately at the same time with another *Monte* (the nobles) which derived from the institutionalisation of all the magnate families, even though memory of their exclusion from town offices was retained.[34]

The situation in Rome was also quite complicated. Two areas of participation were formed around the communal government during the early decades of the fourteenth century: the *milites* or *nobiles viri* and the *populares*; the distinction here too was tied to the relationship between the greater and lesser guilds and the *militia*. This distinction tended to diminish during the Quattrocento after the reaffirmation of the pope's authority and when the city elite attempted to construct its own community structures: confraternities, for example (the Società dei raccomandati del Salvatore). The demarcation of the urban nobility was still uncertain, however, because its ranks remained open, leaving the 'popular' space not well defined, and above all because it remained clearly separated from the great nobility of the barons: that is, a narrow circle of well-defined lineages whose power derived partly from their relationship to the city, but mostly from their own seigneurial lands (often freeholds) and from their close relation to the legitimising authority of the pope.[35]

The Roman barons, territorial lords who were tied to the pope but who were not necessarily his vassals, in the fourteenth and fifteenth centuries represented the case of a grand aristocracy that could play in diverse theatres and assume varying roles. They in fact constituted a

---

[33] Bowsky, *A Medieval Italian Commune*, 52ff.   [34] Shaw, *Popular Government*, 4–6.
[35] Carocci, 'Una nobiltà bipartita'; Mineo, 'Nobiltà romane e nobiltà italiane'.

bridge between the aristocratic world of central Italy and the southern mainland as they were often also the barons of the king of Naples: but in this instance they were the king's vassals.

The variation of meaning of 'baron' between the pontifical territories and the Neapolitan kingdom takes us into a still different world. Without doubt here the feudal reality of the king's vassals emerges clearly in comparison to some central-northern areas distinguished by communal origins; the southern barons might be similar in some traits to lords in many other parts of Italy, beginning with Lazio, and then ducal Lombardy, Emilia and the Romagna, but certainly the nature of their presence and their institutional role within a great monarchy put them a world apart. Backed by the law and a function that had clear correspondents in the common lexicon of European 'feudalism', one may not claim, however, that the Neapolitan barons constituted a real body nor that they represented *the* nobility of the kingdom (just as we cannot say, strictly, that even the extremely powerful Roman barons were *the* nobility of the pontifical state). In Naples, instead, an urban aristocracy was formed which was distinct from the barons, that is a space of pre-eminence produced by the city's politics. This space assumes the form of the so-called *sedili*, which may be interpreted as corporate territorial groups which developed between the thirteenth and fourteenth centuries in the midst of the administrative experience and were consolidated in middle of the fourteenth century. Once again it is a hierarchy that emerges and tends to codify the relations between the two more noble seats, Capuana and Nido, the less prestigious ones, and that of the *popolo*: a hierarchy that included, even here, the *popolo* as a corporate and politically active subject in as much as it held a minor quota of privilege.[36]

The case of Naples, whose institutional model would be imitated by other centres of the kingdom, confirms that the political urban systems, that is, the practices of citizenship and representation, produced powerful mechanisms of hierarchisation even where there was a tradition of institutionalised feudalism. The case of Sicilian cities is analogous. As we have seen, they experienced the same processes, but naturally there were feudal lands, and in fact the politics of the Aragonese crown in the fifteenth century tended to favour the growth of baronial space. In both of these kingdoms there was an attempt to co-ordinate these differing claims of political legitimacy: the establishment of the parliaments, which in this context should be interpreted as further signs of the effort to formalise the political arenas that had

---

[36] Vitale, *Elite burocratica e famiglia*.

developed through the fourteenth and fifteenth centuries. The emergence of the parliaments confirms a point that I have already touched on: that is, that the practice of representation began to take on the mark of privilege. As in many councils in central and northern Italy, and in those of southern cities as well, or in the Neapolitan system of *sedili*, participation in the parliaments (generally reserved to the barons, prelates and urban elite) began to be a strong indicator of pre-eminence. Strong but not exclusive: the court and the king's council, the central offices and the representative systems of the larger cities also generated aristocracy.

This short digression serves only to underline the necessity of singling out a common institutional denominator in the plurality of aristocratic processes; in other words, the meanings of pre-eminence look functional for the concrete definition of institutions and politics. For this reason the comparison between different political worlds, the southern kingdoms and the states originating from a communal tradition is useful: it shows how the specific local forms of prestige and pre-eminence undergo comparable metamorphoses and some convergences in the midst of institutional changes at the end of the Middle Ages.

Between learned reflection and common sense

What evidence do we have of contemporary realisation of the evolutions that I have described? The multiplicity of points of view is quite obvious: on the one hand there was a basic common sense, a sort of almost unconscious and universal mechanism of representation of the social world founded on the naturalisation of the elementary opposition between nobles and non-nobles (like that, outside Italy, between *noblesse* and *roture*, lords and commoners, and so forth) or on the reproduction of ancient functionalistic models, such as that of a tripartite society. At the same time many of those who moved in the public sphere elaborated very different analyses, in which the nobility was seen as having strictly institutional significance.

A concrete case comes out of early fifteenth-century Milan, a controversy that takes us directly to the problem. As we have seen, the cathedral chapter already constituted a closed aristocratic community. Strong in its recognised right, the chapter contested the nomination by the apostolic see of an important person of the town to the position of *canonico ordinario*. The reason for the protest was explicit and connected to the fundamental common sense mentioned above: the person in question was not '*de nobili genere procreatus*' and might not be awarded the privilege that had been denied '*multis doctoribus et viris excellentibus*', on the basis of the principle according to which '*inter nobiles et ignobiles non potest esse commertium*'. Notwithstanding this, duke Filippo Maria Visconti, to whom the chapter appealed, confirmed the privilege.[37] This is not a case of the princely power of ennoblement, given that the case touched on the relationships between the Milanese chapter and the Roman curia. Nevertheless, called upon to resolve the controversy, the duke indirectly demonstrated that the terms defining aristocratic superiority were not as obvious as some members of the chapter would have liked.

The Milanese case is important because it shows how deeply rooted and legitimate a feudal-aristocratic language could be in an urban environment with a great communal tradition. The customs to which the cathedral chapter referred in effect protected the right of the *nobiles* organised in the chapter community: they appealed to the duke defending an exclusive vision of superiority based on the natural and self-sufficient character of nobility. Nevertheless the duke did not react arbitrarily; on the contrary, his decision was perfectly understandable to contemporary public opinion. The idea of nobility in fact rested on the awareness of the polysemy of the words that designated social superiority: the criterion adopted by the Milanese canons could have been justly claimed as the resolution of the question, but in truth it was only one of many possibilities. The duke's action showed that another criterion was equally valid in relation to the legitimising function of the prince and all 'sovereign' authorities such as, in our case, the pope. In the light of a criterion of this kind, the social distinction did not seem to be a fact of nature but rather an effect of the political use of privilege.

Now, there is a clear correspondence between the different ways of being noble (the social practices) and the theoretical work that develops from the middle of the fourteenth century.[38] Previously – it is known and must be underscored – these reflections had appeared sporadically and unsystematically, at least those that dwelt on the juridical and political dimensions of 'nobility'. Those concerning nobility as virtue – a literary and philosophical motif used frequently at least from the time of Dante (and of Jean de Meun, author of the *Roman de la Rose*) – were part of another, more abstract conceptual order. The later type of analysis followed closely on the reinforcement of the states; so much so that the institutional changes may be considered the real motive for these reflections, or at least for the more meaningful ones. At the same time

---

[37] Besozzi, 'La "matricula" delle famiglie nobili', 280.
[38] Donati, *L'idea di nobiltà*, ch. 1; Castelnuovo, 'L'identità politica'.

this signalled an uncertainty that was not perceived earlier: disorientation in the face of the multiple foundations for legitimacy.[39]

I will consider briefly only two kinds of reply to the question 'what is nobility?' Two types of explanation of the congenital polysemy of the word were drawn from the public discussion that developed at the end of the Middle Ages and were not always of a strictly theoretical and erudite nature. The fundamental source of the first type of analysis is Bartolo da Sassoferrato, and the second may be traced to Machiavelli.

Bartolo introduced a new departure point in the debate over nobility because he brought to light a rather common way of understanding social superiority in Italy,[40] attributing to it a systematic-doctrinal form. In fact we find for the first time in his writings an organic elaboration of the theme based on the principle according to which the prince is the normal source of nobility, where '*princeps*' means not only the emperor and the pope (or a king) but corresponds in general to an abstract concept, to the titular of sovereignty. Thus an independent Italian *civitas* might carry out its functions. Nobility, then, appeared to be a local political phenomenon which should not be confused with other possible meanings of the word, for example the theological and moral ones. It is the local context which fixes the meaning of 'nobility' and its relative signs: the *militia*, a public office, a certain type of conduct and so on.[41]

Once the political foundation was in place, Bartolo could easily state that nobility is not a natural condition, but a relative quality that one may acquire or lose ('*adesse vel subesse*'); when he speaks of '*naturalis nobilitas*' he in fact means a generic disposition towards power (a '*habitus electivus*'),[42] and when he treats the most delicate theme of blood-lines he has no difficulty in stating that the sons or grandsons of a non-noble (*rusticus*) may become noble just as farmers can become citizens: '*unde ex patre ignobili sed tamen valente nascitur filius vel nepos nobilis*'. It is the holder of sovereignty who may effect the operation and confer nobility: the virtue and will of the individual have little effect on this end.

Bartolo was continuously taken up and cited, projecting a very long shadow over later tradition and amplifying the ambiguities that we have seen in practice. His proposal in fact helped to fix an explicitly political

---

[39] Jones, *The Italian City-State*, 315.
[40] Donati, *L'idea di nobiltà*, 3–7: Bartolo's text is part of the comment on the constitution XII, 1.1 *Si ut proponitis*, C. *De dignitatibus* of the Giustinian *Codex*; the edition referred to is in Schnerb-Lièvre and Giordanengo, 'Le songe de Vergier'.
[41] Beginning with the conceptual difficulty introduced by the anti-magnate legislation, Bartolo (*ibid.*) adds at the end that, in certain situations, '*qui nobilis appellatur vel reputatur*' is noble.
[42] *Ibid.*, 223.

criterion in formalising nobility, but it did not impede a contemporary reinforcement of the sense of inheritance and blood. In the case of the Florentine Lapo da Castiglionchio we see clearly that the two perspectives were not mutually exclusive. Between 1377 and 1381 Lapo wrote a long memoir on the origins of his own family,[43] explicitly applying Bartolo's thoughts in the light of a specific aim: to use the family's past and its memory as a political resource in the communal context.[44] It is true that magnate families were often defined, in the communal statutes, on the basis of their belonging to a dynastic heritage, a blood-line:[45] Lapo, however, makes us understand that this type of distinction acquired sense in relation to a given political community, its specific institutional lexicon and its law. It needed a context to activate it and establish its efficacy.

Little more than a half century later, at the end of the 1450s, the Veronese jurist Bartolomeo Cipolla had not distanced himself from this position. After having enumerated twenty-six different definitions of nobility, drawing on a range of authors from Plato to Poggio Bracciolini, he provided a version that confirmed the substantial ambiguity of the word: 'true nobility is that which derives from ancestors of wealth and *virtù* conjoined with honour and public responsibilities'.[46] A definition of this kind – generic and anodyne but realistic – may serve as a frame for the concrete network of privileges that varied from place to place according to political constitution.

Conclusion

Bartolo da Sassoferrato's undertaking had thus established a new cultural balance destined to last a long time, and not only in Italy. He offered a key that served to bring order to the chaotic universe of privileges and also to unveil their origins. Representing a tendency common to western Europe, but perhaps more explicitly to Italy, his proposal was standardised between the fourteenth and sixteenth centuries. The Bartolian scheme allowed, in fact, the understanding of the paradox of the communal magnates, that is, of a 'nobility' of seigneurial origins that could be excluded from governing for precisely that reason, and that, in as much as it was removed from offices, it could not be considered really 'noble': '*et sic diffinitio nobilitatis eis non congruit*'. In this way the magnates are our litmus papers, revealing a decisive nucleus in the mechanism of distinction: they undergo (and propagate) a real

---

[43] Sznura (ed.), *Antica possessione*.   [44] Castelnuovo, 'Vivre dans l'ambiguïté', 105–16.
[45] *Ibid.*, 103–4.   [46] Donati, *L'idea di nobiltà*, 14ff.

cultural shock – excluded *because* they are noble (and because they are classified as such)[47] in a context marked by the total absence of ideological dissimulation of the political character of pre-eminence. But this is true even in the southern kingdoms – directly comparable to other European monarchies – where the original subordination of the baronial universe to the crown was clear as early as the Norman foundation and where, then, the way to legitimacy was always transparent.

There is, therefore, in this entire reflection, the establishment of the local character of privileged superiority with, however, the singling out of the thread that unifies the various nobilities: the discovery that social limits of privilege were constructed inside the institutional borders fixed by the new states. In this discovery the processes of institutionalisation and legalisation of nobilities came not only from a political need but also from the revelation of the newly increased insecurity about the very meaning of *nobilitas*; it came also, in the face of this insecurity, from the need for legitimacy expressed by the political elites made fluid and renewed by demographic and political crises that had radically changed their composition during the last two centuries of the Middle Ages.

There is in fact no doubt that noble ideology sought a more solid centre of gravity in the principle of the birth of the nobility *before* (or *beyond*) politics, as a phenomenon tied to the transmission of blood and honour. Already the most influential of Bartolo's students, Baldo degli Ubaldi, had modified his *maestro*'s point of view by emphasising the value of blood as the source of nobility,[48] and developing the theme of natural nobility that we have seen present also in the urban environment.

But the longevity of the Bartolian methodology is demonstrated by the famous Machiavellian argument with which we started. Chapter I, 55, of the *Discorsi* proposes, as we know, the kingdom–republic opposition and describes nobility as a phenomenon exclusive to monarchies; it is not this that overturns the realistic logic developed in the fourteenth century. The idea that a king is destined to failure if he does not destroy the *equality* of citizens in the republics, and does not elevate to privilege 'many of ambitious spirit and unquiet spirit' by making them gentlemen 'in fact, and not in name', seems to hide, for example, from the Venetian patriciate the awareness of what the citizenry had become and the prospect of its dynastic prerogatives. In other places, though, the argument is different. 'In every republic there are great and popular men', as he says in *Discorsi* I, 5; and, in I, 16, as we already know, he adds that 'in all republics, ordered in whatever mode, never do even forty or fifty

---

[47] Castelnuovo, 'L'identità politica', 199.
[48] Grubb, 'Patriziato', 246; see Gilli, *La noblesse du droit*, 43, on the idea of *nobilitas perfecta*.

citizens reach the ranks of command'. Finally, the true nature of the Venetian constitution is unveiled in I, 6.

Thus it is relevant to recall that Machiavelli, in taking for granted the existence of ranks, subordinates them to the historical moment and to the variability of local political factors: the phenomenon of interdependence of princes and nobility (a theme that will often be taken up again, as for example in Chapter XIV of Francis Bacon's *Essays*) had a trait in common with the experience of the republican senates, that is, a style of legitimisation directly tied to the form of the institutions. At the beginning of the sixteenth century, in sum, the image of natural nobility had not yet replaced the realistic perspective the medieval jurists had previously proposed: rather it is from their alchemy that many of the later schemes of stratification will be produced.[49]

---

[49] Salvemini, 'Le "impossibili tavole dei ranghi"'.

17 Women and the state

Serena Ferente

Introduction

'Feminism does not have a theory of the state', wrote Catharine MacKinnon in 1989, and the claim has been repeated more recently.[1] Is this perhaps why, despite a traceable tradition of feminist interest in the state, 'women' and 'the state' are terms not often seen together in historical writing? Historiography on the state remains, in Italy as elsewhere, a privileged ground to observe how a persistent lack of interest in the history of women can indeed become a form of blindness. Yet one just needs to subsume women under 'family' or dilute the state into 'politics' to come to two objects of study that sound compatible enough. If the resulting wider picture is considered, then the historiography on late medieval and early modern Italy seems to offer a partial exception to the traditional gender-blindness of institutional history. The history of the state – even while being contested – has long been the *via regia* in the Italian context and historians interested in women and gender have found themselves addressing the issue of the state in a remarkably explicit way over the past thirty years. In fact, there might well be something about late medieval Italian states that made women's issues, if not women themselves, unavoidable for historians.

The binomial 'women and the state' presents problems of its own (including the viability of its two components, a singular 'state' and an all-encompassing 'women') but, perhaps more than 'the family and the state', has the advantage of questioning past and present assumptions about the interplay between 'the private' and 'the public', and offering a different perspective on the famous monopoly of violence, on the state's duties of protection and justice, and on legitimacy, discipline and institutions, three elements that have been indicated as the 'necessary conditions' of state-building.

---

[1] MacKinnon, *Toward a Feminist Theory*, 157.

The caveats that apply to any treatment of 'Italy' as a whole in the late Middle Ages need to be stressed even more strongly when looking at women's and gender history. The dramatic imbalance between studies available for Florence and Venice and studies on other Italian areas should not tempt historians to conclude that one case can be easily taken as representative – but it should also not thwart all attempts to identify trends that go beyond local and regional differences. The abstract distinction between 'monarchical' and 'republican' constitutions dear to historians of political thought appears in some respects surprisingly reinforced, but must in other respects be replaced by a more meaningful distinction between dynastic and oligarchic forms of government, which in most central and northern Italian *signorie* mingled quite comfortably.

Historiography on women and gender in Italy has often treated the centuries between 1300 and 1800 together – in part influenced, no doubt, by the American understanding of the 'early modern' – but the resulting picture is not always one of continuity throughout the period. The two or three decades around 1400 mark in many geographical areas a change of pace in state-building processes, and there seems to be a widespread, if not always explicit, consensus that the new politico-religious order implemented after the Council of Trent changed profoundly important aspects of the lives of women in Italy. Occasionally historians have not shied away from an assessment of the nature of such changes in terms of improvement or worsening of women's condition, but virtually no one has followed Joan Kelly in asking whether 'the Renaissance state' was co-responsible for 'a contraction of [women's] social and personal options'.[2] Much more influential than the latter have been research questions typical of the history of the family in the 1960s and 1970s, such as the respective weight of agnatic and cognatic kinship links or the origins of an idea of the nuclear family as a community of love. The question of women and the state has been, in many ways, a byproduct of an extraordinarily productive season of studies on the family.

Today there is no disputing that the Renaissance state was concerned with women; that women were concerned with the state may be a more adventurous statement, but it is certainly not a preposterous one. This chapter will try to point to the most interesting areas of research that have connected women's and gender history with the category 'state' between, roughly, 1350 and 1550; inevitably, this will remain a partial overview, and much work of importance and creativity will be left out.

---

[2] Kelly Gadol, 'Did women have a Renaissance?', 138.

Property, or the state as the father

The question of women's inheritance and property rights is an old and crucial one. Although it did not account for all the ways in which women could acquire goods, the dowry has rightly been seen as the most characteristic institution reifying the asymmetry between the sexes; intrinsically gendered and universally adopted, it was such a staple of late medieval Italian society that it is no surprise to find it a very early object of historical attention, particularly among legal historians.[3] The dowry was an endowment attached to a daughter by her natal family as part of the marriage process, meant to be administered by the husband during the years of marriage but to revert to the woman once she became a widow, in order to ensure her maintenance and preserve her honour. These basic rules, enshrined in Roman law, have to be understood as a template that local customs, written statutes and a growing body of jurisprudence could transform into a multifaceted juridical object, whose appearance in each context changed considerably when the presence of children, a subsequent marriage, the choice of residence, the woman's provenance and other circumstances were taken into account.

Dowries, which in Roman law did not automatically exclude daughters from the *legitima*, or portion of paternal inheritance due to each of the children, were often the sole part of the natal family's patrimony that went to daughters. Other transfers of property to women, however, took place (*donationes propter nuptias, morgincap, antefato,* wedding gifts and trousseaux, as well as testamentary bequests), and could involve substantial amounts of wealth, complementing or counterbalancing the dowry.[4]

A dowry was indispensable to marriage, and marriage remained in pre-Tridentine Italy a contract between laypeople. In most central and northern Italian cities a notary, not a priest, guaranteed the publicity of the act. In the kingdom of Naples in 1332, Robert of Anjou had imposed a blessing *in facie Ecclesiae* and the hearing of a mass, in addition to the '*conventiones et pacta*' between the parents, as necessary for the validity of the marriage, but even there the extent to which the law was applied remains to be verified.[5]

Two trends, particularly well studied in the cases of Florence and Venice, are evident in the period between 1350 and 1550: on the one hand the irresistible inflation of the cost of dowries for elite women, on

---

[3] Bellomo, *Ricerche*; on Florence, see Kuehn, *Law, Family and Women*; in general, see Guerra Medici, *L'aria di città*.
[4] Klapisch-Zuber, *Women, Family and Ritual*, 213–46; for an overview, see Calvi and Chabot (eds.), *Le ricchezze delle donne*.
[5] Vitale, *Élite burocratica e famiglia*, 99–101.

the other an equally irresistible increase in legislation concerning those dowries. The two phenomena are obviously related but must be seen against a complex background, of which the population crises of the fourteenth century and subsequent processes of aristocratic closure of the urban elites were two main elements.

In fifteenth-century Venice, the trend took the form of successive attempts to cap the amounts that fathers were allowed to pay for dowries and the accompanying trousseau (*corredo*): 1,600 ducats, of which at least two-thirds formed the dowry, in 1420; 3,000 ducats inclusive of all gifts and trousseau in 1505; 4,000 ducats in 1525 with added fines and sanctions for the receiving husbands – yet throughout the period many patrician fathers paid amounts that were twice as high. Each bout of legislation elicited extensive debates in which ideas of liberty (for fathers to form marriage alliances) and equality (among members of the patrician group, irrespective of differences in wealth) in the republic were rehearsed on opposite sides, and the conflict of identities for those fathers/legislators manifested itself openly.[6]

The Florentine government followed a different route, establishing what is probably the most impressive institutional connection between dowries and state-building in late medieval Europe, with the foundation in 1425 of the *Monte delle Doti*. This Dowry Fund aimed to address the needs of those fathers who could not afford to marry off their daughters, while at the same time helping to offset the ballooning public debt consolidated in the *Monte Comune*: Florentine fathers who invested in the Dowry Fund would receive back a dowry once their daughters' marriage was consummated.[7] The link between dowries and public debts is confirmed, in a less macroscopic yet explicit way, in fifteenth-century Genoa, where shares in the Casa di San Giorgio became an increasingly important part of dowries.[8]

In the Florentine case, the need to repopulate the city, which had been ravaged by the plague, is explicitly mentioned in both the recorded debates and the wording of the law as the inspiration behind new legislation and new institutions, and demanded that marriages be encouraged and the spiralling cost of dowries brought under control. In Florence as in Venice, however, the conflict of interest between those ruling fathers that aimed to encourage as many younger men as possible to get married but kept bidding higher on the dowry market to enhance the social standing of their family remained unresolved.

---

[6] Chojnacki, *Women and Men*, 53–75.   [7] Molho and Kirshner, 'The dowry fund'.
[8] Kamenaga Anzai, 'Attitudes towards public debt'.

Dowry inflation has been observed in other city-states, such as Siena – where the trend seems to have started well before 1350 – and Ragusa.[9] By the beginning of the sixteenth century, inflation is evident wherever records have allowed historians to make estimates, including cities that enjoyed much lower levels of autonomy such as Parma, Rome and Naples.[10] The few studies of dowries in the lower urban classes seem to confirm that the inflationary trend was typical of the elite (and in fact partly constitutive of that elite). The idea of a 'dowry market', as suggestive as it is, must be used with great caution, however. A dowry 'speaks' first and foremost about the specific marriage to which it is attached, its social context *and* its immediate circumstances (including the physical bodies of the bride and the groom, whose concrete importance Venetian legislation took into account, for example, when it provided dispensations from the dowry cap for blind patrician women).

Larger dowries, in any case, meant that widowed elite women found themselves titular of very substantial amounts of wealth, an ambiguous position that exposed them to the potentially aggressive courting of both their natal and marital families, and could deprive them of any agency: this was very much the law and the social convention in Florence, where young widows with large dowries were often forced to remarry and abandon their existing children.[11] A large dowry in widowhood, however, could also become a unique opportunity for independence and power, and historians of Venice have produced several examples of patrician widows enjoying a relatively ample freedom of initiative, for instance as patrons and benefactors.[12]

More complex, but not altogether incongruent, are the cases of the civic and landed nobilities of the kingdoms of Naples and Sicily. As early as 1351–3 the members of the urban *seggi* of Capuana and Nido in the city of Naples produced autonomously a set of written rules concerning dowries, which slowly gained ground as an informal standard of noble behaviour in marriage matters and were finally imposed on the rest of the kingdom in 1598. Compared to the *mos* detailed in the written *consuetudines* of 1305, which contemplated the possibility of the wife's inheriting from the husband and vice versa, the new pact, clearly intended as a mark of aristocratic distinction for the members of the two most prestigious *seggi* of Naples, hardened the boundaries between maternal and

---

[9] On Siena, see Reimer, 'Women, dowries, and capital investment'; on Ragusa, see Mosher Stuard, 'Dowry increase'.
[10] On Parma, see Arcangeli, 'Un'aristocrazia territoriale al femminile'; on Rome, see Esposito, 'Li nobili huomini di Roma'; on Naples, see Vitale, *Modelli culturali*.
[11] Klapisch-Zuber, *Women, Family and Ritual*, 117–31.
[12] Chojnacki, *Women and Men*.

paternal portions of the patrimony, easing the return of the dowry to the wife's natal family.[13]

In Sicily the civic *consuetudines*, produced in abundance in the fourteenth century, acknowledged the prevalence of a custom, a *mos latinorum*, by which the dowry brought by the wife and the husband's properties merged to form an indistinct unity, for which husband, wife and children were communally responsible. Few fathers opted for a different dotal regime, called *mos graecorum*, which in accordance with Roman–Byzantine law kept the dowry separate from the rest of the family patrimony without depriving women of their right to the *legitima*. It is only with the beginning of the fifteenth century that a clear trend in the direction of a more widespread preference for the *mos graecorum* is identifiable, coinciding with the formation of a 'state nobility' largely defined by office-holding within the structures of royal government.[14]

In both southern kingdoms, however, the monarchy, rather than as a validator of successoral practices in a sustained direction, remained a source of dispensations and exceptions (especially in feudal-law matters of female exclusion and primogeniture), which favoured or disrupted family strategies responding to individual male or female pleaders. Supposedly weak and certainly unstable royal government under the late Anjous of Naples or the early Aragonese in Sicily, in fact, did not translate into a stronger nobility, and produced instead great instability and dramatic renewal in both the feudal and urban aristocracies of the two kingdoms, where new lineages (often of foreign origin) emerge frequently in the fourteenth century, while old family names die out or fall into disgrace.

Dowries were central in processes of social distinction, which in turn interacted with state-sanctioned rules defining the nobility, such as office-holding. The difference between (broadly republican) states (or state instances) that univocally represent the interests of an oligarchy of fathers and (broadly monarchical) states where the prince and the aristocracies are distinct (albeit not always conflicting) entities is a factor that deserves to be examined when determining the extent to which the state supported the patriarchs' agnatic strategies.

Women's property shaped their identities within and between families, intended as the constituent units of the political community. This connection between property and political identity may seem self-evident when property and jurisdiction over people coincide, as in the case of the *dominae* of lands, but is also helpful in understanding the problematic notion of women's citizenship. The consideration of citizenship from a

---

[13] Visceglia, 'Linee per uno studio'. [14] Mineo, *Nobiltà di stato*.

gender perspective brings into relief not only the disaggregation of the constitutive elements of citizenship produced by patrician closure, but also the persistent nature of late medieval states as communities of households, not individuals. Since the mechanisms of both political inclusion and political exclusion always applied to family groups, women could become the channel though which men transformed their political status.

Women in late medieval Italy were citizens-as-opposed-to-foreigners, not citizens-as-opposed-to-subjects, since they were categorically excluded from office-holding. They were part of the citizenry with respect to their *origo*, their origin, the laws and privileges that defined their economic activities and also their fiscal responsibilities when heads of households. Jurists generally deemed women unable to transmit citizenship to their children – *origo* derived from fathers, except in cases when the father was unknown – and bound to acquire that of their husbands. The latter point, however, generated a good amount of learned controversy concerned with women 'married elsewhere', in a different place from that of their *origo*, who had to deal with justice for criminal or property matters: which local statute applied to them? If jurists and legislators recognised that women had a sort of dual citizenship, it was often in order to ensure fiscal control over their properties and, more generally, to contain the erosion of the citizenry's properties located in the city and its district – another instance of the recurrent identification of civic legislators with the fathers, not the husbands.[15]

Occasionally, though, and interestingly, city policies aiming at favouring immigration configured the marriage to a woman citizen as a way for foreign husbands to obtain citizenship. This happened, for example, in Venice in 1407, when the government issued a law offering the status of *cittadini* – a category that was distinct from that of patricians and that did not enjoy membership of the political councils – to immigrant men who married Venetian women.[16]

Government, or the state as a household

Women rulers in fourteenth- and fifteenth-century Italy are easy to encounter, yet they have begun to attract sustained attention only very recently. (There may well be interesting historiographical reasons behind this neglect, which have to do with the weight of republican traditions in the construction of Italian history from the nineteenth century

[15] Kirshner, '"Women married elsewhere"'.
[16] Bellavitis, *Identité, mariage, mobilité sociale*.

onwards.) Laywomen governing large or very large states in their own right, with or without husbands – in Naples queens Giovanna I and Giovanna II, in Sicily queen Maria I, in Sardinia the *giudichessa* Eleonora of Arborea, in the principality of Taranto countess Maria of Enghien – are quite numerous but today almost entirely overlooked. The mothers, wives and daughters of central and northern Italian *signori* are instead beginning to emerge not only as powerful patrons of literary and artistic activity (a role that had already gained them some historical visibility) but also as prominent political agents whose collaboration was indispensable to the *signorile* version of dynastic rule.

Studies on queenship in medieval and early modern Europe have emphasised the formal political role of consorts and the normality of female regencies for minor, absent or incapacitated kings in dynastic regimes. Similar mechanisms are in place in the *signorie* of central and northern Italy, where ladies regent are a common occurrence. Jacob Burckhardt had already famously pointed to the parallel illegitimacies – of birth and of political authority – that characterised the Italian despots of the Renaissance, and it is clear that fourteenth- and fifteenth-century ruling families of *signori* were far from adopting rigid dynastic rules. Primogeniture, for example, remained frequently contested, and illegitimacy seemed to become an obstacle to succession only well into the sixteenth century – the Este dynasty of lords and then dukes of Ferrara is a paradigmatic example.[17] Hypergamy was one of the means through which these lords enhanced their status and their legitimacy in state systems that were expanding and becoming increasingly interconnected; thus a great number of *signori*'s wives in the fifteenth century were nobler than their husbands.

The relative success of some Renaissance women rulers acting as regents – the benevolence and admiration that surrounded some of them – could only partially balance the intrinsic precariousness of their authority, challenged by their husbands' brothers or their own sons. The short-lived but intense conflict between Bianca Maria Visconti and her son Galeazzo Maria Sforza between 1466 and 1468 (when the duchess died) affected the Milanese ducal council, state officials, the chancery and diplomatic relations, and would have threatened the integrity of the territorial dominion, since Bianca Maria had decided to separate her dotal city, Cremona, from the rest of the state.[18]

Many children, male *and* female, legitimate *and* natural, were decidedly understood as a resource in *signorile* families and their

---

[17] Bestor, 'Bastardy and legitimacy'.
[18] Covini, 'Tra cure domestiche, sentimenti e politica'.

marriages to political allies used as a crucial component of foreign politics. Despite some recurring exceptions (not only heiresses but also many sons destined for an ecclesiastical career), the rule was of course that men stayed and women left. Shifting the attention from the men who stay to the women entering and exiting a ruling family naturally creates a picture of state-building as the product of infra- and interstate networks of alliance (urban, regional, Italian, Mediterranean and/or European); these networks were also family relations that the travelling princesses embodied, together with the people, objects, tastes and traditions they brought with them. The Medici transition from a political hegemony over republican Florence in the first half of the fifteenth century to the grand ducal title in 1569, its ups and downs, accelerations, crises, and hazards, can be followed with impressive clarity through the Medici women's comings and goings: the pious and pragmatic Florentine Lucrezia Tornabuoni in 1467 wanted a woman from the highest nobility for her son Lorenzo, and succeeded in obtaining the hand of Clarice Orsini; the rich Florentine Maria Salviati was an excellent match for the illegitimate *condottiero* Giovanni de' Medici, but their son, duke Cosimo I, marked the dynasty's newly found stability under the Habsburg wing by marrying the daughter of the viceroy of Naples, Eleonora of Toledo; in 1560 Caterina de' Medici became queen regent of France, reaching much higher than planned when her recent, doubtful nobility had to be counterbalanced with an enormous dowry for Henry of Valois.

In the second half of the fifteenth century, princely marriages reveal diplomatic developments with impressive precision. The delicate and frustrating negotiations about the annulment of the betrothal of Galeazzo Maria Sforza and Dorotea Gonzaga (who was finally rejected because of an alleged physical defect) preoccupied the rulers of Milan and Mantua between 1463 and 1467 as much as a league or a war, since they signalled a new hierarchical relationship between the larger state and its satellite. During that half-century, so characterised by the growth of a new diplomacy, princesses such as Ippolita Sforza or Eleonora of Aragon became informal but crucial diplomatic resources, observers, intermediaries, representatives, in their new courts in Naples and Ferrara.[19]

The court, as an image of the princely household where public and private are eminently confused, was, unlike city councils and assemblies, a political space where women were present, visible and fulfilled formal

---

[19] On Ippolita, see Welch, 'Between Milan and Naples', and Bryce, 'Between friends?'; on Eleonora's diplomatic role, see Folin, 'La corte della duchessa'.

roles. Within the court women had tasks, spaces and competences that complemented the male ones – but occasionally competed with them – and consorts were surrounded by dedicated retinues (sometimes including chancellors who produced written documents exclusively on their behalf) that varied in size and degree of financial independence. In fact the female court both reflected and influenced the effective power of the consort, which changed with her life-cycle: the birth of an heir could turn isolation into centrality and the heir's own marriage turn centrality into marginality. The presence of a stable lover of the prince – who in the fourteenth and fifteenth centuries was often, unlike the consort, a woman (or man) from the local civic aristocracy, with ties and interests that were precious to the prince himself – could dispossess the legitimate wife of much of the political power that she derived from her unique access to the prince.

Among Renaissance courts the papal curia is obviously anomalous, not only because of its specific mixture of government and religion, or its unparalleled cosmopolitanism, but because it was a court where women had no place. It seems all the more significant, therefore, that the transformation of the lands of the church into an Italian state among other states coincided with the explosion of the old practice of papal nepotism, which put family relations at the centre of the papal court, sometimes scandalously. From the last decade of the fifteenth century, papal women (daughters, much more than concubines) not only did have some visibility during ceremonies such as marriages or baptisms, albeit in a context of complete informality, but were also crucial elements, together with their brothers, of nepotistic strategies that aimed at gaining a landed power base (itself a *stato*) and political alliances for the papal family, while in the short term consolidating the disparate collection of lordships and self-governing communities subject to the sovereign pontiff. The most notorious great lady of Renaissance Rome, Lucrezia Borgia, daughter of Alexander VI, married a vassal of the pope, Alfonso d'Este. Caterina Cybo, granddaughter of Innocent VIII, niece of Leo X and Clement VII, married another papal vassal, Giovanni Maria da Varano. Both women were entrusted with small or large jurisdictions – Lucrezia was made governor of Spoleto and other Umbrian towns in 1499, Caterina governed Camerino as regent for her daughter from 1527 to 1535.[20]

Courts, then, required the presence of women, and women acquired political prominence in the court. In the Italian *signorie* the formation of

---

[20] On Lucrezia Borgia and Caterina Cybo, see, respectively, the essays by S. Feci and G. Zarri, in Arcangeli and Peyronel (eds.), *Donne di potere*, 465–79 and 575–93.

a court had been, throughout the late medieval period, a manifest sign of the transition from communal to *signorile* governments. Perhaps the most telling case of hostility to a woman ruler that was connected with republican resistance involved Alfonsina Orsini: only three years after the end of the republican resurgence in Florence, the aristocratic widow of Piero de' Medici found herself informally regent for her son Lorenzo and *de facto* ruler of Florence between 1515 and 1519, a unique period of female government – not surprisingly surrounded by vitriolic misogyny – in the most rigidly agnatic political system in Italy.[21]

Many Renaissance ladies and princesses proved to be remarkably successful investors and administrators of their personal fortunes, confirming that propertied women were comfortable exercising economic initiative, even on a large scale, as a legitimate prosecution of their household role. When the household was the princely one, this gendered economic role could be integrated within the princely duties, as in the mirror for the princess that Diomede Carafa wrote for Eleonora of Aragon when she left Naples to become duchess of Ferrara in 1471.[22] In Carafa's guide to government, the management of *stato* and *casa*, fiscal policies and household administration, are distinct but inseparable concerns of the prince – third after the military duties and the judicial ones; Carafa's detail and emphasis on the government of state finances are uncommon in traditional mirrors for the prince, including Machiavelli's otherwise very non-traditional one, and may well have something to do with the gender of the dedicatee.

Together with the growing number of art objects commissioned by female princely patrons, writings such as Carafa's treatise are perhaps the most significant cultural reflection of the reality of female rule in late medieval and Renaissance Italy. A new genre was inaugurated by Boccaccio's *De mulieribus claris*, written in 1362 for Giovanna I of Naples, and evolved especially after 1450 into a typically appropriate literary offering to female ruler-patrons. Despite their moral and social conservatism, even their irony or playfulness, Italian fifteenth-century books on famous women, such as the *Gynevera* by Sabadino degli Arienti or Jacopo Foresti's *De claris mulieribus*, attempted the relatively new task of producing historical models of female virtue in a secular context and were among the earliest voices in the European '*querelle des femmes*'.[23] Unlike Boccaccio's, many of the heroines featured in these collections of lives were 'modern', not ancient, women, rulers such as Teodolinda or

---

[21] Tomas, *The Medici Women*, 164–84.   [22] Carafa, *Memoriali*.
[23] Kolsky, *The Ghost of Boccaccio*. See also the essays by D. Zancani and M. Ajmar in Panizza (ed.), *Women in Italian Renaissance*.

Matilda of Canossa, but also the illustrious mothers, sisters or relatives of the female dedicatee of the book, who formed a sort of female pantheon where prestige and traditions ran along the female lines. Real women exercising real power in the public realm both required and inspired new models of virtuous political agency.

Protection, or the state as a surrogate family

Providing support for poor women became in the late Middle Ages the principal occupation of public assistance – 'poor' being a complex category that went beyond economic circumstances to include the many weak members of the Christian community, beginning with orphans and widows. The mixture of ecclesiastical and lay control of public charity characterising the period between 1200 and 1550 is the background to the wave of state-sponsored initiatives that mark the fifteenth and early sixteenth centuries. If compared to northern Europe, Italy appears remarkable for the preponderant role of the laity in creating, staffing and autonomously administering institutions of public assistance (chiefly in urban contexts), even if these enterprises were always framed within the parameters of religious devotion, and jurisdiction over them was sometimes a matter of conflict, often one of collaboration, between lay corporations and the church (typically the bishop or mendicant religious orders).

Between the thirteenth and the sixteenth centuries central governments not only continued to agree to requests of fiscal privileges or conveyed resources to charitable institutions, but increasingly took the initiative to found, reform or co-manage them. This process did not produce a 'welfare state' – it lacked systematic and sustained commitment and it was never entirely distinct from religious devotion – but government initiative, which translated at a higher level the Christian duty of charity always felt by powerful individuals and corporate bodies (such as guilds or confraternities), did launch several instances of state-managed public assistance.

Naples offers very early examples not only of royal hospital foundations, but also patronage and special sponsorship on the part of royal women. Taken together they seem to delineate both an Angevin dynastic tradition of public charity and, within it, a gendered tradition, mirrored in the numerous important donations and bequests to hospitals by women from the civic aristocracy or the merchant class of Naples. The foundations and initiatives of Giovanna I from the 1360s onwards are particularly impressive, including the hospital of the Incoronata, with the annexed church, and the hospitals of Santa Elisabetta and of San

Nicola al Molo (the latter primarily devoted to the assistance of sailors). All these royal foundations were managed in complete autonomy by religious orders or male lay confraternities, frequently representing the Neapolitan *popolo* of merchants and professionals; it was the second Giovanna, in the 1420s, the first Neapolitan sovereign who reformed the governance of the hospital of the Annunziata and San Nicola al Molo, but neither the queen, nor her successor Alfonso of Aragon, went so far as to directly appoint the hospitals' officials.[24]

The appointment of the rector of the hospital of Santa Maria della Scala in Siena – one of the largest hospitals of the late Middle Ages and a model for many later foundations – fell instead under the jurisdiction of the commune of Siena in 1404.[25] The Florentine Ospedale degli Innocenti, specialising in the care of abandoned children and funded by the government on a large scale, was administered from 1445 by the Silk Guild (Arte della Seta, which had an institutional role in the commune), maintaining this kind of semi-governmental supervision until grand duke Cosimo I brought all Florentine hospitals under state supervision in 1542.[26] Shortly after becoming dukes of Milan in 1450, Francesco Sforza and Bianca Maria Visconti promoted a reform of the city's many hospitals, regrouping the majority of them under a single administration, in part appointed by the dukes, and commissioning to the architect Filarete the grandiose building of the Ospedale Maggiore – but duke Gian Galeazzo Visconti had already initiated a reform in 1401 that went in the same direction.[27]

If hospitals that were increasingly specialised, such as those providing for the sick or taking in abandoned children, can illustrate the nature of state initiative in charitable institutions, then women become an integral part of the history of the expansion of state competences in this sector, which encompassed very rich establishments. Women's activities overall appear, here as elsewhere, less valued and less visible than those of men, but there can be little doubt that women's contribution to public assistance in the late Middle Ages was comparable to men's in numerical terms and in the variety of roles.

As benefactors, wives could act together with their husbands, part of a pious couple who created and/or endowed a small new institution, a shelter for sick people, orphaned children or poor widows; women, however, acted also as individuals or in associations – mixed or female-only *societates mulierum*, bound or not by membership in a confraternity – often addressing the needs of other women. Of the myriad small hospital

---

[24] Vitolo and Di Meglio, *Napoli angioino-aragonese*. [25] Infantini and Toti, *Spedale*.
[26] Gavitt, *Charity and Children*. [27] Albini, *Carità e governo*.

houses run by charitable women we know little, since they tended to disappear with their founders. We know more of larger hospitals, where most women within the staff had dedicated themselves to the institution, donating their property (cash, buildings, lands) in exchange for membership in a community that would take care of them once they became unable to work. These devout *oblate*, *bizzocche* or *pizzocchere* were typically older women, since hospitals hesitated to welcome women of fertile age among their staff, because of the supposed disruption their sexuality could bring into the community. Some *oblate* were themselves former patients, and in fact the distinction between those giving care and those receiving it in late medieval and Renaissance hospitals is not always easy to draw. At a lower level in the hierarchy, many women were employed by charitable institutions for a salary, as cooks, laundresses and seamstresses. A multitude of wet-nurses performed a crucial function for hospitals and was employed on the same contract conditions that an ordinary elite *paterfamilias* would seek for his children, working frequently in their own homes in the countryside – the Ca' di Dio of Padua employed 2,279 wet-nurses between 1400 and 1484, of which only 48 lived in the hospital.[28]

Wet-nurses are part of the large percentage – among both hospital staff and patients whose provenance can be ascertained – of women that came from the *contado*, immigrants seeking work, a social and spiritual refuge in cities, where it was very difficult for women to live alone; charitable institutions were among the few central institutions with outreach over the territory that directly affected the lives of many women. It seems clear that the opportunity of an active life coupled with spiritual benefits attracted women; women were in turn necessary to the ideology of the surrogate family that inspired the organisation and dominated the language of charitable institutions. Borrowed from confraternities, the image remained unchanged when secular governments, more or less resolutely, took charge of public assistance.[29]

Large hospitals of all kinds (including foundling hospitals) tended both men and women, and had separate male and female wards. As in the confraternities that run many of them, in hospitals women were generally excluded from the higher administrative or medical functions – they could not be *rectores*, *spedalinghi* or physicians continuously employed by the hospitals and increasingly subject to government approval and control – but the segregation by sex and the structure itself of the hospital meant that prioresses were required to manage the female wards.

---

[28] Bianchi, *La Ca' di Dio di Padova*.   [29] Terpstra, *Abandoned Children*.

Prioresses could in fact be very prominent. The prioress of the foundling hospital of the Pietà in Venice – a hospital run and administered independently, by decree of the Gran Consiglio, by the female confraternity of the Beata Vergine dell'Umiltà since 1354 – was elected by the sisters of the fraternity and officially approved by the doge.[30] The *gubernatrix* of the hospital of Monna Agnese in Siena – founded by the pious Agnese before 1278 and particularly devoted to assisting poor pregnant women – was always a woman (supervising the work of male and female staff), whose appointment was confirmed in a public ceremony by the bishop in the fourteenth century and by the *Priori* of the Commune of Siena in the fifteenth.[31] If such a level of autonomy and state recognition for a female administrator of a public institution is a rare occurrence, the Venetian prioress of the Pietà or the governor of the hospital of Monna Agnese, whose authority was so reminiscent of that of abbesses, was perhaps the closest approximation to the inconceivable notion of a female public official in a late medieval republic.

Women, finally, not men, were the main receivers of public assistance at all points in their life-cycles. Baby girls accounted for an average of two-thirds of all abandoned children; many domestic servants and domestic slaves (around 90 per cent of slaves living in Italy from 1350 to 1500 were women)[32] gave birth to their masters' illegitimate children in hospitals like that of Monna Agnese in Siena or left their children to hospitals; poor mothers from the *contado* were prosecuted for fraudulently abandoning their newborns and later offering themselves as salaried wet-nurses to the same hospitals; from the fourteenth to the sixteenth centuries, and increasingly towards the end of the period, hospices for older women without a family multiplied everywhere in Italy, overwhelmingly sponsored by other women.

Women were regularly the majority of the poor helped by an institution dispensing alms such as Orsanmichele of Florence between the Black Death and 1400. More strikingly, and in parallel with a similar preoccupation among fathers and mothers for their own families, providing dowries to young women became not only one of the main missions but also a source of anxiety and financial instability for confraternities and charitable institutions, large and small. From 1468 to 1500 in Rome two confraternities specialising in dowries for young Roman women were founded, and three more multi-activity charitable foundations added dowries to their charitable provision;[33] after the Council of Trent these same confraternities providing dowries would

---

[30] Grandi, 'L'assistenza all'infanzia abbandonata'. [31] Brunetti, *Agnese e il suo ospedale*.
[32] Cluse, 'Femmes en esclavage'. [33] Esposito, '"Ad dotandum puellas"'.

also become instrumental in state–church policies encouraging the conversion of Jewish women.

Being a woman and being poor – that is, a target for assistance – were concepts easily associated in late medieval Italy. Providing for women and their children was a powerful justification of institution-building and centralisation (a process in which women participated actively, often but not always in subordinate roles); in fact charitable distribution of dowries meant that many men received public assistance through their wives, a maternalist concept of welfare complementing a strongly patriarchal state ideology.

Legitimacy and fiscality, or the moralising state

Legislative and normative texts repeated that women were *fragiles*, weak, prone to 'fall', spiritually, socially, economically. Women's bodies were the repositories of everyone's honour, their husbands' and fathers', their families', their communities', their cities'. A well-ordered sexuality was a chief concern of states and another area where continuity and innovation in institution-building intertwined throughout the late medieval period. Ensuring female modesty and honesty was a long-term public policy.

Italy is where secular governments, as opposed to the church, first passed sumptuary, or spending, laws in Europe (the Genoese *Breve di Compagna*, temporarily prohibiting sable furs to trim hems, dates from 1157) and where the highest number of these kinds of laws was produced in the late Middle Ages. Sumptuary legislation had a variety of goals – including basic economic policies, the regulation of social communication and ritual, and the segregation of marginal groups such as Jews and prostitutes – but consistently targeted women, their clothing and luxury objects, dictating also if they had to wear a veil, or cry at a funeral, and occasionally prefacing dispositions with ample borrowings from the misogynist repertoire on the vanity, lasciviousness and sloth of the *sexo femineo*. Because wedding ceremonies were the most important occasions for public display of wealth, and clothes and other luxury objects were part of the bride's *corredo* or her wedding gifts, sumptuary laws can be considered precedents for the caps on dowries adopted, for example, by the Venetian government in the fifteenth century. Not surprisingly, sumptuary legislation incurred the same difficulties of enforcement as dowry limits, and revealed the same conflicts of identity in the fathers/legislators wanting to rein in luxury spending but also socially promote themselves and their families through their women.

Women, on their part, regularly eluded and sometimes openly resisted sumptuary legislation, which put restrictions on the only type of wealth that was securely theirs to keep or to transmit. Governments, however, were committed to enforcing the laws, recruiting, for example, parish priests among those who could check and denounce, and always deputing one or more existing officials (even the *podestà*) to the task of inspecting men and women on the streets and applying fines, which generally had to be paid from dowries when women were the transgressors (that is, in the overwhelming majority of cases). There are few but interesting instances of governments that, starting in the 1330s, created *ad hoc* magistracies, from the *donnaio* of Siena, to the five *Savii* over inordinate expenses of Venice, to the *Ufficiale delle donne* – from 1427 the *Officiales super ornamentis mulierum* – of Florence, although the competences of such offices tended to shift back and forth and the offices themselves to appear and disappear, not unlike other parts of late medieval judicial apparatuses.[34]

Charles II of Anjou and the parliament of the kingdom of Sicily issued comprehensive sumptuary legislation already in 1290, and so did in 1308 Frederick III of Sicily, and the dukes of Savoy and of Milan in the fourteenth and the fifteenth centuries. It was urban elites, however, both in the north and in the south, who most preoccupied themselves with those aspects of civic order that required a tightening of control over morals; it was to urban audiences that mendicant preachers addressed their virulent condemnations of women's vanity, as well as of sodomy, factionalism and Jewish usury. Where the fullness of state power was held by the urban elite – that is, in republics – legislation and institutional control over moral conduct appear as a coherent attempt to rally the powers of the state to enforce a vision of civic morality.

The municipalisation, topographic segregation and fiscal exploitation of brothels and prostitutes at the beginning of the fifteenth century are a well-known European phenomenon; in Italy such developments can be observed from Naples to Ferrara, from Pavia to Rome to Florence.[35] The prosecution of sodomy in Florence offers a more specific case in point of a coherent wave of reforms and new institutions devised by the city's regime between the 1390s and the 1430s to deal with matters of morality. After decades of legislation punishing sodomy, in 1432 the Florentine *signoria* created the six *Ufficiali di Notte* (the Night Officials), and gave them power to prosecute and convict men engaging in sodomitic practices. Between 1432 and 1502 more than 15,000 individuals were tried before the officials, and roughly 3,000 were convicted. The fines imposed in the quasi-totality of cases were far from intolerable for the rich, could be avoided in some cases and were further reduced in

---

[34] Kovesi Killerby, *Sumptuary Law*. [35] Trexler, 'La prostitution florentine'.

1459, on account of the 'ubiquity' of the sin (well known elsewhere as an especially Florentine vice) among the artisan classes.[36] Throughout the fifteenth century and despite highs and lows of this sort of activity, the state's appropriation of jurisdiction over the crime of sodomy translated into a degree of leniency, turned the promised exemplary punishments into a source of income through fines and reinforced hierarchical differences by punishing 'active' older men more harshly than the 'passive' young (who were also the politically unemancipated), equated to women.

Women's sexuality caused a different sort of anxiety, more pervasive and more complex than any other matter of public morality. In fact any state initiative targeting women – from dowry and sumptuary legislation, to charitable assistance, to the regulation of prostitution or wet-nurses' contracts, to the arbitration of disputes over female slaves and, of course, to the prosecution of sexual violence – presupposed an idea of female worth rooted in sexuality.

Perhaps there is no better illustration of the multiple stakes of state interference in the regimentation of female sexuality than the initiatives for the reform of urban nunneries between the middle of the fifteenth century and the decades of Trent. It may seem curious that in 1433, a year after their establishment, the Florentine Night Officials were given the added responsibility of safeguarding the purity of convents by controlling access of male individuals not related to the nuns. Nunneries and convents grew extraordinarily in membership and number throughout the fifteenth and the early sixteenth centuries. They housed the female scions of all the city's best families, having become the most important outlet for the 'surplus' of elite women generated by the *favor agnationis* and dowry inflation – a function that was explicitly acknowledged by contemporary writers.

Women's entry into religious life was envisioned as another form of marriage, a corollary of the image of the nun as bride of Christ. Prospective nuns received from their families a dowry (often ranging from one-tenth to one-third of a secular bride's dowry), which they brought to the monastery, and made their profession of solemn vows in front of a large audience including their relatives. Their social identity and relationships were not lost inside the cloister. Powerful lineages funded the construction of private quarters (*celle*) in the monastery for their women, who furnished and decorated them, determined to pass them on to younger women of the same family; if a family was the founder and patron of a female religious community it often negotiated

[36] Rocke, *Forbidden Friendships*.

privileges of admission for its women. A girl from the elite would often be able to join an 'aunt' in the family cell, and receive from her an education and special protection. The office of abbess or prioress, as a consequence, could be a matter of remarkable political sensitivity in the city at large, and a cause of heavy interference from the families and factions outside, of which the nuns became the active political terminal. In a city where factions had a high degree of institutional power, such as Parma, female monasteries were in fact an integral part of the dynamics of factional government and conflict.[37]

If practices contravening monastic or convent rules were widespread in late medieval Italy, anxiety about the discipline of female monasteries was equally widespread. As with sumptuary legislation, the republic of Genoa was first in attempting to take charge directly of monastic reform, creating a deputation of four citizens in 1459, then a magistracy in 1462 to oversee the reform of the city's nunneries. By the middle of the sixteenth century cities enjoying varying degrees of political autonomy, such as Venice, Bologna, Parma, Piacenza, Florence, Lucca and Siena, had instituted magistracies presiding over female monasteries, with or without a sharing of competences with the church. In the kingdom of Naples the viceroy Pedro of Toledo granted requests to the same effect to the *universitates* of Lecce and Nocera, but denied them to Chieti (where the local patriciate was perhaps already too strong in the eyes of the central government).[38]

Interest in female monasteries and convents was motivated by the opportunity to manage or financially exploit their properties: urban elites were keen to control Italian nunneries, which could be rich proprietors. Religious women, however, had a deeper relation to the identity of the city. The city and its inhabitants, rich and poor, needed the power of the nuns' prayers, a power dependent on the virginal purity of the nuns themselves. So, after the catastrophic defeat of Agnadello, in 1509, a writer felt that the prayers of the Venetian nuns – *meretrices* rather than virgins – had failed the city. Nunneries not only hosted plenty of the patricians' own 'blood', they were also a reason for civic pride and a symbol of the city. The civic meaning of urban nunneries was enacted clearly in the Venetian ritual where the prince doge 'married' the abbess of the Monastero delle Vergini in a symbolic wedding: the doge offered two rings to the newly elected abbess, in a public ceremony that marked his unmediated patronage over the monastery as well as the sacrality of the doge's authority. This Venetian

---

[37] On Parma, see Arcangeli, 'Ragioni politiche'.
[38] On the kingdom of Naples, see Novi Chavarria, *Monache e gentildonne*.

sposalizio resembled several similar ceremonies marking the new bishop's 'wedding' with his diocese, often represented by the abbess of an urban monastery, while at the same time echoing the ceremonial stages of the consecration of a nun.[39]

There were women whose religious charisma was such that both civic communities and lords were ready to fight to appropriate it. The 'living saint' Lucia Broccadelli was invited by duke Ercole I d'Este to relocate to Ferrara, in a new convent the prince had built for her, but the people and the priors of Viterbo, where Lucia lived, rose against the decision. Lucia reached Ferrara at the end of a period of diplomatic pressure between the duke, the pope and the city of Viterbo, and her prayers and prophecies supported the Este ducal family until Ercole's death; the family in turn sponsored her cult and deflected ecclesiastical suspicions about her stigmata. Another living saint, the mystic Osanna Andreasi, became the spiritual mother of the marquises of Mantua, establishing a mutually beneficial link between her own following and the political consensus enjoyed by the Gonzaga. Living saints such as Lucia, Osanna or the peacemaker Colomba da Rieti, protected by the Baglioni lords of Perugia, appear in Italian towns and courts with particular frequency during the uncertain years of the Italian Wars, and they sometimes temporarily assumed the function of local patron saints, protectors and protected, becoming a formidable source of civic identity and princely legitimacy.[40]

The reforms of female religious communities requested by urban governments underwent a dramatic acceleration with the dispositions of the Council of Trent. The enforcement of strict seclusion of nuns and the extension of the bishop's jurisdiction over all religious communities, including exempt ones, contained in the *Decretum super regularibus et monialibus*, changed quite abruptly the life inside most female communities, including those of laywomen modelled on the monastic ones. High walls, small windows and gratings transformed the external and internal appearance of nunneries and convents everywhere in Italy; the whole monastic building fervour of the late sixteenth century accompanied a drastic reduction in contacts with the world outside now permitted to the nuns; family identities within the convent were weakened.

The many women who had entered religious life as more or less willing partners in a family strategy found themselves forced to accept different, much more severe terms. Some welcomed the changes and even made themselves promoters of a reform that aimed to restore authenticity to the religious vocation of women, even if the reform seemed capable of

---

[39] Zarri, *Recinti*, 251–388; Lowe, 'Secular brides and convent brides'.
[40] Zarri, *Le sante vive*.

conceiving such a vocation, obsessively, only as a complete segregation from the world. Other women resisted what they saw as an incarceration, with vigour and occasionally desperation – like the Roman nuns who fled or committed suicide shortly after the closing of the Council's sessions. A number of nuns resorted to tribunals, both those of the church and those of the states, to obtain the annulment of their vows and the restoration of their share of their family's patrimonies, fighting legal battles against everyone, their own relatives and their religious communities, generally with little success.

Despite the magnitude and the ideological urgency of Tridentine reforms, and the great restrictions imposed on orthodox religious experience, in the following centuries many women continued to seek and find forms of religious life that did not exclude active membership in the larger civic community; cloistered nuns continued to read and write, to make music, even theatre, finding in religious life what appears, still, to be a privileged space of self-expression. The Council did not change everything, but certainly stopped and inverted the trend towards an ever increasing interference of states (via urban magistracies) in matters of religious discipline. It had espoused long-held aspirations of noble fathers, and avoided some of their contradictions.

Concluding remarks: women's agency and the state

Italian states between 1350 and 1550 seem to serve and embody the interests of the fathers/rulers who were serving and embodying the state; the protagonists and the beneficiaries of state-building were the same.

Women too, however, held official roles, even if they were excluded from that category of individuals that best represented the state, the *officiali*. Women too could be princes, even if a female sovereign remained a highly problematic juridical category and a highly contested political one. Women too were tax-paying subjects, even if state legislation tended to reduce their legal personality to that of a minor under guardianship. Women's fertility was both a blessing and a threat, as long as fathers were involved in the construction of the fiction of a male lineage necessary for admission to full political membership of their communities. Women were weak *and* dangerous; it was the state's duty to protect *and* enclose them.

These contradictions mark institutional structures and state ideologies throughout the Italian late Middle Ages, and seem to be the logical consequence of a state that is not only gendered but sees women with the eyes of fathers. Women taking masculine roles often, but not always, exercised them as champions of the same male strategies that generally marginalised them but occasionally gave them great power. This seems to be, for example, the attitude of pugnacious widows such as Giovanna Rasponi, who became the head of factions, engaged in feuds and envisaged their own families accordingly in rigidly agnatic ways.[41] Yet exactly because the state was a state of citizens/fathers or a prince/father, the image of the family or the household enabled women to participate in state-building in roles that were typically theirs, as mothers, mediators, carers, administrators and even special intermediaries between God and the civic community.

The strengthening of states (as exemplified, for instance, by the increase in legislation and the coherence of its enforcement) undoubtedly multiplied the limits to women's public agency, but could occasionally become for women a source of authority external and alternative to their families. The proliferation in fifteenth-century Italy of statutory limits to women's capacity to enter into contracts or appear in court, for example, imposed the presence of a guardian (still called *mundualdus* in some statutes) or a procurator in virtually all legal acts involving women; judges or magistrates, however, could replace family members as the women's guardians, and in some cases had to, because of women's vulnerability to family pressure, which the law recognised.[42] In so doing, statutes established a direct relationship between women and state officials, a relationship that women could occasionally use to their advantage. In Florence this very mechanism transformed the legal bond between widowed mothers and their children after the establishment of the Ufficio dei Pupilli (Office of Wards) in 1393: the Florentine state greatly limited widows' claims to their families' patrimonies and their own dowries, and, as a consequence, assisted them as the more disinterested parties to whom the wardship of children could be entrusted, provided that the mothers did not remarry. The office did not privilege mothers as guardians as a matter of principle, but did succeed in becoming the third party in a previously binary relationship between the children's maternal and paternal kin.[43]

The single most important area of direct interaction between the state and women (as well as a majority of men) was obviously justice. The encounters between women and courts of justice offer the opportunity to evaluate the extent to which late medieval states were capable of positing themselves as neutral arbitrators, if necessary deciding against the vested interests of individual members of the state's ruling elite. Matrimonial disputes or, more ambiguously, state prosecutions of sexual

[41] Casanova, 'Mogli e vedove di condottieri'. [42] Feci, *Pesci fuor d'acqua*.
[43] Calvi, *Il contratto morale*; Fisher, 'Guardianship'.

violence offer some of the most significant cases. Judicial sources do not easily allow us to disentangle women's interests from those of the people supporting them, but it is not impossible to follow individual strategies of legally savvy women, like the Venetian patrician Cateruzza Vitturi, who in 1464–5 overcame the resistance of her profligate husband Niccolò and obtained in court the annulment of her marriage.[44] The attitudes of civil courts towards women who sued their husbands illustrate how fully the state had embraced the paternal model, and how, despite the legal framing of women as needy of protection, courts protected the rights of husbands/fathers more than those of wives (most explicitly in cases of adultery).[45] The same cases confirm that a degree of domestic violence on wives was deemed normal, even beneficial, and the state never desired to interfere with that.

Women's active involvement with 'the state', however, is in late medieval Italy a historical object to be sought with cautious optimism. Judicial records confirm that age and social networks (perhaps even more than class) are the most important factors in determining women's public agency. Female legislators, public administrators or women founders of public institutions are, or should be, obvious actors in stories of state-building. Women acting in courts, producing legal precedents, commissioning juridical *consilia*, opting for church tribunals instead of state tribunals or vice versa, ought to be included too. An analysis of the state from the perspective of women and gender has already considerably changed our understanding of late medieval and Renaissance Italy, and is likely to continue to do so.

---

[44] Chojnacki, 'Il divorzio di Cateruzza'.
[45] See for example Dean, 'Fathers and daughters'.

18 Offices and officials

Guido Castelnuovo

Introduction

One of the main characteristics of the developing state, in terms of its internal organisation, is the importance acquired by the prince's officials. This, along with the development of the art of war and the growth of diplomacy, is one of the greatest novelties of the Renaissance state. '[T]he state is now concentrated about [...] two poles: the power of the sovereign and the hierarchy of "officials"' – or so Federico Chabod put it in 1956, when the binomial 'state–officials' was first introduced in contemporary Italian historiography.[1] But what state and which officials was Chabod talking about? And what has changed in historians' interpretations of the evidence over the past fifty years? In Chabod's view, the world in which officials assumed importance belonged to a precise time, and it took place within a particular political geography. Chabod's officials were characteristic of the 'state of the Renaissance', which he thought existed from the middle of the fifteenth century to the middle of the sixteenth. The Italy he was concerned with was above all princely and mainly Lombard, with a Milanese and Sforza bias. The result of Chabod's influential work was what might be called an 'Italian way' of studying officials in the later Middle Ages and early modern period, and I should like to begin this overview by pointing to three problematic aspects of this scholarship as it has developed subsequent to Chabod.

To begin with, an overwhelming desire to periodise has impinged on our interpretation of the evidence. Research into administrative history has long adopted a modernistic and princely perspective, presenting officials as the protagonists of a 'new' Italy, no longer centred on communes and their itinerant magistrates, such as the *podestà*, but rather on regional states dominated by kings and princes possessed of governing apparatus that were tendentially bureaucratic. Seen from this perspective, the networks of both central and territorial officials in the late

---

[1] Chabod, 'Esiste uno stato del Rinascimento', 604.

medieval and early modern periods, with their increasingly administrative profile, ought to be distinguished from the more political urban magistrates of communal origin. The point is crucial. On one hand it confirms the existence of a historiographical link between the rise of officials and the premises of the state; on the other it has actually fostered a historiographical divide between research on urban political society and the study of officials in kingdoms, *signorie* and principalities. Thus most present-day scholars of the cities and communes of late medieval Italy, whatever their historiographical background, have been shunning the lexicon of the state for more than a decade now. They have been minimising and in some cases denying that there was any form of 'stateness' in the political regimes that came into being in the medieval 'Italy of the cities'. And studies of offices and officials have been relegated to the margins of the socio-institutional historiography of late medieval communal Italy. The historiography has emphasised the gap between the territorial states of communal origin and the French-style principalities (such as Savoy) or the southern kingdoms (particularly the kingdom of Sicily), which have recently received much fresh attention in studies of offices and officials. In a wide-ranging research programme headed by Jean-Philippe Genet, on the genesis of the modern state, the parts regarding the Italian city-states are focused on written culture and civilisation, while the universe of offices and the prosopography of office-holders are absent.[2]

A second problematic feature of this historiography regards an increasing distinction within the old and established world of the communes, beginning at least from the start of the fourteenth century, between republican regimes and princely *signorie*. The communal magistrate of the thirteenth century is idealised as *homo politicus*, whereas the official of the prince-*signore* is treated either as an executor of his lord's wishes or as member of a developing courtly entourage. The official is a mere instrument, with no political background or agenda of his own beyond the earning of a salary. As an administrative representative, or as a loosely defined member of the prince's domestic staff, he loses his specific professional profile and his personal political agency. This leads to a further problem with the way Italian offices have been studied: the growth of a host of new officials is thought not to have begun until late in the fourteenth century and to have been restricted to the royal and princely sphere. Not by chance, the planning statement of one comparative study of Italian offices announced that it aimed to 'study the governing machinery of regional states'[3] in a royal or princely context

---

[2] See the contents page in Genet (ed.), *L'État moderne. Genèse*.
[3] Leverotti, 'Le ragioni di un seminario', 283.

only, insisting on the considerable difference between a princely official chosen directly by his lord and a republican magistrate usually chosen through the drawing of lots.

A third problem with Italian studies of the world of offices regards the selective approach favoured by numerous recent politico-institutional studies. Once the threshold of the Trecento has been crossed, the communal experience tends not to be read in a unitary manner: diversity becomes a driving concept. The result has been a series of refined, exemplary analyses of single urban, territorial or regional contexts, more intent on emphasising what is special about these contexts than on a broad or even comparative reading of the forms of government as a whole. Documentary and historiographical categories have become so differentiated that for the second half of the Trecento, and then for the Quattrocento, there is no research comparable to the *summa* on the world of the *podestà* edited by Jean-Claude Maire Vigueur.[4] Few recent surveys of Renaissance Italy have bothered to look at the larger theme of the rise of officials. What has emerged instead is a highly diversified picture, with regard both to states of communal origin and to kingdoms or principalities. Much is known, for example, about Sicilian offices, but very little about Neapolitan offices in the Quattrocento. Moreover, while we are very familiar with state policy, we often lack precise prosopographical information about the officials who carried it out. For the duchy of Milan, to name but one example, the classic works of Caterina Santoro remain our only resource.[5]

Italian historians of offices and officials work within a relatively narrow timeframe that does not correspond well with other European contexts (such as France or England). They look mostly at case studies from the Quattrocento. They have failed to overcome Italy's diversified political geography, whose differences they accentuate and rarely compare (kingdoms and cities; republics and *signorie*). And, because the study of officialdom and its history is necessarily linked to the *vexata questio* – at least in Italy – of the definition of the 'modern' state,[6] there have been ideological and professional reasons for avoiding it. These are the main difficulties confronted by anyone who strives to come up with a consistent survey of the history of offices and officials in the Italian Renaissance states.

Yet matters are beginning to change. For some years now there have been seminars and conferences in which the theme of the official has

---

[4] Maire Vigueur (ed.), *I podestà dell'Italia comunale*.
[5] Santoro, *Gli uffici del dominio sforzesco*; Santoro, *Gli offici del comune di Milano*.
[6] Chittolini, Mohlo and Schiera (eds.), *Origini dello stato*.

become significant. The 'Florentine territorial state' is so named partly because it actually had specific offices. The princely chanceries could also be seen as administrative training grounds. It has also become somewhat easier to work comparatively, whether by studying offices with similar functions in different fifteenth-century Italian states[7] or by comparing officials' work on different sides of the Alps, both in princely/ *signorili* contexts and in republics of communal origin.[8]

Let me attempt, therefore, a broad-based reading of the changing shape of offices and officials in Renaissance Italy, without denying the particular features found in each territory and each city. I shall start with the model most open to extra-peninsular European influences – that of royal and princely officials. I shall then move on to the Italy of cities and communes, while also taking a close look at the numerous differences between the *signorie* and the republics, presenting at the same time a synthesis that will also try to highlight some of the similarities between all these various central and territorial officials. And I shall conclude by briefly considering administrative and cultural changes that took place during the Quattrocento.

Kings' and princes' officials: from Sicily to Europe?

The years from the last decades of the fourteenth century to the middle of the fifteenth appear to have been a time of exponential growth for officials in the kingdom of Sicily. At the apex of power, the central offices became more and more specialised, setting them apart from the courtly entourage: such was the case for the treasurers, or *maestri razionali* (masters of accounts), followed, after 1414, by the *conservatore del real patrimonio*. In the territory, the 'justiciars', legal experts who also connected the centre to Sicilian elites, oversaw the administering of justice, whereas the city captains and *viceportulani* co-ordinated the lower levels of royal control in the towns.[9] Although a general reappraisal of fifteenth-century urban autonomy and growth is still needed for Sicily,[10] the nature of the connections between centre and territory is reasonably clear. These were defined by a political-administrative framework focused on the interplay of three interconnected poles with a reciprocal conditioning effect: royal legitimacy, government machinery and local political society. The urban elites at that time considered a post at the

---

[7] Leverotti (ed.), *Gli officiali*.
[8] Castelnuovo and Mattéoni (eds.), *De part et d'autre des Alpes*.
[9] Corrao, *Governare un regno*, 307–422; Corrao and D'Alessandro, 'Geografia amministrativa e potere'.
[10] Corrao, 'La difficile identità'; Mineo, *Nobiltà di stato*; Titone, *Governments*.

heart of a central administrative network so close to royal favour a principal source of income, prestige and status. Hence the perception of a political society in which offices and officials played an essential role. On the island, officials were placed on at least the same social plane as court entourages, ruling urban groups and aristocratic elites, families and nobility. We can thus present Sicily as an almost exemplary case of a royal and regional society strongly conditioned by its officials.

What is more, the example of Sicily has many parallels. Notwithstanding the duly noted differences, the kingdom of Naples and the principality of Savoy, to name but two, also appear as case studies of supra-regional powers with a markedly administrative character. These are most certainly states in the making. They are not models of bureaucratic rationality, the uniformisation of rules, administrative centralisation and a clear separation between public and private. Yet in Naples, as in Chambéry and Turin, the world of officials, with its central and territorial machineries, played an extremely prominent role in constructing political society and shaping governmental choices.[11] In both cases there were fundamental thirteenth-century inputs: in the south, the Frederician *Constitutiones* of Melfi (1231) and the early Angevin actions (ca. 1268–90); in the north, the statutes of Peter of Savoy in the 1260s. In each instance the governmental machinery proved to be tentacular, and towards the beginning of the Quattrocento it became markedly formalised. In the Savoyard principality, just as in the Angevin-Aragonese kingdom, the central administration developed around the classical triad of offices with fiscal, judicial and auditing functions. The administrative areas tended, moreover, to develop internal hierarchies and to become more specialised from the fourteenth century onwards. This led to the development of career paths within specific areas of government, permitting officials to detach themselves from court structures.

The professionalisation of these central offices did not result in their becoming separate from the territorial staffs. On the one hand, intermediate offices were developed, both military and judicial, be they Savoyard bailiffs or Angevin-Aragonese justiciars and, on the other, circulation between centre and territory was widespread and generalised. The officials, appointed, paid and controlled by the sovereign and his or her machinery, acted at the same time as both politicians and administrators. For this reason, recruitment was wide, drawing from the several groups which acted as protagonists in the regional political society, from the old (and recent) rural and urban aristocracies to the

---

[11] Ryder, *The Kingdom of Naples*; Morelli, 'Gli ufficiali del regno di Napoli'; Castelnuovo, *Ufficiali e gentiluomini*; Barbero, *Il ducato di Savoia*.

various city elites. Thus, as in Sicily, there is a three-pole virtual model: the royal or princely centre (court and administration), the baronial aristocracies and the urban elites. Within this model, while power relations were certainly variable (a greater emphasis on the urban component in Sicily, for example, or far-reaching seigneurial supremacy in Savoy), the offices are prominent everywhere as important social and political safety valves. They are by now considered essential tools of internal social and geographical mobility within a kingdom or principality; they are thus harbingers of prestige and status, both personally and in the family and community.

This by no means implies that officials and their machinery are the prince-sovereign's only tool for political action, nor that their activities are reducible primarily to the sphere of administrative rationality and political planning ability. Sovereigns and their elites also use other methods of politico-social control, including pardons, favours, immunities, court bonds, enfeoffments and ennoblements. Besides, the '*sovrano tutore* [guardian sovereign]'[12] is never the only one to benefit from the active presence of offices, which grow in cities, *signorie* and rural communities as well.[13] Finally, the administrative growth goes together with the establishment of highly significant non-formalised links, ranging from inheritability and venality trends in offices to important networks of patronage and mediation.

The undoubted complexity of each Renaissance polity justifies the great volume of studies that have contributed to broadening and at the same time modifying interpretations of Italian Renaissance states. I, however, shall dwell on two crucial points. The first, a more general point, is that no protagonist must be excluded from the dynamics and languages of power, especially the officials, who were one of the main actors in the Renaissance authority and political legitimation process. The second point, more specific, is that offices and officials in kingdoms or principalities have many technical and social characteristics in common: this feature makes them important protagonists in overall Italian political society, not just in the prevalent urban context. The Italy of cities of communal origin is far removed from the royal and princely model – broadly applicable to Europe beyond the Alps – to the point of being almost ontologically different to it. This singularity, at first sight, appears as much chronological as institutional and historiographical.

---

[12] Mannori, *Il sovrano tutore*.
[13] Chittolini, *La formazione dello stato regionale*; Chittolini, 'Organizzazione territoriale e distretti urbani'.

In the land of the communes: a general picture

Let us start from time-scale, which points to a somewhat late and often imperfect politico-territorial recomposition. The Renaissance states are often considered as still *in fieri* for a good part of the fifteenth century, even after the peace of Lodi (1454). Only at the dawn of the sixteenth century, in a period of crisis that also affects other European polities, do we see a more shared political evolution that prefigures the building of modern Italy. In this context, the descent of the foreign armies gave rise to a process whereby Renaissance Italy drew politically closer to the rest of Europe.

The succession of events in the states of communal origin, rarely linear, greatly favoured a plurality of administrative methods and a diversity of institutional outcomes. Present-day scholars thus talk of principalities and republics, *stati monocittadini* (single-city states) and supra-regional governments. From Isabella Lazzarini's 'phenomenology of differences'[14] to Ann Katherine Isaacs's Quattrocentesque and Italic 'polyvalent symbiosis',[15] the praise of diversity – every single city or prince seems to be a case history itself – is at the centre of recent Italian research. Not by chance, the coexistence of a complex set of 'modular structures' never uniform but always connected appears as a part of the specific character of the Italian way to the Renaissance state.[16]

From this perspective, the most recent research has mostly focused on the theme of the control of the territory, with special regard to city districts and rural *contadi*. The centre, its history and its social and institutional transformations, on the other hand, have been neglected, and only now the central mechanisms of government, the documentary choices and the careful prosopography of public agents and officials in different states have started to be evaluated with a comparative approach. We thus can count on many analyses of fiefs and cities (or communities) or studies on statutory rivalries and changes in justice rather than actual research about the central administrative machinery, as in the French context, or about the role and importance of officials in the framework of the political societies in question.[17]

The existence of an Italian 'singularity' is beyond doubt. It is a primarily urban singularity that can be read from a dual perspective: we face on one hand the 'Italy of the city' and on the other an 'Italy of many cities'.

---

[14] Lazzarini, *L'Italia degli stati territoriali*, 154.
[15] Isaacs, 'Sui rapporti interstatali in Italia', 119, 128.
[16] Ginatempo, 'Le città italiane, XIV–XV secolo', 160; Lazzarini, 'I domini estensi', 22.
[17] Details in Castelnuovo, 'Uffici e ufficiali'.

The Italy of the city refers to a common substrate of extremely long duration, the survival of an irreducible urban *libertas* that culminates in the fundamental and shared experiences of the thirteenth-century commune.[18] Urban setting and organisation and a communal political language were the bases of this common pattern in the twelfth and thirteenth centuries. Fourteenth-century proto-*signorile* developments varied the model without calling into question the long-standing pre-eminence of the values and the political languages of the city. The lasting vitality of communal roots in the fifteenth-century 'Italy of the city' is, after all, a fully acknowledged fact: recent historiography still emphasises the importance of this substantially homogeneous cultural, documentary and administrative *humus*. At the same time, however, a second Italy is revealed, an Italy of many cities and territories. Here, recent research mostly emphasises diversity, especially in the fourteenth and fifteenth centuries. The communal *reductio ad unum* thus risks being transformed into a kind of spring fair of Renaissance-inspired differences. Here, as we have seen, lie the roots of the historiographical image of Italy as a reality fractioned into countless forms of government, sometimes competing, sometimes superimposed over one another and sometimes statically juxtaposed. As well as the by now classical dualism between republics and principalities, what comes to mind is the distinction between simple state and composite state,[19] or the recent yearning to go 'beyond the city' in search of political, social and institutional peculiarities which do not derive from an urban background. This image of a 'de-urbanised' territory, as recent studies seem to present late medieval Lombardy,[20] aims to put the city out of focus: legitimate as it looks, this perspective cannot save from amazement every scholar used to investigating European regions – as most of France and England – where urbanisation was not so advanced.

This exaggerated drive towards typologisation has contributed significantly to the difficulty in comparisons. It also raises the risk of developing a chronological, interpretative paradox. In this paradox, the thirteenth century's Italy of the city offers a substantial degree of homogeneity represented no longer by the Frederician *Constitutiones* or the older Savoy statutes but rather by the communal political choices and the *signorile* options of the early fourteenth century. From the middle of the fourteenth century to the peace of Lodi, the overall picture apparently becomes much more fragmented. Finally, at the dawn of the

---

[18] Crouzet-Pavan, *Enfers et paradis*; Maire Vigueur, *Cavaliers et citoyens*; Artifoni, 'I governi di "popolo"'.
[19] Discussed in Castelnuovo, 'Uffici e ufficiali', 310–11.   [20] Gamberini, *Oltre le città*.

modern age, the crises and regroupings take on the appearance, by then, of a process more European than Italian.

We shall dig deeper on this topic, trying to understand how and how much this supposed coming together of an original widespread homogeneity (the Italy of the city) and a subsequent, more accentuated diversity (the Italy of many cities) influenced over the long term the establishment of governmental machineries and the nature of officials in urban and communal Italy. I shall start from the most striking and well-known fact of all: the multiplicity of institutional and administrative forms of government, exemplified, among other things, by the republics/principalities hendiadys of communal origin.

In the land of communes: officials in republics and principalities

In the multi-centric Italy of the cities, the centres and forms of power are so numerous that it becomes essential to analyse their political and institutional points of intersection, be they between the authority of the prince (and his court) and the power of the communal magistracies; the seigneurial nuclei and the princely machineries; the elites of the *dominante* and the political societies of the dominated cities; the administrative centres and the territorial protagonists. Moreover, the various factions in the cities – highly active in many *contadi* too – appear, with their deeply rooted and carefully coded administrative structures, to be just as much political protagonists as the territories, with their villages, seigneurial fiefs and rural (local or valley) communities.[21]

The different fiscal and financial strategies of republics and principalities further strengthen the impression that Renaissance Italy of communal lineage has its very own brand of administrative plurality. I shall limit myself to dealing briefly with the range of 'republican' choices.[22] The existence, in both Florence and Venice, of a consolidated public debt (*Monte*) has important consequences for the profile of the governmental machinery and some of the characteristics of its officials. Thus, from at least the middle of the fourteenth century onwards, wherever a *Monte* was established, controlling bodies of magistrates developed, the equivalents of which were not to be found anywhere else. Furthermore, these particular forms of public funding greatly limited the technical recourse to venality by offices and officials in the republics. As well as having technical-administrative effects, the *Monte* tended to lead to a more

---

[21] Gentile (ed.), *Guelfi e ghibellini*.
[22] Ginatempo, 'Spunti comparativi'; Ginatempo, 'Finanze e fiscalità'.

general political involvement of the *cives* of the *dominante* and a preferential recourse to their elites, these being the only groups with the right/duty to contribute to it.

The comparison between republics and principalities also concerns the provenance and recruitment of officials. In the republics, the choice of officials appointed by the centre is mostly geographically and socially restricted to the ruling groups of the *dominante*.[23] Many principalities, on the other hand, draw on a broader pool of administrative recruitment, involving in the competition for offices not only members of the subject urban elites, but also men who, while of proven princely loyalty, were extrinsic to the country, such as the fellow adventurers of long-time *condottiere* Francesco Sforza. The upward mobility opportunities for individual officials thus appear more ample and lasting, being able to count not only on their familiarity with the court but also their own professional attitudes: Cicco Simonetta, first secretary and councillor of Francesco Sforza, is an outstanding example of this phenomenon.[24]

Regarding this, historians have often underlined that political knowhow is brought to the fore rather than purely administrative action. Among others, the Florentine *dominio* was indeed safeguarded by magistrates elected by the Florentine regime, provided with political rather than administrative duties, and much more interested in conserving the city's territorial hegemony than administering it in the technical sense.[25] However, according to more recent studies, the development of magistracies and offices in the Florentine state, both central and peripheral, had reached a level of complexity almost analogous to that of the more celebrated Sicilian kingdom, and many of its officials were actually more urban or territorial administrators than political agents of the Florentine regime.[26]

In summarising these institutional and administrative diversities, we should take into account that Italian officials in the late Middle Ages acted in greatly different environments. Not only were the various polities composed of a plurality of centres of power, especially in urban and communal contexts, but they also showed a great array of governmental practices related to the specificity of each political structure. The classical example is the distinction between republics and principalities: they differed both technically (regarding financial, fiscal and documentary

---

[23] De Angelis, 'Ufficiali e uffici'. A partly different picture for the Venetian Terraferma emerges in Viggiano, *Governanti e governati*.
[24] Fubini, *Italia quattrocentesca*, 107–35; Leverotti, '*Diligentia, obedientia, fides*'.
[25] Zorzi, 'Gli ufficiali territoriali', 192, 198, 204, discussed in Mannori, 'Lo stato di Firenze'.
[26] Zorzi and Connell (eds.), *Lo stato territoriale*.

practices) and on the socio-administrative level (regarding geopolitical origins, recruitment methods and professional privileges of officials).

An initial, partial meeting point between these marked institutional divergences can be found in the politico-administrative choices linked to the organisation of the territory. Regarding territorial control, both republican and princely states elaborated three common strategies. First, a simple recovery, *pro domo sua* by the prince or the *dominante*, of previous administrative networks of communal origin through which local political practices are legitimised: the long-term survival of the *podestà* and/or the persistence of the statutory pre-eminence of the city over the territory. A broader-based reorganisation of the districts, as in Florence, for example, is a second option, aiming to make each dominated city and its district directly subject to the *dominante* by sending into the territory agents acting under central command and with wide-ranging powers. The last option is to develop some intermediate control mechanisms, as princely commissioners (*commissari*) or provincial governors, as partly set up, for example, by the fifteenth-century papal states.[27]

Whatever the preferred strategy, still one really essential fact remains: urban and communal (at times proto-*signorile*) based politico-administrative models can continue to play a decisive role in the late medieval development of offices and officials well into the Quattrocento. Vercelli is a peripheral, and yet exemplary, case in point. The city, dominated by the Visconti of Milan since the previous century, was taken by Savoy in 1427: Vercelli should have been rapidly included in the administrative structures of the Alpine principality. Nevertheless, fifteen years later, the situation was still complex. Technically speaking, the Vercelli officials were integrated into the Savoy territorial administration. The duke appointed them, the general treasury paid them, and yet their organisation reflected that of the city's previous institutions. Whereas in other Savoy lands the territorial agents were few and homogeneous (bailiff, squire, judge and, in Piedmont, also *podestà*, vicar and *clavario*), in Vercelli the officials receiving a ducal payment numbered more than twenty. Here, as in other post-communal environments, the administrative memory was two-fold: the original layer was represented by the communal offices (*podestà*, chancellor, judges and notaries); the fourteenth-century addition can be referred to as the first *signorile dominio*, with its Viscontian referendaries, captains and military squires.[28] Thus, in Vercelli, well into the Quattrocento, there were three

---

[27] Carocci, 'Governo papale e città', 165–7, 197–9.
[28] Castelnuovo, 'Quels offices', 13, 36–7.

superimposed institutional models: the commune, the first *signore* and the last prince. In Vercelli, as in the papal states or the Venetian Terraferma, the officials are an institutional and administrative vector capable of both attenuating established diversities and fostering new affinities in the very heart of the Italy of the city. These analogies, at the very least, concern the methods of controlling the territory and the long-standing flexible profile of the central administrative structures.

Communes, principalities, kingdoms: central and territorial officials

More recently, historiography has dwelt greatly on an apparent paradox represented by the dialectic between the opportunity for close control of the territory and the modest scale of the interventions into local government practices still strongly conditioned by communal and rural-seigneurial systems in the Italian states in the making from the Trecento onwards. What could be the profile of the territorial officials, considering that the politico-military expansion of the Renaissance states was recent and that, in the subject cities and their districts, it was accompanied by hardened institutional and administrative rivalries, often legally sanctioned in surrender pacts made by the citizens? Without question, the territorial interventionist mindset of principalities and *dominanti* maintains a strong communal *habitus* for a long time: as in Florence, a city/*contado* dialectic could be transferred to a broader geographical setting to make 'a single big *contado* out of the territorial state'[29] with reference to both the direct control of the territory and the development of a multi-form hierarchy of subject cities. In global terms, the importance of social mediations and territorial political pluralism does not exclude increased administrative action by the centre. The joint interest of princes (or *dominanti*) and subject cities often comes back to the taming of the *contado*, its villages and its *signori*, to avoid the marked political and demographic regression experimented by some cities in the Po valley. This crisis in Parma had got to the point where no man from the Apennines *contado* intended to obey 'either the signore, or the *podestà* or the officials of Parma' any more.[30]

Hence, the role of the territorial agents, as 'local terminals of power',[31] was far from simple. Above all, they had to deal with what existed

---

[29] Zorzi, 'L'organizzazione del territorio', 348.
[30] Varanini, 'Governi principeschi', 119. On the dynamics between the commune, the seigneurial powers and the Visconti, see Gentile, *Terra e poteri*; Gamberini, *La città assediata*.
[31] Varanini, 'Gli ufficiali veneziani', 162.

already, as the late medieval ambiguity surrounding the figures of the *podestà* or commissioner/rector clearly shows. The *podestà*, having a centuries-old pedigree of urban and even rural institutional deep-rootedness, was still an expression of municipal autonomy and acted as an intermediary between the city he operated in and the centre that was making every effort to dominate it. Even if he was ever more frequently appointed, or at least controlled, by the centre, his institutional physiognomy had forcefully communal connotations: a wide-ranging geographical-administrative circulation, an essential representative function in the communities (urban, village, rural, valley) and a daily obligation to respect their statutes.[32] The second, more recent figure, the commissary (Milan, Mantua, Ferrara)[33] or the 'rector' (Venice, Florence, papal states),[34] designated a temporary agent appointed by the centre and generally recruited from within its elites.

With the introduction of commissaries and rectors, principalities and *dominanti* strove to loosen the very strong bond between each city and its territory or, rather, between commune and *contado*. This separation was pursued by divergent methods, but for a long time its effectiveness was limited; its scope, however, was almost always the same: to lessen the original autonomy at the municipal and local level. And so, the old urban magistracies were flanked by new agents (among them referendaries)[35] directly delegated from the centre. Princes and *dominanti* also started to take over the appointing of local control officials, and the number of interventions on city statutes multiplied, although without necessarily changing the hierarchies of the sources of law.

Furthermore, these 'connecting' officials had to deal with a not always entirely legitimised regional centre (urban, *signorile* and princely) and, locally, with a city whose councils and magistrates often paid their salaries. They were officials that both parties expected to control. This is attested, in the whole of Italy, by the existence of a practice technically unknown north of the Alps: the *sindacato*. This procedure, of evident communal origin, had been established to allow the city councils to scrutinise the actions of magistrates and officials at the end of their mandate. It is interesting to note that the *sindacato*, in the fourteenth

---

[32] Maire Vigueur (ed.), *I podestà dell'Italia comunale*; Leverotti, 'Gli officiali del ducato', 36–9, 46–51, 56–7; Folin, 'Note sugli officiali', 110–13; Varanini, 'Gli ufficiali veneziani', 159–61; Grillo, 'La selezione del personale', 41–51.

[33] Leverotti, 'Gli officiali del ducato', 34–6; Folin, 'Principi e città', 33–7; Varanini, 'Governi principeschi', 117–20.

[34] Viggiano, 'La disciplina dei rettori'; De Angelis, 'Ufficiali e uffici', 81–8; Gardi, 'Gli "officiali" nello stato pontificio', 243–5. On the Florentine commissaries, see Connell, 'Il commissario'.

[35] Leverotti, 'Gli officiali del ducato', 40–2; Varanini, 'Gli ufficiali veneziani', 160–1.

and fifteenth centuries, was also implemented in lands with very few or no communes, from Savoyard Piedmont to Sicily via Naples, whereas it was totally absent in the transalpine areas of the Savoy principality, a world of lords and officials but certainly not a world of cities.[36] So, if the *sindacato* brings together various Italian Renaissance states, the insistence on the professional separation between central offices and territorial careers differentiates the administrative practices of the regional states of urban and communal origin from those greatly favoured in monarchies and principalities and the like, where the administrative upward mobility, linked to the territory, takes second place to a horizontal professional *cursus*, more inclined towards the inheritability of offices than to their accumulation.

Let us now look at the centre and its machinery, where, according to classical schemes, public functions are in the hands of specialists in finance, justice and administrative control. Apart from the technical nature of the individual offices, the low level of institutional formalisation of the central governmental apparatus until well into the sixteenth century is striking. In the republics, the central magistracies, largely unrenewed, retained more socio-political than professional-administrative characteristics, in a kind of 'symbiosis between government structures and *dominante* ruling classes'.[37] Florence very clearly shows this phenomenon, defining the two most important groups of magistrates and officials chosen by the *dominante* both in documents and chronicles as *offici di onore e utile*.[38] In the principalities, on the other hand, administrative success can be linked as much to the personal loyalty owed to the prince-*signore* as to the typical professionalism of career officials.

In general, the lower cohesion of the central administration and its officials seems to be the long-lasting administrative pendant of the urban memory and the persistent vigour of the structures of local control. However, Renaissance Italy shows various signs of a growth in the social role and political importance of professional officials. We shall look more closely at three aspects: the forms of administrative documentation; the models of institutional legitimacy; and the patterns of culture.

Administration, institutions and culture: some fifteenth-century transformations

The Quattrocento is a century noteworthy for increasing uniformity in the production, consumption and archiving of public written records.[39]

---

[36] On the late medieval *sindacato*, see many examples in Leverotti (ed.), *Gli officiali*.
[37] Chittolini, 'Di alcuni aspetti della crisi', 25.
[38] Brown, 'Uffici di onore e utile'.   [39] Lazzarini (ed.), *Scritture e potere*.

In Florence, the Archivio delle Riformagioni is expanding rapidly and producing many inventories.[40] More generally, diplomatic and administrative correspondence, political letters (such as those of Lorenzo the Magnificent), *cahiers de doléances* – with countless complaints put into writing by Sforza officials[41] – appointment records, sets of legislative documents and lists of offices are increasing almost everywhere. In princely Ferrara, pontifical Rome, Gonzaga Mantua, the Venetian republic, the Florentine *dominio* and the duchy of Milan, written public records directly connected to the world of officials grow ceaselessly. In around the middle of the fifteenth century, the traditional and lively urban-centric model that connected 'documentary tradition and the history of the city'[42] combined, in a decisive way, with new written records of a purely administrative character. These more concentrated and more efficiently preserved written records of and for the office are connected to a general growth in the cultural skills supplied by officials to their governments.

Throughout the whole of the Quattrocento, princes and *dominanti* felt the urgent need to legitimise their new powers. To get around the lack of a deep-rooted dynastic legitimacy or a lasting communal *libertas* whose limits were just starting to be considered (or feared), comparisons and reassurance were increasingly sought in imperial, royal or princely external models. In the quest for the necessary 'order' for 'governing the kingdoms and the powerful cities', to cite a proem to the Albizzeschi statutes of 1409,[43] what better example to follow, at least for an urban *signore*, than that of the '*serenissimi e augusti*' princes admired by the young Borso d'Este and referred to when legitimising the establishment of a new magistracy, the council of justice, in 1452?[44]

In satisfying this demand for politico-institutional legitimacy, the cultural professionalism of the officials takes on decisive importance. The Quattrocento was indeed the century of gradual change from the notary-chronicler to the (notary-)chancellor-humanist. This process at the apexes of political power is well known, be it with reference to the renowned Florentine chancellors or the grand Milanese secretary/chancellors. The two famous Simonetta brothers were ideologues of the new Sforza power, one of them, Cicco, being the right-hand man of Francesco Sforza in the role of first secretary and secret adviser, the

---

[40] Fasano Guarini, 'Gli statuti delle città soggette', 70–4.
[41] Chittolini, 'L'onore dell'officiale'.
[42] Cammarosano, *Tradizione documentaria e storia cittadina*.
[43] Fubini, *Storiografia dell'umanesimo*, 137–46; Tanzini, *Statuti e legislazione*, 50–60 (quotation at 54).
[44] Folin, 'Note sugli officiali', 102.

other, Giovanni, as chancellor, secretary and, above all, biographer of the prince.[45] This phenomenon arose in response to a specific request from the central authorities, and often derived from their immediate control. A new intellectual *koine* involves the whole set of administrative personnel engaged in cultural activities, both in the republics and in the principalities, at a higher and a lower level. These officials are the new holders of an actual monopoly of information and bring together the different political and cultural experiences of fifteenth-century Italy. Thus, alongside the more famous intellectuals-humanists who were often also officials,[46] the Ferrarese notary-official Ugo Caleffini is the author of a chronicle that incorporates both urban tradition and administrative practices,[47] and the notary-chancellor-humanist Antonio Ivani, a Sarzana- and Florence-based theoriser, writes of the 'decline of the communal autonomies'.[48]

These officials shared a common nature of itinerant medium of administrative techniques, professional practices and political cultures as well as documentary and cultural activities. They also enjoyed great opportunities for political success and upward social mobility and participated in the construction of reference models that were no longer merely inter-city but also courtly and, in perspective, inter-state. Could these officials, then, be the new *podestà* of Renaissance Italy? If this were so, we find here, in the circulation of collective experience and the establishment of common cultural *humus*, a clear sign of convergence between the secretaries of Palermo and the commissaries of Milan, between the judges of Savoy and the rectors of Florence.

Conclusion

The thirteenth-century foundations of the variegated universe of Italian Renaissance officials emphasise the differences in their points of departure: we find in the communes, the magistrates, that is, officials established in a strongly participative urban context; in other places, officials from more hierarchical, *signorile* or court-oriented models. These original distinctions, however, tend to be blurred from the fourteenth century onwards. The universe of the city cast off its politico-institutional unity, giving life not only to urban-centric *signorie* and future *monocittadini* or regional principalities but also to a new republican hierarchy in which the *dominanti* cities were clearly different to the

---

[45] Ianziti, *Humanistic Historiography*, 151–61, 210–30.
[46] Connell, 'Il cittadino umanista'.   [47] Folin, 'Le cronache a Ferrara'.
[48] Fubini, 'Antonio Ivani da Sarzana'.

dominated communes; at the same time, in the southern kingdoms, just as in the transalpine principalities, the role of the urban centres became ever stronger. Everywhere, moreover, the administration of territory emphasised the changing profile of a myriad of officials that were active between centre and periphery. It is here that the fourteenth-century premises for the political and social growth of individual officials were to be found, and these officials began to emerge, in the course of the fifteenth century at the very latest, as a group aware of its own institutional and cultural identity. Thus, a vigorous bond formed between the administrative post held (office or magistracy, at the centre even earlier than in the territory) and the social eminence of the official appointed there. Grafted on to this bond, in turn, was the increased prestige of the office itself, seen not as a salaried job but as a benefice. Certainly, we are still a long way from the sixteenth century's shared conviction in the almost boundless power of officials, who in the future will become nobles *de robe*, *letrados* or judges. However, already by the end of the Quattrocento, offices and officials, be they Sicilian, Milanese, Venetian or Ferrarese, seem to pre-announce their modern successors, who, according to the much reiterated *doléances* of subjects against their administrators, will live off a form of robbery that is known, public and unpunished. During the sixteenth century, after a period of much acclaimed growth and specialisation, the Italian office-holding class entered a phase of devolution in which both its effectiveness and its public image, by then fully European, corresponded well with the portrait François Hotman paints of the officials of the Paris Parlement in 1574, who, 'on setting foot' in the royal institution, wasted no time in amassing goods and riches, so that they came to behave 'just like little kings'.[49]

---

[49] In Descimon, 'La vénalité des offices', 90–1.

19 Public written records

Gian Maria Varanini

Introduction

As with European monarchies, so with Italian states of the Renaissance (from the fourteenth century to the beginning of the sixteenth), abstract models of a homogeneous sovereignty exerted over a territory by a central power cannot be imposed. In the 'long Renaissance', the form these states took is rather that of a composite reality, an open field in which different institutional subjects, dealing at the same time with the centre and each other, are apportioned significant quotas of sovereignty and important public functions. Simply put, this is one of the innovations of the past thirty to forty years which this book intends to demonstrate.

No reminders are needed of the close connection between 'written records and power';[1] any public authority, if it is to be considered legitimate and exercise social control adequately, must rigorously conserve, order and verify its written information. But rigour, exclusiveness and secrecy are what characterise the modern or contemporary state on achieving sovereignty. In the Italian Renaissance state, every different territorial institution corresponds specifically to the documentary sources it produces and preserves. There are many 'public' archives, and their characteristics reflect the actual structure of the state.

Thus, recent research has drawn not only on the archives of capital cities – Florence, Venice, Rome and Milan – and the better-known courts (Ferrara, Mantua), but on records of rural communities, subject towns and major seigneurial families, together with previously neglected ecclesiastical sources. In addition, traditional sources such as diplomatic correspondence (now back in favour) are viewed in a new way to study the 'informal' aspects of power and not just the diplomatic and military relations between states.

---

[1] Lazzarini (ed.), *Scritture e potere*.

The aim of this essay is to construct a 'map' of these archives and their characteristics to envision the overarching and varying nature of these politico-territorial formations. The chronological limits of this study extend from the second half of the fourteenth century, when the major urban communes began to expand and stabilise their supremacy in several regions of Italy (Tuscany, Lombardy and the Veneto), to the end of the fifteenth century, with the Italian Wars. Two circumstances influenced the shape of these archives in the fourteenth and fifteenth centuries – and the possibility of 'reading' them – at both ends of the time-scale: on the one hand, the transformations of the archives in the nineteenth and twentieth centuries; on the other hand, the communal and thirteenth-century origins of the documentary system of Italian Renaissance states. These two considerations have also focused on historical and archival research in recent decades.

Archives in the nineteenth and twentieth centuries

With this subject (to which I will return briefly in the conclusion of this chapter) I will now deal quickly. The institutional transformations of the French revolution irreversibly altered the relationship between institutions and archives of the *ancien régime* in Italy. Ever since the nineteenth-century state took over medieval and modern archives, making them accessible and encouraging their preservation, they have been profoundly manipulated. The marked contrast between the private and the public and, in the public sphere, between the 'political' and the 'legal' is reflected in the organisation of public records: a different concept of sovereignty, which characterises the modern (nineteenth-century) state, determines a different reading of the past and its evidence. In the Jacobean era, the principles of the separation of powers were applied to the peripheral archives of an *ancien régime* state, uniting court funds 'as office "precedents" [...] [with the archives] of the new state courts'.[2] It comes as no surprise, therefore, to discover that in the nineteenth century funds could be – and frequently were – reorganised and amalgamated, with the creation of new archives *a posteriori* – as happened with the *Carteggio sforzesco* in the State Archives of Milan, the result of combining the deposits of five separate collegial bodies,[3] or with the *Grande archivio*, created by the Bourbon kingdom in Palermo, which also included records originating from the city.

---

[2] The example quoted regards the papal state: Gardi, 'Gli archivi periferici', 798.
[3] Covini, 'Scrivere al principe', 8 and n. 31, with references to previous studies.

From the second half of the nineteenth century, the spread of the historical method in archival studies, still now substantially in vogue, emphasised, in contrast, the correspondence between the characteristics of an institution and the records pertaining to it, working in the opposite direction and sometimes resulting in the dismembering of previously united archives and the reconstruction of the previously broken physiological relationship between the institution and the records that reflect it.

Sensitivity to this problem is even greater now than in the past. The actual structure of the archive itself and its internal organisation are seen as bearers of precious information.[4] In any event, dedicating great attention to the panorama of documentary sources pertaining to a territorial state, as it appears now to the present-day researcher, with all its possibilities and problems, concatenations and ruptures, resulting from the decisions of nineteenth- and twentieth-century archivists, is now a precondition of any new historical study. In many cases, at the beginning of the more thorough research monographs, there is a chapter on the organisation of the documentary sources. As regards Renaissance Italy, the dialogue between archivist and historian has rarely been as alive and fruitful as it is today.

Thirteenth-century archives in communal Italy

What happened 'after' the territorial states, whose internal organisation survived until the seventeenth century, were swept away by the French revolution thus affects the possibility of our being able to interpret how they were organised in the late Middle Ages. Of equal importance, however, is identifying the basic lines of the mechanism that produced the sources and seeing how they were preserved in the archives 'before' the fourteenth- and fifteenth-century stage with the incessant flow of institutionalised power studied here. As the periodisation after this stage cannot be clearly defined, nor can the periodisation before it (i.e. from the communal and *signorile* age to the origins of the Renaissance state). Indeed, as we shall see, institutions and documentation then established a relationship that lived on for a long time.

The 'documentary revolution'[5] of the Italian urban commune has been a focal point for the analysis of the relationship between Western societies – in which literacy increased vigorously throughout the twelfth and thirteenth centuries – and pragmatic writing (*'pragmatische*

---

[4] Bartoli Langeli, 'Premessa'.
[5] Maire Vigueur, 'Révolution documentaire', 177–85. For the records of the Italian communal cities, see Cammarosano, *Italia medievale*, 113–203.

388 Gian Maria Varanini

Schriftlichkeit', to quote the familiar expression of Keller in his proposal for a grand collective research project).[6] As research into Italian communal written records continues to prove, the protagonists of this revolution were the notaries. By using their *fides publica* for the benefit of the commune, these professionals of the written word ushered in its political growth and institutional consolidation, creating a form of 'communal diplomatics' 'that proved itself capable of breaking down the canonical dichotomy between purely chanceresque and purely notarial documents, thus bringing to the fore a composite group of written records [...] highly dynamic and rich in variations in both time and space, which reflected the changing relationships between institutions and notaryship and between political forms and documentary forms'.[7] Collegial body reports, lists of citizens drawn up for various purposes, fiscal and judicial sources, *libri iurium* and statutes (no longer on unbound parchment but in *quaterni* and *registri*, adopting the serial documentation principle): all these were important novelties, giving substance and form to documents with remarkably homogeneous characteristics in the years ca. 1170–1220, which were then to differ partly from city to city and when, especially around the middle of the thirteenth century, the documentation increased impressively. Notaries were perfectly aware of their own centrality, and continued to be so for centuries. The statutes of the college of Genoa of 1470 stated with pride that all had to submit to the *fides* of the notary.[8]

In the commune led by the *podestà* and the *popolo*, the development of the city-state archive started as a simple deposit of documents (*munimina*), soon branched out into office archives and different documentary series divided by subject (fiscal, legal and military), and then kept pace with the increasing complexity in the bureaucratic organisation of public institutions and the growth of a strong identity and conciousness. Many are the increasing symbolic expressions of this self-awareness in city governments, such as that of the *biccherne* (fiscal volumes) of the commune of Siena being decorated by the most sought-after painters,[9] or the elegance and precision of many statute codes or *libri iurium*; and, on another level, the widespread practice of keeping statutes or accounts in the monasteries of the mendicant orders. But recent research has confirmed and substantiated above all that the creation and development of

---

[6] Keller, Grubmüller and Staubach (eds.), *Pragmatische Schriftlichkeit*. For a full picture of the research carried out in this project (1986–99), see www.uni-muenster.de/Geschichte/MittelalterSchriftlichkeit/ProjektA/litera.htm.
[7] Bartoli Langeli, 'Premessa', ix.   [8] Quotation *ibid.*, at xiii.
[9] Pierini, *Arte a Siena*.

communal archives was not merely a consequence, but rather an integral part, of the urban commune's institutional consolidation. Some of its main cornerstones were laid in the second half of the thirteenth century. These regarded not only the physical structure of the archives ('*archivum publicum*', '*camera librorum*' and '*camara actorum*'),[10] usually kept in the communal palace, but more significantly their functions, starting with the distinction between 'archive-*thesaurus*' and 'current archive' (or 'sedimentation' archive), one for the *Urkunden*, the other for the *Akten*, a basic distinction also applicable to individual office archives.

The laws made by an urban commune such as Padua, for example, allow us to reconstruct this process of distinction. Preservation must be orderly and in a specific place ('colligere omnes libros rationes et iura et protestationes comunis [...] in armario distincta per canzellos', where *canzellus* means 'shelf'), with the discarding of archival rejects ('ubi plura invenientur volumina unius tenoris sufficiat eis unum colligere'), and rules for withdrawal and replacement 'semper in promptu possit haberi memoria'. There are also specific regulations on the different types of documents (in particular, for diplomatic correspondence: 'acta et legaciones et relaciones ambaxatorum, litteras missivas et responsivas'), on the work of the *conservatores* who must 'create tools for accessing the documents' and on public use and consultation (with citizens having the right to a free copy of the documents that interest them).[11]

And then, in another crucial area, urban communes made use of notaries and their archives for the certification of private citizens' acts of which they were guarantors. In the 1260s in Bologna the *Memoriali* office was created, with similar offices being set up in other Italian communes towards the end of the century and the beginning of the 1300s,[12] showing that there was a widespread demand for these facilities. In general, it became the established view, later to be sanctioned by Baldo degli Ubaldi, that 'an "*ex archivo publico*" document is authenticated "*propter auctoritatem archivii*"'.[13]

With a few differences, the evolution briefly outlined here was homogeneous throughout the whole of communal Italy, which included central-eastern Piedmont, Liguria, Lombardy, Emilia, the Romagna, Tuscany, Umbria, the Marche and Lazio, to as far as Viterbo.

---

[10] Romiti, *L'armarium comunis della* Camara Actorum.
[11] Bonfiglio Dosio, *La politica archivistica*, 11–17.
[12] Tamba, 'I memoriali', 235ff.; Cammarosano, *Italia medievale*, 276.
[13] Bartoli Langeli and Irace, 'Gli archivi', 403.

In Renaissance states: public archives in subject towns

Why dedicate so much space to the records and archiving policy of thirteenth-century city communes? The answer is that not only the logic – what we could call the DNA – but also the actual administrative bodies formed at that time and, consequently, the documentary deposits derived from them, remained active and basically effective for a very long time, with some features lasting (*mutatis mutandis*) to the eighteenth century, the end of the *ancien régime*. In the fourteenth and especially fifteenth centuries, in fact, it was the cities of communal origin, both capital and subject towns, that formed the backbone of the Italian territorial states: not only in Florentine Tuscany, Lombardy of the Visconti and the Sforza and Venetian Terraferma, but also in Liguria under the commune of Genoa, the papal states, Emilia of the *signorie* and minor principalities, and even Savoy in Piedmont.

A large number of Italian cities lost their independence in the complicated series of political and military events around the second half of the fourteenth and beginning of the fifteenth centuries, but the archival materials of the communes, more or less controlled by an elite that acted as interpreter of the municipal identity, did not lose their importance. The administrative system remained the essential link through which power manifested itself concretely to the citizens and rural communities of the territory. The ordering of the documents reflected an urban-centric approach, varying in strength but constant, and never really called into question.

The town hall (*palazzo comunale*), sometimes rebuilt, especially in the fifteenth century, as in the case of the loggias of Brescia and Verona, continued to house the records of the city councils, the judicial archives and the fiscal surveys of the city and the territory. The city chancellor was often a renowned humanist, and the notarial colleges continued to be decisive. Communes promoted important archival innovations: in some towns in the Venetian Terraferma – Treviso in the fourteenth century and Verona and Vicenza at the start of the fifteenth century – offices (the *uffici del registro*) were established for the registration and preservation of private acts and wills, sometimes reviving fourteenth-century ideas.[14] These institutes developed independently along their own trajectories and, for a long time, the *dominante* government did not interfere with them. In 1571 Venice introduced a tax on the registration of documents in all the Terraferma towns – not because of a new-found awareness of its

---

[14] Rossi, '*Volentes falsitatibus obviare*', also for the fifteenth century. For Mantua in the fifteenth century, see Lazzarini, *Fra un principe*, 80–1.

public functions in the obligatory certification and preservation of documents, but simply to increase its revenues to pay for the defence of Cyprus.[15] Furthermore, communal archives continued to play a crucial role in civic identity even in places where the central government's pressure on the subject towns was much greater (such as in Florentine Tuscany).

Relations with central government obviously had important consequences in terms of archives, differing from place to place. As a general rule, city communes kept documents originating from the central power separated from their own. These documents could either be executive and regulatory, in the form of letters (ducal letters) transcribed in a register, or current correspondence, or formal documents drafted by the chancery (bulls, decrees or other authoritative documents). Documents also originated from the 'capital' for the central government's peripheral institutions, which were required not only to receive and file them but also to produce them independently. The paradox of the continuity and consistency of the archives being greater where subject towns were stronger and more aware of their prerogatives is only apparent and not real. In these cases, reciprocal relations were clearer and there was therefore more order and regularity; this is demonstrated by the example of the *Camere fiscali* of the Veneto Terraferma towns, as compared to the archives of the Visconti commissaries or the peripheral representatives of the papal government.

Archives in capital cities: communal tradition and new functions – Florence and Venice

In oligarchic capitals, such as Florence, Venice and Genoa, the commune-based archive system, dependent on notaries, retained their characteristics for a long time.[16] It adapted to the new functions of producer and collector of documents pertaining to (or coming from) a vast subject territory; it was modified and obliged to perform new tasks and, while being considerably reshaped, was not radically transformed. This could not have been otherwise, however, as the documentary culture and practice of notaries continued to be irreplaceable, and the communes of the capital cities kept a firm grip on the important functions of ordinary fiscal, judicial and military administration, in a not always peaceful interaction with executive power (the Florentine *signoria*, the Genoese doge or the Venetian Council of Ten).

---

[15] Sancassani, 'L'archivio dell'antico ufficio', 482.
[16] Roccatagliata, 'L'archivio del governo', 427ff.

The documentary and archival history of the commune of Florence in the first half of the fourteenth century is highly complex. We do not know exactly where the main storage place for public records – the *Camera del comune*, located in the offices of the *podestà* and hence in the offices of whoever held executive power – actually was: with the disorder created by the expulsion of the duke of Athens (1343) a great number of records were destroyed. This was the age of the first Florentine territorial expansion in Tuscany (Prato, San Gimignano, Pistoia and Arezzo and their territories were conquered in few decades). The equilibrium changed. In 1352 the office of the *Regolatori delle entrate e delle uscite* was established. As the name suggests, this was a financial magistracy, but actually pursued the typically political objective of breaking down the relationships between the cities and their *contadi*. It is not surprising therefore that the preserved records, although not abundant, consist mainly of correspondence, intended for the Florentine officials sent into the towns. The later expansion of the state, and in particular the conquest of the great city of Pisa (1406), altered even more deeply the mechanism of producing and preserving public written records. It was then perhaps that the Florentine government became aware of the complexity of the problems it faced, and this new-found awareness generated greater attention to the documents produced by the subject towns. An important role was played by the Ufficio delle riformagioni, which, from 1415 onwards, checked and approved the statutes of the state's communities (the *terre*, in Florentine administrative jargon), began keeping copies of them, and also conserved the *capitoli*, or rather 'territorial jurisdiction titles'.[17] Very soon, this magistracy accumulated a core of *munimina* – an 'archive-*thesaurus*' – of the territorial state.

Also of great importance were the material and physical characteristics of the documents conserved in the Florentine archives in the first decades after the creation of the territorial dominion. For a long time, the predominant form was unbound paper or parchment documents (*instrumenta*), *fasciculi* and *quaterni* (sometimes but not always bound together, *simul ligati*), that is, material that was often handled, moved, bound and renumbered, while well-organised registers were rarer. In the fourteenth and fifteenth centuries, there were frequent 'retrievals and selections of grouped unbound records for subsequent documentary sedimentation'.[18] Finding one's way in these highly diversified and scattered records could not have been easy and, in fact, halfway through the fifteenth century (perhaps earlier) an inventory of the *Riformagioni*

---

[17] Klein, 'Costruzione dello stato', 3ff. (quotation at 4). [18] *Ibid.*, 10.

archive was drawn up. This was ordered on a topographical basis (arranged by subject towns), as far as the territory was concerned, but structured by series with reference to the internal constitutional organisation of the Florentine republic.

All in all, the management of Florence's public written records regarding the government of the territory has strongly centripetal tendencies, which fit well with the guiding philosophy of the Albizzesco and proto-Medicean period, that of making the dominion a simple big city district. The archival consequences of the creation of the state are considerable, as borne out by the tens of thousands of *polizze* (individual records) reaching Florence from every corner of Tuscany with the *Catasto* of 1427.

Finally, in a very different context, further proof of the variety and complexity of the documentary consequences of the creation of the state can be seen in the importance assumed by the private archive of the leading family in the age of Lorenzo de' Medici. With its hypertrophic correspondence,[19] this archive reflects (as intensive studies over the last decades have brought to light) an exercise of power that goes even beyond the informal channels of personal and patronage relationships, and not just through institutions – but always relating to Florence and the Medici palace in via Larga.

In Venice, on the other hand, the strong communal tradition of documentary awareness – entirely city-based – had difficulty in projecting itself on the dominion. The archival consequences of governmental activity which, from 1428, was exercised over the most extensive state in Italy (about 30,000 km^2) emerged more slowly, and, by the fifteenth century, were relatively limited.

For one thing, the Venetians would not have even dreamt of dishonouring subject towns by carting records as war trophies, as the Florentines had done after the conquests of Pisa and the lands of Guidi counts.[20] Above all, however, in the archives of the main Venetian Terraferma offices, in the first decades of the fifteenth century, records regarding the Terraferma simply sedimented in existing documentary deposits. Certainly, in the senate deliberation registers, the *Senato-Terra* series can be seen as from 1440; and an appeals' magistracy, the *Auditores novi sententiarum*, was purposefully created, with a resulting independent archival series. But there was no active control over the subject towns' production of statutes, and nor was an office set up to store them; an archival series that already existed, the *Commemoriali*, was judged adequate and sufficient for the preservation of the *signoria* titles (*munimina*).

---

[19] Salvadori, *Dominio e patronato*.   [20] Klein, 'Costruzione dello stato', 14.

Basically, the function of the Venetian communal magistracy's archives was predominantly that of a passive collector of Terraferma government records; for example, the creation of *ad hoc* institutes (and archives) for new and crucial functions, such as military administration, was not felt to be necessary. Nor did the Council of Ten attribute much importance or dedicate much energy to these relationships, despite occasionally keeping up correspondence (as did the capital's other governmental bodies) with the rectors representing the Venetian government in the individual towns (*podestà*, captain and *camerlengo*). The magistracy assigned to controlling the most important peripherally located government institutions, the *Camere fiscali*, was not formed until 1449 (Provveditori sopra le Camere di Terraferma). Finally, it is significant that no offices with the specific task of governing the territory in extremely important economic fields (the *Provveditori sopra i beni inculti*, the *Provveditori sopra feudi* and the *Provveditori sopra i beni comunali*) were formed before the middle of the sixteenth century.[21] Often their documentary series began with sets of rules from the past in the form of *munimina* and guiding principles taken from the records of the Senate or other bodies.

These observations fit well with the philosophy and characteristics of the first-known Venetian archival inventory. It was drawn up no earlier than the 1530s – significantly later than in other states – by the *cancellier grande* Andrea Franceschi, probably acting on an impulse of the doge, Andrea Gritti, in the context of a *renovatio urbis* plan which was also *renovatio civitatis*, with great emphasis on self-consciousness. It was a detailed and extremely thorough piece of work but it took into consideration only the more prestigious series of registers of the more venerable colleges in the Venetian republic. The purposes it served were commemorative rather than practical and, the registers of the *Senato-Terra* being obviously included, it demonstrated how slowly the Venetian patriciate metabolised the growing economic and political centrality of the Terraferma.[22]

Signorie, principalities and kingdoms in the fourteenth and fifteenth centuries

We have seen above that the archival system of Italian cities and towns fell into a regular pattern in the thirteenth century. It comes as no surprise, therefore, to see that at the beginning of the following century

---

[21] Varanini and Viggiano, 'Gli archivi giudiziari'.
[22] Lazzarini, 'Materiali per una didattica', 54.

Public written records 395

the communal legacy was strong in cities and towns ruled by *signori* as well. The *signori*, established only recently, moreover, and not yet legitimised by imperial or papal vicariates, employed some of the *dictatores comunis* (notaries) who soon became their chancellors.[23] All the stable *signorie* (Visconti, Scaligeri, Bonacolsi, Gonzaga, Estensi, da Carrara and so on) soon began to apply princely models to the production or administration of certain kinds of documents, especially letters patent (or 'diplomas') – i.e. the chancery authoritative document[24] – and documents about pleas (*supplicae*) and pardons (*gratiae*). Thus, in each city or town, in a more or less consistent and regular way, chancery documentary series were formed. Furthermore, as from the fourteenth century, princely families started keeping administrative documents regarding not only their family estates but also public functions taken over or developed by the court. Although sometimes preserved separately, these records were frequently mixed and overlapping, as was more often the case in single-city *signorie*, where the greater proximity of the *signore* and the communal notaries simplified the merging of the two traditions. The actual 'chemistry', or balance, between communal records and princely records, produced and preserved in either the 'court' or the prince's household – where the *arcana imperii* are administered – differed from case to case. In Treviso in the 1330s, for example, it was in the communal archive that the extensive correspondence between the city's *podestà*, Pietro Dal Verme, and the della Scala *signori* was preserved.[25]

Mantua offers a well-known and significant example of a tendentially all-comprehensive princely archive.[26] Here the long reign of the Gonzaga *signoria* over the city (from 1328 to the beginning of the eighteenth century) and the completeness of the records (unharmed by the 'targeted' destructions that frequently occur in popular uprisings or revolts)[27] allow us to trace the physiological development of a princely archive. From the fourteenth century onwards, Gonzaga chancellors and notaries appropriated all public records from the commune, the previous dynasty (the Bonacolsi) and ecclesiastical bodies and stored them in the urban castle. From the fourteenth century general descriptions appeared, followed halfway through the fifteenth century by systematic inventories.[28] The *signore* was interested in 'documents attesting to his

---

[23] Varanini, 'I notai e la signoria cittadina', 44ff.
[24] Bartoli Langeli, 'La documentazione', 51ff. [25] Varanini, 'Pietro Dal Verme'.
[26] See the wide-ranging analysis by Lazzarini, *Fra un principe*, 1–88 (with references to Luzio, Torelli and Behne).
[27] De Vincentiis, *Memorie bruciate* (regarding the fourteenth century).
[28] Behne, *Das Archiv der Gonzaga*.

rights, his properties and the more significant political acts (treaties, leagues, peaces, etc.)';[29] anything escaping this pervasive influence, such as the archives of some public offices (the Masseria, the communal council), is lost.

Starting from the second half of the fourteenth century, in Milan and Lombardy the Visconti *signoria* acted differently. The political and territorial setting was more complicated than the 'simple state' of the Gonzaga and the communal documentary heritage more difficult to manage. The dominion was divided up several times from 1360 to the 1380s between Bernabò, Galeazzo II and Gian Galeazzo, which meant different residences, chancellors and archives. These various archives retained their autonomy even when Gian Galeazzo, by then the only *signore*, assembled them in the castle of Pavia.[30] But putting records together does not necessarily mean knowing about them or 'using' them. Sometimes, officials of what was actually a highly organised chancery, instead of looking at the archives, would ask the rectors or subjects themselves for information. The Visconti *signoria*, in fact, was 'weak' in comparison to the 'strong archival consciousness' of republics such as Florence and Venice.[31]

Just a half-century later, at the beginning of the Sforza reign (post-1450), the new duke Francesco I (known as the '*signore* of the news' because of the frenetic sorting of the news of his diplomats all over Italy) proposed 'governing with documents'. Francesco acted decisively on the archives inherited from Filippo Maria Visconti (whose daughter he married). Disregarding the previous fourteenth-century records, he regrouped, selected and recreated a *post factum* continuity, and ordered several inventories to be redacted[32] in the very years when thorough inventories and reorganisations were being created in the archives of Florence and Mantua. From then on, the Sforza archive was used regularly and frequently, with ever more refined methods and knowledge.

A new approach emerged, significantly, at the end of the century. Not only government officials but also humanists (such as Bernardino Corio) began to use the 'scripture di moltissima importantia [very important documents]' to support pro-Sforza historiographical propaganda. The divide between literary skills on the one hand and archival and diplomatic skills on the other was now becoming evident. When Lodovico il Moro needed an archivist capable of finding the documents

---

[29] Lazzarini, *Fra un principe*, 6.   [30] Leverotti, 'L'archivio dei Visconti', 3ff.
[31] Gamberini, *Lo stato visconteo*, 58ff., also for the comparison with Venice and Florence.
[32] Leverotti, 'L'archivio dei Visconti', 11ff.

deposited in the archives, a literary figure of worth such as Tristano Calco was rejected without hesitation.[33]

Also, in the marquisate of Monferrato, the chronicler Benvenuto di Sangiorgio used records for history, referring to documents from the marquis's archive in the castle (yet again, in a castle) in Casale in his *Cronica del Monferrato*.[34] Finally, for the same period in Ferrara, the multi-talented Pellegrino Prisciani, *conservator iurium ducalis camere et comunis Ferrarie* (in charge of both a ducal office and a communal office!) demonstrated his ability to combine archival-diplomatic skills with historical and propaganda interests, as well as with iconographic ones. He inspired the iconography of the frescoes in the palazzo di Schifanoia, and drew up the inventory of the Este archive in 1488: the arrangement of the archive reveals his various interests, as some of the cabinets contained both books and manuscripts.[35]

The growing importance princes attached to archives with ready reference of written records is demonstrated by the large number of inventories available for the fifteenth century, as mentioned previously. Their aim was to enable documents to be found: rather than 'achieving a goal of order, [these inventories] photograph disorder in progress'.[36] There was, however, an internal logic to them. In the nine cabinets of the Visconti archives at the time of their transfer to the Sforza, the order was: privileges (so the archive-thesaurus comes first of all), matrimonial records, oaths of subject towns, relations with the church and then on to the archives of the various lords. Occasionally, quantitative estimates are possible. In the archive of the Franco-Italian Savoy dynasty, which had introduced and regularised archiving procedures as from 1379, there were forty-five cabinets.[37] In the fourteenth century there were 12,000 archive units in the castle of Chambéry, whereas in the Florentine Ufficio delle riformagioni archive around 1440 there were only 2,900.[38] For the more important types of documents, the identification methods (common to different situations) based on 'figures, coats of arms or signs of ideogrammatic value'[39] (the 'book of the *Colonna*' or the 'red register') indicate an emphasis on single items rather than inclusion in series.

The archives of taxes and accounts offices were clearly quite crucial, being *pecunia nervus rei publicae*, and the *signori* had been aware of this for a long time. In the second half of the fourteenth century, the poet

---

[33] *Ibid.*, 14.   [34] Del Bo, *Uomini e strutture di uno stato feudale*, 117.
[35] Folin, *Rinascimento estense*.   [36] Rück, *L'ordinamento degli archivi ducali*, 146.
[37] Barbero, *Il ducato di Savoia*, 38–9.   [38] Klein, 'Costruzione dello stato', 15.
[39] *Ibid.*

Fazio degli Uberti notes, in *Dittamondo*, deploring the 'signor moderni/ che stan co' suoi quaterni/en camera dì e notte a far ragioni [modern lords/with their notebooks/in the chamber doing accounts day and night]', unlike the *signori* of old of the golden spur (*spiron aurato*) with their aristocratic and knightly traits. The form of these archives, however, is less recognisable in the fifteenth century than previously. In the princely chambers (at least in Mantua and Ferrara), there had been a gradual merging of the functions of the communal bodies (the Masseria, administration of indirect taxes, etc.) and those of the *signorile fattoria*, originally a private body which gradually took on a public role.

Also worthy of attention is that very singular monarchical state, the papal state, reorganised from the time of the pontificate of Martin V (1417–31). This reorganisation was influenced by many factors (differences in the relationship between Roman power and the *immediate* or *mediate subiectae* towns, various decisions made by popes, the extreme variety of political conditions at different places and times, etc.),[40] and its results were highly varied. For many cities, decisions were reissued constantly (the building of fortresses, stationing of governors or legates, etc.). On the other hand, the Roman church inherited a highly advanced and mature body of administrative practice from the fourteenth century, which compares favourably with any other state in Europe. The consequences can be seen clearly on a documentary level. Offices specifically linked to the pope as sovereign (the *dataria* and *segreteria*) were kept separate from those under the *immediate subiectae* towns and, in particular, from the apostolic chamber, which had authority over the peripheral officials. Thus, already in the first half of the fifteenth century, and with greater regularity with papacies in the second half of the century, a new kind of record was produced – *libri officiorum*, *libri officialium*, *tabula officiorum* (the latter under Paul II, 1464–71)[41] – which provided a systematic picture of the election (or rather, of the swearing of oaths) of papal officials sent out to the periphery. Towns and castles are listed in alphabetical order, a factor that is not irrelevant.

Significantly, the archive of the apostolic chamber became the collection point for the archives of the provincial treasuries: these documentary series, centralised on a regular basis, are now partly preserved in the state archives of Rome. In addition to this, in various towns, the archives of the legates and governors became remarkable (even if their wealth was achieved mainly in the sixteenth century) and they sometimes interfered and overlapped with the archives of the subject towns.[42] Thus, all things

---

[40] Carocci, 'Governo papale e città'.   [41] Petrini, 'La *tabula officiorum*'.
[42] Gardi, 'Gli archivi periferici', especially 810ff. for Bologna.

considered, of all the Italian powers it was the papal state that had the most 'modern' and organised archival structure.

As regards the southern Italian kingdom, research over the past few decades into the archival sources has on the whole depicted a scenario that is more nuanced and varied, and less empty at the 'periphery' than generally assumed. Clearly, the thirteenth-century Hohenstaufen and then Angevin sovereigns laid the foundations of the later organisation. The rules on notarial practice were gradually integrated but substantially confirmed up to the Aragonese age. The tradition of grand chancery registers (*Liber donationis, Liber inquisitionis*) was rooted in the Angevin archive, whose impressiveness was matched only by the destruction it suffered in the Second World War. Moreover, in the kingdom of Sicily, a solid documentary system established in the royal court, which has been studied in detail. The Sicilian urban system was polycentric, and Palermo (in particular, with the judicial fonds of the *Corte pretoriana*) and other demesnial towns, through their own efforts, produced and preserved important groups of documents, especially from the late fourteenth century onwards. These clusters of documents surpassed even the very widespread production of registers of privileges ('red books' – in Sicily, in the towns of Agrigento, Marsala, Noto, Salemi and Piazza Armerina). In the mainland kingdom, on the other hand, the archival framework of the cities and towns, for a somewhat longer period, was weak, because of a highly tortuous and confused political situation that lasted well into the fifteenth century. It was hard to get beyond the stage of the mere preservation (in a chest, or in a 'red' or 'green' register, as mentioned above) of the royal privileges and develop a current archive for routine administration purposes. In the late fifteenth century, however, the archives of southern Italian cities and towns (*universitates*) appear to have become more dynamic and alive.

Relations between states: foreign policy and the archives of diplomacy

As previously mentioned, the revival of political-diplomatic history (also with regard to the publication of sources) is one of the most interesting features of research during the past twenty years.[43] This revival has not been limited to the main protagonists of Italian politics (the largest states: Venice, Florence, Milan, the papacy and the kingdom of the south) or to international relations with France and the empire. It has

---

[43] Here, Lazzarini, 'Renaissance diplomacy', in this volume, and the bibliography quoted therein; '*Diplomazia edita*'.

focused on the practices of the 'system', looking also at the Italian powers that were significant only on a regional level (Gonzaga, Este and Montefeltro, etc.) and the complicated array of smaller *signorie* (in Emilia, the Romagna, the Marche, etc.) with their constant interplay of supplying professional armies, forming matrimonial alliances and entering or exiting from the spheres of influence of the major states.

Treaties and documents regarding inter-state relations were stored in the state archives, as can be seen, for example, in the *Libri pactorum* or the previously quoted *Commemoriales* of the republic of Venice (updated throughout the fifteenth century with the bilateral agreements made with external powers), or other sets of documents, often listed in hierarchical order by contracting party, starting with the emperor or pope. Increasingly intense political relations, however, gradually gave rise to new archival series. Again in Venice, in 1425, the Senate created the (now lost) *Relazioni* series in the ducal chancery, and at about the same time there are the additional fragmentary records of the *Segreti e lettere segrete* (1382–5) and *Commissioni* (1408–13).

Although historiography has for centuries focused on everyday diplomatic correspondence, recent research is looking, among other things, at the 'letter' as a text whose documentary flexibility and variety emphasise its use and significance.[44] The analysis of the growing mass of fifteenth-century dispatches, produced by resident or temporary ambassadors and sent to governments, still preserved in the archives of some Italian states (especially Mantua, Milan, Florence and, to a lesser extent, Venice), allow us to reconsider both diplomatic practices and sources. The practice of providing regular information was already widespread by the second half of the fourteenth century, both in times of crisis (see, for example, the Venetian dispatches at the time of the war of Chioggia, in 1379), and in 'normal' periods, as the Mantuan records or the *copialettere* of the da Carrara family (*signori* of Padua, 1402) clearly show.[45] But the real boom is in the fifteenth century. The Gonzaga archive contains thousands of foreign letters (and also many letters of the reigning family, together with internal correspondence),[46] as do the Sforza and Medici archives. The *signori* had their 'home' correspondence preserved and archived also because they were fully aware of the extreme importance of patronage and private relationships with their aristocracies, their own officials and followers, as well as with other reigning families.[47]

---

[44] Lazzarini, 'Introduzione', and the bibliography quoted therein.
[45] Pastorello (ed.), *Il copialettere marciano*; Lazzarini (ed.), *Dispacci di Pietro Cornaro*.
[46] Lazzarini, *Fra un principe*.   [47] Lazzarini (ed.), *I confini della lettera*.

In some cases – especially that of Lorenzo de' Medici (see above) – these 'informal' relationships attested by the correspondence reflect actual characteristics of the Renaissance state, almost to the point of overshadowing the institutional aspects of the letters and hinting at new and intriguing interpretative perspectives.[48]

Circulation of models and imitation of practices on the periphery of states: the archives of minor centres, small seigneurial states and rural communities

The strong emphasis on the importance of the powers on the 'periphery', either geographical (mountain and marginal areas, i.e. a long way from the capital) or institutional (sometimes in the form of allies or *accomandatari*), of the territorial states of the fifteenth century, or in the interstices between the different states (in the Apennines or Alps, in Emilia, Piedmont, etc.), is one of the more significant novelties of recent research. Two 'key concepts' can be used to explain the origins and characteristics of the archives of these minor centres: on the one hand, there is a general process of 'administrative intensification', regarding all social and political life and making it ever more necessary to revert to documents; on the other hand, there is a process of 'imitation'. I shall focus on these two different aspects separately.

Regarding the 'intensification', it is important to ascertain the consistency of the public archives in these minor centres (or 'almost-towns', quasi-*città*),[49] which, in Florentine Tuscany, Lombardy and the Venetian Terraferma or in the Este and Mantuan state, were looked after by a *podestà* from the central government (or sometimes from the provincial capital, even if subject to a *dominante*). Addressing this question means ascertaining the homogeneous dissemination of a shared administrative culture, and hence going to the very essence of the concept of state as a territory in which public functions are homogeneously exercised.

Many small centres, even when politically independent and resisting the expanding force of the major cities – up to the middle and sometimes final decades of the fourteenth century – converged spontaneously on the powerful documentary and archival model that had matured in the communal cities during the thirteenth century. Examples of this are Monselice in the territory of Padua, Conegliano in the territory of Treviso, and Colle Val d'Elsa, San Miniato and San Gimignano in Florentine and Sienese Tuscany. But the main interpretative problem

---

[48] Klein, 'Costruzione dello stato'.   [49] Chittolini, *Città, comunità e feudi*, 85–104.

is assessing the point at which the local archives were forced to change (in the fourteenth century they had generally been entrusted to the *camerlengo* in addition to his other duties) because of the rise of a new dominant city other than the provincial capital, in terms of both the depth and the consistency of these changes across archives.

Highly significant in this context is a Florentine measure of 1447 that forbade the election of non-Florentine citizens or subjects as chancellors in subject communities (be they *civitates*, castles or simple communities); but this centralising trend certainly did not stop the subject communities from actively pursuing the 'treasuring of their [own] written records for self-documentation purposes', a process in which the chancellor was made responsible for looking after the archive.[50] As regards the interaction between unifying inputs and a variety of concrete local situations, a good test for the Terraferma was the set of *formulae* devised by a Paduan notary, Giovanni da Prato della Valle, chancellor of the Venetian *podestà* in the Terraferma and the *da Mar* state (Istria and Dalmatia).[51] He listed twenty or so types of documents for which separate *quaterni* were to be created and stored in the archive in the *podestà*'s office. Political-military records were fully covered by the castle *registri munitionum* (stocks of cereals, as well as arms) and the *copialettere* (*littere misse et recepte*). The other *quaterni* covered justice (summonses, setting of terms, proclamations, examination of witnesses, civil and criminal sentences and damages awarded) or administrative matters (*fideiussiones*, distraints, dowries and so on). Other *quaterni*, on different topics, could be created, provided that they did not damage '*mores et consuetudines* [local uses and customs]'. And so public attitudes in these centres were strongly conditioned by coding, arranging and formalising. From then on into the sixteenth and seventeenth centuries, the practice of binding together the many documents (*avvolumare*) produced during the administrative mandate of a *podestà* in a single archiving unit also became widespread. Thus, in the archives of some minor *podestà*, a series known as the *Reggimento* was created. The elites of the local communities, both then and in the centuries to follow, had a strong interest in preserving these documents, as can be seen in a request to the Venetian authorities to 'obtain the old scriptures of the chancery [*ottenire le scritture vechie de la cancelleria*]' to create a deposit archive.[52]

In the network of institutions that formed the territorial state of central-northern Italy, archives – or rather 'depositaries of documents [...]

---

[50] Mineo, 'La dimensione archivistica', 383, 394–5 (for the quotation) and 410–12.
[51] Pagnin, *I formulari di un notaio*. [52] Varanini and Viggiano, 'Gli archivi giudiziari'.

or network[s] of traceable written records'[53] – became more evident in rural communities, similar to practice in minor urban centres. From the thirteenth century onwards, the increasingly positive attitude to literacy, promoted by the city government but also encouraged by the internal social and political evolution, inevitably affected the rural world. In the fourteenth and fifteenth centuries, the need to preserve routine administration documents as well as statutes, of great importance also from a symbolic point of view, intensified, as relations with more distant centres of power gradually became more frequent. In the Alps, archives were generally kept by notaries by both small *contrade* and rural communities and also, on a larger territorial scale, by communities further down valleys and the federations of rural communes. Written records were also kept by the so-called *Territori* or *Contadi*, institutions representing the whole of the communities in one urban district that became established in the fifteenth and sixteenth centuries and managed fiscal matters, whereas the points of reference for the seigneurial 'small states' were the grand courts of the princely states in the Po plain (the Este, the Gonzaga and, obviously, the Visconti and the Sforza). In all places, notaries exercised an all-pervasive hegemony by privately preserving public records thanks to the transmission of deeds and drafts (*imbreviature*) from father to son, a practice widespread in urban communes as well right up to the fourteenth century.[54]

The disappearance of a good number of these statelets – ironically termed *'spicciolati d'Italia'* by Niccolò Machiavelli (with specific reference to the Emilia area)[55] – was one of the most significant changes to the political map of Italy after the Italian Wars. It resulted, inevitably, in an accentuated scattering of records. The archives followed the course of dynastic, hereditary and matrimonial events and are not often easily reconstructable in their entirety. Even though the marquisate of Monferrato survived as an autonomous political entity, from the 1660s to the nineteenth century, its archive travelled from Casale to Mantua to Turin via Vienna.[56] The documents of the Pio family, lords of Carpi, near Modena, until 1523, are now spread between Ferrara, Carpi, Rome and the Biblioteca Ambrosiana in Milan;[57] those of the Dal Verme, *signori* of an extensive dominion near Piacenza in the fifteenth and

---

[53] Della Misericordia, 'Mappe di carte', 155.
[54] For all this, see *ibid.*; for southern Italy, see Senatore, 'Gli archivi delle universitates'.
[55] Chittolini, 'Ascesa e declino', 475 and n. 6.
[56] Del Bo, *Uomini e strutture di uno stato feudale*, 19.
[57] Clough, 'The Pio di Savoia Archives', 197ff.; Fiorina (ed.), *Inventario dell'archivio Falcò Pio*.

sixteenth centuries, are in Verona, Milan and elsewhere;[58] those of the Rossi of Parma are also scattered.[59] The archives of the grand seigneurial families of the southern Italian kingdom (Orsini, Caracciolo, Carafa) are partly in public archives, partly still with the families. The attitude towards records in these great aristocratic families, so important in the military and political life of the Renaissance, thus merits careful reconstruction.

There was no lack of specific awareness in the way seigneurial families managed their archive documents, as borne out by the allocation of *ad hoc* storage areas in the castle (*'in arce in camarino archivii scripturarum'*). Sometimes the archive was in the studio frescoed with portraits of orators and poets, as in the case of the Rossi castle in Torrechiara near Parma.[60] Sometimes in the organisation of archive material, an important role preserving the documents as a sort of *'archivum-thesaurus'* was played by the dynastic cartulary,[61] which lists and states the value of all the privileges and concessions obtained by the dominant family. For routine administration the small state made use of basic offices for the production of documents (the chancellor, specially appointed notaries, etc.) often in remarkable proximity to the notarial offices of the local capital.

Conclusion

The middle of the sixteenth century can be singled out as a significant turning point in the archival organisation of Italian states. What emerged, albeit slowly and in different ways in different cases, was a drive towards homogeneity, the ability of the 'centre' (either the capital or a strengthened princely court) to introduce practices applicable to the whole territory that would confer a recognisable physiognomy to the 'documentary landscape' in the different regions. On the other hand, at this time in the whole of Europe the *trésor* archive finally gave way to the 'sedimentation' archive.[62]

The signs of this process are many. In 1565 in the papal state Pius IV 'instituted a wide deposit to collect "everything pertaining to the Holy See"'.[63] In 1570 the grand duchy of Tuscany created a public archive of contracts to preserve notarial contracts, and important collections were built up in various centres in the territory, maintaining the distinction

---

[58] Savy, 'La famiglia Dal Verme'.
[59] Nori, '"Nei ripostigli delle scanzie"'; Zanichelli, 'La committenza dei Rossi', 207.
[60] Zanichelli, 'La committenza dei Rossi', 205.
[61] Gamberini, 'La memoria dei gentiluomini'. [62] Bautier, 'La phase cruciale', 139ff.
[63] Poncet, 'Les archives de la papauté', 742.

between the 'old state' and the former Sienese territories, annexed in 1555.[64] In the cities and towns of the Veneto, at the end of the sixteenth and beginning of the seventeenth centuries, public notarial archives were created and at about the same time the '*notarius veneta auctoritate*'[65] came into existence, with a notarial license issued by the doge and not by the emperor or his delegate. Thus, in both cases, a territorial network of archives was created; the same occurred in Liguria and Lombardy.[66]

In the eighteenth century, at the dawn of the upheavals of the Napoleonic period, the original impulses (in particular, the care taken by the cities of communal origin over their 'own' documents) prove to be lasting. The old protagonists, the urban communes, still have a role to play and put the task of reorganising and registering the judicial archives in the hands of notaries, as at Verona in 1770 with the appointment of Francesco Menegatti '*nodaro fornito di probità ed esperimentata abilità in tali materie*'.[67] He ordered the records '*per reggimento*', that is to say, on the basis of *podestarile* succession, as would have been done centuries earlier.

Despite radically altering the geography of archived documents and their accessibility, not even the French revolution marked a sharp caesura from the point of view of the city's centrality and documentary awareness. In fact, in the second half of the nineteenth century, after Italian unification, the documents pertaining to the Florentine and Venetian governments in many towns were deposited in the municipal archives.[68] It did not, however, happen everywhere. In southern Italian towns the post-Bourbon nineteenth century proved to be a period of neglect for fifteenth-century civic records.[69] But, in central-northern Italy, at least, these records, pertaining mainly to the archives of the kingdom and seen as an integral part of the institutional identity of each individual town, were of special interest to students of the municipality. There could be no more eloquent recognition of the irrepressible vitality of Italian towns and cities. The circle was closing.

---

[64] Giorgi and Moscadelli, 'Gli archivi delle comunità dello stato senese', 81–2.
[65] Pedani, '"Veneta auctoritate notarius"', 15ff.
[66] Giorgi and Moscadelli, '*Ut ipsa acta illesa serventur*', 93–4.
[67] Varanini and Viggiano, 'Gli archivi giudiziari'.   [68] *Ibid.*
[69] Airò, 'L'inventario dell'archivio che non c'è più', particularly 536 (for Taranto).

20 The language of politics and the process of state-building: approaches and interpretations

Andrea Gamberini

Introduction

The theme of 'political languages' is not only one of those most frequently discussed in recent historiography, but is also probably among the most difficult to outline, since it appears to include so much. Understood as a system for conveying political content, as a code of communication of which social actors know the rules, the meanings, the potential to generate new realities, such language can indeed be verbal, but also figurative, musical or ritual. Nor can there be any doubt that each of these forms was used during the early Renaissance to express ideals, to create consensus, to delimit membership, to establish hierarchies, to produce legitimacy, to shape identity and to define the contents of a new sense of the state.

In reality not all these codes were accessible to the same degree to all social actors; some seem in fact to have circulated among quite restricted groups, as in the case of some musical expressions of political language. Think of the music of courts: with texts in Latin or French and generally requiring complex groups of musicians, these musical expressions of ideas constituted a form of communication better adapted to horizontal and vertical circulation, among members of an elite (the only ones able to grasp the message conveyed by the complex relation between the musical and vocal elements) rather than among the many components of political society. Other sorts of music would be open to wider comprehension, in particular, sonorities understood by all and associated with a specific political message (as in the case of the sound of bells, which in late medieval cities and in the countryside were used to summon heads of families to communal assemblies or to call men to arms).[1]

Perhaps because of their particularities, these systems of political communication have generally been the object of studies restricted to a

---

[1] Bordone, 'Campane, trombe e carrocci'.

specific field, to their own terms of reference, and not always concerned to connect the results of the research to ideas about the later medieval state. And yet from the perspective of state-building, for example, such enquiries can be stimulating for political and institutional historians, above all since the profound methodological renewal they have undergone has brought to light the significance, not merely as propaganda, but also dialectical and constitutional, of political communication.

Such outcomes have been made possible by the increasing emphasis on key elements and concepts made by quite distinct disciplines (such as iconology, the history of ideas, political history, etc.) in exchanges of suggestions and methodological borrowings that have led to some converging results. First of all, they have in common recognition of the ample spectrum of persons capable of producing and employing political languages, of expressing the ideals orienting their actions: not only the holders of power, but also the social and territorial bodies of the dominion (communities, aristocratic lineages, factions, social groups, etc.), which engaged in a continuing dialogue with the holders of power. What seems to emerge from many fields of research is a new attention to bringing out the plurality of voices and positions confronting each other within the political bodies of the later medieval and early modern periods: a true dialectical confrontation, finally, which demonstrates genuine capability to shape social and political structures and the relations of authority between the governors and the governed. It is probably in these aspects that the principal outcome of the passage from the study of 'political propaganda' to that of 'political communication' resides:[2] not a mere change of label, but a real change of approach, which has substituted for an analytical perspective focused on the individual producer of the message and the connection of the message to metahistorical categories of thought (the contribution of Leonardo Bruni to republicanism, for example) a different perspective, focused rather on the relation of the message to those to whom it was addressed, and the interaction with them (what did Bruni mean when he referred to republicanism?). This is a perspective from which questions about the persuasive power of the message and its real meaning seem to be answered – as will be shown below – within the horizon of the notion of 'context', understood not simply as an element that makes sense of political discourse, that historicises the concepts and the vocabulary that articulate the language, but in a wider sense as political and institutional space pervaded by the representations of the actors, and influencing them in turn.

[2] Cammarosano (ed.), *Le forme della propaganda politica*, is indicative of this historiographical ferment, considering together diverse aspects of political communication.

At this point, it is worth recalling the cultural matrices that are the foundation of these orientations. It is not difficult to spot ideas deriving from strands, some interwoven, of the recent debate, from the *Begriffsgeschichte* to the New Cambridge School of political thought, from linguistic post-modernism to the iconic turn.[3]

In this chapter, I propose to focus on the areas of political and institutional historiography that have benefited most from these influences. In particular, I shall investigate the contribution of political languages – essentially the verbal, but with some consideration of the iconographic and the ritual, when necessary – to the construction of a new kind of state in the late Middle Ages. At the centre of the discussion will be both the content of the language – the various ideals advanced by the social actors, the principal themes of political debate – and the functions of the language, which political actors made use of not only to 'communicate', but also to 'act'.

The language of politics: producers and matrices

One of the most widely accepted interpretations of developments in the Italian peninsula at the end of the Middle Ages is that which sees the transformations in the political sphere as 'simplification': between the fourteenth and fifteenth centuries new forms of co-ordination and dominion (regional states) were overlaying the plurality of powers that had come into being independently from the eleventh century in the countryside (rural lordships) and in the cities (communes), noticeably reducing the number of recognised actors on the chessboard of international relations.

This is a reading which has become in some way 'classic', and does certainly have the merit of grasping one salient aspect of the constitution of the new regional states: their tendency to rein in the autonomy of those social and territorial entities incorporated in various ways into the state, but never losing their separate identity within it. Hence that characteristic of the later medieval state that has been demonstrated so clearly in numerous studies, the stratification of institutional levels, to which corresponded the subjects (cities, communities, rural lordships, etc.) that were linked directly or indirectly to the prince or the dominant city.

The aspect of these dynamics that has perhaps been most overshadowed – in part because much research has been principally concerned with

---

[3] The literature on this topic is vast: for recent works of synthesis, see Mampsher-Monk, Tilmans and Von Vree (eds.), *History of Concepts*; Chignola and Duso (eds.), *Sui concetti giuridici e politici*; Pagden (ed.), *The Languages of Political Theory*; Richter, 'Reconstructing the history of political languages'.

institutions – is the parallel process of sedimentation that also affected the political cultures of the dominion. The advent of the regional states, in fact, did not extinguish the traditional values and principles of political cohabitation that had been developed by civic communes, rural communities, rural lords and factions in the twelfth and thirteenth centuries. On the contrary, they remained as vital as ever, continuing to inspire the actions of wide sectors of society and not infrequently conflicting with one another, and with the new ideals put forward by the prince or the dominant city.[4]

These are aspects which have only recently been brought to light, thanks to the meeting of a renewed institutional history, concerned to emphasise the plurality of bodies and groups present in late medieval entities, and an equally renewed history of ideas, ever more attentive to the connection between political confrontation and ideological debate, between positions of principle and purposeful action by those enunciating them.

Clearly, aspects such as conceptions of power and the ideological content of relations of subordination are not a novelty in the field of the history of ideas. From at least the second half of the nineteenth century some famous moments of Renaissance political debate have attracted the attention of scholars interested in the political orders and cultures of those distant centuries. One exemplary instance is the literary duel between Antonio Loschi and Coluccio Salutati at the end of the Trecento, against the background of the great conflict between Milan and Florence. The apparently explicit character of the texts composed by the two chancellors – on one side the impassioned exaltation of the principality as guarantor of order and peace, on the other the defence of republican government as the sole expression of liberty – seemed to lend itself not only to introducing the discussion about the two most widely diffused constitutional forms of the late Middle Ages, but also to formulating principles postulated as being general. And it mattered little that the positions taken by Loschi and Salutati (and then those of Bruni, Decembrio and other celebrated authors) were in reality the offspring of particular circumstances, elaborated to achieve particular ends and directed to a specific audience. It is only relatively recently that there has arisen a new awareness of the social and discursive context in which ideas are formed, of their cultural traditions, of the careers of their authors, of the relations between the authors and the intended recipients of their works. Thanks to this awareness it has been possible to dismantle

---

[4] Della Misericordia, 'Principat, communauté et individu'; Gamberini, *Lo stato visconteo*, 11–30; Folin, *Rinascimento Estense*.

the nineteenth- and twentieth-century 'grand narrative', which had been responsible for the hypostasis of some elements of those distant debates: for example, crystallising the rich and varied elaborations of Florentine humanists into an indistinct and atemporal category of thought, 'civic republicanism', the expression of a no less idealised 'civic humanism'.[5]

Behind this rereading is the same new awareness that, in a related field, that of figurative languages, has permitted a contextualised interpretation of some celebrated political paintings. Take, for example, the most famous cycle of Good Government painted by Lorenzetti in the *palazzo pubblico* of Siena, and works with analogous themes to be found in Venice and elsewhere: in-depth studies have shown that these iconographic documents, although expressing similar subjects (the effects of good and bad government), did not constitute convergent contributions to the same abstract idea of civil coexistence, but were instead only the expression of the ideology of the regime that commissioned them and were directed to quite limited ends, which have to be investigated at a local level, in the light of features of the political and cultural context.[6]

These few examples will suffice to demonstrate an aspect that became ever more evident over the years: the impossibility of restricting political language to a single field of meaning, to an unambiguous political message.

This is a crucial point, which is worth emphasising. On one hand, the efforts above all of English-speaking scholars to identify some specific languages (theological, Aristotelian, that of classical republicanism, of civil law, etc.), each of them defined on the basis of a more or less coherent ensemble of tropes, rhetorical figures, *topoi* and forms of argument, should be called to mind.[7] On the other hand, however, those who have studied the concrete use of these same languages by political actors have observed that there were many ways in which they could be used: in fact, a different context, a particular selection of sources, an emphasis on some authorities rather than on others, perhaps chosen with the projected audience in mind, would suffice to change the logic of the discourse and to influence its purpose. Within certain limits, related to the original nature of these discursive materials which made them more consonant with some aims rather than others, the expressive

---

[5] See Fubini, *L'umanesimo italiano e i suoi storici*, in opposition to Baron, *The Crisis of the Early Renaissance*, and Hankins (ed.), *Renaissance Civic Humanism*; but see also Skinner, *The Foundations of Modern Political Thought*, and Skinner, *Visions of Politics*.

[6] Pavanello (ed.), *Il buono e il cattivo governo*.

[7] See the different suggestions on what political languages might be in the collective volume, Pagden (ed.), *The Languages of Political Theory*; see also Black, 'Political languages'; Lambertini, 'La diffusione della "politica"'.

potential of political languages was indeed very wide.[8] Thus it can be noted that biblical language was used by governments and governors to provide the foundations of a concept of ascending power (power derives from the people), as well as one of descending power (power derives from God);[9] similarly, recourse was had to Aristotelianism – a veritable mine of arguments – to provide foundations for antithetic models of government (monarchical/republican).[10] As for the language of humanism, that was no less versatile: if in fifteenth-century Florence it could be employed to legitimate a series of regimes lacking real ideological continuity, in the Venetian *Stato da Terra* it offered, in the same period, a lexicon for the affirmation of identity on the part of subject cities and the arguments by which *la Serenissima* claimed full *dominium* over the Terraferma.[11]

In a way political languages can be compared to bricks, with which very different buildings can be constructed. Nor was this the case only with verbal languages. If attention is turned to the language of ritual, analogous dynamics of resignification can be found. Civic Christianity, for example, was a potent ideological glue developed by the city-states from the thirteenth century, and was readily taken up by some regional states. As in the Visconti duchy, too, where the annual ceremony during which subject cities sent offerings to the cathedral of Milan, in token of submission to the *civitas* and its lords, revived – bringing it up to date and endowing it with new significance – a ritual that in the communal era the rural communities of some districts had observed towards their respective cities.[12]

The content of political language

If these were the discursive materials, the arsenal of vocabulary and arguments available for political communication, what ideas were they embodying? What principles of political cohabitation were they expressing? The historiography has recently tried to free the debate on political

---

[8] Lambertini, 'La diffusione della "politica"', 678. It should perhaps be emphasised that some linguistic registers and some ideals might be peculiar to certain actors and to certain social ambits (officials or communities, for example), rather than others. Compare Airò, 'Luci e balestre'; Corrao, '*De la vostra gran senyoria*'; Della Misericordia, 'Per non privarci de nostre raxone'; Senatore, 'La cultura politica'.
[9] Buc, *L'ambiguïté du livre*.
[10] Lambertini, 'La diffusione della "politica"'; Meier, *Mensch und Bürger*, 106–7.
[11] Fubini, *Italia quattrocentesca*; Viggiano, *Governanti e governati*, 22–5.
[12] Chittolini, 'Civic religion and the countryside'; Gamberini, *Oltre le città*, 89–91; Cengarle, 'I Visconti e il culto della Vergine'. For Florence, see also Ricciardelli, 'Le forme rituali', 20–1.

languages in Renaissance states from the confines into which the discussion of abstract constitutional models (republic vs principality) has forced it. To appreciate fully the meaning of the appeals to principle transmitted by the languages – beginning with that of princes and sovereigns – it seems necessary to begin by restoring their original polemic and assertive weight, recalling that these formulations were affirmed not in the context of a generic confrontation of opinions, but in that of practical politics, to bring about concrete effects. While some general institutional co-ordinates inherent in the new political formations – constructed sometimes around the central role of the prince, sometimes around that of a dominant governing elite – remained fixed, it was clear that the actual characteristics of the principality, and of the republic, were not set in the abstract, once and for all, but would be developed (and realised) in the ambit of a frequently lively dialogue between the top levels of the state, who were the bearers of an autonomous political proposal, and a series of subjects who repeatedly invested the governors with their own expectations, projecting on to them their own ideals of the *bonum commune*, of equity, of social peace and so on.

Among the many planes of this dialectic, two in particular are worth recalling for their intensity of communication and for their constitutional and ideological effects. The first, common to all the states of the time, is that of the exchange between the governed and the governors, between the prince (or the dominant city) and the social and territorial bodies of the dominion. In this case the frequent clashes on the political scene were accompanied by a tendency on the part of the actors themselves to formulate ideal principles, models of co-operation, most often expressed in response to precise demands (such as the request for a tax on behalf of the prince, which could give rise to a response from the community referring to ideals of political co-operation, to equality in the distribution of the fiscal burden, to the just prince who cannot violate custom, etc.).

The second level, which has been studied carefully with reference to some state formations – the dominions of the crown of Aragon, including Sicily; the duchy of Savoy in the time of Amedeo VIII – is that of the exchange between the mendicant orders and political society (the prince, therefore, but not the prince alone). Franciscans above all expended great efforts in developing new languages of rule, which could give birth to a mystic evangelical community in which the sovereign would be the guarantor of the new political and economic ethics of the kingdom.[13]

---

[13] Evangelisti, *I Francescani*.

In the complexity of these dynamics reside the reasons that explain why it is not possible to identify a single language of the principality, nor a single language of republics: each has its own peculiar story and its own characteristics. Furthermore, it may be doubted whether it would be possible even to identify a single language for a single prince: detailed research into the dominion of Azzone, the founder of the Visconti regional state, for example, has shown that the lord of Milan constructed his own legitimacy using different languages in turn, in accordance with changes in the political and cultural context within which he was operating (shifting relations with the empire, the arrival in Milan of Marsilius of Padua, etc.) and to which different styles of government corresponded.[14]

Rather than search for coherence and permanence over the long term, therefore, with the risk of reverting to ideal-types and metatemporal categories (the language of republics, the language of principalities, and so on), it has seemed more useful to historians of politics and institutions to study political languages using the riches of communicative exchange between the actors, thus bringing to light above all the plurality of political cultures flourishing in the fourteenth and fifteenth centuries, some of them circulating only in restricted social or territorial ambits.

To bring this confrontation between voices and positions to light, it has been necessary first to clear the terrain of analyses based on 'great authors', on celebrated pictorial cycles, on classic works of political and juridical reflection, to concentrate attention on the so-called pragmatic writings (letters, prefaces to decrees, preambles to statutes, testimonials, etc.), sources usually overlooked by historians of political thought. This has revealed the tendency, shared by all persons who were acting politically, to accompany their political initiatives with more or less articulate appeals to the ideals behind them: as the prince did when, for example, the motivation for his intervention was set out in the preamble to one of his decrees, and as communities did, when in their petitions to the prince they did not forbear to express their own ideals.

Historians of the early Renaissance have therefore begun to examine the texts of these appeals with great care: their rhetorical structure and choice of words.[15] As might be expected, these enquiries have revealed different degrees of awareness in the use of language: the conditions of political obligation expressed by peasants and recorded indirectly in the

---

[14] Cengarle, 'La signoria di Azzone Visconti'.
[15] Petralia, 'Stato e moderno'; but see also the contributions in Gamberini and Petralia (eds.), *Linguaggi politici*.

report of an official or the testimony of a judicial deposition were one thing; the preamble to a civic statute or the petition drawn up by a municipal council with the help of a learned lawyer or a scribe trained in the great tradition of formulating municipal documents was quite another.[16] Yet beyond these significant differences, what emerges is a confrontation of positions often based on ideals that were not shared. To the question 'on what does obedience to a superior power rest?', these persons expressed positions that were not only different, but often founded on heterogeneous and mutually incompatible principles of political culture. This is a crucial aspect, which has permitted a new reading of political conflict in late medieval states, within which were opposed persons motivated not only by conflicting interests, but often also by very diverse elements of political culture. Let us look at some examples.

That collection of values traditionally labelled 'civic republicanism' (equal political rights for all members of the community, decisions by majority vote, respect for procedure understood as one of the guarantees of correct functioning of the political system, etc.) has now been clearly delimited in the historiography.[17] Although a confirmed historical tradition usually relates these experiences to the urban world, some recent studies have shown that they were also firmly rooted in rural contexts such as the mountains of Lombardy, where they continued to inspire a vigorous political praxis even while in cities factors such as the 'crisis of communal liberties' and incipient oligarchical closures were rendering the distance between ideals and practice ever more evident.[18]

Yet with the advent of the regional states, the political role of the community within the new institutional architecture of the dominion became one of the points of most heated ideologicial conflict. Both the oligarchical republics (Florence, Venice) and the princely governments (the dukes of Milan) were in fact bearers of a political culture who preferred to prioritise – above all when it came to the government of the territory – efficiency and rapidity of execution over the observance of those highly formalised procedures that constituted one of the most characteristic traits of public life in communities. Hence the tendency of central governments (and of their local representatives, the officials) to bypass the mediation of local institutions (in the first place the

---

[16] For the importance of rhetoric in school curricula before the late Middle Ages as well, see Black, *Humanism and Education*.
[17] On the origin of republican ideas, see Skinner, 'Machiavelli's Discorsi', and Adorni Braccesi and Ascheri (eds.), *Politica e cultura*.
[18] Della Misericordia, 'Decidere e agire', 378. For a civic example, see Shaw, 'The language'.

assembly of heads of households) and to establish contact with socially prominent figures of the locality, privileging the individual, chosen for his personal qualities, over the community as a collective subject. But hence also the systematic discrediting by the state of the political culture of communities, whose practices of collaboration were condemned in a language of religious moralism, which represented as sinful some traits of local public life (insubordination became a manifestation of *superbia*; rivalry between groups or communities attributed to *invidia* or *ira*; etc.), while a new vocabulary of excellence recognised individuals whom the prince had chosen as interlocutors (the *meliores*, the *principales*).[19]

In this battle of ideas that took place in the states of the late Middle Ages, the weapon of discredit was often employed against those who appealed to political cultures perceived as antagonistic. Governors regarded as particularly dangerous the culture that inspired the Guelf and Ghibelline factions, who became the target of negative propaganda. Historiography has also fallen victim to this propaganda as, following in the track of representations furnished by governors and also of the homilies of mendicant friars, it has nourished a negative myth, in which the parties were reduced to a mere manifestation of violence and disorder. By contrast, an analysis of the language and the self-representation of the parties and the factions has revealed the capacity of the Guelfs and Ghibellines to construct an ideology of *equalitas* – balance and parity between the parties – as a condition for good government of the city and the territory.[20]

Closely entwined with the debate about the forms of associative life (and the difficult cohabitation of such divergent models) was that about the foundations of subordination to a superior power. Even on this terrain, there was heated debate at all levels of society. In some rural areas, for example, it was conflict between lords and their dependent peasants that revealed the existence of different cultural hinterlands which were not shared. To the culture of territoriality, which theorised an impersonal subordination to the holder of the *iurisdictio* (according to the Roman law formula, *iurisdictio cohaeret territorio*), the peasants opposed an idea of obedience founded on personal fidelity, activated exclusively by a decision freely taken – and that

---

[19] For the duchy of Milan, see Della Misericordia, 'Principat, communauté et individu'. But concerning Florentine intolerance of community formalisms, see Fubini, *Italia quattrocentesca*, 136ff.
[20] Gentile, 'Discorsi sulle fazioni, discorsi delle fazioni'; Della Misericordia, 'Dividersi per governarsi'. For the language of Guelfs, see Ferente, 'Guelphs!'

could therefore be reversed at any moment – by the individual villein to *confugere* in the *castrum* of the lord.[21]

But in reality the polemic over the foundations of obedience cut across the whole of society, fostered by the diffusion of principles of pactism which offered strong bases for argument. Between the fourteenth and fifteenth centuries it was not rare to encounter communities that opposed the power of local lords and of the prince himself, invoking respect for obligations sanctioned by the deed of submission or feudal subordination.[22] Local lords in their turn claimed of the prince an obligation to respect privileges granted to them or their ancestors. In effect, in some polities, such as the kingdom of Sicily, the culture of pactism had become shared by the governed and the governors, almost as a cornerstone of the constitution. Elsewhere, however, the picture was less clearly delineated, and appeals on the part of territorial entities for obligations to be respected that were not defined in terms of reciprocity, or that the communities themselves placed within a vague, almost mythical, temporal horizon, constituted a weapon used in the ambit of confrontation with superiors, like the threat of exercising that right of resistance whose contents were being worked out at the time *in puncto iuris*.[23] In this vision of political relations the foundations of obedience resided in fact in the observance of a (real or mythical) pact, which all the contracting parties must observe, beginning with the prince, who was also invested with the function of guarantor of the contractual obligations. It was over just this point that there was one of the most heated ideological conflicts. Because although the idea of the prince as the dispenser of justice, *executor iustitiae*, according to the formula of Thomas Aquinas, was widely shared in the society of the time, interpretations of the content of princely justice varied. What is a just prince? He who disposes scrupulous respect for pacts and custom, as the territorial bodies called for, or he who smoothes the way for their evasion according to the superior claims of equity, as some princes asserted? He who refers the people to statutary legislation, to local ordinances, guaranteeing their careful observance, or he who in the name of the efficiency of the system reserves to himself *arbitrium* to derogate from pacts, from laws and from tradition? In the confrontation with territorial bodies, not a few princes advanced this latter thesis, to accompany the development of more authoritarian traits of government.[24] Moreover,

---

[21] Gamberini, *Lo stato visconteo*, 203–30.   [22] De Benedictis, *Repubblica per contratto*.
[23] Della Misericordia, 'Per non privarci de nostre raxone'; De Benedictis, *Rebellare – resistere*.
[24] Gamberini, *La città assediata*, 249–58.

the tendency of governors to override the logic of pactism was matched in these years by another phenomenon, visible in the mirror of language: the absorption of relations of vassalage – contractual relations by definition – within the sphere of subjection. Changes to the formularies of investiture are quite revealing, in Milan and also in Naples.[25]

Political language as a form of political action

At the end of the 1980s, in a weighty essay, Roger Chartier lamented the enduring lack of communication between factual history, which 'uses massive amounts of quantifiable documentary data to reconstruct societies as they really were', and the history of representations, 'devoted to the illusions of discourse and far removed from reality'.[26] Provocatively, therefore, objectivity versus subjectivity, but also the history of practice versus the history of ideas. Evidently, this is not a new problem: Georges Duby had already demonstrated his dissatisfaction with a history of society too often understood by historians as solely a history of practices, of actions – hence the invitation to consider as well the systems of ideas through which social actors filtered reality and elaborated representations that in some way shaped action.[27]

Precious hints, which the historiographical storms at that time did not allow to be fully appreciated: not until at least the mid-1980s can a significant change be observed, when the wind of the *linguistic turn* began to blow over the terrain of other human sciences, showing, for example, how it was possible effectively 'to do things with words' and thus making evident a possible point of contact between the plane of discourse and that of action.[28]

It is worth observing how around the same years in which these theses began to circulate in the ambit of historiography, cultural history also came, albeit by a different road, to test how a different language, that of ritual, far from being the mere representation of practices or expression of ideas, might in reality itself be a way of concretely realising these principles.[29] Moreover, even among historians of iconology, questions about the communicative efficacy of images, about their capacity to structure social and political reality, have found a positive answer through investigations that have focused on the reactions aroused by the images themselves.[30]

---

[25] Cengarle, *Immagine di potere*, 54; Vitolo, 'Linguaggi', 57.
[26] Chartier, *Cultural History*, 5–6. [27] Duby, 'Ideologies in social history'.
[28] Austin, *How to Do Things with Words*; Searle, *Speech Acts*.
[29] A good perspective on this topic can be found in Visceglia, *La città rituale*.
[30] Freedberg, *The Power of Images*.

On several sides, in sum, the idea has begun to spread that language – whether written, ritual or figurative – could be not simply an instrument to communicate a message but also a mode of translating it into practice, to affect the social and political context. This is an important observation, which appears to throw a bridge over the gulf that has long seemed to exist between idealism and practice.

Within the historiography on the polities of the early Italian Renaissance, we owe much to the pioneering research of Edward Muir on Venice and of Richard C. Trexler on Florence, both of which appeared in the early 1980s,[31] the opening up of a new road in the interpretation of those ceremonial moments – such as processions, coronations, funerals, weddings, tournaments – that saw the governed and the governors position themselves (and reposition themselves) in relation to one another through the language of ritual, in what appeared to be a confrontation between different ideals but at the same time a way of translating them into practice. Behind this reading is the conviction that political space might not be a rigidly defined reality, but on the contrary constitutes a structure that is ever changing, one permeable to the interpretations of reality of the actors themselves.[32] In consequence, there has been a series of investigations that have demonstrated the capacity of ritual to sanction important aspects of the construction of a new political order, such as the principle of the continuity of the state (through, for example, the funeral of the prince), the pactist character of political obligation (as in the thoroughly studied example of the marriage of Venice to the sea), the unity of the body of society (through the celebration of *Corpus Domini* in Venice and Genoa, and of the Virgin in Milan), the primacy of public justice over other forms of conflict resolution (through the ceremonial of punishments) and so on.[33]

Besides these studies, which have focused above all on the role of those holding power, their ability to communicate, there are others that have emphasised the initiative of different subjects. Rendering confrontation within Italian states in the late Middle Ages particularly lively was the familiarity of so many actors with this type of language: long before the princes developed their own, cities, for example, had accrued experiences and traditions in the field of ritual that they did not

---

[31] Muir, *Civic Ritual in Renaissance Venice*; Muir (ed.), *Ritual in Early Modern Europe*; Trexler, *Public Life in Renaissance Florence*.
[32] Rexroth, 'Politische Rituale', 79; Fantoni, 'Simbologia e ritualità', 9.
[33] Gaffuri and Ventrone (eds.), *Images, cultes, liturgies*; Gaffuri (ed.), '*Monasticum regnum*'; Zorzi, 'Rituali di violenza'; Casini, *I gesti del principe*; Gentile, *Riti ed emblemi*; Crouzet-Pavan, *Venice Triumphant*.

hesitate to deploy in dialogue with the new governors.[34] In the middle of the fifteenth century, in the principalities and in the kingdom of Naples, the *joyeuse entrée* of the *princeps* into a city constituted one of the principal occasions for the affirmation of status and prerogative for all those involved. In general, this happened in peaceful and agreed forms, as in the carefully studied example of Capua, where the entry of the king of Naples sanctioned the primacy of the *civitas* over the other urban centres of the kingdom. Nevertheless, there were also instances of confrontation, which revealed a conflict of ideas. At Reggio Emilia, for example, where the arrival of duke Borso d'Este saw the civic community sabotage the ritual organised by the Ferrarese courtiers and prepare a rather different one that, in a setting of the exaltation of republican ideals, challenged the autocratic profile of the duke and affirmed full participation by the *civitas* in the sphere of jurisdiction (in which the duke claimed the monopoly).[35] Nor were cities the only subjects to interact with the prince (or with the dominant city) through the language of ritual, a mode of communication particularly familiar to territorial aristocracies as well.[36] In Visconti and Sforza Lombardy, for example, attempts by the duke to confirm the state monopoly of war brought quick reaction from noble lineages that not only claimed the status of *bellum* for clashes between *milites*, but above all fought (or were concerned to represent their conflicts) according to those rituals (throwing down the gauntlet to open hostilities, respecting certain customs in the treatment of enemies and civilians, etc.) that the princes themselves made use of in their military campaigns, to signify a common cultural horizon and therefore full parity of rank.[37]

As determined to oppose the hegemonic designs of the prince and to affirm their own role in binding together the dominion were the parties, who, for instance in the ritual of May Day – when in many regions trees were planted that were traditionally associated with the Guelfs (such as elms) and Ghibellines (oaks) – saw an important moment of reaffirmation of their distance from the principles of political cohabitation of the state.[38]

An impression of lively communication by several voices, the carrier of ideals and at the same time an instrument to realise them, can also be gained by glancing at the considerable body of studies that have dealt – at their heart or tangentially – with the theme of figurative and

---

[34] Bertrand and Taddei (eds.), *Le destin des rituels*; Vauchez (ed.), *La religion civique*; Ricciardelli (ed.), *I luoghi del sacro*; *Simboli e rituali*.
[35] Senatore, 'Cerimonie regie'; Turchi, 'Una piccola modifica'.
[36] Arcangeli, 'Piccoli signori lombardi'.   [37] Gamberini, *Oltre le città*, 109–31.
[38] Gentile, 'Discorsi sulle fazioni, discorsi della fazioni'.

symbolic languages. In the field of architecture, for example, it has been pointed out that the interventions of the prince were inserted into an urban fabric profoundly affected by the communal experience, generating a sometimes heated dialogue, in which appropriations and resignifications (of spaces, single buildings, city walls, etc.) on the part of the lord (or the dominant *civitas*) provoked reaction from subject cities, jealous of the government of their own spaces no less than of the testimony of their monuments, the bulwark of their residual autonomy.[39]

It is well known that to the intimidatory message conveyed by the construction of new urban fortresses – with the Este and the Gonzaga, the Scaligeri and the Visconti showing the way – *cives* sometimes responded in as violent a manner by destroying the castle (as happened in 1306 at Reggio, following the expulsion of the Este, or in 1447 at Milan, after the death of duke Filippo Maria Visconti).[40] Perhaps less well known is the attempt by some lords to share the concerns of the *cives* and to make their new urban refuges less invasive by attributing a more reassuring significance to them, linked to that widespread need for pacification to which the institution of the *signoria* was itself intended to be a response. This was what Luchino Visconti did at Parma, where the fortification of the *piazza* – the political space *par excellence* – was accompanied by its redesignation as '*Sta' in pace* [Be at peace].' A simple and direct message, this, like all those that architecture could convey, according to the lucid theory put forward by Leon Battista Alberti in *De re aedificatoria*, a real 'grammar of the language of architecture current in Quattrocento Italy'.[41] And few things, in effect, were more clear and more comprehensible than interventions to beautify the city, an expression of that persuasive *magnificentia* that had its roots in a celebrated passage of the *Nicomachean Ethics* and on which so many lords sought to rely, above all in their capitals: as the Visconti and Sforza did at Milan (where the artistic patronage of Azzone was such that for a long time tradition attributed to him the building of city walls which in fact were a century older), the Gonzaga at Mantua, the Este at Ferrara (which long before the famous '*addizione erculea*' had cast off its reputation as a malodorous and muddy city, courtesy of the interventions by Niccolò II in the fourteenth century), the Scaligeri at Verona (a city that for good reason came to be called '*marmorina* [the city of marble]'), the Carraresi at Padua, pope Nicholas V at Rome, the Angevins at Naples and so on.[42]

---

[39] Ciccaglioni, 'La costruzione'.   [40] Covini, 'Aspetti della fortificazione urbana'.
[41] Boucheron, *Le pouvoir de bâtir*; Boucheron, 'L'architettura come linguaggio politico'.
[42] Calzona et al. (eds.), *Il principe architetto*; Boucheron and Chiffoleau (eds.), *Les palais dans la ville*; Varanini, 'Propaganda dei regimi signorili'.

Once more, however, it is worth noting that, if these interventions affected the context (architectural as well as political), they were also shaped by the context in their turn: even the placing of the prince's residence in a particular zone of the urban fabric – now in a central position, now in a more peripheral one – was the outcome of compromises, negotiations, careful assessments of suitability, translating the debate over forms and limits of power in terms of space. In this sense, the impossibility of establishing a firm connection between urbanistic choices and the prevailing form of government (republican or princely), like the difficulty in detecting a thread of continuity in the attitudes of a single dynasty (such as the Visconti and Sforza), tells more clearly than many words could do of an unending dialectic, which brought political actors continually to change the positions they took up in relation to one another.

Nor, what is more, did this political confrontation *sub specie architecturae* take place solely in an urban context. In some areas of the Po valley, for example, the transformation of some noblemen's castles into little courts reflected the ambitions of a territorial aristocracy who refused to see themselves as subjects and presented themselves as being on the same level as the prince. But in the late medieval countryside other subjects also expressed their own ideals of political life through the language of building: in many regions of the peninsula the construction of the palace of the commune or the village church was an important stage in the maturation of a shared and deeply felt community ideal.[43] The paintings that decorated the residences of princes often contributed to making the message of architecture more incisive, just as public buildings did. The very numerous studies on this theme have grasped some characteristic aspects, like the tendency to politicise religious motifs or the emphasis on certain iconographic motifs, as in the case of portraits of famous men, of galleries of heroes, which lent themselves so readily to conveying the ideals of those in power.[44] Once again, however, rather than lingering over self-legitimising discourses of governors (as is generally done), it can be interesting to link these representations with those elaborated in the same area of communication by the governed: as in the case of Venetian subject cities, where during the fifteenth century images of eagles or even portraits of emperors could be found in private houses and in public places, in what appears to be the assumption of a strong position against the sovereignty claimed by Venice.[45]

---

[43] Della Misercordia, *Divenire comunità*, 341–50.
[44] Welch, *Art and Authority*; Di Donato, 'Cose morali'; Campbell (ed.), *Artists at Court*; Pavanello (ed.), *Il buono e il cattivo governo*.
[45] Viggiano, *Governanti e governati*, 8–10.

With respect to a panorama of studies that has been prematurely polarised by research on the languages of ritual and on architectural and figurative languages, it is worth emphasising the ever greater space that political historians have reserved in recent years for verbal languages, for the rhetorical dimension of the word, for the discourses elaborated through it. These have a central importance within the ambit of systems of political communication because of their tendency to be entwined, sometimes inextricably, with other codes of communication: as in the case of musical languages, where the message is entrusted to the complex relation between words and music; or as in the case of figurative languages, in which cartouches and inscriptions are an integral part of the documentary value of the image.[46] Sometimes, as in the records of community meetings or in letters, even before the tenor of the documents, it is the forms in which they were written (in which lists, sketches and frames were beginning to appear) that suggest taxonomies, create hierarchies, imply logical connections: in brief, express contents.[47] Sometimes, the form of the document represents the medium of an ideological confrontation: the choice by a lord to swear fidelity to the prince not through a notarial deed (a private deed by definition), but through a patent letter promulgated by the lord himself (a public deed, reserved for authorities) is only one among many examples on which the attention of Italian historians has concentrated recently.[48]

It appears that written language becomes, by its very nature, the most accessible to a wide spectrum of political subjects, above all after the epistolary revolution of the early fourteenth century, with the diffusion of a new, particularly flexible medium, the *litterae clausae* (closed letters, so called because of how they were folded after they had been drawn up).[49] If in fact the thirteenth-century city-states in their relations with their respective territories made use above all of judicial orders and notarial instruments – extremely dry documents, directed only one way – succeeding governments, above all those of the *signori*, introduced a new written form, the closed letter, which not only lent itself well to transmitting the commands of the authorities, but which soon began to be used in the other direction as well, to send the voices of the periphery to the centre. Above all in the second half of the thirteenth century, its narrative contents became more complex and detailed, thanks to the

---

[46] Bolzoni, *The Web of Images*.
[47] Della Misericordia, *Figure di comunità*; Lazzarini, *Il linguaggio del territorio*.
[48] Gamberini, *Lo stato visconteo*, 55–6; Lazzarini (ed.), *Scritture e potere*.
[49] Gamberini, *Lo stato visconteo*, 40–52; Della Misericordia, 'Principat, communauté et individu'; Lazzarini, 'Materiali per una didattica'; Bartoli Langeli, 'La documentazione degli stati italiani'.

increasing cultural level of the prince's chancellors, but also to the ever more frequent recourse by communities to *scriptores* trained in law or in the *ars dictaminis*. These writings became, in short, the bearer of an intense political communication, which registered the tendency of all the actors involved to give ever more space to the ideals behind their actions. Witness to that is, for example, the common inclination of protagonists to situate their own claims within an idealised, imaginary picture of relations and politics. This can be found in the petition of a small Alpine community (which indeed appealed to a mythical pact as the foundation of their obedience to the prince, as has been noted) or in the pompous exhortation of a *signorile* decree (which might supply a philosophical basis for the proto-absolutist traits of the *dominus*). With respect to this tendency, recent historiography, far from limiting itself to establishing the gap between plan and action, beween the plane of ideals and that of current dynamics, has instead accentuated the practical constitutional worth of this exchange of models, remarking once again that the political context within which the subjects matured their own ideal positions – that is the state, with its institutional dynamics, its practices – would not constitute a reality fixed in the abstract, once and for all, but would in some way be transformed by the model of how it should function that the social and territorial entities proposed. From this perspective, the right of resistance flourished in the petitions of the Alpine communities to the duke of Milan or the pactist memory that pervaded the cartulary of a great aristocratic family (to strengthen the thesis of contractual relations with the prince, which he could not alter unilaterally) were nothing other than potent ideological filters, representations elaborated in moments of particular tension and intended to shape the political context, to define (or redefine) its contours.[50]

Within this line of research, concerned with the relation between language and action, it is worth mentioning some studies that have stressed verbal communication from a linguistic perspective, successfully exploring the possibility of applying to some types of documents the 'theory of speech acts'. Thus, for example, a close analysis of the methods of constructing the diplomas of the king of Naples (inclusion in the diploma of the text of the petition that originated the royal intervention, the use of illocutory words on behalf of the king, their taking immediate effect and producing a new status for the recipient of the privilege) has clearly demonstrated the authentically performative capacity of language.[51]

---

[50] Compare Della Misericordia, 'Per non privarci de nostre raxone'; Gamberini, *Lo stato visconteo*, 231–44; Cengarle, 'La comunità di Pecetto'.
[51] Airò, 'L'architettura istituzionale e territoriale'.

Conclusion

The spreading into constitutional history of experiences and methods developed in other disciplines has been an operation conducted with a high degree of empiricism, which has certainly not barred errors or ingenuousness. Nevertheless, at least in the case of research into the early Renaissance states, some dangers inherent in the matrices of these new approaches have been avoided, beginning with those represented by some misdirections from post-modernism and the linguistic turn. This is not an allusion to the doubts about the scientific status of history, to questions of how it differs from fiction – provocations which Italian historiography and, more generally, that on polities between the medieval and the early modern period have not taken up – as much as to the more subtle and concrete risks inherent in deconstructionism and culturalism. On one hand, the identification of a large number of subjects capable of elaborating a political message has not led to a new hierarchy of historiographical importance, and still less to the renunciation of investigating institutional transformations from the perspective of the prince (or the dominant city); on the contrary, these new approaches, making it possible to overcome the 'top-down' approach that has long dominated studies of political communication, have introduced into the plane of languages the pluralistic principle that has for some time enriched constitutional history.[52]

On the other hand, the very entry of political languages into the precinct of institutional historiography has permitted a bridge to be constructed between theoretical elaboration and praxis, overcoming one of the deepest gulfs that has opened up in the terrain of historical research. The interest of Italian constitutional historiography has not in fact been oriented to the reconstruction of different linguistic or discursive traditions, but has focused on the pragmatic dimension of languages.[53] Thanks to a closer interaction between the planes of power and the ideological elaboration capable of justifying them, between the negotiation of political roles and the battle of ideologies, it has been possible to launch a new season of studies about the genesis of the late medieval state, which is beginning to yield significant results.

---

[52] Blockmans, Holenstein and Mathieu (eds.), *Empowering Interactions*.
[53] Gamberini and Petralia (eds.), *Linguaggi politici*; Delle Donne, 'Regis servitium nostra mercatura'.

21 Renaissance diplomacy

Isabella Lazzarini

Introduction

The beginnings of permanent diplomacy and the emergence of resident ambassadors have been usually associated by European scholars with growth of territorial powers in Italy between the fourteenth and fifteenth centuries: the time-scale of these developments has tended to be telescoped by historians looking for the first resident ambassadors, and their consistency and rationality have been considerably exaggerated in the search for a rather anachronistic continuity in diplomatic practices between Renaissance and modern nation-states.[1] Since Garrett Mattingly's more accurate and systematic research into Italian diplomacy in the 1950s, a new generation of scholars has pointed out that the process was less dramatic and much more nuanced, even though resident embassies were still regarded as the key element in the transition from medieval to modern diplomacy.[2]

In recent decades, the publication of a large number of systematically edited diplomatic records and closer attention to the mechanisms of power and legitimation within the Italian states have enabled scholars to focus on innovative approaches to the theme of Renaissance diplomacy. Riccardo Fubini has stressed that new governments' need for internal and external legitimation caused a major change in the nature of the ambassadorial role, transforming the *nuntius* or proctor into a public official not limited by a strict mandate, and deeply and autonomously involved in the conservation of the state for which he acted both in prolonged and temporary assignments to mediate conflicts, achieve peace, gather information and strengthen the institutional role of his government.[3] The prosopography of diplomatic envoys has revealed the deep link between central chanceries – that is, the heart of

---

[1] For the origins of this historiographical debate, see Senatore, *'Uno mundo de carta'*, 28–50.
[2] Mattingly, *Renaissance Diplomacy*; Queller, *The Office of Ambassador*; Ilardi, *Studies in Italian Renaissance Diplomatic History*.
[3] Among Fubini's works, see Fubini, 'Diplomacy and government'.

political decision-making – and diplomacy,[4] and analysis of the symbiotic relations upon which the political balance of the Italian peninsula was built in the middle of the Quattrocento has shown the complementarity between diplomacy and war.[5] In recent years, research has focused on communication networks, the crucial role of intelligence-gathering, the practices of negotiation, and the sophisticated balance between oral and written communication within a *mundo de carta* where letters represented the biggest part of a growing quantity of public written records.[6]

With closer attention to a long chronology, and a broader spectrum of case studies,[7] Italian diplomacy has become a highly articulated research subject, offering to scholars an open field of investigation without disowning the claim to its originality, but basing it upon something more than the growth of resident embassies in the age of the Lega Italica.

Sources, chronology and geography

During the fifteenth century, diplomatic sources multiplied at an unprecedented rate: this explosion was the documentary result of a crucial change in medieval diplomacy, linked to the evolution of the peninsular system of power and to the complementary change in public written communication.[8] This growth was mostly due to the massive volume of diplomatic dispatches exchanged between governments and envoys sent abroad for increasingly prolonged missions. Nevertheless, despite the significance of dispatches, in both quantitative and qualitative terms, the diplomatic sources as a whole comprised different groups of texts, whose growth goes back to the middle of the fourteenth century.

The body of Italian diplomatic sources at the end of the Middle Ages presents a considerable homogeneity across the peninsula, despite the institutional differences among the Italian states which produced them. We count as diplomatic sources both the documents produced *for* the ambassadors, and those produced *by* them: empirically, they may be divided into three different groups. First and foremost are the letters, written either by public authorities to their ambassadors or by other correspondents abroad, and vice versa. Both groups of letters (*missive* and *responsive*) may be preserved in rough copies or loose originals, or in

---

[4] Leverotti, *Diplomazia e governo dello stato*; Lazzarini, 'L'informazione politico-diplomatica'; Senatore, *'Uno mundo de carta'*.
[5] Isaacs, 'Sui rapporti interstatali in Italia'; Mallett, 'Diplomacy and war'.
[6] Bullard, 'The language of diplomacy'; Senatore, *'Uno mundo de carta'*; Lazzarini (ed.), *Scritture e potere*; Dover, 'The resident ambassador'.
[7] Duranti, *Diplomazia e autogoverno*; Pibiri, *En voyage*.
[8] Fubini, *Italia quattrocentesca*, 19–21; Lazzarini (ed.), *Scritture e potere*.

specific registers: the volumes of letters sent may also include general or specific instructions to the ambassadors (although these documents too were sometimes collected in separate registers); the volumes of the letters received may contain in turn final reports, though they may have been copied into separate volumes as well. Secondly, we have the various collections of documents gathered by the ambassador or his chancellor during the mission. Basically these documents are not too different from the previous ones: the core of the personal documentation of the envoy was represented by original letters and rough copies, variously collected and reordered for personal use, but we may also find among them accounts of expenses or journals with personal memoirs about travelling and accommodation. Finally, we may classify as diplomatic sources different documents linked both to the main aims of the embassy (such as council records of political debates arising from the public reading of the ambassadors' letters) and to its practical, day-to-day aspects (such as ambassadors' appointments, payments, travels, accommodation).[9] The amount of these sources is highly variable according more to preservation than to production, and reaches its peak around 1450–70, continuing quite regularly afterwards, in spite of regional differences and local chronological fluctuations. Before this date, we can find here and there considerable quantities of documents but, despite their individual significance, we cannot rely on them as a homogeneous basis for systematic research.[10]

This last statement introduces also the complementary themes of chronology and geography in Italian diplomacy: when did the supposed transition from 'medieval' to 'Renaissance' diplomacy begin? And was the process linear in time and in space?

We should consider a chronology both longer and finer than the traditional turning point in the middle of the fifteenth century, as the key elements of the evolving institutional and geopolitical scenario followed unequal rhythms. The first examples of prolonged missions abroad emerged both in principalities and in republics after the middle of the fourteenth century, in connection with territorial wars and the displacement of the papal court to Avignon; on the other hand, an ordinary network of resident embassies was barely in place before 1480. Chronology should not only be longer, but also attentive and flexible: we do not see a linear and general process from temporary and occasional envoys to permanent and regular ambassadors, or from

---

[9] Lazzarini, 'Materiali'; Senatore, 'Callisto III'.
[10] Ilardi, 'Fifteenth-century diplomatic documents'; Ilardi, 'Index of microfilms on Italian diplomatic history, 1454–1494'.

irregular negotiating practices to a more systematic communication network, but instead the slow building of a much more fragmented pattern, with highs and lows according to different local rhythms and specific circumstances.

This cautious attitude towards unambiguous models must be adopted also as regards the geography of transformation: not only were the rhythms of change various and irregular, but also different states chose different strategies at different times. The most important territorial states – the principalities from the 1460s and the republics from the 1480s – developed a reciprocal negotiating system quite regularly based upon ambassadors who stayed abroad for long periods and became part of the inner circles of political decision-making. The second-rank powers (such as Mantua, Monferrato, Ferrara, Siena, Lucca, Bologna) developed in a more nuanced way, starting to employ long-term envoys earlier, but finding it hard to consolidate this practice on a regular basis, and instead taking advantage of various networks in turn to gather vital information and to keep open every possible negotiating channel to guarantee their survival.[11]

Conflicts, authority and legitimacy

Prolonged stays, communication networks and information-gathering are some of the most analysed features of Renaissance Italian diplomacy: first and foremost, however, we need to investigate the inner development of power and legitimacy at the root of this 'diplomatic revolution'.

The major changes in Italian diplomacy in the fourteenth and fifteenth centuries stemmed in fact from a complex political process of concentration and legitimation of power deeply connected to the conflicts of the late fourteenth century and their related processes of territorial expansion. Prolonged territorial wars – and the increasing financial pressure which came with them – pushed the Italian powers towards oligarchical channels and autocratic innovations. However, the growing effectiveness in political decision-making and the concentration of authority and power in the hands of princes and narrower elites that resulted from these innovations could not avoid a dangerous lack of internal legitimacy and external recognition. In the first half of the fifteenth century, this situation generated a need for mutual bonds between regimes, to supply by reciprocal acknowledgement a formal and public recognition of their internal hegemony and external role.

---

[11] Lazzarini, 'News from Mantua'.

The Sforza–Medici semi-private, even collusive, relationship from 1434 is one of the clearest examples of this tendency.[12]

According to Fubini, this is the crucial focus of the whole transformation of Italian diplomacy. The need for self-produced legitimation led to the growth of the political autonomy of the ambassador: his growing similarity to a public official made concretely possible the reciprocal recognition of substantially illegitimate regimes through bilateral and multilateral pacts and leagues that required a prolonged negotiating effort. Diplomatic activity became such an integral part of the existence of the Italian states of the fifteenth century 'that it modified their constitutional order': ambassadors took part in the political decision process, and their choice became a crucial element in the balance of power in courts and councils, as soon as the first attempt at a general league (the Lega Italica in 1455) showed its limits and failed to prevent a succession of local and less local crises whose intensity and frequency worsened from the period 1476–8.[13] Therefore, in the second half of the fifteenth century a more and more political and constitutional diplomacy provided the inner mechanism of a system dominated by a state not of semi-permanent peace, but on the contrary of semi-permanent war, due to the fragility of the various regimes and their growing 'thoughtless bellicoseness'.[14] As Galeazzo Maria Sforza clearly explained to Charles the Bold of Burgundy in 1476, the Italians, 'when in conflict with three people, try to make peace with one, truce with another, war with the last, to attend easier to the rest of their businesses and achieve their purposes'.[15]

The analysis of Italian diplomacy in the last couple of decades of the fifteenth century has suffered in some ways the effect of retrospection: in the light of the Italian Wars, historians tended to judge diplomatic practices and political mechanisms at the end of the Quattrocento as a comprehensive failure. Despite these dramatic events, the whole process should be considered by itself: it did in fact produce a political system – albeit a somewhat fragile one – where conflicts were kept under some kind of control by means of pacts aiming more to cause damage to the others by excluding them from negotiating dynamics than to prevent war or resolve conflicts. These practices emphasised the political role of the ambassadors, prolonged their stay and strengthened their influence. At the same time they increased mutual bonds among regimes facing

---

[12] Lazzarini, *L'Italia degli stati territoriali*. [13] Fubini, 'Diplomacy and government', 30–1.
[14] *Ibid.*; Mallett, 'Diplomacy and war', 269.
[15] G. M. Sforza to G. P. Panigarola, Villanova, 12 April 1475, in *Carteggi diplomatici fra Milano sforzesca e la Borgogna*, I, 460 ('quando hanno una controversia con tre, si sforzano de fare con l'uno pace, et con l'altro tregua et con l'altro guerra, acciò che più facilmente possano attendere alle altre cose et adimpire li soy disigni').

potential crises and endorsed the recourse to multiple solutions instead of an unqualified resort to a military response. Successful or not in providing an efficient solution to the damage caused by the French armies, they did at least establish an innovative practice of diplomacy.[16]

Nature and forms of diplomatic assignments

It is time now to turn our attention to the most characteristic elements of this innovative practice. At the end of the fifteenth century, the ambassador was supposed to represent his masters, gather information, negotiate alliances, keep open vital communication networks as an alternative to war and eventually (but not mainly) settle conflicts: all of these functions may be reduced to three main duties, that is, representation, negotiation and information. The ambassadorial role assumed a public character, and the *legatio* became an *officium*, thanks both to a process of concentration of power within the state, and to the increasing politicisation of diplomacy. However, this was a process in the making and far from unambiguous. This assumption leads us back to the nature of diplomatic assignments during the late Middle Ages, putting the traditional problem of resident embassies in a new light. Even though this famous topic has been subject to revision by historians, two crucial points should still be stressed: the habit of sending envoys abroad for more or less prolonged periods had multiple rather than single origins in the late Middle Ages, and different types of envoys for different purposes were dispatched in many various ways to deal with a wide spectrum of tasks.[17]

The figure of the envoy evolved between the thirteenth and the fifteenth centuries: his prerogatives multiplied, his autonomy increased and he was transformed from a simple instrument of his master's authority (*nuntius*) first to an agent provided with autonomy defined by mandate (*procurator*), and finally to an official with a public role and full decision-making autonomy (*orator* or *ambassador*) and with a wide and changeable variety of competencies (diplomatic, legal, political) according to the situation and the purpose of his mission.[18] The end result of this development was, as Ermolao Barbaro pointed out clearly for the very first time, that 'the purpose of the *legatus* is the same as all the others who work for the republic, that is to do, say,

---

[16] Fubini, 'Diplomacy and government', 32; Lazzarini, 'News from Mantua'.
[17] Fubini, 'La "résidentialité de l'ambassadeur"'.
[18] Mattingly, 'The first resident embassies'; Queller, 'Thirteenth-century diplomatic envoys'; Gilli, 'La fonction d'ambassadeur'.

counsel and think everything they judge useful to maintain and increase the good state of their city'.[19]

This evolution was actually far from being progressive and unilateral: looking for the right path to the 'modern' ambassador, we face an uneasy, if not misleading task. The crucial point in this process does not lie in finding out who, among merchant consuls, papal collectors, proctors at the pontifical court in Avignon, or envoys sent to bond feudal and military *adhaerentiae*, played the key role in the evolution towards a single model of resident ambassador.[20] A side effect of late medieval political development was in fact the increasing interconnection of states and communities. Growing networks turned different governments to intelligence-gathering and reciprocal dialogue: in this sense, all the figures just mentioned were sides of the same coin. Their specific nature and goals could be different case by case, and the formal definition of their role was distinct, but they all shared a hunger for information and a clearer tendency to prolong their missions. In this perspective, the length of ambassadors' long, and in principle unlimited, stay abroad does not make a clear-cut difference to the nature of their professional and public identity; it rather characterises a practice and represents an increasingly common feature of a growing political, economic and social symbiosis.[21]

As a practice, it was neither simple nor definite. Principalities and republics chose different strategies, the former openly preferring the residential option, the latter – tied by collegiality and turnover, and already relying on different and well-established information networks such as merchant consulates – retained the habit of sending temporary envoys at least until the 1480s.[22]

As a practice, however, prolonged stays slowly became crucial, and saw a turning point with Francesco Sforza: this *condottiere*-prince's obsession with information made him the most coherent supporter of residential practice in the middle of the fifteenth century.[23] Regular flows of information, local know-how and the possibility of intervening promptly in case of emergency provided the rationale for a prince to keep one man permanently abroad. The Florentine Antonio Cenni da

---

[19] Barbaro, *De coelibatu, de officio legati*, 159 ('Finis legato idem est qui et caeteris ad Rempublicam accedentibus, ut ea faciant, dicant, consulant et cogitent quae ad optimum suae civitatis statum et retinendum et amplificandum pertinere posse iudicent').

[20] Mattingly, *Renaissance Diplomacy*, 71–5; Blet, *Histoire de la représentation diplomatique de la Saint Siège*; Ashtor, 'Levant trade'; Fubini, 'Classe dirigente'.

[21] Fubini, 'Classe dirigente',125. [22] Lazzarini, 'Materiali'.

[23] Ilardi, 'The banker-statesman and the condottiere-prince'; Senatore, *'Uno mundo de carta'*, 25–84, 251–63.

Ricavo was clear in suggesting to Ludovico Gonzaga in 1451 that he keep a man in Florence: 'Besides, my very distinguished lord, I wrote already to your excellence that I consider it not only useful, but also necessary that your excellence keeps here one man permanent and stable [*uno continuo et fermo*] who could develop a full knowledge of our customs and habits, to look after your businesses and possible needs.'[24] At the end of this process, Barbaro could conclude that 'the ambassadorial office [the *legatio*] does not have a predefined expiry date'.[25]

Despite the growing importance of the prolonged stay, however, residentiality not only had multiple origins, but was far from an uninterrupted and overwhelming practice, either in time or space. Small and large states chose from time to time to retire their permanent ambassadors from their usual postings, because of lack of business, or thanks to alternative and less expensive solutions represented by dynastic links (endogamy among princes reached a peak in the last decades of the fifteenth century) or ecclesiastical and military networks (mostly focused on cardinal-princes or *condottieri*).[26] The papal court relied on the old framework of papal collectors and opted for a flexible use of legates and *nuntii* in more or less temporary assignments until the beginning of the sixteenth century, when we can find the first signs of permanent *nunziature*.[27] For the whole of the fifteenth century, Genoa resorted mostly to its broad network of commercial consulates rather than developing a diplomatic system based on regular ambassadors.[28] Even Naples continued to rely on a complex pattern of multiple solutions: diplomatic missions were conceived more as a class of political assignment given by the king to his faithful officers, courtiers, even relatives, according to the Aragonese tradition, than as a distinct function entrusted to a selected corps of professionals and run according to specific rules.[29]

Communication networks and political leagues

The Italian late medieval political system needed negotiation, information, communication: in sum, it needed a common discourse of

---

[24] A. Cenni to L. Gonzaga, Florence, 16 December 1451, ASMn, AG, b. 1099 ('Praeterea signore illustrissimo, altra volta scripsi alla vostra excellentia che a me parebbe non solamente utile, ma necessario che la vostra excellentia havesse qui uno continuo et fermo, el qual havesse notitia piena delle consuetudine et observantie nostre, per vacare a facti et occorrenti bisogni della vostra signoria').

[25] Barbaro, *De coelibatu*, 159 ('Non habet praefinitum aliquod tempus huiusmodi legatio').

[26] Covini *et al.*, 'Pratiche e norme'.

[27] Blet, *Histoire de la représentation diplomatique de la Saint Siège*, 175–202; Gaeta, 'Origine e sviluppo'; Barbiche, 'Les "diplomates" pontificaux'.

[28] Olgiati, 'Diplomatici e ambasciatori'. [29] Covini *et al.*, 'Pratiche e norme'.

diplomacy.[30] So, between the fourteenth and the fifteenth centuries, diplomatic practice transformed itself from an episodic way of solving problems by means of an intermediate or a meeting between the parties, to a mutual communication network whose common political language could contain every conflict within a negotiated framework.[31]

Information was one of the main duties of a late medieval envoy – perhaps the most important, surely the most innovative. Francesco Sforza knew very well the crucial role played by intelligence-gathering. He wanted openly to be a 'master of news':

> Do not write to anybody about state matters apart from us, because sometimes some troubles could happen, and I advise you that we want to be the master, and if someone wants to have news, we want him to have it from us first, and only what we want him to know and nothing more, and in this matter we do not make exceptions for anyone, even our children or brothers, and we want this rule to be forever.[32]

The crucial need for information was both a cause and an effect of more prolonged stays by ambassadors and envoys, and went together with a global increase in documentation.[33] Lay professionals of written communication – chancellors, secretaries, notaries – built day by day a body of documentary practices whose purpose was to elaborate political information, government techniques, negotiating practices: their careful preservation is a symptom of an increasing documentary consciousness.[34] The huge amount of letters produced by the daily activity of ambassadors is one of the most conspicuous results of this process,[35] and it is deeply linked to the very nature of diplomatic commitment: as the Florentines Pandolfini and Sacchetti declared, in fact, 'the ambassadors' office [...] is to report to their masters everything they know hour by hour, day by day, telling them also how they gained knowledge of it, and from whom they got the information, and how'.[36]

---

[30] Grubb, 'Diplomacy in the Italian city-state'.
[31] Ferrer Mallol et al. (eds.), Negociar en la Etad Media.
[32] F. Sforza to A. da Trezzo, Milan 22 July 1458, in Senatore, 'Uno mundo de carta', 429 ('Non scrivere a veruno di cose de stato se non ad nuy, perché alle volte nasce de li inconvenienti, avisandoti che nuy vogliamo essere el patrone, et chi vorrà sapere novelle vogliamo le sapiano prima da nuy che da altri, et quelle ne paia che sapiano et non più, et in questo non ne exceptamo persona, se'l fusse ben nostro figliolo o nostro fratello, et intende essere questa regula per sempre').
[33] Lazzarini, L'Italia degli stati territoriali, 2.   [34] Lazzarini (ed.), Scritture e potere.
[35] Petrucci, Scrivere lettere.
[36] G. Pandolfini and F. Sacchetti to the Signoria, Aversa, 5 May 1450, Dispacci sforzeschi da Napoli, I, 51 ('L'uficio degli imbasciatori [...] è giorno per giorno, hora per hora, secondo che intendono, et da chi et in che modo, dare notitia a chi gli manda').

The ambassador could fulfil his duty of collecting the requested news first and foremost from the mouth of the prince during daily audiences, in private conversations or through the official mediation of the chancery. Chanceries were very attentive in trying to keep the flow of information under surveillance, and many princes required ambassadors to report to their masters only what they themselves or their chancellors told them. Losing control of words and news could prove itself dangerous, dramatising disputes or fuelling suspicion between fragile allies. Nevertheless, an ambassador could – and usually did – obtain information also from members of the political elite, from fellow ambassadors and finally from different sources, more or less reliable: friends, anonymous voices, public rumours, secret informers.[37] His duty was to consider – and register – them all. The abundance of news was often so confusing that the ambassador gave up trying to produce any coherent version of the facts, and limited himself to reporting everything, leaving the final judgement to his master, and justifying the obscurity of his reports:

> I do the opposite of many among those who write to your Sublimity, who look to their register before writing, to avoid contradicting what they had already written to you. I swear to your Sublimity that I have never looked at my register in writing all my letters to you, because I think that my office and my duty are to write what I get from the royal Majesty and from his men day by day.[38]

The collection of information was then a sort of game of fools, as the recurrent use of rhetorical *topoi* of game and madness demonstrates very well. In the face of these contradictions, the ambassador took refuge in a gambling attitude: 'therefore, I simply *play* the role of the *fool*, I just try to *guess*'.[39]

Given the flood of information, we may wonder who actually read these reports and how this raw material was used in determining political choices. Chancellors usually prepared brief summaries of letters to enable their masters to understand the situation more easily and to divulge information in a controlled way between allies and friends.

---

[37] Mallett, 'Ambassadors and their audience'; Lazzarini, 'L'informazione politico-diplomatica'; Dover, 'The resident ambassador'.

[38] Z. Barbaro to the Venetian Senate, Naples, 10 March 1472, in *Dispacci di Zaccaria Barbaro*, 93 ('Io fo el contrario de quello fanno molti quando scriveno a la Sublimità vostra che, prima scrivano a quella, guardano el suo registro per non se contradir de quello havesseno scripto. Prometto a vostra Sublimità che de tante lettere quante ho scripto a quella mai ho voluto vedere el registro mio, perché mi pare l'officio et debito mio sia scriver quello ho da la regia Maestà et da i suo' de zorno in zorno').

[39] M. Andreasi to L. Gonzaga, Milan, 24 November 1460, in *Carteggio degli oratori mantovani*, II, 307 ('Et perhò me limito a farla da pazzo, a zugare ad indovinare').

Nevertheless, some statesmen used to read the letters personally every day: Lorenzo de' Medici apparently based his decisions on the attentive analysis of the rich but sometimes inconclusive or incoherent information gathered by Florentine ambassadors.[40] Therefore, councils, governors and princes could be confused by the contradictory and changeable flow of news, and all this almost frantic intelligence-gathering resulted in confusion rather than clarity, deepening conflicts rather than resolving them. As Melissa Bullard underlined, ambassadors, by feeding a 'tremendous appetite for news', helped by considering every political situation with *ragione* and *iudicio*, but they also heightened anxiety and complicated relationships.[41]

All these communications networks were also meant to prepare the general or particular agreements upon which were based all the leagues, treaties, pacts, *intelligentiae* that bound together – publicly or secretly – the Italian powers with an increasing pace towards the last decades of the fifteenth century. Since the first general treaties of peace or alliance in the second half of the fourteenth century which had gathered together dozens of cities, lords and states in a complex hierarchy of alliances and *adherentiae*, the preparatory work required by the establishment of these agreements fuelled endless negotiations and gave birth to the first experiments with ambassadors holding proctorial authority for prolonged stays.[42] This tendency grew during the conflicts of the first decades of the fifteenth century, and in the preparation of the Lega Italica in 1455. The successive revisions of this first alliance, the contemporary overlapping of treaties of differing scope, and finally the secret overthrow of formal leagues through hidden and smaller *intelligentiae* generated a continuous flux of men and news. This complex framework was also complicated by the frequent crossing of the interests of the single states and those of the general league.[43] The Florentine case was even more articulated by Lorenzo's unofficial political and diplomatic hegemony: in this case, the layers to consider were three – the league, the city, the

---

[40] Bullard, 'The language of diplomacy', 104.   [41] *Ibid.*, 95.
[42] Fubini, '"Potenze grosse" e piccolo stato'.
[43] In 1483 the Florentine *Priori* explained to their ambassadors to France: 'Your mission [*legatione*] should have a double commission, because you are acting in behalf of two instances, that is the matters important to our city, and those that you will negotiate together with the ambassadors of our league, that are relevant to the other allies as well as to us' (the *Priori* to Florentine ambassadors to France, Florence, 8 November 1483, in *Négotiations diplomatiques*, I, 200) ('La vostra legazione è necessario che abbi commissione bipartita, come sono ancora di due ragioni le cose che arete a eseguire: cioè le proprie della nostra città, et quelle che harete a trattare insieme cogli imbasciadori della nostra Lega, che appartengono agli altri confederati nostri come a noi').

regime.⁴⁴ The need to bring up to date these close webs of changeable alliances was also partially responsible for the politicisation of diplomatic staff: the inner circle of ambassadors from the major states of the peninsula, integrated at the end of the century with envoys from France, Spain or the empire, gradually and informally ended up in constituting in Milan, Venice and Rome a sort of closed council that altered the traditional balance of internal power and external hierarchies. In this process, in fact, a widening gulf opened out between the most important members of the Italian political system and the others. What used to be a space of relatively free access to the major powers for every envoy with reliable credentials became a more disciplined and closed world, where only a few powers achieved unlimited reciprocal access to the person of the prince or the ruling elite, and all the others were forced to get second-hand information.⁴⁵

Practices and men

Daily diplomacy was concretely composed of a series of acts, rituals and conventions that defined the ambassador's rank, his authority and the limits of his action, both abroad and at home, and slowly became standardised practices. The ambassador's activity was marked by some key moments: arrival and welcome, presentation of credentials, the daily work of negotiating and intelligence-gathering, the end of the mission and official permission to leave. Daily life on duty previewed, then, a succession of acts that embedded the ambassador fully into local political society: if he did not reside at the inn or in a palace owned by his masters, he enjoyed local hospitality at court, or stayed with 'friends', sharing their private lives; he exchanged presents, and acted as a provider of many sorts of goods; finally, he participated in public events such as religious and civil ceremonies, festivities and tournaments, hunts and travels. Culture, good temper, flexibility, the ability to switch from *domesticheza* to formalism when needed and physical fitness were the personal qualities mostly required for the job.⁴⁶ The ambassador should

---

[44] Just one example – in 1485, Lorenzo wrote to Francesco Gaddi, the Florentine ambassador in Milan: 'besides what you have by commission from the Ten, you need to understand the true reason of your mission, that is [...]' (L. de' Medici, *Lettere*, IX *(1485–1486)*, 3, Lorenzo to F. Gaddi, Florence, 14 October 1485) ('Oltre a quanto havete in commissione da' Dieci, è necessario che intendiate la vera cagione dell'andata vostra, la quale è perché [...]'). See Rubinstein, 'Lorenzo de' Medici'; Fubini, 'La "résidentialité de l'ambassadeur"'.

[45] Lazzarini, 'News from Mantua'.

[46] Senatore, *'Uno mundo de carta'*; Folin, 'Gli oratori estensi'.

also be rich: salaries were neither high nor secure, and he needed to be able to survive without financial support from his masters even for long periods; moreover, anticipating money to pay goods for his lord or settling his debts was often part of the office.[47] All social events were organised according to a complex hierarchy of rank and importance: chanceries elaborated and preserved orders regulating the ambassadors' participation in public events in the city and at the court, and the correspondence and the chronicles are full of accounts of disputes and fierce discussions about rank.[48]

The ambassadors' daily activity within local political society was mostly oral: negotiation, information-gathering and sociability required a display of various skills derived from extensive control over the spoken word, both as a common language (vernacular, Latin, eventually foreign languages) and as a set of linguistic instruments.[49] On the other hand, all this world needed to be reported, that is, to be 'translated' into a written text, compiled by the ambassador himself or by his chancellor. The written version is the only one we have: this fact partially biases our understanding of most of the social and political exchanges at the basis of diplomatic practice, presenting to us material that had passed through a process of conscious and unconscious selection of what to write, and how to write it, even though the richness and the vivacity of the diplomatic letters often enchant the reader with their supposed immediacy. Moreover, we should not underestimate the long-lasting survival of rhetorical techniques for the organisation of discourse, such as the *ars dictaminis*, or the force and the hold of a standardised chancery style of letter-writing, and finally the heavy legacy of humanistic studies.[50]

In particular, the gestural and/or emotional dimension of negotiations is often rigidified or underestimated in written reports that emphasise an argumentative attitude and aim at giving a precise interpretation of reality and human behaviour.[51] This attitude towards a rational organisation of news and events grew up during the fifteenth century: it was not very developed at the beginning of the century, when the narrative style of diplomatic dispatches was more concise and less speculative, and it started to lose its grip in the face of the traumatic events of the end of the century, when anxiety fed by uncontrolled events opened a way to

---

[47] Dover, 'The economic predicament'.   [48] Maspes, 'Prammatica'.
[49] Noflatscher, 'L'"Italia" nella percezione politica'.
[50] Senatore, *'Uno mundo de carta'*, 161–250; 'Diplomazia edita'; Lazzarini, 'La nomination'; Lazzarini, 'Argument and emotion'.
[51] Lazzarini, 'Il gesto diplomatico'.

more emotional expression. Lorenzo de' Medici in examining rationally the main problems facing Italy, formulated a diagnosis:

I have often thought about the situation of the whole of Italy [...] and it looks to me that if we observe state after state we see that everyone is unhappy and in danger for various reasons. And if it is true, it looks certainly very unreasonable [*fuori d'ogni ragione*] not to try some remedies, because in my opinion there are many solutions that should please and secure everyone.[52]

Some sixty years earlier, Rinaldo degli Albizi, leader of the regime that governed Florence until the rise of Cosimo de' Medici, drily and vividly told stories, related verbal exchanges and gave orders:

From Venice, nothing good, I believe, from news I have from there; and I listen also to what news you sent to me. Vieri, ensure that the company [*brigata*] find you in peace: let that peace be what we can have for now, you understand me – traps sometimes close around the ones who set them. You will be sought out again, if you will know how to govern yourselves: everybody has his own time.[53]

Less than fifteen years after Lorenzo's letter, Pandolfo Collenuccio resorted to a totally different narrative vein to describe the reaction of pope Alexander VI as the French armies approached Rome. The astonishment of the pope – and the ambassador's emotional description – reflected also the amazement of a whole world, at odds facing a reality which acted through a different logic: 'he is doubtful and as one stunned, poor in advice and counsel. I believe that he does not know what to do, or to deliberate, and that in moaning, and complaining, and talking he will not be able to do anything else but notice that he has the king close on his back, and will finally submit.'[54]

---

[52] Lorenzo to N. Michelozzi, 1 January 1481, L. de' Medici, *Lettere*, V, 128 ('Io ho molte volte pensato in che termine si truova tutta Italia [...] Parmi in effetto, ricercando a potentia ad potentia, che ciascuna d'epse sia et male contenta, et in qualche pericolo per diverse cagioni. Et se così è, per certo pare cosa molto fuori d'ogni ragione che non ci si pigli qualche rimedio, che a mio parere ce ne è di quelli che doverebbono et contentare et assecurare ciascuno').

[53] R. degli Albizi to V. Guadagni, Rome, 4 November 1424, in *Commissioni*, III, 278 ('Di Vinegia niente credo di buono, per ora, per aviso che io ho di là; e quanto di nuovo mi avete mandato, anche sento. Fate, Vieri, che la brigata vi truovi in pace: sia ella pace quale avere si puote per ora. Tu m'intendi: le trappole scoccano alle volte a dosso a chi le tende. Voi sarete ancora ricercati, se vi saprete governare: ognuno ha il tempo suo'): Lazzarini, 'Argument and emotion'.

[54] P. Collenuccio to Ercole d'Este, Rome, 13 November 1494, in Negri, 'Le missioni di Pandolfo Collenuccio', 422 ('Dubioso sta e como stupefacto, commo povero de partiti e de consiglio. Io credo ch'el non sappia che fare, né che deliberare, e che querelando e dolendo e parlando non si saperà se non accorgere ch'el harà il re adosso, e starà a obedientia finalmente'): Martines, *Strong Words*, 249–63.

These extracts from letters written both by professional diplomats and statesmen and their apparent incoherence well describe the characters of the composite diplomatic corps in late medieval Italy. Generally, its physiognomy was very flexible and varied, according to the nature of missions and the time of stay: for official occasions, the social standing of the temporary envoys was high, but the daily work of prolonged embassies was fulfilled by political and diplomatic practitioners, possibly with a good education, and mostly with proven negotiating skills. All these men shared both a political specialisation and qualified competence in oral and written communication: some of them had had a humanistic education, some of them were clerics. The link between diplomacy and the chancery's world was crucial: in some cases, such as Milan or Mantua, the ambassadors came straight from the chancery's ranks; in other cases, such as Venice and, in the end, also Florence, chancellors and secretaries accompanied the ambassadors, selected from among the patricians. The choice of an ambassador was personal and arbitrary in principalities, where the ambassador was nominated by the prince and dealt directly with him and his chancery, and more regulated and formal in republics, where the coexistence of several offices with diplomatic responsibilities complicated and slowed diplomatic action, and a far-reaching control system was combined with election by sortition.[55]

Laws, theories and tales

Diplomacy was a flexible and pragmatic practice, and its evolution was far from over by the 1500s; it is not surprising, then, that a search for theoretical reflections or legal rules on this topic brings only uncertain results.[56]

Diplomacy was regulated only slightly by legislation: laws and rules, where they existed, were concerned more with the economic treatment of the ambassadors, the cases when it was possible to refuse a diplomatic mission, and the regulation of gifts than with the building of a coherent and comprehensive body of law on the matter.[57] Nevertheless, a set of shared habits and skills was developing, and the political importance of diplomatic practice was growing fast: after 1480, this cumulative process was strong enough to produce various texts devoted to the ambassador.

---

[55] Leverotti, *Diplomazia e governo dello stato*; Lazzarini, 'Materiali'.
[56] Gilli, 'La fonction d'ambassadeurs'.
[57] Queller, *Early Venetian Legislation*; Fubini, 'Classe dirigente'; Senatore, *'Uno mundo de carta'*, 47–50.

Above all stands the first theoretical description of diplomatic office, that is, Ermolao Barbaro's treaty *De officio legati*, written around 1490.[58] Barbaro (1453–93) was a Venetian patrician, a renowned humanist, an ambassador and son of an ambassador, and he ended up as patriarch of Aquileia. Of course, Barbaro's short text was not the first theoretical analysis of diplomacy in western Europe: its novelty, nevertheless, was precisely in defining the elusive nature of the 'new' office of the ambassador through a pragmatic analysis of its prerogatives and duties, freeing it from the limits of the old jurisprudence.[59] Barbaro's ambassador was a public official, whose duty was to work autonomously for the good of his city, with no time limits and no mandate: the picture emerging from this (probably unfinished) treaty, written by a fine humanist and experienced statesman, is a good portrait of a changing era.[60] At a more practical level, some short texts were composed on specific occasions and devoted to reminding a generic ambassador of some rules and instructions about diplomatic missions; these *Memoriali* or *Ricordi*, halfway between a chancery's aide-mémoire (such as Niccolò Machiavelli's *Notula per uno che va ambasciatore in Francia*) and a more organised consideration of ambassadorial work (such as Diomede Carafa's *Memoriale per un ambasciatore*) were pragmatic texts written and used in chanceries, where they circulated in manuscript copy.[61]

This inclination towards empirical description rather than abstraction produced another interesting group of texts. Ambassadors travelled for work and placed themselves in different environments, languages and cultures; a memorialistic mode developed towards the end of the fifteenth century, evolving from the bare enumeration of stops on a journey (usually included in final reports to justify travel expenses), and producing several examples of travel journals where personal memories combined with an increasing interest in geography, *ante litteram* ethnology and even literature.[62] In Rinaldo degli Albizi's *Commissioni* we find the first steps of this process; here, personal notes are frequently mixed with formal reports, and some of them resound with details more worthy of a novella by Boccaccio than of a diplomatic account:

Today 9th of May, on Sunday, I left Florence: in the evening I arrived at the inn at San Piero a Sieve, with 10 horses. Miles 12 [...]

---

[58] Barbaro, *De coelibatu*; Figliuolo, *Il diplomatico e il trattatista*.
[59] Hrabar, *De Legatis et Legationibus Tractatus Varii*; Behrens, 'Treatises on the ambassador'.
[60] Fubini, 'L'ambasciatore'.
[61] Machiavelli, *Notula per uno che va ambasciadore in Francia*, 54–5; Carafa, *Memoriali*, 371–3.
[62] Hyde, 'The role of diplomatic correspondence'.

Today 11th of May 1423, resting near Bologna half a mile [...] I found at the door of her farmhouse a gentlewoman called madonna Doratea, the wife of Marino di ser Goro, Bolognese draper, a shapely woman, who seemed decent, nice and charming [*formosa et in aspetto onesta, cara e vaga*], who with courtesy and much humanity asked through two of my servants if I would like to take breakfast and to rest, etc. It was around midday.[63]

The outcome is left to the reader, with a rather literary effect. To move from such texts to Francesco Vettori's description of the pleasure of travelling in 1507, the distance is great in time and subtlety, but short in self-awareness. From Albizi's brief notes to Vettori's literary masterpiece through the travel journals of Felice Brancacci to Egypt in 1422, Giovanni Ridolfi to Milan in 1480, Andrea Franceschi to Germany (1492) and England (1497), Francesco Guicciardini and Andrea Navagero to Spain (1511, 1519), the ambassadors took pleasure in observing men and facts and telling stories, comparing their reality with others, and exercising their professionally trained eye in spotting details of a wider world.[64]

On a more literary note, Vespasiano da Bisticci's *Vite* offers a different perspective on diplomacy, giving us the unforgettable portrait of the ambassador in action on at least two occasions, that is, in the lives of the Neapolitan ambassador Antonio Cicinello and of the Florentine humanist and statesman Giannozzo Manetti. Cicinello's carrier displayed a full range of practical skills, from a controlled use of violence and shrewdness when necessary, to the mixture of courtesy, gentility and aristocratic behaviour expected from a Neapolitan noble and the ambassador of a great king.[65] Manetti, on the other hand, was a champion of republican civic humanism: his rhetorical performance in front of the Venetian Senate and the doge, Francesco Foscari, is a hymn to the power of the spoken and learned word:

[The doge] gave him a public audience in the Senate, and over five hundred gentlemen attended; all those who could come were there, drawn by the fame of his special talents. Messer Giannozzo spoke for an hour or more in the morning,

---

[63] *Commissioni*, I, 414 ('A dì 9 magio 1423, in domenica, partì da Firenze: la sera venni ad albergo a San Piero a Sieve, con dieci cavalli, miglia 12 [...] A dì 11 di maggio 1423, posando presso a Bologna un mezzo miglio [...] trovai all'uscio di un suo luogo una gentildonna per nome chiamata madonna Doratea, moglie di Marino di ser Goro drappiere bolognese, formosa e in aspetto onesta, cara e vaga; la quale per sua cortesia e con tanta umanità per due de' miei famigli mi fe' dire mi piacessi far collazione e se posare io voleva, ec. Era in sul mezo dì').
[64] Catelacci, 'Diario di Felice Brancacci'; Jones, 'Travel notes'; *The Travel Journal of Antonio de Beatis*, 1–56.
[65] Bisticci, *Le vite*, II, 101–25; Fubini, 'L'ambasciatore'.

and was listened to with such attention that not one person moved or spoke. When he finished, everyone was astounded at the great power of his speaking.[66]

Conclusion

From the 1480s contacts and crossings between Europe and Italy deepened and became regular and reciprocal. In 1495, Ludovico Sforza was fully aware of the novelty – and the potential danger for the Italian states – of such a change when, in his vacillating politics, he proposed in vain to Venice to stipulate a 'new league among Italian princes only'.[67] The French invasion transformed the tensions among Italian states from the level of hypothetical internal and/or external diplomatic alliances to a succession of military leagues and real wars. Nevertheless, it was not only a matter of pure violence: the redefinition in terms of military aggression of the intermittent influence of the European powers over Italy actually dismantled the political symbiosis upon which the Italian system was precariously built, as Guicciardini sharply pointed out when he wrote that with the French armies 'there entered into Italy a flame and a plague that not only changed the states, but also the ways of government, and the ways of war'.[68] Italians were totally unused to such a non-communicative way of defining conflict and solving disputes: the breakdown of the Italian political balance revealed the weaknesses of the common discourse of diplomacy which had ensured since the 1450s a certain autonomy to the Italian system of territorial states, but had also accelerated its evolution.

The broadening of the political network and the partial changing of the rules of the competition transformed the hierarchies of negotiation, reducing the protagonists of the diplomatic dialogue to a closed circle of major powers, and forcing everybody else to rely on second-hand circuits or dynastic alliances to stay involved, or to survive by avoiding involvement. However, this change led to two other crucial consequences. The transformation of diplomatic dynamics gradually involved in a single arena a wide range of first- and second-rank protagonists in Italy and in Europe, and implemented a common language made out of the

---

[66] Bisticci, *Le vite*, I, 485–538, 504 ('Giunto a Vinegia, gli fu fatto grandissimo onore dal doge, ch'era messer Francesco Foscari, uomo di grandissima autorità. Dettegli udienza publica nel Consiglio di Pregati, vi si trovò più 500 gentiluomini, e vennonvi tutti quegli che si potevano venire, mossi dalla fama de le due singulari virtù. Parlò messer Giannozzo la matina una ora o più, e fu istato audire con tanta atentione che non fu mai ignuno si muovessi né parlassi. Parlato ebe, istavano tuti come ismariti, veduta la gran forza aveva nel parlare'); Gilli, 'De l'importance'.
[67] Catalano, 'La fine della signoria sforzesca', 478.   [68] Guicciardini, *Opere*, I, 117.

combination of different habits within a general pattern developed mostly in an Italian context. Secondly, this common language, once standardised and recognisable, became progressively more rigid and formally defined: the ambassador's profile focused on professionality and social status; chancellors stepped back to a merely supportive role; treatises flourished, defining the characters of both an aristocratic corps and an established function.[69]

[69] Frigo (ed.), *Politics and Diplomacy*.

22 Regional states and economic development

Franco Franceschi and Luca Molà

Introduction

In recent historiography on the Italian regional states, a political-institutional perspective has taken centre stage, while markedly less space has been allotted by historians to economic change. Among the first to deal with the topic that interests us here was David Herlihy, who in the late 1960s began to reflect on the birth of a 'Tuscan regional economy'[1] and to wonder to what degree the creation of the Florentine territorial state had conditioned the economic structure of Tuscany.[2] Some fifteen years later, his insights were arranged more systematically in the thesis of Paolo Malanima, who held that Florence's demographic and economic-financial supremacy over the other cities of Tuscany maintained its military dominance, which in turn enabled its territorial expansion and the achievement of a regional state.[3]

The study of the formation and makeup of the 'economic regions' was soon extended to Lombardy and the Veneto[4] and received a significant boost in the 1990s with Stephan R. Epstein's innovative research. Engaging in a constant critical dialogue with the positions of Douglass C. North[5] and the English-speaking New Institutional Economics school, Epstein broadened the field of observation from north-central Italy to Aragonese Sicily and subsequently to a comparison between Italian and European states in a long-term perspective.[6] The central core of Epstein's thesis, which approached the problem from many sides, is that economic growth in the pre-industrial age depended essentially on

---

Franco Franceschi wrote pp. 444–53 of this chapter, Luca Molà pp. 453–63; the text and the conclusion are the result of a common work of research and collaboration.

[1] Herlihy, *Medieval and Renaissance Pistoia*, 155–60.
[2] Herlihy, 'Le relazioni economiche', 79. [3] Malanima, 'La formazione'.
[4] Mirri, 'Formazione'; Ciriacono, 'Venise'; Ciriacono,'L'economia regionale'; Knapton, 'City wealth'.
[5] See North, *Institutions*.
[6] See Epstein, *Freedom*, the bibliography of which includes also most of this scholar's previous works.

market integration; this process, in turn, was closely tied to the reinforcement of the sovereignty of the states and their increased capacity to reduce the obstacles to development represented by monopolies and rent-seeking positions, in particular by reducing transaction costs.

While the 'regionalist approach' encountered a certain success in European historiography, in the case of Italy Epstein's work was flanked by that of a small group of scholars who dealt with the general theme from different, and sometimes contrasting, angles.[7] The scholarship on this topic in most recent years has been more episodic, even though interest has not totally waned.[8] One aspect that should be emphasised is that, for specialists in the fourteenth to sixteenth centuries, the discussion on economic regions has constantly been intertwined with renewed interpretations of the 'crisis' of the late Middle Ages, which spotlighted mainly its positive effects: increased per capita income, the growth and diversification of consumption, the birth of new manufacturing centres, often located in smaller towns and rural villages, the reduction of production costs – all processes which in turn were able to stimulate the formation of more integrated regional markets.[9]

In general, this season of research and debate has left to those who want to analyse the relationship between the formation of regional states and the development of the economy a legacy of a broad range of topics, issues and even unresolved problems. Still debated are aspects such as the degree of division of labour on a territorial scale, the spread of proto-industry, the relationship between regional and extra-regional economic circuits, the correspondence between political and economic regions, the real impact of measures enacted by governments, and the diversity of results obtained in the different institutional contexts. Without aspiring to deal with such a vast host of questions here, we shall concentrate in these pages on a specific aspect of the relationship between politics and the economy: the role of public policies in the development of production and exchange in the regional states of Italy. We know that a number of scholars nourish substantial scepticism on the cohesiveness and organic nature of these interventions;[10] nonetheless we feel that the topic

---

[7] Tangheroni, 'Il sistema economico'; Franceschi, 'Istituzioni'; Malanima, 'Teoria economica'; Frangioni, 'La politica economica'; Corritore, 'Una fondamentale discontinuità'; Knapton, 'Tra dominante e dominio'; Lanaro, *I mercati*.
[8] La Roncière, 'Dalla città', especially 18–29; Faugeron, 'De la commune'; Sakellariou, 'Elementi'.
[9] For an overview of these theses and the changes in historiographical approach they reflect, see Franceschi and Molà, 'L'economia'.
[10] See, for example, Epstein, *An Island*, 122–3; Knapton, 'City wealth', 189; Frangioni, 'La politica economica', 256.

deserves further reflection, and not only on the 'territorial' perspective of the governments' strategies, but also on their ability to influence the economic trend *tout court*.

Commercial policy and development of the domestic market

Can it be maintained that in Renaissance Italy, with the formation of the regional states, the role of the public authority in the organisation of the infrastructure of exchange becomes more crucial? To answer this question, we shall analyse first of all the case of the Florentine territory, currently the best-known, and then go on to offer some elements of comparison with the republic of Venice, the duchy of Milan and the kingdoms of southern Italy.

Before the most intense phase of territorial expansion, Florentine policy concerning customs and food administration was inspired by three basic objectives: to increase tax income, to ensure the food supply in Florence and to foster trade in a city that based its prosperity on cloth-manufacturing and mercantile activity. These orientations, not always easy to harmonise with each other, were implemented by means of the development of an efficient road system, surveillance of the number and functions of the marketplaces, the establishment of customs duties designed to encourage the influx of food and raw materials into Florence and discourage the opposite movement, an attempt to standardise weights and measures, and control of the distribution of agricultural products in case of a food crisis. These same objectives can be seen in the policies implemented on a regional level, based on accords with neighbouring towns aimed at introducing reciprocal facilitations and toll franchises. With Pisa, Lucca and Siena in particular, Florence negotiated access to the Tyrrhenian ports in the possession of these city-states.[11]

The subjection of Arezzo, Pisa and Cortona, joined in 1421 by the acquisition of Livorno and Porto Pisano, changed, at least partially, the perception the Florentines had of their dominion, increasing the need to adapt their economic policies to the new territorial picture. As soon as they achieved their desired outlet on the Tyrrhenian sea, they therefore created the magistracy of the Sea Consuls, whose purpose was to manage the outfitting of a merchant fleet and at the same time to act as a sort of general economic 'ministry'. In 1426, the office was split into two

---

[11] La Roncière, *Firenze*, parts II–III; Franceschi, 'Intervento', 865–76; Epstein, 'Stato territoriale', 880–1; Goldthwaite, *The Economy*, 489.

sections: besides the task of defining the entire organisation of the system of galleys, the Florentine consuls assumed full jurisdiction over any juridical dispute connected with the activity of the fleet and partial jurisdiction over litigation between Florentines and foreigners which earlier had been the province of the Mercanzia, the merchants' court. The Pisan consuls, among their other offices, obtained a sort of supervision over the taxes and duties that concerned the city of Pisa and its former territory but also the task of regulating export licenses for wheat.[12]

Customs and marketplaces, together with the roads and seaways, remained at the centre of public policy interventions also in subsequent decades. In the course of the fifteenth century and the first half of the sixteenth, the Tower Officials, the magistracy with the greatest responsibility for the roads, operated both in the *contado* and in the district with initiatives of building, repair and maintenance of roads and bridges. Assisted by the *Viai*, officials charged with inspecting the road network and pointing out critical problems, and in constant contact with territorial officials, they often had to deal, however, with local communities' resistance to carrying out the operations they were required to do.[13] With the intent of extending to the entire state the relations already established with its *contado*, the Florentine government deprived the subject cities, with the partial exception of Pistoia, of the right to fix duties and tariffs independently. This new sovereignty was sometimes utilised to reduce and even abolish the customs barriers between Florence and its adjoining municipalities, above all to the advantage of the dominant city, but not in order to create a unified system, given that different circumscriptions continued to exist, with their own administration and different regulations, marked by the persistence of special franchises and exemptions.[14] Some progress was represented by the establishment in 1448 of the *Dogana dei Traffici* (Trade Customs), which was supposed to simplify the forms of payment and step up the fight against smuggling.[15] This action was followed in 1451 by other measures concerning commerce in Livorno and Porto Pisano, in 1458 by the proposal, never carried out, to channel the Arno from Pisa to Florence as a stimulus to internal exchange,[16] and above all in 1461 by the so-called *Legge dei Passeggieri*. This law aimed at redistributing the costs of maintenance of the infrastructure among the various communities in the

---

[12] Franceschi, 'Intervento', 902–5.   [13] Franceschi, 'Istituzioni', 99–101.
[14] Epstein, 'Stato territoriale', 882–3; Epstein, 'Strutture', 102; Fasano Guarini, 'Città soggette', 16–17.
[15] Dini, 'Le vie', 289–90.   [16] Franceschi, 'Industria', 552.

dominion, but also at rationally organising the territorial tariff system by redesigning the geography of the collection points and channelling all the traffic along pre-set routes. The new tax-collection arrangement, nonetheless, did not completely do away with the passes located in the interior areas of the state and in any case continued to be adjusted in the following decades,[17] until in 1545 the entire customs apparatus was reformed as part of the revision of taxes and tariffs ordered by Cosimo I.[18]

The picture is not too different if we look at Florentine policy concerning fairs and markets. Between the middle of the fourteenth century and 1560, at least thirty-eight fairs were founded or reactivated, seventeen of which obtained total exemption from tariffs on the merchandise offered for sale. In that same period, at least thirty-four new weekly markets were opened, of which twelve with toll franchises. The distribution of the new establishments, more numerous between the 1430s and the 1480s, shows that the Florentine authorities intended above all to encourage the formation of a web of fairs and markets along its borders, in particular with Siena, Umbria and Marche, in order to stimulate the import of agricultural products and livestock.[19] At the origin of the creation of a fair or market was the request of the community where it was to be located, but the Florentine government had the right to accept the proposal or not. With the advent of the Medici principality, the procedure became more formalised, and among the variables considered was the impact that the opening of a new market might have on the business of neighbouring ones and thus on the income from the taxes this business generated.[20]

Stephan Epstein expresses a mixed judgement on these developments. In the case of Florence, territorial expansion and political centralisation fostered a decrease in indirect taxes, rationalisation of the regional road network (resulting in decreased internal transportation costs) and the chance also for politically weak communities to have their own fairs and markets despite the opposition of the cities to which they had been subject in the past. On the other hand, the Florentines remained essentially incapable of identifying the real benefits of the process of formation of a regional economy; they were too eager to control internal trade and were motivated above all by political and fiscal concerns.[21]

Where the Florentine ruling class, albeit with its contradictions and inconsistencies, showed a certain overall vision and a 'territorial' strategy, the Venetian aristocracy, or at least a large portion of it, set up

---

[17] Epstein, 'Strutture', 97–9, 117; Dini, 'Le vie', 290–2.
[18] Brown, 'Concepts', 283, 286.   [19] Epstein, *Freedom*, 153–4.
[20] See Pult Quaglia, *'Per provvedere'*, 101–7.   [21] Epstein, 'Strutture', 118–19.

strong resistance to the very idea of expansion on to the mainland. Venice, as Gian Maria Varanini effectively summed up, was and remained the fulcrum of the ideology of the city's elite, and this assumption was the bedrock from which two fundamental objectives of their commercial policy derived: to foster the flow into the city of consumer products for the people and the raw materials necessary for the 'state' industries such as the arsenal; and to make the port and the market of Venice obligatory stops for the commerce of the Terraferma (mainland) cities, so as to control the payment of duties and encourage the use of Venetian ships.[22]

The application of these directives, however, did not happen without conflicts, exceptions and adjustments. On the food-supply front – according to recent research – the formation of a dominion did not set in motion great transformations initially: every Terraferma city kept its procurement system, the territory remained fragmented by multiple interior customs points, and almost no new fairs were created, with the exception of a few border fairs in the area of Bergamo, set up to attract agricultural products from Lombardy. Very little was invested in strengthening the road system, which had in any case traditionally been neglected in favour of water transport.[23] Nonetheless, under this apparent continuity, something began to change: while the Collegio alle Biave (office in charge of the grain supply) became the court of appeal for litigation between subjects and communities on the mainland, the Council of Ten assumed greater power in the decision-making process in matters of food supply. The intervention of this magistracy later became essential during the wars with Milan, and in particular in the years around the peace of Lodi (1454), when Venice had to deal with an authentic food crisis, distributing grain to many rural municipalities abandoned by their urban centres. The food-supply policy therefore became a means to legitimise the superiority of the dominant city and to reinforce its authority over the subject lands, even if no 'substantial changes'[24] came about until the next century due to Venice's reluctance to enter into conflict with the Terraferma cities, which especially in unfavourable years tried to keep the agricultural production of their respective territories for themselves, raising the spectre of famine.[25]

The issue of obligatory passage of goods through the port of Venice is multifaceted as well. A cornerstone of the republic's economic policy, it was extended starting in 1407 to the newly subjected territories. In the

---

[22] Varanini, 'Le politiche', 248; Varanini, 'Élites cittadine', 158–9.
[23] Faugeron, 'De la commune', 106–7.   [24] *Ibid.*, 107–11.
[25] Collodo, 'Il sistema annonario', 400–1.

meantime, it should be said that the measure was applied only to exchange with foreign countries and not to domestic trade; furthermore, as the relations with Verona and Brescia demonstrate, the conduct of the Venetian government was not at all univocal.[26] On the basis of the pacts of submission drawn up in 1405, Veronese merchants were allowed to avoid the stop in Venice and its tariffs: the products manufactured in Verona, first and foremost wool cloth, could thus be sent over land to Mantua and Ferrara and then, through the Apennine passes, reach the distribution centres and fairs of central and southern Italy, or could follow the Adige and Po rivers as far as Ravenna, and there set sail for the East or the Adriatic ports. The privilege was revoked, however, in 1421, and then reintroduced in 1437 as a result of the protests of the Veronese, cancelled again in 1455 but immediately reinstated, and cancelled yet again in 1475. On this occasion, the Veronese maintained that the passage through Venice may indeed have increased the revenues of tariffs collected on the lagoon, but it reduced the income from those on the mainland and encouraged contraband. The result was that, in 1485, Venice backed down once more.[27] With Brescia, on the other hand, the Venetian government applied a dual policy: substantially *laissez-faire* with regard to land trade with the Germanic regions, and much less flexible for the trade that used maritime routes and ports. These choices are exemplified by the decree that in 1519 permitted the free entry of wax coming from German countries to Brescia, but required that the wax imported by sea transit through the port of Venice.[28]

In addition, in the same period, marked by the effects of the defeat at Agnadello and the initiation of a 'gradual move towards the mainland of the political and economic equilibrium [...] of the entire state',[29] Venetian trade policy, too, began to show greater attention to the economy of the dominion and less tolerance for the prerogatives of the subject cities. This tendency, exemplified also by the institution of the Cinque Savi alla Mercanzia (1517), the magistracy with very broad jurisdiction over both land and sea traffic, took the form in the central decades of the century of more incisive initiatives aimed at restoring centrality to the port of Venice and a constant 'drainage of money towards the capital'. The definitive abolition in 1581 of the privilege granted to Verona can be seen in this perspective.[30] The fact remains, underlined by Paola Lanaro, that the republic's decision to let 'transportation networks independent of the obligatory passage through the port

---

[26] Lanaro, *I mercati*, 58–9. [27] On this issue, see Demo, *L''anima'*, 252–5.
[28] Lanaro, *I mercati*, 70–4. [29] Knapton, '"Nobiltà"', 186.
[30] Lanaro, *I mercati*, 68, 86–7 (quotation at 123).

of Venice' survive for a long time – along with that of normally allowing the subject towns to keep their fairs – contributed to the 'maintenance of the ancient economic basins'.[31]

If the efforts at integration of the regional market made by the Florentine government had only partial success and the trade policy of Venice towards its dominion wavered for a long time, what were the scenarios outside the major republican states?

In Lombardy from the early fourteenth century, the Visconti, well aware of the function of Milan and its region as a zone of transit, focused on developing inter-regional commerce. The treaties contracted in the first half of the century with Venice, the house of Savoy and Bellinzona, but above all the *Provisiones Januae* of 1346, can be explained in this perspective. The peculiarity of this last-mentioned agreement, destined to stimulate trade among the Lombard plain, Genoa and northern Europe, lay in the fact that it did not concern just Milan but also Como, Cremona, Lodi and Pizzighettone[32] (to which were later added Novara, Bergamo and Brescia) as centres joined together in a customs union. In essence, these towns gave up, at least in principle, their right to impose restrictions on trade or variations of tariffs in favour of the lords of Milan, who in exchange committed to guaranteeing peaceful trade relations in the entire region.[33] In the subsequent decades the Visconti, who had been only partially sensitive to the conditioning of the interests of merchants and entrepreneurs,[34] strengthened economic relations between Lombardy and its more important interlocutors (first and foremost, the house of Savoy, the dukes of Burgundy, and Genoa),[35] while from the early fifteenth century they claimed full authority to institute new fairs and markets and to establish road tolls.

Similar policies were enacted by the Sforza, who in the second half of the century approved the institution of fairs, especially in smaller towns.[36] In 1454, in the meantime, duke Francesco had prescribed, for the transport of goods to Milan, 'obligatory itineraries, established with precise aims of securing taxes and public safety'.[37] Certainly, the efficacy of these measures was limited; as in the above-mentioned reform of the road and customs system undertaken a few years later in Tuscany, the Sforza measure as well was haunted by the spectre of evasion and smuggling.[38] Another meaningful aspect of the Visconti–Sforza policy on trade concerns the waterways, a fundamental resource in a region

---

[31] Lanaro, 'Periferie', 24–5. [32] Frangioni, *Milano*, 39–41.
[33] Epstein, *Freedom*, 124–5. [34] See Mainoni, *Economia*, 6.
[35] Frangioni, *Milano*, 41–2. [36] Epstein, *Freedom*, 79, 125.
[37] Frangioni, 'La politica economica', 266. [38] *Ibid.*

that contained one of the most impressive hydrographic systems in Europe. The importance of initiatives such as the creation of the Navigliaccio between Milan and Pavia in the years 1339–65, the digging of the Bereguardo canal around 1420 and the building of the inland waterway of Martesana, begun in 1457 and intended to link the capital city with the Adda river, is well known,[39] but the evolution of the institutions in this sphere should also be highlighted. Through the figure of the judge of the waters, introduced permanently in 1346, and in 1396 through the office of the roads, waters and bridges, the management of the rivers and canals was gradually broadened to encompass the entire state. This geographic extension acted in concert with the political extension, given that the assigned magistracy no longer limited itself to fulfilling functions of arbitration, as had been the case in the age of the communes, but also had powers of control and coercion. Water management – as Patrick Boucheron has pointed out – was one of the essential factors in the construction of the regional state.[40]

Overall, the most peculiar characteristic of Milanese policy with regard to the infrastructure of commerce seems to have been the ability to unite a capacity for intervention on a regional scale with the awareness of the irrepressibly polycentric physiognomy of the dominion. In a region in which the cities, 'albeit subject', had not lost 'their power as political and administrative centres, as city-states, nor their capacity for territorial control',[41] first the Visconti and then the Sforza gave up plans of centralisation on the Florentine model and aimed instead at weakening the larger cities by guaranteeing fiscal, commercial and jurisdictional privileges to the rural communities and smaller towns. 'At the same time, they were careful to ensure that grants of territorial franchise did not include market and excise rights. Devolution of local power seems therefore to have gone hand in hand with a reduction of institutional barriers to regional trade.'[42]

A similar result was reached in the kingdom of Naples by means of different policies. According to Eleni Sakellariou's research, in the course of the fifteenth century the Aragonese monarchy, albeit not in a systematic manner and, what is more, in response to requests from the local communities, carried out a series of reforms that fostered economic integration: standardisation of weights and measures, promotion of a single currency, improvement of the road system, but above all the creation of new fairs on a regional level and the reduction of indirect taxes on internal trade. Of the 290 fairs documented in the kingdom

---

[39] Fantoni, *L'acqua*, 61–74.   [40] *Ibid.*, 123–31; Boucheron, *Le pouvoir*, 289–99.
[41] Chittolini, 'Alcune note', 428.   [42] Epstein, 'Town', 464.

between the thirteenth and the sixteenth centuries, a good 190 were instituted in the fifteenth and early sixteenth centuries. Located primarily in the smaller towns of all twelve provinces of the state, these represented a fundamental tool for interchange among the various areas of the dominion. Equally positive for the development of the kingdom's economy was relief in several categories of tariffs and the frequent concession of exemptions and customs franchises to individual communities, measures that Alfonso the Magnanimous could afford thanks to the increased revenue collected by equipping the crown property with two sure sources of income: direct taxation and payment for use of communal pasturelands.[43]

At least in the period between 1416 and 1458, when Alfonso ruled over Sicily, this island, too, benefited from similar policies: the customs exemptions proliferated (to the point that at the end of the fifteenth century they concerned more than forty demesnial towns), the number of fairs grew as never before, and the system of weights and measures was partially standardised. The effects of these measures can be recognised, starting in the second half of the century, above all in the improvement in the grain distribution network, an improvement demonstrated by more uniform prices and less frequent food-supply crises, even in a phase of great population growth. As in the kingdom of Naples, the pressure of local communities was a determining factor, a fact that has been judged, however, perhaps too severely, as the demonstration that 'state intervention on the regional market was largely random and opportunist'.[44]

Strategies of redistribution of productive activities on a regional scale

The distribution of manufacturing activities in the Italian states of the Renaissance presents the same picture as that of commercial policies. For the entire fifteenth century and the first part of the sixteenth, we find no regional-scale strategies of redistribution of production except ones in favour of the dominant city, which were often only *ad hoc* measures designed to meet contingent needs. In any case, this type of regional strategy could have been adopted with success only where the relations of power with the subject communities permitted it.

The case of Tuscany is exemplary in this sense. The weight of industry, capital and population in Florence seems to have permitted it to harmonise the individual economies of the region, moving – as posited

---

[43] Sakellariou, 'Elementi'.   [44] Epstein, *An Island*, 85–123 (quotation at 123).

by Paolo Malanima – from 'a model of growth founded on a multiplicity of competing towns' in the thirteenth century to one in which Florence functioned as the central node, with the smaller towns specialising in production that did not compete with that of the capital city.[45] Thus in Colle di Val d'Elsa the paper industry grew, in Pistoia metallurgy and weapons-manufacturing, and in Arezzo the weaving of cotton cloth. This 'natural' evolution of the economy, however, was counterbalanced by Florence's strong intervention in the dominion's wool industry, which was reorganised in the 1420s in a three-part hierarchy: the capital city naturally remained the principal manufacturing pole, holder of the monopoly on the creation of luxury fabrics using English wool. There were other towns, such as Prato, where any wool except English could be worked; and the rural wool manufactures, which were authorised only to make low-quality cloth using exclusively local material. The inclusion of the wool industry of Pisa in this latter category was unquestionably intended as a punitive measure, only partially attenuated by the fact that in those same years the building of the state galleys relaunched the Pisan ship-building industry and that in the following decades other sectors of its economy – soap production, leather processing, and hat manufacturing – obtained support.[46] All in all, Stephan Epstein seems to be right when he says that Florentine 'industrial policy' penalised the main cities of the state in favour of the smaller towns and outlying areas. The most evident case is Pescia, where the production of raw silk and the spinning of threads prospered as a result of the demand for raw materials and partly finished goods on the part of the silk industry in Florence.[47]

It is a less simple matter to identify a consistent orientation in the economic policy of the duchy of Milan. A capital city teeming with different activities, with peaks of excellence in the textile sector, in the production of gold and silver thread, and in weapons manufacturing, was flanked by numerous towns of various sizes and rural villages devoted mainly to the cloth industry. The spread and expansion of the manufacture of linen cloth, fustians and woollens that took place between the middle of the fourteenth and the middle of the fifteenth centuries were not the effect of homogeneous, unified growth but, paradoxically, drew benefit from institutional and jurisdictional fragmentation caused by the ducal policy of granting privileges to the minor settlements against the interests of the urban centres. During the fifteenth century, however, both in the woollens and in the fustian industries an extreme protectionism of local origin arose, which the

---

[45] Malanima, 'Politica'. [46] Franceschi, 'Industria', 547–53.
[47] Epstein, 'Stato territoriale', 883–90.

dukes, forced to mediate between contrasting interests, did not try or were not able to harmonise.

Nonetheless, it was Milanese industry, as might be expected, that received particular protection. Francesco Sforza, for example, in 1454 limited the entrance into Milan of cloth made in other towns and areas of the duchy, while even earlier measures had been taken to force the concentration in Milan of the linen warps (*cavezzi*) traditionally used to make fustians and to forbid the export of these semi-finished goods beyond the borders of the duchy without a special licence, measures that had created tension with the rural producers. To this protectionist policy the dukes added meticulously detailed legislation in defence of the quality of Milanese products, reaching the point in 1517 of threatening to cut off the right hand of anyone who counterfeited gold thread by gilding it with copper and orichalc.[48] At any rate, starting in the fifteenth century, protectionism and quality control were common to the majority of the Italian states.

The Venetian government, having to compete with large and medium-sized producers, here too chose to follow a line of compromise. In the 'pacts of devolution', the government did not in any way limit wool-manufacturing, in rapid expansion from the thirteenth century in Verona and from the fourteenth in Padua, Vicenza and Brescia. This substantial autonomy facilitated the growth of the industries on the mainland, which in the course of the fifteenth century saw a significant increase in the number of goods produced: Vicenza and Verona, for example, which in the middle of the fifteenth century each manufactured about 3,000 bolts of cloth per year, went to producing towards the end of the century 4,000 and 11,000 pieces, respectively.[49] At the moment of its territorial expansion, conversely, Venice had not yet developed a strong interest in wool-manufacturing, which grew at a steady rate only after the early decades of the sixteenth century.[50] As a consequence, production in the mainland cities was not in competition with Venice, but rather fit well into its mechanism of trade, providing a prestigious item to add to the products exported to the East. Furthermore, the human capital of the subject territories gave a fundamental boost to manufacturing in the capital city: if in the fourteenth century the textile industries of Venice were almost monopolised by experts from Tuscany and the Milan area, in the next two centuries artisans and workers from Brescia, Bergamo and all over the Venetian mainland predominated.[51]

---

[48] Barbieri, *Economia*; Mazzaoui, 'The Lombard cotton industry'; Mazzaoui, 'La diffusione', 163–8; Frangioni, 'La politica economica'; Epstein, 'Manifatture'.
[49] Demo, *L''anima'*.   [50] Mozzato, 'The production'.
[51] Molà and Mueller, 'Essere straniero'.

But Venice did not always act as it did in the case of the wool industry. When it was a question of key sectors, ones important for its own international image, the capital city gave priority to its own interests over those of its subjects. This is the case of the glass and silk industries. As early as the fourteenth century, Padua, Vicenza and Verona had successfully devoted their efforts to the production of glass, entering into competition with the Venetians, who had protected the Murano industry by forbidding the export of soda ash (sodium carbonate) coming from Syria, essential for the production of fine glass, on which they held a semi-monopoly thanks to their merchant fleet. Precisely in order to have a supply of this material, in 1394 the glass-makers of Vicenza and Verona, in that period under the dominion of Milan, asked Gian Galeazzo Visconti to block the export to Venice of equally indispensable raw materials coming from their territories or the Milan area, which the Murano glass-makers needed to make their glass paste and kiln tools. After it had acquired almost all of the Veneto at the beginning of the fifteenth century, and despite the fact that the pacts of devolution confirmed the rights of the subject towns to manufacture glass, starting in 1408 Venice adopted a protectionist stance: it limited the quantity of soda ash from the East that could be exported to the subject towns; prohibited the building of new kilns in these cities; forbade the circulation of glass-makers inside the state, persecuting the Murano glass-makers who, during the months of forced inactivity in the summer and autumn, would go to work on the mainland; and imposed the free export of Murano products to the entire dominion. In some cases the Venetian directives were not effective, whether because in the following decades the glass-makers emigrated illegally to other towns on the mainland, or because soda ash was often smuggled, but they succeeded at least in limiting internal competition, which was subsequently completely defeated when Murano, starting in the middle of the fifteenth century, began to specialise in the production of high-quality glass, a sector in which it had no competitors for almost two centuries.[52]

For silk fabrics, protectionism was even more pronounced. The working of silk in Venice, dating from the thirteenth century, had been transformed by the immigration of skilled workers from Lucca in the early fourteenth century, making it one of the major European silk-manufacturing centres of the Renaissance. By contrast, even in the fifteenth century none of the mainland cities had established this industry; nonetheless, the growing consumption of silk cloth, with the

---

[52] Jacoby, *Raw Materials*; Varanini, 'Élites cittadine', 165–6.

concomitant increase in the demand for raw materials, led Vicenza, Verona and other districts to focus on raising silkworms, to the point that, at the end of the sixteenth century, the annual production of raw silk in the Venetian state was close to a half million pounds. The capital city supported the development of sericulture with a non-punitive fiscal and tariff policy; in the meantime, Vicenza and Verona were left free to build throwing machines for transforming their silk into semi-finished goods that were exported to markets in Italy and northern Europe. This approach, however, was counterbalanced by the prohibition, reiterated a number of times, on producing luxury fabrics (brocade, velvet, satin, damask). The supplications of the representatives of many mainland city councils were often in vain, obtaining only temporary concessions. Meanwhile, Venetian silk cloth was imposed on the entire state by means of the ban on the import of foreign fabrics, thus giving the capital city a monopoly in a vast market.[53]

The choice to give priority to the silk industry of the capital city was common to other states. In 1474, a petition to the duke of Milan to introduce velvet-manufacturing into Pavia was rejected by the Milanese magistrates because this concession would have caused a sharp decline in production in Milan, and consequently also in fiscal revenues, given that the move of skilled workers elsewhere would have reduced the income from taxes on consumption. The officials, moreover, reminded the duke that in the states where the main city produced silk velvet, as in Venice, Florence or Ferrara, this industry was not permitted in other towns.[54] This assertion could have been applied not long afterwards also to the kingdom of Naples, where, besides the capital, only Catanzaro, because of an ancient tradition, could produce luxury fabrics. In 1488, king Ferdinand, worried about the plots of some individuals who, in league with other cities, wanted to have artisans move there in order to begin a silk industry, issued a decree prohibiting the departure of skilled labour and the transfer of materials from Naples, carrying a fine of 1,000 ducats.[55]

In reality, it was the state of Ferrara, used by the Milanese as one of their examples of protectionism, that opened the gates of the subject cities to silk-manufacturing. They began with Modena in 1480, to which Ercole I d'Este granted various privileges for starting up this industry, while silk-manufacturing was introduced to Reggio Emilia by duchess Lucrezia Borgia in person, who sponsored before the elders a Genoese silk worker resident in Ferrara, thus founding the leading early modern

[53] Molà, *The Silk Industry*, 217–94. [54] Verga, *Il Comune*.
[55] Pescione, 'Gli statuti', 64–5.

industrial activity of Reggio.⁵⁶ These were very different approaches from those adopted by other Italian states, which can be explained perhaps by the absence in Ferrara of a strong core of entrepreneurs capable of determined resistance to the spread of the most valuable technical knowledge outside the capital city.

Support for manufacturing

In the fifteenth century, the most successful new silk industries were precisely those of Milan, Ferrara and Naples, all supported by their respective governments. In Milan, Filippo Maria Visconti entered in 1442 into a contract with the Florentine Pietro di Bartolo to start up a cloth-weaving industry. In Ferrara, Borso d'Este did the same in 1462 with the Genoese Urbano Trincherio, subsequently reaching agreements with dyers, gold-beaters and other experts who could guarantee the launch of a high-quality industry. King Ferrante signed three contracts (an unusually and significantly high number) with different entrepreneurs – a Venetian, a Florentine and a Genoese – between 1465 and 1475 in order to set the silk industry of Naples on a solid foundation. In these contracts, the rulers offered the innovators facilitation that ranged from fiscal privileges to interest-free loans, receiving in exchange the commitment to activate a given number of looms and produce a specified amount of fabric. The silk industry thus created, and favoured later with numerous decrees and the institution of guilds with extended jurisdictional privileges, remained for centuries the principal manufacturing activity in these three cities, as evidence of the degree to which public intervention influenced their economic development. But many other examples of state intervention in the establishment of silk industries could easily be given, including Siena in 1438, Perugia in 1459, Messina in 1486 and Mantua in 1523, as well as the cities in Emilia already mentioned and others still, some of which limited themselves to introducing the spinning of thread in order to supply the industries of nearby towns. These policies, moreover, were joined by others aimed at increasing the production of raw material, such as the requirement to plant a certain number of mulberry trees, whose leaves were the food for silkworms, on private and public property, and the real establishment of some plant nurseries run by the government (in the states of Mantua, Milan and Savoy) to supply growers with young trees.⁵⁷

---

⁵⁶ Fiorenzi, *Le arti*, 112–13; Rombaldi, 'L'arte', 43–7.
⁵⁷ For an overview with bibliographical references, see Molà, 'The Italian silk industry'.

If the development of the silk industry, which throughout the early modern age was the driving force of the Italian economy, is the most sensational example of the crucial role played by governments in the economic growth of their states, rulers and city councils acted in similar ways to develop other sectors. Using all the tools at their disposal – from bids to attract technicians to incentives for opening workshops and acquiring citizenship, tax exemptions, and bans on the import of the products of competing industries[58] – but focusing above all on agreements with individual entrepreneurs, they succeeded in broadening the productive base in a phase of expanding demand for goods. Pre-eminence was always given to textiles, capable of creating jobs and thus functioning as a stimulus for the entire economy and a guarantor of social peace. But the range of activities introduced into the cities thanks to the efforts of the institutions was vast and tended to grow wider over time. These included tapestry-weaving, printing, glass-making, the manufacture of paper, wax, soap, and pottery, metallurgy and the making of metal objects, and the working of semi-precious stones and of precious metals. The registers of city councils or the princely chanceries include numerous contracts signed with entrepreneurs and artisans for an ever widening range of activities.[59] In some cities, such as early fifteenth-century Florence, where the political weight of the corporations was significant, these were the ones who pursued the start-up of new productions or the perfecting of existing ones through the contribution of foreign technicians. For twenty years, starting in 1418, the Florentine wool guild (Arte della Lana) promoted the production of a lightweight fabric originating in southern France and Catalan-Aragonese Spain, called *'perpignan'*, making agreements with artisans from those regions to emigrate to Tuscany for this purpose.[60] In those same years, three Florentine entrepreneurs were rewarded by the government for having brought to the city Genoese and Venetian experts in the production of gold and silver thread and in this way given a crucial boost to the manufacturing of *auroserico* cloth.[61]

Institutional intervention in favour of innovations could be more complex. As early as the first half of the fifteenth century the governors of some Italian states were showing evidence of a broader vision of the world of production, which took the form not only of measures benefiting specific sectors, but also of an attempt to reorganise the entire manufacturing apparatus of a city or district. Thus it was that in 1422 the Florentine government assigned the sea consuls the task of analysing

---

[58] Mazzaoui, 'Artisan migration'.   [59] On this theme in general, see Molà, 'States'.
[60] Franceschi, 'La grande manifattura', 380–2.   [61] Franceschi, 'I forestieri', 410–11.

the situation of all the state manufacturing industries for the purpose of introducing the activities still lacking and of supporting the sectors in difficulty. The task kept the consuls busy until 1426, when they presented a plan of intervention based mainly on a protectionist excise policy. Conversely, the assignment given in 1447 to the *Monte* officials to scout out foreign artisans and technicians and bring them to Florence to start up activities unknown until then was aimed exclusively at innovation.[62]

The republic of Siena embarked in 1459 on an even more ambitious project to reorganise the urban production system – which like the Florentine efforts involved also the republic's territory – with the establishment of a special body appointed to 'attract crafts to the city and there organise, support, augment and preserve them'. Composed of eighteen members, for more than two years this commission met in the town hall and issued decrees in support of the industries that already existed, made contracts with artisans and entrepreneurs willing to start up new forms of production, and introduced protectionist regulations to shield these industries from foreign competition. Thus it was decided to relaunch glass-making, to support the production of leather and furs, and to initiate the weaving of linen cloth and woollen *perpignan*, the manufacture of white soap and of hats, the dyeing of leather in a red colour, and even the making of lanterns. At the same time, the commission granted a monopoly on the planting of dyer's woad, promoted the construction of forges for working iron, offered financing to the producers of silk cloth, and paid the salary of a dyer invited to settle in Siena for this purpose. This was clearly a broad-ranging strategy to revitalise industrial production, whose final goals were very clear to the group, whose members in one of their first meetings, with a lucid comment reflecting a proto-mercantilist slant, specified that they were acting 'considering the great utility that every republic draws from having an abundance of trades and skills in its city, by means of which the poor men find work and earnings, and goods are obtained at the best price, the city becomes more populated and in the end wealthy, because foreign money comes in and its own money does not go out'.[63]

A few years after these statements were made, some court officials and intellectuals began to theorise the importance of supporting industries and the commerce connected with them for economic, fiscal and social reasons. Among the first was Diomede Carafa, supervisor of the militia and finances for the kingdom of Naples and closely tied to king Ferrante.

---

[62] Franceschi, 'Intervento', 904–7; Franceschi, 'Istituzioni', 109–11, 115–16.
[63] Archivio di Stato di Siena, *Arti*, 166 (quotation at fol. 3v).

As a counsellor he had closely followed the creation of the wool industry in Naples in 1473, an initiative strongly desired by Ferrante – as was the contemporary one in favour of silk-manufacturing – which was similarly entrusted to a team of experts from Florence.[64] This enterprise was praised by Carafa in a memoir on the good government of the state addressed to Eleonora of Aragon and written shortly afterwards, in which he maintained also that among the greatest duties of a ruler was to provide incentives to commercial, industrial and agricultural enterprises, which were indispensable for developing the local economy.[65] Other terminology, but the same substance, was used a few years later by one of the kingdom's leading humanists, Giovanni Pontano, in his *De Principe Heroe*, while in the following century the necessity of endowing cities and states with manufacturing activities became a *topos* of treatises on the state.[66]

Protection of technical innovation

Venice, in contrast with other capitals and smaller cities, never worried much about setting up new industries through direct agreement with foreign specialists. From its position of strength as the home of a highly diversified system of production as early as the fourteenth century, in synergetic relation with its commercial network, the city was a natural magnet for anyone wanting to start up a new business, with no need for special efforts on the part of the institutions. It is true that at the beginning of the fourteenth century the government had mobilised to take in silk workers fleeing from Lucca, and that in the second half of the century, during a phase of demographic decline, it had provided substantial incentives for artisans immigrating there. Nonetheless, the industries that developed in Venice starting in the fifteenth century did not need state support. The only exception was the introduction of printing presses by John of Spyre, to whom the Senate granted a five-year monopoly in 1469 for setting up this new industry. This privilege, however, lasted only a very short time, due to John's death, and was followed by a liberalisation of the printing market, which soon became a point of pride for Venetian manufacturing.[67]

The concession of an exclusive grant on a technical innovation, however, recalls a trait that distinguished Venice from other Italian states,

[64] Del Treppo, 'Il regno', 158–62.
[65] Carafa, *Memoriali*, 193–9; Persico, *Diomede*, 147–50, 165–8.
[66] Persico, *Diomede*, 176–7. For an analysis of Carafa's text, see Abulafia, 'The crown', 129–33.
[67] Plebani, *Venezia*.

because it aimed above all at compensating inventors by protecting the rights to commercial use of their creativity. Up to the middle of the fifteenth century, Venetian privileges for inventions were episodic in nature, but they served to spread gradually a spirit of trust in state protection of innovation, reinforced in 1453 by a decree in favour of inventors of machines useful in public works, which from that moment on took precedence in contracts assigned by the state. Probably also as a result of the rapid success of printing in the city, in March 1474 the Senate decided to regulate the matter of innovations, issuing the first general law on patents and the protection of intellectual property in history, preceding by a century and a half the English Statute of Monopolies of 1624.

The text of the Venetian legislation mentioned the large number of men from different places 'able to think up and find various ingenious devices' who converged on Venice and would be happy to make their inventions public if given government protection. To encourage these individuals to study new technical solutions useful to the public, they were guaranteed a ten-year privilege in the entire dominion on their new discoveries – by 'new' was meant any invention never adopted before in the state of Venice – and protection from plagiarists, whom the inventor could sue in any court in the capital city.[68] The law was a success and led to a proliferation of requests for patents presented to the Venetian government, which in the course of the sixteenth century totalled more than 1,000. In just a few decades, the practice of granting industrial patents spread to all the Italian states, even without a general set of rules and regulations, and was then imitated after the middle of the sixteenth century by most European governments and even applied in Spain's American colonies.[69]

In Italy, and subsequently in other regions of Europe, machines of various types were registered, as were technical and chemical procedures. But what characterised the Italian peninsula was the request for protection for a vast range of unprecedented products and objects. Numerous innovations regarded textile products, often imitations of successful foreign fabrics. In Venice, the glass industry asked for a substantial number of privileges, having to do with articles that became very successful in later centuries (such as glass with a 'web' or 'net' effect, made by placing very thin white and colored canes inside the crystalline mass to form spirals and other geometric designs, patented by the Serena glassworks on Murano in 1527) or items destined for the

---

[68] Mandich, 'Le privative'.   [69] Molà, 'Stato e impresa', 549–72.

lower end of the market, such as rosary beads, bijouterie and imitation pearls, for which a woman inventor applied for a patent in 1501.[70]

An interesting element in the history of Renaissance patents is its extra-urban dimension, since the defence of innovation extended to the entire territory of the state. Thus the mechanism of a fulling-mill patented in Venice in 1497 by Francesco degli Uberti and his sons, Venetian citizens originally from Florence, but invented by a technician from Verona, had to be set up in workshops located in the district of Padua.[71] Many other similar examples could be cited for the machines and techniques which received privileges in the course of the sixteenth century. The possibility of applying for patents induced artisans, merchants, architects, engineers and technicians from the subject cities to propose innovative technologies, fostering the transmission of knowledge and creating a virtuous circle of experts who often ended up communicating and doing business with each other. The list of those applying for patents in Venice included Venetian noblemen and citizens as well as foreigners from various regions of Italy and Europe, but much more preponderant was the number of subjects who found the legislation of the capital to be a spur to promoting their discoveries and consequently their technical creativity. Similarly, patent applicants in the grand duchy of Tuscany in the closing decades of the sixteenth century were of course Florentines, but also people from Pisa, Livorno, Prato, Pistoia, Siena, Empoli, Cortona and Pescia.[72]

Conclusion

Even with their diversity of approaches, the economic policies implemented by the governments of the principal Italian states in the Renaissance show at least three significant aspects in common.

The first was that economic policies were conditioned by an increasing fiscal burden: a virtually foregone fact in an era that saw a dizzying rise in the cost of political and military competition and also that of the ordinary administration of the territories, but which has to be placed in context. In the course of the fifteenth century, the tax burden was quite different in aspect from that during the age of the communes. As a rule, the importance of direct taxes increased with regard to overall revenues, while the incidence of indirect taxes diminished. Within this latter

---

[70] Zecchin, 'Famiglie vetrarie', 212–13; Archivio di Stato di Venezia, *Collegio, Notatorio*, reg. 23, fol. 39v.
[71] Archivio di Stato di Venezia, *Senato Terra*, reg. 13, fol. 26r.
[72] Lamberini, '"A beneficio dell'universale"'.

category, the reduction mainly concerned excise taxes on urban consumption, while the revenues from customs duties remained quite high (around one-sixth of the total in Tuscany and in the Po valley, just taking into account the main commercial tariffs). These tendencies mark the difficulty governments encountered in carrying out significant reductions in the taxation of production and exchange, which, indeed, were easier to implement in places – such as the kingdom of Naples – where the central authority relied more on alternative fiscal resources.[73]

The second aspect was the will to use economic decisions as a negotiating tool with cities, rural communities and various pressure groups, a practice displayed by the strategies followed in the concession of fairs and markets to subject towns, but also by commercial policies that, in individual cases, often betrayed the principles that inspired them. The cut in or cancellation of taxes on tools and raw materials indispensable for certain activities, the reduction of entrance and transit duties, and conversely the concession of protectionist tariffs in defence of specific types of production were the most tangible manifestations of the growing recourse to privileges. Such privileges, in the towns and cities of post-communal Italy which by this point had lost their fiscal autonomy to a lord or a dominant city, became a means by which the elites tried to limit the consequences of the 'confiscation of the city finances' by deflecting its costs on to other subjects, in particular the inhabitants of the countryside.[74]

The third point was the tenacious survival of a municipal vision of the management of the economy, the tendency to protect the interests of the city as a priority and especially those of the capital city, a choice that was not necessarily aimed at damaging the subject towns, but certainly at preventing, at least in the sectors of the economy that were considered strategic, the development of smaller towns and communities and areas of the territory from coming into conflict with the development of the capital.

These aspects should not relegate to the background the fact that, over time, greater public control was exercised over the infrastructure of production and exchange, the creation or strengthening of specialised magistracies, and more vigilant attention to the territorial dimension of economic policies. From the duchy of Milan to the republic of Florence, from the Aragonese kingdom of Naples to the republic of Venice, the role of the central authority in decision-making and arbitrage concerning

---

[73] On these issues, see the fundamental works by Ginatempo, 'Spunti comparativi' and 'Finanze'.
[74] Ginatempo, 'Finanze', 284–91 (quotation at 285).

food supply, excise and customs duties, communications links, fairs and markets, manufacturing, and innovation grew stronger. This is a process that it does not seem right to dismiss *in toto* solely as the 'unintended consequence of attempts to extend state sovereignty'.[75] At least as far as support for productive activities is concerned, as early as the fourteenth century resolute intervention on the part of governments can be observed, which in the next two centuries would turn into a real policy of innovation, a policy aimed at harmonising and enriching the manufacturing aggregate, shared by all the Italian states, independently of their size and form of constitution. To be sure, these strategies mainly concerned individual cities, above all the capitals, but they contributed nonetheless to the valuing and optimal use of human capital in the Italian peninsula, stimulated the spread of know-how and, precisely by virtue of their mercantilist and protectionist slant, spurred cities and states in competition with each other to seek out ever new solutions for defeating the competition. Among these, unquestionably, starting in the sixteenth century the granting of patents for inventions stands out, a practice that, even though still limited and incapable of real impact on economic development, shows the degree to which technical innovation had become valuable both to governments and to the entrepreneurial and artisan classes.

Returning to the territorial dimension of economic policies, it is right to recall that the initiatives of the governments had to deal with an ineliminable fact characterising the economies of the Renaissance states, that is to say, the survival of basins and circuits of production and commerce which did not correspond fully with the political borders. This was true – as we have seen – for the districts of Bergamo and Brescia, which maintained strong economic ties with Milan and western Lombardy even after decades of political subordination to Venice. But it was equally true, to cite just one example, in the case of Arezzo and other zones of southern and eastern Tuscany which gravitated towards Perugia, Ancona and Rome.[76] The coincidence between political space and economic region, therefore, cannot be considered axiomatic, also because the efforts of the Renaissance states to make the most of their internal resources did not detract from their interest in inter-regional and international commerce. If in the middle of the sixteenth century Italy still possessed a very solid productive base, had Europe's highest average product per capita, and remained pre-eminent in world trade,[77]

---

[75] Epstein, *Freedom*, 169.
[76] See Dini, 'Le vie', 286; Ginatempo, 'Gerarchie demiche', 379, n. 108.
[77] See Malanima, *La fine*, ch. 1.

this was perhaps also due to the willingness of governments to focus their efforts on development across the economy as a whole: whether it came from exchange within the Aragonese 'common market' or from Venice's trade across the sea, the exploitation of the mines of Volterra or the creation of a silk industry in Modena, the increase in wealth was a guarantee both of well-being for the collectivity and of substantial tax revenues.

23 The papacy and the Italian states

Giorgio Chittolini

Introduction

The history of developments in the relations between Rome and the Italian states between the fourteenth and the sixteenth centuries had much in common with that of many other European states: the papacy tended to assert its primacy in the government of the whole of Christendom, and the states tended in turn to strengthen their institutions and their authority – in matters of taxation and jurisdiction – over their ecclesiastical institutions. Characteristic of the Italian situation, as compared with that of other countries, was the particularly close relation between the papacy, states and society: on the one hand because of the strong authority that the pope was able to exercise over the peninsula, on the other hand because of the influence that the popes, the court of Rome and ecclesiastical institutions felt from their close connection with Italian society and states. This characteristic was very evident in the period of transition from the Middle Ages to the early modern era, when the papacy, after the residence in Avignon, after the schism and the conflict with the conciliar movement, could exert greater authority towards the middle of the Quattrocento, while Italy, far from constituting a united state, remained bent on marked political fragmentation, not overcoming the particularism of little territorial formations centred largely on cities, above all in the centre and the north.

It is a crucial period, of whose significance – in religious life and in aspects of society – contemporaries were well aware, although they gave different interpretations of it. Machiavelli noted, for example: 'We Italians are obliged to the church and to priests for this, first of all: for having become bad, without religion; but we have another, greater obligation to them, which is the second cause of our ruin: that the church has kept and continues to keep this province divided.' To Guicciardini, that Italy lacked a great monarchy, which had always been obstructed by the papacy, seemed a positive thing, a condition of the development of so many prosperous cities, yet he agreed about the inauspicious influence of 'priests' on moral and civil life. The debate on the role of the papacy grew during and after the Reformation: for some it was the primary cause of a sound religious life, of the protection, including political protection, of Italy in the Europe of the great powers; for others it was the primary cause of the divergence of Italian cultural and political history from that of the rest of western Europe. It is a debate to which historiographical reflection has often returned, from the nineteenth century to the present day – through, for example, Sismondi, Gioberti, De Sanctis and Gramsci – as one of the fundamental pivots of the political and social history of Italy.

Some 'original characteristics'

The history of the close relations between church and society in Italy, moreover, goes much further back, originating in the widely ramified presence of ecclesiastical institutions in Italian territory from the earliest centuries of the Christian era. The number of bishoprics – the pillars of secular ecclesiastical organisation – had been and remained high, despite discontinuities in the early Middle Ages which were compensated for only in part in the centuries after 1000 by the creation of new dioceses in the Norman south and, in more limited numbers, in the centre and the north. It has been calculated that in the fifteenth century there were over 300 Italian dioceses (compared with around 130 in France, 55 in the Holy Roman empire and about 30 in England, Scotland and Wales), dioceses that were on the whole comparatively small, in some cases in the south limited to a few parishes, although some, particularly in the north, extended for thousands of square kilometres.[1]

The grafting of episcopal sees on to the existing network of cities, on the model of 'each diocese a city, each city a diocese', established a two-way relation between civic institutions and urban religious institutions, between clergy and laity, the premise for continuous, reciprocal influence. Thus in Italy the primary sphere for the local church was above all the city: the development of great institutions outside cities was relatively limited (the network of large rural monasteries in the early and central Middle Ages was sparser, less dense, compared to other European countries, their areas of economic and ecclesiastical influence less extensive, except perhaps in southern Italy).[2]

The connection between ecclesiastical institutions and cities proved an enduring one, even more significant because of the prominence of

---
[1] Hay, *The Church in Italy*, 9–25.
[2] Brentano, *Two Churches*; De La Roncière, 'L'église en Italie', 730–4.

cities in the general history of Italy. Churches were strongly influenced by civic society, above all after the great urban expansion, the 'Renaissance of the eleventh century' and the establishment of the communes. After the triumph of the communes, above all, the ancient tradition of a close symbiosis between ecclesiastical and municipal institutions became a process of the 'veritable deconstruction of ecclesiastical organization', with a weakening of the church's own institutions, and in particular of the episcopate (its ecclesiastical and religious influence as well as its economic foundations),[3] and at the same time the commingling of citizens and clergy. While normally in Europe the clergy appeared 'as a specific extraneous body in the city, especially after the split between church and state in the struggle over investitures' (M. Weber), in Italy there was instead integration of clerics and citizens, an assimilation of the local ecclesiastical hierarchy to the groups who governed the city, without profound contrasts. If there were, as everywhere, confrontations between clerics and laymen (over questions of jurisdiction, taxation and ecclesiastical property), the contrasts were in fact less rigid and lasting than elsewhere. Clerics and laymen continued to form a relatively homogeneous and united body, which identified with civic institutions and with those of the urban church (the chapters of cathedrals and the major churches, convents, confraternities, hospitals):[4] a commingling that, as we shall see, also found expression in the elaboration of religious values profoundly permeated by civic values.

A related aspect of this Italian church, constituted of the sum of the city churches, was the ample space for the influence of the apostolic see, that was not only geographically close and rooted in the very fabric of the peninsula, but which did not even have to face there those limitations on its action posed elsewhere in Europe by strong state institutions or strong regional or national churches. After the so-called Gregorian reform and the concordat of Worms (which had consolidated pontifical authority over the Italian episcopate to the detriment of the empire), with the weakening of the episcopate itself in consequence of the affirmation of the commune, there was substantial agreement between the papacy and the communal movement, confirmed at the end of the thirteenth century by the affirmation of Guelfism. Already in the second half of that century the majority of Italian bishops were nominated by the pope; nor did the lukewarm sense of belonging to a national church (of which the pope himself was the primate) feed anti-Roman sentiment in

---

[3] Jones, *The Italian City-State*, 429ff.
[4] See, for example, for the fifteenth century, Chittolini, 'Stati regionali e istituzioni ecclesiastiche', 181–2, and Bizzocchi, 'Clero e chiesa', 28ff.

Italy. Papal control over the regular clergy was quite strong, in particular over those mendicant orders which, above all in the thirteenth century, were major protagonists of religious life.

Cities also had an important role in southern Italy, from Lazio to Calabria to Sicily. Nevertheless the evolution of ecclesiastical institutions there was not characterised by the same close, two-way relation with the cities, whose mesh, originally even closer than in the centre and north, showed itself to be more fragile. Many centres disappeared; numerous others were already reduced to little more than villages in the period between the end of the Roman empire and the early Middle Ages. At the end of the tenth century some coastal cities saw notable development, but on the whole southern Italy and the islands remained outside, or scarcely touched by the great urban revival evident in many regions of Europe in the eleventh and subsequent centuries, and indeed the cities' autonomy was limited within the powerful Norman kingdom.

The network of dioceses – despite the disappearance of many of them, and the rearrangements caused by occupation by the Byzantines, Lombards, Arabs and Normans – remained quite dense in the south of the peninsula, so much so that in the fifteenth and sixteenth centuries there were more than 130 of them. But the diocesan seats did not usually correspond, as in the north, to major cities, but rather to centres that were then quite small, and the dioceses often had a limited area, some tens or few hundreds of square kilometres. In short, that interaction between strong urban entities, civic society and municipal ecclesiastical institutions did not become established in the south. Not by chance, great monasteries such as Montecassino, San Vincenzo al Volturno and Farfa, with their vast properties and numerous dependent churches, forming huge exempt areas in the system of the diocesan churches, had a more important role in the south than in the north.

Also limiting the development of a robust system of civic churches was the authority of the kingdom, Norman and then Swabian, with its powerful feudal institutions and a policy of containment of urban autonomy. Added to this was the dependence of the southern crown on the papacy. It was a dependence that dated from the formation of the kingdom of Sicily, when the papacy had granted the royal title to the Norman dynasty, reserving to itself a kind of feudal 'suzerainty' over the kingdom; a dependence that the Hohenstaufens had sought in vain to contest and reduce, and which had been consolidated when the popes had favoured the advent of the Angevin dynasty. Charles I d'Anjou in particular, having conquered the kingdom, had recognised it as a true fief held for the pope, undertaking to pay a large annual *census*, to provide troops and ships on request and to guarantee ample liberty to ecclesiastical functions, persons and property.[5]

From the Avignonese exile to the victory of the papacy over conciliarism

This picture, delineated during the communal era, was modified from the beginning of the fourteenth century. The papacy in its Avignonese 'exile' appeared intent on concentrating functions and prerogatives, creating a new, vast apparatus of curial government. Many European states energetically opposed papal 'interference', above all in matters of taxation and jurisdiction, and seemed inclined to support national churches, which were easier to control. The schism and the conciliarist movement at the end of the century were the resounding manifestations of this malaise.

In Italy the papacy did not have to confront great monarchies; it did, however, have to engage with powerful communes (such as Florence, Genoa and Venice, on the way to becoming territorial powers), and with enterprising lords, such as the Visconti, Scaligeri and Estensi, who tended to put a brake on both ecclesiastical interference and the temporal interests of the papacy. The ambition of the popes to maintain extensive political influence over the peninsula, as had happened in the second half of the thirteenth century thanks to the Angevins and the Guelf party, was seen to be excessive: the idea, aired from time to time, of a kingdom of 'Alta Italia', a vassal of the apostolic see, could not be realised. Particularly violent was the clash with the Visconti, who were at the head of Italian Ghibellinism, and were engaged in an effort of vast territorial expansion: they were struck with a series of excommunications and interdicts. Guelf Florence, where papal authority continued to be associated with the sovereignty of the commune, waged against the pope an actual war (known as the War of the Eight Saints, from the ironic nickname given to the Florentine magistracy charged with its conduct), notwithstanding the interdict launched against it.[6]

Nor did the more limited objective of strengthening the papal states meet with success, despite the temporary successes of campaigns by legates such as cardinal Albornoz and Bertrand du Pouget. For over a century, it was a field of conflict between local lords (the Roman barons,

---

[5] Galasso, *Il regno di Napoli*, 16–26, 91–5, 456–7.
[6] Somaini, 'Processi costitutivi'; Trexler, 'Ne fides communis diminuatur'; Trexler, *The Spiritual Power*; Becker, 'Church and State in Florence'.

the Romagnol 'tyrants', the Montefeltro, the Malatesta), cities (such as Bologna, Perugia and Rome itself, endowed by Cola da Rienzo with ephemeral republican institutions) and *condottieri* (from John Hawkwood to Braccio da Montone and the Sforza). Not even the return of the papacy to Rome (1378), complicated immediately by the schism, rendered the task of the Roman pontiffs simpler: indeed in the divisions between the various obediences states and cities found room for greater freedom of movement (as the Savoia and Visconti did), thanks to their relations with the Council of Basle. Naples, however, did not profit from the schism, under the close tutelage of a series of popes and a numerous band of Neapolitans in the curia.[7]

Only after the failure of the council, in effect, did a period of relative stability begin. It was during the decades from 1430 to 1450 that the popes succeeded in stemming the external interference of other powers and of *condottieri*, in having an army at their disposal, in disciplining to some extent the autonomies that cities and lords had enjoyed within the papal states, and in increasing tax yields.[8] It was also in this period that the political system of the peninsula stabilised, with the five large regional states of Milan, Venice, Florence, Rome and Naples and the constellation of minor states, in a reciprocal equilibrium that was maintained without major upsets until the end of the century, just as the internal order of these states remained relatively stable.

The solemn celebration of the jubilee in 1450 was intended to show the faithful of the whole of Europe the image of a restored and strong papacy. Rome itself, for long centuries sparsely peopled and much reduced from its old extent, a city 'of ruins and shepherds', began to grow in importance and in population, to acquire the appearance of a great monumental centre, a worthy seat of the pontiffs, the capital of Christianity. In its dealings with the European states (alarmed by the excesses of the conciliar movement), the papacy could take the role of guarantor of the discipline of the entire church, and make agreements and concordats with them, which on the one hand sanctioned its prerogatives and on the other recognised the sphere of authority and influence that princes and sovereigns intended to exercise over the churches of their states.[9]

---

[7] On Milanese ecclesiastical policy during the conciliar era, see Prosdocimi, *Il diritto ecclesiastico*, 62ff.; on Naples, see Galasso, *Il regno di Napoli*.
[8] Partner, *The Pope's Men*.
[9] Stieber, *Pope Eugenius IV*; Rapp, 'Le rétablissement de la papauté'; Thomson, *Popes and Princes*; Oakley, *The Western Church*, 61–77, 169–74, 291ff., 394ff.

Rome, the 'capital city'

In Italy the papacy found itself confronted by an ecclesiastically and politically disjointed framework, a sum of medium-sized and small states, a myriad of local churches, civic and episcopal, which gravitated directly towards Rome without being inserted in other political and ecclesiastical structures that organised them and watched over them.[10] In this situation of long-standing fragmentation the instruments of intervention developed by the new papal monarchy could operate more effectively.

As for provision to benefices, the pope, who had already in the fourteenth century established in Italy the practice of papal provision to major abbacies and bishoprics and to more than a few minor benefices (through papal 'reservations'), declared himself to be henceforth the *dominus beneficiorum* of the entire peninsula. From papal interventions derived extensive curial competence over the very frequent judicial disputes through the ample possibilities of appeal and recourse to the major Roman tribunals (in matters concerning benefices as in other questions of jurisdiction): appeals and recourse that the states did not succeed in impeding. Papal taxation on churches and religious houses was also increased.[11] The religious orders, especially the mendicants, were an effective instrument for the papacy, because of the influence they exerted through their preaching and direction of cults and devotional practices, and their role in the tribunals of the inquisition, directly dependent on the apostolic see.[12]

The reinforcement of the pope's power over his Italian dominions weighed heavily on the relation of the Roman church to Italian society: the ancient 'patrimony of St Peter' was transformed into the 'state of the church', a real temporal principality, which was also seen as a guarantee of the spiritual authority of the papacy. To Lorenzo Valla's irrefutable demonstration of the falsity of the donation of Constantine, Enea Silvio Piccolomini (the future Pius II) opposed historical reasons and the law of nations (*ius gentium*) to justify the temporal dominion; and besides, according to the conviction shared by all popes of this epoch, it was legitimate to have recourse to terrestrial power, to riches and arms, in order to realise the kingdom of God.[13] The 'lands of the church' became one Italian principality among others, tied up with the rest of the peninsula.

---

[10] Prosperi, 'L'Italie'; Fragnito, 'Istituzioni ecclesiastiche'.
[11] Prosperi, 'Dominus beneficiorum'. [12] Brambilla, *Alle origini del Sant'Uffizio.*
[13] Prodi, *The Papal Prince,* 28–40.

The closeness between the apostolic see and Italy became still more marked and freighted with greater implications than in the past. This change was noted by contemporaries, above all Italians (Guicciardini, among others, pointed out that since the beginning of the Quattrocento the popes 'began to appear secular princes rather than pontiffs'); and many denounced that 'temporal' logic as in marked opposition to the idea of a spiritual and Christian government, and the distortions that derived from the confusion between the responsibilities of the universal pontiff and those of an Italian prince.

Another important element in the rooting of the papacy in the peninsula was the so-called Italianisation of the curia, because of the closer relations that were established through the osmosis between Italian aristocracies and curial offices. The fourteenth- and especially fifteenth-century phenomenon of the growth of the apparatus of papal government has been described – of papal government in the widest sense: from the true administrative apparatus, to the court and household that burgeoned around the pope, the cardinals and the great prelates of the curia. Between 250 and 300 people on average were employed in the curia at Avignon; just under 500 at the beginning of the fifteenth century and around 560 at the beginning of the sixteenth century.

From this marked growth in members of the curia and the household the clergy of the peninsula profited notably, thanks also to the fact that nearly all the popes from 1417 to 1521 were Italian (except for the two Borgia, Callixtus III and Alexander VI). A spell in the papal court became a normal stage in the career of major Italian prelates (from a sample of thirty dioceses, over a century one bishop in three had been at the curia); and even more numerous were those clerics who played the Roman card without enjoying equal good fortune. There were many who flocked to the courts of the cardinals: courts that were ever more crowded, cardinals that were ever more Italian, and ever more numerous (not least because to the Italian orientation of the popes' choices were added the pressures of the princely courts and of the great families of the peninsula to have a representative in the Sacred College).[14]

Besides these figures linked more organically to the institutions of government and the great Roman prelates, there moved a variegated world of ecclesiastics and laymen: in the guise of solicitors, fiduciaries, procurators, men of business, acting independently or as representatives of cities or of great seigneurial families. There were also, of course, financiers and merchants acting in Rome on behalf of their companies,

---

[14] Partner, *The Pope's Men*.

or holding contracts on offices and revenues of the curia; or bishops, claiming rightly to be more use to their prince and their church by being resident in Rome rather than in their dioceses. And with the pope there were envoys and ambassadors from the major Italian states: the role of the papacy in maintaining the political and diplomatic equilibrium of Italy and the role of Rome in consolidating the use of continuous diplomatic representation are well known.

In short, Rome was the place where the major questions were dealt with, including those connected only indirectly with the government of the church: transactions concerning ecclesiastical benefices (*resignationes*, exchanges, pensions), careers and alliances, contracts and licences; strategies for the advancement of families, the great and the not so great, were put in train; factional alliances, matrimonial agreements, financial understandings were concluded; political affairs and private affairs, ecclesiastical and civil. And from Rome the effects of the negotiations, the agreements, the confrontations spread out, through family ties, factional links, relations between clients and patrons, municipal allegiances, to reach remote places, great families, various classes and social groups. Rome was seen to be an ever more important meeting point, a central junction in the system of relations by which Italian society was organised; the clerics and laymen who crowded the palaces of the pope and the cardinals came to constitute a kind of order, an aristocracy governing Italian society.[15] And Rome, owing to the flow of news and information coming from throughout Italy and Christendom, was also the centre for news (residents at Rome, as they found themselves at the nerve centre of the circulation of information, were generally expected to pass on such news to their correspondents).

Yet this centrality of Rome had two faces. On one side it multiplied the instruments of intervention by the popes, made their influence, and that of the magistracies in Rome, increasingly pervasive. On the other side, however, it opened up ways giving easy access to Rome for the benefit of the Italian states, of various 'bodies' and local societies. This dense and convoluted system of relations did not function in one direction only – from Rome towards Italy; it could also serve to open up the curia to Italian churches, local aristocracies, states, clerics and laymen.

The Roman world did not appear to Italians as an alien, closed, refractory world, intent only on the defence of papal prerogatives. The court of Rome was, in the end, one of the great Italian courts, the state of the church, one state among the others of the peninsula, tied to them by close diplomatic, military and financial connections.

---

[15] Gensini (ed.), *Roma capitale*.

If the world of the curia was expressing a corporate self-awareness, it nevertheless kept its character as a heterogeneous aggregate of different groups, of the seat where the aspirations, interests and ambitions directed at Rome from the various societies of the peninsula, seeking satisfaction, were represented. A curial office, clerical robes, would not break the links that the many 'foreigners' in Rome maintained with their places of origin and with their fellow citizens, ecclesiastics or laymen, private or public as they might be.

These intertwined threads, ecclesiastical and political, are essential to the understanding of the relations between the church and Italian society in the Renaissance. The solution of the conciliar crisis, which in other European states brought a more precise distinction of the respective powers of church and state, in Italy led to what has been defined as a condominium between Rome and the civil authorities (the regional states, urban corporations, communities, seigneurial and noble families): a condominium derived from the broad sharing of people and interests between the world of political power and that of the ecclesiastical hierarchy, from the lack of prominence of lines of contrast and conflict between the rights 'of the state' (or the city, or the community) and the rights of the church or, at least, the ease with which it was possible to arrive at general political grounds for agreement.[16]

The regional states

In the light of this situation it can be understood how the reciprocity of the relations between the regional states of the peninsula and Rome worked. Usually, there were no strong claims, general, formal agreements or concordats, like those that different European powers stipulated with the papacy. The prevailing tone of their relations was of negotiation, of diplomacy, of a search for understandings concerning the various questions that arose – the assignation of a benefice, the imposition of a tax, the appointment of a cardinal, a diplomatic agreement: negotiations in which the curia and the states sought to manipulate to their own advantage the close interconnection that has been described. Thanks to representation by ambassadors, and to the presence of less formal agents and fiduciaries, relations were close and continuous; there was no shortage at the court (in the offices of the curia, in the Sacred College, in the various *familie* of the cardinals in Rome) of friendly prelates, clients, 'creatures' of the major princely families. And beyond this system of relations, above all in dealings with

[16] Bizzocchi, 'Clero e chiesa', 43–4.

Italian states, were valid those more general political reasons which also applied in the negotiation of ecclesiastical matters: reasons felt even more forcefully in that 'Italian system' in which the temporal dominion of the pope constituted an integral part. In Italy, the threads of ecclesiastical politics could be disentangled from the complex fabric of political relations less easily than elsewhere in Europe.

The different states took various positions in relation to Rome. The connections appeared strongest with Florence and also Siena, because of their vicinity and a long-standing tradition, because of the close financial relations with the major banking companies.[17] At the opposite extreme was Venice: to some degree because the republic for a long time kept its distance from Italian affairs, to some degree because of the tradition of control over ecclesiastical institutions by the political authorities (which was also expressed in the sacral connotations of the figure of the doge). Rome appeared from the lagoon to be a different world, even when the popes were Venetian (indeed the families who maintained relations with Rome were regarded with suspicion, and those who were in contact with the Roman curia because of benefices they held or because of family ties were excluded from deliberations concerning relations with Rome as '*papalisti*', as they were called).[18] In the history of the Visconti–Sforza state, too, there were signs of 'regalist' and jurisdictionalist orientations, partly in consequence of the political conflict between the papacy and the Visconti in the Trecento.[19] The position of the kingdom of Naples, however, remained weak, due to the long tradition of dependence on Rome inherited by the Aragonese dynasty (and whose force they felt, for example, at the time of the conspiracy of the barons).[20]

On the whole, however, the prevailing tone of relations was that of negotiation, ever more akin to diplomacy, of a search for agreements in which states put forward their demands, without taking up a position that was antagonistic in principle to those from the papacy and the curia.

In appointments to bishoprics – quite a delicate matter, even if the bishops of Italy were weaker than in other European churches – states could claim a sort of right of presentation: by custom, as in Venice, Florence and Visconti Milan; or thanks to an indult, as in Sforza Milan. At Venice, candidates were named by a vote in the Senate; at Florence, lists of names were drawn up to submit to the pope; the duke of Milan put forward his candidates through diplomatic channels. This right also

---

[17] Trexler, 'Florence'; Bizzocchi, *Chiesa e potere*, 202ff.
[18] Prodi, 'The structure and organisation of the church'; Cozzi, 'Politica, società, istituzioni', 233ff.; Del Torre, 'Stato regionale e benefici ecclesiastici'.
[19] Prosdocimi, *Il diritto ecclesiastico*; Chittolini (ed.), *Gli Sforza*.
[20] Galasso, *Il regno di Napoli*, 457ff.; Vitolo, 'Il regno angioino', 60–7.

aimed to reserve to governments a kind of control or monopoly of relations with Rome, in the most important matters, and to discourage direct petitions from individual candidates. When the pope did not accept the candidate, presentations could be followed by bargaining and negotiations: with outcomes that might differ from those originally foreseen but not without the choice falling on persons acceptable to both parties (many of them, as mentioned above, had spent time at the curia), and not without a new opportunity for negotiation soon presenting itself.

The results obtained by the Venetian government for the sees of the Terraferma, for example, were significant. It has been calculated that of the 111 bishops nominated between 1405 and 1550, 85 were Venetian patricians or citizens; and it should be noted that in the richest sees, such as the patriarchate of Aquileia (with an income of 20,000 ducats) or the bishopric of Padua (6,000–8,000 ducats), and in the other sees of greatest political importance, Venetian prelates succeeded one another without a break. In the republic of Florence, too, in the Quattrocento two-thirds of the bishops nominated in the cities of the dominion (twenty of thirty-one) were of Florentine origin, and fourteen came from the chapter of the cathedral of Florence.[21] In the duchy of Milan – as in the other principalities – it was not so much the candidates' provenance that counted as their relations with the prince, and in fact the Visconti and Sforza (like the Este and the Montefeltro) usually succeeded in providing to their sees men who were faithful or at least not hostile.[22] In any case, the role and effective presence of bishops at the head of their dioceses remained limited: absent, far away, perhaps resident for long periods at Rome or with political and diplomatic (or ecclesiastical) horizons that transcended the confines of their dioceses, they often relied on vicars-general, frequently chosen by governments, and certainly more malleable, not least because they could be dismissed with relative ease.[23]

Not much different was the picture as regards provision to other major benefices (abbacies, canonries, commendams) which were also the object of prolonged diplomatic negotiations, because they were coveted by cardinals, Roman prelates and clerics from other states. In these cases, too, the result was often a compromise, perhaps with wider and growing spaces for members of the curia, above all when the benefice was not of any particular political moment. Regional states had a freer hand in matters of church properties (which were often huge, despite the spoliations of earlier centuries), claiming further control – beyond the

---

[21] Del Torre, 'Stato regionale e benefici ecclesiastici'; Bizzocchi, *Chiesa e potere*, 202ff.
[22] Somaini, *Un prelato lombardo*.
[23] Bizzocchi, *Chiesa e potere*, 245ff.; Belloni, *Francesco della Croce*, 59ff.

indirect control derived from influence over the choice of bishops and commendatories – over how they were acquired, alienated or leased, to the benefit of those social classes and groups that were asserting themselves in the new regional states. There were also instances of violent occupation and seizure, and not a few of the great families, with the complicity of ecclesiastics as well as of princes, acquired vast possessions, which were then broadly integrated into their private patrimonies and then kept – in the renewed order of the regional state and the Counter-Reformation – with full title, except perhaps for a few dues of recognition.

Nevertheless, these processes did not lead to an irreparable impoverishment of the ecclesiastical patrimony, as happened in other European states with secularisations. The very control that princes claimed to exercise showed itself to be gradually less lenient towards occupiers and despoilers: considerations of indulgence towards clients were balanced by more general considerations of the defence of an internal order in which ecclesiastical institutions also had to find security and protection: above all those that were increasingly affirming themselves (such as the monasteries that were part of the major reformed congregations). Already in the Quattrocento, a phase of consolidation and of a new expansion of ecclesiastical property began to be evident, suggesting to various states interventions to limit the possibility for acquisition of property by ecclesiastical entities.

The revenues of the church continued to be subject to taxation. Without the principle of the immunity of ecclesiastical property being explicitly denied in theory, authorisation or at least tolerance was obtained from the apostolic see, nevertheless, for extraordinary taxes (tenths, forced loans, contributions for the crusade, etc.), part of which could be reserved for the papacy. The levies appeared to be substantial and growing throughout the Quattrocento, even though they seemed to preserve a less routine and systematic character compared with those in other European states; nor did they reach the levels found in the sixteenth century and into the early modern era.[24]

In equally delicate and pressing questions of jurisdiction, the customs and laws of Italian states asserted the competence of civil tribunals over clerics, and tended to circumscribe the competence of ecclesiastical courts, curial and local; as elsewhere in Europe, they sought to limit the interventions of Roman tribunals. Yet the principle of ecclesiastical immunities and liberties was certainly not contested, nor were there formal impediments – as there were in other European states

---

[24] Landi, *Storia economica del clero in Europa*.

(*appel comme d'abus* in France, the statute of *Praemunire* in England) – to the jurisdictional intervention of Rome, which indeed was accentuated during the fifteenth century, although in the usual climate of diplomacy and negotiation, or to the growing recourse to judges-delegate.[25]

There were significant interventions by states in relation to religious orders. More limited perhaps were those directed towards older, Benedictine orders, which tended to concern major foundations intended to dignify the 'religion of the prince' (such as the Carthusian foundations) or the management of the vast landed patrimonies through rich monastic commendams.

Governments paid more attention to the mendicant orders, or to movements such as the 'observant' reforms, which expressed sentiments that were widespread among the laity too, and which were expanding and exerting influence over the faithful through preaching, pastoral activities and charitable initiatives: a sector that responded not only to the demands of lay piety but also (and indeed because of this) to the intentions of the government authorities. In fact, these were movements that sometimes deliberately sought the support of princes for their actions, and that could be more easily oriented to more directly political ends.[26]

Enjoying notable support were the observants in particular, whose new foundations were favoured, and who were generally supported against the conventuals, if need be, and against the recurring projects of the old orders to reabsorb them. Observant congregations, in their new organisation, detached from traditional hierarchies and old provincial regulation, arranged themselves according to a new ecclesiastical geography which often reflected the political geography of the regional states.[27] And the 'protection' of princes and governments could be manifested in the nomination of vicars and provincials, in the choice of friars authorised to preach, in the orientation of numerous charitable activities.

The princes and civic authorities appear to have directed their efforts above all to using the institutions, the men and the property of the church for essentially political ends, to procure financial resources, to reward families and persons most bound to the new regimes. But sometimes they had a wider perspective, which might lead them when necessary to take initiatives aimed at a 'reform' of ecclesiastical institutions in

---

[25] Prosdocimi, *Il diritto ecclesiastico*, 295–305; Brucker, *Renaissance Florence*, 181ff.; Bizzocchi, *Chiesa e potere*, 145ff.
[26] Chittolini and Elm (eds.), *Ordini religiosi e società politica*.
[27] Zarri, 'Aspetti dello sviluppo'.

their organisation and discipline, in harmony with widely diffused aspirations shared by their subjects; the image of a religious, pious government was important for garnering the approval and support of the faithful.

This did not happen only in Italy: the intersection of aspirations for the reform of the kingdom with aspirations for the reform of the church,[28] sometimes the active promotion of reforms (the so-called reformation of the princes) was manifest throughout Europe. Petitions to civic authorities for the amelioration of religious institutions and religious life were numerous. Particular attention was reserved for benefices with cure of souls (perhaps partly because they were smaller and less desirable); in appointments to these benefices, however, considerations of politics and clientage took second place, and attention was paid to what was required and the suitability of candidates, and to the requests of the communities (also to avoid those protests and disorders against unworthy priests that *podestà* and officials not infrequently had to report). Equally governments did not neglect a measure of control over the behaviour of priests, intervening to punish or remove the unworthy, at times at the request of the ecclesiastical authorities themselves: a function of control that came to form a kind of state jurisdiction parallel to the ecclesiastical jurisdiction, replacing it, and able to take more incisive action.

Support for the observant movement was along these lines, in their activities that responded more to the religious requirements of the faithful and supplied the pastoral failings of the secular clergy, with preaching, the offer of cults and devotional practices pleasing to the faithful, with works of charity and almsgiving. And along the same lines was the support reserved for those numerous charitable and welfare initiatives of the laity that flanked the parallel initiatives by governments for welfare and poor relief. All these interventions, which not infrequently were inspired by a genuine religious spirit, had significant effects: on the one hand, because they accredited and strengthened the position of the state authorities in their promotion of social discipline; on the other hand because they contributed to the slow renewal of the institutions of the church in the fifteenth century, laying the groundwork for many sixteenth-century developments.

Local churches and the civic church

The framework of relations between church and society was not limited to those between ecclesiastical institutions and the state. As the state

---

[28] Contamine, 'Réformation'; Rapp, 'Le rétablissement de la papauté'.

structures in the Renaissance encompassed, alongside the powers of the prince, those of other bodies, territorial and non-territorial, that enjoyed wide margins of autonomy, so the system of relations between church and society was expressed in a series of connections with the various bodies and social groups: the city, the communities, the territorial lordships, the great families.

What may be defined as the 'civic church' stood out prominently on the map of ecclesiastical institutions: a prominence analogous to that with which the city stood out in the panorama of Italian polities, above all, where there were urban centres of political and economic significance, ruled by strong and autonomous local aristocracies.

By civic church should be understood not an actual institution that possessed formal functions of ecclesiastical government: not the bishop, often far away, not the cathedral, which nevertheless remained the most representative institution; but rather that system of power and influence that was centred on the principal institutions of the urban church or, more precisely, on that civic and 'ecclesiastic elite' that presided over them. That group of ecclesiastics, drawn from among the citizens, possessed the richest and most prestigious benefices and dignities in the city (the stalls in the cathedral, therefore, but also those in other illustrious collegiate churches, provostships, abbacies). They formed a kind of 'ecclesiastical patriciate' that tended to identify with and be integrated into the families of the civic establishment, from whose ranks they were in very large measure recruited, and whose aims, interests and political influence they shared; they were not greatly disturbed by the claims of the princes in ecclesiastical matters, nor by the interventions of the pope or the curia, nor by the actions of the bishops.

Nor did the civic churches suffer particularly in the Quattrocento from renewed pressure by the Roman curia. Indeed the traditional direct connection with Rome was consolidated during the century in consequence of the 'pact' between the aristocracies of Italy and the papal court, and of the presence in Rome of so many clerics from the cities of the peninsula who maintained close links with their places of origin, becoming ambassadors or representatives for them at the court: a connection with Rome that could often be used to the advantage of the citizens in their relations with the prince or the government of the republic.[29]

Hence the picture presented by urban churches in the Quattrocento, of institutions that were an organic element of urban society, of a clergy profoundly integrated with the urban aristocracies. Prosopographical

---

[29] Pellegrini, *Ascanio Maria Sforza*; Gensini (ed.), *Roma capitale*.

research into the composition of the chapters of cathedrals and the major urban collegiate churches – at Florence, Milan or Turin, as in the cities of the Terraferma, or the papal states, at Naples as in the Sicilian cities (even if in a situation in which the cities were weaker) – confirms this broad identification: the fruit of customary mechanisms of co-option, sometimes formalised in the fourteenth and fifteenth centuries by statutes and norms that prescribed membership of a noble family or, more precisely, as at Milan, of a register of noble families, for the acquisition of a cathedral canonry. And research on the role of canons in urban life has shed light on the community of interests with the governing elite of the city, as much in devotional or religious or welfare initiatives as in, for example, control of the mechanisms of provision to benefices, or in the administration of church property.[30]

There was no lack of motives for conflict between the civic clergy and urban society and government. Such conflicts could turn bitter in particular circumstances, as in the well-known case of the interdict launched against Florence during the War of the Eight Saints (1375–8), when the necessity for a clear choice between ecclesiastical and civic obedience provoked unease and confrontation. These were, however, exceptional situations compared with the normal regime of relations in which conflicts concerned, periodically, the problem of fiscal impositions, or, occasionally, some trial of a cleric or some dispute over the property of a church. These latter conflicts, when they were not simply reflections of confrontations with the governing city elite, were on the whole circumscribed and open to mediation, because the civic clerics appeared not so much in the character of a separate caste of priests extraneous to the city as in that of *filii communis*, members of the urban body, sharing the ideals, the practices and rites of civic religion, closely linked to the laity in a joint, collaborative administration of ecclesiastical affairs.

And it is difficult, in fact, to find in Italy those forms of anti-clericalism that were so diffused in so many European cities in the fifteenth and sixteenth centuries, in keeping with a much more bitter state of conflict that saw *Bürger* and *Kleriker* take up positions that were often opposed (in part owing to the composition of the urban clergy, among whom were nobles from outside the city): questions still open and unresolved and much in evidence during the Reformation.[31]

---

[30] Berengo, *L'Europa della città*, 675ff.
[31] On the clearer separation north of the Alps between *Kleriker* and *Bürger* – the premise sometimes for confrontations and occasionally bitter conflicts that resulted in clashes between clerics and burgers, between churches and urban governments, and that could

The canons and prelates of the 'civic church' – and those social groups from which they came – maintained a marked influence over provisions to local benefices, following one or other of the ways open to them (direct access to Rome, bargaining with the authorities of the state, intimidation of outsiders). From this came the strongly municipal character and the broad uniformity shown by the clergy of a city – from the canonries, to the network of parochial rectors, to the complex system of chaplaincies and patronage. From this came ample possibilities for influence over the methods of administration and the revenues of the property of local churches. They were not wealthy properties like those of the great monasteries, of the abbeys in commendam, or the bishoprics (the hunting ground of a different social group, from the curia or put forward by princes); but they were still notable, as a whole; and the citizens were indeed the principal beneficiaries of their revenues, as the holders of leases, of tithes, above all of long-term grants in emphyteusis. And there also came, naturally, the function of vigilance over the female convents, where lived the sisters and daughters of those same patricians who governed the commune, and the close connections with the mendicants and observants. And the participation in the various forms of devotional life and charity that sprang from urban society: hospitals, *monti di pietà*, confraternities.

A 'civic church', therefore, and beside it, also a sort of 'civic religion', as has often been emphasised: a complex of religious values, that is to say, strongly permeated with lay and civil, indeed, more properly civil, values.[32] Civic religion 'made sacred' ethical and civil values expressed and produced in the ambit of the social and political experience of urban life and of the commune, recognised in them a religious valence. The love of God became love of the community in which one lived, charity became urban philanthropy, sainthood useful works for one's fellow citizens, love of the poor a civic responsibility; a religiosity of the citizen, directed to the common good of the city, to the urban religion of good works, to the *cura civium* as well as to the *cura animarum*. The church of the commune, the cathedral, the churches of the corporations were sustained by the same municipal or corporate spirit with which political and civil objectives were pursued. The identification of urban society with the church found its 'representation' in an imposing series of

---

generate a diffused sentiment of hostility towards the clergy as a whole, of *Pfaffensturm*, see Moeller, 'Kleriker als Bürger'; Scribner, 'Anticlericalism and the cities'. The distinction between 'rural clergy' and 'civic clergy' that does not always appear in other areas of Europe (see Swanson, 'Le clergé rural anglais') seems to me to be clearly evident in Lombardy.

[32] Chittolini, 'Religione cittadina e chiese di comune'.

ceremonies, of rites and symbols: the procession of the patron saint, not merely the patron, but also the *specialis protector* or *defensor civitatis*, the festivals and devotions for citizen 'saints', linked to the anniversaries and solemnities of the history of the commune. It was an orientation that perhaps still returned in the Quattrocento to a specific trait of Italian urban culture, less noble, more 'democratic' or communal than elsewhere in Europe. And the potential symbiosis between civil values and religious values tended, after its culmination in the thirteenth and fourteenth centuries, to favour the former, 'fruit of a process of deprivation of authority and of mortification to which the church was subject in the ambit of the city':[33] a church that was judged to be good when it was reduced to an extension of good government or, worse, the church as *instrumentum regni*, in the manner of Machiavelli. And, in effect, except during the brief experience of Savonarolan Florence, expressions of a 'reforming communalism' such as would be manifested a little later in German cities were not to be found in Italy.

The influence of the civic church was not confined within the circle of the city walls: it spread out into the countryside, expressing in the ambit of ecclesiastical institutions as well the pervasiveness and capacity for expansion into the *contado* that the great episcopal and urban centres of northern and central Italy had shown in the economic and political spheres. Rural benefices, at least in the areas nearest the urban centre, above all parishes without cure of souls, benefices that owing to their relatively limited value were usually not the concern of high-level negotiations between Rome and the governments of the regional states and remained within reach of local forces – these constituted the hunting preserves of the families of the civic oligarchies (with the associated possibility of getting their hands on the patrimonies of these churches, through investitures and leases). In part this was thanks to the formal patronal rights of single families and clans, sometimes the legacy of ancient local hegemonies of lineages that had then transferred to the city, sometimes the fruit of the more recent penetration by citizens into landed property.[34]

Hence that difficulty many rural communities had to emancipate themselves from the influence of the city in ecclesiastical affairs. The lack of a strong community structure and the absence or weakness of

---

[33] Cracco, 'Habitare secum'; Miccoli, 'La storia religiosa', 592–8; Bullard, 'L'altra "anima" della chiesa'.

[34] Chittolini, 'Civic religion and the countryside'. On the difficulties that urban ecclesiastical institutions encountered in carving out their own space in the cities, within a territorial organisation based not on cities but on lordships and principalities, as in Germany or France, faced by the antagonism of monastic, or episcopal, seigneurial or princely powers, see Berengo, *L'Europa delle città*, 689–95.

minor local and village aristocracies were translated into the weakness or absence of control over rural parishes and churches. If for other areas of Europe it has been emphasised that, at the close of the Middle Ages, a strong parochial network was developed and there were energetic initiatives by many rural communities to 'communalise' their churches, assuming the associated burdens and rights,[35] this phenomenon was not so evident in Italy, where a process of anti-seigneurial 'communalisation' had already been widely manifest, but where the rural communities subject to the dominion of the cities appeared weak and defenceless in ecclesiastical affairs in the later Middle Ages.

Structures and nuclei of rural churches of some substance could exist where local communities had the strength to resist the civic and regional governments, and could even enjoy political and administrative autonomy that protected them from external interference. This was the case in the Alpine valleys, with their deep-rooted liberties in relation to the cities and the regional states: the Val d'Aosta in Savoyard territory, the Valsesia, l'Ossola, the 'Swiss' valleys and the Valtellina in the duchy of Milan; the whole area of the Tyrol and the Trentino, or regions such as Carnia or the Altopiano dei Sette Comuni in the republic of Venice. Here parochial structures that had disappeared in other areas still persisted, extensive rights of the faithful in the election of parish priests, and in general a strong capacity to control and influence the ecclesiastical institutions of their lands: the fruit and consequence of the support that the communities gave to their churches, bolstered by offerings and tribute, enriched by donations and the endowment of benefices.[36]

This was also the case in large townships and villages in the plain that, if they did not enjoy the status and prerogatives of a town, did have a certain economic and demographic substance, could be the administrative centres of small districts, and sometimes profited from an ample autonomy on the political and administrative level, up to being treated as 'separate' from the *contado* of the city, and as 'immediately dependent' on the prince or the republic: centres such as San Miniato, Pescia or Colle Val d'Elsa in Tuscany; *terre separate* such as Monza, Vigevano or Borgo San Donnino (Fidenza) or Voghera in the duchy of Milan; centres such as Salò, Legnano, Bassano or Castelfranco in the Venetian Terraferma; or even smaller, less important townships, which might still be shielded by some fiscal or jurisdictional privilege, and had a little local aristocracy. That condition of autonomy, which gave their civic life a

---

[35] Blickle, *Gemeindereformation*; Blickle, 'Einführung'.
[36] See, for example, Ostinelli, *Il governo delle anime*; Canobbio, 'Preti nelle visite pastorali'; De Vitt, *Istituzioni ecclesiastiche e vita quotidiana*.

tone and substance unknown to the greater part of other non-urban communities, allowed them an efficacious defence of their ecclesiastical institutions (which often already had an ancient and by no means mediocre tradition), sustained by that same strong municipal spirit that they displayed in the defence of their civic liberties. They claimed rights of election and patronage for churches and chapels of local foundation, supported the churches of the regular clergy or promoted their foundation. They also exercised a vigilant and careful supervision over the ecclesiastical life of the community, over the behaviour of the clergy, over the buildings and property of the churches; they favoured the assignment of benefices to native, resident clerics. The largest of these centres also sought to remove themselves from the authority of the bishop – and of the urban church at his side – claiming exemptions, to belong to no diocese (*nullius diocesis*), or even the dignity of an episcopate, which sometimes they managed to achieve.[37]

Finally, lordships and fiefs could also constitute areas of autonomous organisation of local ecclesiastical life, of resistance to outside interference. Feudatories and rural lords who wished to exercise some ecclesiastical influence over their lands had ways to make their voices heard – among the many voices soliciting privileges and benefices – at the court of the prince and of the pope. Ancient forms of influence over the nomination of clerics were formalised by obtaining rights of patronage, and new rights of patronage could be gained for the price of foundations or even donations to already extant entities: chapels, but also churches with care of souls (*cura animarum*), collegiate churches. The influence of the feudatories spread to monasteries and religious houses as well, extending over their possessions, which sometimes came to be absorbed in the family patrimony. Some lordships, the most important ones, sought to obtain exemptions and autonomies for their territories, like little ecclesiastical provinces, detached from the rest of the diocese.[38]

This picture of ecclesiastical organisations centred not on the 'city' but on communities of various kinds, was particularly detailed in the regions of central Italy, and in those of the south where the strong influence of the feudal nobility and the barons was an additional factor.

Concluding remarks: continuities and transformations in the early Cinquecento

The beginning of the Cinquecento marked a turning point. Following the sudden bursting into the peninsula of the great European powers,

[37] Nencini (ed.), *Colle Val d'Elsa*.   [38] Chittolini, 'Note sui benefici rurali', 458ff.

the relations of the Italian states with Rome changed, becoming weaker. The states that were becoming provinces of European monarchies, such as Milan and Naples, weakened because the forceful politics of the kings of France and Spain towards Rome did not apply to their Italian provinces. On the other hand, the states that maintained their independence were shaken by profound crises as was Venice, or by institutional changes, as was Florence, which moreover had to face two Medici popes, Leo X and Clement VII. And this condition of weakness inevitably had repercussions on the lesser political entities (cities, communities) and on the Italian aristocracies who were bound into that political system.

By contrast, the position of the papacy was strengthened because of its political role in the peninsula and its role in ecclesiastical government – the disturbances provoked by reform themselves stimulated the consolidation thereof. Moreover the curia, grown stronger as a structure of government as well as an ecclesiastical body, had become less permeable, less open to Italian aristocracies and states, who saw their weight and capacity for influence reduced, while a growing number of ecclesiastics from the curia secured benefices for themselves in the different dioceses. And the strengthening of the papal state, reorganised along more centralised lines, helped to reinforce the papacy in Italy.

In short, the influence of Rome over the Italian church – a church of ever more 'limited sovereignty' in the face of the apostolic see – was more evident. It was at this time that the court of Rome began to appear to be the only major centre of power in the peninsula, the only court with a European dimension left in Italy, and the church as the last hope for the uncertain fortunes of Italian aristocracies. It was the moment of the bitter reflections of Guicciardini, who was full of malice and disdain for 'priests', a 'pack of villains', but who at the same time was forced to serve them all his life, in a career spent in the employment of the papacy. It was the moment in which a large number of scholars and men of culture abandoned civil robes and princely courts to enter the service of the pope or to take refuge under the protection of ecclesiastical robes and benefices; the moment in which the idea of a community of cultured men forming around the lay courts of princes was replaced by a society of men of the church gathered around Rome.[39]

If, therefore, reform in Italy (that is, the Catholic Reformation, the most lasting and substantial outcome of the unrest in the sixteenth century) constituted a crucial phase in the process of moral renewal and reform of the ecclesiastical apparatus, it did not represent a real break in the history of the presence of the church in civil society, and its

---

[39] Prosperi, 'L'Italie', 328–9; Dionisotti, 'Chierici e laici'.

relations with lay power: if anything, those relations were reorganised following the logic of the accord with the states and their ruling elites. If in the rest of Europe the political context for the affirmation of a new religiosity and disciplined models of life was that of the creation of state churches, in Italy the context, no less important, was that of the interpenetration of church, political institutions and society:[40] with more space for the Roman church and for an episcopate that was on the road to renewal, in the face of a weakened and centralised Italian political system.

[40] Bizzocchi, 'Clero e chiesa', 43–4.

24 Justice

Andrea Zorzi

Introduction

Justice in late medieval Italy has, in recent years, been a subject of considerable interest to historians and of a profound interpretative revision. This has been due, in part, to a spread of historiographic tendencies, including studies in Italy, which, since the 1970s, have favoured judicial sources, making this one of the principal areas of international research. Furthermore, the administration of justice has proved a rich area of research in the branch of studies concerning the formation of the state, which has characterised research on political history in Renaissance Italy. Overall, this research has brought forward new knowledge and has played a part in building an often original profile of criminality, judicial institutions and trial courts. A shift in direction has also been of fundamental importance, and research has moved away from studies chiefly centred on analyses of the administration of public justice. Emphasis has now been placed on the plurality of judicial systems, which result not only in court actions, but also in various measures for solving disputes that may operate outside the courts.

In the 1970s scholars' attention was still focused on violence and the transition from 'community-based' methods of social control and judicial order to more strictly 'state' structures. A change can be seen in the 1980s, when research explored the dimensions of the public function of justice, underlining the centrality of court procedures, the advisory role of jurists, and the plurality of jurisdictions. From the 1990s, understanding of the plurality of judicial practices (violent and peaceful, extra-procedural and sanctionary) for conducting and settling disputes increased. Research also highlighted that practices previously considered marginal or 'pathological', such as vendettas, feuds, peace-making, arbitrations and the entire range of non-procedural methods of resolving conflicts, were in fact widely and commonly used. These practices indeed constituted the largest sphere of justice in late medieval Italy. Not only, then, was there a plurality of judicial fora, but also of judicial systems. With the aim of overcoming traditional notions of the public function of justice and the progressive rise of the state, the understanding of medieval justice has considerably broadened. An important result of this change in perspective has been a widening of the range of documentation used by scholars. In addition to court documents, legal sources and statutes, other documents are now used including notary sources, council deliberations, written *ricordanze* and chronicles. A profitable enhancement in the methodological use of the documentation thus corresponds to a conceptual renewal of the notions of justice.

This chapter aims to see a unitary coherence in this judicial pluralism. It will explore the practices that became established in the political experience of the communes, which were then reconfigured in the territorial states.

Communitary justice: conflicts, peaces and vendettas

One of the greatest historians of criminal law, Mario Sbriccoli, has suggested a reconsideration of the nature of late medieval justice, drawing a distinction between 'negotiated' justice and 'hegemonic' justice. The first appears 'marked out by a distinct community-based character based on belonging, chiefly directed towards compensating for the offence, regulated by shared rules and practices, and in an environment where oral [methods of communication] dominate'. The second is characterised instead 'by a distinct character of apparatus, based on submission, chiefly directed towards punishing the guilty party, regulated by legislative rules, notably and consistently more formalised, and in an environment where writing dominates'. Consequently, according to Sbriccoli, 'vendettas and retaliations, negotiations and agreements, transactions and settlements, mediation and private peace-making, pacts, condescendences, renunciations, pardons and forgiveness' would have been set out 'in the name of "justice". All of this would not be the result of "state" justice, in the sense of the state apparatus, conducted by public bodies assigned to this purpose [...] Reflecting on these cultures and mentalities, historians should perhaps say "justice first, repression second", and would thus be much nearer the mark.'[1]

Judicial pluralism should be understood, therefore, not only as a plurality of courts, but also as a plurality of ways of resolving conflicts. Indeed, social actors had a range of judicial resources at their disposal in which to carve out – according to individual, family and collective possibilities – their own strategies for managing and settling disputes.

---

[1] Sbriccoli, *Storia del diritto penale e della giustizia*, 1236ff.

Recourse to trial, to the courts and magistracies, was, for the most part, a stage in the dynamics of a conflict, which went before the judge only to be resolved largely out of his presence. Some of the reasons for recourse to judicial seats included to move out of a position of stalemate, to intimidate the opposing party or to restore the balance of a confrontation. In turning to different fora, the litigants based their decision on a careful judgement regarding the type of laws each was able to exercise, and the most suitable place in which to call on them.

An example worthy of consideration is the ecclesiastical courts. Laymen often turned to the bishops' courts for their ability to offer a judicial seat for the formal settlement, either in or out of court, of conflicts. The analysis of judicial practices has revealed the highly negotiatory nature of episcopal justice, that is, as with lay justice, their disposition for offering settlement and peace-making tools for long-running conflicts in society. Recourse to episcopal arbitration was frequent for resolving disputes between ecclesiastics, and between ecclesiastics and laymen, but also between laymen with regards to usurped goods, unpaid tithes, exchanges of insults, etc. Peace being made between the parties is also attested and was sometimes demanded by the same episcopal vicars. This could put an end to ongoing actions, mitigate the punishments imposed, or lead to the absolution of the accused. A negotiatory practice specific to the ecclesiastical court was the swearing of an oath in the case of insufficient or flawed evidence through which one of the interested parties recovered the estimated amount of compensation from the other (generally in cases concerning marriages or for debts or the removal of goods). The adversary's oath, which was obviously agreed on, became a sort of settlement capable of deciding the terms of the case.[2]

Practical alternatives were therefore offered to the parties, and the *consilium* and *auxilium* of relatives, friends and neighbours proved pivotal in suggesting ways of handling, and coming out of, a conflict. These went from violent solutions to institutional triangulation, and routes to settlement and peace-making.

In this environment, the culture of the vendetta was central. It was informed by the guiding concepts of 'friendship' and 'enmity', which steered the logic behind the vendetta between 'enemies'. The conflicts that innervated relationships of enmity wove throughout the social fabric, from eminent lineages to individuals of more modest means. The practice of vendetta was not peculiar to a single social group, much less to the knights and magnates. Various local situations, at different

---

[2] Della Misericordia, 'Giudicare con il consenso'.

times, confirm the social diffusion of vendetta over a long period. For example, the involvement of different social groups can be seen in Mantua in the early thirteenth century, in Parma in the middle of the thirteenth century and in Siena at the end of the century. In Florence at the time of Dante Alighieri, from a sample of almost 100 conflicts between families, popular families (i.e. lineages without *milites*) were involved in almost half of the cases (forty-seven of ninety-eight). In more than one in four of these cases (twenty-five of ninety-eight), the feud concerned only kinships who were not magnates.[3]

A vendetta or a feud could be started by those who could afford it, regardless of background or social group. When these were started, however, they would shake the city and put the lives and emotions of the individuals and families involved at stake. It is not difficult to understand, then, why the moral stance regarding these practices was ambivalent – both one of legitimation and condemnation. Indeed, there is not a writer, poet or treatiser from the communal period who writes positively about vendettas without highlighting negative aspects and a preference for peace and pardon.

Individuals and family groups weighed up the choice of whether to avenge themselves of harm done and, above all, whether to enter into conflict on the basis of the resources available to them. This explains why lineages that were more powerful, in terms of demographic structures, social relations, political influence, and symbolic and economic resources, turned more frequently to starting vendettas. Starting a vendetta was not an impulsive act but a strategically thought-out decision, the outcome of a *consilium*. In 1246, a judge, Albertano da Brescia, dedicated the *Liber consolationis et consilii*, a moral treatise which represented a lucid and careful examination of the options for conflicts, precisely to the subject of 'advice' regarding vendettas or justice.

Recourse to the *consilium* made education on vendettas one of the primary aspects of the political education of the citizen. Important testimony of this can be found, for example, in manuals that gave instruction on holding public speeches, and particularly in collections of texts written by certain notaries (the *Arringhe* by Matteo de' Libri, the *Flore de parlare, çoè somma d'arengare* by Giovanni da Vignano, and the *Dicerie da imparare a dire a huomini giovani et rozzi* by Filippo Ceffi). In each of these collections there are some examples of discourses on 'Come si dee adomandare consiglio e aiuto agli amici per fare sua vendetta', 'Come si dee dire e confortare gli amici a fare vendetta', 'Come si dee dire a' consorti per l'amico offeso' and so

---

[3] Zorzi (ed.), *Conflitti, paci e vendette nell'Italia comunale*.

on. The education of the citizen of a commune therefore involved education on vendettas.

Moreover, juridical legitimation of these practices appears to have been important. Indeed, there are no texts in the statutes and laws of Italian communes that ban vendettas. In fact, fundamentally, the normative *ratio* considered the practice of retaliation legitimate. Laws, therefore, were limited simply to defining the congruity of the vendetta with regard to the people who could carry it out and be subject to it, its extent, the places involved, etc. The intention was to contain indirect retaliation and avoid larger alliances joining the conflict.[4]

Legislative intervention also allowed for making mediation official. This could be carried out by institutions to favour those moments – truces, arbitrations, agreements – which could put an end to a conflict and bring about its peaceful resolution. Central among the acts intended to bring conflicts to an end was peace, publicly endorsed and attested juridically by a notary. Peace could be made outside the courtroom, to prevent further offence or to seal a restored balance following a compensatory act of revenge, or in line with the more defined aim of calling off judicial proceedings or reducing the penalties. Those who reconciled themselves with the offended party could, in fact, secure adjournment of the case or a reduction of the sanction.[5]

Public authorities were active in adopting measures for containment and peace-making. They recognised the existence of conflict in society and sought to remedy such conflicts without repression or sanctions, but rather by aiming to contain the effects. There are countless examples of peace being made between individuals and families, fostered and mediated by communal rectors, committees of peace-makers, etc. Collective appeasements were frequent and were fostered by communal authorities, often working with papal legates. This is true of a time-span which, broadly speaking, lasted from the 1270s until the 1320s: the great peace settlements reached in Bologna, Florence, Siena, Lucca and so on are well known. As *signore* of Florence in 1342–3, Walter VI of Brienne forced more than 400 families in conflict, a total of some thousands of individuals from every social condition (from lineages of *milites* to families of merchants to common craftsmen), to swear peace publicly. In Rome, in 1347, the leader of the *popolo* regime, Cola di Rienzo, promoted the creation of a '*casa della iustizia e della pace* [house of justice and peace]' where he claimed to have brought about the reconciliations of 1,800 cases of enmity between citizens over the years.

[4] Zorzi, 'La cultura della vendetta'. [5] Padoa Schioppa, 'Delitto e pace privata'.

Peace was an integral part of conflict, and it always constituted a political objective. It is precisely the public nature of acts of peace that suggests a reconsideration of the concepts of 'private' and 'public' in practices surrounding conflict. The actors were private, but their practices were public: from patent and mortal enmity to proclaiming a vendetta, from public peace-making to obligations made by the notarial *instrumentum publicum* and so on.

Trials and procedures

The normality of judicial pluralism is shown in an analysis of its proceedings which were established to some extent in all of the Italian communes in the second quarter of the thirteenth century around the figure of the *podestà*, who assumed an executive role of co-ordination not only in the judicial field, but also more generally in the political arena. Professional courts, with curie of specialists (the *podestà*'s judges and notaries), represented the new element in the judicial system of the Italian cities during the thirteenth century. Almost everywhere these worked alongside, and then replaced, the judicial practices that had developed, from the middle of the twelfth century, from the first political magistrates (*consoli*) of the Italian communal regime. This therefore marked an important discontinuity in the public administration of justice.

In the *podestà*'s curie there developed a substantially triadic procedure – defined by some, somewhat approximately, as accusatory – which moved the confrontational grounds of the conflict on to the level of formal confrontation before a judge (a confrontation of positions, with ample recourse to legal and oratory techniques).[6] The public judicial system pursued mediatory rather than punitive ends. The penal dimension was minor, consisting of the *bannum pro contumacia* – a sentence of banishment. It was not so much the wrongdoings that were punished as evading court or failing to answer to the *podestà*'s injunctions. In reality, banishment was the only imposable sanction in this court system. Therefore defaulting (not appearing at court) became the crime, and the *bannum pro contumacia* was sanctioned in many statutes. For this reason, from the 1210s and 1220s, lists of those punished, *libri bannitorum*, began to be produced. These were registers that kept a record of those banished, primarily *pro maleficio* and for debt. Banishment could be revoked after the person in question had served the sentence, had answered to the *podestà*'s

---

[6] Vallerani, *Il sistema giudiziario del comune di Perugia*.

injunctions, or if peace had been granted by the injured party. In these cases, the names were removed from the books.[7]

Alongside these books, the judicial records took shape in the form of a register, which came to be progressively differentiated according to the procedural stages: from a single, large register where notaries recorded all stages, to an increasingly differentiated range of books on charges, inquisitions, testimonies, actions, sentences and prosecution inquests. It is therefore in the middle of the thirteenth century that we can place the creation of the communal judicial archives within the more general context of the passage from a set of documentation consisting of single records, mostly recording laws, to one in the form of a register, which bore witness to the new practical use of writing for administrative and certification purposes, with a considerable development of notarial practices of production and archiving.

A new stage began in the middle of the thirteenth century when the judicial system of the *podestà* was thrown into crisis. Although it had guaranteed access to justice for a wide range of citizens, due to its cost not everybody could have access to this form of mediation to solve conflicts. Indeed, trials had come to function as a system progressively used by wealthy *cives*, i.e. by those who could afford procurators, sureties, bail and court costs. A profound change in power structures began in the middle of the thirteenth century and developed in almost all the communes over the second half of the century. This change followed the emergence on to the political stage of new family groups who had grown in riches and status through trade, banking, craftsmanship and the juridical professions themselves. Rising with them were policies based on penal law and its negotiation, and on an extraordinary ideological mobilisation around the themes of *pax* and *iustitia*. The principal stages of development of these processes were: (1) the political and judicial measures adopted against the *magnates* or *potentes* (in practice, the old ruling group of the commune); (2) the development of judicial practices based on *ex officio* procedures, the expansion of penal law, and the diffusion of extraordinary measures; and (3) the political use of judicial banishment.

With regard to the measures against the magnates, firstly, of particular note was the conjunction between the exclusion from the most important political offices of lineages that had dominated the political scene of the communes since the consular age (an exclusion that is attested more or less everywhere) and their inequality before the law in comparison to citizens considered of the *popolo*. This immediate and explicit

---

[7] Milani, 'Prime note su disciplina e pratica del bando'.

connection between politics and justice substantially consisted of a kind of 'hyper-penal law', a substantial discrimination, corroborated by extraordinary measures in terms of judicial procedures. Beginning with the probatory system which in many communes had been reduced to an oath by the injured party or the descendants thereof, these measures also included instrumental use of the notion of *fama publica* (public reputation), and the weakening of guarantees of fair-trial procedures for the accused – with the shortening of trial duration, immediate conviction, payment in cash only and the negation of the right to appeal.[8]

There are also similarities to be found in ordinary judicial practices. In the second half of the thirteenth century, these seem to be characterised by the considerable expansion of the sphere of penal law, which may also be seen simply by analysing the statutes. From the late thirteenth century and early fourteenth century onwards an entire volume of the statutes began to be dedicated to criminal law. By this time, criminal matters seemed to have expanded to cover an ever larger range of behaviour subject to penal sanctions. The *ex officio* procedures were brought alongside the *per accusationem* procedures and supplemented them, very often creating mixed court proceedings. In quantitative terms, inquests that began *ex officio* always remained, broadly speaking, less numerous than traditional ones. However, the new purposes attributed to the judicial activity of the courts mattered: no longer were they only for the formal mediation of conflicts, but they also increasingly became an instrument for punishing offenders. The *inquisitio ex officio* essentially emerged as a more effective means of producing evidence in relation to the *publica fama* of the accused. As a direct result of this feature, judicial practices of the communes developed new institutions such as torture, which is attested in the statutes precisely from the middle of the thirteenth century.

The rationale of this system lay, on the whole, more in its negotiatory rather than its coercive nature. Indeed, most of the analyses of the documentation, from all those communes in which some survived, attest to two fundamental elements in the judicial practice of the communes from the late thirteenth and early fourteenth centuries: the structural default of those under investigation and the negotiation of its related punishment. Exceptional powers of inquest and persecution were periodically conferred upon judicial rectors. The additional powers gave rise to an expansion of the sphere of criminalised behaviour and an increase in *ex officio* actions. However, those being investigated very rarely presented themselves at, or were brought before, court; the default rate was

---

[8] Fasoli, 'Ricerche sulla legislazione antimagnatizia'.

extremely high (up to 70 per cent). On the one hand, this absence served those interested in negotiating a reduction in, if not the cancellation of, the sentence and, on the other, served the highest political bodies, which received the requests, to legitimise their position on the political stage and implement policies of pardon. The physiological nature of default should therefore be recognised, as it served the processes of social reintegration and legitimisation of power. The administration of the courts by foreign rectors generally proceeded in the absence of the accused, and most often condemned him to banishment – banishment *pro maleficio* even more than banishment for exile – on the grounds of default considered as evidence of guilt. This approach gave political bodies the power to negotiate the reversal of the sentence with the banished defaulter, thus remitting the punishment and readmitting the offender into the political framework.

This mechanism, which can be clearly seen in the anti-magnate measures as well as in the political use of banishment, spread in a fairly systematic way in the decades at the end of the thirteenth and the beginning of the fourteenth centuries. The Bolognese banishments against the Lambertazzi faction between the 1270s and 1280s are well known, as are those in Florence against the Bianchi and the Ghibellines of 1302 and 1311.[9] The way in which exclusion by judicial means worked resided in the chance, for some families and some individuals, to exclude others from offices and from the city, and to strike them at the very foundation of their patrimony. The process of negotiating banishment and readmission into political society of the communes was fundamental.

Hegemonic justice: criminal law

The development of the criminal trial 'to charge the alleged perpetrator of a crime; to prove, according to the laws, his guilt; to impose the penalty according to the law or another deemed appropriate by the *ius*' was one of the characteristics of 'hegemonic justice'. Trials of this nature moved 'the aim of jurisdiction from justice to repression', responding to political imperatives such as '*ne crimina remaneant impunita*', '*ne ludibrium fiat principi vel legibus*'.[10] It was in the early fourteenth century that practices of justice and legal doctrine began to devise the notion that the violation of the law and penal obligations overall corresponded to a form of insubordination, and to point towards identifying disobedience with rebellion.

---

[9] Milani, *L'esclusione dal comune*.
[10] Sbriccoli, *Storia del diritto penale e della giustizia*, 1240ff.

In this sense, the conflict that, between 1312 and 1313, pitted Henry VII against Robert of Anjou, supported by Clement V, was decisive in that the trial promoted by the emperor against the king of Naples and some Italian Guelf cities attributed a legal value to the notion of *rebellio*. This value was clearly defined by the imperial constitutions, enacted at Pisa in 1313, *Ad reprimenda* and *Quis sit rebellis*. Henry VII established the possibility of acting quickly in the case of lese-majesty and also of judging in the absence of the accused. This laid the foundation for activating systematic judicial procedures which, under the veil of persecuting rebels, aimed at protecting and restoring sovereignty. This was not only an Italian tendency. Indeed, between the 1280s and 1350s, Christian Europe saw a wave of trials without precedent, promoted by both secular and ecclesiastical jurisdictions. These trials were not only against political enemies but also against powerful court members, prelates, important financiers, intellectuals and men of faith. Underlying these political charges and accusations of heresy was a single strategy of repression. In Italy, even mere communes held large judicial proceedings. This was the case in Treviso where, in 1314–15, some supporters of the da Camino *signoria*, which had dominated the city for some decades, were put under inquest. Many citizens were called to give evidence about the family's legitimacy and its deeds, even answering explicit questions on its 'tyrannical' nature.[11]

In Italy, with a programme of restoration aiming to reaffirm Guelf predominance in the territories around the Po valley and over church lands, pope John XXII, in particular, launched in the 1320s an armed crusade and a series of trials for rebellion and heresy against numerous *signori* – Matteo, Galeazzo and other members of the Visconti dynasty, Rinaldo and Obizzo d'Este, Federico da Montefeltro, the Gozzolini family of Osimo and their supporters from Recanati – and against intellectuals and men of faith such as Francesco Stabili (known as Cecco) of Ascoli or Muzio di Francesco of Assisi. In these cases, as in others, the accusation of heresy was instrumental in the conspicuously political use of judicial procedures against rival powers that undermined the *plenitudo potestatis* demanded by the pontificate. In the large cases brought by the pope, and by other sovereigns of the age, the fundamental issue was the defence of sovereignty and the will to impose, through the unusual use of established instruments, obedience to a legitimate order.

Their common element was the adoption of the form of trial that included the preparation of the inquest, the examination of witnesses, the presentation of pleas, the deliberation, the issuing of a sentence, etc.

---

[11] Cagnin (ed.), *Il processo Avogari*.

These mobilised the repertoire of judicial practices which had matured in the twelfth century at the time in which the *ordines iudiciarii* had been defined. This evolution drew on the reflections on the criminal trial and the political function of the judge as stipulated by canonist and civil jurists such as Guillaume Durand or Alberto da Gandino. The latter was a judge, active in the courts of the *podestà* in various Italian cities between 1280 and the early fourteenth century, and the author of *Tractatus de maleficiis*, the first theoretical account of criminal law. In the productive exchange of models and practices between ecclesiastical and ordinary courts, the large criminal trials of the fourteenth century saw play a defining role the inquisitorial method, non-formalised denunciations, the *fama publica* of the crime, recourse to confession (procured by torture if necessary) as supreme proof, and the development of the *ex officio* procedure. These trials were often characterised by the speeding-up of the penal sentence, the shortening of the *ordo iudiciarius*, and the extension of the judge's *arbitrium*. They became extraordinary procedures justified by invoking the *crimen lesae maiestatis*. In some respects, these procedures consolidated, leading to the emergence of tendencies also at work in the ordinary courts, such as the orientation towards defence, by the judicial route too, of the public interests, of the republic or of the *signore*, which was typical of the emergence of the public penal system.[12]

Social control and public order

Alongside the emergence of a public penal system and the development of court procedures, the methods of social control and public order underwent a profound transformation. Between the thirteenth and fifteenth centuries the general phenomenon of loosening the mechanisms of control can be observed, which until this point had been centred on the activities of local communities (neighbourhood, parish, district, village, etc.).

In Venice, for example, the *capi contrada*, who from the thirteenth century had been in charge of monitoring taverns and foreigners, were stripped of this authority in 1319 when the *capi sestiere* were created. The *capi sestiere*, whose job it was to register the names of foreigners present in the city, expel suspects and monitor inns and taverns, were nominated by the Maggior Consiglio and were directly subordinate to the Consiglio dei Dieci (Council of Ten). In other cities, too, social control was organised around officials active at *vicinia* or parish level: in Bologna, Imola and Forlì, for example, these were called *ministeriales*, in Milan

---

[12] Rigon and Veronese (eds.), *L'età dei processi*.

and Bergamo they were *anziani*, in Siena *sindaci*, and in Padua, Pistoia and Florence *cappellani*. The organisation of the community was regulated by the communal structures, beginning with the obligation to denounce crimes. This structure was thrown into crisis during the fourteenth century; this is true of Bergamo, for example, but also of Milan, where, towards the end of the fourteenth century, the *anziani* of the parishes were increasingly being accused of no longer reporting crimes committed in their own district. In Florence, the activity of the *cappellani* waned and eventually ceased in the middle of the fourteenth century. In the second half of the fourteenth century, the decline of community methods of social control is also confirmed by the increased frequency of sentences imposed on entire communities for not having fulfilled their collective obligation to pursue and capture wrongdoers or, for rural communities, for having offered refuge and shelter to *publici et famosi latrones*.[13]

The crisis of community structures also struck the militias, which, in the thirteenth century, had kept order at territorial level. There was a more general transition towards the creation of 'police' forces, a phenomenon common to many areas of the medieval West sometime in the fourteenth and fifteenth centuries. In Florence, for example, the number of officials (*bargelli, capitani di custodia e balìa, difensori del contado e distretto*) together with their own contingents of *berrovieri*, joining the patrols of communal rectors grew over the fourteenth century. In the same way, the numbers working within police forces operating in the city saw a significant increase. This increase in police forces brought about an appreciable change in the proportion of policemen to inhabitants, which was impressive almost everywhere. In Siena, for example, the ratio between *berrovieri* and inhabitants was 1 *berroviere* to 145 inhabitants in the 1330s; in Venice, in the second half of the fourteenth century, this ratio was 1 to 250–350 inhabitants. In Florence, between the beginning and the end of the century, this ratio went from 1 to approximately 2,000 inhabitants at the height of the communal age (when the city had 100,000–110,000 inhabitants) to a ratio of 1 to 150 at the time of the rise of the oligarchic regime (when the population was reduced to fewer than 60,000 inhabitants).[14]

New judicial bodies

The transformations in methods of social control and public order were only one aspect of the overall tendency to tighten relationships between

---

[13] Zorzi, 'Contrôle social, ordre public et répression judiciaire'.
[14] Manikowska, 'Il controllo sulle città'.

political power and judicial apparatus. New institutional arrangements directly linked judicial policies to the action of governments, progressively entrusting these policies to bodies directly linked to the governments. These bodies were composed of eminent members of ruling groups, who had no understanding of law and performed their judicial duties as well as having a deterrent effect outside the court itself as part of the new, and more concentrated, structures of power.

In Venice, for example, the institution of the Council of Ten in 1310 was a reaction to a conspiracy, thus creating this magistracy that, by its immediate connection with the Maggior Consiglio, well expressed the tendency towards the explicit politicisation of the judicial function. Initially charged with extraordinary functions so as to restore order to the city by punishing rebels who had taken part in the plot hatched by Baiamonte Tiepolo and Marco Querini, the Ten were then confirmed in their investigative and judicial roles concerning factions, conspiratorial activity, and manifestations of dissent, thus progressively eroding the prerogatives of those bodies previously in charge of criminal justice, beginning with the *Quarantia criminal*.

In the other republics, the transfer of judicial functions to new magistracies directly enacted by government was particularly evident and resulted in the progressive divestiture of the authority of the judicial bodies of the communal tradition. In Siena, for example, the transition took place at the fall of the regime of the Nine in 1355. In 1355, the activity of all courts and judicial offices centred upon the *capitano del popolo* (captain of the people), a post that was given no longer to a foreigner but to a prominent citizen. From 1371, to work alongside the communal *podestà*, *defensores status pacifici comunis Senarum* were brought in who were charged with, among other things, co-ordinating the forces of order and had full judicial powers when it came to matters of security. In Lucca, in 1374, the *conservatores libertatis*, a magistracy composed of citizens, was instituted 'ad conservandum libertatem civitatis Lucane et pacificum et bonum statum ipsius', which placed the *podestà*'s actions under tight control and directly intervened in security matters with judicial decrees and modifications to the city statutes. In 1392, the offices (held by foreigners) of the *maggior sindaco*, the *giudice degli appelli* and the *ufficiale delle gabelle* were abolished and their powers concentrated in the re-established captain of the people. In Florence, the repression of the revolt of the Ciompi in September 1378 was entrusted to a new body, the *Otto di Guardia*, a commission appointed by the *Priori*, charged with the task of co-ordinating the activity 'circa custodiam civitatis et attentantes aliquod contra statum in civitate vel extra', and soon endowed with increasing judicial powers. The *Otto di Guardia* acquired, *de facto* before *de iure*, the power to punish any wrongdoing, to take over a case from any court, to direct courts in what sentences to issue and to modify the sanctions of any court. Thus, they progressively divested communal rectors of judicial authority, leading to their definitive suppression during the fifteenth century.

The supersession of the judicial structure of the communes came about in specific ways in the *signorie*. Over the roles of the *podestà*, which nonetheless remained almost everywhere the courts of reference for both the criminal and civil justice of the cities, were superimposed new magistracies and councils with competences that took away the *podestà*'s most important functions. New central magistracies situated in the court were the centre of the territorial state administration of justice: in the Visconti–Sforza duchy, for example, these were the ducal councils, masters of the chamber and fiscal lawyers. The councils, secret council (also known as the senate in the Sforza period) and council of justice were set up as advisory bodies for the duke, who would submit matters to them which, in the judicial context, oversaw jurisdictional controversies between cities, fiefs and communities, the control of territory and public order, the repression of dissidents, and the drafting of new laws. Three 'masters' were in charge of bringing in extraordinary revenues to the ducal chamber; their responsibility was to ensure that sentences and confiscations were carried out, as well as to manage the goods and lands confiscated from the banished and the guilty through expropriation and sales. Given the many disputes this subject caused, these specialist accountants were supported by the stable presence of a jurisconsult in the office. There were also fiscal lawyers, a role always undertaken by jurisprudents, to protect the legal interests of the chamber and its income from trials and cases.

It must be observed that, with the exception of the kingdom of Naples, other contemporary states did not experience the ample involvement of jurists in the roles of the judicial administration (and beyond) of the Milanese duchy, in which men of law in the cities of the dominion found many career opportunities. In other princely states, such as the duchy of the Este or the marquisate of the Gonzaga, the presence of jurisprudents in the judicial offices was very limited. The Este privileged other practical skills and other professional profiles when recruiting their officers, mainly setting aside a place for jurists in the consulting role reserved to the council of ducal justice. The Gonzaga concentrated real powers and decision-making positions in the chancery, in which literati and notaries outnumbered the jurists.

The role of jurisprudents in the public administration of justice was also marginal in the republican states, in which the direct involvement of ruling groups prevailed. In the Florentine dominion, for example, the number of men of law progressively dwindled in the territorial courts, while the central offices were monopolised by the Florentine *cives* with the technical support of notaries. In the Venetian state, however, the different legal tradition between the dominant city and the Terraferma barred jurists from the dependent cities from being organically involved in roles of state. These remained firmly in the hands of the Venetian patriciate, with conspicuous exceptions such as that of the Veronese jurist Bartolomeo Cipolla. In other words, jurists everywhere, and especially the *doctores*, maintained a significant role in the function of giving top-level judicial advice in the affairs of state and diplomatic activity, and continued to monopolise the judicial professions. However, they were far less present in the operational roles of judges in the central magistracies and in the peripheral courts.[15]

The pragmatic nature of judicial policies

The new judicial bodies adopted procedures that were not exactly complete innovations, but which signalled a profound discontinuity in investigative and judicial action, above all highlighting procedural flexibility. Particularly evident are aspects such as the legitimation of secret denunciations, the secret nature of documents and the greater speed of the court *ordo*.

Indeed, growing recourse to secret and anonymous denunciations was one of the most significant elements of the transformation that took place in judicial systems. Unlike accusations made formally before a judge in ordinary courts, which carried the burden of following guarantee procedures (publication of the accusation, nomination of fidejussors, etc.), secret denunciators could not be punished for slander. In fact, often they were incentivised by rewards and cash prizes. It was immediately following the institution of the new magistracies that recourse to secret information became systematic and the principal means of starting a court action. In Florence, for example, the *Otto di Guardia* acted almost exclusively on the basis of notifications delivered in special boxes and on sources of information from spies and secret informers, who also operated inside the corporate world. From 1382, the Venetian Ten had funds at their disposal for 'secret' payments that did not have to be justified to any other council and were used for paying informers and spies. Princely regimes also incentivised people with cash rewards for bringing in a wealth of secret information: in Ferrara in 1472, for

---

[15] Covini, '*La balanza drita*', 15–28.

example, to deal with a fresh wave of 'homicidi, robarie et altri gravi et enormi delicti [murders, thefts and other serious and terrible crimes]' duke Ercole I d'Este allocated as many as 25 gold ducats for anyone who denounced a homicide or 10 gold ducats for the denunciation of theft. Informer anonymity was assured.

The social and political legitimation given to anonymity was a sign of new power structures which increasingly turned towards secrecy in judicial action too. The Venetian Council of Ten, for example, carried out investigations, took decisions and issued sentences within the strict silence of the ducal palace. In Florence, the *Otto di Guardia* worked in the same way: the secrecy of their activities is mirrored in the brevity of their written records. The secret nature of procedures was often screened by the lack, or vagueness, of the rules the new judicial bodies had to adhere to. The authority of the Milanese *capitano di giustizia* (captain of justice), for example, was not controlled by the statutes, but answered to the duke's discretion ('non è sottoposto alli statuti et ha larga baylia [is not subject to the statutes and has significant power]'). It is known that the *capitano di giustizia* in Ferrara could operate 'nullo iuris ordine servato nec servatis statutis aliquibus'. An *ordo non servatus* was also typical of the Council of Ten. In practice, meanwhile, the Florentine *Otto di Guardia* acted for a century without normative regulation of their authority. When these regulations were laid down in 1478, they were nevertheless given 'pienissimo arbitrio [total arbitrary power]' to judge and sentence 'in quel modo et forma che giudicassino convenirsi [in the way and by whichever means they saw fit]'. The new magistracies' arbitrary power was yet another reconfiguration of the *arbitrium* of judicial power, which had been one of the fundamental elements of the *ius commune* law system.[16]

Colleges such as the Venetian Ten or the Florentine *Otto* were not true courts but rather political judicial bodies. They did not prepare regular trials; instead their members discussed cases as a college. For the activities of the *Otto*, for example, no typical judicial documentation (registers of inquests, witness examinations, and sentences) remains, but only volumes of deliberations, which constitute exceptional evidence of a 'political' method of solving conflicts, consisting, above all, of mediations, arbitrations and compromises. This flexibility of intervention allowed the *Otto*, and similar magistracies in other cities, to carry out a policy of both repression and reintegration. Alongside harsh pecuniary punishments, capital punishment and condemnation to exile, the majority of their measures consisted of admonitions, orders, precepts and

[16] Meccarelli, *Arbitrium*.

absolutions. It was, therefore, a process in which forms of mediation and settling problems prevailed, and which, in a certain sense, brought these institutions closer to the pluralism of means of resolving conflicts which was always the most common and widespread judicial practice in the old regime.[17]

Justice under the princely regimes also appears characterised by a strongly pragmatic orientation. In the penal sphere, the interest in punishment was largely determined by fiscal needs, with repressive and targeted interventions intended to set an example. The everyday nature of interventions was formed by a plurality of actions which bent the work of magistrates, courts and officials to the image of the clement and peace-making ruler capable of righting wrongs, settling disputes and conflicts and, where necessary, using the severity of force. This underlying principle was interpreted by each prince, often according to different styles. Recent research on the judicial policies of the Sforza dukes of Milan has revealed precisely this: the founder of the dynasty, Francesco Sforza, operated with prudence, mediating conflicts and aiming to legitimise his authority through approval; his successor, Galeazzo Maria, stressed, in a despotic sense, the arbitrary aspects of the power of judicial intervention, while Ludovico il Moro knew how to use juridical instruments in an unscrupulous manner so as to reinforce his supremacy.[18]

Ruling with mercy, ruling with the gallows

One of the signs of the 'change' of the powers of *signori* in the autocratic sense was the spread, from the middle of the fourteenth century, of the system of pleas and granting of mercy: concessions on request to private individuals and institutions for exemptions and privileges in derogation or in exception to the statutes, decrees and municipal customs. Ruling with 'mercy', a long-standing prerogative of universal sovereignties and monarchical powers, also became an attribute of the new Italian urban powers in the fourteenth century. Acts of grace were propagandistically branded as manifestations of the total readiness of the *signori* to listen to their subjects, hailing supplication as a means of communicating requests, needs and wrongs which could be granted or solved by the prince, the source of accessible justice for all, in the certainty of being heard and understood.

In Bologna, the system of pleas to the *signore* was systematically introduced between 1326 and 1334 when the papal legate Bertrand du

---

[17] Zorzi, *L'amministrazione della giustizia penale*, 83–9.
[18] Leverotti, *'Governare a modo e stillo de' Signori . . .'*; Covini, *'La balanza drita'*.

Pouget ruled. He granted mercies and derogations that were, up until that time, impossible under the regime of the commune, and this practice was subsequently taken up and developed by Taddeo Pepoli between 1337 and 1347. A jurist by training, Pepoli portrayed himself ideologically to the citizens as the merciful lord, protector of the poor and needy (according to an image going back to the first councils of Christianity), able to place princely *potestas*, by exercising grace, on the same level as the coercive power of the ordinary laws of the commune.

In Milan under the Visconti, especially from the 1350s during the rule of Bernabò, the use of mercy spread systematically: from collective pardons, like the one granted in 1368 to all those who had been sentenced for a series of crimes, with the aim of reinforcing territorial defence in a time of war, to individual pardons, such as the one granted in 1382 to the Schiaffenati family of Pavia, with the aim of revoking various sentences imposed for acts of sedition and violence. The procedure was relatively simple: after a plea was drawn up, the prince's chancery would produce a letter patent that ended trials, allowed the brief cognisance of long-running court cases, revoked sentences and banishments, and showed mercy for a wide variety of crimes. The revocation of the punitive effects of sentences was justified as the prince bestowing his favour on a chosen few, as a generous and magnanimous gift, as a benevolent concession, which built up the image of a special, selective justice which rewarded the prince's beneficiaries. At the same time, since these pardons called into question the principle of the necessary punishment of crimes, the prince's clemency was justified by the need to restore the 'original legality', which had been violated by excessively severe punishments, and by the prince's desire for equal treatment for all, which led to his intervention to correct and mitigate the work of the judges.

However, the unchecked and indiscriminate recourse to mercy – chiefly motivated by fiscal necessities – could provoke discontent and tension when it resulted in harm being done to the rights and interests of third parties. This happened, for example, in cases where mercy being granted allowed the guilty party to recover goods and rights which had, in the meantime, been confiscated and redistributed. Furthermore, the remission of sentences and fines was not looked upon favourably by the judges who had imposed them: it diminished their work, put their 'honour' at stake and, above all, reduced their income (which was partly based on the collection of pecuniary sanctions).[19]

---

[19] Covini, 'De gratia speciali'.

Over the fourteenth and fifteenth centuries, the judicial policies implemented by the new powers balanced the mildness of pardon with the harshness of repression, aiming both for the reintegration of the social groups on which their consensus was founded and for the refinement of the exemplary function of punishment. During the thirteenth century, penal coercion was marked by the extension of specific typologies of punishment to an ever greater range of criminal cases. There was a proliferation of painful, ignominious and corporal sanctions, which characterised the communal era, with its intense and harsh forms of repression. On reaching maturity, the system of punishments underwent an appreciable transformation, which showed itself above all in the reduction of the variety of executive methods and in the extension of pecuniary sanctions in place of corporal and ignominious punishments.

Indeed, the concentration on a few penal typologies was accompanied by a reduction in the frequency of executions. This can be clearly seen with regard to capital punishments: little evidence has been analysed; however, it is known, for example, that in Ferrara the average annual number of executions between 1441 and 1577 was 5–6, with oscillations depending on attempts at conspiracy and on which member of the Este family was ruling (Leonello's early rule was more benevolent, while Ercole I's and Alfonso II's were more severe). In Florence, capital punishment decreased from an annual average of 11–13 cases in the fourteenth century to a rate of 7–8 in the fifteenth, and was destined finally to collapse with the rise of the grand duke. In Rome a rise in the second half of the sixteenth century has been noted, followed by a rapid decrease in the subsequent two centuries. Executions were generally by hanging or decapitation, with a progressive discontinuation in the use of other forms such as burning at the stake.

A reduction in the variety of penal typologies did not mean that the violence of executions grew less severe. Indeed, the decrease in the number of capital punishments corresponded to their increased sensationalism. The establishment of regimes which, like those of the *signori*, emphasised the search for consensus reinforced the admonitory features of the execution, connoting its ritual as a growing expression of the power assuring order and the vendetta against and the protection of the community from enemies.[20]

The ferocity of death penalty was concentrated on the body. The suffering of the condemned was a particularly essential element of the execution: from simple public exhibition, to the range of tortures associated with different penalties, to the mangling of the corpse that

---

[20] Zorzi, *Pene e rituali di giustizia*.

sometimes followed execution. By recomposing and burying the limbs, and, in more general terms, by offering aid and comfort to the condemned, the church set itself against these slaughters in the name of public justice, proposing a Christian softening of its cruelty and atrocities. The *compagnie di giustizia* (confraternities who comforted criminals condemned to execution) played a role of recognised importance in the city communities and developed a function of supporting the stability of regimes. Persons of prestige were part of these *compagnie*: their activity was not only to implement the intention of reaffirming the link of solidarity between the community of the living and the world of the dead, but also to demonstrate the possibility of social reconciliation.[21]

Justice in the territorial states

With the establishment of the territorial states, justice became a field of debate between the ruling city or the prince, who laid claim to ever larger areas of intervention, and the subjugated cities, which did not resign themselves to losing their control over a crucial aspect of community life. The appointment of judges was appropriated by the centre. In the republican states, such as Florence and Venice, it was the members of the ruling groups who took the posts of *podestà* in the subject cities, while in the principalities it was the prince who sent his own officials to the dominion. Everywhere the cities lost the faculty to elect their own rectors autonomously. This created entirely new situations for cities, causing tensions that would long endure. These were, on the one hand, over the responsibility of the officials and which law to apply in the administration of justice and, on the other, over the protection of the urban patriciates' interests and the prerogatives of the city curie as regards their respective *contadi*.

In the construction of their own dominion, for example, the Florentines did not limit themselves to controlling the role of the rectors in the subjugated cities (Arezzo, Pistoia, Pisa, etc.), but also directly assumed the jurisdictions of the *podestà* in the minor centres and rural communes in their *contadi*. This created a marked discontinuity at local level. Indeed, the Florentine government paid little attention to those aspects of the administration of justice that did not directly affect public order or the protection of the patrimonial and landed interests of its citizens: matters in which the ruling city's law was involved. Even in civil matters, justice did not seem to satisfy local needs. Unlike other states – the Venetian state, for example, where some subject cities maintained

---

[21] Terpstra (ed.), *The Art of Executing Well*.

their own courts of first instance, such as the consulates of Verona and Vicenza, the similar offices in Brescia or the *giudici pedanei* in Padua – in the Florentine state, the subjugated cities neither had nor retained courts run by the eminent local group.

From the subject centres, therefore, there came requests for a level of professionalism in the judges that was in some ways comparable to that enjoyed during the communal period. Pursuing a policy of preservation rather than the administration of the dominion, Florence consistently reduced (by at least twenty) the number of those professional judges who accompanied its rectors. A legal expert also meant a differentiation of privileges compared with the less urbanised areas of the dominion and the protection of a more appropriate administration of civil justice. There were, therefore, numerous complaints put forward by the cities to raise the quality of the judges sent by Florence. It was only during the Medici regime, which was more attentive to a policy of consensus even outside Florence, that some cities – Pisa, Arezzo and Pistoia, but also centres such as Cortona, Montepulciano or Borgo San Sepolcro – succeeded in making certain that rectors were always accompanied by judges who were not generic *iurisperiti*, as was widespread in the early years of domination, but rather equipped with degrees or doctorates in civil law.[22] By contrast, in the Venetian Terraferma, the political system, oriented to allying with subjugated urban oligarchies, was based on the ability to moderate two traditions of law. Thus, respect for the autonomy and privileges of the subject cities and communities, which followed the learned law of local tradition, was moderated with interventions based on equitable justice by Venetian rectors, who were instead accustomed to Venetian local law. The policy of the law of the Venetian authorities was, however, invested in the *arbitrium*, that is, on rapid and equitable solutions, in which the *Auditori nuovi* stood out. The *Auditori nuovi* were created in 1410 and had the function of appeal in the civil cases of the dominion's courts.[23]

In the duchy of Milan, the application of civil justice remained the prerogative of the cities, overseen by local colleges of *doctores*, which monopolised the judicial *consilia* and the appeals. But the prince retained the right to appoint local *podestà*, aiming to give them responsibility – for example, in the eventual abolition of the *consilium sapientis iudiciale* in penal matters during the Visconti era – and always considering them as his own points of reference in the dominion. In turn, the communities looked to constrain the work of the rectors, obliging

---

[22] Connell and Zorzi (eds.), *Florentine Tuscany*.
[23] Cozzi (ed.), *Stato società e giustizia nella Repubblica veneta*.

them stringently to observe city statutes – often in open conflict with the ducal decrees – and local judicial procedures (*stylus uriae*). In some cases, as in Reggio at the end of the fourteenth century, the city came to the economic rescue of the *podestà*, whose salary the prince did not pay on time, inveigling him in an ambiguous relationship and one that was not without consequences, for example, in the progress of certain trials. The demand for the co-partnership of the *civitas* in the judicial sphere was also expressed on a symbolic level, as happened, for example, again in Reggio in 1453. As the new lord, Borso d'Este, made his triumphal entrance, the city brought, alongside the chariots of the duke and the patron saint, its own chariot of justice, thus demanding shared administration of justice between the local patricians and the prince.[24]

On the other hand, during the fifteenth century, commissioners made their appearance in various territorial states. Commissioners were plenipotentiary officials who worked alongside, and sometimes took over from – as happened in certain circumstances in the Florentine dominion – the cities' *podestà*. They were initially charged with carrying out individual missions and then became increasingly established, but they were not bound to respect city statutes, nor were they subject to local review of their behaviour (*sindacato*), but rather answered directly to the ruling city or the prince. The commissioners' actions undermined the centrality of local law and challenged the hierarchy of the sources of law, favouring the prevalence of the laws of the ruling city or the ducal decrees over the city statutes.

The cities were also careful to preserve the primacy of their respective courts with regard to the new administrative circumscriptions (fiefs, vicariates, rural areas controlled by a *podestà*) which the prince or ruling city marked out over the territory, and which undermined, also in the judicial sphere, the privilege – unchallenged until now – of the *cives* as regards the *comitatini*. In the Florentine dominion, for example, the jurisdiction of the urban *podestà* was limited to the few miles of countryside surrounding the city walls, the *contado* being returned to the dependency of the new circumscriptions of *podestà* and vicars, carved from the *contadi* of the subjugated centres. Everywhere the *cives* submitted themselves, always rather unwillingly, to the jurisdiction of the rural officials, seeking to retain, wherever possible, the privilege of being judged in the cities, including in cases which set them against the inhabitants of the respective *contado*. At the end of the fourteenth century, in the Visconti duchy, the cities were successful in making sure

---

[24] Gamberini, *La città assediata*, 27–36, and Turchi, 'Una piccola modifica'.

that the *capitano del divieto*, who operated as though he were a *podestà* of the *contado*, lost the *merum et mixtum imperium* and retained only the power to control contraband, but nevertheless in a subordinate position relative to the urban curie.

Analogies with certain aspects of the administration of justice in the territorial states can be gathered from the analyses of the judicial structures of the kingdoms of Naples and Sicily. In the kingdom of Sicily, judicial authority was shared between the crown, the demesnial centres and the aristocracy. In this system, certain privileged legal fora were also recognised: the citizens of the main cities (Palermo, Messina) benefited from these, just as mercantile curie and ecclesiastic courts had their own fora. In the enfeoffed territories the lords presided over local courts composed of members appointed by them. The central court was the royal Grand Court, set up by Frederick II and still active at the time of Alfonso V of Aragon, which did not have a fixed seat but followed the sovereign wherever he went. Composed of jurists (four at the time of Alfonso the Magnanimous), the Grand Court acted as a court of appeal and a privileged forum for lords. It also had exclusive authority regarding crimes of lese-majesty and feudal cases, and it heard pleas directed to the sovereign and passed judgement on legal disputes. In 1433, Alfonso also established the royal commissioners, charged with special cases of particular complexity, who often came to replace ordinary magistrates.

At a local level, however, the system integrated elected magistracies with magistracies of royal appointment. Mixed bodies administered justice in the demesnial cities. These were composed of local officials elected by the communities and presided over by officials appointed by the king. These courts were generally composed of a captain of royal appointment, a judge, always a *iurisperitus*, and an elected notary, the last two being elected and salaried by the *universitates*. The captain – who had the title *giustiziere* in Palermo and *stratigoto* in Messina – acted as the sovereign's direct representative, often in opposition to the city institutions, and was the object of the cities' constant and widespread discontent. This was exacerbated by the fact that the captain, besides having criminal jurisdiction, was responsible for public order, supported by patrols which often came into conflict with the patrols organised within the quarters of the cities. Civil justice was also administered in the kingdom by elected local magistracies: the *curie baiulari* consisting of a *baiulus* and three judges, made up of jurists and laymen. Of Norman origins and later reformed by Frederick II, these curie strengthened the *iurisdictio* after the revolt of the Vespers in 1282, permanently establishing their local nature, although the *baiulus* retained the title of *regius*, as he was, at one time, both the king's representative at local level and the manifestation of city authority.[25]

Concluding remarks

If there is, then, a common element in the research conducted on justice in recent years, this appears to return to the impossibility of interpreting the process of the formation of the Italian Renaissance states in Max Weber's terms of the progressive 'monopolisation of violence'. On the contrary, the action of public powers was oriented towards the use of instruments of justice as a resource in the political struggle, as systems of government and systems of defining new power structures, as sources of legitimation, and as a means of organising consensus.

Judicial practices were characterised by a wide sphere of negotiatory procedures, capable – as has been shown – of permeating even the procedures of public justice. Ideal processes of justice themselves oscillated between the language of arbitrariness and that of respecting the law. In the middle of the fourteenth century, for example, in the Visconti duchy, the two models embodied respectively by Bernabò and Galeazzo II can be contrasted. The former demanded a wider *arbitrium* for the prince, and the power to depart from procedures and the law in order to rectify distortions within the judicial system, acting as *executor iustitiae*. The latter, however, embodied the *iustus* prince as guarantor of the statutes and customs, sparing as he was in granting mercy so as not to depart from the law, and supreme custodian of the legal system.[26]

The two opposing ideals of justice continued. In fifteenth-century republican Florence, for example, the Medici chancellor Bartolomeo Scala was the author of a *De legibus et iudiciis dialogus* (dated to 1483) which aimed to replace the centrality of the notions of *iustitia* and *libertas* with those of *utilitas* and *equitas*, which were more flexible as regards varying policies. Returning to the humanistic polemic against the doctrinarianism of legal science, Scala declared himself an advocate of a justice founded on fairness and the natural law, opposed to the obscurity of the law of jurists, who made use of its immutability to impose unjust and cruel sentences, against nature and equity. Examining the nature of the law – whether it should be eternal or whether it ought to change according to the times and circumstances – in the *Dialogus*, Scala entrusts the argument regarding the flexibility and ability to adapt to different and daily 'occurrences' to himself, and the defence of the

---

[25] Pasciuta, *'In regia curia civiliter convenire'*, 41–68.
[26] Gamberini, *La città assediata*, 253–5.

sacred nature of the law and its immutability to his friend Bernardo Machiavelli (a man of the law and father of Niccolò).[27]

Reflected in the various languages of justice, therefore, are tensions based around creating a more liberal justice system and more discretional sentences, a law capable of changing according to the times and circumstances, and a law able to adapt itself in a flexible manner to the processes of legitimising power during the Renaissance.

---

[27] Brown, *Bartolomeo Scala*, 288–96.

Bibliography

1. *The kingdom of Sicily* (Fabrizio Titone)

Abulafia, D., 'Signorial power in Aragonese southern Italy', in E. Nicholas and N. Terpstra (eds.), *Sociability and Its Discontents: Civil Society, Social Capital, and Their Alternatives in Late Medieval and Early Modern Europe*, Turnhout: Brepols, 2009, 173–92.

The Two Italies: Economic Relations Between the Norman Kingdom of Sicily and the Northern Communes, Cambridge University Press, 1977.

Arcifa, L., 'La città nel Medioevo. Sviluppo urbano e dominio territoriale', in L. Scalisi (ed.), *Catania. L'identità urbana dall'Antichità al Settecento*, Catania: Domenico Sanfilippo Editore, 2009, 72–111.

Aymard, M., 'Il commercio dei grani nella Sicilia del '500', *Archivio Storico della Sicilia Orientale* 72 (1976), 7–40.

Barberi, G. L., *Il 'Magnum Capibrevium' dei feudi maggiori*, G. Stalteri Ragusa (ed.), 2 vols., Palermo: Società siciliana per la Storia patria, 1993.

Baviera Albanese, A., 'L'istituzione dell'ufficio del Conservatore del Real Patrimonio e gli organi finanziari del regno di Sicilia nel sec. XV (Contributo alla storia delle magistrature siciliane)', Palermo, 1958, republished in A. Baviera Albanese, *Scritti minori*, Messina: Rubbettino, 1992, 3–107.

'Studio introduttivo', in L. Citarda (ed.), *Acta Curie Felicis Urbis Panormi*, Palermo: Municipio di Palermo, 1984, III, xv–lxviii.

Benigno, F., and C. Torrisi (eds.), *Rappresentazioni e immagini della Sicilia tra storia e storiografia. Atti del convegno di studi*, Caltanissetta: Sciascia, 2003.

Bresc, H., '1282. Classes sociales et révolution nationale', in *La società mediterranea all'epoca del Vespro*, 4 vols., Palermo: Accademia di Scienze Lettere e Arti, 1983–84, I, 241–58.

Un monde méditerranéen. Économie et société en Sicilie 1300–1450, 2 vols., Rome and Palermo: École française de Rome, 1986.

Cancila, O., *Baroni e popolo nella Sicilia del grano*, Palermo: Palumbo, 1983.

Corrao, P., *Governare un regno. Potere, società e istituzioni in Sicilia fra Trecento e Quattrocento*, Naples: Liguori, 1991.

'Uomini d'affari stranieri nelle città siciliane del tardo Medioevo', *Revista de Historia Medieval* 11 (2000), 139–62.

Cosentino, G., *Codice diplomatico di Federico III d'Aragona re di Sicilia*, Palermo: Società Siciliana per la Storia Patria, 1866.
D'Alessandro, V., *Politica e società nella Sicilia aragonese*, Palermo: Manfredi, 1963.
  Terra, nobili e borghesi nella Sicilia medievale, Palermo: Sellerio, 1994.
Del Treppo, M., *I mercanti catalani e l'espansione della Corona d'Aragona nel secolo XV*, 2nd edn, Naples: Giannini, 1972.
Epstein, S. R., *Freedom and Growth: The Rise of States and Markets in Europe, 1300–1750*, London: Routledge, 2000.
  An Island for Itself: Economic Development and Social Change in Late Medieval Sicily, Cambridge University Press, 1992.
Evangelisti, P., *I francescani e la costruzione di uno stato. Linguaggi politici, valori identitari, progetti di governo in area catalano-aragonese*, Padua: Editrici Francescane, 2006.
Fodale, S., 'Federico III d'Aragona e la genesi del Parlamento siciliano', in A. Romando (ed.), *'De curia semel in anno facienda'. L'esperienza parlamentare siciliana nel contesto europeo*, Milan: Giuffrè, 2002, 61–71.
Genuardi, L., *Il comune nel Medioevo in Sicilia. Contributo alla storia del diritto amministrativo*, Palermo: Società Orazio Fiorenza, 1921.
Giambruno, S., and L. Genuardi (eds.), *Capitoli inediti delle città demaniali di Sicilia*, Palermo: Boccone Del Povero, 1918.
Giardina, C., 'Unione personale o unione reale fra Sicilia e Aragona e fra Sicilia e Napoli durante il regno di Alfonso il Magnanimo?', in *Atti del congresso internazionale di studi sull'età aragonese*, Bari: Adriatica Editrice, 1972, 191–225.
Giarrizzo, G., 'La Sicilia dal cinquecento all'unità d'Italia', in G. Galasso (ed.), *Storia d'Italia*, XVI *La Sicilia dal Vespro all'Unità*, Turin: Utet, 1989, 99–785.
Gregorio, R., *Considerazioni sopra la storia di Sicilia dai tempi normanni sino ai presenti*, Palermo: Edizioni della Regione Siciliana, 3 vols., 1972.
Gulotta, P., '*In unum corpus et unam societatem*. I capitula iuratorum del 1309 (Testa 1324) e l'assetto istituzionale della città di Palermo durante il regno di Federico III', *Archivio Storico Siciliano* 26 (2000), 19–56.
Hillgarth, J. N., *The Spanish Kingdoms 1250–1516*, 2 vols., Oxford University Press, 1976–8.
Ligresti, D. (ed.), *Il governo delle città. Patriziati e politica nella Sicilia moderna*, Catania: Cuemc, 1990.
Küchler, W., *Les finances de la Corona d'Aragó al segle XV (regnats d'Alfons V i Joan II)*, V. Farías Zurita (transl.), Valencia: Edicions Alfons el Magnànim, 1997.
Marrone, A., *Repertorio della feudalità siciliana, 1282–1390*, Palermo: Mediterranea, 2006.
Mazzarese Fardella, E., 'Osservazioni sul suffeudo in Sicilia', *Rivista di storia del diritto italiano* 34 (1961), 99–183.
Mineo, E. I., 'Città e società urbana nell'età di Federico III. Le élites e la sperimentazione istituzionale', in M. Ganci, V. D'Alessandro and R. S. Guccione (eds.), *Federico III d'Aragona re di Sicilia (1296–1377)*, Palermo: Società Siciliana di Storia Patria, 1997, 109–49.

Nobiltà di stato. Famiglie e identità aristocratiche nel tardo Medioevo. La Sicilia, Rome: Donzelli, 2001.

Moscati, R., *Per una storia della Sicilia nell'età dei Martini (Appunti e documenti: 1396–1408)*, Messina: Università degli Studi di Messina, 1954.

Pace, G., *Il governo dei gentiluomini. Ceti dirigenti e magistrature a Caltagirone tra Medioevo ed età moderna*, Rome: Il Cigno Galileo Galilei, 1996.

Pasciuta, B., *Placet regie maiestati. Itinerari della normazione nel tardo Medioevo*, Turin: Giappichelli, 2005.

Peri, I., 'Per una storia della vita cittadina e del commercio nel Medioevo. Girgenti porto del sale e del grano', in *Studi in onore di Amintore Fanfani*, 2 vols., Milan: Giuffrè, 1962, I, 3–87.

Restaurazione e pacifico stato in Sicilia 1377–1501, Rome and Bari: Laterza, 1988.

La Sicilia dopo il Vespro. Uomini, città e campagne. 1282/1376, Rome and Bari: Laterza, 1990.

Uomini, città e campagne dall'XI al XIII secolo, Rome and Bari: Laterza, 1978.

Villani e cavalieri nella Sicilia medievale, Rome and Bari: Laterza, 1993.

Petralia, G., *Banchieri e famiglie mercantili nel Mediterraneo aragonese. L'emigrazione dei Pisani in Sicilia nel Quattrocento*, Pisa: Pacini Editore, 1989.

'Sui Toscani in Sicilia fra Due e Trecento. La penetrazione sociale e il radicamento nei ceti urbani', in M. Tangheroni (ed.), *Commercio, finanza, funzione pubblica. Stranieri e realtà urbane in Sicilia e Sardegna nei secoli XII–XV*, Naples: Liguori, 1989, 129–218.

Romano, A., *'Legum doctores' e cultura giuridica nella Sicilia aragonese. Tendenze, opere, ruoli*, Milan: Giuffrè, 1984.

Silvestri, G. (ed.), *I Capibrevi di Giovanni Luca Barberi*, 3 vols., Palermo, 1879–88, repr., Palermo: Società Siciliana per la Storia Patria, 1985.

(ed.) *De Rebus Regni Siciliae. Documenti inediti estratti dall'Archivio della Corona d'Aragona*, 2 vols., Palermo, 1882, repr., Palermo: Società Siciliana per la Storia Patria, 1982.

Sorrenti, L., 'Le istituzioni comunali di Troina nell'età aragonese', *Archivio Storico Siciliano* 4 (1978), 111–67.

Starrabba, R., and L. Tirrito (eds.), *Assise e consuetudini della terra di Corleone*, Palermo: Società Siciliana per la Storia Patria, 1880.

Testa, F. M., *Capitula regni Siciliae*, 2 vols., Panormi: A. Felicella, 1741–3.

Titone, F., *Governments of the Universitates: Urban Communities of Sicily in the Fourteenth and Fifteenth Centuries*, Turnhout: Brepols, 2009.

'Il tumulto popularis del 1450. Conflitto politico e società urbana a Palermo', *Archivio Storico Italiano* 603 (2005), 43–86.

Varvaro, A., *Le chiavi del castello delle Gerbe. Fedeltà e tradimento nella Sicilia trecentesca*, Palermo: Sellerio, 1984.

2. *The kingdom of Naples* (Francesco Senatore)

Abulafia, D., 'Southern Italy and the Florentine economy, 1265–1370', *Economic History Review* 34, 3 (1981), 377–88.

The Two Italies: Economic Relations Between the Norman Kingdom of Sicily and the Northern Communes, Cambridge University Press, 1977.

The Western Mediterranean Kingdoms 1200–1500: The Struggle for Dominion, London: Addison Wesley Longman, 1997.

Airò, A., 'L'inventario dell'archivio che non c'è più. I privilegi aragonesi come deposito della memoria documentaria dell'università di Taranto', in A. Bartoli Langeli, A. Giorgi and S. Moscadelli (eds.), *Archivi e comunità tra Medioevo ed età moderna*, Rome: Ministero per i beni e le attività culturali, 2009, 521–58.

Cadier, L., *Essai sur l'administration du Royaume de Sicilie sous Charles I et Charles II d'Anjou*, Paris: Thorin, 1891.

Calabria, A., *The Cost of Empire: The Finances of the Kingdom of Naples in the Time of Spanish Rule*, Cambridge University Press, 1991.

Calasso, F., *La legislazione statutaria nell'Italia meridionale. Le basi storiche. Le libertà cittadine dalla fondazione del regno all'epoca degli statuti*, Rome and Bari: Biblioteca della rivista di storia del diritto italiano, 1929.

Capitani, O., 'Medioevo', in 'Storiografia', *Enciclopedia italiana di scienze, letteratura ed arti*, Appendix V, *1979–1992*, vol. V, *SO–Z*, Rome: Istituto dell'Enciclopedia italiana, 1995, 286–92.

Cassandro, G. I., *Lineamenti del diritto pubblico del regno di Sicilia Citra Farum sotto gli aragonesi*, Bari: Cressati, 1934.

Corrao, P., 'Centri e periferie nelle monarchie meridionali nel tardo Medioevo. Note sul caso siciliano', in G. Chittolini, A. Mohlo and P. Schiera (eds.), *Origini dello stato. Processi di formazione statale in Italia fra Medioevo ed età moderna*, Bologna: Il Mulino, 1994, 187–205.

Croce, B., *Storia del regno di Napoli*, Bari: Laterza, 1924.

Cruselles, E., *El mestre racional de Valencia. Función política y desarrollo administrativo del oficio pùblico en el siglo XV*, Valencia: Ed. Alfons el Magnànim, 1989.

Cutolo, A., *Margherita d'Enghien*, Naples: ITEA, 1929.

Re Ladislao d'Angiò Durazzo, 2nd edn, Naples: Berisio, 1969.

Dalena, P., *Ambiti territoriali, sistemi viari e strutture del potere nel Mezzogiorno medievale*, Bari: Adda, 2000.

De Montagut i Estrangués, T., *El mestre racional a la Corona d'Aragó (1283–1419)*, 2 vols., Barcelona: Fundació Noguera, 1987.

Del Treppo, M., 'Alfonso il Magnanimo e la Corona d'Aragona', in G. D'Agostino and G. Buffardi (eds.), *La Corona d'Aragona ai tempi di Alfonso il Magnanimo. I modelli politico-istituzionali. La circolazione degli uomini, delle idee, delle merci. Gli influssi sulla società e sul costume. Celebrazioni alfonsine*, 2 vols., Naples: Paparo, 2000, I, 1–17.

'I catalani a Napoli e le loro pratiche con la corte', in G. Vitolo and C. Carlone (eds.), *Studi di storia meridionale in memoria di Pietro Laveglia*, Salerno: Laveglia, 1994, 31–112.

La libertà della memoria. Scritti di storiografia, Rome: Viella, 2006.

I mercanti catalani e l'espansione della Corona d'Aragona nel secolo XV, 2nd edn, Naples: L'arte Tipografica, 1972.

'Mezzogiorno, Nord mancato', *Itinerario* 3 (December 1987), 129–31.

'Prospettive mediterranee della politica economica di Federico II', in A. Esch and N. Kamp (eds.), *Friedrich II.*, Tagung des Deutschen Historischen Instituts in Rom im Gedenkjahr 1994, Tübingen: Niemeyer, 1996, 316–38.

'Il re e il banchiere. Strumenti e processi di razionalizzazione dello stato aragonese di Napoli', in G. Rossetti (ed.), *Spazio, società e potere nell'Italia dei Comuni*, Napoli: Liguori-GISEM, 1986, 229–304.

'Il regno aragonese', in G. Galasso and R. Romeo (eds.), *Storia del Mezzogiorno*, IV/1, Rome: Editalia, 1986, 87–201.

'Un ritrovato libro del Percettore generale del regno di Napoli', in P. Corrao and E. I. Mineo (eds.), *Dentro e fuori la Sicilia. Studi di storia per Vincenzo D'Alessandro*, Rome: Viella, 2009, 295–318.

Delle Donne, R., 'Alle origini della Regia Camera della Sommaria', *Rassegna Storica Salernitana* 8 (1991), 25–61.

'Le cancellerie dell'Italia meridionale (secoli XIII–XV)', *Ricerche Storiche* 25 (1994), 361–88.

Durrieu, P., *Les archives angevines de Naples. Étude sur les registres du roi Charles I (1265–1285)*, 2 vols., Paris: Thorin, 1886–7.

Epstein, S. R., *An Island for Itself: Economic Development and Social Change in Late Medieval Sicily*, Cambridge University Press, 1992.

'Storia economica e storia istituzionale dello stato', in G. Chittolini, A. Mohlo and P. Schiera (eds.), *Origini dello stato. Processi di formazione statale in Italia fra Medioevo ed età moderna*, Bologna: Il Mulino, 1994, 97–111.

Faraglia, N. F., *Storia della lotta tra Alfonso d'Aragona e Renato d'Angiò*, Lanciano: Carabba, 1908.

Storia della regina Giovanna II d'Angiò, Lanciano: R. Carabba, 1904.

Figliuolo, F., 'Profilo di storia dell'organizzazione territoriale nel Mezzogiorno medioevale', in G. Chittolini and D. Willoweit (eds.), *L'organizzazione del territorio in Italia e Germania. Secoli XIII–XIV*, Bologna: Il Mulino, 1994, 373–94.

Galasso, G., *Il Mezzogiorno nella storia d'Italia*, Florence: Le Monnier, 1977.

Il Mezzogiorno angioino e aragonese (1266–1494), in G. Galasso (ed.) *Storia d'Italia*, XV, *Il regno di Napoli*, I, Turin: Utet, 1992.

Gentile, P., 'Lo stato napoletano sotto Alfonso I d'Aragona', *Archivio Storico per le Province Napoletane* 62 (1937), 1–56; 63 (1938), 1–56.

Kiesewetter, A., 'La cancelleria angioina', in N. Coulet and J.-M. Matz (eds.), *L'état angevin. Pouvoir, culture et société entre XIIIe et XIVe siècle*. Rome: Ecole française de Rome, 1998, 361–415.

Léonard, E. G., *Les Angevins de Naples*, Paris: PUF, 1954.

Histoire de Jeanne Ière reine de Naples, comtesse de Provence (1343–1382), 3 vols., Paris and Monaco: Picard, 1932–6.

Leone, A., *Ricerche sull'economia meridionale dei secoli XIII–XV. Saggi e note critiche*, Naples: Athena, 1994.

Licinio, R., *Masserie medievali. Masserie, massari e carestie da Federico II alla dogana delle pecore*, Bari: Adda, 1998.

Morelli, S., 'Il controllo delle periferie nel Mezzogiorno angioino alla metà del XIII secolo. Produzione e conservazione di carte', in I. Lazzarini (ed.), *Scritture e potere. Pratiche documentarie e forme di governo nell'Italia*

tardomedievale (XIV–XV secolo), *Reti Medievali Rivista* 9 (2008), 1–29 (www.retimedievali.it).
'I giustizieri nel regno di Napoli al tempo di Carlo I d'Angiò. Primi risultati di un'analisi prosopografica', in N. Coulet and J.-M. Matz (eds.), *L'état angevin. Pouvoir, culture et société entre XIIIe et XIVe siècle*, Rome: Ecole française de Rome, 1998, 491–517.
'Tra continuità e trasformazioni. Su alcuni aspetti del Principato di Taranto alla metà del XV secolo', *Società e Storia* 73 (1996), 487–525.
'Note sulla fiscalità diretta e indiretta nel regno angioino', in C. Massaro and P. Petracca (eds.), *Territorio, culture e poteri nel Medioevo e oltre. Scritti in onore di Benedetto Vetere*, Galatina: Confedo, 2011, 389–413.
Nunziante, N., 'I primi anni di Ferdinando d'Aragona e l'invasione di Giovanni d'Angiò', *Archivio Storico per le Province Napoletane* 17–23 (1892–8).
Palmieri, S., *La cancelleria del regno di Sicilia in età angioina*, Naples: Accademia Pontaniana, 2006.
Petraccone, C., *Le 'due Italie'. La questione meridionale tra realtà e rappresentazione*, Rome and Bari: Laterza, 2005.
Putnam, R. D., with R. Leonardi and R. Y. Nanetti, *Making Democracy Work: Civic Tradition in Modern Italy*, Princeton University Press, 1993.
Ryder, A., *Alfonso the Magnanimous, King of Aragon, Naples and Sicily (1396–1458)*, Oxford: Clarendon Press, 1990.
The Kingdom of Naples Under Alfonso the Magnanimous: The Making of a Modern State, Oxford: Clarendon Press, 1976.
Sáiz Serrano, J., *Caballeros del rey. Nobleza y guerra en el reinado de Alfonso el Magnánimo*, Valencia: PUV, 2008.
Scarton, E., 'La congiura dei baroni del 1485–87 e la sorte dei ribelli', in F. Senatore and F. Storti (eds.), *Poteri, relazioni, guerra nel regno di Ferrante d'Aragona. Studi sulle corrispondenze diplomatiche*, Naples: Cliopress, 2011 (www.storia.unina.it/cliopress/senatore-storti.html), 213–90.
'Il parlamento napoletano del 1484', *Archivio Storico per le Province Napoletane* 124 (2006), 113–36.
Senatore, F., 'Gli archivi delle *universitates* meridionali. Il caso di Capua ed alcune considerazioni generali', in A. Bartoli Langeli, A. Giorgi and S. Moscadelli (eds.), *Archivi e comunità tra Medioevo ed età moderna*, Rome: Ministero per i beni e le attività culturali, 2009, 447–520.
'Cerimonie regie e cerimonie civiche a Capua (secoli XV–XVI)', in G. Petti Balbi and G. Vitolo (eds.), *Linguaggi politici e pratiche del potere. Genova e il regno di Napoli nel tardo Medioevo*, Salerno: Laveglia, 2007, 151–205.
'Parlamento e luogotenenza generale. Il regno di Napoli nella corona d'Aragona', in Á. Sesma Muñoz (ed.), *La Corona de Aragón en el centro de su historia 1208–1458. La Monarquía aragonesa y los reinos de la Corona*, Zaragoza: Grupo de investigaciòn de excelencia CEMA, 2010, 435–78.
'Le scritture delle *universitates* meridionali', in I. Lazzarini (ed.), *Scritture e potere. Pratiche documentarie e forme di governo nell'Italia tardomedievale (XIV–XV secolo)*, *Reti Medievali Rivista* 9 (2008), 1–32 (www.retimedievali.it).
Senatore, F., and F. Storti, *Spazi e tempi della guerra nel Mezzogiorno aragonese. L'itinerario militare di re Ferrante (1458–1465)*, Salerno: Carlone, 2002.

Somaini, F., and B. Vetere (eds.), *I domini del principe di Taranto in età orsiniana (1399–1463)*. *Geografie e linguaggi politici alla fine del Medioevo*, Galatina: Congedo, 2009.
Sthamer, E., 'Die Hauptstraßen des Königreichs Sicilien im 13. Jahrhundert', in *Studi di storia napoletana in onore di M. Schipa*, Naples: ITEA, 1926, 97–112.
Storti, F., *L'esercito napoletano nella seconda metà del Quattrocento*, Salerno: Laveglia, 2007.
Tabacco, G., 'Il potere politico nel Mezzogiorno d'Italia dalla conquista normanna alla dominazione aragonese', in P. De Leo (ed.), *Il Mezzogiorno medievale nella storiografia del secondo dopoguerra. Risultati e prospettive*, Soveria Mannelli: Rubbettino, [1985], 65–111.
Tramontana, S., *Il Mezzogiorno medievale. Normanni, svevi, angioini, aragonesi nei secoli XI–XV*, Rome: Carocci, 2000.
Vallone, G., *Istituzioni feudali dell'Italia meridionale tra Medioevo ed antico regime. L'area salentina*, Rome: Viella, 1999.
Vitale, G., *Elite burocratica e famiglia. Dinamiche nobiliari e processi di costruzione statale nella Napoli angioino-aragonese*, Naples: Liguori, 2003.
Ritualità monarchica, cerimonie e pratiche devozionali nella Napoli aragonese, Salerno: Laveglia, 2006.
'Sul segretario regio al servizio degli aragonesi di Napoli', *Studi Storici* 49 (2008), 293–321.
Vitolo, G. (ed.), *Città e contado nel Mezzogiorno tra Medioevo ed età moderna*, Salerno: Laveglia, 2005.
'*In palatio communis*. Nuovi e vecchi temi della storiografia sulle città nel Mezzogiorno medievale', in G. Chittolini, G. Petti Balbi and G. Vitolo (eds.), *Città e territori nell'Italia del Medioevo. Studi in onore di Gabriella Rossetti*, Naples: Liguori, 2007, 243–94.
'Il regno angioino', in G. Galasso and R. Romeo (eds.), *Storia del Mezzogiorno*, IV/1, Rome: Editalia, 1986, 9–86.
'Storiografie parallele. Mario Del Treppo, Gabriella Rossetti e il Gisem', *Studi Storici* 49 (2008), 391–494.
Wickam, C., 'City Society in Twelfth-Century Italy and the Example of Salerno', in P. Delogu and P. Peduto (eds.), *Salerno nel XII century. Istituzioni, società, cultura*, Salerno: Provincia di Salerno, Centro Studi salernitani Raffaele Guariglia, 2004, 12–26.
Yver, G., *Le commerce et les marchands dans l'Italie méridionale au XIIIe et au XIVe siècle*, Paris: Bibliothèques des Écoles françaises d'Athène et de Rome, 1903.

3. *The kingdom of Sardinia and Corsica* (Olivetta Schena)

Abulafia, D., *The Western Mediterranean Kingdoms 1200–1500: The Struggle for Dominion*, London: Longman, 1997.
Anatra, B., 'Corona e ceti privilegiati nella Sardegna spagnola', in B. Anatra, R. Puddu and G. Serri, *Problemi di storia della Sardegna spagnola*, Cagliari: EDES, 1975, 9–132.
'Dall'unificazione aragonese ai Savoia', in G. Galasso (ed.), *Storia d'Italia*, X, *La Sardegna medioevale e moderna*, Turin: Utet, 1984, 191–663.

'Economia sarda e commercio mediterraneo nel basso Medioevo e nell'età moderna', in B. Anatra, A. Mattone and R. Turtas, *Storia dei Sardi e della Sardegna*, III, *L'Età moderna. Dagli Aragonesi alla fine del dominio spagnolo*, M. Guidetti (ed.), Milan: Jaca Book, 1989, 109–32.

Arribas Palau, A., *La conquista de Cerdeña por Jaime II de Aragón*, Barcelona: Horta-Instituto Español de Estudios Mediterráneos, 1952.

Bologna, F., *Napoli e le rotte mediterranee della pittura. Da Alfonso il Magnanimo a Ferdinando il Cattolico*, Naples: Società napoletana di Storia Patria, 1977.

Boscolo, A. (ed.), *I Parlamenti di Alfonso il Magnanimo (1421–1452), Aggiornamenti, apparati e note*, O. Schena (ed.), Cagliari: Consiglio Regionale della Sardegna, 1993.

Brook, L. L., F. C. Casula, M. M. Costa, A. M. Oliva, R. Pavoni, and M. Tangheroni (eds.), *Genealogie medievali di Sardegna*, Cagliari and Sassari: Deputazione di Storia Patria per la Sardegna–Due D Editrice Mediterranea 1984.

Cadeddu, M. E., 'Giacomo II d'Aragona e la conquista del regno di Sardegna e Corsica', *Medioevo. Saggi e Rassegne* 20 (1995), 251–316.

Carbonell, J., 'La lingua e la letteratura medievale e moderna', in Carbonell and Manconi (eds.), *I Catalani in Sardegna*, 93–8.

Carbonell, J., and F. Manconi (eds.), *I Catalani in Sardegna*, Cagliari and Barcelona: Consiglio Regionale della Sardegna-Generalitat de Catalunya, 1984.

Carrère, C., *Barcelone 1380–1462, centre économique à l'époque des difficultés*, 2 vols., Paris: La Haye, 1967.

Casula, F. C., *La Sardegna aragonese*, 2 vols., Sassari: Chiarella, 1990.

La storia di Sardegna, Pisa and Sassari: ETS-Carlo Delfino Editore, 1992.

La storiografia sarda ieri e oggi, Sassari: Carlo Delfino Editore, 2009.

Conde y Delgado de Molina, R., 'Il ripopolamento catalano di Alghero', in Mattone and Sanna (eds.), *Alghero, la Catalogna e il Mediterraneo*, 75–103.

Conde y Delgado de Molina, R., and A. M. Aragó Cabañas, *Castell de Càller. Cagliari catalano-aragonese*, Cagliari: Edizioni dell'Istituto sui rapporti italo-iberici del CNR, 1984.

La Corona d'Aragona e il Mediterraneo. Aspetti e problemi comuni da Alfonso il Magnanimo a Ferdinando il Cattolico (1416–1516), 3 vols., Congresso di storia della Corona d'Aragona, 9, I–II, Naples: Società napoletana di Storia Patria, 1978–82; III, Palermo: Accademia di Scienze Lettere e Arti, 1984.

La Corona d'Aragona in Italia, 5 vols., Congresso di storia della Corona d'Aragona, 14, Sassari, 1996.

Corrao, P., 'Il nodo mediterraneo. Corona d'Aragona e Sicilia nella politica di Bonifacio VIII', in *Bonifacio VIII*, Spoleto: Centro italiano di studi sull'alto Medioevo, 2003, 145–70.

D'Agostino, G., and G. Buffardi (eds.), *La Corona d'Aragona ai tempi di Alfonso il Magnanimo. I modelli politico-istituzionali. La circolazione degli uomini, delle idee, delle merci. Gli influssi sulla società e sul costume*, 2 vols., Naples: Paparo, 2000.

Day, J., *Uomini e terre nella Sardegna coloniale (XII–XVIII secolo)*, Turin: CELID, 1987.

De la Torre, A., *Documentos sobre relaciones internacionales de los Reyes Católicos (1479–1483)*, I, Barcelona: Consejo Superior de Investigaciones Científicas, 1949.

Del Treppo, M., 'Alfonso il Magnanimo e la Corona d'Aragona', in D'Agostino and Buffardi (eds.), *La Corona d'Aragona ai tempi di Alfonso il Magnanimo*, I, pp. 1–17.

'La "Corona d'Aragona" e il Mediterraneo', in *La Corona d'Aragona e il Mediterraneo*, I, 301–31.

'L'espansione catalano-aragonese nel Mediterraneo', in *Nuove Questioni di Storia Medievale*, Milan: Marzorati, 1964, 259–300.

I mercanti catalani e l'espansione della Corona d'Aragona nel secolo XV, 2nd edn, Naples: L'arte Tipografica, 1972.

'Il regno aragonese', in G. Galasso and R. Romeo (eds.), *Storia del Mezzogiorno*, IV/1, Rome: Editalia, 1986, 87–201.

Di Tucci, R., *Il Libro Verde della città di Cagliari*, Cagliari: Società Editoriale Italiana, 1925.

Era, A., *Il Parlamento sardo del 1481–1485*, Milan: A. Giuffrè Editore, 1955.

Gallinari, G., 'Guglielmo III di Narbona', *Medioevo. Saggi e Rassegne* 18 (1993), 91–121.

'Gli ultimi anni di esistenza del regno giudicale d'Arborea. Riflessioni e prospettive di ricerca', *Medioevo. Saggi e Rassegne* 25 (2002), 155–90.

Gallinari, L., 'Alcuni "discorsi" politici e istituzionali nello scontro tra Pietro IV d'Aragona e Mariano IV d'Arborea', in *Sardegna e Mediterraneo*, 149–83.

Galoppini, L., *Ricchezza e potere nella Sassari aragonese*, Cagliari: Edizioni dell'Istituto sui rapporti italo-iberici del CNR 1989.

Hillgarth, J. N., 'Mallorca e Italia. Relaciones culturales durante la baja Edad Media', in M.G. Meloni and O. Schena (eds.), *La corona d'Aragona in Italia, 5. Comunicazioni, 4. Incontro delle culture nel dominio catalano-aragonese in Italia*, Pisa: ETS, 1998, 337–45.

Iradiel, P., 'Introduzione', València i la Mediterrània medieval, *Revista d'Història Medieval* 3 (1992), 7–9.

Koenigsberger, H. G., 'Parlamenti e istituzioni rappresentative negli antichi Stati italiani', in Storia d'Italia, *Annali I, Dal feudalesimo al capitalismo*, Turin: Einaudi, 1978, 573–613.

Lalinde Abadía, J., *La Corona de Aragón en el Mediterráneo medieval (1229–1479)*, Zaragoza: Institución Fernando el Católico, 1979.

Livi, C., 'La popolazione della Sardegna nel periodo aragonese', *Archivio Storico Sardo* 34, 2 (1984), 23–130.

Manca, C., *Aspetti dell'espansione economica catalano-aragonese nel Mediterraneo occidentale. Il commercio internazionale del sale*, Milan: A. Giuffrè Editore, 1966.

'Colonie iberiche in Italia nei secoli XIV e XV', *Anuario de Estudios Medievales* 10 (1980), 505–38.

Manconi, F., 'Catalogna e Sardegna. Relazioni economiche e influssi culturali fra Quattrocento e Cinquecento', in P. Maninchedda (ed.), *La Sardegna e la presenza catalana nel Mediterraneo*, 2 vols., Cagliari: CUEC, 1998, I, 35–54.

'L'identità catalana della Sardegna', *Isole nella storia, Cooperazione Mediterranea. Cultura, economia, società*, 1–2 (Jan.–Aug. 2003), 105–12.

Marongiu, A., *I parlamenti sardi. Studio storico, istituzionale e comparativo*, Milan: A. Giuffrè Editore, 1979.

'Il Reggente la Reale Cancelleria, primo ministro del governo viceregio (1487–1847)', in A. Marongiu, *Saggi di storia giuridica e politica sarda*, Padua: CEDAM, 1975, 185–201.

Mattone, A., 'I privilegi e le istituzioni municipali di Alghero', in Mattone and Sanna (eds.), *Alghero, la Catalogna e il Mediterraneo*, 281–310.

Mattone, A., and P. Sanna (eds.), *Alghero, la Catalogna e il Mediterraneo. Storia di una città e di una minoranza catalana in Italia (XIV–XX secolo)*, Sassari: Gallizzi, 1994.

Meloni, G., 'Contributo allo studio delle rotte e dei commerci mediterranei nel basso Medioevo', *Medioevo. Saggi e Rassegne* 3 (1977), 117–30.

Genova e Aragona all'epoca di Pietro il Cerimonioso. 1338–1387, 3 vols., Padua: CEDAM, 1971–82.

(ed.), *Il parlamento di Pietro IV d'Aragona (1355)*, Cagliari: Consiglio Regionale della Sardegna, 1993.

Meloni, M. G., 'Alfonso il Magnanimo e la Corsica. Attività militare, politica e diplomatica tra il 1416 e il 1422', in D'Agostino and Buffardi (eds.), *La Corona d'Aragona ai tempi di Alfonso il Magnanimo*, I, 483–513.

Oliva, A. M., 'Il consiglio regio nel regno di Sardegna. Prime ricerche', in M. T. Ferrer i Mallol, J. Mutgé Vives and M. Sánchez Martínez (eds.), *La Corona catalano-aragonesa i el seu entorn mediterrani a la baixa edat mitjana*, Barcelona: CSIC, 2005, 205–38.

'March Jover uomo del re e uomo dei Consiglieri di Cagliari nella Sardegna del Tre e Quattrocento', in *Sardegna e Mediterraneo*, 283–327.

'*Memorial de totes les coses que ha a fer, dir, applicar per la Universitat de Càller d'anant lo senyor Rey*. Ambasciatori della città di Cagliari alla corte catalano-aragonese nel Quattrocento. Prime note', in R. Narbona Vizcaíno (ed.), *La Mediterrània de la Corona d'Aragó, segles XIII–XVI. VII Centenari de la sentència arbitral de Torrellas, 1304–2004*, Valencia: Universitat de Valencia-Fundació Jaume II el Just, 327–48.

'*Rahó es que la Magestat vostra sapia*. La Memoria del sindaco di Cagliari Andrea Sunyer al sovrano', *Bullettino dell'Istituto Storico Italiano per il Medio Evo* 105 (2003), 336–84.

Oliva, A. M., and O. Schena (eds.), *I parlamenti dei viceré Giovanni Dusay e Ferdinando Girón de Rebolledo (1495, 1497, 1500, 1504–1511)*, Cagliari: Consiglio Regionale della Sardegna, 1998.

'Il regno di Sardegna tra Spagna ed Italia nel Quattrocento. Cultura e società. Alcune riflessioni', in Luciano Gallinari (ed.), *Descubrir el Levante por el Poniente. I viaggi e le esplorazioni attraverso le collezioni della Biblioteca Universitaria di Cagliari*, Cagliari: Edizioni dell'Istituto sui rapporti italo-iberici del CNR, 2002, 101–34.

'I Torrella, una famiglia di medici tra Valenza, Sardegna e Roma', in M. Chiabò, A. M. Oliva and O. Schena (eds.), *Alessandro VI. Dal Mediterraneo all'Atlantico*, Rome: RR, 2004, 115–46.

Olla Repetto, G. (ed.), *La Corona d'Aragona. Un patrimonio comune per Italia e Spagna (secc. XIV–XV)*, Milan and Cagliari: Deputazione di Storia Patria per la Sardegna, 1989.

'La società cagliaritana nel '400', in *Cultura quattro-cinquecentesca in Sardegna. Retabli restaurati e documenti*, Cagliari: Soprintendenza BAAAS s.a., 1985, 19–24.

Studi sulle istituzioni amministrative e giudiziarie della Sardegna nei secoli XIV e XV, Cagliari: Deputazione di Storia Patria per la Sardegna, 2005.

Olla Repetto, G., and G. Catani, 'Cagliari e il mondo atlantico nel '400', *Rassegna degli Archivi di Stato* 48, 3 (1988), 677–85.

Salavert y Roca, V., *Cerdeña y la expansión mediterránea de la Corona de Aragón. 1297–1314*, 2 vols., Madrid: Consejo Superior de Investigaciones Científicas-Escuela de Estudios Medievales, 1956.

Sanna, M. G., 'Papa Giovanni XXII, Giacomo II d'Aragona e la questione del *Regnum Sardinie et Corsice*', in *Tra diritto e storia. Studi in onore di Luigi Berlinguer promossi dalle Università di Siena e di Sassari*, 2 vols., Soveria Mannelli (Catanzaro): Rubbettino Editore 2008, II, 737–52.

Sardegna e Mediterraneo tra Medioevo ed età moderna. Studi in onore di Francesco Cesare Casula, M. G. Meloni and O. Schena (eds.), Genoa: Brigati Editore, 2009.

Schena, O., 'Notai iberici a Cagliari nel XV secolo. Proposte per uno studio prosopografico', in M. T. Ferrer i Mallol, J. Mutgé i Vives and M. Sánchez Martínez (eds.), *La Corona catalanoaragonesa i el seu entorn mediterrani a la baixa edat mitjana*, Barcelona: CSIC, 2005, 395–412.

'Pietro IV il Cerimonioso re d'Aragona', in *I personaggi della storia medioevale*, Milan: Marzorati, 1987, 457–512.

Simbula, P. F., *Corsari e pirati nei mari di Sardegna*, Cagliari: Edizioni dell'Istituto sui rapporti italo-iberici del CNR, 1993.

'Il porto di Cagliari nel Medioevo. Topografie e strutture portuali', in *Dal mondo antico all'età contemporanea. Studi in onore di Manlio Brigaglia offerti dal Dipartimento di Storia dell'Università di Sassari*, Rome: Carocci editore, 2001, 287–307.

Sale e saline nel XV secolo. Aspetti della politica catalano-aragonese nel regno di Sardegna, Cagliari: AM&D, 2004.

Suárez Fernández, L., *Claves históricas en el reinado de Fernando i Isabel*, Madrid: Real Academia de la Historia, 1998.

Tangheroni, M., *Aspetti del commercio dei cereali nei Paesi della Corona d'Aragona*, I, *La Sardegna*, Cagliari: Edizioni dell'Istituto sui rapporti italo-iberici del CNR, 1981.

La città dell'argento. Iglesias dalle origini alla fine del Medioevo, Naples: Liguori, 1985.

'Il feudalesimo', in Carbonell and Manconi (eds.), *I Catalani in Sardegna*, 41–6.

'Il "*Regnum Sardiniae et Corsicae*" nell'espansione mediterranea della Corona d'Aragona. Aspetti economici', in G. Meloni and O. Schena (eds.), *La Corona d'Aragona in Italia*, Sassari: Carlo Delfino Editore, 1993, I, 47–88.

'Trasporti navali e commercio marittimo nell'Italia del Quattrocento', in *València i la Mediterrània medieval, Revista d'Història medieval* 3 (1992), 27–53.

Tasca, C., *Ebrei e società in Sardegna nel XV secolo. Fonti archivistiche e nuovi spunti di ricerca*, Florence: Giuntina, 2008.

Gli Ebrei in Sardegna nel XIV secolo. Società, cultura, istituzioni, Cagliari: Deputazione dei Storia Patria per la Sardegna, 1992.

'Portoghesi in Sardegna nell'età delle scoperte', *Archivio Storico Sardo* 37 (1992), 145–80.

Todde, G., 'Maestro razionale e amministrazione in Sardegna alla fine del '400', in *La Corona d'Aragona e il Mediterraneo*, II, *Comunicazioni*, 147–55.

Tramontana, S., *Il Mezzogiorno medievale. Normanni, svevi, angioini, aragonesi nei secoli XI–XV*, Rome: Carocci, 2007 (1st edn, 2000).

Turtas, R., *Storia della chiesa in Sardegna dalle origini al Duemila*, Rome: Città Nuova, 1999.

Urban, M. B., *Cagliari aragonese*, Cagliari: Edizioni dell'Istituto sui rapporti italo iberici del CNR, 2000.

Vicens Vives, J., *Manual de historia económica, 7a ed.*, Barcelona: Rafael Dalmau Editor, 1976.

Vilar, P., *La Catalogne dans l'Espagne moderne. Recherches sur les fondaments économiques des structures nationales*, Paris: La Haye, 1962.

Vita e morte dei villaggi rurali tra Medioevo ed Età Moderna, M. Milanese (ed.), Florence: All'Insegna del Giglio, 2006.

Zedda, C., *Cagliari. Un porto commerciale nel Mediterraneo del Quattrocento*, Naples: Istituto per l'Orientamento C.A. Nallino, 2001.

4. *The papal state* (Sandro Carocci)

Burckhardt, J., *The Civilization of the Renaissance in Italy*, London: Penguin, 1990.

Caravale, M., *Ordinamenti giuridici dell'Europa medievale*, Bologna: Il Mulino, 1994.

'Lo stato pontificio da Martino V a Gregorio XIII', in G. Galasso (ed.), *Storia d'Italia*, XIV, *Lo stato pontificio da Martino V a Pio IX*, Turin: Utet, 1978, 1–371.

Carocci, S., 'Governo papale e città nello stato della chiesa. Ricerche sul Quattrocento', in S. Gensini (ed.), *Principi e città alla fine del Medioevo*, Pisa: Pacini, 1996, 151–224.

Il nepotismo nel Medioevo. Papi, cardinali, famiglie nobili, Rome: Viella, 1999.

'Patrimonium Sancti Petri', in *Federico II. Enciclopedia fridericiana*, Rome: Istituto della Enciclopedia italiana, 2005, II, 483–91.

'Regimi signorili, statuti cittadini e governo papale nello stato della chiesa (XIV e XV secolo)', in R. Dondarini, G. M. Varanini and M. Venticelli (eds.), *Signori, regimi signorili e statuti nel tardo Medioevo*, Bologna: Pàtron, 2003, 245–69.

'Vassalli del papa. Note per la storia della feudalità pontificia (secoli XI–XVI)', in G. Barone, L. Capo and S. Gasparri (eds.), *Studi medievali in onore di Girolamo Arnaldi*, Rome: Viella, 2001, 55–90.

Vassalli del papa. Potere pontifico, aristocrazie e città nello stato della chiesa nel Medioevo, Rome: Viella, 2010.

Chittolini, G., 'Papato, corte di Roma e stati italiani dal tramonto del movimento conciliarista agli inizi del Cinquecento', in G. De Rosa and G. Cracco (eds.), *Il papato e l'Europa*, Soveria Mannelli: Rubettino, 2001, 191–217.

'Per una geografia dei contadi alla fine del Medioevo', in G. Chittolini, *Città, comunità e feudi negli stati dell'Italia centro-settentrionale (secoli XIV–XVI)*, Milan: Unicopli, 1996, 1–17.

Colliva, P., 'Bologna dal XIV al XVII secolo. "Governo misto" o signoria senatoria?', in *Storia dell'Emilia-Romagna*, Bologna: 1977, II, 13–34.

De Benedictis, A., *Repubblica per contratto. Bologna. Una città europea nello stato della chiesa*, Bologna: Il Mulino, 1995.

De Vicentiis, A., *Battaglie di memoria. Gruppi, intellettuali, testi e la discontinuità del potere papale alla metà del Quattrocento*, Rome: RR, 2002.

'Papato, stato e *curia* nel XV secolo. Il problema della discontinuità', *Storica* 24 (2002), 91–115.

'La sopravvivenza come potere. Baroni di Roma e papi nel XV secolo', in S. Carocci (ed.), *La nobiltà romana nel Medioevo*, Rome: École française de Rome, 2006, 551–613.

Dessì, R. -M., 'Predicare e governare nelle città dello stato della chiesa alla fine del Medioevo', in G. Barone, L. Capo and S. Gasparri (eds.), *Studi sul Medioevo per Girolamo Arnaldi*, Rome: Viella, 2001, 125–54.

Esch, A., 'Un bilancio storiografico della ricerca su Roma in età rinascimentale (dal 1970 circa)', *RR. Roma nel Rinascimento. Bibliografia e note*, 2007, 87–101.

Bonifaz IX. und der Kirchenstaat, Tübingen: Max Niemeyer, 1969.

Gardi, A., 'La fiscalità pontificia tra Medioevo ed età moderna', *Società e storia* 9 (1986), 509–57.

'Gli officiali nello stato pontificio del Quattrocento', *Annali della Scuola Normale superiore di Pisa*, ser. IV, Quaderni, 1 (1997), 225–91.

Lo stato in provincia. L'amministrazione della legazione di Bologna durante il regno di Sisto V (1585–1590), Bologna: Istituto per la storia di Bologna, 1994.

Guicciardini, F., *Maxims and Reflections (Ricordi)*, Philadelphia: University of Pennsylvania Press, 1992.

Jamme, A., 'De la république dans la monarchie? Genèse et développements diplomatiques de la contractualité dans l'état pontifical (fin XIIe–début XVIe siècle)', in F. Foronda (ed.), *Avant le contrat social. Le contrat politique dans l'Occident médiéval (XIIe–XVe siècle)*, Paris: Publications de la Sorbonne, 2011, 37–80.

'Forteresses, centres urbains et territoire dans l'état pontifical. Logiques et méthodes de la domination à l'âge albornozien', in É. Crouzet-Pavan (ed.), *Pouvoir et édilité. Les grands chantiers dans l'Italie communale et seigneuriale*, Rome: Ecole française de Rome, 2003, 375–417.

'Le Languedoc en Italie? Réseaux politiques et recrutement militaire pendant la légation du cardinal Bertrand du Pouget (1319–1334)', in *Jean XXII et le Midi*, 45e Cahier de Fanjeaux: Fanjeaux, 2010, 121–44.

Jamme, A., and O. Poncet (eds.), *Offices, écrit et papauté (XIIIe–XVIIe siècle)*, Rome: Ecole française de Rome, 2007.

(eds.), *Offices et papauté (XIVe–XVIIe siècle). Charges, hommes, destins*, Rome: Ecole française de Rome, 2005.

Lazzarini, I., *L'Italia degli stati territoriali. Secoli XIII–XV*, Rome and Bari: Laterza, 2003.
Maccarrone, M., *Studi su Innocenzo III*, Padua: Italia Sacra (Studi, 17), 1972.
Machiavelli, N., *The Prince*, transl. by W. K. Marriott, Rockville: Arc Manor, 2007.
Maire Vigueur, J. -C., *Les pâturages de l'église et la Douane du bétail dans la province du patrimonio (XIVe–XVe siècles)*, Rome: Istituto di studi romani, 1981.
Mascioli, P., *Viterbo nel Quattrocento. Politica, istituzioni, poteri nella periferia pontificia*, Manziana: Vecchiarelli, 2004.
Monacchia, P. (ed.), *'Ut bene regantur'. Politica e amministrazione periferica nello stato ecclesiastico*, Modena, 2000.
Nico Ottaviani, M. G. (ed.), *Rocche e fortificazioni nello stato della chiesa*, Naples: ESI, 2004.
Palermo, L., *Mercati del grano a Roma tra Medioevo e rinascimento*, Rome: Il Centro di ricerca, 1990.
Partner, P., *The Lands of St Peter: The Papal State in the Middle Ages and the Early Renaissance*, London: Eyre Methuen, 1972.
The Papal State Under Martin V: The Administration and Government of the Temporal Power in the Early Fifteenth Century, London: British School at Rome, 1958.
The Pope's Men: The Papal Civil Service in the Renaissance, Oxford: Clarendon, 1990.
Petrucci, E., 'Il cardinale Egidio di Albornoz e la riconquista del patrimonio di S. Pietro in Tuscia', in A. Vasina (ed.), *La storiografia di Eugenio Duprè Theseider*, Rome: Istituto storico italiano per il Medio Evo, 2002, 81–197.
'Innocenzo III e i comuni dello stato della chiesa. Il potere centrale', in *Società e istituzioni dell'Italia comunale. L'esempio di Perugia (secoli XII–XIV)*, Perugia: Deputazione di storia patria per l'Umbria, 1988, 91–136.
Prodi, P., *Il sovrano pontefice. Un corpo e due anime. La monarchia papale nella prima età moderna*, Bologna: Il Mulino, 1982.
Robertson, I., *Tyranny Under the Mantle of St Peter: Pope Paul II and Bologna*, Turnhout: Brepols, 2002.
Shaw, C., *The Political Role of the Orsini Family from Sixtus IV to Clement VII: Barons and Factions in the Papal States*, Rome: Istituto storico italiano per il Medio Evo, 2007.
'The Roman barons and the Guelf and Ghibelline factions in the papal states', in M. Gentile (ed.), *Guelfi e ghibellini nell'Italia del Rinascimento*, Rome: Viella, 2005, 475–94.
'The Roman barons and the popes', in M. Gentile and P. Savy (eds.), *Noblesse et états princiers en Italie et en France au XVe siècle*, Rome: École française de Rome, 2009, 101–24.
'The Roman barons and the security of the papal states', in M. Del Treppo (ed.), *Condottieri e uomini d'arme nell'Italia del Rinascimento*, Naples: Liguori, 2001, 311–25.
Sommerlechner, A. (ed.), *Innocenzo III. Urbs et orbis*, Rome: Istituto storico italiano per il Medio Evo, 2003.

Soranzo, G., 'Collegati, raccomandati e aderenti negli stati italiani dei secoli XIV e XV', *Archivio Storico Italiano* 99 (1941), 3–35.
Vallerani, M., 'La supplica al signore e il potere della misericordia. Bologna 1337–1347', *Quaderni storici* 44 (2009), 411–42.
Volpi, S., *Le regioni introvabili. Centralizzazione e regionalizzazione nello stato pontificio*, Bologna: Il Mulino, 1983.
Waley, D., *The Papal State in the Thirteenth Century*, London: Macmillan, 1961.
Zenobi, G. B., *Le 'ben regolate città'. Modelli politici nel governo delle periferie pontificie in età moderna*, Rome: Bulzoni, 1994.

5. Tuscan states: *Florence and Siena* (Lorenzo Tanzini)

Angiolini, F., *I cavalieri e il principe. L'ordine di S. Stefano e la società toscana in età moderna*, Florence: Edifir, 1996.
Ascheri, M., 'Siena nel primo Quattrocento. Un sistema politico tra storia e storiografia', in M. Ascheri and D. Ciampoli (eds.), *Siena e il suo territorio nel Rinascimento*, Siena: Il Leccio, 1986, I, 1–53.
 Siena nel Rinascimento. Istituzioni e sistema politico, Siena: Il Leccio, 1985.
 'Statuti, legislazione e sovranità. Il caso di Siena', in G. Chittolini and D. Willoweit (eds.), *Statuti città territori in Italia e Germania tra Medioevo ed età moderna*, Bologna: Il Mulino, 1991, 145–94.
Ascheri, M., G. Mazzoni and F. Nevola (eds.), *L'ultimo secolo della repubblica di Siena. Arti, cultura e società*, Siena: Accademia degli Intronati, 2008.
Ascheri, M., and F. Nevola (eds.), *L'ultimo secolo della repubblica di Siena. Politica e istituzioni, economia e società*, Siena: Accademia degli Intronati, 2007.
Astorri, A., 'Note sulla Mercanzia fiorentina sotto Lorenzo de' Medici. Aspetti istituzionali e politici', *Archivio Storico Italiano* 150 (1992), 965–93.
Baron, H., *The Crisis of the Early Italian Renaissance*, Princeton University Press, 1966.
Becker, M., *Florence in Transition*, Baltimore: Johns Hopkins University Press, 1967–8.
Berengo, M., *Nobili e mercanti nella Lucca del Cinquecento*, new edn, Turin: Einaudi, 1999.
Black, R., *Education and Society in Florentine Tuscany: Teachers, Pupils and Schools*, Leiden and Boston: Brill, 2007.
Boisseuil, D., 'La Toscane siennoise. Territoire et ressources (XIV–XV siècle)', in Boutier, Landi and Rouchon (eds.), *Florence et la Toscane*, 147–59.
Boutier, J., S. Landi and O. Rouchon (eds.), *Florence et la Toscane, XIVe–XIXe siècles. Les dynamiques d'un état italien*, Rennes: Presses Universitaires, 2004.
Bowsky, W., *A Medieval Italian Commune: Siena Under the Nine, 1287–1355*, Berkeley: University of California Press, 1981.
Bratchel, M. E., *Lucca 1430–1494. The Reconstruction of an Italian City-Republic*, Oxford: Clarendon Press, 1995.
 Medieval Lucca and the Evolution of the Renaissance State, Oxford University Press, 2008.
Brown, A., *Bartolomeo Scala, 1430–1497, Chancellor of Florence*, Princeton University Press, 1979.

'De-masking Renaissance republicanism', in Hankins (ed.), *Renaissance Civic Humanism*, 179–99.
Brucker, G. A., *Florentine Politics and Society (1343–1378)*, Princeton University Press, 1962.
Caferro, W., *Mercenary Companies and the Decline of Siena*, Baltimore and London: Johns Hopkins University Press, 1998.
Chabot, I., 'Le gouvernement des pères. L'état florentin et la famille (XIVe–XVe siècles)', in Boutier, Landi and Rouchon (eds.), *Florence et la Toscane*, 241–63.
Chittolini, G., 'Ricerche sull'ordinamento territoriale del dominio fiorentino agli inizia del secolo XV', in G. Chittolini, *La formazione dello stato regionale e le istituzioni del contado*, Turin: Einaudi, 1979, 292–352.
Ciappelli, G., *Fisco e società a Firenze nel Rinascimento*, Rome: Storia e Letteratura, 2009.
Cohn, S. K., *Creating the Florentine State: Peasants and Rebellion, 1348–1434*, Cambridge University Press, 1999.
Connell, W. J. (ed.), *Society and Individual in Renaissance Florence*, Berkeley: University of California Press, 2002.
Connell, W. J., and A. Zorzi (eds.), *Florentine Tuscany: Structures and Practices of Power*, Cambridge University Press, 2000.
Epstein, S. R., 'Market structures', in Connell and Zorzi (eds.), *Florentine Tuscany*, 93–134.
Fasano Guarini, E., *L'Italia moderna e la Toscana dei prìncipi. Discussioni e ricerche storiche*, Florence: Le Monnier, 2008.
Ferente, S., 'Guelphs! Factions, liberty and sovereignty: inquiries about Quattrocento', *History of Political Thought* 28, 4 (2007), 571–89.
Findlen, P., M. M. Fontaine and D. J. Osheim (eds.), *Beyond Florence: The Contours of a Medieval and Early Renaissance Italy*, Stanford University Press, 2003.
Franceschi, F., 'I "Ciompi" a Firenze, Siena e Perugia', in G. Pinto, M. Bourin and G. Cherubini (eds.), *Rivolte urbane e rivolte contadine nell'Europa del Trecento. Un confronto*, Florence: Firenze University Press, 2008, 277–303.
Fubini, R., *Politica e pensiero politico nell'Italia del Rinascimento. Dallo stato territoriale al Machiavelli*, Florence: Edifir, 2009.
  'Il regime di Cosimo de' Medici e Firenze', in R. Fubini, *Italia quattrocentesca. Politica e diplomazia nell'età di Lorenzo il magnifico*, Milan: F. Angeli, 1994, 62–86.
  'Renaissance historian: the career of Hans Baron', *Journal of Modern History* 64 (1992), 541–74.
Ginatempo, M., *Crisi di un territorio. Il popolamento della Toscana senese alla fine del Medioevo*, Florence: Olschki, 1988.
  'Uno "stato semplice". L'organizzazione del territorio nella Toscana senese del secondo Quattrocento', in *La Toscana al tempo di Lorenzo il Magnifico, Politica economia cultura arte*, Pisa: Pacini, 1996, III, 1073–1101.
Goldthwaite, R., *The Building of Renaissance Florence: An Economic and Social History*, Baltimore: Johns Hopkins University Press, 1980.

The Economy of Renaissance Florence, Baltimore: Johns Hopkins University Press, 2009.
Green, L., 'Florence and the republican tradition', in M. Jones (ed.), New Cambridge Medieval History, VI, *c. 1300–c. 1415*, Cambridge University Press, 2000, 469–87.
Guidi, A., *Un segretario militante. Politica, diplomazia e armi nel Cancelliere Machiavelli*, Bologna: Il Mulino, 2009.
Hankins, J. (ed.), *Renaissance Civic Humanism: Reappraisals and Reflections*, Cambridge University Press, 2000.
Kent, D., *Cosimo de' Medici and the Florentine Renaissance*, New Haven and London: Yale University Press, 2000.
 Friendship, Love and Trust in Renaissance Florence, Cambridge, MA: Harvard University Press, 2009.
 The Rise of the Medici: Faction in Florence, 1426–1434, Oxford University Press, 1978.
Kent, F. W., *Lorenzo de' Medici and the Art of Magnificence*, Baltimore and London: Johns Hopkins University Press, 2004.
Kent, F. W., and P. Simons (eds.), *Patronage, Art and Society in Renaissance Italy*, Oxford University Press, 1987.
Kirshner, J., 'Family and marriage: a socio-legal perspective', in J. M. Najemy (ed.), *Italy in the Age of the Renaissance, 1300–1550*, Oxford University Press, 2004, 82–102.
Kuehn, T., *Law, Family and Women: Toward a Legal Anthropology of Renaissance Italy*, University of Chicago Press, 1991.
Lantschner, P., 'The "Ciompi revolution" constructed', *Annali di Storia di Firenze* 4 (2010), 277–97.
Medici, Lorenzo de', *Lettere*, 12 vols., Florence: Giunti, 1977–2007.
Mannori, L., 'Effetto domino. Il profilo istituzionale dello stato territoriale toscano nella storiografia degli ultimi trent'anni', in M. Ascheri and A. Contini (eds.), *La Toscana in età moderna (secoli XVI–XVIII). Politica, istituzioni, società. Studi recenti e prospettive di ricerca*, Florence: Olschki, 2005, 59–90.
 Il sovrano tutore. Pluralismo istituzionale e accentramento amministrativo nel principato dei Medici, Milan: Giuffré, 1994.
Martines, L., *April Blood: Florence and the Plot Against the Medici*, London: Jonathan Cape, 2003.
 Lawyers and Statecraft in Renaissance Florence, Princeton University Press, 1968.
Molho, A., 'The state and public finance: a hypothesis based on the history of late medieval Florence', in A. Molho, *Firenze nel Quattrocento*, Rome: Storia e Letteratura, 2006, I, 165–202.
Najemy, J., *Corporatism and Consensus in Florentine Electoral Politics, 1280–1400*, Chapel Hill: University of North Carolina Press, 1982.
 A History of Florence, 1200–1575, Oxford: Blackwell, 2006.
Peterson, D. S. (ed.), *Florence and Beyond: Culture, Society and Politics in Renaissance Italy*, Toronto: Centre for Reformation and Renaissance Studies, 2008.

'The War of the Eight Saints in Florentine memory and oblivion', in Connell (ed.), *Society and Individual*, 173–214.

Petralia, G., 'Fiscality, politics and dominion in Florentine Tuscany at the end of the Middle Ages', in Connell and Zorzi (eds.), *Florentine Tuscany*, 65–89.

Prodi, P., 'Gli affanni della democrazia. La predicazione di Savonarola durante l'esperienza del governo popolare', in G. C. Garfagnini (ed.), *Savonarola e la politica*, Florence: Edizioni del Galluzzo, 1998, 27–74.

Rubinstein, N., *The Government of Florence Under the Medici*, new edn, Oxford University Press, 1997.

Salvadori, P., *Dominio e patronato. Lorenzo dei Medici e la Toscana nel Quattrocento*, Rome: Storia e Letteratura, 2000.

Savelli, A., *Siena. Il popolo e le contrade (XVI–XX secolo)*, Florence: Olschki, 2008.

Shaw, C., *Popular Government and Oligarchy in Renaissance Italy*, Leiden: Brill, 2006.

Tanzini, L., *Alle origini della Toscana moderna. Firenze e gli statuti delle comunità soggette*, Florence: Olschki, 2007.

  Statuti e legislazione a Firenze dal 1355 al 1415. Lo statuto cittadino del 1409, Florence: Olschki, 2004.

Tognetti, S., *Da Figline a Firenze. Ascesa economica e politica della famiglia Serristori (secoli XIV–XVI)*, Figline: Opuslibri, 2003.

  Un'industria di lusso al servizio del grande commercio. Il mercato dei drappi serici e della seta nella Firenze del Quattrocento, Florence: Olschki, 2002.

  '"Tra compagni palesi e ladri occulti". Banchieri senesi del Quattrocento', *Nuova Rivista Storica* 88 (2004), 27–101.

Trexler, R., 'Il parlamento fiorentino del 1378', *Archivio Storico Italiano* 143 (1985), 437–75.

von Albertini, R., *Firenze dalla repubblica al principato. Storia e coscienza politica*, new edn, Turin: Einaudi, 1970.

Witt, R., *Hercules at the Crossroads: The Life, Work and Thought of Coluccio Salutati*, Durham, NC: Duke University Press, 1983.

Zorzi, A., *L'amministrazione della giustizia penale nella Repubblica fiorentina. Aspetti e problemi*, Florence: Olschki, 1988.

  'The "material constitution" of the Florentine dominion', in Connell and Zorzi (eds.), *Florentine Tuscany*, 6–31.

6. *Ferrara and Mantua* (Trevor Dean)

Blockmans, W., 'Patronage, brokerage and corruption in symptoms of incipient state formation in the Burgundian–Habsburg Netherlands', in A. Maczak (ed.), *Klientelsysteme im Europa der Frühen Neuzeit*, Munich: R. Oldenbourg, 1988, 117–26.

Bocchi, F., 'La "Terranuova" da campagna a città', in G. Papagno and A. Quondam (eds.), *La corte e lo spazio. Ferrara estense*, Rome: Bulzoni, 1982, 167–92.

Bratchel, M. E., *Medieval Lucca and the Evolution of the Renaissance State*, Oxford University Press, 2008.

Cardini, F., 'Il libro e il potere. Le università e i signori d'Italia', in P. Castelli (ed.), 'In supreme dignitatis . . .'. *Per la storia dell'università di Ferrara, 1391–1991*, Florence: Olschki, 1995, 297–307.
Carpeggiani, P., 'Traccia per una storia di Mantova dalle origini all'Ottocento', in P. Carpeggiani and I. Pagliari, *Mantova. Materiali per la storia urbana dalle origini all'Ottocento*, Mantua: Arcari, 1983, 9–54.
Castiglione, Baldesar, *Il libro del cortigiano*, B. Maier (ed.), 2nd edn, Turin: UTET, 1964.
Cattini, M., and M. A. Romani, 'Le corti parallele. Per una tipologia delle corti padane dal XIII al XVI secolo', in *Lo stato e il potere nel Rinascimento, per Federico Chabod (1901–1960)*, in *Annali della facoltà di Scienze politiche, Materiali di storia*, 1980–1, 57–87.
Chabod, F., 'Lo stato di Milano e l'impero di Carlo V', in *Lo stato e la vita religiosa a Milano nell'epoca di Carlo V*, Turin: Einaudi, 1971, 5–230.
Chambers, D. S., and T. Dean, *Clean Hands and Rough Justice: An Investigating Magistrate in Renaissance Italy*, Ann Arbor: University of Michigan Press, 1997.
Chittolini, G., 'Infeudazioni e politica feudale nel ducato visconteo-sforzesco', in G. Chittolini, *La formazione dello stato regionale e le istituzioni del contado*, Turin: Einaudi, 1979.
  'L'onore dell'officiale', in S. Bertelli, N. Rubinstein and C. H. Smith (eds.), *Florence and Milan: Comparisons and Relations*, 2 vols., Florence: La Nuova Italia, 1989, I, 101–33.
  'Stati padani, "stato del rinascimento". Problemi di ricerca', in G. Tocci (ed.), *Persistenze feudali e autonomie comunitative in stati urbani fra Cinque e Settecento*, Bologna: CLUEB, 1988, 9–29.
  'Le "terre separate" nel ducato di Milano in età sforzesca', in *Milano nell'età di Ludovico il Moro*, Milan: Archivio storico civico e Biblioteca Trivulziana, 1983, I, 115–28.
Dean, T., 'After the war of Ferrara: relations between Venice and Ercole d'Este, 1484–1505', in D. S. Chambers, C. H. Clough and M. E. Mallett (eds.), *War, Culture and Society in Renaissance Venice*, London: Hambledon, 1993, 73–98.
  'Ferrarese chroniclers and the Este state, 1490–1505', in D. Looney and D. Shemek (eds.), *Phaethon's Children: The Este Court and Its Culture in Early Modern Ferrara*, Tempe: Arizona Center for Medieval and Renaissance Studies, 2005, 169–88.
  Land and Power in Late Medieval Ferrara: The Rule of the Este, 1300–1450, Cambridge University Press, 1988.
  'Venetian economic hegemony: the case of Ferrara 1200–1500', *Studi Veneziani* 12 (1986), 45–98.
Epstein, S. R., *Freedom and Growth: The Rise of States and Markets in Europe, 1300–1750*, London and New York: Routledge, 2000.
Folin, M., 'Ferrara 1385–1505. All'ombra del principe', in D. Calabi (ed.), *Fabbriche, piazze, mercati. La città nel Rinascimento*, Rome: Officina, 1997, 354–88.

'Note sugli officiali negli stati estensi, secoli XV–XVI', in F. Leverotti (ed.), *Gli officiali negli stati italiani del Quattrocento*, Pisa: Annali della Scuola Normale Superiore di Pisa, Quaderni, 1 (1997), 99–125.

Rinascimento estense. Politica, cultura, istituzioni di un antico stato italiano, Rome and Bari: Laterza, 2001.

'Studio e politica negli stati estensi fra Quattro e Cinquecento. Dottori, ufficiali, cortigiani', in P. Castelli (ed.), *Giovanni e Gianfrancesco Pico. L'opera e la fortuna di due studenti ferraresi*, Florence: Olschki, 1998, 59–90.

Franceschini, A., 'Il sapore del sale. Ricerche sulla assistenza ospedaliera nel sec. XV in una città di punta. Ferrara', *Atti e memorie della Deputazione ferrarese di storia patria*, 4th ser., 1 (1981), 5–165.

Gamberini, A., 'Una città e la sua coscienza comunitaria. Reggio Emilia fra Trecento e Quattrocento', in Gamberini, *Oltre le città*, 83–108.

Oltre le città. Assetti territoriali e culture aristocratiche nella Lombardia del tardo Medioevo, Rome: Viella, 2009.

Grignani, M. A., A. M. Lorenzoni, A. Mortari and C. Mozzarelli (eds.), *Mantova 1430. Pareri a Gianfrancesco Gonzaga per il governo*, Mantua: G. Arcari, 1990.

Grubb, J. S., *Firstborn of Venice: Vicenza in the Early Renaissance State*, Baltimore and London: Johns Hopkins University Press, 1988.

Guerzoni, G., 'The Italian Renaissance courts' demand for the arts: the case of d'Este of Ferrara (1471–1560)', in M. North and D. Ormrod (eds.), *Art Markets in Europe, 1400–1800*, Aldershot: Ashgate, 1998, 61–80.

Gundersheimer, W. L., *Ferrara: The Style of a Renaissance Despotism*, Princeton University Press, 1973.

'Toward a reinterpretation of the Renaissance in Ferrara', *Bulletin d'humanisme et de Renaissance* 30 (1968), 267–81.

Jones, P. J., 'Communes and despots: the city state in late-medieval Italy', *Transactions of the Royal Historical Society*, 5th ser., 15 (1965), 71–96.

Lazzarini, I., 'I domini estensi e gli stati signorili padani. Tipologie a confronto', in G. Fragnito and M. Miegge (eds.), *Girolamo Savonarola da Ferrara all'Europa*, Florence: SISMEL, 2001, 19–50.

Fra un principe e altri stati. Relazioni di potere e forme di servizio a Mantova nell'età di Ludovico Gonzaga, Rome: Istituto storico italiano per il Medio Evo, 1996.

'La nomination des officiers dans les états italiens du bas Moyen Âge (Milan, Florence, Venise). Pour une histoire documentaire des institutions', *Bibliothèque de l'Ecole des Chartes* 159 (2001), 389–412.

'Gli officiali del marchesato di Mantova', in F. Leverotti (ed.), *Gli officiali negli stati italiani del Quattrocento*, Pisa: Annali della Scuola Normale Superiore di Pisa, Quaderni, 1 (1997), 79–97.

'*Palatium juris e palatium residentie*. Gli offici e il servizio del principe a Mantova nel Quattrocento', in C. Mozzarelli, R. Oresko and L. Ventura (eds.), *La corte di Mantova nell'età di Andrea Mantegna. 1450–1550*, Rome: Bulzoni, 1997, 154–64.

'*Sub signo principis*: political institutions and urban configurations in early Renaissance Mantua', *Renaissance Studies* 16 (2002), 318–29.

Leverotti, F., 'Ricerche sulle origini dell'Ospedale Maggiore di Milano', *Archivio storico lombardo*, 10th ser., 6 (1981), 77–113.
Lubkin, G., 'Strutture, funzioni e funzionamento della corte milanese nel Quattrocento', in J.-M. Cauchies and G. Chittolini (eds.), *Milano e Borgogna. Due stati principeschi tra Medioevo e Rinascimento*, Rome: Bulzoni, 1990, 75–84.
Malacarne, G., *I Gonzaga di Mantova*, 5 vols., Modena: Il Bulino, 2000–8.
Miglio, M., 'L'immagine del principe e l'immagine della città', in S. Gensini (ed.), *Principi e città alla fine del Medioevo*, Pisa: Pacini, 1996, 315–32.
Mozzarelli, C., 'Corte e amministrazione nel principato gonzaghesco', *Società e storia* 16 (1982), 245–62.
  'Lo stato gonzaghesco. Mantova dal 1382 al 1707', in G. Galasso (ed.), *Storia d'Italia*, XVII, *Ducati padani, Trento e Trieste*, Turin: Utet, 1979, 357–495.
Patetta, L., 'Milano. XV–XVII secolo. La difficoltà di costruire piazza', in D. Calabi (ed.), *Fabbriche, piazze, mercati. La città nel Rinascimento*, Rome: Officina, 1997, 60–74.
Romani, M., *Una città in forma di palazzo. Potere signorile e forma urbana nela Mantova medievale e moderna*, Mantua: Quaderni di Cheiron, 1, 1995.
Rosenberg, C., *The Este Monuments and Urban Development in Renaissance Ferrara*, Cambridge University Press, 1997.
Salmons, J. (ed.), *The Renaissance in Ferrara and Its European Horizons / Il Rinascimento a Ferrara e i suoi orizzonti europei* (Italian part, W. Moretti (ed.)), Cardiff: University of Wales Press, 1984, and Ravenna: Edizioni dei Girasole, 1984.
Sestan, E., 'La storia dei Gonzaga nel Rinascimento', in *Mantova e i Gonzaga nella civiltà del Rinascimento*, Segrate: Edigraf, 1977, 17–27.
Soldi Rondinini, G., 'Le strutture urbanistiche di Milano durante l'età di Ludovico il Moro', in *Milano nell'età di Ludovico il Moro*, Milan: Archivio storico civico e Biblioteca Trivulziana, 1983, II, 553–73.
Storia di Ferrara, 3 vols., Ferrara: Corvo, 1987–2000.
Tarducci, F., 'Gianfrancesco Gonzaga signore di Mantova (1407–1420)', *Archivio storico lombardo*, 3rd ser., 17–18 (1902), 310–60, 33–88.
Tuohy, T., *Herculean Ferrara: Ercole d'Este (1471–1505) and the Invention of a Ducal Capital*, Cambridge University Press, 1996.
Turchi, L., 'Istituzioni cittadine e governo signorile a Ferrara (fine sec. XIV–prima metà sec. XVI)' in *Storia di Ferrara*, VI, *Il Rinascimento, situazioni e personaggi*, Ferrara: Il Corbo, 2000, 128–58.
  'Una piccola modifica. Il linguaggio della negoziazione politica fra principe e città', in G. Badini and A. Gamberini (eds.), *Medioevo reggiano. Studi in ricordo di Odoardo Rombaldi*, Milan: F. Angeli, 2007, 343–73.
  'Riflessioni su statuti e politica signorile del diritto. Il caso estense fra XV e XVI secolo', in R. Dondarini, G. M. Varanini and M. Venticelli (eds.), *Signori, regimi signorili e statuti nel tardo Medioevo*, Bologna: CLUEB, 2003, 367–96.
Welch, E. S., *Art and Authority in Renaissance Milan*, New Haven: Yale University Press, 1995.

7. Venice and the Terraferma (Michael Knapton)

Preference has gone to studies specific to Venice and its dominions, and to more recent publications. Many titles listed refer to further research. Single pieces in multi-authored volumes or in essay collections by the same author are generally not listed individually.

Bellavitis, A., 'Quasi-città e terre murate in area veneta. Un bilancio per l'età moderna', in E. Svalduz (ed.), *L'ambizione di essere città. Piccoli, grandi centri nell'Italia rinascimentale*, Venice: Istituto Veneto di Scienze, Lettere ed Arti, 2004, 97–114.

Casini, M., *I gesti del principe. La festa politica a Firenze e Venezia in età rinascimentale*, Venice: Marsilio, 1996.

Castagnetti, A., and G. M. Varanini (eds.), *Il Veneto nel Medioevo. Le signorie trecentesche*, Verona: Banca popolare di Verona, 1995.

Cavalieri, P., *'Qui sunt guelfi et partiales nostri'. Comunità, patriziato e fazioni a Bergamo tra XV e XVI secolo*, Milan: Unicopli, 2008.

Chojnacki, S., *Women and Men in Renaissance Venice*, Baltimore: Johns Hopkins University Press, 2000.

Collodo, S., *Società e istituzioni in area veneta. Itinerari di ricerca (secoli XII–XV)*, Fiesole: Nardini, 1999.

Cozzi, G., M. Knapton and G. Scarabello, *La Repubblica di Venezia nell'età moderna*, 2 vols., Turin: Utet, 1986–92.

D'Andrea, D., *Civic Christianity in Renaissance Italy: The Hospital of Treviso, 1400–1530*, Rochester: University of Rochester Press, 2007.

Del Torre, G., *Patrizi e cardinali. Venezia e le istituzioni ecclesiastiche nella prima età moderna*, Milan: F. Angeli, 2010.

Venezia e la Terraferma dopo la guerra di Cambrai. Fiscalità e amministrazione (1515–1530), Milan: F. Angeli, 1986.

Finlay, R., *Venice Besieged: Politics and Diplomacy in the Italian Wars, 1494–1534*, Aldershot and Burlington: Ashgate, 2008.

Fortini Brown, P., *Venice and Antiquity: The Venetian Sense of the Past*, New Haven and London: Yale University Press, 1996.

Grubb, J., *Firstborn of Venice: Vicenza in the Early Renaissance State*, Baltimore and London: Johns Hopkins University Press, 1988.

'When myths lose power: four decades of Venetian historiography', *Journal of Modern History* 58, 1 (1986), 43–94.

Humfrey, P. (ed.), *Venice and the Veneto*, Cambridge University Press, 2007.

Intorno allo stato degli studi sulla terraferma veneta, Verona, 2000 (*Terre d'Este* 17).

Ivetic, E., *L'Istria moderna. Un'introduzione ai secoli XVI–XVII*, Trieste and Rovigno: Centro di ricerche storiche, Rovigno, 1999.

Knapton, M., '"Nobiltà e popolo" e un trentennio di storiografia veneta', *Nuova Rivista Storica* 82, 1 (1998), 167–92.

Labalme, P., L. Sanguineti White and L. Carroll (eds.), Città excelentissima: *Selections from the Renaissance Diaries of Marin Sanudo*, Baltimore and London: Johns Hopkins University Press, 2008.

Lanaro, P. (ed.), *At the Centre of the Old World: Trade and Manufacturing in Venice and the Venetian Mainland, 1400–1800*, Toronto: Centre for Reformation and Renaissance Studies, 2006.
Lane, F. C., *Venice, a Maritime Republic*, Baltimore and London: Johns Hopkins University Press, 1973.
Law, J. E., *Venice and the Veneto*, Aldershot: Ashgate, 2000.
Mallett, M., and J. Hale, *The Military Organization of a Renaissance State: Venice c. 1400 to 1617*, Cambridge University Press, 1983.
Martin, J. and D. Romano (eds.), *Venice Reconsidered: The History and Civilization of an Italian City-State, 1297–1797*, Baltimore and London: Johns Hopkins University Press, 2000.
Muir, E., *Mad Blood Stirring: Vendetta and Factions in Friuli During the Renaissance*, Baltimore and London: Johns Hopkins University Press, 1993.
Orlando, E., *Altre Venezie. Il dogado veneziano nei secoli XIII e XIV (giurisdizione, territorio, giustizia e amministrazione)*, Venice: Istituto Veneto di Scienze, Lettere ed Arti, 2008.
Ortalli, G., and M. Knapton (eds.), *Istituzioni, società e potere nella Marca trevigiana e veronese (secoli XIII–XIV). Sulle tracce di G. B. Verci*, Rome: Istituto storico italiano per il Medio Evo, 1988.
Pezzolo, L., 'Stato, guerra e finanza nella Repubblica di Venezia fra Medioevo e prima età moderna', in R. Cancila (ed.), *Mediterraneo in armi (secc. XV–XVIII) (Quaderni – Mediterranea. Ricerche storiche*, 4 (2007)), 67–112.
Povolo, C., 'Un sistema giuridico repubblicano. Venezia e il suo stato territoriale (secoli XV–XVIII)', in I. Birocchi and A. Mattone (eds.), *Il diritto patrio tra diritto comune e codificazione (secoli XVI–XIX)*, Rome: Viella, 2006, 297–353.
Raines, D., *L'invention du mythe aristocratique. L'image de soi du patriciat vénitien au temps de la Sérénissime*, Venice: Istituto Veneto di Scienze, Lettere ed Arti, 2006.
Romano, D., *The Likeness of Venice: A Life of Francesco Foscari, 1373–1457*, New Haven and London: Yale University Press, 2007.
Storia di Venezia. Dalle origini alla caduta della Serenissima, 14 vols., Rome, 1991–2002 (III, G. Arnaldi, G. Cracco and A. Tenenti (eds.), *La formazione dello stato patrizio*, 1997; IV, A. Tenenti and U. Tucci (eds.), *Il Rinascimento. Politica e cultura*, 1996; V, A. Tenenti and U. Tucci (eds.), *Il Rinascimento. Società ed economia*, 1996; XII, A. Tenenti and U. Tucci (eds.), *Il Mare*, 1992).
Varanini, G. M., *Comuni cittadini e stato regionale. Ricerche sulla Terraferma veneta nel Quattrocento*, Verona: Libreria Editrice Universitaria, 1992.
  'Nelle città della Marca Trevigiana. Dalle fazioni al patriziato (secoli XIII–XV)', in M. Gentile (ed.), *Guelfi e ghibellini nell'Italia del Rinascimento*, Rome: Viella, 2005, 563–602.
  'La Terraferma veneta nel Quattrocento e le tendenze recenti della storiografia', *Ateneo Veneto* 197 (2010: numero monografico: *1509–2009. L'ombra di Agnadello: Venezia e la Terraferma*, G. Del Torre and A. Viggiano (eds.)), 13–63.
  'Gli ufficiali veneziani nella Terraferma veneta quattrocentesca', Annali della Scuola Normale Superiore di Pisa, ser. 4, Quaderni, 1 (1997), 155–80.

Ventura, A., *Nobiltà e popolo nella società veneta del '400 e '500*, Bari: Laterza, 1964; Milan: Unicopli, 1993.
Viggiano, A., *Governanti e governati. Legittimità del potere ed esercizio dell'autorità sovrana nello stato veneto della prima età moderna*, Treviso: Canova, 1993.
Zamperetti, S., *I piccoli principi. Signorie locali, feudi e comunità soggette nello stato regionale veneto dall'espansione territoriale ai primi decenni del '600*, Venice: Il Cardo, 1991.

8. Lombardy under the Visconti and the Sforza (Federico Del Tredici)

Due to restrictions of space, it is not possible to provide a complete bibliography of the extensive studies into the themes of this chapter. With particular reference to works published after 1998, this bibliography aims to provide a useful resource that can be integrated with the excellent bibliography found in Francesco Somaini's essay *Processi costitutivi*.

Albini, G., *Carità e governo delle povertà. Secoli XII–XV*, Milan: Unicopli, 2002.
Andenna, G., and G. Chittolini (eds.), *Storia di Cremona. Il Trecento. Chiesa e cultura (VIII–XIV secolo)*, Azzano San Paolo: Bolis, 2007.
Andreozzi, D., *Nascita di un disordine. Una famiglia signorile e una valle piacentina tra XV e XVI secolo*, Milan: Unicopli, 1993.
Arcangeli, L., 'Aggregazioni fazionarie e identità cittadina nello stato di Milano (fine XV–inizio XVI secolo)', in G. Chittolini and P. Johanek, *Aspetti e componenti dell' identità urbana in Italia e in Germania secoli XIV–XVI*, Bologna: Il Mulino, 2003, 277–350.
  Gentiluomini di Lombardia. Ricerche sull'aristocrazia padana nel Rinascimento, Milan: Unicopli, 2003.
  'Milano durante le guerre d'Italia (1499–1529). Esperimenti di rappresentanza e identità cittadina', *Società e Storia* 104 (2004), 225–66.
  (ed.), *Milano e Luigi XII. Ricerche sul primo dominio francese in Lombardia (1499–1512)*, Milan: F. Angeli, 2002.
Arcangeli, L., and M. Gentile (eds.), *Le signorie dei Rossi di Parma tra XIV e XVI secolo*, Florence: Firenze University Press, 2007.
Barni, G., 'La formazione interna dello stato visconteo', *Archivio Storico Lombardo* 68 (1941), 3–66.
Baroni, M. F., 'La formazione della cancelleria viscontea da Ottone a Giangaleazzo', *Studi di Storia Medioevale e Diplomatica* 2 (1977), 97–118.
Bellosta, R., 'Le "squadre" in consiglio. Assemblee cittadine ed élite di governo urbana a Piacenza nella seconda metà del Quattrocento tra divisioni di parte ed ingerenze ducali', *Nuova Rivista Storica* 87 (2003), 1–54.
Black, J., *Absolutism in Renaissance Milan: Plenitude of Power Under the Visconti and the Sforza 1329–1535*, Oxford University Press, 2009.
  'Double duchy: the Sforza dukes and the other Lombard title', in P. Guglielmotti, I. Lazzarini and G. M. Varanini (eds.), *Europa e Italia. Studi in onore di Giorgio Chittolini/Europe and Italy. Studies in honour of Giorgio Chittolini*, Florence: Firenze University Press, 2011, 15–28.

Boucheron, P., *Le pouvoir de bâtir. Urbanisme et politique édilitaire à Milan (XIVe–XVe siècles)*, Rome: École française de Rome, 1998.
Cadili, A., *Giovanni Visconti arcivescovo di Milano (1342–1354)*, Milan: Biblioteca Francescana, 2007.
Cariboni, G., 'Comunicazione simbolica e identità cittadina a Milano presso i primi Visconti (1277–1354)', *Reti Medievali Rivista* 9 (2008) (www.storia.unifi.it/_RM/rivista/dwnl/saggi_cariboni_08_1.pdf).
Cengarle, F., 'Le arenghe dei decreti viscontei (1330ca.–1447). Alcune considerazioni', in Gamberini and Petralia (eds.), *Linguaggi politici*, 55–88.
  Immagine di potere e prassi di governo. La politica feudale di Filippo Maria Visconti, Rome: Viella, 2006.
Cengarle, F., G. Chittolini and G. M. Varanini (eds.), *Poteri signorili e feudali nelle campagne dell'Italia settentrionale fra Tre e Quattrocento. Fondamenti di legittimità e forme d'esercizio*, Florence: Firenze University Press, 2005.
Chiappa Mauri, L., L. De Angelis and P. Mainoni (eds.), *L'età dei Visconti. Il dominio di Milano tra XIII e XV secolo*, Milan: Unicopli, 1993.
Chittolini, G., 'Ascesa e declino di piccoli stati signorili (Italia centro-settentrionale, metà Trecento). Alcune note', *Società e Storia* 121 (2008), 455–80.
  Città, comunità e feudi negli stati dell'Italia centro-settentrionale (XIV–XVI secolo), Milan: Unicopli, 1996.
  'Considerazioni conclusive', in A. Zorzi and W. Connell (eds.), *Lo stato territoriale fiorentino (secoli XIV–XV). Ricerche, linguaggi, confronti*, Pisa: Pacini, 2001, 591–604.
  '"Crisi" e "lunga durata" delle istituzioni comunali in alcuni dibattiti recenti', in L. Lacchè, C. Latini, P. Marchetti and M. Meccarelli (eds.), *Penale, giustizia, potere. Per ricordare Mario Sbriccoli*, Macerata: Eum, 2007, 125–54.
  La formazione dello stato regionale e le istituzioni del contado, Turin: Einaudi, 1979.
  'Un paese lontano', *Società e Storia* 100–1 (2004), 331–54.
  (ed.), *Gli Sforza, la chiesa lombarda, la corte di Roma. Strutture e pratiche beneficiarie nel ducato di Milano (1450–1535)*, Naples: Liguori, 1989.
  (ed.), *Storia di Cremona. Il Quattrocento. Cremona nel ducato di Milano (1395–1535)*, Azzano San Paolo: Bolis, 2008.
Cognasso, F., 'Note e documenti sulla formazione dello stato visconteo', *Bollettino della Società Pavese di Storia Patria* 23 (1923), 23–169.
  'Ricerche per la storia dello stato visconteo. I–II', *Bollettino della Società Pavese di Storia Patria* 22 (1922), 121–88; 26 (1926), 1–63.
Covini, M. N., '*La balanza drita*'. *Pratiche di governo, leggi e ordinamenti nel ducato sforzesco*, Milan: F. Angeli, 2007.
  L'esercito del duca. Organizzazione militare e istituzioni al tempo degli Sforza (1450–1480), Rome: Istituto storico italiano per il Medio Evo, 1998.
  'La trattazione delle suppliche nella cancelleria sforzesca. Da Francesco Sforza a Ludovico il Moro', in Nubola and Würgler (eds.), *Suppliche*, 107–46.
De Benedictis, A., *Repubblica per contratto. Bologna. Una città europea nello stato della chiesa*, Bologna: Il Mulino, 1995.

Del Tredici, F., 'Comunità, nobili e gentiluomini nel contado di Milano del Quattrocento,' Ph.D. thesis, Università degli Studi di Milano, 2009.
Della Misericordia, M., 'La "coda" dei gentiluomini. Fazioni, mediazione politica, clientelismo nello stato territoriale. Il caso della montagna lombarda durante il dominio sforzesco (XV secolo)', in Gentile (ed.), *Guelfi e ghibellini*, 275–389.
'Decidere e agire in comunità nel XV secolo (un aspetto del dibattito politico nel dominio sforzesco)', in Gamberini and Petralia (eds.), *Linguaggi politici*, 291–378.
La disciplina contrattata. Vescovi e vassalli tra Como e le Alpi nel tardo Medioevo, Milan: Unicopli, 2000.
Divenire comunità. Comuni rurali, poteri locali, identità sociali e territoriali in Valtellina e nella montagna lombarda nel tardo Medioevo, Milan: Unicopli, 2006.
'La Lombardia composita. Pluralismo politico-istituzionale e gruppi sociali nel secoli X–XVI (a proposito di una pubblicazione recente)', *Archivio Storico Lombardo* 124-5 (1998-9), 601–48.
'"Per non privarci de nostre raxone, li siamo stati desobidienti". Patto, giustizia e resistenza nella cultura politica delle comunità alpine nello stato di Milano (XV secolo)', in Nubola and Würgler (eds.), *Suppliche*, 147–215.
Ferente, S., *La sfortuna di Jacopo Piccinino. Storia dei bracceschi in Italia (1423-1465)*, Florence: Olschki, 2005.
Fubini, R., *Italia quattrocentesca. Politica e diplomazia nell'età di Lorenzo il Magnifico*, Milan: F. Angeli, 1994.
Gamberini, A., *La città assediata. Poteri e identità politiche a Reggio in età viscontea*, Rome: Viella, 2003.
'Il contado di fronte alla città', in R. Greci (ed.), *Storia di Parma. Parma medievale. Poteri e istituzioni*, Parma: MUP, 2010, 169–211.
Oltre le città. Assetti territoriali e culture aristocratiche nella Lombardia del tardo Medioevo, Rome: Viella, 2009.
Lo stato visconteo. Linguaggi politici e dinamiche costituzionali, Milan: F. Angeli, 2005.
Gamberini, A., and G. Petralia (eds.), *Linguaggi politici nell'Italia del Rinascimento*, Rome: Viella, 2007.
Gazzini, M., 'Patriziati urbani e spazi confraternali in età rinascimentale. L'esempio di Milano', *Archivio Storico Italiano* 158 (2000), 491–514.
Gentile, M., 'Aristocrazia signorile e costituzione dello stato visconteo-sforzesco', in Gentile and Savy (eds.), *Noblesse*, 125–55.
Fazioni al governo. Politica e società a Parma nel Quattrocento, Rome: Viella, 2009.
(ed.), *Guelfi e ghibellini nell'Italia del Rinascimento*, Rome: Viella, 2005.
'Leviatano regionale o forma-stato composita. Sugli usi possibili di idee vecchie e nuove', *Società e Storia* 89 (2000), 561–73.
'"*Postquam malignitates temporum hec nobis dedere nomina* ...". Fazioni, idiomi politici e pratiche di governo nella tarda età viscontea', in Gentile (ed.), *Guelfi e ghibellini*, 249–74.

Terra e poteri. Parma e il parmense nel ducato visconteo all'inizio del Quattrocento, Milan: Unicopli, 2001.

Gentile, M., and P. Savy (eds.), *Noblesse et états princiers en Italie et en France au XVe siècle*, Rome: École française de Rome, 2009.

Grillo, P., 'Un'egemonia sovracittadina. La famiglia Della Torre di Milano e le città lombarde (1259–1277)', *Rivista Storica Italiana* 120 (2008), 694–730.

'Rivolte antiviscontee a Milano e nelle campagne fra XIII e XIV secolo', in G. Pinto, M. Bourin and G. Cherubini (eds.), *Rivolte urbane e rivolte contadine nell'Europa del Trecento. Un confronto*, Florence: Firenze University Press, 2008, 197–216.

Leverotti, F., *Diplomazia e governo dello stato. I 'famigli cavalcanti' di Francesco Sforza (1450–1466)*, Pisa: ETS, 1992.

'Governare a modo e stillo de' Signori ...'. *Osservazioni in margine all'amministrazione della giustizia al tempo di Galeazzo Maria Sforza (1466–1476)*, Florence: Olschki, 1994.

'Leggi del principe, leggi della città nel ducato visconteo-sforzesco', in R. Dondarini, G. M. Varanini and M. Venticelli (eds.), *Signori, regimi signorili e statuti nel tardo Medioevo*, Bologna: Patron, 2003, 143–88.

'Gli officiali del ducato sforzesco', *Annali della Classe di Lettere e Filosofia della Scuola Normale Superiore*, 4th ser., Quaderni I (1997), 17–77.

Lubkin, G. P., *A Renaissance Court: Milan Under Galeazzo Maria Sforza*, Berkeley: University of California Press, 1994.

Mainoni, P., *Economia e politica nella Lombardia medievale. Da Bergamo a Milano fra XIII e XV secolo*, Milan: Gribaudo, 1994.

(ed.), *Politiche finanziarie e fiscali nell'Italia settentrionale (secoli XIII–XV)*, Milan: Unicopli, 2001.

Merlo, G. G., 'Ottone Visconti arcivescovo (e "signore"?) di Milano. Prime ricerche', in G. G. Merlo (ed.), *Vescovi medievali*, Milan: Biblioteca Francescana, 2003, 25–71.

Milano nell'età di Ludovico il Moro, Milan: Comune di Milano, 1983.

Nubola, C., and A. Würgler (eds.), *Suppliche e 'gravamina'. Politica, amministrazione, giustizia in Europa (secoli XIV–XVIII)*, Bologna: Il Mulino, 2002.

Santoro, C., *Gli uffici del dominio sforzesco (1450–1500)*, Milan: Fondazione Treccani degli Alfieri, 1948.

Senatore, F., *'Uno mundo de carta'. Forme e strutture della diplomazia sforzesca*, Naples: Liguori, 1998.

Soldi Rondinini, G., *Saggi di storia e storiografia visconteo-sforzesche*, Bologna: Cappelli, 1984.

Somaini, F., 'Il binomio imperfetto, Alcune osservazioni su guelfi e ghibellini a Milano in età visconteo-sforzesca', in Gentile (ed.), *Guelfi e ghibellini*, 131–215.

Un prelato lombardo del XV secolo. Il card. Giovanni Arcimboldi, vescovo di Novara, arcivescovo di Milano, 3 vols., Rome: Herder, 2003.

'Processi costitutivi, dinamiche politiche e strutture istituzionali dello stato visconteo-sforzesco', in *Storia d'Italia*, G. Galasso (ed.), VI, *Comuni e signorie nell'Italia settentrionale. La Lombardia*, Turin: Utet, 1998, 681–825.

Storia di Milano, V, *La signoria dei Visconti (1310–1392)*; VI, *Il Ducato visconteo e la Repubblica ambrosiana (1392–1450)*; VII, *L'età sforzesca dal 1450 al 1500*; VIII, *Tra Francia e Spagna (1500–1535)*, Milan: Fondazione Treccani degli Alfieri, 1955–7.

Storti Storchi, C., *Scritti sugli statuti lombardi*, Milan: Giuffrè, 2007.

Tabacco, G., *Egemonie sociali e strutture del potere nel Medioevo italiano*, Turin: Einaudi, 1979.

Vaglienti, F. M., *Sunt enim duo populi. Esercizio del potere ed esperimenti di fiscalità straordinaria nella prima età sforzesca (1450–1476)*, Milan: CUEM, 1997.

Welch, E., *Art and Authority in Renaissance Milan*, New Haven: Yale University Press, 1995.

9. *The feudal principalities: the west (Monferrato, Saluzzo, Savoy and Savoy-Acaia)* (Alessandro Barbero)

Andenmatten, B., and A. Paravicini Bagliani (eds.), *Amédée VIII – Félix V, premier duc de Savoie et pape (1383–1451)*, Lausanne: Bibliothèque Historique Vaudoise, 1992.

Barbero, A., 'Appannaggi, infeudazioni, riacquisti. La politica feudale dei marchesi di Saluzzo nel Quattrocento', in Gentile and Savy (eds.), *Noblesse*, 335–63.

'La corte ducale sotto Carlo II (1504–1553)', in Barbero, *Il ducato di Savoia*, 197–256.

'Corti e storiografia di corte nel Piemonte tardomedievale', in *Piemonte medievale. Forme del potere e della società. Studi per Giovanni Tabacco*, Turin: Einaudi, 1985, 249–77.

Il ducato di Savoia. Amministrazione e corte di uno stato franco-italiano, Rome and Bari: Laterza, 2002.

'Le fazioni nobiliari alla corte di Ludovico (1446–1451)', in Barbero, *Il ducato di Savoia*, 163–83.

'Un governo per il Piemonte. L'evoluzione del consiglio cismontano e del "Consilium cum domino residens" (1419–1536)', in Barbero, *Il ducato di Savoia*, 121–44.

'Il mutamento dei rapporti fra Torino e le altre comunità del Piemonte nel nuovo assetto del ducato sabaudo', in R. Comba (ed.), *Storia di Torino*, II, *Il basso Medioevo e la prima età moderna (1280–1536)*, Turin: Einaudi, 1997, 373–419.

'L'organizzazione militare del ducato sabaudo durante la guerra di Milano (1449)', in Barbero, *Il ducato di Savoia*, 68–97.

'Progetti di riforma della tesoreria ducale (1448–1452)', in Barbero, *Il ducato di Savoia*, 98–120.

'Savoiardi e Piemontesi nel ducato sabaudo all'inizio del Cinquecento: un problema storiografico risolto', *Bollettino Storico-Bibliografico Subalpino* 87 (1989), 591–637.

'I soldati del principe. Guerra, stato e società nel Piemonte sabaudo (1450–1580)', in C. Dipper and M. Rosa (eds.), *La società dei principi nell'Europa moderna (secc. XVI–XVII)*, Bologna: Il Mulino, 2005, 169–205.

'La storia ufficiale nel XV secolo. Perrinet Dupin, segretario e cronista della duchessa Iolanda', in Barbero, *Il ducato di Savoia*, 184–96.

'La struttura amministrativa del ducato', in Barbero, *Il ducato di Savoia*, 3–47.

'La venalità degli uffici. L'esempio del vicariato di Torino (1360–1536)', in Barbero, *Il ducato di Savoia*, 48–67.

Barbero, A., and T. Brero, 'Genre et nationalité à la cour de Béatrice de Portugal, duchesse de Savoie (1521–1538)', in L. Arcangeli and S. Peyronel (eds.), *Donne di potere nel Rinascimento*, Rome: Viella, 2008, 333–60.

Bianchi, P., and L. C. Gentile (eds.), *L'affermarsi della corte sabauda. Dinastie, poteri, élites in Piemonte e Savoia fra tardo Medioevo e prima età moderna*, Turin: Zamorani, 2006.

Biolzi, R., *Avec le fer et la flamme. La guerre entre la Savoie et Fribourg (1447–1448)*, Lausanne: Université de Lausanne, 2009.

Bozzola, A., 'Appunti sulla vita economica, sulle classi sociali e sull'ordinamento amministrativo del Monferrato nei sec. XIV e XV', *Bollettino Storico-Bibliografico Subalpino* 25 (1923), 211–61.

Parlamento del Monferrato, Bologna: Forni, 1926.

Castelnuovo, G., 'Cancellieri e segretari fra codificazione amministrativa e prassi di governo. Il caso sabaudo (metà Trecento-metà Quattrocento)', *Ricerche Storiche* 24 (1994), 291–303.

'Les maréchaux en Savoie au bas Moyen Âge', in *La société savoyarde et la guerre. Huit siècles d'histoire, XIIIe–XXe siècles*, Chambéry: Société savoisienne d'histoire et d'archéologie, 1997, 91–9.

'Nobles des champs ou nobles de cour? Princes et noblesse dans les chroniques savoyardes du XVe siècle', in Gentile and Savy (eds.), *Noblesse*, 191–208.

'Omaggio, feudo e signoria in terra sabauda (metà '200–fine '400)', in F. Cengarle, G. Chittolini and G. M. Varanini (eds.), *Poteri signorili e feudali nelle campagne dell'Italia settentrionale fra Tre e Quattrocento. Fondamenti di legittimità e forme di esercizio*, Florence: Firenze University Press, 2005, 175–201.

'Principi e città negli stati sabaudi', in S. Gensini (ed.), *Principi e città alla fine del Medioevo*, Pisa: Pacini, 1996, 77–93.

'Quels offices, quels officiers? L'administration en Savoie au milieu du XVe siècle', *Études Savoisiennes* 2 (1993), 3–43.

Ufficiali e gentiluomini. La società politica sabauda nel tardo Medioevo, Milan: F. Angeli, 1994.

Castelnuovo, G., and B. Andenmatten, 'Produzione documentaria e conservazione archivistica nel principato sabaudo, XIII–XV secolo', *Bullettino dell'Istituto italiano per il Medio Evo e Archivio Muratoriano* 110 (2008), 279–348.

Cengarle, F., *Immagine di potere e prassi di governo. La politica feudale di Filippo Maria Visconti*, Rome: Viella, 2006.

Chittolini, G., 'I principati italiani alla fine del Medioevo', in *Poderes públicos en la Europa medieval. Principados, reinos y coronas*, Pamplona: Gobierno de Navarra, 1997, 235–59.

Comba, R. (ed.), *Ludovico I marchese di Saluzzo. Un principe tra Francia e Italia (1416–1475)*, Cuneo: Società per gli studi storici, archeologici ed artistici della provincia di Cuneo, 2003.

(ed.), *Ludovico II marchese di Saluzzo. Condottiero, uomo di stato e mecenate (1475–1504)*, Cuneo: Società per gli studi storici, archeologici ed artistici della provincia di Cuneo, 2005.

'Il progetto di una società coercitivamente cristiana. Gli Statuti di Amedeo VIII di Savoia', *Rivista Storica Italiana* 103 (1991), 33–56.

Corio, B., *Storia di Milano*, A. Morisi Guerra (ed.), Milan: Utet, 1978.

Del Bo, B., *Uomini e strutture di uno stato feudale. Il marchesato di Monferrato (1418–1483)*, Milan: LED, 2009.

Demotz, B., 'Une clé de la réussite d'une principauté aux XIIIe et XIVe siècles. Naissance et développement de la Chambre des comptes de Savoie', in P. Contamine and O. Mattéoni, *La France des principautés. Les Chambres des comptes, XIVe–XVe siècles*, Paris: Comité pour l'histoire économique et financière de la France, 1996, 17–26.

Gentile, G., 'Le carriere di Galeazzo e Francesco Cavassa all'ombra dei marchesi di Saluzzo', in Comba (ed.), *Ludovico II marchese di Saluzzo*, 115–49.

Gentile, L. C., 'Il cerimoniale come linguaggio politico nelle corti di Savoia, Acaia, Saluzzo e Monferrato', in Bianchi and Gentile (eds.), *L'affermarsi della corte sabauda*, 55–76.

Riti ed emblemi. Processi di rappresentazione del potere principesco in area subalpina (XIII–XVI secc.), Turin: Zamorani, 2008.

Gentile, M., and P. Savy (eds.), *Noblesse et états princiers en Italie et en France au XVe siècle*, Rome: École française de Rome, 2009.

Grillo, P., 'Comunità e signori del Saluzzese nell'età di Ludovico I', in Comba (ed.), *Ludovico I marchese di Saluzzo*, 207–50.

'I gentiluomini del marchese. Ludovico II e i suoi ufficiali', in Comba (ed.), *Ludovico II marchese di Saluzzo*, 17–56.

Koenigsberger, H. G., 'The Parliament of Piedmont during the Renaissance', in H. G. Koenigsberger, *Estates and Revolutions*, Ithaca and London: Cornell University Press, 1971, 19–79.

Marini, L., *Savoiardi e Piemontesi nello stato sabaudo (1418–1601)*, I, *1418–1536*, Rome: Istituto storico italiano per l'età moderna e contemporanea, 1962.

Mongiano, E., '"*Predecessorum suorum imitando vestigia*". Autorità del principe e autonomie locali sotto il governo di Ludovico II', in Comba (ed.), *Ludovico II marchese di Saluzzo*, 79–114.

Moriondo, G. B., *Monumenta Aquensia*, Bologna: Forni, 1967 (1st edn, Turin, 1789).

Patriarca, P. G., *La riforma legislativa di Carlo II di Savoia. Un tentativo di consolidazione agli albori dello stato moderno, 1533*, Turin: Deputazione Subalpina di Storia Patria, 1988.

Raviola, B. A., *Il Monferrato gonzaghesco. Istituzioni ed élites di un micro-stato (1536–1708)*, Florence: Olschki, 2003.

Savy, P., 'Gli stati italiani del XV secolo. Una proposta sulle tipologie', *Archivio Storico Italiano* 163 (2005), 735–59.

Settia, A. A. (ed.), 'Quando venit marchio Grecus in terra Montisferrati'. *L'avvento di Teodoro I Paleologo nel VII centenario (1306–2006)*, Casale: Associazione Casalese Arte e Storia, 2008.

'*"Sont inobediens et refusent servir"*. Il principe e l'esercito nel Monferrato dell'età avignonese', in *Piemonte medievale. Forme del potere e della società. Studi per Giovanni Tabacco*, Turin: Einaudi, 1985, 85–121.

Tallone, A., *Parlamento sabaudo*, 13 vols., Bologna: Zanichelli, 1928–46.

Varanini, G. M., 'Governi principeschi e modello cittadino di organizzazione del territorio nell'Italia del Quattrocento', in S. Gensini (ed.), *Principi e città alla fine del Medioevo*, Pisa: Pacini, 1996, 95–127.

10. *The feudal principalities: the east (Trent, Bressanone/Brixen, Aquileia, Tyrol and Gorizia)* (Marco Bellabarba)

Algazi, G., *Herrengewalt und Gewalt der Herren im späten Mittelalter. Herrschaft, Gegenseitigkeit und Sprachgebrauch*, Frankfurt am Main and New York: Campus Verlag, 1996.

Austro-Friulana. Sammlung von Actenstücken zur Geschichte des Conflictes Herzog Rudolfs IV. von Österreich mit dem Patriarchate von Aquileja. 1358–1365, collected and ed. by J. V. Zahn, Vienna: Commission bei Karl Gerold's Sohn Buchhändler der Kais. Akademie der Wissenschaften, 1877.

Bellabarba, M., 'Statuti, "Landrecht", leghe aristocratiche. Diritti e potere nello spazio trentino-tirolese del primo Quattrocento', in M. Gentile and P. Savy (eds.), *Noblesse et états princiers en Italie et en France au XVe siècle*, Rome: École française de Rome, 2009, 231–51.

Bellamy, J. G., *Bastard Feudalism and the Law*, London: Routledge, 1989.

Bettotti, M., 'L'aristocrazia nel tardo Medioevo', in A. Castagnetti and G. M. Varanini (eds.), *Storia del Trentino*, III, *L'età medievale*, Bologna: Il Mulino, 2004, 417–59.

Bianco, F., *1511. La 'crudel zobia grassa'. Rivolte contadine e faide nobiliari in Friuli tra '400 e '500*, Pordenone: Biblioteca dell'Immagine, 1995.

Brunettin, G., 'Una fedeltà insidiosa. La parabola delle ambizioni goriziane sul Patriarcato di Aquileia (1202–1365)', in S. Cavazza (ed.), *Da Ottone III a Massimiliano I. Gorizia e i conti di Gorizia nel Medioevo*, Gorizia: Edizioni della Laguna, 2004, 281–338.

Cammarosano, P., 'L'alto Medioevo. Verso la formazione regionale', in P. Cammarosano, F. De Vitt and D. Degrassi (eds.), *Storia della società friulana. Il Medioevo*, Udine: Casamassima, 1988, 9–155.

Casella, L., *I Savorgnan. La famiglia e le opportunità del potere*, Rome: Bulzoni Editore, 2003.

Chittolini, G., *Città, comunità e feudi negli stati dell'Italia centro-settentrionale (XIV–XVI secolo)*, Milan: Unicopli, 1996.

'Signorie rurali e feudi alla fine del Medioevo', in *Comuni e signorie. Istituzioni, società e lotte per l'egemonia*, Turin: Utet, 1981 (*Storia d'Italia*, G. Galasso (gen. ed.), IV), 597–676.

Corbellini, R., 'Udine capitale della Patria del Friuli. La costruzione di un'identità cittadina per un ruolo di governo', in M. Bellabarba and

R. Stauber (eds.), *Identità territoriali e cultura politica nella prima età moderna. Territoriale Identität und politische Kultur in der Frühen Neuzeit*, Bologna: Il Mulino, 1998, 239–54.

Cusin, F., *Il confine orientale d'Italia nella politica europea del XIV e XV secolo*, Trieste: Edizioni Lint, 1977 (1st edn, 1937).

Degrassi, D., 'Frontiere, confini e interazioni transconfinarie nel Medioevo. Alcuni esempi nell'area nordorientale d'Italia', *Archivio Storico Italiano* 160 (2002), 195–220.

Haushofer, A., *Pass-Staaten in den Alpen*, Berlin-Grunewald: K. Vowinckel, 1928.

Holenstein, A., 'Introduction. Empowering interactions: looking at the statebuilding from below', in W. Blockmans, A. Holenstein and J. Mathieu (eds.), *Empowering Interactions: Political Cultures and the Emergence of the State in Europe 1300–1900*, Farnham, UK: Ashgate, 2009, 1–31.

Lattimore, O., *Studies in Frontier History: Collected Papers, 1928–1958*, Oxford University Press, 1962.

Lazzarini, I., *L'Italia degli stati territoriali. Secoli XIII–XV*, Rome and Bari: Laterza, 2003.

Leicht, P. S., *Il parlamento friulano nel primo secolo della dominazione veneziana*, Milan: Giuffrè, 1948.

Mallet, M. E., 'La conquista della Terraferma', in A. Tenenti and U. Tucci (eds.), *Storia di Venezia dalle origini alla caduta della Serenissima*, IV, *Il Rinascimento. Politica e cultura*, Rome: Istituto dell'Enciclopedia italiana, 1996, 159–236.

Morsel, J., 'Die Erfindung des Adels. Zur Sociogenese des Adels am Ende des Mittelalters – das Beispiel Franken', in O. G. Oexle and W. Paravicini (eds.), *Nobilitas. Funktion und Repräsentation des Adels in Alteuropa*, Göttingen: Vandenhoeck and Ruprecht, 1997, 313–75.

Muir, E., *Mad Blood Stirring: Vendetta and Factions in Friuli During the Renaissance*, Baltimore and London: Johns Hopkins University Press, 1993.

Niederstätter, A., *Die Herrschaft Österreich. Fürst und Land im Spätmittelalter, 1278–1411*, Vienna: C. Ueberreuter, 2001.

Ortalli, G., 'Federico IV Tascavuota. Venezia e il principe-vescovo. Alleanze, sospetti e prestiti nel Quattrocento trentino', *Bullettino dell'Istituto Storico Italiano per il Medio Evo* 102 (1999), 141–66.

'Le modalità di un passaggio. Il Friuli e il dominio veneziano', in *Il Quattrocento nel Friuli occidentale*, 2 vols., Pordenone: Provincia, 1996, I, 13–33.

Paschini, P., *Storia del Friuli*, II, *Dalla seconda metà del Duecento alla fine del Settecento*, Udine: Libreria editrice Aquileia, 1954.

Porcia, G. di, *Descrizione della patria del Friuli fatta nel secolo 16, dal conte Girolamo di Porcia*, Udine: Tip. Del Patronato, 1897.

Riedmann, J., 'Vescovi e avvocati', in C. G. Mor and H. Schmidinger (eds.), *I poteri temporali dei vescovi in Italia e in Germania nel Medioevo*, Bologna: Il Mulino, 1979, 35–76.

Rokkan, S., *State Formation, Nation-Building, and Mass Politics in Europe: The Theory of Stein Rokkan Based on His Collected Works*, Kuhnle, S., P. Flora and D. Urwin (eds.), Oxford University Press, 1999.

Sassen, S. *Territory, Authority, Rights: From Medieval to Global Assemblages*, Princeton University Press, 2006.
Spruyt, H., *The Sovereign State and Its Competitors*, Princeton University Press, 1994.
Varanini, G. M., 'Il principato vescovile di Trento nel Trecento: lineamenti di storia politico-istituzionale', in A. Castagnetti and G. M. Varanini (eds.), *Storia del Trentino*, III, *L'età medievale*, Bologna: Il Mulino, 2004, 345–83.
'Venezia e l'entroterra (1300 circa–1420)', in G. Arnaldi, G. Cracco and A. Tenenti (eds.), *Storia di Venezia dalle origini alla caduta della Serenissima*, III, *La formazione dello stato patrizio*, Rome: Istituto dell'Enciclopedia italiana, 1997, 159–236.
Viggiano, A., 'Politica e giustizia. Per uno studio del tribunale del luogotenente della Patria del Friuli a metà Quattrocento', in L. Casella (ed.), *Rappresentanze e territori. Parlamento friulano e istituzioni rappresentative territoriali nell'Europa moderna*, Udine: Forum, 2003, 391–432.
Wiesflecker, H., 'Die politische Entwicklung der Grafschaft Görz und ihr Erbfall an Österreich', *Mitteilungen des Instituts für österreichische Geschichtsforschung* 56 (1948), 329–84.
Zacchigna, M., 'Il patriarcato di Aquileia. L'evoluzione dei poteri locali (1250–1420)', in L. Ferrari (ed.), *Studi in onore di Giovanni Miccoli*, Trieste: Edizioni Università di Trieste, 2004, 91–113.
'L'inclinazione signorile delle aristocrazie friulane nello sviluppo della normativa locale (secoli XIV–XV)', in R. Dondarini, G. M. Varanini and M. Venticelli (eds.), *Signori, regimi signorili e statuti nel tardo Medioevo*, Bologna: Patròn editore, 2003, 191–203.
Zamperetti, S., *I piccoli principi. Signorie locali, feudi e comunità soggette nello stato regionale veneto dall'espansione territoriale ai primi decenni del '600*, Venice: Il Cardo, 1991.
Zmora, H., *State and Nobility in Early Modern Germany: The Knightly Feud in Franconia, 1440–1567*, Cambridge University Press, 1997.
'Feuds for and against princes. Politics, violence and aristocratic identity in early modern Germany', in J. Leonhard and C. Wieland (eds.), *What Makes the Nobility Noble? Comparative Perspectives from the Sixteenth to the Twentieth Century*, Göttingen: Vandenhoeck & Ruprecht, 2011, 121–41.

11. Genoa (Christine Shaw)

Airaldi, G., *Genova e la Liguria nel Medioevo*, Turin: Utet, 1986.
Argenti, P., *The Occupation of Chios by the Genoese and Their Administration of the Island, 1346–1566*, 3 vols., Cambridge University Press, 1958.
Basso, E., 'Antoniotto Adorno e la dominazione francese', in L. Borzani, F. Ragazzi and G. Pistarino (eds.) *Storia illustrata di Genova*, II, *Genova nel Quattrocento*, Milan: Sellino, 1993, 289–304.
'Tommaso Campofregoso e la dominazione milanese', in L. Borzani, F. Ragazzi and G. Pistarino (eds.) *Storia illustrata di Genova*, II, *Genova nel Quattrocento*, Milan: Sellino, 1993, 321–36.
Borlandi, A., 'Ragione politica e ragione di famiglia nel dogato di Pietro Fregoso', *La Storia dei Genovesi*, IV, Genoa: Copy-Lito, 1984, 353–402.

Epstein, S. A., *Genoa and the Genoese, 958–1528*, Chapel Hill: University of North Carolina Press, 1996.
Felloni, G. (ed.), *La Casa di San Giorgio. Il potere del credito, Atti della Società ligure di storia patria* 120 (2006).
Franzini, A., *La Corse du XVe siècle. Politique et société, 1433–1483*, Ajaccio: Piazzola, 1997.
Grendi, E., 'Problemi di storia degli alberghi genovesi', in *La Storia dei Genovesi*, I, Genoa: Copy-Lito, 1981, 183–97.
'Profilo storico degli alberghi genovesi', *Mélanges de l'Ecole Française de Rome. Moyen Âge Temps Modernes* 87 (1975), 241–302.
Heers, J., *Le clan familial au Moyen Âge. Études sur les structures politiques et sociales des milieux urbains*, Paris: PUF, 1974.
'Consorterie et alberghi à Gênes. La ville et la campagne', in *La storia dei Genovesi*, IX, Genoa: Copy-Lito, 1989, 45–63.
Gênes au XVe siècle. Activité économique et problèmes sociaux, Paris: SEVPEN, 1961.
Hughes, D. Owen, 'Kinsmen and neighbors in medieval Genoa', in H. A. Miskimin, D. Herlihy and A. L. Udovitch (eds.), *The Medieval City*, New Haven and London: Yale University Press, 1977, 95–111.
Lopez, R., *Storia delle colonie genovesi nel Mediterraneo. Prefazione e aggiornamento bibliografico a cura di M. Balard*, Genoa: Marietti, 1996.
'Venise et Gênes. Deux styles, une réussite', *Diogène*, 71 (1970), 43–51.
Marengo, E., C. Manfroni and G. Pessagno, *Il Banco di San Giorgio. L'antico debito pubblico genovese e la Casa di S. Giorgio, la Marina di Genova, S. Giorgio e i possedimenti coloniali di terraferma, il palazzo della società e le sue dipendenze*, Genoa: A. Donath, 1911.
Musso, R., 'Il dominio sforzesco in Corsica (1464–1481)', *Nuova rivista storica* 78 (1994), 531–88; 79 (1995), 27–76.
'Le istituzioni ducali dello "Stato di Genova" durante la signoria di Filippo Maria Visconti (1421–1435)', in L. Chiappa Mauri, L. De Angelis Cappabianca and P. Mainoni (eds.), *L'età dei Visconti. Il dominio di Milano fra XIII e XV secolo*, Milan: Unicopli, 1993, 65–111.
'Lo "stato cappellazzo". Genova tra Adorno e Fregoso (1436–1464)', *Studi di Storia Medioevale e di Diplomatica* 17 (1988), 223–88.
'"El stato nostro de Zenoa". Aspetti istituzionali della prima dominazione sforzesca su Genova (1464–1478)', in *Serta antiqua et mediaevalia*, V, *Società e istituzioni del Medioevo ligure*, Rome: G. Breitschneider, 2001, 199–236.
Ortalli, G. and D. Puncuh (eds.), *Genova, Venezia, il Levante nei secoli XII–XIV, Atti della Società ligure di storia patria*, 115 (2001).
Pacini, A., *La Genova di Andrea Doria nell'Impero di Carlo V*, Florence: Olschki, 1999.
I presupposti politici del 'secolo dei genovesi'. La riforma del 1528, Atti della Società ligure di storia patria 30 (1990).
'La tirannia delle fazioni e la repubblica dei ceti. Vita politica e istituzioni a Genova tra Quattro e Cinquecento', *Annali dell'Istituto Storico Italo-Germanico in Trento* 18 (1992), 57–119.
Pandiani, E., *Un anno di storia genovese (giugno 1506–1507) con diario e documenti inediti, Atti della Società ligure di storia patria*, 37 (1905).

Petti Balbi, G., 'Dinamiche sociali ed esperienze istituzionali a Genova tra Tre e Quattrocento', in *Italia 1350–1450. Tra crisi, trasformazione, sviluppo*, Pistoia: Centro italiano di studi dei storia e d'arte, 1993, 113–28.

'Élites economiche ed esercizio del potere a Genova nei secoli XIII-XV', in G. Petti Balbi (ed.), *Strutture del potere ed élites economiche nelle città europee dei secoli XII–XVI*, Naples: Liguori, 1996, 29–39.

'L'opzione su Cipro', in G. Petti Balbi, *Una città e il suo mare. Genova nel Medioevo*, Bologna: CLUEB, 1991, 186–99.

Simon Boccanegra e la Genova del '300, Genoa: Marietti, 1991.

Pistarino, G., 'La caduta di Costantinopoli. Da Pera genovese a Galata turca', in *Storia dei Genovesi*, V, Genoa: Copy-Lito, 1985, 7–47.

'Genova e la Sardegna: due mondi a confronto', in *Storia dei Genovesi*, IV, Genoa: Copy-Lito, 1984, 191–236.

'Genova medievale tra Oriente e Occidente', in G. Pistarino, *La capitale del Mediterraneo. Genova nel Medioevo*, Bordighera: Istituto internazionale di studi liguri, 1993, 69–104.

Scovazzi, I., and F. Noberasco, *Storia di Savona*, 3 vols., Savona: Società savonese di storia patria, 1926–8.

Shaw, C., 'Bartolomea Campofregoso: a woman's claim to power in fifteenth-century Genoa', in L. Arcangeli and S. Peyronel (eds.), *Donne di potere nel Rinascimento*, Rome: Viella, 2008, 465–79.

'Concepts of libertà in Renaissance Genoa', in J. Law and B. Paton (eds.), *Communes and Despots in Late Medieval and Renaissance Italy*, Farnham: Ashgate, 2010, 177–92.

'Counsel and consent in fifteenth-century Genoa', *English Historical Review* 116 (2001), 834–62.

'The French signoria over Genoa', in M. Schnettger and C. Taviani (eds.), *Libertà e dominio. Il sistema politico genovese. Le relazioni esterne e il controllo del territorio*, Rome: Viella, 2011, 39–54.

'The language of Genoese political pragmatism in the Quattrocento', in A. Gamberini and G. Petralia, *Linguaggi politici nell'Italia del Rinascimento*, Rome: Viella, 2007, 171–86.

Popular Government and Oligarchy in Renaissance Italy, Leiden: Brill, 2006.

'Principles and practice in the civic government of fifteenth-century Genoa', *Renaissance Quarterly* 58 (2005), 45–90.

Sieveking, H., *Studio nelle finanze genovesi nel Medioevo e in particulare sulla Casa di S. Giorgio*, 2 vols., *Atti della Società ligure di storia patria*, 35 (1905–6).

La storia dei Genovesi (Atti dei Convegni internazionali di studi sui ceti dirigenti nelle istituzioni della Repubblica di Genova), 12 vols., Genoa: Copy-Lito, 1981–91.

Surdich, F., *Genova e Venezia fra Tre e Quattrocento*, Genoa: Flli. Bozzi, 1970 (shorter version published as *Atti della Società ligure di storia patria* 81 (1967), 205–327).

Taviani, C., *Superba discordia. Guerra, rivolta e pacificazione nella Genova di primo Cinquecento*, Rome: Viella, 2008.

12. The collapse of city-states and the role of urban centres in the new political geography of Renaissance Italy (Francesco Somaini)

For editorial reasons and constraints, the bibliography for this chapter includes only the secondary sources quoted in the notes. It is possible to construct a more comprehensive bibliography, attesting to the vast quantities of works on this theme, from the works listed below.

Ascheri, M., *Le città-stato*, Bologna: Il Mulino, 2006.
Berengo, M., *Città italiana e città europea. Ricerche storiche*, M. Folin (ed.), Reggio Emilia: Diabasis, 2010.
  L'Europa delle città. Il volto della società urbana europea tra Medioevo ed età moderna, Turin: Einaudi, 1999.
Bertelli, S., *Il potere oligarchico nello stato-città medievale*, Florence: La Nuova Italia, 1978.
Bresc, H. *Un monde méditerranéen. Économie et societé en Sicile 1300–1450*, 2 vols., Rome: École française de Rome, 1993.
Capitani, O., R. Manselli, G. Cherubini, A. I. Pini and G. Chittolini, *Comuni e signorie. Istituzioni, società e lotte per l'egemonia*, in G.Galasso (ed.), *Storia d' Italia*, IV, Turin: Utet, 1981.
Chittolini, G., 'Cities, "city-states", and regional states in north-central Italy', in W. P. Blockmans and C. Tilly (eds.), *Cities and States in Europe, 1000–1800*, Boulder: Kluver Academic Publishers, 1989, 689–706.
  Città comunità e feudi negli stati dell'Italia centro-settentrionale (XIV–XVI secolo), Milan: Unicopli, 1996.
  (ed.), *La crisi degli ordinamenti comunali e le origini dello stato del Rinascimento*, Bologna: Il Mulino, 1979.
  '"Crisi" e "lunga durata" delle istituzioni comunali in alcuni dibattiti recenti', in L. Lacché, C. Latini, P. Marchetti and M. Meccarelli (eds.), *Penale, giustizia, potere. Per ricordare Mario Sbriccoli*, Macerata: Edizioni Università di Macerata, 2007, 125–54.
  La formazione dello stato regionale e le istituzioni del contado, Turin: Einaudi, 1979.
  'Poteri urbani e poteri feudali-signorili nelle campagne dell'Italia centro-settentrionale fra tardo Medioevo e prima età moderna', *Società e Storia* 21, 81 (1998), 473–510.
  'Gli stati cittadini italiani', in R. C. Schwinges, C. Hesse and P. Moraw (eds.), *Europa im späten Mittelalter. Politik, Gesellschaft, Kultur*, Munich: Oldenbourg, 2006, 153–64.
Chittolini, G., and P. Johanek (eds.), *Aspetti e componenti dell'identità urbana in Italia e in Germania (secoli XIV–XVI)*, Bologna: Il Mulino, 2003.
Chittolini, G., G. Petti Balbi and G. Vitolo (eds.), *Città e territori nell'Italia del Medioevo. Studi in onore di Gabriella Rossetti*, Naples: Liguori, 2007.
Chittolini, G., and D. Willoweit (eds.), *L'organizzazione del territorio in Italia e in Germania. Secoli XIII–XIV*, Bologna: Il Mulino, 1994.

Bibliography

Cirillo, G., 'Città e contado nel Mezzogiorno. La *vexata quaestio* di un recente dibattito storiografico', *L'Acropoli* 7, 1 (2006), 72–84.

Corrao, P., *Governare un regno. Potere, società e istituzioni in Sicilia fra Trecento e Quattrocento*, Naples: Liguori, 1991.

Crouzet-Pavan, E., *Enfer et paradis. L'Italie de Dante et de Giotto*, Paris: Albin Michel, 2001.

Crouzet-Pavan, E., and E. Lecuppre-Desjardin (eds.), *Villes de Flandre et d'Italie (XIIIe–XIVe siècle). Les enseignements d'une comparaison*, Turnhout: Brepols, 2008.

Dean, T., 'The rise of *signori*', in *The New Cambridge Medieval History*, V, *1198c.–1300*, D. Abulafia (ed.), Cambridge University Press, 1999, 458–78.

Dean, T., and C. Wickham (eds.), *City and Countryside in Late Medieval and Renaissance Italy: Essays Presented to Philip Jones*, London and Ronceverte: Hambledon Press, 1990.

Epstein, S. R., *An Island for Itself: Economic Development and Social Change in Late Medieval Sicily*, Cambridge University Press, 1992.

Franceschi, F., and I. Taddei, *Les villes d'Italie du XIIe siècle au milieu di XIVe siècle. Économie, societés, pouvoir, cultures*, Paris: Bréal, 2004.

Fubini, F., '"Potenze grosse" e piccolo stato nell'Italia del Rinascimento. Consapevolezza della distinzione e dinamica dei poteri', in L. Barletta, F. Cardini and G. Galasso (eds.), *Il piccolo stato. Politica, storia, diplomazia*, San Marino: AIEP, 2003, 91–126.

Gamberini, A., *Oltre le città. Assetti territoriali e culture aristocratiche nella Lombardia del tardo Medioevo*, Rome: Viella, 2009.

Gentile, M. (ed.), *Guelfi e ghibellini nell'Italia del Rinascimento*, Rome: Viella, 2005.

Ginatempo, M., 'Le città italiane, XIV–XV secolo', in *Poderes pùblicos en la Europa modioval*, Pamplona: Gobierno de Navarra, 1997, 149–209.

Ginatempo, M., and L. Sandri, *L'Italia delle città. Il popolamento urbano tra Medioevo e Rinascimento (secoli XIII–XVI)*, Florence: Le Lettere, 1990.

Grillo, P., *Cavalieri e popoli in armi. Le istituzioni militari nell'Italia medievale*, Rome and Bari: Laterza, 2008.

Hay, D., and J. Law, *Italy in the Age of Renaissance: 1380–1530*, London: Longman, 1989.

Heers, J., and C. Bec (eds.), *Exil et civilisation en Italie (XIIe–XIVe s.)*, Nancy: Presses Universitaires, 1990.

Hyde, J. K., *Society and Politics in Medieval Italy: The Evolution of the Civil Life, 1000–1350*, London: St Martin's Press, 1973.

Jones, P., *The Italian City-State: From Commune to Signoria*, Oxford University Press, 1997.

Larner, J., *Italy in the Age of Dante and Petrarch, 1216–1380*, London: Longman, 1980.

Law, J., L. Green and D. Abulafia, 'Italy in the age of Dante and Petrarch', in *The New Cambridge Medieval History*, V, *c. 1300–c. 1415*, M. Jones (ed.), Cambridge University Press, 2000, 442–524.

Lazzarini, I., *L'Italia degli stati territoriali. Secoli XIII–XV*, Rome and Bari: Laterza, 2003.
Mallett, M., *Mercenaries and Their Masters*, London: Bodley Head, 1974.
The Northern Italian States, in *The New Cambridge Medieval History*, VII, *1415–1500*, C. Allmand (ed.), Cambridge University Press, 1998, 547–70.
Milani, G., *I comuni italiani. Secoli XIV–XV*, Rome and Bari: Laterza, 2005.
Najemy, J. (ed.), *Italy in the Age of the Renaissance*, Oxford University Press, 2004.
Pellegrini, M., *Le guerre d'Italia, 1494–1530*, Bologna: Il Mulino, 2009.
Simeoni, L., *Le signorie*, Milan: Vallardi, 1950.
Somaini, F., 'Henri VII et le cadre italien. La tentative de relancer le *Regnum Italicum*. Quelques réflexions préliminaires', in *Europäische Governance in Spätmittelalter. Heinrich VII. von Luxembourg und die grossen Dynastien in Europas – Gouvernance européenne au bas moyen âge. Henri VII de Luxembourg et l'Europe des grandes dynasties*, M. Pauly (ed.), Luxembourg: Publications de la Section historique de l'Institut Grand Ducal, Publications du CLUDEM, 2010, 397–428.
'The political geography of Renaissance Italy', in M. Folin (ed.), *Courts and Courtly Arts in Renaissance Italy: Art, Culture and Politics, 1395–1530*, Woodbridge: Antique Collectors' Club, 2010, 35–61.
Tabacco, G., *Egemonie sociali e strutture del potere nel Medioevo italiano*, Turin: Einaudi, 1979.
Titone, F., *Governments of the* Universitates*: Urban Communities of Sicily in the Fourteenth and Fifteenth Centuries*, Turnhout: Brepols, 2009.
Valeri, N., *L'Italia nell'età dei principati. Dal 1343 al 1516*, Milan: Mondadori, 1949.
Varanini, G. M., 'Aristocrazie e poteri nell'Italia centro-settentrionale dalla crisi comunale alle guerre d'Italia', in R. Bordone, G. Castelnuovo and G. M. Varanini, *Le aristocrazie dai signori rurali al patriziato*, Rome and Bari: Laterza, 2004, 121–93.
Vitolo, G. (ed.), *Città e contado nel Mezzogiorno tra Medioevo ed età moderna*, Salerno: Laveglia, 2007.
Zorzi, A., and W. J. Connell (eds.), *Lo stato territoriale fiorentino (secoli XIV–XV). Ricerche, linguaggi, confronti*, Pisa: Pacini, 2001.

13. *The rural communities* (Massimo Della Misericordia)

Adami, R., M. Bonazza and G. M. Varanini (eds.), *Volano. Storia di una comunità*, Rovereto: Nicolodi, 2005.
Alfani, G. and R. Rao (eds.), *La gestione delle risorse collettive nell'Italia settentrionale (secoli XII–XVIII)*, Milan: F. Angeli, 2011.
Barlucchi, A., *Il contado senese all'epoca dei Nove. Asciano e il suo territorio tra Due e Trecento*, Florence: Olschki, 1997.
Bartoli Langeli, A., A. Giorgi and S. Moscatelli (eds.), *Archivi e comunità tra Medioevo ed età moderna*, Rome and Trent: Ministero per i Beni e le attività culturali – Editrice Università degli Studi di Trento, 2009.

Bianco, F., *1511. La 'crudel zobia grassa'. Rivolte contadine e faide nobiliari in Friuli tra '400 e '500*, Pordenone: Biblioteca dell'Immagine, 1995.
Bicchierai, M., *Ai confini della Repubblica di Firenze. Poppi dalla signoria dei conti Guidi al vicariato del Casentino*, Florence: Olschki, 2005.
Blickle, P., *Kommunalismus. Skizzen einer gesellschaftlichen Organisationsform*, Munich: Oldenbourg, 2000.
Bordone, R., P. Guglielmotti, S. Lombardini and A. Torre (eds.), *Lo spazio politico locale in età medievale, moderna e contemporanea*, Alessandria: Edizioni dell'Orso, 2007.
Bourin, M., G. Cherubini and G. Pinto (eds.), *Rivolte urbane e rivolte contadine nell'Europa del Trecento. Un confronto*, Florence: Firenze University Press, 2008.
Braccia, R., *Diritto della città, diritto del contado. Autonomie politiche e autonomie normative di un distretto cittadino*, Milan: Giuffrè, 2004.
Cherubini, G. (ed.), *Protesta e rivolta contadina nell'Italia medievale*, Annali dell'Istituto 'Alcide Cervi' 16 (1994).
Chittolini, G., *Città, comunità e feudi negli stati dell'Italia centro-settentrionale (XIV–XVI secolo)*, Milan: Unicopli, 1996.
Cohn, S. K., *Creating the Florentine State: Peasants and Rebellion, 1348–1434*, Cambridge University Press, 1999.
Comba, R. (ed.), *Storia di Cuneo e del suo territorio. 1198–1799*, Cuneo: Editrice artistica piemontese, 2002.
Cortonesi, A. and F. Viola (eds.), *Le comunità rurali e i loro statuti (secoli XII–XV)*, Rivista storica del Lazio 13–14 (2005–6).
Cozzetto, F., *Città e contado nel Mezzogiorno. La 'grande' università di Cosenza e casali*, I, Rubbettino: Soveria Monnelli, 2005.
Dani, A., *I comuni dello stato di Siena e le loro assemblee (secc. XIV–XVIII). I caratteri di una cultura giuridico-politica*, Siena: Cantagalli, 1998.
Del Tredici, F., 'Comunità, nobili e gentiluomini nel contado di Milano nel Quattrocento', Ph.D. thesis, Università degli studi di Milano, 2009.
Della Misericordia, M., 'I confini della solidarietà. Pratiche e istituzioni caritative in Valtellina nel tardo Medioevo', in L. Chiappa Mauri (ed.), *Contado e città in dialogo. Comuni urbani e comunità rurali nella Lombardia medievale*, Milan: Cisalpino, 2003, 411–89.
  Divenire comunità. Comuni rurali, poteri locali, identità sociali e territoriali in Valtellina e nella montagna lombarda nel tardo Medioevo, Milan: Unicopli, 2006.
  Figure di comunità. Documento notarile, forme della convivenza, riflessione locale sulla vita associata nella montagna lombarda e nella pianura comasca (secoli XIV–XVI), Morbegno: Ad fontes, 2008 (www.adfontes.it/biblioteca/scaffale/notarile/copertina.html).
  'La mediazione giudiziaria dei conflitti sociali alla fine del Medioevo. Tribunali ecclesiastici e resistenza comunitaria in Valtellina', in M. Bellabarba, G. Schwerhoff and A. Zorzi (eds.), *Criminalità e giustizia in Germania e in Italia. Pratiche giudiziarie e linguaggi giuridici tra tardo Medioevo ed età moderna*, Bologna: Il Mulino, 2001, 135–71.

'I nodi della rete. Paesaggio, società e istituzioni a Dalegno e in Valcamonica nel tardo Medioevo', in E. Bressan (ed.), *La magnifica comunità di Dalegno. Dalle origini al XVIII secolo*, Breno: Tipografia camuna, 2009, 81–320.

'"Per non privarci de nostre raxone, li siamo stati desobidienti". Patto, giustizia e resistenza nella cultura politica delle comunità alpine nello stato di Milano (XV secolo)', in C. Nubola and A. Würgler (eds.), *Forme della comunicazione politica in Europa nei secoli XV–XVIII. Suppliche, gravamina, lettere*, Bologna: Il Mulino, 2004, 147–215.

'Principat, communauté et individu au bas Moyen Âge', *Médiévales* 57 (2009), 93–112.

Di Tullio, M., *La ricchezza delle comunità. Guerra risorse, cooperazione nella Geradadda del Cinquecento*, Venezia: Marsilio, 2011.

Favaretto, L., *L'istituzione informale. Il territorio padovano dal Quattrocento al Cinquecento*, Milan: Unicopli, 1998.

Ferrante, C., and A. Mattone, 'Le comunità rurali nel diritto statutario della Sardegna medievale', in Cortonesi and Viola (eds.), *Le comunità rurali*, 133–69.

La formation des communautés d'habitants au Moyen Âge. Perspectives historiographiques, Xanten, June 2003 (http://lamop.univ-paris1.fr/W3/lamopII.Communautes.htm).

Grendi, E., *Il Cervo e la repubblica. Il modello ligure di antico regime*, Turin: Einaudi, 1993.

Guglielmotti, P., *Comunità e territorio. Villaggi del Piemonte medievale*, Rome: Viella, 2001.

Ricerche sull'organizzazione del territorio nella Liguria medievale, Florence: Firenze University Press, 2005).

Lazzarini, I., *Il linguaggio del territorio fra principe e comunità. Il giuramento di fedeltà a Federico Gonzaga (Mantova 1479)*, Florence: Firenze University Press, 2009 (www.storia.unifi.it/_RM/e-book/titoli/Lazzarini.htm).

Mannori, L., *Il sovrano tutore. Pluralismo istituzionale e accentramento amministrativo nel principato dei Medici*, Milan: Giuffrè, 1994.

Massaro, C., *Potere politico e comunità locali nella Puglia tardomedievale*, Lecce: Congedo, 2004.

Ortu, G. G., *Villaggio e poteri signorili in Sardegna. Profilo storico della comunità rurale medievale e moderna*, Rome and Bari: Laterza, 1998.

Ostinelli, P., *Il governo delle anime. Strutture ecclesiastiche nel Bellinzonese e nelle Valli ambrosiane (XIV–XV secolo)*, Locarno: Dadò, 1998.

Per una storia delle comunità (Ricordando i primi anni '80), Este, April 2002 (http://venus.unive.it/riccdst/sdv/saggi/saggi.html).

Pirillo, P., *Creare comunità. Firenze e i centri di nuova fondazione della Toscana medievale*, Rome: Viella, 2007.

Politi, G., 'Rivolte contadine e movimenti comunali. Una tesi', in S. Gasparri, G. Levi and P. Moro (eds.), *Venezia. Itinerari per la storia della città*, Bologna: Il Mulino, 1997, 159–91.

Poloni, A., '*Ista familia de Fine audacissima, presumptuosa et litigiosa ax rixosa*'. *Una lite tra la comunità di Onore e i da Fino nella Val Seriana superiore*

degli anni '60 del Quattrocento, Fino del Monte: Comune di Fino del Monte, 2009.
Scharf, G. P. G., *Borgo San Sepolcro a metà del Quattrocento. Istituzioni e società. 1440–1460*, Florence: Olschki, 2003.
Titone, F., *Governments of the Universitates: Urban Communities of Sicily in the Fourteenth and Fifteenth Centuries*, Turnhout: Brepols, 2009.
Tocci, G., *Le comunità in età moderna. Problemi storiografici e prospettive di ricerca*, Rome: Carocci, 1997.
Torre, A., *Il consumo di devozioni. Religione e comunità nelle campagne dell'Ancien Régime*, Venice: Marsilio, 1995.
Vianello, F., *La politica nella comunità rurale. Bassano e l'Università di Rosà tra ricerca di autonomia e conflitti interni*, Padua: Il Poligrafo, 2004.
Vitolo, G. (ed.), *Città e contado nel Mezzogiorno tra Medioevo ed età moderna*, Salerno: Laveglia, 2005.
  Organizzazione dello spazio e comuni rurali. San Pietro di Polla nei secoli XI–XV, Salerno: Laveglia, 2001.
Wickham, C., *Comunità e clientele nella Toscana del XII secolo. Le origini del comune rurale nella Piana di Lucca*, Rome: Viella, 1995.
Zannini, A., '*L'identità urbana in Toscana*. Fine di una ricerca, inizio di una riflessione', *Società e storia* 23 (2000), 575–97.

14. *Lordships, fiefs and 'small states'* (Federica Cengarle)

Abulafia, D., 'Signorial power in Aragonese southern Italy', in E. Nicholas and N. Terpstra (eds.), *Sociability and Its Discontents: Civil Society, Social Capital, and Their Alternatives in Late Medieval and Early Modern Europe*, Turnhout: Brepols, 2009, 173–92.
Allegrezza, F., *Organizzazione del potere e dinamiche familiari. Gli Orsini dal Duecento agli inizi del Quattrocento*, Rome: Viella, 1998.
Arcangeli, L., *Gentiluomini di Lombardia. Ricerche sull'aristocrazia padana nel Rinascimento*, Milan: Unicopli, 2003.
  'I Pallavicini. Un lignaggio padano tra autonomia signorile e corte principesca', in Gentile and Savy (eds.), *Noblesse*, 29–100.
  'Piccoli signori lombardi e potenze grosse', in A. Gamberini and G. Petralia (eds.), *Linguaggi politici nell'Italia del Rinascimento*, Rome: Viella, 2007, 409–43.
  'Principi, *homines* e "partesani" nel ritorno dei Rossi', in Arcangeli and Gentile (eds.), *Le signorie dei Rossi*, 231–306.
Arcangeli, L., and M. Gentile (eds.), *Le signorie dei Rossi di Parma tra XIV e XVI secolo*, Florence: Firenze University Press, 2007.
Barbero, A., 'Appannaggi, infeudazioni, riacquisti. La politica feudale dei marchesi di Saluzzo nel Quattrocento', in Gentile and Savy (eds.), *Noblesse*, 335–63.
  'Da signoria rurale a feudo. I possedimenti degli Avogadro fra il distretto del comune di Vercelli, la signoria viscontea e lo stato sabaudo', in Cengarle, Chittolini and Varanini (eds.), *Poteri signorili e feudali*, 31–45.

'Principe e nobiltà negli stati sabaudi. Gli Challant in Valle d'Aosta tra XIV e XVI secolo', in C. Mozzarelli (ed.), *'Familia' del principe e famiglia aristocratica*, 2 vols., Rome: Bulzoni, 1988, II, 245–76.

Bazzoli, M., *Il piccolo stato nell'età moderna. Studi su un concetto della politica internazionale tra XVI e XVIII secolo*, Milan: Jaca Book, 1990.

Bettotti, M., *La nobiltà trentina nel Medioevo (metà XII–metà XV secolo)*, Bologna: Il Mulino, 2002.

Bordone, R., G. Castelnuovo and G. M. Varanini, *Le aristocrazie dai signori rurali al patriziato*, Rome and Bari: Laterza, 2004.

Canzian, D., 'Signorie rurali nel territorio trevigiano al tempo della prima dominazione veneziana (1338–1381)', in Cengarle, Chittolini and Varanini (eds.), *Poteri signorili e feudali*, 227–41.

Carocci, S., *Baroni di Roma. Dominazioni signorili e lignaggi aristocratici nel Duecento e nel primo Trecento*, Rome: École française de Rome, 1993.

'Vassalli del papa. Note per la storia della feudalità pontificia (secoli XI–XVI)', in G. Barone, L. Capo and S. Gasparri (eds.), *Studi sul Medioevo per Girolamo Arnaldi*, Rome: Viella, 2001, 55–90.

Castelnuovo, G., 'Omaggio, feudo e signoria in terra sabauda (metà '200–metà '400)', in Cengarle, Chittolini and Varanini (eds.), *Poteri signorili e feudali*, 175–201.

Ufficiali e gentiluomini. La società politica sabauda nel tardo Medioevo, Milan: F. Angeli, 1994.

Cengarle, F., *Feudi e feudatari del duca Filippo Maria Visconti. Repertorio*, Milan: Unicopli, 2007.

'Gerarchie e sfere d'influenza nella pace di Milano del 1420. Il Reggiano tra Filippo Maria Visconti e Niccolò III d'Este', in G. Badini and A. Gamberini (eds.), *Medioevo reggiano. Studi in ricordo di Odoardo Rombaldi*, Milan: F. Angeli, 2007, 306–25.

Immagine di potere e prassi di governo. La politica feudale di Filippo Maria Visconti, Rome: Viella, 2006.

'La riduzione dei diritti feudali di Ludovico I di Saluzzo in un fascicolo di fidelitates prestate a Filippo Maria Visconti (1431–1432)', in R. Comba (ed.), *Ludovico I marchese di Saluzzo. Un principe tra Francia e Italia (1416–1475)*, Cuneo: Saste, 2003, 235–50.

'Vassalli et subditi. Una proposta d'indagine a partire dal caso lombardo (XV–XVI secolo)', *Rechtsgeschichte* 13 (2008), 117–32.

Cengarle, F., G. Chittolini and G. M. Varanini (eds.), *Poteri signorili e feudali nelle campagne dell'Italia settentrionale fra Tre e Quattrocento. Fondamenti di legittimità e forme di esercizio*, Florence: Firenze University Press, 2005.

Chittolini, G., 'Ascesa e declino di piccoli stati signorili (Italia centro-settentrionale, metà Trecento). Alcune note', *Società e Storia* 121 (2008), 455–80.

Città, comunità e feudi negli stati dell'Italia centro-settentrionale (XIV–XVI secolo), Milan: Unicopli, 1996.

La formazione dello stato regionale e le istituzioni del contado, Turin: Einaudi, 1979.

'Guerre, guerricciole e riassetti territoriali in una provincia lombarda di confine. Parma e il parmense, agosto 1447–febbraio 1449', *Società e Storia* 108 (2005), 221–49.

'Signorie rurali e feudi alla fine del Medioevo', in G. Galasso (ed.), *Storia d'Italia*, IV, *Comuni e signorie. Istituzioni, società e lotte per l'egemonia*, Turin: Utet, 1981, 597–676.

(ed.), *La crisi degli ordinamenti comunali e le origini dello stato del Rinascimento*, Bologna: Il Mulino, 1979.

Chittolini, G., and D. Willoweit, *L'organizzazione del territorio in Italia e in Germania. Secoli XIII–XIV*, Bologna: Il Mulino, 1994.

Corrao, P., *Governare un regno. Potere, società e istituzioni in Sicilia fra Trecento e Quattrocento*, Naples: Liguori, 1991.

Covini, M. N., *L'esercito del duca. Organizzazione militare e istituzioni al tempo degli Sforza (1450–1480)*, Rome: Istituto storico italiano per il Medio Evo, 1998.

'In Lomellina nel Quattrocento. Il declino delle stirpi locali e i "feudi accomprati"', in Cengarle, Chittolini and Varanini (eds.), *Poteri signorili e feudali*, 127–74.

Dean, T., 'The dukes of Ferrara and their nobility: notes on language and power', in Gentile and Savy (eds.), *Noblesse*, 364–74.

Land and Power in Late Medieval Ferrara: The Rule of the Este, 1350–1450, Cambridge University Press, 1988.

Del Bo, B., 'Un itinerario signorile nel crepuscolo angioino. I Falletti di Alba', in R. Comba (ed.), *Gli Angiò nell'Italia nord-occidentale (1259–1382)*, Milan: Unicopli, 2006, 313–30.

Uomini e strutture di uno stato feudale. Il marchesato di Monferrato (1418–1483), Milan: LED, 2009.

Del Tredici, F., 'Comunità, nobili e gentiluomini nel contado di Milano del Quattrocento', Ph.D. thesis, Università degli studi di Milano, 2008.

Della Misericordia, M., *La disciplina contrattata. Vescovi e vassalli tra Como e le Alpi nel tardo Medioevo*, Milan: Unicopli, 2000.

'Dal patronato alla mediazione politica. Poteri signorili e comunità rurali nelle Alpi lombarde tra regime cittadino e stato territoriale (XIV–XV secolo)', in Cengarle, Chittolini and Varanini (eds.), *Poteri signorili e feudali*, 203–9.

Divenire comunità. Comuni rurali, poteri locali, identità sociali e territoriali in Valtellina e nella montagna lombarda nel tardo Medioevo, Milan: Unicopli, 2006.

Dondarini, R., G. M. Varanini and M. Venticelli (eds.), *Signori, regimi signorili e statuti nel tardo Medioevo*, Bologna: Patròn editore, 2003.

Folin, M., 'Feudatari, cittadini, gentiluomini. Forme di nobiltà negli stati estensi fra Quattro e Cinquecento', in L. Antonielli, C. Capra and M. Infelise (eds.) *Per Marino Berengo. Studi degli allievi*, Milan: F. Angeli, 2000, 34–75.

'Officiali e feudatari nel sistema politico estense (secoli XV–XVII)', in E. Fregni (ed.), *Poteri signorili, patriziati e centri urbani minori nell'area Estense in antico regime*, Rome: Bulzoni, 1999, 81–120.

Fubini, R., '"Potenze grosse" e piccolo stato nell'Italia del Rinascimento. Consapevolezza della distinzione e dinamica dei poteri', in L. Barletta, F. Cardini and G. Galasso (eds.), *Il piccolo stato. Politica, storia, diplomazia*, San Marino: AIEP, 2003, 91–126.

Galasso, G., *Il Mezzogiorno angioino e aragonese (1266–1494)*, in G. Galasso (ed.), *Storia d'Italia*, XV, *Il Regno di Napoli*, 1, Turin: Utet, 1992.

Gamberini, A., *La città assediata. Poteri e identità politiche a Reggio in età viscontea*, Rome: Viella, 2003.

 Oltre le città. Assetti territoriali e culture aristocratiche nella Lombardia del tardo Medioevo, Rome: Viella, 2009.

 Lo stato visconteo. Linguaggi politici e dinamiche costituzionali, Milan: F. Angeli, 2005.

Gentile, M., '"*Cum li amici et seguaci miei, quali deo gratia non sono puochi*". Un aspetto della costituzione dei piccoli stati signorili del Parmense (XV secolo)', in R. Greci and D. Romagnoli (eds.), *Uno storico e il territorio. Vito Fumagalli e l'Emilia occidentale nel Medioevo*, Bologna: CLUEB, 2005, 125–44.

 'Giustizia, protezione, amicizia. Note sul dominio dei Rossi nel Parmense all'inizio del Quattrocento', in Cengarle, Chittolini and Varanini (eds.), *Poteri signorili e feudali*, 89–104.

 Terra e poteri. Parma e il parmense nel ducato visconteo all'inizio del Quattrocento, Milan: Unicopli, 2001.

Gentile, M., and P. Savy (eds.), *Noblesse et états princiers en Italie et en France au XVe siècle*, Rome: École française de Rome, 2009.

Greci, R., *Parma medievale. Economia e società nel Parmense dal Tre al Quattrocento*, Parma: Battei, 1992.

 'Gli stati minori della Padania: un anacronismo funzionale', in *Storia della società italiana*, VIII, *I secoli del primato italiano. Il Quattrocento*, Milan: Teti, 1988, 203–32.

Jones, P., *Economia e società nell'Italia medievale. La leggenda della borghesia*, in *Storia d'Italia*, Annali, I, *Dal feudalesimo al capitalismo*, Turin: Einaudi, 1979, 187–372.

Lazzarini, I., 'Un'Italia di feudi e di città? Alcune considerazioni attorno al caso ferrarese', *Società e Storia* 51 (1991), 125–52.

Maire Vigueur, J.-C., *Comuni e signorie in Umbria, Marche e Lazio*, in G. Galasso (ed.), *Storia d'Italia*, VII/2, *Comuni e signorie nell'Italia nord-orientale e centrale*, Turin: Utet, 1987, 323–606.

Marrone, A., *Repertorio della feudalità siciliana, 1282–1390*, Palermo: Mediterranea (Quaderni 1), 2006.

Massaro, C., *Potere politico e comunità locali nella Puglia tardomedievale*, Galatina: Congedo, 2004.

Mineo, E. I., *Nobiltà di stato. Famiglie e identità aristocratiche nel tardo Medioevo. La Sicilia*, Rome: Donzelli, 2001.

Morelli, S., 'Tra continuità e trasformazioni. Su alcuni aspetti del principato di Taranto alla metà del XV secolo', *Società e Storia* 73 (1996), 487–525.

Nico Ottaviani, M. G., '*Statuta sie leges municipales ordinatae a Domino et Patrono*. Signorie e statuti in Umbria nei secoli XIV–XVI', in Dondarini, Varanini and Venticelli (eds.), *Signori, regimi signorili*, 289–306.

Pirillo, P., 'Controllare e proteggere. L'organizzazione della difesa del contado fiorentino tra esigenze locali e centralizzazione', in É. Crouzet-Pavan (ed.), *Pouvoir et édilité. Les grands chantiers dans l'Italie communale et seigneuriale*, Rome: École française de Rome, 2003, 439–59.

'La Romagna fiorentina', in M. G. Muzzarelli and A. Campanini (eds.), *Castelli medioevali e neo-medievali in Emilia-Romagna*, Bologna: CLUEB, 2006, 191–6.

'Signorie dell'Appennino tra Toscana ed Emilia-Romagna alla fine del Medioevo', in Cengarle, Chittolini and Varanini (eds.), *Poteri signorili e feudali*, 211–26.

Un principato territoriale nel regno di Napoli? Gli Orsini del Balzo principi di Taranto (1399–1463), Atti del convegno di studi (Lecce, 20–2 October 2009), forthcoming.

Raviola, B. A., *L'Europa dei piccoli stati. Dalla prima età moderna al declino dell'antico regime*, Rome: Carocci, 2008.

Regni, C., 'I Gabrielli di Gubbio. Una precoce esperienza signorile umbra? Prime riflessioni', in M. Donnini and E. Menestò (eds.), *Studi sull'Umbria medievale e umanistica. Studi in onore di Olga Marinelli, Pier Lorenzo Meloni, Ugolino Nicolini*, Spoleto: Cisam, 2000, 397–417.

Shaw, C., *The Political Role of the Orsini Family from Sixtus IV to Clement VII: Barons and Factions in the Papal States*, Rome: Istituto storico italiano per il Medio Evo, 2007.

'The Roman barons and the popes', in Gentile and Savy (eds.), *Noblesse*, 101–24.

Sisto, A., *Banchieri-feudatari subalpini nei secoli XII–XVI*, Turin: Giappichelli, 1963.

Somaini, F., 'Le *declarationes colligatorum, adherentium et recomendatorum* delle potenze italiane nei trattati della Lega italica del 1454–1455. Una lettura geopolitica (e alcune proposte cartografiche) sull'Italia di metà Quattrocento', in *Il sistema degli stati italiani e la ricerca dell'equilibrio politico. La pace di Lodi del 1454*, Atti del convegno Lodi, 27–28 febbraio 2004, forthcoming.

'Una storia spezzata. La carriera ecclesiastica di Bernardo Rossi tra il "piccolo stato", la corte sforzesca, la curia romana e il "sistema degli stati italiani"', in Arcangeli and Gentile (eds.), *Le signorie dei Rossi*, 109–86.

Somaini, F., and B. Vetere (eds.), *I domini del principe di Taranto in età orsiniana (1399–1463). Geografie e linguaggi politici alla fine del Medioevo*, Galatina: Congedo, 2009.

Vallone, G., *Feudi e città. Studi di storia giuridica e istituzionale pugliese*, Galatina: Congedo, 1993.

Istituzioni feudali dell'Italia meridionale tra Medioevo ed antico regime. L'area salentina, Rome: Viella, 1999.

Varanini, G. M., 'Aristocrazie e poteri nell'Italia centro-settentrionale dalla crisi comunale alle guerre d'Italia', in Bordone, Castelnuovo and Varanini, *Le aristocrazie*, 121–93.

'I Pio di Carpi e la signoria carpigiana nel sistema politico italiano (1336–1500 ca.)', in M. Cattini and A. M. Ori (eds.), *Storia di Carpi*, II, *La città ed il territorio dai Pio agli Estensi (secc. XIV–XVIII)*, Modena: Mucchi, 2009, 3–24.

Qualche riflessione conclusiva, in Cengarle, Chittolini and Varanini (eds.), *Poteri signorili e feudali*, 249–63.

Visceglia, M. A., *Territorio, feudo e potere locale. Terra d'Otranto tra Medioevo ed età moderna*, Naples: Guida, 1988.
Vitale, G., *Elite burocratica e famiglia. Dinamiche nobiliari e processi di costruzione statale nella Napoli angioino-aragonese*, Naples: Liguori, 2003.
Vitolo, G., 'Linguaggi e forme del conflitto politico nel Mezzogiorno angioino-aragonese', in G. Petti Balbi and G. Vitolo (eds.), *Linguaggi e pratiche del potere*, Salerno: Laveglia, 2007, 41–69.
Zacchigna, M., 'L'inclinazione signorile delle aristocrazie friulane nello sviluppo della normativa locale (secoli XIV–XV)', in Dondarini, Varanini and Venticelli (eds.), *Signori, regimi signorili*, 191–203.
Zamperetti, S., *I piccoli principi. Signorie locali, feudi e comunità soggette nello stato regionale veneto dall'espansione territoriale ai primi decenni del '600*, Venice: Il Cardo, 1991.

15. *Factions and parties: problems and perspectives* (Marco Gentile)

Abbondanza, R., 'Franco Gaeta, Il vescovo Pietro Barozzi e il trattato *De factionibus extinguendis*', *Bollettino dell'Istituto di Storia della Società e dello Stato Veneziano* 1 (1959), 241–56.
Andreozzi, D., *Nascita di un disordine. Una famiglia signorile e una valle piacentina tra XV e XVI secolo*, Milan: Unicopli, 1993.
Ansell, C., and J. Padgett, 'Robust action and the rise of the Medici, 1400–1434', *American Journal of Sociology* 98 (1993), 1259–1319.
Arcangeli, L., 'Appunti su guelfi e ghibellini in Lombardia nelle prime guerre d'Italia (1494–1530)', in Gentile (ed.), *Guelfi e ghibellini*, 391–472.
  'Un'aristocrazia territoriale al femminile. Due o tre cose su Laura Pallavicini Sanvitale e le contesse vedove nel parmense', in Arcangeli and Peyronel (eds.), *Donne di Potere*, 595–654.
  Gentiluomini di Lombardia. Ricerche sull'aristocrazia padana nel Rinascimento, Milan: Unicopli, 2003.
  'Tra Milano e Roma. Esperienze politiche nella Parma del primo Cinquecento', in G. Periti (ed.), *Emilia e Marche nel Rinascimento. L'identità visiva della 'periferia'*, Azzano S. Paolo: Bolis, 2005, 89–111.
  '*Les Ytaulx qui désirent franchise*. Invasione francese, permanenze e mutamenti nell'Italia del primo Cinquecento', *Atti e Memorie della Società Savonese di Storia Patria* 44 (2008), 137–54.
Arcangeli, L., and S. Peyronel (eds.), *Donne di potere nel Rinascimento*, Rome: Viella, 2008.
Artifoni, E., *Salvemini e il Medioevo. Storici italiani fra Otto e Novecento*, Naples: Liguori, 1990.
Ascheri, M., 'Siena nel Quattrocento. Una riconsiderazione', in K. Christiansen, L. B. Kanter and C. B. Strehlke (eds.), *La pittura senese nel Rinascimento 1420–1500*, Siena: Monte dei Paschi di Siena, 1989, xix–lvi.
Ascheri, M., and P. Pertici, 'La situazione politica senese del secondo Quattrocento', in *La Toscana al tempo di Lorenzo il Magnifico*, III, 995–1012.

Baja Guarienti, C., 'Le "guerre civili" di Reggio. Una faida tra guelfi e ghibellini all'inizio del XVI secolo', in G. Bebbi, *Reggio nel Cinquecento. Le guerre civili tra Guelfi e Ghibellini del secolo XVI*, Reggio Emilia: Antiche Porte, 2007, 11–61.
Baron, H., *The Crisis of the Early Italian Renaissance*, Princeton University Press, 1966.
Bellosta, R., 'Le "squadre" in consiglio. Assemblee cittadine ed élite di governo urbana a Piacenza nella seconda metà del Quattrocento tra divisioni di parte ed ingerenze ducali', *Nuova Rivista Storica* 87 (2003), 1–54.
Benigno, F., '*Reductio ad unum*. Il fascino discreto dell'assolutismo', *Storica* 29 (2004), 79–110.
Berengo, M., *L'Europa delle città. Il volto della società urbana europea tra Medioevo ed età moderna*, Turin: Einaudi, 1999.
Bianco, F., *1511. La 'crudel zobia grassa'. Rivolte contadine e faide nobiliari in Friuli tra '400 e '500*, Pordenone: Biblioteca dell'Immagine, 1995.
Blok, A., *The Mafia of a Sicilian Village: 1860–1960*, Oxford: Blackwell, 1974.
Boissevain, J., *Faction, Parties and Politics in a Maltese Village*, in Schmidt, Scott, Landé and Guasti (eds.), *Friends, Followers and Factions*, 279–87.
Bombardini, S., *Il diavolo nel tamburo. Lotte e tragedie nella storia di una città romagnola e nel diario di un guelfo imolese (1500–1525)*, Imola: Santerno Edizioni, 1982.
Bosco, J., 'Faction versus ideology: mobilization strategies in Taiwan's elections', *China Quarterly* 137 (1994), 28–62.
Briquet, J., 'Clientelismo e processi politici', *Quaderni storici* 97 (1988), 9–30.
Brown, A., *The Medici in Florence: The Exercise and Language of Power*, Perth: University of Western Australia Press, 1992.
Brucker, G., *The Civic World of Early Renaissance Florence*, Princeton University Press, 1977.
Bruni, F., *La città divisa. Le parti e il bene comune da Dante a Guicciardini*, Bologna: Il Mulino, 2003.
Casanova, C., 'Ai vertici della città', in A. Prosperi (ed.), *Storia di Cesena*, III, *La dominazione pontificia (secoli XVI–XVII–XVIII)*. Rimini: Bruno Ghigi, 1989, 63–100.
Comunità e governo pontificio in Romagna in età moderna, Bologna: CLUEB, 1981.
'Da "parziale" a "buono ecclesiastico". Continuità o rottura?', in G. Tocci (ed.), *Persistenze feudali e autonomie comunitative in stati padani fra Cinque e Settecento*, Bologna: CLUEB, 1988, 246–61.
'Mogli e vedove di condottieri in area padana fra Quattro e Cinquecento', in Arcangeli and Peyronel (eds.), *Donne di potere*, 513–34.
'Potere delle grandi famiglie e forme di governo', in L. Gambi (ed.), *Storia di Ravenna*, IV, Venice: Marsilio, 1994, 39–129.
Cavalieri, P., *'Qui sunt guelfi et partiales nostri'. Comunità, patriziato e fazioni a Bergamo fra XV e XVI secolo*, Milan: Unicopli, 2008.
Chittolini, G., A. Molho and P. Schiera (eds.), *Origini dello stato. Processi di formazione statale in Italia fra Medioevo ed età moderna*, Bologna: Il Mulino, 1994.

Commynes, P. D., *Mémoires* (Joël Blanchard, ed.), Paris: Le Livre de Poche, 2001.
Connell, W. J., *La città dei crucci. Fazioni e clientele in uno stato repubblicano del '400*, Florence: Nuova Toscana Editrice, 2000.
Connell, W. J., and A. Zorzi (eds.), *Florentine Tuscany: Structures and Practices of Power*, Cambridge University Press, 2000.
Corrao, P., *Governare un regno. Potere, società e istituzioni in Sicilia fra Trecento e Quattrocento*, Naples: Liguori, 1991.
Dedola, M., '"Tener Pistoia con le parti". Governo fiorentino e fazioni pistoiesi all'inizio del '500', *Ricerche Storiche* 22 (1992), 239–59.
Delille, G., 'Marriage, faction and conflict in sixteenth-century Italy: an example and a few questions', in T. Dean and K. J. P. Lowe (eds.), *Marriage in Italy, 1300–1650*, Cambridge University Press, 1998, 155–73.
Della Misericordia, M., 'La "coda" dei gentiluomini. Fazioni, mediazione politica, clientelismo nello stato territoriale. Il caso della montagna lombarda durante il dominio sforzesco (XV secolo)', in Gentile (ed.), *Guelfi e ghibellini*, 275–389.
Divenire comunità. Comuni rurali, poteri locali, identità sociali e territoriali in Valtellina e nella montagna lombarda del tardo Medioevo, Milan: Unicopli, 2006.
'Dividersi per governarsi. Fazioni, famiglie aristocratiche e comuni in Valtellina in età viscontea', *Società e Storia* 86 (1999), 715–66.
Dessì, R. M., 'I nomi dei guelfi e ghibellini da Carlo I d'Angiò a Petrarca', in Gentile (ed.), *Guelfi e ghibellini*, 3–78.
Ferente, S., 'Guelphs! Factions, liberty and sovereignty: inquiries about the Quattrocento', *History of Political Thought* 28, 4 (2007), 571–98.
La sfortuna di Jacopo Piccinino. Storia dei bracceschi in Italia 1423–1465, Florence: Olschki, 2005.
'Gli ultimi guelfi. Passioni e identità politiche nell'Italia del secondo Quattrocento', Ph.D. thesis, European University Institute, 2007.
Fubini, R., *Italia quattrocentesca. Politica e diplomazia nell'età di Lorenzo il Magnifico*, Milan: F. Angeli, 2002.
L'umanesimo italiano e i suoi storici. Origini rinascimentali – critica moderna, Milan: F. Angeli, 2001.
Gamberini, A., *La città assediata. Poteri e identità politiche a Reggio in età viscontea*, Rome: Viella, 2002.
Oltre le città. Assetti territoriali e culture aristocratiche nella Lombardia del tardo Medioevo, Rome: Viella, 2009.
Lo stato visconteo. Linguaggi politici e dinamiche costituzionali, Milan: F. Angeli, 2005.
Gardi, A., *Lo stato in provincia. L'amministrazione della legazione di Bologna durante il regno di Sisto V (1585–1590)*, Bologna: Istituto per la storia di Bologna, 1994.
Gentile, M., 'Bartolo in pratica. Appunti su identità politica e procedura giudiziaria nel ducato di Milano alla fine del Quattrocento', *Rivista internazionale di Diritto Comune* 18 (2007), 231–51.
'Casato e fazione nella Lombardia del Quattrocento. Il caso di Parma', in A. Bellavitis and I. Chabot (eds.), *Famiglie e poteri in Italia tra Medioevo ed età moderna*, Rome: École française de Rome, 2009, 151–87.

'Discorsi sulle fazioni, discorsi delle fazioni. "Parole e demonstratione partiale" nella Lombardia del secondo Quattrocento', in A. Gamberini and G. Petralia (eds.), *Linguaggi politici nell'Italia del Rinascimento*, Rome: Viella, 2007, 381–408.

Fazioni al governo. Politica e società a Parma nel Quattrocento, Rome: Viella, 2009.

'From commune to regional state: political experiments in fourteenth-century Cremona', in J. E. Law and B. Paton (eds.), *Communes and Despots in Medieval and Renaissance Italy*, Farnham, UK: Ashgate, 2010, 91–104.

'Guelfi, ghibellini, Rinascimento. Nota introduttiva', in Gentile (ed.), *Guelfi e ghibellini*, vii–xxv.

(ed.) *Guelfi e ghibellini nell'Italia del Rinascimento*, Rome: Viella, 2005.

'"*Postquam malignitates temporum hec nobis dedere nomina* ...". Fazioni, idiomi politici e pratiche di governo nella tarda età viscontea', in Gentile (ed.), *Guelfi e ghibellini*, 249–74.

Terra e poteri. Parma e il parmense nel ducato visconteo all'inizio del Quattrocento, Milan: Unicopli, 2001.

Gilli, P., 'Guelfisme et mémoire urbaine. Un discours inédit de Coluccio Salutati au cardinal Philippe d'Alençon (Juin 1381)', in J. Chiffoleau and P. Boucheron, *Réligion et société urbaine au Moyen Âge. Mélanges offerts à Jean Biget*, Paris: Publications de la Sorbonne, 2000, 499–509.

Green, D., B. Palmquist and E. Schickler, *Partisan Hearts and Minds: Political Parties and the Social Identities of Voters*, New Haven and London: Yale University Press, 2002.

Heers, J., *Parties and Political Life in the Medieval West*, Amsterdam: North-Holland, 1977.

Hespanha, A. M., *Introduzione alla storia del diritto europeo*, Bologna: Il Mulino, 1999.

Isaacs, A. K., 'Cardinali e "spalagrembi". Sulla vita politica a Siena fra il 1480 e il 1487', in *La Toscana al tempo di Lorenzo il Magnifico*, III, 1013–50.

'Cesena agli inizi del Cinquecento', in A. Prosperi (ed.), *Storia di Cesena*, III, *La dominazione pontificia (secoli XVI–XVII–XVIII)*, Rimini: Bruno Ghigi, 1989, 17–61.

Kent, D., *The Rise of the Medici: Faction in Florence, 1426–1434*, Oxford University Press, 1978.

Landé, C., 'Group politics and dyadic politics: notes for a theory', in Schmidt, Scott, Landé and Guasti (eds.), *Friends, Followers and Factions*, 506–10.

Law, J. E., 'Guelfs and Ghibellines in Belluno, c. 1400', in Gentile (ed.), *Guelfi e ghibellini*, 603–24.

Lewellen, T. C., *Antropologia Politica*, Bologna: Il Mulino, 1987 (1983).

Mainoni, P., *Le radici della discordia. Ricerche sulla fiscalità a Bergamo tra XIII e XV secolo*, Milan: Unicopli, 1997.

March, J. G, and J. P. Olsen, *Rediscovering Institutions: The Organizational Basis of Politics*, New York: Free Press, 1989.

Mascioli, P., *Viterbo nel Quattrocento. Politica, istituzione, poteri nella periferia pontificia*, Rome: Vecchiarelli, 2004.

Mazzoni, V., 'Dalla lotta di parte al governo delle fazioni. I guelfi e i ghibellini del territorio fiorentino nel Trecento', *Archivio Storico Italiano* 160 (2002), 455–513.

Merici, G., 'Luigi Avogadro. Un signore e un feudo nella congiura antifrancese del 1512', *Civiltà Bresciana* 3–4 (2009), 137–81.

Milner, S. J., 'Rubrics and requests: statutory division and supra-communal clientage in Pistoia', in Connell and Zorzi (eds.), *Florentine Tuscany*, 312–32.

Mineo, E. I., *Nobiltà di stato. Famiglie e identità aristocratiche nel tardo Medioevo. La Sicilia*, Rome: Donzelli, 2001.

Muir, E., *Mad Blood Stirring: Vendetta and Factions in Friuli During the Renaissance*, Baltimore and London: Johns Hopkins University Press, 1993.

Musso, R., 'I "colori" delle Riviere. Fazioni politiche e familiari a Genova e nel suo dominio tra XV e XVI secolo', in Gentile (ed.), *Guelfi e ghibellini*, 523–62.

Najemy, J. M., 'Politics, class and patronage in twentieth-century Italian Renaissance historiography', in A. J. Grieco, M. Rocke and F. Gioffredi Superbi (eds.), *The Italian Renaissance in the Twentieth Century*, Florence: Olschki, 2002, 119–36.

Nicholas, R. W., *Factions: A Comparative Analysis*, in Schmidt, Scott, Landé and Guasti (eds.), *Friends, Followers and Factions*, 55–73.

Ottokar, N., *Il comune di Firenze alla fine del dugento*, E. Sestan (ed.), Turin: Einaudi, 1962.

Pacini, A., 'La tirannia delle fazioni e la repubblica dei ceti. Vita politica e istituzioni a Genova tra Quattro e Cinquecento', *Annali dell'Istituto Storico Italo-Germanico in Trento* 18 (1992), 57–119.

Pagnoni, F., '"Il trattato che fessemo cum la Illustrissima Signoria". Gian Giacomo Martinengo e la congiura antifrancese del 1512 a Brescia', *Civiltà Bresciana* 3–4 (2009), 97–136.

Palumbo, B., 'Scuola, scala, appartenenza. Problemi di identità tra storia e antropologia', in J. Revel (ed.), *Giochi di scala. La microstoria alla prova dell'esperienza*, Rome: Viella, 2006, 251–300.

Partner, P., 'Florence and the papacy in the earlier fifteenth century', in N. Rubinstein (ed.), *Florentine Studies: Politics and Society in Renaissance Florence*, Evanston, IL: Northwestern University Press, 1968, 381–402.

Pertici, P., 'Uno sguardo in avanti. Il soggiorno di Sigismondo di Lussemburgo e le ultime manifestazioni di ghibellinismo a Siena', in G. Piccinni (ed.), *Fedeltà ghibellina, affari guelfi. Saggi e rilettura intorno alla storia di Siena nel Trecento*, Pisa: Pacini, 2008, 617–49.

Quaglioni, D., *Politica e diritto nel Trecento italiano. Il 'De tyranno' di Bartolo da Sassoferrato (1314–1357)*, Florence: Olschki, 1983.

Raggio, O., *Faide e parentele. Lo stato genovese visto dalla Fontanabuona*, Turin: Einaudi, 1990.

Rehberg, A., *Clientele e fazioni nell'azione politica di Cola di Rienzo*, Rome: Union Printing, 2004.

Rokkan, S., *State Formation, Nation-Building and Mass Politics in Europe: The Theory of Stein Rokkan, Based on His Collected Works*, P. Flora, S. Kuhnle and D. Urwin (eds.), Oxford University Press, 1999.

Salvemini, G., *Magnati e popolani in Firenze dal 1280 al 1295. Seguito da La dignità cavalleresca nel Comune di Firenze*, E. Sestan (ed.), Turin: Einaudi, 1960.
Schiera, P., 'Il *Buongoverno* melancolico di Ambrogio Lorenzetti e la "costituzionale faziosità" della città', *Scienza and Politica* 34 (2006), 93–108.
Schmidt, S. W., J. C. Scott, C. Landé and L. Guasti (eds.), *Friends, Followers and Factions: A Reader in Political Clientelism*, Berkeley, Los Angeles and London: University of California Press, 1977.
Serio, A., *Una gloriosa sconfitta. I Colonna tra papato e impero nella prima età moderna*, Rome: Viella, 2008.
Shaw, C., 'Bartolomea Campofregoso: a woman's claim to power in fifteenth-century Genoa', in Arcangeli and Peyronel (eds.), *Donne di potere*, 465–79.
  'Counsel and consent in fifteenth-century Genoa', *English Historical Review* 116 (2001), 834–62.
  Popular Government and Oligarchy in Renaissance Italy, Leiden: Brill, 2006.
  The Political Role of the Orsini Family from Sixtus IV to Clement VII: Barons and Factions in the Papal States, Rome: Istituto storico italiano per il Medio Evo, 2007.
  'Principles and practice in the civic government of fifteenth-century Genoa', *Renaissance Quarterly* 58 (2005), 45–90.
  'The Roman barons and the Guelf and Ghibelline factions in the papal states', in Gentile (ed.), *Guelfi e ghibellini*, 475–94.
  'The Roman barons and the security of the papal states', in M. Del Treppo (ed.), *Condottieri e uomini d'arme nell'Italia del Rinascimento*, Naples: Liguori, 2001, 311–25.
Somaini, F., 'Il binomio imperfetto. Alcune osservazioni su guelfi e ghibellini a Milano in età visconteo-sforzesca', in Gentile (ed.), *Guelfi e ghibellini*, 131–215.
Spruyt, H., *The Sovereign State and Its Competitors*, Princeton University Press, 1994.
Tabacco, G., *Egemonie sociali e strutture del potere nel Medioevo italiano*, Turin: Einaudi, 1979.
Taviani, C., *Superba discordia. Guerra, rivolta e pacificazione nella Genova di primo Cinquecento*, Rome: Viella, 2008.
Titone, F., *Governments of the Universitates: Urban Communities of Sicily in the Fourteenth and Fifteenth Centuries*, Turnhout: Brepols, 2009.
Torre, A., 'Faide, fazioni e partiti, ovvero la ridefinizione della politica nei feudi imperiali delle Langhe tra Sei e Settecento', *Quaderni storici* 63 (1986), 775–810.
La Toscana al tempo di Lorenzo il Magnifico. Politica economia cultura arte, 3 vols., Pisa: Pacini, 1996.
Valeri, N., *La libertà e la pace. Orientamenti politici del rinascimento italiano*, Turin: Società Subalpina Editrice, 1942.
Varanini, G. M., 'Nelle città della Marca trevigiana. Dalle fazioni al patriziato (secoli XIII–XV)', in Gentile (ed.), *Guelfi e ghibellini*, 563–602.

Visceglia, M. A., 'Farsi imperiale. Faide familiari e identità politiche a Roma nel primo Cinquecento', in F. Cantù and M. A. Visceglia (eds.), *L'Italia di Carlo V. Guerra, religione e politica nel primo Cinquecento*, Rome: Viella, 2003, 477–508.

Vitolo, G., '*In palatio communis*. Nuovi e vecchi temi della storiografia sulle città del Mezzogiorno medievale', in G. Chittolini, G. Petti Balbi and G. Vitolo (eds.), *Città e territori nell'Italia del Medioevo. Studi in onore di Gabriella Rossetti*, Naples: Liguori, 2007, 243–83.

'Linguaggi e forme del conflitto politico nel Mezzogiorno angioino-aragonese', in G. Petti Balbi and G. Vitolo (eds.), *Linguaggi e pratiche del potere*, Salerno: Laveglia, 2007, 41–69.

Zorzi, A., 'I conflitti nell'Italia comunale. Riflessioni sullo stato degli studi e sulle prospettive di ricerca', in Zorzi (ed.), *Conflitti, paci e vendette nell'Italia comunale*, Florence: Firenze University Press, 2009, 7–41.

'*Fracta est civitas magna in tres partes*. Conflitto e costituzione nell'Italia comunale', *Scienza and Politica* 39 (2008), 61–87.

'The "material constitution" of the Florentine dominion', in Connell and Zorzi (eds.), *Florentine Tuscany*, 6–31.

16. *States, orders and social distinction* (E. Igor Mineo)

Arcangeli, L., *Gentiluomini di Lombardia. Ricerche sull'aristocrazia padana nel Rinascimento*, Milan: Unicopli, 2003.

Besozzi, L., 'La "matricula" delle famiglie nobili di Milano e Carlo Borromeo', *Archivio storico lombardo* 110 (1984), 273–330.

Bordone, R., 'L'aristocrazia territoriale tra impero e città', in Bordone, Castelnuovo and Varanini, *Le aristocrazie*, 1–36.

Bordone, R., G. Castelnuovo and G. M. Varanini, *Le aristocrazie dai signori rurali al patriziato*, Rome and Bari: Laterza, 2004.

Bowsky, W. M., *A Medieval Italian Commune: Siena Under the Nine, 1287–1355*, Berkeley: University of California Press, 1981.

Cammarosano, P., 'Élites sociales et institutions politiques des villes libres en Italie de la fin du XIIe au début du XIVe siècle', in *Les élites urbaines au Moyen Âge*, Rome: Ecole française de Rome, 1997, 193–200.

Carocci, S., 'Una nobiltà bipartita. Rappresentazioni sociali e lignaggi preminenti a Roma nel Duecento e nella prima metà del Trecento', *Bullettino dell'Istituto Storico Italiano per il Medio Evo* 95 (1989), 1–52.

Castelnuovo, G., 'L'identità politica delle nobiltà cittadine', in Bordone, Castelnuovo and Varanini, *Le aristocrazie*, 197–243.

Ufficiali e gentiluomini. La società politica sabauda nel tardo Medioevo, Milan: F. Angeli, 1994.

'Vivre dans l'ambiguïté. Être noble dans la cité communale du XIVe siècle', in A. Bellavitis and I. Chabot (eds.), *Famiglie e poteri in Italia tra Medioevo ed età moderna*, Rome: Ecole française de Rome, 2009, 95–116.

I ceti dirigenti nella Toscana del Quattrocento, Monte Oriolo (Impruneta): F. Papafava, 1987.

Chojnacki, S., 'La formazione della nobiltà dopo la Serrata', in *Storia di Venezia*, III, *La formazione dello stato patrizio*, Rome: Istituto dell'Enciclopedia Italiana, 1998, 641–728.

Collavini, S., *'Honorabilis domus et spetiosissimus comitatus' gli Aldobrandeschi da 'conti' a 'principi territoriali' (secoli IX–XIII)*, Pisa: ETS, 1998.

De Vio, *Felicis et fidelissimae urbis panormitanae selecta aliquot privilegia*, Palermo, 1706.

Della Misericordia, M., *Divenire comunità. Comuni rurali, poteri locali, identità sociali e territoriali in Valtellina e nella montagna lombarda nel tardo Medioevo*, Milan: Unicopli, 2006.

Donati, C., *L'idea di nobiltà in Italia. Secoli XIV–XVIII*, Rome and Bari: Laterza, 1988.

Epstein, S. R., *An Island for Itself: Economic Development and Social Change in Late Medieval Sicily*, Cambridge University Press, 1992.

Fasoli, G., and Q. Sella, *Statuti di Bologna dell'anno 1288*, Rome, 1937.

Gaudenzi, A. (ed.), *Statuti delle società del Popolo di Bologna*, II, *Società delle Arti*, Rome, 1896.

Gentile, M., 'Aristocrazia signorile e costituzione del ducato visconteo-sforzesco', in M. Gentile and P. Savy (eds.), *Noblesse et états princiers en Italie et en France au XVe siècle*, Rome: École française de Rome, 2009, 125–55.

Gilli, P., *La noblesse du droit. Débats et controverses sur la culture juridique et le rôle des juristes dans l'Italie médiévale. XIIe–XVe siècles*, Paris: Honoré Champion, 2003.

Grubb, J., 'Patriziato, nobiltà, legittimazione: con particolare riguardo al Veneto', in G. Ortalli and M. Knapton (eds.), *Istituzioni società e potere nella Marca Trevigiana e veronese (secoli XIII–XV). Sulle tracce di G. B. Verci*, Rome: Istituto storico italiano per il Medio Evo, 1988, 235–51.

Jones, P., *The Italian City-State: From Commune to Signoria*, Oxford University Press, 1997.

Klapisch-Zuber, C., 'Kinship and politics in fourteenth-century Florence', in D. I. Kertzer and R. Saller (eds.), *The Family in Italy from Antiquity to the Present*, New Haven and London: Yale University Press, 1991, 208–28.

Retour à la cité. Les magnats de Florence, 1343–1434, Paris: EHESS, 2006.

La Mantia, V., *Antiche consuetudini delle città di Sicilia*, Palermo, 1900.

Magnati e popolani nell'Italia comunale, Pistoia: Centro italiano di studi di storia e di arte, 1997.

Maire Vigueur, J.-C., *Cavaliers et citoyens. Guerre, conflits et société dans l'Italie communale, XIIe–XIIIe siècles*, Paris: Éditions de l'École des hautes études en sciences sociales, 2003.

Milani, G., *L'esclusione dal comune. Conflitti e bandi politici a Bologna e in altre città italiane tra XII e XIV secolo*, Rome: Istituto storico italiano per il Medio Evo, 2003.

Mineo, E. I., 'Morte e aristocrazia in Italia nel tardo Medioevo. Alcuni problemi', in F. Salvestrini, G. M. Varanini and A. Zangarini (eds.), *La morte e i suoi riti in Italia tra Medioevo e prima età moderna*, Florence: Firenze University Press, 2007, 153–80.

Nobiltà di stato. Famiglie e identità aristocratiche nel tardo Medioevo. La Sicilia, Rome: Donzelli, 2001.

'Nobiltà romane e nobiltà italiane, 1300–1500' in *La nobiltà romana nel Medioevo*, Rome: Ecole française de Rome, 2006, 43–70.

Najemy, J. M., 'Civic humanism and Florentine politics', in J. Hankins (ed.), *Renaissance Civic Humanism: Reappraisals and Reflections*, Cambridge University Press, 2000, 75–104.

'The dialogue of power in Florentine politics', in A. Molho, K. Raaflaub and J. Emlen (eds.), *City-States in Classical Antiquity and Medieval Italy: Athens and Rome, Florence and Venice*, Stuttgart: Franz Steiner Verlag, 1991, 269–88.

A History of Florence 1200–1575, Oxford: Blackwell, 2006.

Palmieri, M., *Vita civile*, G. Belloni (ed.), Florence: Sansoni, 1982.

Salvemini, B., 'Le "impossibili tavole dei ranghi". La costruzione sociale del territorio del principe (Italia, Francia ed Inghilterra, XV–XVIII secolo)', in B. Salvemini, *Il territorio sghembo. Forme e dinamiche degli spazi umani in età moderna. Sondaggi e letture*, Bari: Edipuglia, 2006, 311–52.

Schnerb-Lièvre, M., and G. Giordanengo, 'Le songe de Vergier et le traité des dignités de Bartole, source des chapitres sur la noblesse', *Romania* 110 (1989), 214–30.

Shaw, C., *Popular Government and Oligarchy in Renaissance Italy*, Leiden: Brill, 2006.

Statuti del comune di Padova dal secolo XII all'anno 1285, Padua, 1873.

Sznura, F. (ed.), *Antica possessione con belli costumi. Due giornate di studio su Lapo da Castiglionchio il Vecchio*, Florence: Aska, 2005.

Titone, F., *Governments of the* Universitates*: Urban Communities of Sicily in the Fourteenth and Fifteenth Centuries*, Turnhout: Brepols, 2009.

'Il tumulto popularis del 1450. Conflitto politico e società urbana a Palermo', *Archivio Storico Italiano* 163 (2005), 43–86.

Todeschini, G., *Visibilmente crudeli. Malviventi, persone sospette e gente qualunque dal Medioevo all'età moderna*, Bologna: Il Mulino, 2007.

Varanini, G. M., 'Aristocrazie e poteri nell'Italia centro-settentrionale dalla crisi comunale alle guerre d'Italia', in Bordone, Castelnuovo and Varanini, *Le aristocrazie*, 121–93.

Vitale, G., *Elite burocratica e famiglia. Dinamiche nobiliari e processi di costruzione statale nella Napoli angioino-aragonese*, Naples: Liguori, 2003.

17. *Women and the state* (Serena Ferente)

Albini, G., *Carità e governo delle povertà. Secoli XII–XV*, Milan: Unicopli, 2002.

Arcangeli, L., 'Un'aristocrazia territoriale al femminile. Due o tre cose su Laura Pallavicini Sanvitale e le contesse vedove del parmense', in Arcangeli and Peyronel (eds.), *Donne di potere*, 595–654.

'Ragioni politiche della disciplina monastica. Il caso di Parma tra Quattro e Cinquecento', in G. Zarri (ed.), *Donna, disciplina, creanza cristiana dal XV al XVI secolo*, Rome: Edizioni di Storia e Letteratura, 1996, 165–87.

Arcangeli, L., and S. Peyronel (eds.), *Donne di potere nel Rinascimento*, Rome: Viella, 2008.
Bellavitis, A., *Identité, mariage, mobilité sociale. Citoyennes et citoyens à Venise au XVIe siècle*, Rome: École française de Rome, 2001.
Bellavitis, A., and I. Chabot (eds.), *Famiglie e poteri in Italia tra Medioevo ed età moderna*, Rome: École française de Rome, 2009.
Bellomo, M., *Ricerche sui rapporti patrimoniali tra coniugi*, Milan: Giuffré, 1961.
Bestor, J., 'Bastardy and legitimacy in the formation of a regional state in Italy: the Estense succession', *Comparative Studies in Society and History* 38 (1996), 549–85.
Bianchi, M., *La Ca' di Dio di Padova nel Quattrocento. Riforma e governo di un ospedale per l'infanzia abbandonata*, Venice: Istituto veneto di scienze, lettere ed arti, 2005.
Brunetti, L., *Agnese e il suo ospedale. Siena, XIII–XV secolo*, Pisa: Pacini, 2006.
Bryce, J., 'Between friends? Two letters of Ippolita Sforza to Lorenzo de' Medici', *Renaissance Studies* 21 (2007), 340–65.
Calvi, G., *Il contratto morale. Madri e figli nella Toscana moderna*, Rome: Laterza, 1994.
Calvi, G., and I. Chabot (eds.), *Le ricchezze delle donne. Diritti patrimoniali e poteri familiari in Italia (XIII–XIX secc.)*, Turin: Rosenberg & Sellier, 1998.
Calvi, G., and R. Spinelli (eds.), *Le donne Medici nel sistema europeo delle corti, XVI–XVIII secolo*, 2 vols., Florence: Polistampa, 2008.
Carafa, D., *Memoriali*, F. Petrucci Nardelli (ed.), Rome: Bonacci, 1988.
Casanova, C., 'Mogli e vedove di condottieri in area padana fra Quattro e Cinquecento', in Arcangeli and Peyronel (eds.), *Donne di potere*, 513–34.
Chojnacki, S., 'Il divorzio di Cateruzza. Rappresentazione femminile ed esito processuale (Venezia 1465)', in Quaglioni and Seidel Menchi (eds.), *Coniugi nemici*, 371–416.
Women and Men in Renaissance Venice, Baltimore: Johns Hopkins University Press, 2000.
Cluse, C., 'Femmes en esclavage. Quelques remarques sur l'Italie du Nord (XIVe–XVe siècles)', in *Medieval Mediterranean Slavery (8th–15th Centuries)*, http://med-slavery.uni-trier.de:9080/minev/MedSlavery/publications/Femmes.pdf.
Cohn, S. K., *Women in the Streets: Essays on Sex and Power in Renaissance Italy*, Baltimore and London: Johns Hopkins University Press, 1996.
Covini, M. N., 'Tra cure domestiche, sentimenti e politica. La corrispondenza di Bianca Maria Visconti (1450–1468)', in I. Lazzarini (ed.), *I confini della lettera. Pratiche epistolari e reti di comunicazione in Italia tra tardo medioevo e prima età moderna (secoli XIV–XV)*, *Reti Medievali-Rivista* 10 (2009) (www.retimedievali.it).
Dean, T., 'Fathers and daughters: marriage laws and marriage disputes in Bologna and Italy. 1200–1500', in Dean and Lowe, *Marriage in Italy*, 85–106.
Dean, T., and K. Lowe, *Marriage in Italy, 1300–1650*, Cambridge University Press, 1998, 41–65.
Esposito, A., '"Ad dotandum puellas virgines, pauperes et honestas": social needs and confraternal charity in Rome in the fifteenth and sixteenth centuries', *Renaissance and Reformation* 18 (1994), 5–18.

'"Li nobili huomini di Roma". Strategie familiari tra città, curia e municipio', in S. Gensini (ed.), *Roma capitale (1447–1527)*, Pisa: Pacini, 1994, 373–88.

Feci, S., *Pesci fuor d'acqua. Donne a Roma in età moderna, diritti e patrimoni*, Rome: Viella, 2004.

Fisher, G., 'Guardianship and the rise of the Florentine state, 1368–1393', in Bellavitis and Chabot (eds.), *Famiglie e poteri*, 265–82.

Folin, M., 'La corte della duchessa. Eleonora d'Aragona a Ferrara', in Arcangeli and Peyronel (eds.), *Donne di potere*, 481–512.

Gavitt, P., *Charity and Children in Renaissance Florence: The Ospedale degli Innocenti, 1410–1536*, Ann Arbor: University of Michigan Press, 1990.

Gazzini, M., *Studi confraternali. Orientamenti, problemi, testimonianze*, Florence: Firenze University Press, 2009.

Grandi, C., 'L'assistenza all'infanzia abbandonata veneziana. I "fantolini della pietade" (1346–1548)', in Grieco and Sandri (eds.), *Ospedali e città*, 67–106.

Grieco, A., and L. Sandri (eds.), *Ospedali e città. L'Italia del Centro-Nord, 13–16 secolo*, Florence: Le Lettere, 1997.

Guerra Medici, M. T., *L'aria di città. Donne e diritti nel comune medievale*, Naples: Edizioni Scientifiche, 1996.

Henderson, J., *Piety and Charity in Late Medieval Florence*, Oxford: Clarendon, 1994. *The Renaissance Hospital: Healing the Body and Healing the Soul*, New Haven: Yale University Press, 2006.

Infantini, C., and E. Toti, *Spedale di Santa Maria della Scala*, Siena: Monte dei Paschi, 1988.

Kamenaga Anzai, Y. 'Attitudes towards public debt in medieval Genoa: the Lomellini family', *Journal of Medieval History* 29 (2003), 239–63.

Kelly Gadol, J., 'Did women have a Renaissance?', in R. Bridenthal *et al.* (eds.), *Becoming Visible: Women in European History*, Boston: Houghton Mifflin, 1977, 137–74.

Kirshner, J., '"Women married elsewhere": gender and citizenship in Italy', in A. Jacobsen Schutte, T. Kuehn and S. Seidel Menchi (eds.), *Time, Space, and Women's Lives in Early Modern Europe*, Kirksville, MO: Truman State University Press, 2001, 117–49.

Klapisch-Zuber, C., *Women, Family and Ritual in Renaissance Italy*, University of Chicago Press, 1985.

Kolsky, S., *The Ghost of Boccaccio: Writings on Famous Women in Renaissance Italy*, Turnhout: Brepols, 2005.

Kovesi Killerby, C., *Sumptuary Law in Italy: 1200–1500*, Oxford University Press, 2002.

Kuehn, T., *Law, Family and Women: Toward a Legal Anthropology of Renaissance Italy*, University of Chicago Press, 1991.

Lowe, K., 'Secular brides and convent brides: wedding ceremonies in Italy during the Renaissance and Counter-Reformation', in Dean and Lowe, *Marriage in Italy*, 41–65.

MacKinnon, C., *Toward a Feminist Theory of the State*, Cambridge, MA: Harvard University Press, 1989.

Mineo, E. I., *Nobiltà di stato. Famiglie e identità aristocratiche nel tardo Medioevo. La Sicilia*, Rome: Donzelli, 2001.

Molho, A., and J. Kirshner, 'The dowry fund and the marriage market in early Quattrocento Florence', *Journal of Modern History* 50 (1978), 403–38.

Mosher Stuard, S., 'Dowry increase and increments in wealth in medieval Ragusa (Dubrovnik)', *Journal of Economic History* 41 (1981), 795–811.
Novi Chavarria, E., *Monache e gentildonne. Un labile confine. Poteri politici e identità religiose nei monasteri napoletani, secoli XVI–XVII*, Milan: F. Angeli, 2001.
Panizza, L. (ed.), *Women in Italian Renaissance Culture and Society*, Oxford: Legenda, 2000.
Quaglioni, D., and S. Seidel Menchi (eds.), *Coniugi nemici. La separazione in Italia dal XII al XVIII secolo*, Bologna: Il Mulino, 2000.
(eds.), *Matrimoni in dubbio. Unioni controverse e nozze clandestine in Italia dal XIV al XVIII secolo*, Bologna: Il Mulino, 2001.
(eds.), *I tribunali del matrimonio (secoli XV–XVIII)*, Bologna: Il Mulino, 2006.
Reimer, E., 'Women, dowries, and capital investment in thirteenth-century Siena', in M. Kaplan (ed.), *The Marriage Bargain: Women and Dowries in European History*, New York: Haworth Press, 1985, 59–79.
Rocke, M., *Forbidden Friendships: Homosexuality and Male Culture in Renaissance Florence*, Oxford University Press, 1996.
Terpstra, N., *Abandoned Children of the Italian Renaissance: Orphan Care in Florence and Bologna*, Baltimore: Johns Hopkins University Press, 2005.
The Politics of Ritual Kinship: Confraternities and Social Order in Early Modern Italy, Cambridge University Press, 2000.
Tomas, N., *The Medici Women: Gender and Power in Renaissance Florence*, Aldershot: Ashgate, 2003.
Trexler, R., 'La prostitution florentine au XVe siècle. Patronages et clientèles', *Annales. Histoire, Sciences Sociales* 36 (1981), 983–1015.
Visceglia, M. A., 'Linee per uno studio unitario dei testamenti e dei contratti matrimoniali dell'aristocrazia feudale napoletana tra fine Quattrocento e Settecento', *Mélanges de l'Ecole française de Rome. Moyen Âge, Temps modernes* 95 (1983), 393–470.
Vitale, G., *Elite burocratica e famiglia. Dinamiche nobiliari e processi di costruzione statale nella Napoli angioino-aragonese*, Naples: Liguori, 2003.
Modelli culturali e nobiliari nella Napoli aragonese, Salerno: Carlone, 2002.
Vitolo, G., and R. Di Meglio, *Napoli angioino-aragonese. Confraternite, ospedali, dinamiche politico-sociali*, Salerno: Carlone, 2003.
Welch, E., 'Between Milan and Naples: Ippolita Maria Sforza, duchess of Calabria', in D. Abulafia (ed.), *The French Descent into Renaissance Italy: Antecedents and Effects*, Aldershot: Variorum, 1995, 123–36.
Zarri, G., *Recinti. Donne, clausura e matrimonio nella prima età moderna*, Bologna: Il Mulino, 2000.
Le sante vive. Cultura e religiosità femminile nella prima età moderna, Turin: Rosenberg & Sellier, 1990.

18. *Offices and officials* (Guido Castelnuovo)

Artifoni, E., 'I governi di "popolo" e le istituzioni comunali nella seconda metà del secolo XIII', *Reti Medievali – Rivista* 9 (2003/2) (www.dssg.unifi.it/_RM/rivista/saggi/Artifoni.htm).

Barbero, A., *Il ducato di Savoia. Amministrazione e corte di uno stato franco-italiano*, Rome and Bari: Laterza, 2002.
Barletta, L., F. Cardini and G. Galasso (eds.), *Il piccolo stato. Politica storia diplomazia*, San Marino: AIEP, 2003.
Brown, A., 'Uffici di onore e utile: la crisi del repubblicanesimo a Firenze', *Archivio Storico Italiano* 161 (2003), 285–321.
Cammarosano, P., *Tradizione documentaria e storia cittadina. Introduzione al 'Caleffo Vecchio' del Comune di Siena*, Siena: Accademia senese degli Intronati, 1988.
Carocci, S., 'Governo papale e città nello stato della chiesa. Ricerche sul Quattrocento' in Gensini (ed.), *Principi e città*, 151–224.
Castelnuovo, G., 'Quels offices, quels officiers? L'administration en Savoie au milieu du XVe siècle', *Études Savoisiennes* 2 (1993), 3–43.
  'Uffici e ufficiali nell'Italia del basso Medioevo', in Gensini (ed.), *L'Italia alla fine del Medioevo*, 295–332.
  Ufficiali e gentiluomini. La società politica sabauda nel tardo Medioevo, Milan: F. Angeli, 1994.
Castelnuovo, G., and C. Guilleré, 'Les finances et l'administration de la Maison de Savoie au XIIIe siècle', in B. Andenmatten, A. Paravicini-Bagliani and E. Pibiri (eds.), *Pierre II de Savoie, 'le petit Charlemagne'*, Lausanne: Université de Lausanne, 2000, 33–125.
Castelnuovo, G., and O. Mattéoni (eds.), *Chancelleries et chanceliers des princes à la fin du Moyen Âge*, forthcoming.
  (eds.), *De part et d'autre des Alpes. Les châtelains des princes à la fin du Moyen Âge*, Paris: Publications de la Sorbonne, 2005.
Chabod, F., 'Esiste uno stato del Rinascimento?', in Chabod, *Scritti*, 591–623.
  Scritti sul Rinascimento, Turin: Einaudi, 1967.
Chittolini, G., 'Di alcuni aspetti della crisi dello stato sforzesco', in J. M. Cauchies and G. Chittolini (eds.), *Milano e Borgogna. Due stati principeschi tra Medioevo e Rinascimento*, Rome: Bulzoni, 1990, 21–34.
  La formazione dello stato regionale e le istituzioni del contado, Turin: Einaudi, 1979.
  'L'onore dell'officiale', in S. Bertelli, N. Rubinstein and C. H. Smith (eds.), *Florence and Milan: Comparisons and Relations*, 2 vols., Florence: La Nuova Italia, 1989, I, 101–33.
  'Organizzazione territoriale e distretti urbani nell'Italia del tardo Medioevo', in Chittolini and Willoweit (eds.), *L'organizzazione del territorio*, 7–26.
Chittolini, G., and P. Johanek (eds.), *Aspetti e componenti dell'identità urbana in Italia e in Germania (secoli XIV–XVI)*, Bologna: Il Mulino, 2003.
Chittolini, G., A. Mohlo and P. Schiera (eds.), *Origini dello stato. Processi di formazione statale in Italia fra Medioevo ed età moderna*, Bologna: Il Mulino, 1994.
Chittolini, G., and D. Willoweit (eds.), *L'organizzazione del territorio in Italia e Germania. Secoli XIII–XIV*, Bologna: Il Mulino, 1994.
Chojnacki, S., 'Il divorzio di Cateruzza. Rappresentazione femminile ed esito processuale (Venezia 1465)', in Quaglioni and Seidel Menchi (eds.), *Coniugi nemici*, 371–416.

Connell, W. J., 'Il cittadino umanista come ufficiale nel territorio. Una rilettura di Giannozzo Manetti', in Zorzi and Connell (eds.), *Lo stato territoriale*, 359–83.
  'Il commissario e lo stato territoriale fiorentino', *Ricerche storiche* 18 (1988), 591–617.
Corrao, P., 'La difficile identità delle città siciliane', in Chittolini and Johanek (eds.), *Aspetti e componenti*, 97–122.
  Governare un regno. Potere, società e istituzioni in Sicilia fra Trecento e Quattrocento, Naples: Liguori, 1991.
Corrao, P., and V. D'Alessandro, 'Geografia amministrativa e potere sul territorio nella Sicilia tardomedievale', in Chittolini and Willoweit (eds.), *L'organizzazione del territorio*, 411–25.
Crouzet-Pavan, É., *Enfers et paradis. L'Italie de Dante et de Giotto*, Paris: Albin Michel, 2001.
  Renaissances italiennes, Paris: Albin Michel, 2007.
De Angelis, L., 'Ufficiali e uffici territoriali della repubblica fiorentina tra la fine del secolo XIV e la prima metà del XV', in Zorzi and Connell (eds.), *Lo stato territoriale*, 73–92.
Dean, T., 'Fathers and daughters: marriage laws and marriage disputes in Bologna and Italy. 1200–1500', in Dean and Lowe, *Marriage in Italy*, 85–106.
Dean, T., and K. Lowe (eds.), *Marriage in Italy, 1300–1650*, Cambridge University Press, 1998.
Descimon, R., 'La vénalité des offices et la construction de l'état dans la France moderne', in R. Descimon, J.-F. Schaub and B. Vincent (eds.), *Les figures de l'administrateur. Institutions, résaux, pouvoirs en Espagne, en France et au Portugal, 16e–19e siècle*, Paris: EHESS, 1997, 77–93.
Fasano Guarini, E., 'Gli statuti delle città soggette a Firenze tra '400 e '500. Riforme locali e interventi centrali', in G. Chittolini and D. Willoweit (eds.), *Statuti, città, territori in Italia e Germania tra Medioevo ed età moderna*, Bologna: Il Mulino, 1991, 69–124.
Folin, M., 'Le cronache a Ferrara e negli Stati estensi (secoli XV–XVI)', in A. Prosperi (ed.), *Storia di Ferrara*, VI, *Il Rinascimento*, Ferrara: Corbo, 2000, 459–92.
  'Note sugli officiali negli stati estensi, secoli XV–XVI', in Leverotti (ed.), *Gli officiali*, 99–125.
  'Principi e città fra Medioevo ed età moderna. Note a margine del caso ferrarese', in Chittolini and Johanek (eds.), *Aspetti e componenti*, 25–43.
Fubini, R., 'Antonio Ivani da Sarzana. Un teorizzatore del declino delle autonomie comunali', in Fubini, *Italia quattrocentesca*, 136–82.
  Italia quattrocentesca. Politica e diplomazia nell'età di Lorenzo il Magnifico, Milan: F. Angeli, 1994.
  Storiografia dell'umanesimo in Italia da Leonardo Bruni ad Annio da Viterbo, Rome: Bulzoni, 2003.
Gamberini, A., *La città assediata. Poteri e identità politiche a Reggio in età viscontea*, Rome: Viella, 2003.
  Oltre le città. Assetti territoriali e culture aristocratiche nella Lombardia del tardo Medioevo, Rome: Viella, 2009.

Gardi, A., 'Gli "officiali" nello stato pontificio del Quattrocento', in Leverotti (ed.), *Gli officiali*, 225–91.
Genet, J. P. (ed.), *L'état moderne. Genèse*, Paris: CNRS, 1990.
Gensini, S. (ed.), *Principi e città alla fine del Medioevo*, Pisa: Pacini, 1996.
Gentile, M., '"*Cum li amici et sequaci mei, qualli deo gratia non sono puochi*". Un aspetto della costituzione dei piccoli stati signorili del Parmense (XV secolo)', in R. Greci and D. Romagnoli (eds.), *Uno storico e un territorio. Vito Fumagalli e l'Emilia occidentale nel Medioevo*, Bologna: CLUEB, 2005, 125–44.
  (ed.), *Guelfi e ghibellini nell'Italia del Rinascimento*, Rome: Viella, 2005.
  Terra e poteri. Parma e il parmense nel ducato visconteo all'inizio del Quattrocento, Milan: Unicopli, 2001.
Ginatempo, M., 'Le città italiane, XIV–XV secolo', in *Poderes públicos en la Europa medieval*, Pamplona: Gobierno de Navarra, 1997, 149–209.
  'Finanze e fiscalità. Note sulle peculiarità degli stati regionali italiani e delle loro città', in Salvestrini (ed.), *L'Italia alla fine del Medioevo*, 241–94.
  'Spunti comparativi sulle trasformazioni della fiscalità nell'Italia post-comunale', in P. Mainoni (ed.), *Politiche finanziarie e fiscali nell'Italia settentrionale, secoli XIII–XIV*, Milan: Unicopli, 2001, 125–220.
Grillo, P., 'La selezione del personale politico. Podestà e vicari nelle signorie sovracittadine a cavallo fra Due e Trecento', in M. Vallerani (ed.), *Tecniche di potere nel tardo Medioevo. Regimi comunali e signorie in Italia*, Rome: Viella, 2010, 25–51.
Ianziti, G., *Humanistic Historiography Under the Sforzas: Politics and Propaganda in Fifteenth-Century Milan*, Oxford University Press, 1988.
Isaacs, A. K., 'Sui rapporti interstatali in Italia dal Medioevo all'età moderna', in Chittolini, Mohlo and Schiera (eds.), *Origini dello stato*, 113–32.
Kölzer, T., '*Magna imperialis curia*. Die Zentralverwaltung im Königreich Sizilien unter Friedrich II', *Historisches Jahrbuch der Görres-Gesellschaft* 114 (1994), 287–311.
Lazzarini, I., 'I domini estensi e gli stati signorili padani. Tipologie a confronto', in G. Fragnito and M. Miegge (eds.), *Girolamo Savonarola da Ferrara all'Europa*, Florence: SISMEL, 2001, 19–50.
  L'Italia degli stati territoriali. Secoli XIII–XV, Rome and Bari: Laterza, 2003.
  (ed.), *Scritture e potere. Pratiche documentarie e forme di governo nell'Italia tardomedievale (XIV–XV secolo)*, *Reti Medievali Rivista* 9 (2008) (www.storia.unifi.it/_RM/rivista/2008–1.htm#S_monografica).
Leverotti, F. (ed.), *Cancelleria e amministrazione negli stati italiani del Rinascimento*, Ricerche Storiche 24, 2 (1994), 277–423.
  '*Diligentia, obedientia, fides, taciturnitas cum modestia*. La cancelleria segreta nel ducato sforzesco', in Leverotti (ed.), *Cancelleria e amministrazione*, 305–35.
  'Gli officiali del ducato sforzesco', in Leverotti (ed.), *Gli officiali*, 17–77.
  (ed.), *Gli officiali negli stati italiani del Quattrocento*, Pisa: Scuola normale superiore, 1997.
  'Le ragioni di un seminario', in Leverotti (ed.), *Cancelleria e amministrazione*, 277–289.
Maire Vigueur, J.-C., *Cavaliers et citoyens. Guerre, conflits et société dans l'Italie communale, XIIe–XIIIe siècles*, Paris: EHESS, 2003.

(ed.), *I podestà dell'Italia comunale*, 2 vols., Rome: École française de Rome, 2000.

Mannori, L., *Il sovrano tutore. Pluralismo istituzionale e accentramento amministrativo nel principato dei Medici*, Milan: Giuffré, 1994.

'Lo stato di Firenze e i suoi storici', *Società e Storia* 76 (1997), 400–15.

Martin, J. M., 'L'organisation administrative et militaire du territoire', in *Potere, società e popolo nell'età sveva (1210–1266)*, Bari: Dedalo, 1985, 71–121.

Mineo, I., *Nobiltà di stato. Famiglie e identità aristocratiche nel tardo Medioevo. La Sicilia*, Rome: Donzelli, 2001.

Morelli, S., 'I giustizieri nel regno di Napoli al tempo di Carlo I d'Angiò', in N. Coulet and J.-M. Matz (eds.), *L'état angevin. Pouvoir, culture et société entre XIIIe et XIVe siècle*, Rome: École française de Rome, 1998, 491–517.

'Gli ufficiali del regno di Napoli nel Quattrocento', in Leverotti (ed.), *Gli officiali*, 293–311.

Najemy, J. M. (ed.), *Italy in the Age of Renaissance*, Oxford University Press, 2004.

Quaglioni, D., and S. Seidel Menchi (eds.), *Coniugi nemici. La separazione in Italia dal XII al XVIII secolo*, Bologna: Il Mulino, 2000.

Ryder, A., *The Kingdom of Naples Under Alfonso the Magnanimous: The Making of a Modern State*, Oxford: Clarendon Press, 1976.

Salvestrini, F. (ed.), *L'Italia alla fine del Medioevo. I caratteri originali nel quadro europeo*, Florence: Firenze University Press, 2006.

Santoro, C., *Gli offici del Comune di Milano e del dominio visconteo-sforzesco (1215–1515)*, Milan: Giuffrè, 1968.

Gli uffici del dominio sforzesco (1450–1500), Milan: Fondazione Treccani degli Alfieri, 1948.

Tanzini, L., *Statuti e legislazione a Firenze dal 1355 al 1415. Lo statuto cittadino del 1409*, Florence: Olschki, 2004.

Titone, F., *Governments of the Universitates: Urban Communities of Sicily in the Fourteenth and Fifteenth Centuries*, Turnhout: Brepols, 2009.

Varanini, G. M., 'Governi principeschi e modello cittadino di organizzazione del territorio nell'Italia del Quattrocento', in Gensini (ed.), *Principi e città*, 95–127.

'Gli ufficiali veneziani nella Terraferma veneta quattrocentesca', in Leverotti (ed.), *Gli officiali*, 151–80.

Viggiano, A., 'La disciplina dei rettori nello stato veneto del '400', in Leverotti (ed.), *Gli officiali*, 181–90.

Governanti e governati. Legittimità del potere ed esercizio dell'autorità sovrana nello stato veneto della prima età moderna, Treviso: Canova, 1993.

Zorzi, A., 'L'organizzazione del territorio in area fiorentina tra XIII e XIV secolo', in Chittolini and Willoweit (eds.), *L'organizzazione del territorio*, 73–92.

'Gli ufficiali territoriali dello stato fiorentino', in Leverotti (ed.), *Gli officiali*, 191–212.

Zorzi, A., and W. J. Connell (eds.), *Lo stato territoriale fiorentino (secoli XIV–XV). Ricerche, linguaggi, confronti*, Pisa: Pacini, 2001.

19. Public written records (Gian Maria Varanini)

Airò, A., 'L'inventario dell'archivio che non c'è più. I privilegi aragonesi come deposito della memoria documentaria dell'università di Taranto', in Bartoli Langeli, Giorgi and Moscadelli (eds.), *Archivi e comunità*, 521–58.

Arcangeli, L., and M. Gentile (eds.), *Le signorie dei Rossi di Parma tra XIV e XVI*, Florence: Firenze University Press, 2007.

Barbero, A., *Il ducato di Savoia. Amministrazione e corte di uno stato franco-italiano*, Rome and Bari: Laterza, 2002.

Bartoli Langeli, A., 'La documentazione degli stati italiani nei secoli XIII–XV. Forme, organizzazione, personale', in *Culture et idéologie dans la genèse de l'état moderne*, Rome: École française de Rome, 1985, 35–55.

'Premessa', in Bartoli Langeli, Giorgi and Moscadelli (eds.), *Archivi e comunità*, vii–xiv.

Bartoli Langeli, A., A. Giorgi and S. Moscadelli (eds.), *Archivi e comunità tra Medioevo ed età moderna*, Rome: Ministero per i Beni e le attività culturali, Dir. Gen. per gli archivi, 2009.

Bartoli Langeli, A., and E. Irace, 'Gli archivi', in G. Pugliese Carratelli (ed.), *La città e la parola scritta*, Milan: Scheiwiller, 1997, 401–28.

Bautier, R. H., 'La phase cruciale de l'histoire des archives. La construction des dépôts et la naissance de l'archivistique (XVI siècle–début du XIX siècle)', *Archivum* 18 (1968), 139–49.

Behne, A. J., *Das Archiv der Gonzaga von Mantua in Spätmittelalter*, Ph.D. dissertation, Marburg an der Lahn, 1990.

Bonfiglio Dosio, G., *La politica archivistica del comune di Padova dal XIII al XIX secolo con l'inventario analitico del fondo 'Costituzione e ordinamento dell'archivio'*, Rome: Viella, 2002.

Cammarosano, P., *Italia medievale. Struttura e geografia delle fonti scritte*, Rome: NIS, 1991.

Carocci, S., 'Governo papale e città nello stato della chiesa. Ricerche sul '400', in S. Gensini (ed.), *Principi e città alla fine del Medioevo*, Pisa: Pacini, 1996, 151–224.

Chittolini, G., 'Ascesa e declino di piccoli stati signorili (Italia centro-settentrionale, metà trecento)', *Società e Storia* 121 (2008), 455–80.

Città, comunità e feudi negli stati dell'Italia centro-settentrionale (XIV–XVI secolo), Milan: Unicopli, 1996.

Clough, C. H., 'The Pio di Savoia archives,' in B. Maracchi Biagiarelli and D. E. Rhodes (eds.), *Studi offerti a Roberto Ridolfi*, Florence: Olschki, 1973, 197–222.

Covini, M. N., 'Scrivere al principe. Il carteggio interno sforzesco e la storia documentaria delle istituzioni', in Lazzarini (ed.), *Scritture e potere*, 1–33.

De Vincentiis, A., 'Memorie bruciate. Conflitti, documenti, oblio nelle città italiane del tardo Medioevo', *Bullettino dell'Istituto Storico Italiano per il medio evo* 106 (2004), 167–98.

Del Bo, B., *Uomini e strutture di uno stato feudale. Il marchesato di Monferrato (1418–1483)*, Milan: LED, 2009.

Della Misericordia, M., 'Mappe di carte. Le scritture e gli archivi delle comunità rurali della montagna lombarda nel basso Medioevo', in Bartoli Langeli, Giorgi and Moscadelli (eds.), *Archivi e comunità*, 155–278.

'Diplomazia edita. Le edizioni delle corrispondenze diplomatiche quattrocentesche', *Bullettino dell'Istituto Storico Italiano per il Medioevo* 110 (2008), 1–143.

Dispacci di Pietro Cornaro, ambasciatore a Milano durante la guerra di Chioggia, V. Lazzarini (ed.), Venice: Dep. veneta di storia patria, 1939.

Fiorina, U. (ed.), *Inventario dell'archivio Falcò Pio di Savoia*, Vicenza: Neri Pozza, 1980.

Folin, M., *Rinascimento estense. Politica, cultura, istituzioni di un antico stato italiano*, Rome and Bari: Laterza, 2001.

Gamberini, A., 'La memoria dei gentiluomini. I cartulari di lignaggio alla fine del Medioevo', in Lazzarini (ed.), *Scritture e potere*, 1–16.

Lo stato visconteo. Linguaggi politici e dinamiche costituzionali, Milan: F. Angeli, 2005.

Gardi, A., 'Gli archivi periferici dello stato pontificio. Il caso di Bologna tra XIV e XVII secolo', in Jamme and Poncet (eds.), *Offices, écrit et papauté*, 789–837.

Giorgi, A., and S. Moscadelli, 'Gli archivi delle comunità dello stato senese. Prime riflessioni sulla loro produzione e conservazione (secoli XIII–XVIII)', in P. Benigni and S. Pieri (eds.), *Modelli a confronto. Gli archivi storici comunali della Toscana*, Florence: Edifir, 1996, 63–84.

'*Ut ipsa acta illesa serventur*. Produzione documentaria e archivi di comunità nell'alta e media Italia tra Medioevo ed età moderna', in Bartoli Langeli, Giorgi and Moscadelli (eds.), *Archivi e comunità*, 1–110.

Jamme, A., and O. Poncet (eds.), *Offices, écrit et papauté (XIIIe–XVIIe siècle)*, Rome: École française de Rome, 2007.

Keller, H., K. Grubmüller and N. Staubach (eds.), *Pragmatische Schriftlichkeit im Mittelalter. Erscheinungsformen und Entwicklungsstufen*, Munich: s.n.t., 1992.

Klein, F., 'Costruzione dello stato e costruzione di archivio. Ordinamenti delle scritture della repubblica fiorentina a metà '400', in Lazzarini (ed.), *Scritture e potere*, 1–32.

Lazzarini, I. (ed.), *I confini della lettera. Pratiche epistolari e reti di comunicazione nell'Italia tardomedievale*, Reti medievali, Rivista, 10 (2009) (www.retimedievali.it).

Fra un principe e altri stati. Relazioni di potere e forme di servizio a Mantova nell'età di Ludovico Gonzaga, Rome: Istituto storico italiano per il Medio Evo, 1996.

'Introduzione', in Lazzarini (ed.), *I confini della lettera*, 1–10.

'Materiali per una didattica delle scritture pubbliche di cancelleria nell'Italia del '400', *Scrineum rivista* 2 (2004), (http://scrineum.unipv.it/rivista/2-2004/lazzarini.pdf).

(ed.), *Scritture e potere. Pratiche documentarie e forme di governo nell'Italia tardomedievale (XIV–XV secolo)*, Reti medievali, Rivista, 9 (2008), (www.retimedievali.it).

Leverotti, F., 'L'archivio dei Visconti signori di Milano', in Lazzarini (ed.), *Scritture e potere*, 1–23.

Maire Vigueur, J.-C., 'Révolution documentaire et révolution scripturaire. Le cas de l'Italie médiévale', *Bibliothèque de l'École des Chartes* 153 (1995), 177–85.

Mineo, L., 'La dimensione archivistica di tre terre toscane fra XIV e XV secolo. I casi di Colle Val d'Elsa, San Gimignano e San Miniato', in Bartoli Langeli, Giorgi and Moscadelli (eds.), *Archivi e comunità*, 337–426.

Nori, G., '"Nei ripostigli delle scanzie". L'archivio dei Rossi di Sansecondo', in Arcangeli and Gentile (eds.), *Le signorie dei Rossi di Parma*, 15–22.

Pagnin, B., *I formulari di un notaio e cancelliere padovano del sec. XV*, Padua: Istituto di Storia medievale e moderna, 1953.

Pasciuta, B., In regia curia civiliter convenire. *Giustizia e città nella Sicilia tardomedievale*, Turin: Giappichelli editore, 2003.

Pastorello, E. (ed.), *Il copialettere marciano della cancelleria carrarese (gennaio 1402–gennaio 1403)*, Venice: Deputazione veneta di storia patria, 1915.

Pedani, M. P., 'Veneta auctoritate notarius'. *Storia del notariato veneziano, 1514–1797*, Milan: Giuffré, 1996.

Petrini, A., 'La *tabula officiorum* di Paolo II (1464–1471)', in A. Jamme and O. Poncet (eds.), *Offices et papauté (XIVe–XVIIe siècle). Charges, hommes, destins*, Rome: École française de Rome, 2005, 125–57.

Pierini, P., *Arte a Siena*, Siena and Florence: Monte dei Paschi-Scala, 2004.

Poncet, O., 'Les archives de la papauté (XVIe-milieu XVIIe siècle). La genèse d'un instrument de pouvoir', in Jamme and Poncet (eds.), *Offices, écrit et papauté*, 737–62.

Roccatagliata, A., 'L'archivio del governo della Repubblica di Genova in età moderna', in A. Assini and P. Caroli (eds.), *Spazi per la memoria storica. La storia di Genova attraverso le vicende delle sedi e dei documenti dell'Archivio di Stato*, Rome: Ministero per i Beni e le attività culturali, Dir. Gen. Per gli archivi, 2009, 427–500.

Romiti, A., *L'armarium comunis della Camara Actorum di Bologna. L'inventariazione archivistica nel 13. secolo*, Rome: Ministero per i Beni e le attività culturali, Ufficio centrale per i beni archivistici, 1994.

Rossi, M., '*Volentes falsitatibus obviare ac lites removere occasione testamentorum*. Forme di tutela e pratiche di registrazione degli atti di ultima volontà. Il caso veronese', in A. Castagnetti, A. Ciaralli and G. M. Varanini (eds.), *Medioevo. Studi e documenti*, II, Verona: LEUV, 2007, 351–70.

Rück, P., *L'ordinamento degli archivi ducali di Savoia sotto Amedeo VIII (1398–1451)*, Rome: Ministero per i beni e le attività culturali, 1977.

Salvadori, P., *Dominio e patronato. Lorenzo dei Medici e la Toscana nel Rinascimento*, Rome: Storia e letteratura, 2000.

Sancassani, G., 'L'archivio dell'antico ufficio del registro di Verona', *Vita veronese* 10 (1957), 479–86.

Savy, P., 'La famiglia Dal Verme fra Trecento e Quattrocento. I suoi documenti, i suoi archivi', *Società e storia* 26 (2003), 102, 823–47.

Senatore, F., 'Gli archivi delle *universitates* meridionali. Il caso di Capua e alcune considerazioni generali', in Bartoli Langeli, Giorgi and Moscadelli (eds.), *Archivi e comunità*, 447–520.

Tamba, T., 'I memoriali del comune di Bologna nel secolo XIII. Note di diplomatica', *Rassegna degli archivi di stato* 47 (1987), 235–90.
Varanini, G. M., 'I notai e la signoria cittadina. Appunti sulla documentazione dei Bonacolsi di Mantova fra Duecento e Trecento (rileggendo Pietro Torelli)', in Lazzarini (ed.), *Scritture e potere*, 1–54.
'Pietro Dal Verme podestà scaligero di Treviso (1329–1336)', in M. Knapton and G. Ortalli (eds.), *Istituzioni, società e potere nella Marca trevigiana e veronese (secoli XIII–XIV). Sulle tracce di G. B. Verci*, Rome: Istituto storico italiano per il Medio Evo, 1988, 65–81.
Varanini, G. M., and A. Viggiano, 'Gli archivi giudiziari della Terraferma veneziana', in A. Giorgi and S. Moscadelli (ed.), *La documentazione degli organi giudiziari nell'Italia tardo-medievale e moderna*, Atti del Convegno per il 150° anniversario dell'Archivio di Stato di Siena, forthcoming.
Zanichelli, G. Z., 'La committenza dei Rossi. Immagini di potere fra sacro e profano', in Arcangeli and Gentile (eds.), *Le signorie dei Rossi di Parma*, 187–212.

20. The language of politics and the process of state-building: approaches and interpretations (Andrea Gamberini)

Adorni Braccesi, S., and M. Ascheri (eds.), *Politica e cultura nelle Repubbliche italiane dal Medioevo all'età moderna. Firenze, Genova, Lucca, Siena, Venezia*, Rome: Istituto storico italiano per l'età moderna e contemporanea, 2001.
Airò, A., 'L'architettura istituzionale e territoriale del regno di Napoli nello specchio degli atti linguistici di un privilegio sovrano', in Gamberini and Petralia (eds.), *Linguaggi politici*, 139–67.
 'Luci e balestre. Lessico e metafore della comunicazione politica nella devoluzione del principato di Taranto (1464–1465)', in F. Somaini and B. Vetere (eds.), *I domini del principe di Taranto in età orsiniana (1399–1463)*, Lecce: Congedo, 2009, 107–23.
Arcangeli, L., 'Piccoli signori lombardi e potenze grosse', in Gamberini and Petralia (eds.), *Linguaggi politici*, 409–43.
Artifoni, E., 'Retorica e organizzazione del linguaggio politico nel Duecento italiano', in Cammarosano (ed.), *Le forme della propaganda politica*, 157–82.
Austin, J. L., *How to Do Things with Words*, Cambridge, MA: Harvard University Press, 1962.
Baron, H., *The Crisis of the Early Italian Renaissance*, Princeton University Press, 1966.
Bartoli Langeli, A., 'La documentazione degli stati italiani nei secoli XIII–XV. Forme, organizzazione, personale', in *Culture et idéologie dans la genèse de l'état moderne*, Rome: École française de Rome, 1985, 35–55.
Bertrand, G., and I. Taddei (eds.), *Le destin des rituels. Faire corps dans l'espace urbain, Italia-France-Allemagne*, Rome: École française de Rome, 2008.
Black, A., 'Political languages in later medieval Europe', in D. Wood (ed.), *The Church and the Sovereignty c. 590–1918: Essays in Honour of Michael Wilks*, Oxford: Blackwell, 1991, 313–28.

Black, R., *Humanism and Education in Medieval and Renaissance Italy: Tradition and Innovation in Latin Schools from the Twelfth to the Fifteenth Century*, Cambridge University Press, 2001.

Blockmans, W., A. Holenstein and J. Mathieu (eds.), *Empowering Interactions: Political Cultures and the Emergence of the State in Europe 1300–1900*, Farnham: Ashgate, 2009.

Bolzoni, L., *The Web of Images: Vernacular Preaching from Its Origins to St Bernardino da Siena*, Aldershot: Ashgate, 2004.

Bordone, R., 'Campane, trombe e carrocci nelle città del regno d'Italia durante il Medioevo', in A. Haverkamp (ed.), *Information, Kommunikation und Selbstdarstellung im mittelalterlichen Gemeinden*, Munich: Oldenbourg, 1998, 85–101.

Boucheron, P., 'L'architettura come linguaggio politico. Cenni sul caso lombardo nel secolo XV', in Gamberini and Petralia (eds.), *Linguaggi politici*, 3–53.

Le pouvoir de bâtir. Urbanisme et politique édilitaire à Milan (XIVe–XVe siècles), Rome: École française de Rome, 1998.

Boucheron, P., and J. Chiffoleau (eds.), *Les palais dans la ville. Espaces urbaines et lieux de la puissance publique dans la Méditerranée médiévale*, Lyon: Presses Universitaires de Lyon, 2004.

Brown, A., 'The language of empire', in W. J. Connell and A. Zorzi (eds.), *Florentine Tuscany: Structures and Practices of Power*, Cambridge University Press, 2000.

Buc, C., *L'ambiguïté du Livre. Prince, pouvoir et peuple dans les commentaires de la Bible au Moyen Âge*, Paris: Beauchesne, 1994.

Calzona, A., F. P. Fiore, A. Tenenti and C. Vasoli (eds.), *Il principe architetto*, Florence: L. S. Olschki, 2002.

Cammarosano, P. (ed.), *Le forme della propaganda politica nel Due e Trecento*, Rome: École française de Rome, 1994.

Campbell, S. J. (ed.), *Artists at Court: Image-Making and Identity, 1330–1550*, University of Chicago Press, 2004.

Casini, M., *I gesti del principe. La festa politica a Firenze e Venezia in età rinascimentale*, Venice: Marsilio, 1996.

Cengarle, F., 'La comunità di Pecetto contro i Mandelli feudatari. Linguaggi politici a confronto', in F. Cengarle, G. Chittolini and G. M. Varanini (eds.), *Poteri signorili e feudali nella campagne dell'Italia settentatrionale fra Tre e Quattrocento. Fondamenti di legittimità e forme d'esercizio*, Florence: Firenze University Press, 2005, 105–26.

Immagine di potere e prassi di governo. La politica feudale di Filippo Maria Visconti, Rome: Viella, 2006.

'La signoria di Azzone Visconti tra prassi, retorica e iconografia (1329–1339). Prime note', in M. Vallerani (ed.), *Tecniche di potere nel tardo Medioevo. Regimi comunali e signorie in Italia*, Rome: Viella, 2010, 89–116.

'I Visconti e il culto della Vergine (XIV secolo). Qualche osservazione', in Gaffuri and Ventrone (eds.), *Immagini, culti, liturgie*, forthcoming.

Chartier, R., *Cultural History: Between Practices and Representations*, Cambridge: Polity Press, 1988.

Chignola, S., and G. Duso, *Sui concetti giuridici e politici della Costituzione dell'Europa*, Milan: F. Angeli, 2005.
Chittolini, G., 'Civic religion and the countryside in late medieval Italy', in T. Dean and C. Wickham (eds.), *City and Countryside in Late Medieval and Renaissance Italy: Essays Presented to Philip Jones*, London: Hambledon Press, 1996, 69–80.
Ciccaglioni, G., 'La costruzione e la tutela della memoria di una città suddita nell'Italia del Quattrocento. Osservazioni sul caso pisano', http://municipalia.sns.it.
Corrao, P., '*De la vostra gran senyoria humil e affectuos servidor*. Corrispondenza fra due funzionari iberici in Sicilia e la Corte d'Aragona (1415–1417)', in A. Romano (ed.), *Cultura e istituzioni nella Sicilia medievale e moderna*, Soveria Mannelli: Giappichelli, 1992, 111–63.
Covini, M. N., 'Aspetti della fortificazione urbana tra Lombardia e Veneto alla fine del Medioevo', in A. Turchini (ed.), *Castel Sismondo. Sigismondo Malatesta e l'arte militare del primo rinascimento*, Cesena: Il ponte vecchio, 2003, 59–77.
Crouzet-Pavan, E., *Venice Triumphant: The Horizons of a Myth*, Baltimore: Johns Hopkins University Press, 2002.
De Benedictis, A., 'Rebellare–resistere. Comunicazioni politica come conflitto tra norme in età moderna', in De Benedictis, Corni, Mazohl and Schorn-Schütte (eds.), *Die Sprache des politischen in actu*, 139–62.
  'Rebellion-Widerstand. Politische Kommunikation als Normenkonflikt in der Früzen Neuzeit', in De Benedictis, Corni, Mazohl and Schorn-Schütte (eds.), *Die Sprache des politischen in actu*, 113–38.
  Repubblica per contratto. Bologna, una città europea nello stato della chiesa, Bologna: Il Mulino, 1995.
De Benedictis, A., G. Corni, B. Mazohl and L. Schorn-Schütte (eds.), *Die Sprache des Politischen in Actu. Zum Verhaltnis von politischem Handeln und politische Sprache von der Antike bis ins 20. Jahrhundert*, Gottingen: V&R Unipress, 2009.
Della Misericordia, M., 'Decidere e agire in comunità nel XV secolo (un aspetto del dibattito politico nel dominio sforzesco)', in Gamberini and Petralia (eds.), *Linguaggi politici*, 293–380.
  Divenire comunità. Comuni rurali, identità sociali e territoriali in Valtellina e nella montagna lombarda del tardo Medioevo, Milan: Unicopli, 2006.
  'Dividersi per governarsi. Fazioni, famiglie aristocratiche e comuni in Valtellina in età viscontea (1335–1447)', *Società e Storia* 86 (1999), 715–66.
  Figure di comunità. Documento notarile, forme della convivenza, riflessione locale sulla vita associata nella montagna lombarda e nella pianura comasca (secoli XIV–XVI), Morbegno: Ad fontes, 2008, (www.adfontes.it/biblioteca/scaffale/notarile/copertina.html).
  '"Per non privarci de nostre raxone, li siamo stati desobidienti". Patto, giustizia e resistenza nelle suppliche delle comunità alpine nello stato di Milano (XV secolo)', in C. Nubola and A. Würgler (eds.), *Forme della comunicazione politica in Europa nei secoli XV–XVIII. Suppliche, 'gravamina', lettere*, Bologna: Il Mulino, 2004, 147–215.

'Principat, communauté et individu au bas Moyen Âge', *Médiévales* 57 (2009), 93–112.
Delle Donne, R., 'Regis servitium nostra mercatura. Culture e linguaggi della fiscalità nella Napoli Aragonese', in Petti Balbi and Vitolo (eds.), *Linguaggi e pratiche del potere*, 91–150.
Di Donato, M. M., 'Cose morali, e anche appartenenti secondo e' luoghi. Per lo studio della pittura politica nel tardo Medioevo toscano', in Cammarosano (ed.), *Le forme della propaganda politica*, 491–517.
Duby, G., 'Ideology in social history', in J. Le Goff and P. Nora (eds.), *Constructing the Past: Essays in Historical Methodology*, Cambridge University Press, 1987, 150–65.
Evangelisti, P., *I francescani e la costruzione di uno stato. Linguaggi politici, valori identitari, progetti di governo in area catalano-aragonese*, Padua: EFR, 2006.
Fantoni, M., 'Simbologia e ritualità. Definizione di un campo di studi', in *Simboli e rituali*, 7–16.
Ferente, S., 'Guelphs! Factions, liberty and sovereignty: inquiries about the Quattrocento', *History of Political Thought* 28, 4 (2007), 571–98.
Folin, M., *Rinascimento estense. Politica, cultura, istituzioni di un antico stato italiano*, Rome and Bari: Laterza, 2001.
Freedberg, D., *The Power of Images: Study in the History and Theory of Response*, University of Chicago Press, 1989.
Fubini, R., *Italia quattrocentesca. Politica e diplomazia nell'età di Lorenzo il Magnifico*, Milan: F. Angeli, 1994.
  L'umanesimo italiano e i suoi storici. Origini rinascimentali – critica moderna, Milan: F. Angeli, 2001.
Gaffuri, L. (ed.), *'Monasticum regnum'. Religione e politica nelle pratiche di legittimazione e di governo tra Medioevo ed età moderna*, forthcoming.
Gaffuri, L., and Ventrone, P. (eds.), *Images, cultes, liturgies. Les connotations politiques du message religieux*, forthcoming.
Gamberini, A., *La città assediata. Poteri e identità politiche a Reggio in età viscontea*, Rome: Viella, 2003.
  Oltre le città. Assetti territoriali e culture aristocratiche, Rome: Viella 2009.
  Lo stato visconteo. Linguaggi politici e dinamiche costituzionali, Milan: F. Angeli, 2005.
Gamberini, A., and G. Petralia (eds.), *Linguaggi politici nell'Italia del Rinascimento*, Rome: Viella, 2007.
Gentile, L. C., *Riti ed emblemi. Processi di rappresentazione del potere principesco in area subalpina (XIII–XVI secc.)*, Turin: Zamorani, 2008.
Gentile, M., 'Discorsi sulle fazioni, discorsi delle fazioni. "Parole e demonstratione partiale" nella Lombardia del secondo Quattrocento', in Gamberini and Petralia (eds.), *Linguaggi politici*, 381–408.
Grubb, J., *Firstborn of Venice: Vicenza in the Early Renaissance State*, Baltimore and London: Johns Hopkins University Press, 1988.
Hampsher-Monk, I., K. Tilmans and F. van Vree (eds.), *History of Concepts: Comparative Perspectives*, Amsterdam University Press, 1998.
Hankins, J. (ed.), *Renaissance Civic Humanism: Reappraisals and Reflections*, Cambridge University Press, 2000.

Lambertini, R., 'La diffusione della "Politica" e la definizione di un linguaggio politico aristotelico', *Quaderni Storici* 102 (1999), 677–704.

Lazzarini, I., *Il linguaggio del territorio fra principe e comunità. Il giuramento di fedeltà a Federico Gonzaga*, Florence: Firenze University Press, 2009.

'Materiali per una didattica delle scritture pubbliche di cancelleria nell'Italia del Quattrocento', *Scrineum – Rivista* 2 (2004), (http://scrineum.unipv.it/rivista/2-2004/lazzarini.html).

(ed.), *Scritture e potere. Pratiche documentarie e forme di governo nell'Italia tardomedievale (XIV–XV secolo)*, Reti Medievali Rivista 9 (2008), (www.storia.unifi.it/_RM/rivista/2008-1.htm).

Meier, U., *Mensch und Bürger. Die Stadt im Denken spätmittelalterlicher Theologen, Philosophen und Juristen*, Munich: Oldembourg, 1994.

Mineo, E. I., 'Liberté et communauté en Italie (milieu XIIIe–début XVe s.)', in C. Moatti and M. Riot-Sarcey (eds.), *La république dans tous ses états*, Paris: Payot-Rivages, 2009, 215–50.

Muir, E., *Civic Ritual in Renaissance Venice*, Princeton University Press, 1981.

(ed.), *Ritual in Early Modern Europe*, Cambridge University Press, 1997.

Najemy, J. M., 'The republic's two bodies: body metaphors in Italian Renaissance political thought', in A. Brown (ed.), *Language and Images of Renaissance Italy*, Oxford: Clarendon Press, 1995, 237–62.

Pagden, A. (ed.), *The Languages of Political Theory in Early Modern Europe*, Cambridge University Press, 1987.

Pavanello, G. (ed.), *Il buono e il cattivo governo. Rappresentazioni nelle arti dal Medioevo al Novecento*, Venice: Marsilio, 2004.

Petti Balbi, G., and G. Vitolo (eds.), *Linguaggi e pratiche del potere*, Salerno: Laveglia, 2007.

Petralia, G., 'Stato e moderno in Italia e nel Rinascimento', *Storica* 8 (1997), 7–48.

Rexroth, F., 'Politische Rituale und die Sprache des Politischen in der historischen Mittelalterforshung', in De Benedictis, Corni, Mazohl and Schorn-Schütte (eds.), *Die Sprache des Politischen in actu*, 71–90.

Ricciardelli, F., 'Le forme rituali della politica tra Firenze e le città dominate. Secoli XIV–XV', in *Simboli e rituali*, 17–30.

(ed.), *I luoghi del sacro. Il sacro e la città fra Medioevo ed età moderna*, Florence: Mauro Pagliai, 2008.

Richter, M., 'Reconstructing the history of political languages: Pockock, Skinner and the Geschichtliche Grundbegriffe', *History and Theory* 29/1 (1990), 38–70.

Searle, J. R., *Speech Acts: An Essay in the Philosophy of Language*, Cambridge University Press, 1980.

Senatore, F., 'Cerimonie regie e cerimonie civiche a Capua (XV–XVI sec.)', in Petti Balbi and Vitolo (eds.), *Linguaggi e pratiche del potere*, 151–205.

'La cultura politica di Ferrante d'Aragona', in Gamberini and Petralia (eds.), *Linguaggi politici*, 113–38.

Shaw, C., 'The language of Genoese political pragmatism', in Gamberini and Petralia (eds.), *Linguaggi politici*, 171–86.

Simboli e rituali nelle città toscane tra Medioevo e prima età moderna, in *Annali Aretini* 13 (2005), 7–176.

Skinner, Q., *The Foundations of Modern Political Thought*, Cambridge University Press, 1978.
'Machiavelli's Discorsi and the pre-humanistic origins of republican ideas', in G. Bock, Q. Skinner and M. Viroli (eds.), *Machiavelli and Republicanism*, Cambridge University Press, 1990, 121–41.
Visions of Politics, 3 vols., Cambridge University Press, 2002.
Trexler, R. C., *Public Life in Renaissance Florence*, New York: Academic Press, 1980.
Turchi, L., 'Una piccola modifica. Il linguaggio della negoziazione politica fra principe e città', in G. Badini and A. Gamberini (eds.), *Medioevo reggiano. Studi in ricordo di Odoardo Rombaldi*, Milan: F. Angeli, 2007, 343–73.
Varanini, G. M., 'Propaganda dei regimi signorili. Le esperienze venete del Trecento', in Cammarosano (ed.), *Le forme della propaganda politica*, 311–43.
Vauchez, A. (ed.), *La religion civique à l'époque médiévale et moderne. Chrétienté et Islam*, Rome: École française de Rome, 1995.
Viaggiano, A., *Governanti e governati. Legittimità del potere ed esercizio dell'autorità sovrana nello stato veneto della prima età moderna*, Treviso: Fondazione Benetton, 1993.
Viroli, M., *From Politics to Reason of State: The Acquisition and Transformation of the Language of Politics 1250–1600*, Cambridge University Press, 1992.
Visceglia, M. A., *La città rituale. Roma e le sue cerimonie in età moderna*, Rome: Viella, 2002.
Vitolo, G., 'Linguaggi e forme del conflitto politico nel Mezzogiorno angioino-aragonese', in Petti Balbi and Vitolo (eds.), *Linguaggi e pratiche del potere*, 41–69.
Welch, E. S., *Art and Authority in Renaissance Milan*, New Haven: Yale University Press, 1995.
Zorzi, A., 'Rituali di violenza, cerimoniali penali. Rappresentazioni della giustizia nelle città italiane centro settentrionali (secoli XIII–XV)', in Cammarosano (ed.), *Le forme della propaganda politica*, 395–425.

21. *Renaissance diplomacy* (Isabella Lazzarini)

Ashtor, E., *Levant Trade in the Later Middle Ages*, Princeton University Press, 1983.
Barbaro, E. *De coelibatu, de officio legati*, V. Branca (ed.), Florence: Olschki, 1959.
Barbiche, B., 'Les "diplomates" pontificaux du Moyen Âge tardif à la première modernité. Offices et charge pastorale', in A. Jamme and O. Poncet (eds.), *Offices et papauté (XIVe–XVIIe siècle). Charges, hommes, destins*, Rome: École française de Rome, 2005, 357–70.
Behrens, B., 'Treatises on the ambassador written in the fifteenth and early sixteenth century', *English Historical Review* 51 (1936), 616–27.
Bisticci, V. da, *Le vite*, 2 vols., A. Greco (ed.), Florence: Istituto nazionale di studi sul Rinascimento, 1976.
Blet, P., *Histoire de la représentation diplomatique de la Saint Siège des origines à l'aube du XIXe siècle*, Città del Vaticano: Archivio Vaticano, 1982.
Bullard, M. M., 'The language of diplomacy', in M. M. Bullard, *Lorenzo il Magnifico: Image and Anxiety, Politics and Finance*, Florence: Olschki, 1994, 81–109.

Carafa, D., *Memoriali*, F. Petrucci Nardelli (ed.), Rome: Bonacci, 1988.
Carteggi diplomatici fra Milano sforzesca e la Borgogna, E. Sestan (ed.), 2 vols., Rome: Istituto storico italiano per la storia moderna e contemporanea, 1985–7.
Carteggio degli oratori mantovani alla corte sforzesca (1450–1500), 15 vols., F. Leverotti (gen ed.), Rome: Pubblicazioni degli Archivi di Stato: I *(1450–1459)*, II *(1460)*, III *(1461)*, IV *(1462)*, I. Lazzarini (ed.), 1999, 2000, 2002; V *(1463)*, M. Folin (ed.), 2003; VI *(1464–1465)*, VII *(1466–1467)*, VIII, *(1468–1471)*, M. N. Covini (ed.), 1999, 2000, 2001; X *(1475–1477)*, XII *(1480–1482)*, G. Battioni (ed.), 2007, 2002; XI *(1478–1479)*, M. Simonetta (ed.), 2001; XV *(1495–1498)*, A. Grati and A. Pacini (eds.), 2003.
Il carteggio di Gerardo Cerruti, oratore sforzesco a Bologna (1470–1474), 2 vols., T. Duranti (ed.), Bologna: CLUEB, 2007.
Catalano, F., 'La fine della signoria sforzesca', in *Storia di Milano*, VII, *L'età sforzesca dal 1450 al 1500*, Milan: Treccani, 1956, 431–508.
Catelacci, D., 'Diario di Felice Brancacci ambasciatore con Carlo Federighi al Cairo per il comune di Firenze (1422)', *Archivio Storico Italiano* 8 (1881), 157–88.
Commissioni di Rinaldo degli Albizi per il comune di Firenze dal MCCCXCIX al MCCCCXXXIII, 4 vols., C. Guasti (ed.), Florence: Cellini, 1867–73.
Corrispondenza degli ambasciatori fiorentini a Napoli, 3 vols., B. Figliuolo (gen. ed.), Salerno: Carlone: I, *Giovanni Lanfredini (13.IV.1484–9.V.1485)*, II, *Giovanni Lanfredini (V.1485–X.1486)*, E. Scarton (ed.), 2002, 2005; V, *Francesco Valori e Piero Vettori (VIII.1487–VI.1489)*, P. Meli (ed.), 2011; VI, *Pietro Nasi (IV.1491–XI. 1491), Giovanni Antonio della Valle (XI.1491–I.1492) e Nicolò Michelozzi (I.1492–VI.1492)*, B. Figliuolo and S. Marcotti (eds.), 2004.
Covini, M. N., 'Guerra e relazioni diplomatiche in Italia (secoli XIV–XV). La diplomazia dei condottieri', in *Guerra y Diplomacia en la Europa occidental, 1280–1480*, Pamplona: Gobierno de Navarra, 2005, 163–98.
Covini, M. N., B. Figliuolo, I. Lazzarini and F. Senatore, 'Pratiche e norme di comportamento nella diplomazia italiana: i carteggi di Napoli, Firenze, Milano, Mantova e Ferrara tra fine XIV e fine XV secolo', in J.-C. Waquet (ed.), *Les écrits relatifs à l'ambassadeur et à l'art de négocier de la fin du Moyen Âge a la fin du XVIIIe siècle*, forthcoming.
'Diplomazia edita. Le edizioni delle corrispondenze diplomatiche quattrocentesche', *Bullettino dell'Istituto Storico Italiano per il Medio Evo* 110 (2008), 1–143.
I dispacci di Cristoforo da Piacenza, procuratore mantovano alla corte pontificia (1371–1383), A. Segre (ed.), Florence: Tip. Galileiana, 1909.
Dispacci di Pietro Cornaro ambasciatore a Milano durante la guerra di Chioggia, V. Lazzarini (ed.), Venice: Regia Deputazione di Storia Patria, 1939.
Dispacci di Zaccaria Barbaro (1.11.1471–7.9.1473), G. Corazzol (ed.), Rome: Libreria dello Stato, 1994.
Dispacci sforzeschi da Napoli, 3 vols., M. Del Treppo (gen. ed.), Salerno: Carlone: I *(1444–2.VII.1458)*, II *(4.VII.1458–30.XII.1459)*, F. Senatore (ed.), 1997, 2004; IV *(1.I.–26.XII.1461)*, F. Storti (ed.), 2002.

Dispatches with Related Documents of Milanese Ambassadors in France and Burgundy, 3 vols., Northern Illinois University Press: I *(1450–1460)*, II *(1460–1461)*, P. M. Kendall and V. Ilardi (eds.), Athens, 1970, 1971; III *(1466)*, V. Ilardi (ed.), Dekalb, 1981.

Dover, P. M., 'The economic predicament of Italian Renaissance ambassadors', *Journal of Early Modern History* 12 (2008), 137–67.

'The resident ambassador and the transformation of intelligence gathering in Renaissance Italy', in E. O'Halphin, R. Armstrong and J. Ohlmeyer (eds.), *Intelligence, Statecraft and International Power*, Dublin: Irish Academy Press, 2006, 17–34.

Duranti, T., *Diplomazia e autogoverno a Bologna nel Quattrocento (1392–1466). Fonti per la storia delle istituzioni*, Bologna: CLUEB, 2009.

Ferrer Mallol, M. T., J.-M. Moeglin, S. Péquignout and M. Sánchez Martínez (eds.), *Negociar en la Etad Media, Négocier au Moyen Âge*, Barcelona: CSIC, 2005.

Figliuolo, B., *Il diplomatico e il trattatista. Ermolao Barbaro ambasciatore della Serenissima e il De officio legati*, Naples: Guida, 1999.

Folin, M., 'Gli oratori estensi nel sistema politico italiano (1440–1505)', in G. Fragnito and M. Miegge (eds.), *Girolamo Savonarola da Ferrara all'Europa*, Florence: Il Giglio, 2001, 51–83.

Frigo, D. (ed.), *Politics and Diplomacy in Early Modern Italy: The Structure of Diplomatic Practice, 1450–1800*, Cambridge University Press, 2000.

Fubini, R., 'L'ambasciatore nel XV secolo. Due trattati e una biografia (Bernard de Rosier, Ermolao Barbaro, Vespasiano da Bisticci)', *Mélanges de l'École Française de Rome* 108 (1996), 645–65.

'Appunti sui rapporti diplomatici fra il dominio sforzesco e Firenze medicea. Modi e tecniche dell'ambasciata dalle trattative per la lega italica alla missione di Sacramoro da Rimini', in *Gli Sforza a Milano e in Lombardia e i loro rapporti con gli stati italiani ed europei (1450–1535)*, Milan: Cisalpino-Goliardica, 1979–80, 291–334.

'Classe dirigente ed esercizio della diplomazia nella Firenze quattrocentesca', in *I ceti dirigenti nella Toscana del Quattrocento*, Florence: Papafave, 1987, 117–89.

'Diplomacy and government in the Italian city-states of the fifteenth century (Florence and Venice)', in Frigo (ed.), *Politics and Diplomacy*, 25–48.

Italia quattrocentesca. Politica e diplomazia nell'età di Lorenzo il Magnifico, Milan: F. Angeli, 1994.

'"Potenze grosse" e piccolo stato nell'Italia del Rinascimento. Consapevolezza della distinzione e dinamica dei poteri', in L. Barletta, F. Cardini and G. Galasso (eds.) *Il piccolo stato. Politica storia diplomazia*, San Marino: AIEP, 2003, 91–126.

'La "résidentialité de l'ambassadeur" dans le mythe et dans la réalité. Une enquête sur les origines', in L. Bély (ed.), *L'invention de la diplomatie. Moyen Âge-Temps Modernes*, Paris: PUF, 1998, 27–35.

Gaeta, F. 'Origine e sviluppo della rappresentanza stabile pontificia in Venezia (1485–1533)', *Annuario dell'Istituto Storico Italiano per l'Età Moderna e Contemporanea* 10–11 (1957–8), 3–282.

Gilli, P., 'De l'importance d'être hors-norme. La pratique diplomatique de Giannozzo Manetti d'après son biographe Naldo Naldi', in R. M. Dessì (ed.), *Prêcher la paix et discipliner la société (XIIIe–XVe siècle)*, Turnhout: Brepols, 2005, 413–30.

'La fonction d'ambassadeurs dans les traités juridiques italiens du XVe siècle. L'impossible représentation', *Mélanges de l'École Française de Rome-Moyen Âge* 121, 2 (2009), 173–87.

Grubb, J., 'Diplomacy in the Italian city-state', in A. Molho, K. Raaflaub and J. Emden (eds.), *City-States in Classical Antiquity and Medieval Italy*, Stuttgart: F. Steiner, 1991, 603–17.

Guicciardini, F., *Opere*, I, E. Lugnani Scarano (ed.), Turin: Utet, 1983.

Hrabar, W. E., *De Legatis et Legationibus Tractatus Varii*, Dorpat: Mattiesen, 1905.

Hyde, J. K., 'The role of diplomatic correspondence and reporting: news and chronicles', in J. K. Hyde, *Literacy and Its Uses: Studies on Late Medieval Italy*, Manchester and New York: Manchester University Press, 1993, 217–60.

Ilardi, V., 'The banker-statesman and the condottiere-prince: Cosimo de Medici and Francesco Sforza (1450–1464)', in S. Bertelli, N. Rubinstein and C. H. Smyth (eds.) *Florence and Milan: Comparisons and Relations*, Florence: La Nuova Italia, II, 1989, 217–42.

'Fifteenth-century diplomatic documents in Western European archives and libraries (1450–1494)', *Studies on Renaissance* 9 (1962), 64–112.

'Index of microfilms on Italian diplomatic history, 1454–1494', in D. Abulafia (ed.), *The French Descent into Renaissance Italy 1494–1495: Antecedents and Effects*, London: Aldershot, 1995, 405–83.

Studies in Italian Renaissance Diplomatic History, London: Aldershot, 1986.

Isaacs, A. K., 'Sui rapporti interstatali in Italia dal Medioevo all'età moderna', in G. Chittolini, A. Mohlo and P. Schiera (eds.), *Origini dello stato. Processi di formazione statale in Italia fra Medioevo ed età moderna*, Bologna: Il Mulino, 1994, 113–32.

Jones, P. J., 'Travel notes of an apprentice Florentine statesman, Giovanni di Tommaso Ridolfi', in P. Denley and C. Elam (eds.), *Florence and Italy: Renaissance Studies in Honour of Nicolaj Rubinstein*, London: London Committee for Medieval Studies, Westfield College, 1988, 256–80.

Lazzarini, I., 'Argument and emotion in Italian diplomacy in the early fifteenth century: the case of Rinaldo degli Albizzi (Florence, 1399–1430)', in A. Gamberini, J. P. Genet and A. Zorzi (eds.), *The Languages of Political Society*, Rome: Viella, 2011, 339–64.

'Il gesto diplomatico fra comunicazione politica, grammatica delle emozioni, linguaggio delle scritture (Italia, XV secolo)', in M. Baggio and M. Salvadori (eds.), *Iconografia del gesto. Forme della comunicazione non verbale dall'antico al moderno*, Rome: Quasar, 2009, 75–93.

'L'informazione politico-diplomatica nell'età della pace di Lodi. Raccolta, selezione, trasmissione. Spunti di ricerca dal carteggio Milano–Mantova nella prima età sforzesca (1450–1466)', *Nuova Rivista Storica* 83 (1998), 247–80.

L'Italia degli stati territoriali. Secoli XIII–XV, Rome and Bari: Laterza, 2003.

'Materiali per una didattica delle scritture pubbliche di cancelleria nell'Italia del Quattrocento', *Scrineum-Rivista* 2 (2004), http://scrineum.unipv.it/rivista/2-2004/lazzarini.html.

'News from Mantua: diplomatic networks and political conflict in the age of the Italian Wars', in M. Chisholm, H. Noflatscher and B. Schnerb, *Maximilian I 1459–1519. Wahrnehmung-Übersetzungen-Gender*, Innsbruck: Studien Verlag, 2011, 111–29.

'La nomination d'un cardinal de famille entre l'empire et la papauté. Les pratiques de négociation de Bartolomeo Bonatti, orateur de Ludovico Gonzaga (Rome, 1471)', in *Paroles de négociateurs. L'entretien dans la pratique diplomatique de la fin du Moyen Âge à la fin du XIXe siècle*, S. Andretta, S. Péquignot, M.-K. Schaub, J.-C. Waquet and C. Windler (eds.), Rome: École française de Rome, 2010, 51–69.

(ed.), *Scritture e potere. Pratiche documentarie e forme di governo nell'Italia tardomedievale (XIV–XV secolo)*, RM Rivista 9 (2008), www.storia.unifi.it/_RM/rivista/2008-1.htm#S_monografica.

Leverotti, F., *Diplomazia e governo dello stato. I 'famigli cavalcanti' di Francesco Sforza (1450–1466)*, Pisa: ETS, 1992.

Lutter, C., *Politische Kommunikation an der Wende vom Mittelalter zur Neuzeit. Die diplomatischen Beziehungen zwischen der Republik Venedig und Maximilian 1. (1495–1508)*, Vienna and Munich: Veroffentlichungen des Instituts für Österreichische Geschichtsforschung, 1998.

Machiavelli, N., *Notula per uno che va ambasciadore in Francia*, in N. Machiavelli, *Tutte le opere*, M. Martelli (ed.), Florence: Sansoni, 1971, 54–5.

Mallett, M., 'Ambassadors and their audience in Renaissance Italy', *Renaissance Studies* 8 (1994), 229–43.

'Diplomacy and war in later fifteenth-century Italy', *Proceedings of the British Academy* 67 (1981), 267–88.

Martines, L. *Strong Words: Writing and Social Strain in the Italian Renaissance*, Baltimore: Johns Hopkins University Press, 2001.

Maspes, A., 'Prammatica pel ricevimento degli ambasciatori inviati alla Corte di Galeazzo Maria Sforza, Duca di Milano (1468–10 dicembre)', *Archivio Storico Lombardo* 17 (1890), 146–51.

Mattingly, G., 'The first resident embassies: mediaeval Italian origins of modern diplomacy', *Speculum* 12 (1937), 423–39.

Renaissance Diplomacy, Oxford: Cape, 1955.

Medici, L. de', *Lettere*, 1977–2010, 13 vols., N. Rubinstein and D. V. Kent (gen. eds.), Florence: Giunti: I *(1460–1474)*, II *(1474–1478)*, R. Fubini (ed.), 1977; III *(1478–1479)*, IV *(1479–1480)*, N. Rubinstein (ed.), 1977, 1981; V *(1480–1481)*, VI *(1481–1482)*, VII *(1482–1484)*, M. Mallett (ed.), 1981, 1990, 1998; VIII *(1484–1485)*, IX *(1485–1486)*, H. Butters (ed.), 2001, 2002; X *(1486–1487)*, XI *(1487–1488)*, M. M. Bullard (ed.), 2003, 2004; XII *(II–VII.1488)*, M. Pellegrini (ed.), 2007; XV *(III–VIII.1489)*, L. Boninger (ed.), 2010.

Négotiations diplomatiques de la France avec la Toscane. Documents recueillis par G. Canestrini et publiés par A. Desjardins, 5 vols., Paris: Imprimerie impériale, plus nationale, 1859–75.

Negri, P., 'Le missioni di Pandolfo Collenuccio a papa Alessandro VI (1494–1498)', *Atti e Rendiconti della Società Romana di Storia Patria* 33 (1910), 333–439.
Noflatscher, H., 'L'"Italia" nella percezione politica di Massimiliano I', in L. de Finis (ed.), *La proclamazione imperiale di Massimiliano d'Asburgo (4 febbraio 1508)*, Trento: Studi trentini di scienze storiche 87 (2008), 57–78.
Olgiati, C., 'Diplomatici e ambasciatori della repubblica nel Quattrocento', in *La storia dei genovesi*, XI, Genoa: Copy-Lito, 1991, 353–73.
Petrucci, A., *Scrivere lettere. Una storia plurimillenaria*, Rome and Bari: Laterza, 2008.
Pibiri, E., *En voyage pour Monseigneur. Ambassadeurs, officiers et messagers à la cour de Savoie (XIVe–XVe siècles)*, Geneva: Société d'Histoire de la Suisse Romande, 2011.
Queller, D. E., *Early Venetian Legislation on Ambassadors*, Geneva: Droz, 1966.
The Office of Ambassador in the Middle Ages, Princeton University Press, 1976.
'Thirteenth-century diplomatic envoys: nuncii and procuratores', *Speculum* 35 (1960), 196–213.
Rubinstein, N., 'Lorenzo de' Medici: the formation of his statecraft', *Proceedings of the British Academy* 63 (1977), 71–94.
Schmutz, R., 'Medieval papal representatives: legatus, nuncius, and judges', *Studia Gratiana* 15 (1972), 443–63.
Senatore, F., 'Callisto III nelle corrispondenze diplomatiche italiane. La documentazione sui Borgia nell'Archivio di Stato di Siena', in *I figli del signor Papa, Quinto centenario della morte di Cesare Borgia (1507–2007), Revista Borja. Revista de l'IIEB* 2 (2008–9), 141–86.
'*Uno mundo de carta*'. *Forme e strutture della diplomazia sforzesca*, Naples: Liguori, 1998.
The Travel Journal of Antonio de Beatis: Germany, Switzerland, the Low Countries, France and Italy, 1517–1518, J. R. Hale (ed.), London: Hakluyt Society, 1979.

22. Regional states and economic development (Franco Franceschi and Luca Molà)

Abulafia, D., 'The crown and the economy under Ferrante I of Naples (1458–1494)', in T. Dean and C. Wickham (eds.), *City and Countryside in Late Medieval and Renaissance Italy: Essays Presented to Philip Jones*, London: Humbledon Press, 1990, 125–46.
Barbieri, G., *Economia e politica nel Ducato di Milano, 1386–1535*, Milan: Vita e Pensiero, 1938.
Boucheron, P., *Le pouvoir de bâtir. Urbanisme et politique éditilaire à Milan (XIVe–XVe siècles)*, Rome: École française de Rome, 1998.
Brown, J. C., 'Concepts of political economy: Cosimo I de' Medici in a comparative European context', in *Firenze e la Toscana dei Medici nell'Europa del '500*, 3 vols., Florence: Olschki, 1983, I, 278–93.
Carafa, D., *Memoriali*, F. Petrucci Nardelli (ed.), Rome: Bonacci, 1988.
Chittolini, G., 'Alcune note sul ducato di Milano nel Quattrocento', in S. Gensini (ed.), *Principi e città alla fine del Medioevo*, Pisa: Pacini, 1996, 413–43.

Ciriacono, S., 'L'economia regionale veneta in epoca moderna. Note a margine del caso bergamasco', in *Venezia e la Terraferma. Economia e società*, Bergamo: Comune di Bergamo, 1989, 43–76.

'Venise et ses villes. Structuration et déstructuration d'un marché regional XVIe–XVIIIe siècle', *Revue Historique* 176 (1986), 187–207.

Collodo, S., 'Il sistema annonario delle città venete: da pubblica utilità a servizio sociale (secoli XIII–XVI)', in *Città e servizi sociali nell'Italia dei secoli XII–XV*, Pistoia: Centro italiano di studi di storia e d'arte, 1990, 383–415.

Corritore, P., 'Una fondamentale discontinuità padana. La linea dell'Oglio (secoli XVI–XVIII)', in E. Brambilla and G. Muto (eds.), *La Lombardia spagnola. Nuovi indirizzi di ricerca*, Milan: Unicopli, 1997, 139–53.

Del Treppo, M., 'Il regno aragonese', in G. Galasso and R. Romeo (eds.), *Storia del Mezzogiorno*, IV/I, *Il regno dagli Angioini ai Borboni*, Rome: Editalia, 1986, 87–201.

Demo, E., *L''anima della città'. L'industria tessile a Verona e Vicenza (1400–1550)*, Milan: Unicopli, 2001.

Dini, B., 'Le vie di comunicazione del territorio fiorentino alla metà del Quattrocento', in *Mercati e consumi. Organizzazione e qualificazione del commercio in Italia dal XII al XX secolo*, Bologna: Analisi, 1986, 285–96.

Epstein, S. R., *Freedom and Growth: The Rise of States and Markets in Europe, 1300–1750*, London: Routledge, 2000.

An Island for Itself: Economic Development and Social Change in Late Medieval Sicily, Cambridge University Press, 1992.

'Manifatture tessili e strutture politico-istituzionali nella Lombardia tardo-medievale. Ipotesi di ricerca', *Studi di Storia Medioevale e di Diplomatica* 14 (1993), 55–89.

'Stato territoriale ed economia regionale nella Toscana del Quattrocento', in *La Toscana al tempo di Lorenzo il Magnifico. Politica Economia Cultura Arte*, 3 vols., Pisa: Pacini, 1996, III, 869–90.

'Strutture di mercato', in A. Zorzi and W. J. Connell (eds.), *Lo stato territoriale fiorentino (secoli XIV–XV). Ricerche, linguaggi, confronti*, Pisa: Pacini, 2001, 93–134.

'Town and country in late medieval Italy: economic and institutional aspects', *Economic History Review*, 2nd ser. 46 (1993), 453–77.

Fantoni, G., *L'acqua a Milano. Uso e gestione nel basso Medioevo (1385–1535)*, Bologna: Cappelli, 1990.

Fasano Guarini, E., 'Città soggette e contadi nel dominio fiorentino tra Quattro e Cinquecento. Il caso pisano', in M. Mirri (ed.), *Ricerche di storia moderna*, I, Pisa: Pacini, 1976, 1–94.

Faugeron, F., 'De la commune à la capitale du *Stato di Terra*. La politique annonaire et la constitution de l'état de Terreferme vénitien (Ire moitié du XVe siècle)', in *Les villes capitales au Moyen Âge*, Paris: Publications de la Sorbonne, 2006, 97–111.

Fiorenzi, P., *Le arti a Modena (Storia delle Corporazioni d'Arti e Mestieri)*, Modena: Società Tipografica Modenese, 1962.

Franceschi, F., 'I forestieri e l'industria della seta fiorentina', in L. Molà, R. C. Mueller and C. Zanier (eds.), *La seta in Italia dal Medioevo al Seicento. Dal baco al drappo*, Venice: Marsilio, 2000, 401–22.

'La grande manifattura tessile', in *La trasmissione dei saperi nel Medioevo (secoli XII–XIV)*, Pistoia: Centro italiano di studi di storia e d'arte, 2005, 355–89.

'Industria, commercio, credito', in M. Ciliberto (ed.), *Storia della civiltà toscana*, II, *Il Rinascimento*, Florence: Le Monnier, 2001, 533–60.

'Intervento del potere centrale e ruolo delle Arti nel governo dell'economia fiorentina del Trecento e del primo Quattrocento. Linee generali', *Archivio Storico Italiano* 151 (1993), 863–909.

'Istituzioni e attività economica a Firenze. Considerazioni sul governo del settore industriale (1350–1450)', in *Istituzioni e società in Toscana nell'età moderna*, 2 vols., Rome: Ministero per i Beni Culturali e Ambientali, 1994, I, 76–117.

Franceschi, F., and Molà, L., 'L'economia del Rinascimento. Dalle teorie della crisi alla "preistoria" del consumismo', in M. Fantoni (ed.), *Il Rinascimento Italiano e l'Europa*, I, *Storia e storiografia*, Treviso and Vicenza: Fondazione Cassamarca-Angelo Colla, 2006, 185–200.

Frangioni, L., *Milano e le sue strade. Costi di trasporto e vie di commercio dei prodotti milanesi alla fine del Trecento*, Bologna: Cappelli, 1983.

'La politica economica del dominio di Milano nei secoli XV–XVI', *Nuova Rivista Storica* 71 (1987), 253–68.

Ginatempo, M., 'Finanze e fiscalità. Note sulle peculiarità degli stati regionali italiani e delle loro città', in F. Salvestrini (ed.), *L'Italia alla fine del Medioevo. I caratteri originali nel quadro europeo*, 2 vols., Florence: Firenze University Press, 2006, I, 241–94.

'Gerarchie demiche e sistemi urbani nell'Italia bassomedievale. Una discussione', *Società e Storia* 72 (1996), 347–83.

'Spunti comparativi sulle trasformazioni della fiscalità nell'Italia post-comunale', in P. Mainoni (ed.), *Politiche finanziarie e fiscali nell'Italia settentrionale, secoli XIII–XV*, Milan: Unicopli, 2001, 125–220.

Goldthwaite, R. A., *The Economy of Renaissance Florence*, Baltimore: Johns Hopkins University Press, 2009.

Herlihy, D., *Medieval and Renaissance Pistoia: The Social History of an Italian Town, 1200–1430*, New Haven and London: Yale University Press, 1967.

'Le relazioni economiche di Firenze con le città soggette nel secolo XV', in *Egemonia fiorentina ed autonomie locali nella Toscana nord-occidentale del primo Rinascimento. Vita, arte, cultura*, Pistoia: Centro italiano di studi di storia e d'arte, 1978, 79–109.

Jacoby, D., 'Raw materials for the glass industries of Venice and the Terraferma, about 1370–about 1460', *Journal of Glass Studies* 33 (1993), 65–90.

Knapton, M., 'City wealth and state wealth in northeast Italy, 14th–17th centuries', in N. Bulst and J. P. Genet (eds.), *La ville, la bourgeoisie et la genèse de l'état moderne*, Paris: CNRS, 1988, 183–209.

'"Nobiltà e popolo" e un trentennio di storiografia veneta', *Nuova Rivista Storica* 82, 1 (1998), 167–92.

'Tra dominante e dominio (1517–1630)', in G. Cozzi, M. Knapton and G. Scarabello (eds.), *Storia della Repubblica di Venezia*, Turin: Utet, 1992, 201–549.

La Roncière, Ch. M. de, 'Dalla città-stato allo stato regionale. La costituzione del territorio (XIV–XV secolo)', in J. Boutier, S. Landi and O. Rouchon (eds.), *Firenze e la Toscana. Genesi e trasformazione di uno stato (XIV–XIX secolo)*, updated and revised edn, Florence: La Mandragora, 2010 (2004), 11–30.

Firenze e le sue campagne nel Trecento. Mercanti, produzione, traffici, Florence: Olschki, 2005.

Lamberini, D., '"A beneficio dell'universale". Ingegneria idraulica e privilegi di macchine alla corte dei Medici', in A. Fiocca, D. Lamberini and C. Maffioli (eds.), *Arte e scienza delle acque nel Rinascimento*, Venice: Marsilio, 2003, 47–71.

Lanaro, P., *I mercati della repubblica veneta. Economie cittadine e stato territoriale (secoli XV–XVIII)*, Venice: Marsilio, 1999.

'Periferie senza centro. Reti fieristiche nello spazio geografico della Terraferma veneta in età moderna', in P. Lanaro (ed.), *La pratica dello scambio. Sistemi di fiere, mercanti e città in Europa e in Italia, 1400–1700*, Venice: Marsilio, 2003, 21–51.

Mainoni, P., *Economia e politica nella Lombardia medievale. Da Bergamo a Milano fra XIII e XV secolo*, Milan: Gribaudo, 1994.

Malanima, P., *La fine del primato. Crisi e riconversione nell'Italia del Seicento*, Milan: Bruno Mondadori, 1998.

'La formazione di una regione economica. La Toscana nei secoli XIII–XV', *Società e storia* 20 (1983), 229–69.

'Politica ed economia nella formazione dello stato regionale. Il caso toscano', *Studi veneziani*, ns 11 (1986), 61–72.

'Teoria economica regionale e storia. Il caso della Toscana (XIII–XVI secolo)', in L. Mocarelli (ed.), *Lo sviluppo economico regionale in prospettiva storica*, Milan: CUESP, 1996, 133–48.

Mandich, G., 'Le privative industriali veneziane (1450–1550)', *Rivista di Diritto Commerciale* 34 (1936), 511–47.

Mazzaoui, M. F., 'Artisan migration and technology in the Italian textile industry in the late Middle Ages (1100–1500)', in R. Comba, G. Piccinni and G. Pinto (eds.), *Strutture familiari, epidemie, migrazioni nell'Italia medievale*, Naples: Liguori, 1984, 519–34.

'La diffusione delle tecniche tessili del cotone in Italia nei secoli XII–XVI', in *Tecnica e società nell'Italia dei secoli XII–XVI*, Pistoia: Centro italiano di studi di storia e d'arte, 1987, 157–71.

'The Lombard cotton industry and the political economy of the dukes of Milan in the second half of the fifteenth century', in *Milano nell'età di Ludovico il Moro*, 2 vols., Milan: Comune di Milano, 1983, I, 173–7.

Mirri, M., 'Formazione di una regione economica. Ipotesi sulla Toscana, sul Veneto, sulla Lombardia', *Studi veneziani*, ns 11 (1986), 47–59.

Molà, L., 'The Italian silk industry in the Renaissance', in S. Rauch (ed.), *Le Mariegole delle Arti dei tessitori di seta. I veluderi (1347–1474) e i samitari*

(1370–1475), Venice: Comitato per la Pubblicazione delle Fonti per la Storia di Venezia, 2010, li–lxxxv.

The Silk Industry of Renaissance Venice, Baltimore and London: Johns Hopkins University Press, 2000.

'States and crafts: relocating technical skills in Renaissance Italy', in E. Welch and M. O'Malley (eds.), *The Material Renaissance*, Manchester: Manchester University Press, 2007, 133–53.

'Stato e impresa. Privilegi per l'introduzione di nuove arti e brevetti', in P. Braunstein and L. Molà (eds.), *Il Rinascimento Italiano e l'Europa*, III, *Produzione e tecniche*, Treviso and Vicenza: Fondazione Cassamarca and Angelo Colla Editore, 2007, 533–72.

Molà, L., and R. C. Mueller, 'Essere straniero a Venezia nel tardo Medioevo. Accoglienza e rifiuto nei privilegi di cittadinanza e nelle sentenze criminali', in S. Cavaciocchi (ed.), *Le migrazioni in Europa, secc. XIII–XVIII*, Florence: Le Monnier, 1994, 839–51.

Mozzato, A., 'The production of woollens in fifteenth- and sixteenth-century Venice', in P. Lanaro (ed.), *At the Centre of the Old World: Trade and Manufacturing in Venice and the Venetian Mainland, 1400–1800*, Toronto: Centre for Reformation and Renaissance Studies, 2006, 73–107.

North, D. C., *Institutions, Institutional Change and Economic Performance*, Cambridge University Press, 1990.

Persico, T., *Diomede Carafa. Uomo di stato e scrittore del secolo XV*, Naples: Pierro, 1899.

Pescione, R., 'Gli statuti dell'Arte della seta in Napoli in rapporto al privilegio di giurisdizione', *Archivio Storico per le Provincie Napoletane*, ns 5 (1919), 159–90; 6 (1920), 61–87.

Plebani, T., *Venezia 1469. La legge e la stampa*, Venice: Marsilio, 2004.

Pult Quaglia, A. M., *'Per provvedere ai popoli'. Il sistema annonario nella Toscana dei Medici*, Florence: Olschki, 1990.

Rombaldi, O., 'L'arte della seta a Reggio Emilia nel secolo XVI', in *L'arte e l'industria della seta a Reggio Emilia, dal sec. XVI al sec. XIX*, Modena: Aedes Muratoriana, 1968, 43–73.

Sakellariou, E., 'Elementi di sviluppo regionale nel regno di Napoli del tardo Medioevo', *Archivio storico del Sannio*, ns 4 (1999), 5–28.

Tangheroni, M., 'Il sistema economico della Toscana nel Trecento', in M. Tangheroni, *Medioevo tirrenico. Sardegna, Toscana e Pisa*, Pisa: Pacini, 1992, 107–32.

Varanini, G. M., 'Élites cittadine e governo dell'economia tra comune, signoria e "stato regionale". L'esempio di Verona', in G. Petti Balbi (ed.), *Strutture del potere ed élites economiche nelle città europee dei secoli XI–XVI*, Naples: Liguori, 1996, 135–68.

'Le politiche del dominio. Spunti comparativi', in A. Zorzi and W. J. Connell (eds.), *Lo stato territoriale fiorentino (secoli XIV–XV). Ricerche, linguaggi, confronti*, Pisa: Pacini, 2001, 241–51.

Verga, E., *Il comune di Milano e l'Arte della Seta dal secolo decimoquinto al decimottavo*, Milan: Stucchi Ceretti e C., 1917.

Zecchin, L., 'Famiglie vetrarie famose: i Serena', in L. Zecchin, *Vetro e vetrai di Murano. Studi sulla storia del vetro*, 3 vols., Venice: Arsenale Editrice, 1989, 210–13.

23. *The papacy and the Italian states* (Giorgio Chittolini)

Becker, M. B., 'Church and state in Florence on the eve of the Renaissance (1343–1382)', *Speculum* 37 (1962), 509–27.

'Some economic implications of the conflict between church and state in Trecento Florence', *Medieval Studies* 21 (1959), 1–15.

Belloni, C., *Francesco della Croce. Contributi alla storia della chiesa ambrosiana nel Quattrocento*, Milan: LED, 1995.

Berengo, M., *L'Europa delle città. Il volto della società urbana europea tra Medioevo ed età moderna*, Turin: Einaudi, 1999.

Bizzocchi, R., *Chiesa e potere nella Toscana del Quattrocento*, Bologna: Il Mulino, 1987.

'Clero e chiesa nella società italiana alla fine del Medioevo', in M. Rosa (ed.), *Clero e società nell'Italia moderna*, Rome and Bari: Laterza, 1992, 3–44.

Blickle, P., 'Einführung', in P. Blickle (ed.), *Theorien kommunaler Ordnung in Europa*, Munich: Oldenbourg, 1996, 1–17.

Gemeindereformation. Die Menschen des 16. Jahrhunderts auf dem Weg zum Heil, Munich: Oldenbourg, 1985.

Brambilla, E., *Alle origini del Sant'Uffizio. Penitenza, giustizia e confessione spirituale dal Medioevo al XVI secolo*, Bologna: Il Mulino, 2001.

Brentano, R., *Two Churches: England and Italy in the Thirteenth Century*, Princeton University Press, 1968.

Brucker, G. A., *Renaissance Florence*, New York: Wiley & Sons, 1969.

Bullard, M. M., 'L'altra "anima" della chiesa, nella prima età moderna', in G. Chittolini, A. Molho and P. Schiera (eds.), *Origini dello stato. Processi di formazione statale in Italia fra Medioevo ed età moderna*, Bologna: Il Mulino, 1994, 515–29.

Canobbio, E., *Preti nelle visite pastorali in alta Lombardia alla metà del XV secolo (Como, 1444–1445)*, in G. De Sandre Gasparini (ed.), *Preti nel Medioevo*, Verona: Cierre, 1997, 221–55.

Chittolini, G., 'Civic religion and the countryside in late medieval Italy', in T. Dean and C. Wickham (eds.), *City and Countryside in Late Medieval and Renaissance Italy: Essays Presented to Philip Jones*, London: Hambledon Press, 1996, 69–80.

'Note sui benefici rurali nell'Italia padana alla fine del Medioevo', in *Pievi e parrocchie nel basso Medioevo (secoli XIII–XV)*, Rome: Herder, 1984, I, 415–68.

'Religione cittadina e chiese di comune alla fine del Medioevo', in B. Adorni (ed.), *La chiesa a pianta centrale tempio civico del Rinascimento*, Milan: Electa, 2002, 15–26.

(ed.), *Gli Sforza, la chiesa lombarda e la corte di Roma. Strutture e pratiche beneficiarie nel ducato di Milano (1450–1535)*, Naples: Liguori, 1989.

'Stati regionali e istituzioni ecclesiastiche nell'Italia centrosettentrionale del Quattrocento', in G. Chittolini and G. Miccoli (eds.), *Storia d'Italia. Annali*, IX, *La Chiesa e il potere politico*, Turin: Einaudi, 1985, 147–94.

Chittolini, G., and K. Elm (eds.), *Ordini religiosi e società politica in Italia e Germania nei secoli XIV e XV*, Bologna: Il Mulino, 2001.

Contamine, P., 'Réformation. Un mot, une idée', in P. Contamine, *Des pouvoirs en France, 1300–1500*, Paris: Presses de l'École Normale Supérieur, 1992.

Cozzi, G., 'Politica, società, istituzioni', in G. Cozzi and M. Knapton (eds.), *La repubblica di Venezia nell'età moderna. Dalla guerra di Chioggia al 1517*, Turin: Utet, 1986, 3–271.

Cracco, G., 'Habitare secum. Luoghi dello spirito e luoghi della storia nel Medioevo europeo', in *L'Ateneo* 15, 4 (1999), 51–63.

De La Roncière, Ch. M., 'Dans la campagne florentine au XIV siècle. Le communautés chrétiennes et leurs curés', in J. Delumeau (ed.), *Histoire vécue du peuple chrétien*, Toulouse: Privat, 1979, II, 281–314.

'L'église en Italie', in *Histoire du Christianisme des origines à nos jours*, J.-M. Mayeur, Ch. Petri, A. Vauchez and M. Venard (eds.), Paris: Desclée-Fayard, 1990, V, 720–55.

De Vitt, F., *Istituzioni ecclesiastiche e vita quotidiana nel Friuli medievale*, Venice: Deputazione di storia patria per le Venezie, 1990.

Del Torre, G., 'Stato regionale e benefici ecclesiastici. Vescovadi e canonicati nella Terraferma veneziana all'inizio dell'età moderna', *Atti dell'Istituto veneto di Scienze, Lettere ed Arti* 151 (1992–3), 1171–1236.

Dionisotti, C., 'Chierici e laici', in C. Dionisotti, *Geografia e storia della letteratura italiana*, Turin: Einaudi, 1973, 55–88.

Fragnito, G., 'Istituzioni ecclesiastiche e costruzione dello stato. Riflessioni e spunti', in G. Chittolini, A. Molho and P. Schiera (eds.), *Origini dello stato. Processi di formazione statale in Italia fra Medioevo ed età moderna*, Bologna: Il Mulino, 1994, 531–50.

Galasso, G., *Il Mezzogiorno angioino e aragonese (1266–1494)*, in G. Galasso (ed.) *Storia d' Italia*, XV, *Il Regno di Napoli*, 1, Turin: Utet, 1992.

Gensini, S. (ed.), *Roma capitale (1447–1527)*, Pisa: Pacini, 1994.

Hay, D., *The Church in Italy in the Fifteenth Century*, Cambridge University Press, 1977.

Jones, P., *The Italian City-State: From Commune to Signoria*, Oxford University Press, 1997.

Landi, F., *Storia economica del clero in Europa. Secoli XV–XIX*, Rome: Carocci, 2005.

Miccoli, G., 'La storia religiosa', in R. Romano and C. Vivanti (eds.), *Storia d'Italia*, II, 1, *Dalla caduta dell'impero romano al secolo XVIII*, Turin: Einaudi, 1974, 431–1079.

Moeller, B., 'Kleriker als Bürgher', in *Festschrift für Hermann Heimpel zu 70. Geburtstag, I–II*, Göttingen: Vandenhoeck & Ruprecht, 1971–2, 195–224.

Nencini, P. (ed.), *Colle Val D'Elsa. Diocesi e città fra Cinque e Seicento*, Castelfiorentino: Società Storica della Valdelsa, 1992.

Oakley, F., *The Western Church in the Later Middle Ages*, Ithaca and London: Cornell University Press, 1979.

Ostinelli, P., *Il governo delle anime. Strutture ecclesiastiche nel Bellinzonese e nelle Valli ambrosiane (XIV–XV secolo)*, Locarno: Dadò, 1998.
Partner, P., *The Lands of St Peter: The Papal State in the Middle Ages and the Early Renaissance*, London: Eyre Methuen, 1972.
The Pope's Men: The Papal Civil Service in the Renaissance, Oxford: Clarendon, 1990.
Pellegrini, M., *Ascanio Maria Sforza. La parabola politica di un cardinale-principe del Rinascimento*, Rome: Istituto storico italiano per il Medio Evo, 2002.
Prodi, P., *The Papal Prince: One Body and Two Souls. The Papal Monarchy in Early Europe*, Cambridge University Press, 1997.
'The structure and the organisation of the church in Renaissance Venice', in J. R. Hale (ed.), *Renaissance Venice*, London: Faber & Faber, 1973, 409–30.
Prosdocimi, L., *Il diritto ecclesiastico dello stato di Milano dall'inizio della signoria viscontea al periodo tridentino*, Milan: Edizioni de L'Arte, 1941.
Prosperi, A., 'Dominus beneficiorum. Il conferimento dei benefici ecclesiastici fra prassi curiale e ragioni politiche negli stati italiani tra '400 e '500', in P. Johanek and P. Prodi (eds.), *Strutture ecclesiastiche in Italia e in Germania prima della Riforma*, Bologna: Il Mulino, 1984, 51–86.
'L'Italie', in J.-M. Mayeur, Ch. Pietri, L. Pietri, A. Vauchez and M. Venard (eds.), *De la Réforme à la Réformation (1450–1530)*, VII in *Histoire du christianisme des origines à nos jours*, Paris: Desclée-Fayard, 1994, 328–41.
Rapp, F., 'Le rétablissement de la Papauté. Une victoire imparfaite et coûteuse', in J.-M. Mayeur, Ch. Pietri, L. Pietri, A. Vauchez and M. Venard (eds.), *De la Réforme à la Réformation (1450–1530)*, VII in *Histoire du christianisme des origines à nos jours*, Paris: Desclée-Fayard, 1994, 77–142.
Scribner, B., 'Anticlericalism and the cities', in P. A. Dykema and H. A. Oberman (eds.), *Anticlericalism in Late Medieval and Early Modern Europe*, Leiden: E. J. Brill, 1993, 147–66.
Somaini, F., *Un prelato lombardo del XV secolo. Il card. Giovanni Arcimboldi, vescovo di Novara, arcivescovo di Milano*, 3 vols., Rome: Herder, 2003.
'Processi costitutivi, dinamiche politiche e strutture istituzionali dello stato visconteo-sforzesco', in G. Galasso (gen. ed.), *Storia d'Italia*, VI, *Comuni e signorie nell'Italia settentrionale. La Lombardia*, Turin: Utet, 1998, 681–825.
Stieber, J. W., *Pope Eugenius IV, the Council of Basel and the Secular and Ecclesiastical Authorities in the Empire: The Conflict over Supreme Authority and Power in the Church*, Leiden: Brill, 1978.
Swanson, R. S., 'Le clergé rural anglais au bas Moyen Âge (vers 1300–vers 1530)', in P. Bonassie (ed.), *Le clergé rural dans l'Europe médiévale et moderne*, Toulouse: Presses universitaires du Mirail, 61–100.
Thomson, J. A. F., *Popes and Princes, 1417–1517: Politics and Polity in the Late Medieval Church*, London: Allen & Unwin, 1980.
Trexler, R. C., 'Florence, by the Grace of the Lord Pope', *Medieval and Renaissance Studies* 9 (1972), 115–215.
'*Ne fides communis diminuatur*. Autorità papale e sovranità comunale a Firenze e a Siena fra il 1345 e il 1380', *Rivista di storia della Chiesa in Italia* 39 (1985), 448–501; 40 (1986), 1–25.
The Spiritual Power: Republican Florence Under Interdict, Leiden: Brill, 1974.

Vauchez, A. (ed.), *La religion civique à l'époque médiévale et moderne. Chrétienté et Islam*, Rome: École française de Rome, 1995.
Vitolo, G., 'Il regno angioino', in G. Galasso and R. Romeo (eds.), *Storia del Mezzogiorno*, IV/1, Naples: Editalia, 1986, 11–86.
Zarri, G., 'Aspetti dello sviluppo degli Ordini religiosi in Italia tra Quattro e Cinquecento. Studi e problemi', in P. Johanek and P. Prodi (eds.), *Strutture ecclesiastiche in Italia e in Germania prima della Riforma*, Bologna: Il Mulino, 1984, 207–57.

24. *Justice* (Andrea Zorzi)

Ascheri, M., *Tribunali, giuristi e istituzioni dal Medioevo all'età moderna*, Bologna: Il Mulino, 1989.
Bellabarba, M., *La giustizia nell'Italia moderna. XVI–XVIII secolo*, Rome and Bari: Laterza, 2008.
Bellabarba, M., G. Schwerhoff and A. Zorzi (eds.), *Criminalità e giustizia in Germania e in Italia. Pratiche giudiziarie e linguaggi giuridici tra tardo Medioevo ed età moderna*, Bologna: Il Mulino, 2001.
Boyer, J.-P., A. Mailloux and L. Verdon (eds.), *La justice temporelle dans les territoires angevins aux XIIIe et XIVe siècles. Théories et pratiques*, Rome: École française de Rome, 2005.
Brown, A., *Bartolomeo Scala, 1430–1497, Chancellor of Florence*, Princeton University Press, 1979.
Cagnin, G. (ed.), *Il processo Avogari (Treviso, 1314–1315)*, Rome: Viella, 1999.
Chiffoleau, J., C. Gauvard and A. Zorzi (eds.), *Pratiques sociales et politiques judiciaires dans les villes de l'Occident à la fin du Moyen Âge*, Rome: École française de Rome, 2007.
Connell, W. J., and A. Zorzi (eds.), *Florentine Tuscany: Structures and Practices of Power*, Cambridge University Press, 2000.
Covini, M. N., *'La balanza drita'. Pratiche di governo, leggi e ordinamenti nel ducato sforzesco*, Milan: F. Angeli, 2007.
 '*De gratia speciali*. Sperimentazioni documentarie e pratiche di potere tra i Visconti e gli Sforza', in M. Vallerani (ed.), *Tecniche di potere negli stati italiani (sec. XIV–XV)*, Rome: Viella, 2010, 185–206.
Cozzi, G. (ed.), *Stato società e giustizia nella Repubblica veneta (sec. XV–XVIII)*, 2 vols., Rome: Jouvence, 1980–5.
Dean, T., *Crime and Justice in Late Medieval Italy*, Cambridge University Press, 2007.
Dean, T., and K. J. P. Lowe (eds.), *Crime, Society and the Law in Renaissance Italy*, Cambridge University Press, 1994.
Della Misericordia, M., 'Giudicare con il consenso. Giustizia vescovile, pratiche sociali e potere politico nella diocesi di Como nel tardo Medioevo', *Archivio Storico Ticinese* 38 (2001), 179–218.
Fasoli, G., 'Ricerche sulla legislazione antimagnatizia nei comuni dell'alta e media Italia', *Rivista di storia del diritto italiano* 12, 1939, 86–133; 240–309.

Gamberini, A., *La città assediata. Poteri e identità politiche a Reggio in età viscontea*, Rome: Viella, 2003.
Lo stato visconteo. Linguaggi politici e dinamiche costituzionali, Milan: F. Angeli, 2005.
Gentile, M. (ed.), *Guelfi e ghibellini nell'Italia del Rinascimento*, Rome: Viella, 2005.
Kuehn, T., *Law, Family and Women: Toward a Legal Anthropology of Renaissance Italy*, University of Chicago Press, 1991.
Lazzarini, I., 'Gli atti di giurisdizione. Qualche nota intorno alle fonti giudiziarie nell'Italia del Medioevo (secc. XIII–XV)', *Società e storia* 58 (1992), 825–45.
Leverotti, F., *'Governare a modo e stillo de' Signori …'. Osservazioni in margine all'amministrazione della giustizia al tempo di Galeazzo Maria Sforza duca di Milano (1466–1476)*, Florence: Olschki, 1994.
Manikowska, H., 'Il controllo sulle città. Le istituzioni dell'ordine pubblico nelle città italiane dei secoli XIV e XV', in *Città e servizi sociali nell'Italia dei secoli XII–XV*, Pistoia: Centro Italiano di studi di storia e d'arte, 1990, 481–511.
Martines, L., *Lawyers and Statecraft in Renaissance Florence*, Princeton University Press, 1968.
Meccarelli, M., *Arbitrium. Un aspetto sistematico degli ordinamenti giuridici in età di diritto comune*, Milan: Giuffré, 1998.
Milani, G., *L'esclusione dal comune. Conflitti e bandi politici a Bologna e in altre città italiane tra XII e XIV secolo*, Rome: Istituto storico italiano per il Medio Evo, 2003.
'Prime note su disciplina e pratica del bando a Bologna attorno alla metà del secolo XIII', *Mélanges de l'École française de Rome, Moyen Âges* 109 (1997), 501–23.
Muir, E., and G. Ruggiero (eds.), *History from Crime*, Baltimore: Johns Hopkins University Press, 1994.
Nubola, C., and A. Würgler (eds.), *Suppliche e 'gravamina'. Politica, amministrazione, giustizia in Europa (secoli XIV–XVIII)*, Bologna: Il Mulino, 2002.
Padoa Schioppa, A., 'Delitto e pace privata nel diritto lombardo', in *Diritto comune e diritti locali nella storia dell'Europa*, Milan: Giuffrè, 1980, 555–78.
Pasciuta, B., 'In regia curia civiliter convenire'. *Giustizia e città nella Sicilia tardomedievale*, Turin: Giappichelli, 2003.
Rigon, A., and F. Veronese (eds.), *L'età dei processi. Inchieste e condanne tra politica e ideologia nel '300*, Rome: Istituto storico italiano per il Medio Evo, 2009.
Ruggiero, G., *Violence in Early Renaissance Venice*, New Brunswick, NJ: Rutgers University Press, 1980.
Sbriccoli, M., *Storia del diritto penale e della giustizia*, Milan: Giuffrè, 2009.
Terpstra, N. (ed.), *The Art of Executing Well: Rituals of Execution in Renaissance Italy*, Kirksville, MO: Truman State University Press, 2008.
Turchi, L., 'Una piccola modifica. Il linguaggio della negoziazione politica fra principe e città', in G. Badini and A. Gamberini (eds.), *Medioevo reggiano. Studi in ricordo di Odoardo Rombaldi*, Milan: F. Angeli, 2007, 343–73.
Vallerani, M., *La giustizia pubblica medievale*, Bologna: Il Mulino, 2005.

Il sistema giudiziario del comune di Perugia. Conflitti, reati e processi nella seconda metà del XIII secolo, Perugia: Deputazione di Storia Patria per l'Umbria, 1991.

Zorzi, A., *L'amministrazione della giustizia penale nella Repubblica fiorentina. Aspetti e problemi*, Florence: Olschki, 1988.

(ed.), *Conflitti, paci e vendette nell'Italia comunale*, Florence: Firenze University Press, 2009.

'Contrôle social, ordre public et répression judiciaire à Florence à l'époque communale: éléments et problèmes', *Annales ESC* 45 (1990), 1169–88.

'La cultura della vendetta nel conflitto politico in età comunale', in R. Delle Donne and A. Zorzi (eds.), *Le storie e la memoria. In onore di Arnold Esch*, Florence: Firenze University Press, 2002, 135–170.

Pene e rituali di giustizia nell'Italia del tardo Medioevo, Florence: Nardini, 2011.

Index

Abruzzi, kingdom of Naples 44
absolutism
  rise of 305
  theorised 321
Acaia, principality of 177n, 194
Acciaiuoli, Angelo 97
Acciaiuoli, Niccolò 31
Acciaiuoli family, Florentine bankers 31
Acqui, episcopal city 182
Adige League (1407) 211
administrative records 5, 381, 385–405
  thirteenth-century communes 387–9
  nineteenth- and twentieth-century
    archives 386–7
  archiving of 397
  foreign and diplomatic 399–401, 426–7,
    433
  and intensification of bureaucracy 401
  later treatment of 404–5
  Naples 37, 49
  physical characteristics 392
  Piedmont 187
  political language in 422
  private citizens' 389, 390
  registers 392, 399
  rural communities 277
  Savoy 189
  scattered 403
  small states and rural communities
    401–4
  in subject towns 390–1
  see also archives
Adorno, Antoniotto, doge of Genoa
  226
Adorno, Giorgio, doge of Genoa 226
Adorno family, Genoa 226
Adriatic, Venice and 32, 76, 132
advocati, role in ecclesiastical principalities
  197, 203
  Gorizia 207–8, 209
Agnadello, battle of (1509) 134, 243, 363,
  450

agriculture
  Florentine state 448
  Naples 39, 44
  Sardinia 51
  Sicily 9, 17
  southern Italy 16
Alagón, Leonardo, revolt in Sardinia
  (1478) 62
Alagona, Artale I, vicar of Sicily 20
Alagona family, Catania 257
Alba, acquisition by Milan 157
Albert II, duke of Austria 206, 208
Alberti, Leon Battista 98, 420
Alberto, count of Gorizia and Trent 198
Albizi, Maso degli, Florence 93
Albizi, Rinaldo degli 93, 96, 382
  on diplomacy 438, 440
Albornoz, Gil de, cardinal legate 71, 243,
  471
  Constitutiones Aegidianae (1357) 73
  historiographical view of 71
  and use of apostolic vicariates 84
Aldobrandeschi family 289, 325
Aleramo, marquis 177
Alessandria
  acquisition by Milan 157
  factions 311
  Ghibellinism in 314
Alexander VI, pope (Rodrigo Borgia) 84,
  474
  on French invasion 438
  and Roman aristocracy 82
Alfonso II of Aragon, king of Naples,
  abdication (1495) 33
Alfonso III of Aragon (d. 1291) 13
Alfonso IV of Aragon 223
Alfonso V of Aragon (the Magnanimous),
  king of Aragon and Naples
  claim to Naples 32
  conquest of Naples (1442) 32, 257, 258
  economic policy 33, 38, 453
  and feudal families 34

Index

and government of provinces 44
hospitals in Naples 357
as king of Sicily 23–8, 29, 256
  judicial system 512
and monarchical power 36, 38
reorganisation of *Sommaria* 38
and Sardinia 56, 61–4
  parliament (1421) 59
and Siena 108
standing army 40
Alfonso I d'Este, duke of Ferrara 354
Alfonso II d'Este, duke of Ferrara, use of execution 508
Alghero, Sardinia 54, 55, 58
  port of 61, 62
Alghero, peace of (1354) 55
Alps
  communication routes through 197, 272
  as natural boundary 200
  rural communities 280, 281, 403, 423, 486
Altopascio, battle of (1325) 245
Alviano family 290
ambassadors
  autonomy of 425, 429, 430
  daily practice 436
  facility with language 436
  instructions to 427
  personal qualities 436, 439
  political role of 428, 429, 430, 436
  as public officials 425, 429
  reports by 427, 434, 437
  resident 425, 430, 431, 433
  role of 430
  social standing 439
  tales by 440–2
  see also diplomacy
Amedeo V, count of Savoy 177n
Amedeo VIII, duke of Savoy 177n, 179
  Decreta Sabaudie Ducalia (1430) 193
Anagni, treaty of (1295) 13
Anatra, B. 57, 59, 66
Andreasi, Osanna 364
Andreozzi, D. 306
Anguissola family 290
Anjou, house of
  Durazzo and Provence branches 31
  and Guelfs 90, 313, 319, 322, 324, 471
  Naples 256
  in northern Italy 70, 90
  rivalry with Aragon 11, 12
  in Sicily 13, 19, 350
  war with Aragon 30–3, 37
  see also Charles I; Charles II; Robert of Anjou

anti-clericalism 239, 483
apostolic chamber, papal states 74, 398
apostolic vicars 71, 72, 289
  fiscal obligations 84
  military obligations 84
  policy of revocation 84
  relations with papacy 83–5
appellate court, Sicily 24
Appian Way 44
Appiani family, Piombino 103
Apulia
  agriculture 44
  regulation of pasture land 39
  relations of cities with crown 257
Aquileia, patriarchate 197, 200, 284, 295, 478
  and Friuli 146, 207
  and Gorizia 204
Aquinas, Thomas 330, 416
Aragon
  conquest of Sicily (1282) 9
  and Corsica 50
  expansionism 51, 57
  and Genoa 223
  maximum extension of power (1442) 32
  rivalry with Anjou 11, 12
  and Sardinia 50, 56–60
  and Sicily 12, 13–16, 14–15, 22, 50, 55
  standard government practices 26, 28
  war with Anjou 30–3
  see also Alfonso III, Alfonso IV; Alfonso V; James II; Peter III
Arborea, *giudicato* (kingdom) of, Sardinia 51
  conflict with Aragon 53–6, 57
Arcangeli, L. 167, 320
architecture, political language of 420–1
'archive-thesaurus' 389
archives
  nineteenth- and twentieth-century 386–7
  and civic identity 391
  communal judicial 496
  of conquered towns 392, 393
  of diplomatic documents 433
  of Florentine Terraferma communities 402
  historical method 387
  inventories 397
    Venice 394
  later treatment of 404–5
  organisation of 397, 402
  physical structure 389
  pragmatic writings (and political thought) 413, 422
  public 404
  regulations on 389

archives (cont.)
  storage in castles 395, 397, 404
  tax records 397
  see also administrative records; letters
Arco, Vinciguerra 212
Arezzo 243, 465
  bought by Florence (1384) 95
  cotton textiles 454
  independence from Florence 103
  judges 510
Arienti, Sabadino degli, *Gynevera* 355
aristocracy
  as abstract concept 334
  blood-lines 341
  decline of feudal 324
  excluded from *popolo* 328, 342, 496
  and Guelf or Ghibelline allegiances 314
  institutional value of 328
  and local ruling groups 333–9
  relations with princes 334
  theory and practicality 339–42
  see also oligarchies; rural nobility
aristocracy, eastern Alps
  divisions among 200
  formation of identity 213, 216
aristocracy, Naples
  baronial rebellions (1459–65; 1486–7) 45
  barons as public officials 40
  effect of wars on conquest on 37
  government commissions 42
  new lineages 350
  power of feudal families 33
  shifts in allegiances 35
  urban 42, 338
aristocracy, papal state
  and political communication with towns and state 83
  power of 82
  relations with papacy 71
  relations with popes 81, 82–3
aristocracy, Piedmont, rural magnates 179
aristocracy, Sicily
  and cities 257, 258
  civil war (1330s–60s) 19
  conflict with kings 20, 23
  and Martin I 21
  new lineages 350
  structural reforms by Aragonese kings 14–15, 22, 23, 28
Aristotelianism 411
Aristotle, *Nicomachean Ethics* 420
armies
  financial burden of 247
  mercenary troops 40, 247
  militias 40, 246, 501
  standing 40, 147
art and culture
  motifs 421
  northern Italian cities 248
  political paintings 410, 421
  Siena 106
  strategic use of in Florence 98, 100
  in Venetian Terraferma cities 154
  Venice 136
Asti, acquisition by Milan 157
Attendolo, Muzio 40
Auge, duke d' 319
Avignon popes
  and Bologna 71
  and curial government 471, 474
  effect on diplomacy 427, 431
  and French monarchical model 78
  see also Clement V; Clement VII; Gregory XI; John XXII; Urban V
Avogadro family 289
Azario, Pietro, chronicler of Novara 247

Bacon, Francis, *Essays* 344
Baglioni family, Perugia 252, 289, 364
bagliva (rural policing), Naples 34, 257
balie (special commissions), Florence 93
bande (semi-permanent military force), Florence 103
banishment 495
  political use of 496, 498
bankers
  and kings of Naples 43
  as new feudatories 298, 302
  and papacy 477
banking
  Florence 31, 43, 98, 100
  northern Italian cities 248
  Siena 106
  see also Casa di San Giorgio
Barbaro, Ermolao 430, 432
  De officio legati 440
Barbaro, Francesco 151
Barcelona, as maritime centre 61
Bardi family, Florentine bankers 31
Baron, H., *The Crisis of the Early Italian Renaissance* 94
Bartolo, Pietro di 458
Basle, Council of 319, 472
Bassano 486
  jurisdictions 151
Bavaria, duchy of 198
Beatrice of Camino 204
Beatrice of Portugal, wife of Carlo II of Savoy 191

Index

Beatrice of Wittelsbach 205
Beccuti, Ribaldino, judge of Turin 184
Bellinzona, factions 169
Belluno
  acquisition by Milan 158
  distribution of offices 255
  Guelf and Ghibelline in 317
  Venetian occupation 133
Benedictine order
  reforms 149
  relations with states 480
benefices, church
  assignment of 473, 478
  local 484
  rural 485
  Venice 144, 150
Benevento, Campania 44
Bentivoglio, Giovanni 252
Bentivoglio family, Bologna 252
Bergamo 143, 153, 242
  acquisition by Milan 157
  annexed by Venice 133
  fairs 449
  Guelf and Ghibelline in 314, 317
  social control 501
Bevilacqua family, Verona 154
Bianco, Gioan, Sforza ambassador to Savoy 194
Biella, Piedmont 179, 182
bishoprics 468
  appointments to 477
  relations with smaller townships 487
bishops, nomination by pope 469, 473
Bistici, Vespasiano da, *Vite* 441
Black, J. 159, 172
Black Death (Great Plague)
  effect on city-states 243, 260
  in Sardinia 57
  in Sicily 17, 18, 28
  and Sienese countryside 107
Black Sea, Genoese colonies 220, 222, 228, 229
Blickle, P. 262
Boccaccio, Giovanni, *De mulieribus claris* (1362) 355
Boccanegra, Simone, first doge of Genoa 221, 224, 225
Bodin, Jean 321
Bognetti, G. P. 261
Boiardi family 289
Bologna
  acquisition by Milan 157
  banishment of Lambertazzi faction 498
  capitula agreement with *curia* 86
  papal state and 70–1

  peace settlement 494
  revolt (1334) 71
  Sedici oligarchy 79, 333
  semi-*signore* in 252
  social control 500
  social hierarchy 333
  statutes (1250–80) 327, 330
  system of pleas 506
  territorial influence 75
Bologna, peace of (1529–30) 135
Bolzano/Bozen, Adige League (1407) 211
Bonacolsi family, Mantua 120, 395
Boniface VIII, pope (Benedetto Caetani) 50, 54, 204
Boniface IX, pope (Pietro Tomacelli) 72, 84
Bonifacio, Corsica 65
borghi (larger rural settlements) 264
Borgia, Cesare 84, 309
Borgia, Lucrezia 354, 457
Borgia, Rodrigo *see* Alexander VI
Borgo San Donnino 486
Borgo San Sepolcro 510
Borromeo family 300, 302
Borso d'Este, duke of Ferrara 115, 117, 121, 123, 382
  and Reggio 127, 419, 511
  support for manufacturing 458
Bosa, Sardinia 58
Bosa, siege of (1349) 55
Bosphorus, battle of (1352) 53
Boucheron, P. 452
boundaries, of communes 267, 278
Bracceschi family 319
Bracciolini, Poggio 342
Brancacci, Felice 441
Bratchel, M. 113
Bresc, H. 9, 18
Brescia, Albertano da 493
Brescia 143, 242
  acquisition by Milan 157
  annexed by Venice 133
  Guelf and Ghibelline in 317
  population 143
  trade with Venice 450
  wool industry 455
  written records 390
Bressanone/Brixen, ecclesiastical principality of 197, 200, 206
  assembly of estates (1416) 212
Broccadelli, Lucia 364
Bruni, Leonardo 64, 407, 409
Brünn, Nikolaus von, bishop of Trent 206
Bullard, M. 435
Burckhardt, J. 69, 352

604   Index

bureaucracy
  intensification of 401
  specialisation 115
  see also administrative records; offices and officials
Burgundy, kingdom of 177
  trade with Milan 451
Busca family 289

Cabrera, Bernardo de, Catalan admiral 54
Caetani, Onorato, count of Fondi 36
Caetani family, Naples 33
Caffa, Black Sea 222, 229
Caggese, R. 261
Cagliari, Sardinia 55, 58
  port of 61, 62
Calabria, kingdom of Naples 43, 44
Càlari, *giudicato* kingdom of
    (Sardinia) 51, 52
Calco, Tristano 397
Caldora, Antonio 40
Caldora, Giacomo 40
Caldora family, Naples 33
Caleffini, Ugo, notary-official, Ferrara 383
Callixtus III, pope (Alfonso Borgia) 474
Caltabellotta, treaty of (1302) 13, 19
Cambrai, League of 134
  defeat of Venice 242
  War of 309
Camerino, temporary restoration of republicanism 251
Camino family 289
Campagna-Marittima (Lazio), province of papal state 73
Campania, agriculture 44
Campobasso 257
Campofregoso, Paolo, doge of Genoa 227
Campofregoso, Pietro, doge of Genoa 226, 227, 228, 233
Campofregoso, Pietro, Genoa 232
Campofregoso, Tommaso, doge of Genoa 233
Campofregoso family, Genoa
    226, 233, 234
Camponeschi, Pietro (Lalle I), L'Aquila 258
Camponeschi, Pietro Ludovico (Lalle II), L'Aquila 258
Camponeschi family
  L'Aquila 258
  Naples 33
canals 452
Canavese region 179
captains (officials)
  Florence 100
  Genoa 225, 226, 235
  Piedmont 183
  and *podestà* 126, 151, 394
  Sicily 11, 12, 24, 26, 371, 512
  Siena 502
Capua, Campania 44, 45
  use of ritual 419
Capua, sack of (1501) 44
Caracciolo family, Naples 33, 404
Carafa, Diomede 355, 460
  Memoriale per un ambasciatore 440
Carafa family, archives 404
Caramanico, Martino 297
Cardenas, Gutierre de 65
cardinals
  and diplomacy 432
  Italian 474
  power of 87
Carinthia, duchy of 198, 206
Carlo II, duke of Savoy 177, 195
  court household 191
  statutes 193
Carniola, under patriarch of Aquileia 197
Carrara, Francesco da, Padua 222
Carrara, da (Carraresi) family, Padua 133, 213, 400, 420
Carthusian order, relations with states 480
Casa di San Giorgio (bank), Genoa 220, 227, 231, 348
  and colonies 228, 229
  and Corsica 51
Casale
  commune of 195
  Senate of 186
Caspe, compromise of (1412) 23, 56
Castel di Cagliari, Sardinia, privilege of *Coeterum* 58
Castel di Castro, Sardinia 52
Castel Porpeto family 209
Castelaragonese, Sardinia 58
Castelbarco, Aldrighetto 214
Castelbarco, lords of 213
Castelfranco 486
castellans
  in ecclesiastical principalities
    199, 203, 295
  patria of Friuli 209
  Piedmont rural domain communities
    183, 190
Castelnuovo, G. 192
Castiglionchio, Lapo da 342
Castiglione, Baldassare, *The Courtier* 120
castles 249
  archives in 395, 397, 404
  ecclesiastical principalities 202

Index

on edge of cities 122, 128
Piedmont 179, 182
state of Milan 160, 169
transformed into palaces 421
urban fortresses 85, 420
Castracani, Castruccio, *signore* of
  Lucca 251
Casula, F. C. 50, 57
Catalan aristocracy
  in Sardinia 53, 54
  in Sicily 13
Catalan merchants
  in Naples 32
  Sardinia 63
  Sicily 13
Catalonia
  and Genoa 230
  interests in Sicily 13
  style of government 14, 22
  trade with Sicily 22
Catania 257
  parliament of (1296) 13
Catanzaro, luxury textile production 457
Catasto (Florentine household fiscal
  survey) 95
Cateau-Cambresis, peace of (1559) 241
Catholic Reformation 488
Cattini, M., and M. A. Romani 128
Cavalieri di Santo Stefano, Florence 103
Ceffi, Filippo 493
Cengarle, F. 172
Centelles, Antoni, marquis of
  Crotone 32
Cephalonia, annexed by Venice 134
Cerignola, battle of 44
Cesena
  factions 309
  sack of (1377) 247
Chabod, F. 2, 125, 368
Chambéry, Savoy
  castle 183, 397
  Council of 186
chancellors
  literary abilities 422, 434
  Piedmont 185
chanceries
  Florence 100, 382
  links with ambassadors 425, 434, 439
  Milan 161, 382
  papal states 74
  rise of 382
  Sardinia 66
charitable institutions 356
  fiscal privileges 356
  religious 480, 481

see also hospitals
charity
  and civic religion 484
  control over 356
  provision of 273, 274
  role of laity 356
Charles I of Anjou
  death (1285) 13
  economic interventionism 47
  leader of Guelfs 30, 90
  relations with papacy 470
  and Sicily 10
Charles II of Anjou 361
Charles III of Durazzo 31
Charles IV of Luxembourg, Holy Roman
  emperor 207
  and Carinthia 206
  and Florence 92
  and Gorizia 207, 208
  and Siena 104
  and Tyrol 207
Charles V of Habsburg, Holy Roman
  emperor (1516–56) 33
  coronation in Bologna 177
  and Genoa 226
  'summary' of privileges of Neapolitan
    universitates 35
Charles VI, king of France, and
  Genoa 226
Charles VII, king of France, and
  Genoa 226
Charles VIII, king of France, invasion
  (1494–5) 33, 101, 160
Charles the Bold of Burgundy 429
Charles of Viana, and crown of Sicily 29
Chartier, R. 417
Chiappini, L. 113
Chiaromonte, Isabella di 34
Chiaromonte, Manfredi, count 14
Chiaromonte, Manfredi III, count 20
Chiaromonte family, Palermo
  257, 298, 300
Chicago conference (1993) 3
Chigi family, bankers in Siena 106
children, illegitimate 359
Chioggia, Venice 142
  taken by Genoa (1380) 222
Chioggia, war of (1378–81) 133,
  137, 140, 400
Chios, island 222, 223, 225
  Maona of 229
Chittolini, G. 3, 113, 174, 285, 300, 301
  Città, comunità e feudi negli stati... 164
  La formazione delle stato regionale... 163
Chronicon Spilibergense 208

church
  administration 398
  authority in rural communities 269
  Gregorian reform 469
  and Guelfism 313, 469, 471
  jurisdiction of courts 479
  and legitimacy of power, Naples 41
  reforms 481
  relations of religious orders
    with states 480
  relations with society 481–7
  and use of torture 509
  see also bishoprics; clergy; papacy
church property 478
  alienation of 479
  expansion of 479
  taxation of 479
churches
  local 481–7
  provision by communes and *contrade* 273, 274, 277
  rural 485–7
Cicinello, Antonio 441
Cinque conservatori del Contado, Florence 93
Cipolla, Bartolomeo 342, 504
cities
  built environment 119, 248
  changing relationships with *contadi* 248–50
  conflicts with papal state 472
  and dioceses 468
  ecclesiastic elites in 88, 482
  factions 255
  identity of *popolo* 324
  judicial courts 511
  kingdom of Naples 34, 45
  nature of 116
  papal states 75
  political centrality of 325
  political use of architecture 420
  relationship of princely courts and
    municipality 126–9, 255, 391
  restriction of political participation
    252–5
  Sardinia 66
  Sicily 259
  urban institutions 11, 15, 256–9
  and urbanisation 248
  see also city-states; oligarchies; *signorie*;
    towns
citizens
  marriage of immigrants to women
    citizens 351
  status and privileges of 248
  women as 350

Città di Castello 252
city-states
  collapse of 241–8, 260
  and communal government 374–6
  effect of Black Death on 243, 260
  and impoverishment of rural
    communities 270
  independence regained 242–3
  'military crisis' 246, 260
  and rural representation 271
  submission to major potentates 244–6
  and territorial states 241, 374
  weakening of 488
  see also Florence; Genoa; Milan; Siena;
    signorie; Venice
cives ecclesiastici (urban elites) 88, 482
civic Christianity 411, 482, 484
  and civil values 485
civic council (*consilium civium*)
  kingdom of Naples 258
  reduction in composition of 254
  Sicily 16, 27
  Venetian Terraferma cities 152
Claudia Augusta Roman road 197
Clement V, pope (Bertrand de Got) 499
Clement VII (Robert of Geneva), anti-pope
    31, 102, 247, 316, 488
clergy
  as citizens 469
  conflict with urban society 483
  political influence of 79
  and urban aristocracies 482
  see also mendicants
CNRS (Centre nationale de la recherche
    scientifique) 3
Cognasso, F. 156
Collalto family, and Venice 291
Colle Val d'Elsa 243, 486
  archives 401
  conquered by Florence 92
  paper industry 454
Collenuccio, Pandolfo 438
Colleone family 302
collette, taxes (Naples) 38
Colonna family, Rome 72, 82, 289, 292
  as Ghibellines 316
  military power of 81
  see also Martin V
Commemoriales, Venice 393, 400
commissari
  Naples 41
  supervisory officials in state of Milan 161
  as temporary agent of centre 380
commune Siciliae 11
communes

Index

chronology of development 268–72
conflict within and between 266
and 'crisis of liberties' 414
federations of 265, 271, 272, 281
  and provision of services 273
Florence 90–3
internal tensions 243
membership of 265
Milanese state 163
neighbouring, shared responsibilities 264
oldest form of institutional organisation 264, 375
origins 269
political role in regional states 414
public buildings 276
relations with churches 469
relations with papacy 471
submission to stronger powers 244
Venice 132
communication networks, diplomatic 426, 432–6
Commynes, Philippe de 314, 322
Como
  acquisition by Milan 157
  factions 311
  Ghibellinism in 314
companyes (mercantile societies), Sardinia 63
condottieri (mercenary leaders) 40
  lordships 250, 290, 299, 302
  and papal state 83, 472
  use of in Savoy 178
Conegliano, Treviso, archives 401
conflict
  local factions 310
  within and between communes 266
conflict resolution 490, 491–5
  consilium 493
  official mediation 494
  peace-making 494
Consiglio dei Cento, Florence (1458) 97
Consoli del Mare, Florence 95
Constance of Aragon, wife of Frederick the Simple, king of Sicily 55
Constance, concordat (1418) 72
Constantinople
  fall of (1453) 134
  Venetians in 142
Constitutiones Aegidianae (1357) 73
consulte, Florence 93
consumption 445
  silk cloth 456
Contrari, Uguccione 292
coral, Sardinia 51
Corfù, Venetian occupation 133

Corio, Bernardino 396
Corleone, confederation with Palermo 11
corporations, and guilds 326–33
Corrao, P. 41
Correggio, Manfredo da 292
Correggio family 289
Corsica
  Ferdinand II and 65
  as possession of Genoa 51, 223, 228
  see also Sardinia
Cortona, judges 510
Cosenza, federations of villages 282
Cosimo I, grand duke of Tuscany 103, 110
  and conquest of Siena (1555) 108
Costanzo, Angelo di 48
councils
  local, expansion of 264
  restricted 270
counts
  Sicily 14, 19, 22
  control of revenues 20
courts, ecclesiastical 492
courts, princely (ducal)
  evolution of 128
  Milan 162
  Naples 41
  and public officials 124–6, 190–3
  relationship with cities 126–9, 255, 391
  women in 353, 354
  see also Savoy
Covini, N. 172
Crema 242
  annexed by Venice 133
  Ghibellinism in 314
Cremona 242
  acquisition by Milan 157
  factions 168, 311
Crete, Venice and 132, 142
criminal law 497, 498–500
  heresy 499
  lese-majesty 499
  and rebellion 498
Cubello, Leonardo 56
cultural history 417
Cuneo, acquisition by Milan 157
curia, Rome
  Avignon popes and 471, 474
  character of 476
  Italianisation of 474
  jurisdiction 74, 473
  and local churches 482
  and nepotism 80
  political rhetoric of 78, 88
  power of 488
  relations with cities 85, 86

curia, Rome (*cont.*)
  and Venice 149
  women and 354
curie, judicial 495
currency, single, Naples 452
customs dues
  Florence 435, 447
  Naples 39
  Sicily 24, 25, 453
Cybo, Caterina 354
Cyprus, annexed by Venice 134

Dallo family 289, 294
Dalmatian coast
  Venetian colonies 142
  Venetian occupation 133
Dandolo, Andrea 145
Dandolo family, Venice 140
Dante Alighieri 493
  on nobility 340
Datary, papal office 74
Davidsohn, R., *Geschichte von Florenz* 90
Day, J. 57
de Portis family 209, 289
Decembrio, Pier Candido 409
Decreta Sabaudie Ducalia, Savoy 193
Del Balzo family, Naples 33
Del Bo, B. 188
Del Carretto family, Genoa 223, 289
del maggior magistrato decree (1441 Milan) 163, 174
Del Treppo, M. 33, 43
  on maritime Mediterranean 61, 63
  on southern Italy 45, 49
Della Faggiola, Uguccione, *signore* of Lucca 251
Della Misericordia, M. 165, 170, 310
Della Scala, Antonio, on Friuli 204
Della Scala, Cangrande 205
Della Scala, Mastino, *signore* of Lucca 251
Della Scala family (Scaligeri), Verona 133, 157, 213, 420
  archives 395
  and ecclesiastical interference 471
  and Mantua 242
  territorial consolidation 246
Della Torre, Gastone 205
Della Torre, Napo 156
Della Torre, Pagano 205
Della Torre family 209, 218
  and control over communes 245
  faction in Friuli 209
  Milan 156
Diciotto di Balìa (1435), Naples 42
Dieci di Balìa, Florence 93

diplomacy 425–43
  chronology of change 427–8
  communication networks 432–6
  and geography 428
  language of 442
  and leagues and treaties 435
  Lorenzo de' Medici's personal 100
  nature of assignments 430–2
  politicisation of 436
  practices and men 436–9
  records 399–401
  sources 426–7
  theories of 439–42
  and wars 428–30
  see also ambassadors
discredit, as political weapon 415
d'Isernia, Andrea 297
division of labour 326–33
dohana (duty on trade) 24
doléances, cahiers de (written complaints) 382
dominion, Venetian definitions of 144–7
donativum, voted by parliaments, Sicily 25
Donoratico, *signorie* lands of 51
Doria, Andrea 220
Doria, Brancaleone 55
Doria, Matteo 54
Doria family
  Genoa 223
  signorie lands in Sardinia 51, 223
dowries 347–50
  Florence 99
  inflation 347
  limits on 348, 360
  mos graecorum 350
  mos latinorum 350
  for nuns 362
dualism, in political theory 3
Duby, G. 417
Durand, Guillaume 500
Durazzo family 31, 44
Dusay, Giovanni, viceroy of Sardinia 59

ecclesiastical courts 492
ecclesiastical lords 290
ecclesiastical principalities 197–219, 242
  fifteenth-century power structures 213–19
  conflicting interests of papacy and Holy Roman empire in 201, 204–12
  delayed feudalisation 201–4
  lack of borders 199
  links with neighbouring powers 203
  medieval background 197–8
  as 'pass states' or 'frontier states' 198–200

Index

succession disputes 201
weakness of towns 201
see also Aquileia; Bressanone; Gorizia; principalities; Trent; Tyrol
economic development, regional 444-66
and interests of city 464
protection of technical innovation 461-3, 465
protectionism 455, 456, 464, 465
Florence 460
public policies 445, 446-53, 464
support for manufacturing 458-61, 465
territorial dimension 465
Egypt, Ottoman Turkish control of 134
Eight Saints see War of the Eight Saints
elections
by drawing of lots (*insaculatio*), Sardinia 66
eligibility, Bologna 327
Florence 97, 102
in Paduan commune 327
Eleonora of Aragona 353, 355, 461
Eleonora of Arborea (Sardinia) 55, 352
Eleonora of Toledo, wife of Cosimo de' Medici 353
Elephant, League of the 211
elites, historiography 263
Emanuele Filiberto, duke of Savoy 195
Emilia
factions ('*squadre*') 311
small states in 300, 301
Enghien, Maria d', countess of Lecce and queen of Naples 34, 352
England, Statute of Monopolies (1624) 462
Epstein, Stephan R. 116, 444, 448, 454
on Alfonso V of Aragon 33
on Sicily 10, 17, 43
Epstein, Stephen 221
Ercole d'Este, duke of Ferrara 115, 364
building projects 115, 121, 123
ducal administration 127
judicial administration 505
and silk industry 457
use of execution 508
Escrivá, Ximén Pérez, viceroy of Sardinia 59, 65
Este family (Estensi), Ferrara 112, 115, 242, 352
archives 397
compared with Gonzaga of Mantua 117-18
and court and public officials 125-6
as dukes of Ferrara 116
and ecclesiastical interference 471

and Modena 130
papal campaign against 499
relations with citizenry 114
relations with territories 118-19, 130, 294
urban buildings and spaces 120, 123, 420
see also Alfonso I; Alfonso II; Borso; Ercole; Leonello; Niccoló III
Este, Alberto d' 121
Eugenius IV, pope (Gabriele Condulmer) 84
and Cosimo de' Medici 97
Europe, modern political identity 1
European Science Foundation 3
exports
Naples, monopolies 39
Sicily 17, 22
extromission, exile of opponents from cities 244

factions 304-22
as aggregate of cliques 309
Bellinzona 169
in cities 311
and class struggle 307
composition of 321
criminalisation 305, 321
effect on governments 310-12, 376
emotional attachment to 322
family identity 312
and feuds (vendettas) 312
Genoa 224-6, 228, 233-5
Guelf and Ghibelline identities 310, 311, 313-20
and ideology of *equalitas* 415
individual identity 312
lack of sources 304
legal and political doctrine on 320
at local level 311
Milan 158, 167
and oligarchies 307, 317, 321
Parma 167, 168, 255
Pavia 166
religious condemnation of 415
and ritual of confrontation 419
role of women 322
and rural nobility 255
and social anthropology 308
'*squadre*' 311
in state of Milan cities 166, 167-9
see also Ghibelline factions; Guelf League
fairs and markets 464
Bergamo 449
Florence 448

610   Index

fairs and markets (*cont.*)
  Milanese state 451
  Naples 452
  Sicily 453
Falcon, League of the (Adige League) 211
Falier, Marino, doge of Venice 140
Falletti family 290
Famagusta, Cyprus 222, 223, 228, 229
family, legislation on, Florence 99
Febrer, Andreu, writer 64
Febvre, L. 240
Federico da Montefeltro, duke of
      Urbino 247, 499
Federico I Gonzaga, marquis
      of Mantua 115
Feltre, Bernardino da 321
Feltre
  acquisition by Milan 158
  Venetian occupation 133, 143
feminism 345
Ferdinand I of Aragon, king of Naples
      (Ferrante) 32, 44, 257, 258, 457
  baronial revolts 299
  marriage 34
  and monarchical power 36, 38
  and silk industry 458, 460
  standing army 40
Ferdinand I of Trastámara, king of Aragon
      23, 56
  as king of Sicily 23
  and Sardinia 62
Ferdinand II of Aragon, king of Naples,
      death (1496) 33
Ferdinand II, king of Aragon (the Catholic)
      30, 33
  campaigns in Italy 65
  Mediterranean, Ferdinand II's strategic
      plans for 64
  Sardinia 64–7
    bureaucratic reforms (*redreç*) 66–7
    parliament (1481–5) 59
  strategic plans 64
Ferrara
  castle 123
  civic statutes 127
  and Este dynasty 115
  executions 508
  judicial procedures 503, 504, 505
  new convent 364
  offices and officials 125–6
  Ospedale di Sant' Anna 122, 126
  relations between city and Este family
      114, 123, 126–8
  relations with territory 118–19, 129
  Savi (city council) 126

  silk manufacture 457
  and subject cities 116
  territorial expansion 118
  textile industry 458
  university 115
  urban expansion 121–2
  war with Venice 115, 118, 133, 242
  written records 382
    archives 397
Ferrara, War of (1482–4) 134
festivals 129
  communes 277
feudal principalities *see* ecclesiastical
      principalities; principalities
feudalism
  and communal traditions 340
  feudal contracts 203, 296
  introduced in Sardinia 51, 53
  Naples 33, 46, 256, 297
  and papal authority 77, 470
  and Piedmontese states 177
  reinforcement of 335
  in Sicily 14, 20, 28, 257, 297
  and weakness of towns 202
Ficino, Marsilio 100
fideles, and rural nobility 288, 293
fiefs (fiefdoms)
  ecclesiastical principalities 199,
      202, 203
  and emphyteusis 272, 484
  Saluzzo 180
  and *signorie* 286
  use of 250, 286, 295–300
Fieschi family, Genoa 223, 224,
      234, 289, 301
Filarete, Antonio 357
Filippo Maria Visconti, duke of Milan 158,
      174, 179
  archives 396
  and chapter of the cathedral 340
  and cities of *contado* 165, 166, 173
  death (1447) 242, 420
  economic policy 458
  and Genoa 226
  and Ghibelline allegiance 314
  invasion of papal state (1431) 72
  move to castle 122
Filippo of Savoy, prince of Acaia 177n
Florence
  and appointment of bishops 477
  archives 391–3
  Archivio delle Riformagioni 382
  Cavalieri di Santo Stefano 103
  Ciompi rebellion (1378) 92,
      253, 329, 502

Index

city government
  accoppiatori (electoral officers) 97, 102
  chancery 100, 382, 402
  city statutes 93, 95, 98, 382
  Consiglio Maggiore (Savonarola) 102
  constitutional form of state 102
  Gonfaloniere (chief magistrate) 102
  institutional innovation 93, 95
  monarchical rule of Cosimo I 103
  new ruling elite (1340s) 91
  office of *Monte* 91
  officials 96, 381
  oligarchy 253, 333
  Otto di Guardia 93, 100, 502, 504, 505
  participation government under Savonarola 254
  reforms (1382-7) 254
  Regolatori delle entrate e delle uscite (1352) 392
  under *reggimento* 93-6, 98
economy, trade and finance
  access to sea 95, 446
  commercial policy 446-8
  consolidated public debt (*Monte*) 376
  Dogana dei Traffici (Trade Customs) 447
  Legge dei Passeggieri 447
  Mercanzia (merchants' court) 447
  new manufacturing enterprises 459
  prosperity 91
  and regional manufacturing 453
  Silk Guild 357
  sumptuary laws 361
  taxation 91, 99, 446, 448
  wool guild 459
expulsion of Medici (1494) 254
factions 307
financial and economic crisis (1340s) 91, 96, 392
food supplies 446, 449
foreign policy under Cosimo de' Medici 97
Guelfism 318
imperial vicariate (1355) 92
justice 513
  capital punishment 508
  council of justice (1452) 382
  judges 510
  Ordinamenti di giustizia (1293) 329
  role of jurists 504
  use of banishment 498
and Milan 95, 246
military forces (*bande*) 103
and Naples 31, 32
nature of government
  civic humanism 94, 98, 411

constitutional form of state 102
end of commune era 90-3
establishment of *respublica* 92
as model for *stato del Rinascimento* 94
oligarchy 253, 333
republicanism 91, 94, 251, 332
restoration of republic 101-3
signorie 251
Orsanmichele charity 359
Ospedale degli Innocenti 357
Pazzi conspiracy (1478) 97, 100
peace settlement (1342-3) 494
relations with papal state and papacy 92, 94, 477
rise of Medici 96-9
Sea Consuls 446, 459
social mobility 98
social policies
  Monte delle doti (bank for dowries) 99, 348
  police force 501
  remarriage of widows 349
  social control 501
  sodomy laws 361
  Ufficiali di Notte 361
  Ufficio dei Pupilli (Office of Wards) 366
strategic use of art and culture 98, 100
territorial expansion 92, 95, 109, 158, 249, 392, 446
  and economic policy 446, 453
  towards Pistoia and the Valdarno 91
Tribunale della Mercanzia 98
under Lorenzo de' Medici 99-101
vendetta 493
War of the Eight Saints with papacy 92, 246, 247, 318, 471, 483
wars against Milan 95
see also Florence, territorial state of
Florence, territorial state of 103, 371, 377, 379, 402
  complexity of 95, 96
  justice in 509, 510, 511
  new fairs and markets 448
  and regional manufacturing 453
  Regolatori delle entrate e delle uscite (1352) 392
  relations with rural nobility 293
  and Tuscan regional economy 444
  Ufficio delle riformagioni 392, 397
Fogliani family 289, 294
Folin, M. 114, 124, 125, 129
  'In the shadow of the prince' 119
food supplies
  Florence 446
  Venice 449

foreigners (strangers)
  forenses (outsiders) 279
  in towns and cities 328
Foresti, Jacopo, *De claris mulieribus* 355
Forlì, social control 500
Foscari, Francesco, doge of Venice 134,
    140, 141, 145, 441
Foscarini, Ludovico 151
France
  and Genoa 226
  invasion of Charles VIII (1494–5) 33,
    101, 160, 438, 442
  and Savoy 177
Franceschi, Andrea 394, 441
Francesco I Sforza, duke of Milan 40, 72,
    84, 158, 357
  administration under 161, 377
  control of Milan (1450) 243, 254
  and Cosimo de' Medici 97
  and diplomacy 431, 433
  as duke of Milan 159
  and factional identity in Bellinzona 169
  judicial policy 506
  move to castle 122
  state revenues 162
  and trade 451, 455
  and written records 396
Francesco II Gonzaga, marquis of
    Mantua 115, 117
  church building 120
  and Mantua 114, 115
Francesco II Sforza, duke of Milan 160
Francesco, Muzio di, of Assisi 499
Francis I, king of France 226
Franciscan order 321, 412
Frederic of Arborea 55
Frederick I of Aragon, king of Naples 33
Frederick II of Aragon, king (III of Sicily)
    12, 13, 14, 19
  and aristocratic elites 16
  economic policy 15, 361
  and urban institutions 15
Frederick II of Hohenstaufen (I of Sicily),
    Holy Roman emperor 10, 512
  Liber Augustalis 330
  taxation in Naples 38
Frederick III, Holy Roman emperor
    (Frederick IV of Austria) 211, 212
  claim to Milan 159
  and Sigismund of Luxemburg 212
Frederick IV, king of Sicily 19
Frederick of Habsburg, king of the Romans
    (the Handsome) 205
freedom, language of 94, 111, 146
French revolution, and archives 386, 405

friaries, community provision of 273
friars, political and social homilies 267,
    279, 361, 412, 415
  see also Franciscan Order
Friuli
  fourteenth century 207–10
  decline of parliament 218
  elite families 154, 204
  factions 309
  German interests in 206
  Gorizia and 205
  Guelf and Ghibelline in 317
  internal divisions 215
  political weakness of towns 202
  rural nobility of 202
  and rural representation 271
  under patriarch of Aquileia 197
  uprising (1511) 219
  and Venice 207, 210
Friuli, *Patria* of 200, 209
  Habsburgs as captain-general 208
  Venetian occupation of 133, 143, 146,
    214–16, 217–19
Fubini, R. 425, 429

Gabrielli family 289
Gaddi, Francesco 436*n*
Gaeta, Campania 44
Gaglioffi family, L'Aquila 258
Galasso, G. 48
Galeazzo Maria Sforza, duke of Milan 123,
    159, 161, 252, 352, 353
  and Cremona 168
  on diplomacy 429
  judicial policy 506
Galixi, Tommaso di Pietro 333
Gallura, *giudicato* kingdom of 51, 52
Gamberini, A. 174
Gandino, Alberto da 500
Gatti family, Viterbo 252
Genet, J.-P. 369
Genoa 32, 220–36
  'absence of the state' 220–2
  acquisition by Milan 157
  alberghi 224, 228, 234
  and Aragon 223
  archives 391
  canvassing of public opinion 230
  Casa di San Giorgio (bank) 220, 227,
    231, 348
  colonies 220, 228, 229
  commercial consulates 432
  commercial power of 220,
    222–4, 227, 229
  and Corsica 50, 51

Index   613

factions 224–6, 228, 233–5, 306
forced loans 231
funding of dowries 348
gentes 224
Guelf and Ghibelline alliances 224, 234
institutions of government 235
  Anziani (executive committee) 226, 230, 232, 233
  Captains of the *Libertà* (1442) 235
  'captains of the people' 225, 226, 235
  constitution reformed (1528) 220, 226, 228, 234
  councils 222, 232, 233
  office of doge 224, 225–6, 228, 232–3
  Regulae (1413 constitution) 226, 234
  shared access to political office 232, 234
lack of contemporary chronicles 221
lack of political participation 230–1, 236
monastic reforms 363
and Pisa 223
political instability 220, 235
popolari 224, 234
private fleets 221, 227, 229
public finances (*compere*) 227, 231
public and private spheres 228–35
public records 388
rivalry with Venice 132, 133, 222, 230
and Sardinia 50, 52
submission to external lordships 220, 226, 234, 253
sumptuary laws 360
taxation 231, 234
territory in Liguria 221, 223
trade with Milan 451
uprising of *populari* (1506–7) 234
war with Aragon 53, 55, 57
Gentile, M. 166, 170
Gentiluomini, Siena 104
George of Liechtenstein, prince-bishop 211
Germany
  constitutional history 3
  imperial territorial rights 145
  and routes through Alps 197
  Twelve Articles (1525) 282
Ghibelline factions 245, 313–20, 419
  and allegiance to empire 313
  and change of meaning 319
  in Friuli 218
  Genoa 224
  political attacks on 415
  in state of Milan 168, 313
  see also Guelf League
Gian Francesco Gonzaga, marquis of Mantua 115, 116, 118

Gian Galeazzo Maria Sforza, duke of Milan 159
Gian Galeazzo Visconti, duke of Milan 118, 158, 162, 173, 296, 396
  death (1402) 133, 242
  Florence and 94
  and manufacturing 456
  and Parma 168
  reform of hospitals 357
  and Savoy 179
  as *signore* of Siena 105
  use of fief 296
Giannone, Pietro 48
Giovanni I, marquis of Monferrato 182, 194
Giovanni Maria Visconti, duke of Milan 158, 252
Gippi, Sardinia, *curatori* of 52
Giustinian, Bernardo 145
Giustiniani, Genoese '*popolare*' *alberghi* 225
glass industry
  Siena 460
  Venice 456, 462
Gonfaloniere (chief magistrate), Florence 102
Gonzaga, Dorotea 353
Gonzaga family, Mantua 112, 364
  alliance with Venice 118
  archives 395, 400
  building projects 121, 420
  compared with Estensi of Ferrara 117–18
  and court and public officials 124–5
  and jurists 503
  as marquises of Mantua 116
  relations with city 123
  territorial acquisitions 118
  see also Federico I; Francesco II; Gian Francesco; Ludovico
Gorizia 199
  and Aquileia 204
  counts of 198, 208, 209
  and dukes of Austria 208
  and Friuli 207–8
  and Tyrol 204–7
governance, of cities
  participation in 110, 111, 327
  popolo and 253, 254
  restrictions 252–5
government structures 244
  plurality of 374, 377, 408
Gozzolini family, Osimo 499
Gradenigo, Pietro, doge of Venice 140
grain exports, Sicily 17, 22
grain production, Sardinia 51
Granada, war against 65

Great Plague *see* Black Death
Greece, Venetian territories 142
Gregorio, R. 9
Gregory XI, pope (Pierre Roger de Beaufort), and Florence 92
Grendi, E. 262
Grimaldi family, Genoa 223, 224
Gritti, Andrea, doge of Venice 136, 394
Grubb, J. 113
Guarco, Antonio, Genoa 232
Guarini, E. F., and Chittolini, G. 3
Guelf League (Parte Guelfa) 31, 245, 313–20, 419
   and allegiance to church 313, 469, 471
   and change of meaning 319
   and factions in cities 168, 313
   in Florence 91, 318, 471
   and French allegiance 90, 319
   in Friuli 218
   in Genoa 224, 234
   and Henry VII 245
   northern Italian hegemony 70
   political attacks on 415
   Sicily and 11
   Siena 104
   see also Ghibelline factions
Guerra degli otto santi see War of the Eight Saints
Gui, Bernard, papal legate 246
Guicciardini, Francesco 79, 441, 442
   and Florence 111
   on papacy 467, 474, 488
   on Roman barons 82
Guidi family 289, 293, 393
guilds 326–33
   Florence 91, 329, 459
   hierarchies between 329
   and political participation 330
   and *popolo* 331
   recognition, Palermo 332
   silk industry 458
   and social stratification 329
Guinigi, Paolo, *signore* of Lucca 106, 110, 251
Gundersheimer, W. 113, 115
Guttuari family 290
gypsies 279

Habsburg empire 133, 284
   claim to Trent 207
   and Friuli 207, 208
   and John of Bohemia 206
   and Venice 135
   see also Holy Roman empire
hat making 454

Siena 460
Haushofer, Albrecht 200
Hawkwood, John 472
   English mercenary captain 247
hearth taxes
   Naples 39
   Sicily 17
Heers, J. 221, 304
Henry, count of Tyrol and duke of Carinthia 205, 206
Henry II of Gorizia 204–5, 207
Henry of Valois 353
Henry VII, Holy Roman emperor 245, 313, 499
   and *contadi* 250
   and Genoa 226
heraldry, coats of arms of communes 276
heresy, accusations of 499
Herlihy, D. 444
historiography 2–4
   of collapse of city states 239–41
   and cultural history 417
   of diplomacy 425–6
   economics 444, 445
   of factions 304, 306
   of feudalism and rural nobility 284, 285
   Genoa 220–2
   of justice 490
   of nature of political power in Milan 171
   of offices and officials 368–71
   of political language 406–8
   of 'Renaissance state' 112–14
   and representations 417
   of rural communities 261–8, 280, 281
   Sicily 9–10
   of southern Italy 46–9, 280
   of Tuscany 109, 280
   and view of Albornoz 71
   of women 345
   written records 385, 386–7
Holy Roman empire
   constitutions of Pisa (1313) 499
   and ecclesiastical principalities 197, 201
   and legitimation of Milanese rulers 159
   see also Habsburg empire
hospitals 273, 357–9
   royal, Naples 356
   segregation in 358
   wet-nurses 358, 359
Hotman, F. 384
humanism, language of 411
humanism, civic 1, 382, 390, 410
   Florence 94, 98, 411
   Venice 145, 151, 411
Hungary, kings of, and Venice 133

Index

identity
  civic 324, 391, 408
  factions and 169, 312
  within rural communities 267–8, 277
Iglesias, Sardinia 58
Imola, social control 500
indirect taxes
  Florence 448
  Masseria (administration of) 398
  Naples 44, 452
  Sicily (*gabelle*) 15, 20, 24
  Venice 147
information
  ambassadors' sources 434
  flow into Rome 475
  supplied by ambassadors 433
  transmission of technical knowledge 463
inheritance
  by daughters 347
  and illegitimacy 352
  primogeniture 352, 365
Innocent III, pope (Lotario dei Conti di Segni)
  and papal sovereignty 77
  and papal state 70
  and relationship between curie and towns 85
Inquisition 473
institutions
  civic and ecclesiastical 469
  historiography, rural communities 263–7
  pluralism of 306
  reform of ecclesiastical 480
Iradiel, P. 62
Iron Road (*via vel strata Hungariorum*) 197
Isaacs, A. K. 309, 374
Istria
  under patriarch of Aquileia 197
  Venetian colonies 142
Italian League (Lega Italica) (1455) 159, 302, 319
  diplomacy and 429, 435
Italian Wars (1494–1530) 429
  Genoa and 235
  Guelfs and Ghibellines and 320
  and Milan 175
  Savoy and 195
  Venice 134, 150
Italy
  French invasion (1494–5) 33, 101, 160, 438, 442
  identity and local institutions in modern 262
  legacy of city-states 374–6
  nature of rural communities 280–2

political instability (fourteenth century) 288
  variety of states and forms 4–5
Ivani, Antonio 383

James II of Aragon
  conquest of Sardinia 52
  as king of Sardinia and Corsica 50, 51
  as king of Sicily 13, 15
Jews
  communes and 279
  conversion of women 360
  expulsion of (1492) 66
Joanna I of Anjou, queen of Naples 31, 352, 355, 356
Joanna II of Anjou, queen of Naples 32, 258, 352, 357
John of Anjou 32
John of Aragon, duke, as regent of Sicily 19
John I of Aragon, king of Sardinia 55
John II of Aragon, king of Sicily, economic policy 24, 27
John XXII, pope (Jacques Duèze) 52, 205, 314
  and Bologna 70
  campaign against *signori* 499
  report on Lombardy 246
  and Visconti 157
John of Luxemburg, king of Bohemia 206, 246, 251
John-Henry of Gorizia 205
John-Henry of Luxembourg, king of Bohemia 206
Jones, P. 112, 284
judges
  appointment in territorial states 509
  political function of 500
  political magistrates 495
  professionalism 510
  Venetian Terraferma cities 152
  see also jurists; justiciars
judicial policies
  pragmatic nature of 504–6
  use of mercy and pardons 506–7
judicial procedures 495–8
  and default 497
  ex officio 496, 497, 500
  expansion of penal law 496, 497
  and *fama publica* (public reputation) 497, 500
  professional courts 495
  role of public authorities 494
  Savoy 194
  secret denunciations 504
  trial 492, 499

judicial systems 490–514
  commissioners in territorial states 511
  community-based 490
  and conflict resolution 490
  criminal law 497, 498–500
  new judicial bodies 501–4
  pluralism 490, 491
  political judicial bodies 505
  public justice 490
  registers 495
  in rural communities 273
  Sicily 12, 16, 21, 24
  and social control 500–1
  territorial states 509–13
Julius II, pope (Giuliano della Rovere) 85
jurats, Sicily 16, 258
jurisdictions, Naples 34
  local 34
jurists 503
  Milan 503
  Piedmont 186
  on prince's council, Savoy 185
justice
  hegemonic 491, 498–500
  negotiated 491, 492, 497, 513
  and punishments 495
justiciars
  Naples 37
  Sicily 12, 371

Kelly, J. 346
Kunzmann, Matthäus, bishop of Bressanone/Brixen 206

la Tour, Bertrand de, papal legate 246
labour, division of 326–33, 445
Ladislas of Durazzo 32, 34
Lambertazzi faction, Bologna 498
Lampedusa, Giuseppe Tomasi di, *The Leopard* 47
Lanaro, P. 450
Landi family 289
Landino, Cristoforo 100
Lando, Silvestro, chancellor of Verona 145
landowners, rights and responsibilities 268
language of politics 406–24
  and architecture 420–1
  content of 411–17
  expressive potential of 410
  as form of political action 417–23
  historiography 406–8
  plurality of 413, 424
  pragmatic writings 413

producers and matrices 408–11
and resistance 422
and 'theory of speech acts' 423
L'Aquila, Naples 35, 45
  council of Five 258
  factions 322
  federations of castles 282
  rebellion (1485) 256
laws
  made by papal representatives 73
  on treatment of ambassadors 439
Lazio, region
  factions 316
  papal control 70, 86
  urban development 75
Lazzarini, I. 124, 374
leagues
  and alliances 245, 435
  aristocratic, Tyrol 211
leather processing 454, 460
Lega Italica (1455) *see* Italian League
Legnano 486
Leo X, pope (Giovanni de' Medici) 488
Léonard, E. 47
Leonello d'Este, marquis of Ferrara 115, 117, 122, 508
Lerici, Genoese territory 228
Lesbos, island 223
lese-majesty 499
letters
  closed (*litterae clausae*) 422
  diplomatic 426, 433, 437
  patent 422
Levant, Venetian trade with 134
Levanto, Genoese territory 228
libertà, Guelfism and 319
Libri, Matteo de' 493
Lienz, lordship of 198
Liguria, Genoese territory 223, 229–30
Ligurian republic *see* Genoa
'linguistic turn' 408, 417, 424
literacy, and written records 387, 403
Livorno, commerce regulations 447
'Lo stato territoriale fiorentino' (1996 conference) 3
Lodi 157, 314
Lodi, treaty of (1454) 72, 76, 134, 241, 302, 374, 449
Lodron, Paride 212
Lombardy 156–76
  factional conflicts 310, 311
  and Ghibellinism 314, 319
  and Milanese commercial policy 451
  rural communities 280, 281
  seigneurial and feudal relations 285, 296

Index

see also Milan; Sforza family; Visconti family
Lopez, R. 220
lordships *see* fiefs; rural nobility; *signorie*
Loredan family, Venice 140
Lorenzetti, Ambrogio, frescoes in Siena 104, 410
Loschi, Antonio 409
Louis of Aragon, king of Sicily 19
Louis of Brandenburg 207
Louis I of Anjou 31
Louis II of Anjou 32
Louis III of Anjou 32
Louis IV of Wittelsbach, Holy Roman emperor (the Bavarian) 157, 205, 206
Louis XII, king of France
　expedition (1499) 175, 253, 320
　Milan 160, 226, 253
　Novara 160, 255
Lucca 262
　Florence and 96, 242
　as independent republic 103, 242
　magistracy 502
　peace settlement 494
　sea port 446
　signori 251
　signoria of Paolo Guinigi 106, 110, 251
　silk workers from 456, 461
　as 'simple state' 109
　'war of' (1336–9) 246
Ludovico II Gonzaga, marquis of Mantua 115, 116, 120, 432
Ludovico Sforza (il Moro), duke of Milan 123, 159, 226, 253, 396
　and diplomacy 442
　fall of 168
　government structure 161
　judicial policy 506
Luxemburg, and Friuli 207

Macerata 252
Machiavelli, Bernardo 514
Machiavelli, Niccolò 324
　on church 467
　on discontinuity of papal power 81
　on distinctions between monarchies and republics 323
　and Florence 111
　on nobility 341, 343
　Notula per uno che va ambasciatore in Francia 440
　on papal state 69
　on Roman barons 82
　on small states 403

machinery
　inventions 461, 463
　for silk production 457
MacKinnon, C. 345
Madruzzo family 289
maestri razionali (masters of accounts)
　Naples 37
　Sardinia 66
Maffei family 154
magistracies 501–4
　Sicily 11, 512
magistrates
　arbitrary powers of 505
　peripheral 271, 273
Maire Vigueur, J.-C. 370
Malacarne, G. 114
Malanima, P. 444, 454
Malaspina family, *signorie* lands of 51, 289
Malatesta family, in Romagna 84, 112, 242
　as 'apostolic vicars' 72
Manca, C. 63
Manconi, F. 68
Manetti, Giannozzo 441
Manfred, king of Sicily, defeat by Charles of Anjou (1266) 10
Manfredi family, as 'apostolic vicars' 72
Mantua
　building schemes by Gonzaga 120, 121
　and Casale 195
　castle 123
　Gonzaga archive 395
　hospital 120
　jurists in 503
　merchant families 124
　nature of state 116, 242
　offices and officials 124–5
　period of transition in 114
　popular demands for policy changes 128
　public works 116
　silk industry 458
　street paving 120
　territorial acquisitions 118
　territorial administration 118
　under Gonzaga dynasty 115, 123
　vendetta 493
　and Venice 118
　written records 382
Mantua, marquises of 364
manufacturing
　incentives for entrepreneurs 459
　innovations 459
　new centres 445
　northern Italian cities 248
　protection of technical innovation 461–3
　regional redistribution 453–8

manufacturing (cont.)
  Sicily 17
  state support for 458–61
Marca Trevigiana region 242
  territorial consolidation 246
March, Ausias, poet 64
Marche (Ancona)
  autonomous districts 75
  markets 448
  province of papal state 73
  relations with curia 86
  signoria of Francesco Sforza 72
Maremma region, rural settlements of 107
Margarete of Tyrol 206
Margherita of Durazzo 32
Maria of Enghien, countess of Taranto 34, 352
Maria, wife of Martin the Younger, queen of Sicily 21, 55, 352
Mariano IV of Arborea 53, 54
  war with Peter IV 55
Mariano V of Arborea 55
marketplaces, regulation of 446
markets
  commercial policy and 446–53
  integration 445
marriage
  as civil contract 347
  dynastic 353
  and matrimonial disputes 366
  wedding ceremonies 360
Martin I of Aragon (the Elder) 21
  death (1410) 22
  as king of Sardinia 55, 56
  as Martin II of Sicily 56, 257
Martin I of Aragon, king of Sicily (the Younger) 21–3
  death (1409) 22, 55, 257
  as king of Aragon 22
Martin IV, pope (Simon de Brie) 13
Martin V, pope (Oddone Colonna) 72, 84
  and papal power 72, 81
  and papal sovereign power 78
  written records 398
Martin, J., and D. Romano, on Venice 155
Martinengo family, Brescia 154
Marzano family, Naples 34
Massafiscaglia, Ferrarese settlement 118
Masseria (administration of indirect taxes) 398
Massimiliano Sforza, duke of Milan 160
Matilda of Canossa 293
Mattingly, G. 425
Maximilian of Habsburg, Holy Roman emperor 242

Medici family, Florence 102, 353
  archives 400
  as para-*signorie* 251, 252
  relations with Sforza 429
  rise of 96–9
Medici, Alessandro de' 103
Medici, Caterina de', queen regent of France 353
Medici, Cosimo de' (the Elder) 318, 353, 357
  political power of 97–8
  revision of taxes and tariffs 448
Medici, Giovanni de' 101, 353
Medici, Giuliano de' 100
Medici, Lorenzo de' (the Magnificent) 97, 99–101, 110
  as cultural patron 100
  death 101
  and information from ambassadors 435
  marriage 101, 353
  personal diplomacy 100, 435, 438
  territorial interests 101
  written records (archive) 382, 393, 401
Medici, Piero de' 97, 101, 355
Medici bank 100
Mediterranean
  cultural area 61
  trade and commerce 61, 62
Meinhard III, count of Gorizia 198, 207
Melfi, Constitutions of (1231) 37, 372
Melito, battle of (1349) 44
Meloni, G. 57
Meloria, battle of (1284) 223
mendicant orders
  and charities 356, 480, 484
  'observant' reforms 480, 481
  papal control over 470, 473
  relations with states 480
Menegatti, F. 405
mercantilism 460, 465
mercenaries 247
  Naples 40
  Siena 105
  see also condottieri
merchants
  Catalan 13, 32, 63
  Florence 446
  Mantua 124
  Sardinia 63
Messina 257
  courts 512
  silk industry 458
metallurgy and weapons 454
  Siena 460
Meun, Jean de, *Roman de la Rose* 340

Index

middle classes
  Sardinia 64
  southern Italy 46
Miglio, M. 121
Milan 156–76
  Ambrosian republic (1447–50) 254
  Angera frescoes 156, 157
  and appointment of bishops 477
  canals 452
  castle 121, 122, 420
  cathedral 121
    canons 483
    chapter of 336, 339
    offerings from subject cities 411
  city walls 420
  creation of piazzas 121
  ducal courts 162
  economy
    cloth industry 458
    commercial policy 451–2
    protectionism 457
    Provisiones Januae (1346) 451
    regional manufacturing 454–5
    state finances 161
  expansion under Visconti 157, 158
  factions 158, 167, 310
  and Florence 95, 246
  and Genoa 226
  government structures 160–2, 336
    chanceries 161, 382
    office of auditor 161
    secret council (*consiglio segreto*) 161
  hospitals 357
  judicial systems
    capitano di giustizia (captain of justice) 505
    central 161
    justice council (*consiglio di giustizia*) 161
    use of mercy 507
  nature of political power 171–3, 176, 252
    as consolidated state 158
    and legitimacy of rulers 159
    temporary restoration of republicanism 251
  relations between Visconti and urban populace 122
  relations with papacy 477
  relations with territories 162–3
  social control 500
  under Francesco Sforza 243, 254
  and Venice 134
  written records 382
    State Archives 386
    Visconti archive 396

  see also Milan, state of; Sforza; Visconti
Milan, state of
  administration of justice 503, 510, 511
    ducal councils 503
    fiscal lawyers 503
    master of chambers 503
  apparatus of government 160–5
  communal identity 166
  continuing powers of cities 163
  and death of Filippo Maria Visconti (1447) 242
  diarchy of prince and city 165–71
  divisions within urban society 168
  factions in cities 166, 167–9
  Ghibellinism in 315
  historiography 162–5
  nature of 117
  phases of institutional organisation 164, 174
  political mediation 170–1, 174
  regional maufacturing 454–5
  role of lower classes 168
  rural seigneurs and feudatories 169–70, 174, 175, 250, 336
  and Savoy 177, 188
  and Sforza succession 243, 352
  sumptuary laws 361
militias 501
  communal 246
  feudal 40
Mineo, E. I. 298
Mirandola, Giovanni Pico della 100
Mocenigo, Tommaso, doge of Venice 133
Modena
  Anziano (city council) 127
  city administration 127
  relations with Ferrara 117, 119, 130
  silk industry 457
Molise, kingdom of Naples 44
Monaco 224
Monaldeschi family, Orvieto 252, 289
monarchy
  female regencies 352
  Florence (Cosimo I) 103
  as guarantor of peace and order 409
  methods of politico-social control 373
  and nobilities 323
  papal model 76, 78, 79–81
  in southern Italy 46
  see also monarchy, Naples; monarchy, Sicily
monarchy, Naples
  economic constraints 36
  economic role 42
  incomes 39

620   Index

monarchy, Naples (cont.)
  loans for war 39
  Norman origins 37
  powers of 33–6
  queens 352
  royal court 41
  source of dispensations 350
  use of violence 36
monarchy, Sicily
  queen 352
  role of 9, 19–20, 21, 26
  source of dispensations 350
monasteries
  rural 468, 487
  southern Italy 470
  see also nunneries
Monfalcone, Gorizia 205
Monferrato, marquisate of 177
  administrative structure 182
  archives 397, 403
  auditing of accounts 189
  Councils 186
  court of 192
  decrees 193
  feudal families 180
  officials 186
  parliament 194
  prince's council 185
  records 190
  treasurers 188
Monferrato dynasty 242, 253
monopolies, and patents 461–3, 465
Monselice, Padua, archives 401
Monte delle doti (dowry fund), Florence 99
Monte, office of, Florence 91
Montecatini, battle of (1315) 245
Montefeltro family 120, 242
  as 'apostolic vicars' 72
  in Marche 83
  see also Federico
Montepulciano
  independence from Siena 105
  judges 510
  subdued by Florence (1397) 95
Montone, Braccio da 40, 84, 472
  and expansion in Umbria 72
Monza 486
Mozzarelli, C. 129
Mühldorf, battle of (1322) 205
Muir, E. 217, 309, 418
Mulucci family, Macerata 252
Murano, Venice 142
  glass industry 456, 462
music 406, 422
Musso, R. 222

Najemy, J. 307
Naples, city of 42
  buildings 420
  council of Six 258
  hospitals 356
  luxury textile production 457
  'seat of the People' 258, 338, 349
  silk industry 457, 458
  urban aristocracy 42, 338
  wool industry 461
Naples, kingdom of 30
  and Aragon–Angevin war 30–3
  commercial policy 452–3
  conquest of (1442–3) 24, 28, 65
  control over nunneries 363
  Diciotto di Balia (1435) 42
  diplomatic missions 432
  dowry inflation 349
  economic structure 42–3
  expansionism 72, 245
  government of provinces 44
  historical discourse 48
  judicial foundations 37
  monarchy and local powers 33–6, 256–7
  parliament 38, 41
  political structure 40–3
  rebellions of barons (1458–62; 1485–6) 257
  recurrent instability 33, 35, 44
  relations of cities with crown 257
  relations with papacy 470, 477
  relationship of king and barons 338
  religious aspect of marriage 347
  royal hospitals 356
  rules on dowries 349
  and Siena 108
  standing army 40
  state machinery 37–40, 372
  territory 43–5
  under Angevin rule 32
  use of ritual 419
  written records 399
  see also monarchy; taxation
Naples, sieges of 44
Naples, treaty of (1372) 20
Navagero, Andrea 441
Negroponte
  lost by Venice 134
  Venetian control over 133
nepotism, in papacy 80, 354
Neroni, Dietisalvi 97
New Institutional Economics 444
Niccolò III d'Este, marquis of Ferrara 115
  accords with noblemen 130, 292
  and Modena 119, 127, 130
  statue 121

Niccolò of Luxemburg, patriarch of Gorizia 207, 208
Nicholas V, pope (Tommaso Parentucelli) 84, 420
nobility, as virtue 340
Nono, Giovanni da 325
Norman–Hohenstaufen dynasty 37, 46, 48
North, D. C. 444
notaries 152, 382
  in Alpine communities 403
  Naples 399
  and written records 388, 389
Novara
  acquisition by Milan 157
  Ghibellinism in 314
  rebellion against Sforza (1495) 255
  surrendered to Louis XII 160, 255
nunneries
  controls over 363, 484
  private quarters in 362
  reform of urban 362, 364
  and tribunals 365, 367

obedience, principles of 415
observant Franciscans 321
offices and officials 368–84
  appointment of local 380
  chancellor-humanists 382, 390, 396
  in city governments 376–9
  differences between central and territorial 379–81
  and division of offices 255, 266, 321
  exclusion of women 351
  Ferrara 125–6
  Florence 96, 381
  heritability of 381
  historiography 368–71
  intermediate 372, 378
  Mantua 124–5
  Naples 37, 41
  origins of 125, 377
  Palermo, access to office 332
  papal 474
  papal state 73, 74
  payment for office (Piedmont) 183
  Piedmont 182–5
  recruitment 372, 377
  royal and princely 371–3
  rules of election, Padua 327
  Savoy 186
  social and political role of 381, 384
  specialisation 372, 381
  state of Milan 160
  territorial agents 270, 378, 379, 384
  use of *sindacato* 380

Venice non-patrician 139
  see also captains
oligarchies
  closures (*serrate*) 244, 321, 334, 414
  emergence of 250–5, 260, 332
  and factions 307, 317
  as mediators with ruling powers 254
  popular 253
  and privilege 414
Olla Repetto, G., on Sardinia 60, 61
Ordinamenti di Giustizia (1293, Florence) 91
Oristano, Sardinia 58
  siege of (1410) 56
Orsini, Alfonsina 355
Orsini, Clarice, wife of Lorenzo de' Medici 101, 353
Orsini, Napoleone 53
Orsini family
  Apulia 33, 257
  archives 404
  as Guelfs 316
  Pitigliano 290
  Rome 82, 289, 292
  Taranto 34
Orsini del Balzo, Giovanni Antonio, prince of Taranto 34
Orsini del Balzo, Raimondo, prince of Taranto 34
Orsini del Balzo family 300, 302
Orvieto 252
Ostiglia, acquired by Mantua 118
Otranto, kingdom of Naples 44
  Turkish invasion 44, 65
Otto del Buono Stato (1387), Naples 42
Otto di Guardia, Florence 93, 100, 502, 504, 505
Otto of Habsburg 206
Ottokar, N. 307
Ottoman Turks
  capture of Otranto 65
  conquest of Constantinople (1453) 134, 222
  Venice and 133, 134

Pacini, A. 222
pacts, reciprocal (*pactismo*) 3, 4
  Catalan origins 14, 41
  principles of 416
Padua 133, 242
  acquisition by Milan 158
  bishopric of 478
  Ca' di Dio 358
  civic buildings 153
  glass industry 456

622   Index

Padua (*cont.*)
   laws on written records 389
   monastery of S Giustina 149
   relations with Venice 154
   signorile regime 317, 325
   social control 501
   statutes (1270s) 327
   university 154
   Venetian occupation 133, 144
   wool industry 455
palazzo, urban
   central position 421
   in communes 276
   Siena 106
   superseding *case-torri* 98
palazzo comunale, archives in 390
Palermo 257
   commune civitatis Panormi 11
   courts 512
   revolt (1450) 331
   trades and political participation 330, 331
   written records 399
Palizza family, Messina 257
Pallavicini family 289, 301, 320
Palmieri, Matteo 333
Pandolfini, Giovanni 433
papacy
   apostolic chamber, records 398
   and apostolic vicars 83–5
   attractions of service in 488
   authority of 77, 467, 468, 488
   and conciliarist movement 471, 472
   control over clergy 469
   and Corsica and Sicily 50, 51
   Decretum super regularibus et monialibus 364
   diplomatic networks 432
   influence of ecclesiastical institutions 468–71
   Italian popes 474
   jubilee (1450) 472
   jurisdiction of ecclesiastical courts 479
   monarchical organisation 76, 78
   and nepotism 80, 354
   office of Datary 74
   and peculiarities of sovereign pontiff 79–81, 474
   power of representatives 79
   powers in Naples 35
   primacy over Christianity 76, 472
   and problems of succession 80
   relations with barons of Rome 337
   relations with nobility 81, 82–3
   relations with regional states 476–81
   relations with states 467–89
   return to Rome (1378) 472
   Roman tribunals 365, 367, 473, 479
   and Sardinia 50, 51, 54
   schism (1378) 31, 71, 471, 472
   and Sicily 470
   and vicars-general 478
papal state 69–89, 473
   administrative structures 73–4
   and court in Rome 475
   direct government by 72
   as earliest Italian political entity 70
   and fiefdoms 296
   fluctuations of power 70–2, 471
   geographical extent 75
   growth of 89, 488
   Guelfs and Ghibellines in 315–16
   idiosyncratic nature of 69–70
   nature of power 76–9
   parlamentum (provincial) 74
   plurality of territorial interests 88
   provinces 73, 79
   relations with towns 78, 84
   territorial organisation 74–6, 378
   War of the Eight Saints with Florence 92, 246, 247, 318, 471, 483
   wars with Visconti 246
   written records 382, 398, 404
paper industry 454
Parlamento, Florence 92
parliaments
   Naples 38, 41
   papal states, *parlamentum* (provincial) 74
   Piedmont 194–5
   rural representatives in 271
   Sardinia (Corti) 58–60
   Sicily 25, 259, 338
      (1446) 26
      Catania (1296) 13
      Syracuse (1398) 22
   Trent 212
Parma
   acquisition by Milan 157
   dowry inflation 349
   Este family and 118
   factions 167, 168, 255, 310, 311
   piazza 420
   relations with *contado* 379
   role of convents 363
   temporary restoration of republicanism 251
   vendetta 493
Parte Guelfa *see* Guelf League
parties
   emergence of 305
   see also factions

Index

patents, and monopolies 461–3, 465
Patetta, L. 121
  'The difficulty of constructing piazzas' 119
Patrimonium Petri, province of papal state 73
patronage networks 255
  Florence 94
  papal state 80, 87, 89
  in Venetian Terraferma 150
Paul II, pope (Piero Barbo)
  and papal sovereignty 79
  written records 398
Pavia 175
  acquired by Milan 157
  castle 396
  factions 166, 311
  Ghibellinism in 314
  velvet manufacture 457
Pazzi conspiracy, Florence (1478) 97, 100
peace settlements
  collective 494
  rural nobility as allies 291, 302
Pedro of Toledo, viceroy of Naples 363
Pepoli, Taddeo 507
  signore of Bologna 70
Pera, near Constantinople 222, 229
Peralta, Guglielmo, count 20
percettore generale, office of (Naples) 36
Peri, I. 10, 17
Perugia 75
  Baglioni family 252
  silk industry 458
  under control of Milan 158
Peruzzi family, Florentine bankers 31
Peschiera, acquired by Mantua 118
Pescia 486
  silk industry 454
Peter, count of Savoy 372
Peter II of Aragon, king of Sicily, as co-regent with Frederick III 19
Peter III of Aragon, king of Sicily (Peter I) 11–13
Peter IV, king of Aragon (the Ceremonious) 21
  as king of Sardinia 53–6, 59
petitions 423
Petrucci, Pandolfo, personal rule 108
Petti Balbi, G. 221
Phocaea 223, 229
Piacenza
  acquisition by Milan 157
  factions ('*squadre*') 311
  sack (1447) 247
Piccinino, Giacomo 40, 169

Piccinino, Jacopo 319
Piccinino, Niccolò 40
Piccolomini, Enea Silvio *see* Pius II
Piedmont 177–96
  administrative records 187
  courtiers and officials 190–3
  direct and feudal lordships 180
  institutions of central government 185–90
  jurisdiction of bishops 181
  local offices and officials 182–5
  Milan and 157
  obligation to respect local statutes 193
  relations of local communities with princes 180
  statutory legislation 193
  structure of territory 178–82
  see also Monferrato; Saluzzo; Savoy
Pietracatella, battle of (1383) 44
Pietrasanta, Genoese territory 228
Pio di Carpi family 302, 403
Piombino, enclave of 103
Pirillo, P. 293
Pisa
  conquest by Florence (1407) 95
  economic regulation 447
  and Genoa 223
  imperial constitutions (1313) 499
  judges 510
  migration of elite families 254
  possessions in Sardinia 51, 52
  rebellion against Florence (1494–1509) 103, 243
  role of nobility in 324
  and Sardinia and Corsica 50, 52
  sea port 446, 447
  ship-building 454
  under control of Milan 158
  university 100
  wool industry 454
  written records 392
Pistarino, G. 221
Pistoia 91
  factions 306, 318
  judges 510
  metallurgy and weapons 454
  social control 501
  statutes 328
  surrender to Florence (1401) 95
  under Florentine control 92, 447
Pitti, Luca 98
Pius II, pope (Enea Silvio Piccolomini) 473
  and papal sovereignty 78
  and Roman aristocracy 82
  and Siena 106

624   Index

Pius IV, pope, archives (Giovanni Angelo
    Medici) 404
Po valley, rural settlements 280, 281
podestà
  Ferrara 126
  and magistracies 503
  Mantua 125, 129
  Milan 510
  papal state 85, 87
  Piedmont 183
  Reggio Emilia 511
  role in judicial procedures 495, 496
  survival of 378, 380
  in urban areas of state of Milan 160
  in Venetian mainland cities 151, 394
Poggio a Caiano, Medici villa at 101
police forces 501
political mediation 3
  between rural communities and
    states 270
  central governments and 414
  Milan 170–1
political thought, Renaissance 1
  corporative models 267
  principles of 411
politics, language of 406–24
  and architecture 420–1
  content of 411–17
  as form of political action 417–23
  historiography 406–8
  plurality of 413, 424
  producers and matrices 408–11
  and resistance 422
  and 'theory of speech acts' 423
Poliziano, Angelo 100
Pomposa monastery 118
Pontano, Giovanni, *De Principe Heroe* 461
Ponzone family 289
popolo
  in communal cities 324, 327
  exclusions from 327, 329
  extromission from decision-making 254
  and guilds 331
  political participation 253, 254
  rise of 326
  Sicily
    exemptions from taxation 27
    powers of 28
    relations with kings 12
    and social distinction 332
population
  Brescia 143
  crises 348
  Naples 39
  Sardinia 57

Sicily 17, 18, 28, 453
Venice 132
Verona 143
  see also Black Death
Porcia, Girolamo 218
Pordenone di Cividale 209
Porto Conte, battle of (1353) 53, 54
Porto Pisano, commerce regulations 447
ports and landing places
  access for Florence to 446, 447, 459
  Naples 43
  Sardinia 61, 62
  Venice 449
Portugal, and route to Asia 135
Pouget, Bertrand de, cardinal legate of
    Bologna 70, 471
  use of mercy 506
poverty
  in countryside 270
  relief of, by communes 273, 276
  support for poor women 356
power
  concentration of 430
  conceptions of 409
  legitimation of 428
Prata family, Venice 216
Prato
  sold to Florence 92, 243
  wool industry 454
Prato della Valle, Giovanni da 402
Pretatti family, L'Aquila 258
prince
  as dispenser of justice 416
  dynastic links 432
  as source of nobility 341
  see also monarchy
prince-bishops (Eastern ecclesiastical
    principalities)
  control of feudatories 203
  threats to powers of 199
  and towns 201
  Trent 210–11
principalities 197–219
  characteristics of officials 381
  and concept of *dominium* 131
  contractual state 130–1, 296
  diplomatic strategies 431
  evolution from *signorie* 116
  and factions 316
  feudal origins 242
  financial strategies 376
  institutions 124–5
  and legitimation of powers 382
  local opposition to ducal authority 128
  negotiated power in 119

Index 625

power of princes 119
relations between prince and nobility 334
relations between prince and urban
   society 119, 122, 123, 126–9
relations with rural communities 271
stages in evolution of princely courts 128
territorial control by 378
three views of 119–23
use of fiefdoms 295–300
and weak cities 284
see also Aquileia; Bressanone/Brixen;
   cities; ecclesiastical principalities;
   Ferrara; Gorizia; Mantua;
   'Renaissance state'; Trent; Tyrol
printing, Venice 461
prioresses 359, 363
Prisciani, Pellegrino 397
privilegium fori (privilege of tribunal),
   Sicily 24
prostitutes
   controls over 361
   segregation of 360
public debt, consolidated (*Monte*),
   Florence and Venice 376
punishments 508–9
   banishment 495, 496, 498
   execution 508
   pecuniary 505
   torture 497, 508
Pusteria/Pustertal 197

Queneau, Raymond, *Fleurs bleues* 319
Querini, Marco 502

Raggio, O. 309
Ragusa, dowry inflation 349
Rasponi, G. 366
Ravenna, annexed by Venice 133
Rebolledo, Ferdinando Girón de, viceroy of
   Sardinia 59
rector (governor), papal provinces 73, 86
redreç (reform), Sardinia 66–7
referendari (treasurers), state of Milan 160
Reggio Emilia
   acquired by Milan 157, 166
   city administration 127
   expulsion of Estensi 420
   factions 311
   festival of San Prospero 129
   podestà 511
   relations with Estensi 127, 129, 294
   relations with Ferrara 117, 119
   silk industry 457
   use of ritual 419
regional states

and ecclesiastical jurisdiction 479
effect on identity of subsumed
   entities 408
justice in 509–13
and political relationships 409
and regional economies 444–66
relations with papacy 476–81
relations with rural nobility 249, 284,
   290, 296, 297, 299
see also Florence; Milan; Venice
'Renaissance state'
   assertion of princely authority 112
   and bureaucracy 125
   as fiction 112
   historiography of 112–14
   redistribution of power in 112, 115
   see also cities; principalities
René of Anjou 32
republicanism
   civic 414
   and factions 316
   Florentine ideology of 91, 94, 251, 332
   and liberty 409
   and submission to stronger overlords 245
   temporary restoration in city-states 251
   Tuscan 111
   Venice 132
republics
   characteristics of officials 381
   diplomatic strategies 431
   and 'equality' of citizenry 323
   financial strategies 376
   territorial control by 378
Rhodes 65
Ricavo, Antonio Cenni da 431
Ridolfi, Giovanni 441
Rienzo, Cola da 472
Rieti, Colomba da 364
Rinuccini, Alamanno, *Dialogus de
   Libertate* 100
ritual
   and civic religion 484
   and confrontation 418
   cultural history and 417
   language of 419
   political use of 418
rivolta del Bruco (workers' rebellion, Siena,
   1371) 105
roads and communication routes
   Florence 446, 447, 448
   maintenance 273, 274
   Naples 43, 452
   through Alps 197, 272
Robari, Ottobono de', patriarch of
   Aquileia 205

626   Index

Robert of Anjou, king of Naples 347, 499
  death (1343) 157, 284
  and Genoa 226
Roberti family 289
Roccabruna family 289
Romagna region
  Guelfs and Ghibellines 306, 315
  Malatesta family 84, 112, 242
  papal lands taken by Venice (1503) 141
Roman law, exclusion of women and
    minors 330, 347
Romani, M., 'A city in the form of a palace' 119
Rome, ancient, heritage of 145
Rome, city of 420
  capital punishment 508
  casa della iustizia e della pace (1347) 494
  charities 359
  dowry inflation 349
  growing importance of 472, 475, 488
  nunneries 365
  papacy and 70, 473–6
  papal officials in 474
  political participation 337
  relations with *curia* 86
  urban clergy in 482
Rossellino, Bernardo 98
Rossi family 289, 301, 302
Rossi family, Parma, archives 404
Rossi, Marsilio, *signore* of Lucca 251
Rota, papal office 74
Rottenburg, Heinrich von, League of the
    Falcon 211
Rovereto
  jurisdictions 151
  Venetian occupation 133, 214
Rovigo, annexed by Venice 134
royal council (*sacro collegio*), Sardinia 66
royal officials, Sicily 11, 371
Rubiera, acquired by Ferrara 130
Rubinstein, N., *The Government of Florence
    Under the Medici* 97
Rudolf IV, duke of Austria 207, 210
Ruffo family, Naples 34
rural communities (*contadi*) 261–83
  archives 401–4
  chronology of communalisation 268–72
  collective action 274, 278, 294
  concentration of wealth 270
  and control of resources 272
  crisis in Maremma (Siena) 107
  economic privileges 271
  historiography 261–8
  imposition of regulations 275
  individual and collective identities
      267–8, 275–8

  institutions, historiography 263–7
  leadership 266, 275
  legal formations 266
  and outsiders 278–80
  papal states 75
  Piedmont 178, 181
  political and economic strength of 270, 282
  and provision of services 273–5
  rebellions 282
  relations with Savoy ducal court 193–5
  relations with territorial states 271–2,
      281, 298
  relations with urban governments
      248–50, 269
  and rise of lordships 268
  role of 281
  territories and boundaries 278
  variety of 265–6
  Venetian Terraferma, jurisdictions 152
rural nobility (and seigneurs) 261–83,
    288–94
  absorption into larger states 302
  acceptance of feudal investiture
      291, 295
  as autonomous 'small states' 300, 301
  and bishops of Trent 202
  changing role of 290–2
  and city factions 255
  and *fideles* 288
  and fief 286
  formal recognition of independence 291,
      302, 303
  Friuli 202
  legitimation from emperor 291
  Lombardy 285, 296
  as mediators 294, 299, 303
  Milan 169–70, 174, 175, 250, 336
  origins of 288–90
  and patronage of local churches 487
  Piedmont 179, 183, 190
  provision of protection 288, 303
  recruitment of soldiers 290
  relations with cities 249
  relations with communes 275, 276, 286,
      287
  relations with *homines* and exercise of
      power 169–70, 285, 287, 292–4,
      298, 299
  relations with larger states 249, 284, 290,
      296, 297, 299
  relations with rural communities 286
  return after dispossession 292
  survival of 285, 299
  Tyrol and 210
Rusca family 289

Index

Sabbioneta, acquired by Gonzaga 118
Sabellico, Marcantonio, *Rerum venetarum ab urbe condita...* 145
Sacchetti, F. 433
St Mark, as patron of Venice 135, 144, 149
Saint-Geniès, Bertrand de, patriarch of Aquileia 205, 207, 208, 209
Sakellariou, E. 452
Salerno, Campania 44
  council of Twelve 258
Salimbeni family 290
Salò 486
salt production
  Sardinia 51
  Venice 149
Salutati, Coluccio, chancellor of Florence 94, 409
Saluzzo, marquisate of 177, 295
  council 186
  court of 192
  creation of new fiefs 180
  officials 186
  prince's council 185
  records 190
  statutory legislation 193
Salvemini, G. 261, 307
Salviati, Maria 353
Samo, battle of (1460) 44
San Benedetto Polirone monastery 118
San Gimignano 243
  under Florentine rule 92, 401
San Giorgio castle, Mantua 116
San Miniato 486
  under Florentine rule 92, 401
Sangallo, Giuliano da 98
Sangiorgio, Benvenuto di 397
Sanluri, peace of (1355) 55
Sanseverino family 299, 302
  Naples 33
Sant Jordi, Jordi de 64
Santafiora family, Siena 290
Santhià, Savoy 182
Santoro, C. 370
Sanudo, Francesco 144
Sanudo, Marin, on Venice 135, 139, 144, 150
Sardinia 50–68
  Catalan administrative model 57
  centralisation 51, 67
  cities 58, 66, 257
  constitution (1324) 67
  demographic crisis 57
  economic renewal under Alfonso V 61–4
  economy 51, 63
  effect of Aragonese conquest on 56–60
  effect of feudalism on political structure 53
  feudalism 51
  Genoa and 223
  giudichessa Eleonora 352
  influx of Catalans and Aragonese 58, 60, 63, 65, 67
  introduction of parliamentary assemblies 58–60
  military conquest 51, 52
  parliaments (Corti) 58–60
  in Quattrocento 60–1
  reforms under Ferdinand II 64–7
  reign of Peter IV of Aragon 53–6
  role of rural communities 281
  royal administration 64
Sardinia and Corsica, established as kingdom (1297) 50
Sarzana, Genoese territory 228
Sarzana, Peace of (1353) 92
Sassari, Sardinia 52, 58
Sassoferrato, Bartolo da 241, 342
  on nobility 341
  Tractatus de guelphis et gebellinis 320
Savona, Liguria 223, 230
Savonarola, Gerolamo, Florence 101, 254, 485
Savorgnan family
  Friuli 215, 218
  Udine 209, 218, 289
Savorgnan, Tristano 215
Savoy 177–96
  administrative records 189, 196
  administrative structure 181–2, 296, 372
  archives 397
  Audit Chamber 183
  auditing of accounts 189
  Camera dei Conti 189
  Council of Justice 186
  ducal court 191–2
    relations with officials 192
  as feudal state 177–8, 242, 284, 298, 335
  finances 184, 188
  financial offices 187, 188
  institutions of central government 185–90, 195
  parliament (assemblies) 194
  prince's council 185
  relations with communities 193–5
  Secret (State) Council 186
  secretariat 187
  sumptuary laws 361
  territorial councils 186–7
  Three Estates 184, 188, 196
  trade with Milan 451
  war with Milan 188

Sbriccoli, M. 491
Scala, Bartolomeo, chancellor in Florence 100, 513
Scala (Scaligeri) family *see* Della Scala
Scarampi family 290
Schiaffenati family, Pavia 507
schools, in rural communities 269
Sclafani, Matteo, count 14
Scotti family 289
secrecy, in judicial procedures 504
secretarius domini, Piedmont 187
Segnatura, papal office 74
seigneurs/seigneurial *see* rural nobility
Settanta (senate), Florence 100
Sforza family, Milan 120, 121
    archives 400
    and Genoa 226
    relations with Medici 97, 100, 429
    relations with urban populace 122
    see also Francesco I; Francesco II; Galeazzo Maria; Gian Galeazzo Maria; Ludovico; Massimiliano; Visconti family
Sforza, Ippolita 353
ship-building, Pisa 454
Si aliquem, law of (1286, Sicily) 14
Sicily, kingdom of
    chapter 9–29, 284
    alienation of crown lands 15
    and Aragon 55
    Aragonese conquest (1282) 9
    autonomy (1296–1412) 9, 13
    culture of pactism 416
    demography 16–19
        Black Death 17, 18, 28
        population growth 453
    dependence on papacy 470
    division into four seigneural territories 21
    economy
        crisis (fourteenth–fifteenth century) 19
        policy under Aragon 13–16, 453
        specialisation 28
        sumptuary laws 361
    feudalism 14, 20, 28, 257, 297
    foundation 45
    government by viceroy 23
    judicial authority 512
    jurisdictional districts 12
    officials and offices 11, 371
    parliaments 25, 259, 338
        1446 26
        Catania (1296) 13
        Syracuse (1398) 22
    relations between crown and cities 12, 26, 257, 338, 371
    royal Grand Court 512
    royal role 9, 19–20, 21, 256
    rule of vicars 20–1
    rules on dowries 350
    under Alfonso V 23–8
    under John II 27
    under Peter III 11–13, 28
    urban institutions 15, 256–9
    Vespers revolt (1282) 11
    written records 399
    see also monarchy; taxation
Siena 242, 252, 325
    art and culture 106
    Buon Governo frescoes 104, 410
    city government
        Consiglio Generale 104
        Dodici (closed council) 105
        Gentiluomini 104
        government of *Nove* 104, 253, 336
        magistracy 502
        personal rule of Petrucci 108
        police force 501
        Riformatori coalition 105
        rule of *Monti* 106, 107, 110, 337
        signoria 105
        as 'simple state' 107–8, 109
        statutes (1337–9) 104
        survival of republic 108–9
    conflict with Florence 105, 108
    conquest by Grand Duke Cosimo 108
    Dogana dei Paschi 108
    dowry inflation 349
    elite and landed property 105
    and Ghibelline enthusiasm 314
    medieval legacy of 104–7
    Mercanzia 104
    mercenaries 105
    Monna Agnese hospital 359
    Ospedale della Scala 107
    peace settlement 494
    reforms of manufacturing industries 460
    relations with papacy 477
    relations with territory 107–8
    rivolta del Bruco (workers' rebellion, 1371) 105, 253
    Santa Maria della Scala hospital 357
    sea port 446
    silk industry 458
    social control 501
    sumptuary laws 361
    under control of Milan 158
    university 107, 109
    vendetta 493
    written records 388
Siena, Bernardino da 321

Index

Sigismund of Luxembourg, Holy Roman emperor 182, 212, 214, 314
  truce with Venice 215
signori
  as 'apostolic vicars' 71, 72
  conservatism of 112
  and government of towns 83
  judicial measures against 496
  of long lineage 289
  moved to urban areas 289
  new families 289
  relations with papacy 71, 81
signorie (city-lordships) 112
  and expulsion of opponents 244
  rise of 244, 251–2, 268
  transformed to principalities 116
  written records 394–5
  see also oligarchies
silk industry
  Ferrara 457
  Florence 98, 454
  mulberry trees for 458
  Naples 457, 458
  restrictions on movement of workers 457
  Venice 456
silkworms 457
silver mines, Sardinia 51
Simonetta, Cicco 159, 377, 382
Simonetta, Giovanni 383
sindacato, use of 380
Sindici Inquisitori, Venice 151
Sixtus IV, pope (Francesco della Rovere), and Colonna 82
'small states' 300–3
  de facto and *de jure* recognition 301, 302
  state of Milan and 170
  use of term 287
soap production 454, 460
social anthropology, and factions 308
social control 500–1
social distinctions 323–44
  and dowries 350
social hierarchies, construction of 323, 326, 335
social mobility
  and factions 305
  Florence 98
  Naples, through public office 41
  office as means of 373, 377
  in Savoy court 192
societates mulierum 357
soda ash, imports 456
Soderini, Niccolò 97
sodomy, prosecution of 361
Soldi Rondinini, G. 122

Somaini, F., on Milan 164
sommaria, regia camera della, Naples 37, 41
southern Italy
  agriculture 16
  cities 256–9, 470
  dioceses 468, 470
  factions in 322
  historiography 46–9, 280
  and international economy 43
  later treatment of archives 405
  monasteries 470
  role of urban centres 384
  social distinction 325
  stereotype of underdevelopment 45–9
  strength of monarchy 46, 256
  see also Naples; Sicily
Spain, and Italy (1527) 102
Spanish inquisition, in Sardinia 66
Spannocchi family, bankers in Siena 106
Spaur, George von 212
Spaur, John von 212
Spaur, Peter von 212
Spilimbergo family 209
Spinola family, Genoa 223, 234
Spoleto, duchy of, province of papal state 73
Spyre, John of, printer 461
Stabili, Francesco 499
Starkenburg, Ulrich and Wilhelm von 212
state
  duties of protection and justice 345, 366
  monopoly of legitimate violence 321, 345, 513
  as patrimony 77
  ruling classes in 325
  see also monarchy; republicanism
statecraft, as art, Florence 98
stato del Rinascimento, Florence as model for 94
Stenico family 289
Strozzi, Palla 96
Strozzi family, Florentine bankers 43
Strumieri faction, Friuli 309
Studium, Naples 42
subordination, principle of 415
sumptuary laws 360
Sunyer, Andrea, Cagliari 65
Swabian League 324
Syracuse, parliament of (1398) 22

Tabacco, G. 38, 162
Tagliandi, Luigi, councillor of Savoy 194
Tangheroni, M. 57, 61, 62, 63
Taranto, principality of 32, 34, 352
Taranto, siege of 44

taxation
  of church property 479
  and economic policy 463
  and political participation 327, 328, 329, 331
  see also indirect taxes
taxation, church, papal 473
taxation, Ferrara 130
taxation, Florence 446
  estimo 91
  and family fortunes 99
  new collection system 448
taxation, Genoa 231
  avaria (direct tax) 231, 234
taxation, Naples
  assessment of apprezzo 258
  based on hearths 39
  direct (generalis subventio) 38
  direct royal 34
  indirect 44, 452
  rights of cities and towns 34, 45
taxation, Piedmont, farmed 184, 189
taxation, Sicily 15, 18, 331
  alienation of demesne goods 24, 26
  dohana (duty on trade) 24
  farming of 24
  hearths 17
  new fiscal system 25
  role of civil councils 27
  royal system 24
taxation, Venice
  direct, mainland 147
  indirect, mainland 147
  trade tariffs 149
Tempesta family 289
Terra d'Otranto see Otranto
territoriality, principle of 293
textile industry
  cotton 454
  Florence 31, 446
  fulling-mill patent 463
  gold and silver thread 454, 455, 459
  innovations 462
  luxury fabrics 457
  Mantua 129
  Milan 454
  planting of dyer's woad 460
  Siena 460
  Venice 455
  see also wool industry
Theodorus I Palaeologus, marquis of Monferrato 194
Theodorus II Palaeologus, marquis of Monferrato 226
Theory of Action 308

Thiene family, Vincenza 154
Tiepolo, Baiamonte 502
Tiepolo family, Venice 140
timber, for ship-building, Venice 149
Toledo, Corti of (1480) 65
toll franchises
  Florence 446
  Sicily 25
Toralles, Joan 64
Torella family, Sardinia 65
Tornabuoni, Lucrezia 353
Torre, A. 262, 309
Tortona
  acquisition by Milan 157
  city identity 166
  Ghibellinism in 314
  temporary restoration of republicanism 251
torture, use of 497, 508
towns
  annonary system of control 86
  and autonomy of churches 486
  Dogana dei Pascoli 86
  effect of Great Plague on 116
  relations with princes (principalities) 119, 122, 123, 126–9
  relations with rural communes 248–50, 269
  Sicily 11, 15, 256–9
  and sumptuary laws 361
  weakness in ecclesiastical principalities 201
  see also cities; oligarchies; signorie (city-lordships)
towns, papal state 85–8
  and choice of podestà 85, 87
  direct government 84
  oligarchical groups 87
  papal control over 85
  relations with state 78, 84
  role of church as protector of rights 86
  taxation 85
trade 465
  agricultural products 51, 448
  Mediterranean 61, 62
  Milan 451, 455
  Naples 32, 39
  Venice 132, 133, 134, 142, 149, 450
trade, Sicily 17, 22
  with Catalonia 22
  dohana 24
  effect of civil wars on 19
  regional market 25
  toll franchises 25

Index

trades
  and eligibility for election to councils 327
  and political participation 330, 331
Trani, council of Four 258
Trastámara dynasty, and Sardinia 62
tratte (grants of export), Naples 39
treasurers, Sicily 371
Trent
  bishops of, and rural nobility 202, 284
  relations with aristocracy 210–11, 213
  and Tyrol 204
Trent, Council of, effect on women 346, 359, 364
Trent, ecclesiastical principality of 197, 295
  diocese of 200
  German interests in 206
Trentine revolt (1407) 211
Trentino
  aristocracy 204
  political weakness of towns 202
Treviso
  annexed by Venice (1338) 133, 144
  archives 390, 395
  Battuti hospital 152
  and Gorizia 205
  signorial regime 317, 499
Trexenta, Sardinia, *curatori* of 52
Trexler, R. C. 418
Trieste, Gorizia and 205
Trincherio, Urbano 458
Trinci family 289
Trivulzio, Giacomo 253
Trivulzio, Gian Giacomo 167
Troia, battle of (1441) 44
Tunisia, Alfonso V's expedition against 62
Turin
  as capital of Savoy 186, 195
  Cismontane Council 186
  Studio university 186
Turkish wars
  1463–79 134
  1498–1503 134
Tuscany
  concentrations of powers in cities 110
  decline of feudal aristocracy 324
  demographic crisis, effect on Florence 96
  factions 318
  Guelf league in 245
  poderi (farms) 282
  regional manufacturing 453–4
  republicanism 91, 111
  rural settlements 262, 281
  see also Florence; Lucca; Siena
Tuscany, grand duchy of
  patent applications 463

  public archive 404
Tyrol 199
  aristocratic leagues 211
  counts of 198
  relations with Trentine nobility 210
  transferred to Rudolf IV of Austria 207
  and Trento 204
  vendetta in 217

Ubaldi, Baldo degli 343, 389
Ubaldini family 289, 293, 294
Uberti, Fazio degli 398
Uberti, Francesco degli 463
Ubertini family 289
Udine 202, 208, 215, 218
Ugone II of Arborea (Sardinia) 53
Ugone III of Arborea (Sardinia) 55
Umberto, count of Savoy 177
Umbria
  factions 316
  signoria of Francesco Sforza 72
universitates, defined 264
universitates, communities of Naples
  assessment of hearth taxes 39
  law-making powers 35
  relations with cities 45
  and royal administration 40, 256
universitates, communities of Sicily 11
  direct taxation 15
  indirect taxation 15
  James II's economic guarantees for 15
  privileges 24
  relations with king 24, 256
  sale of 26
  and Vespers revolt 13
universities
  Pisa 100
  Siena 107, 109
Urban IV, pope (Jacques Pantaléon) 10
Urban V, pope (Guillaume de Grimoard), and Sardinia 54
Urban VI, pope (Bartolomeo Prignano) 31
Urbino, under Federico da Montefeltro 120

Val Fontanabuona, factions in 309
Val Nure, factions 306
Valenti, Ferran 64
Valeri, N. 319
Valla, Lorenzo 473
Valperga, Giacomo di, chancellor of Savoy 185
Valtellina 171
  factions 310
Varanini, G. M. 176, 449

Varano, Giovanni Maria da 354
Varano, da, family, Camerino 72, 251
vendetta 490, 491–5
  and conflict resolution 492–4
  education on 493
  and factions 312
  texts on 493
  Tyrol 217
Veneto
  and 'death of factions' 317
  historical research project 261
Venice
  chapter 132–55
  and 1509 crisis 134, 154, 242
  and appointment of bishops 477
  and Aragon 32, 53
  Auditori nuovi 510
  Beata Vergine dell'Umiltà confraternity 359, 363
  and Castelbarco 213
  cittadini (non-patrician officials) 139, 351
  city government
    Camere fiscale (1449) 394
    capi sestiere 500
    Collegio (main executive body) 138, 141
    communal 132
    complexity of 139
    Council of Ten 138, 139, 140, 141
      food supply powers 449
      judicial powers 394, 502, 504
    ducal chancery 139
    The Forty (*Quarantia*) 137, 139, 502
    institutions 136–41
    Maggior Consiglio reforms (1297/1323) (*serrata*) 136, 252, 334
    magistracies 138, 150
    participation in 323
    Savi panels 138
    Senate 137, 138, 139, 141
    signoria 138
    state attorneys 139
    temporary councils 137
    Zonta 141
  defence 147
  doge 139, 363
  economy and finances
    Cinque Savi alla Mercanzia (1517) 450
    Collegio alle Biave 449
    commercial policy 448–51
    consolidated public debt (*Monte*) 376
    finances 147–8
    glass industry 456, 462
    obligatory passage of goods through port 449
    protectionism 456
    and regional manufacturing 455–7
    silk industry 456
    sumptuary laws 361
    wealth from trade 132, 142
  expansion
    aristocratic resistance to 449
    and Friuli 207, 210, 214–16, 217–19
    into Trentino 214
    to mainland 133
  food supply 449
  and Genoa 132, 133, 222, 230
  and Italian Wars 134
  limits on dowries 348, 360
  navy (galley fleets) 132, 134
  nunneries 363
  and Ottoman Turks 134
  overseas dominions 132, 142–3
  patriciate (aristocracy) 136, 137, 140–1, 150–2, 252, 317, 334
  Pietà hospital 359
  political paintings 410
  population 132
  'public historiography' 145
  public ritual 135
  relations with papacy 477
  republicanism 132
    and civic humanism 145, 151, 411
    civic pride 135
    myth and reality of city state 135–6, 144
  role of jurists 504
  social control 500
  taxation 147, 149
    on documents 390
  and technical innovation 461–3
  and Trent region 215
  widows 349
  written records 382, 393–4, 400
    treatment of 393
Venice, regional state (Terraferma) 141–4, 158
  administration of justice 509, 510
  administration of mainland territories 138, 143–4
  definitions of dominion 144–7
  ecclesiastical policy in 149–50
  economic regulation of 449, 455–7
  government activity in 150–2
  imperial investiture with Terraferma lands (1437) 146
  and legitimacy of annexations 145–6
  local decision-making in 152–5
  manufacturing 455–7
  policy and authority in 147–52, 250

Index

terminology of mainland state 146
written records 393–4
Venosta/Vinschgau 197
Ventimiglia, Genoese territory 228
Ventimiglia, Francesco I, count of
    Geraci 14
Ventimiglia, Francesco II, count of
    Geraci 20
Ventimiglia family 298, 300
Vercelli 179, 182
  acquisition by Milan 157
  administration by Savoy 378
  Ghibellinism in 314
Verme, Pietro dal 395
Verme, dal, family 299, 302, 403
Verona 133, 143, 242
  acquisition by Milan 158
  archives 390, 405
  buildings 420
  city statutes 145
  coinage 148
  economic policy in Terraferma 149
  glass industry 456
  Gonzaga family and 118
  justice in Terraferma 148–9
  population 143
  signorial regime 317
  silkworms 457
  trade with Venice 450
  Venetian occupation 133
  wool industry 455
  written records 390
Vespers revolt (1282), Sicily 11, 31, 256, 298
Vettori, Francesco 441
Viadana, acquired by Gonzaga 118
vicars, government of Sicily 20–1
vicars-general 478
Vicenza 242
  acquisition by Milan 158
  archives 390
  glass industry 456
  Gonzaga family and 118
  rural jurisdictions (*Sette Comuni*) 152
  silkworms 457
  Venetian occupation 133
  wool industry 455
viceroys, Sardinia 66
vicini (inhabitants of *contrade* and
    communes) 265, 279
  as active interlocutors 287
  relations with seigneurs 286, 287, 288
Vigevano 486
Vignano, Giovanni da 493
Vilamari, Bernardo de, Aragonese admiral 65
Villa di Chiesa, Sardinia 52

Villani, Giovanni 328, 329
  Cronica 91
Visconti, Azzone 157, 172, 420
  territorial consolidation 246, 413
Visconti, Bernabò 157, 173, 396, 507, 513
Visconti, Bianca Maria 158, 352, 357
Visconti, Galeazzo 157
Visconti, Galeazzo II 157, 173, 396, 513
Visconti, Giovanni, archbishop 157, 158,
    226, 227
Visconti, Luchino 157, 162, 420
Visconti, Matteo 157, 245
Visconti, Ottone, archbishop 156, 157
Visconti family, Milan 72, 92, 112, 133,
    156–62
  archives 396, 397
  branches 289, 294
  building schemes 120
  centralised politics 165
  and control over communes 245
  as dukes of Milan 116, 158
  and ecclesiastical interference 471
  expansion into Veneto 290
  relations with urban populace 122
  and Savoy 178
  territorial consolidation 242, 246
  wars with papacy 246, 499
  see also Filippo Maria; Gian Galeazzo;
    Giovanni Maria
Vitelli family, Città di Castello 252, 289
Viterbo 252
  Priors of 364
Vitturi, Cateruzza 367
Vives, V. J. 57
Voghera 486
Volentes, law of (1298, Sicily) 14
Volpe, G. 261
Volterra
  sack (1472) 247
  under Florentine rule 92, 243

Walter of Brienne, Angevin duke of
    Athens 91
  as *signore* of Florence 251, 392, 494
war, loans for 39
War of the Eight Saints (1375–8) (Florence
    and papacy) 92, 246, 247, 318,
    471, 483
War of the League of Cambrai 309
waterways, Milan 451
Watts, J. 4
wax, trade in 450
wealth
  concentration of 270
  per capita 445, 465

Weber, M. 469, 513
weights and measures, standardisation 446, 452, 453
Welch, E. 121
Wenceslaus, king of Germany 158
Wickham, C. 262
William III, viscount of Narbonne, *giudice* of Arborea 56
Wittelsbachs
  dynastic dispute with Habsburgs 205
  and Friuli 207
women 345–67
  administration of personal wealth 355
  appointment of guardians for 366
  books on 355
  charitable benefactions 357
  and control over morals 361
  at court 353, 354
  and domestic violence 367
  dowries 347–50
    Florence 99, 348
    inflation 347, 349
  and illegitimate children 359
  legal status 279, 360–5
  marriage 347, 351
  and matrimonial disputes 366
  in nunneries 358, 362, 364
  and papal nepotism 354
  as patrons 352
  political identity 350
  political power of 351–6, 364, 365
  as prioresses 359, 363
  property rights 347–51
  in receipt of public assistance 359
  as regents 352
  role in factions 322, 366
  as rulers 351, 365
  segregation of marginal groups 360
  sexuality 360, 362
  and sumptuary laws 360
  support for 356–60, 367
  wet-nurses 358, 359
  widows 349, 366
wool production 454
  Florence 454, 459
  Naples 461
  Sardinia 62
  Venice and 455
wool trade
  Catalonia to Sicily 22
  Naples 39
Worms, concordat of 469

Yver, G. 47

Zamberlani faction, Friuli 309
Zante, annexed by Venice 134
Zonchio, battle of (1499) 134

Printed in Great Britain
by Amazon